Sourcebook on the Foundations of Social Protection Delivery Systems

Sourcebook on the Foundations of Social Protection Delivery Systems

Kathy Lindert,
Tina George Karippacheril,
Inés Rodríguez Caillava, and
Kenichi Nishikawa Chávez,
Editors

WORLD BANK GROUP

1818 H Street NW, Washington, DC 20433
Telephone: 202-473-1000; Internet: www.worldbank.org

1 2 3 4 23 22 21 20

ISBN (paper): 978-1-4648-1577-5
ISBN (electronic): 978-1-4648-1578-2
DOI: 10.1596/978-1-4648-1577-5

Cover illustrations: All illustrations © Shutterstock.com and the following illustrators: Tasty Cat, Unitone Vector, Marina Solva, GoodStudio, Antonov Maxim, Gvardgraph, Atto Stock, Tartila, Anny Murcia, Shirokuma Design, and NotionPic. All illustrations used with permission; further permission required for reuse.
Cover design: Andres de la Roche, A.DELAROCHE DESIGNS; Bill Pragluski, Critical Stages, Inc.
Interior design: Andres de la Roche, A.DELAROCHE DESIGNS; Kirsten Dennison; Nita Congress.
Figure design: Andres de la Roche, A.DELAROCHE DESIGNS.

Library of Congress Control Number: 2020914228

Contents

Chapter 10 A Continuing Journey 419

Margaret Grosh, Tina George Karippacheril, and Inés Rodríguez Caillava

Glossary 427

Boxes

Figures

Tables

Foreword

Social protection delivery systems matter. Policy design and delivery systems have always worked hand in hand to yield meaningful programs and impacts. Countries offer a myriad of social programs, such as cash transfers, subsidies, childcare, training, or labor services, for which delivery is fragmented and navigation not easy for recipients. Simplifying fragmented processes and innovating through a delivery systems approach puts people and families at the center; diffuses complexity; improves inclusion, reach, and coverage; and contributes to efficiencies, quality, and transparency for governments. These benefits, in turn, help to streamline and automate complex eligibility determination processes, facilitate regular feedback on the provision of services to improve their quality, and ultimately contribute to building a relationship of trust between the state and its people.

Some examples illustrate the power of delivery systems. A prime ministerial decree in Turkey shifted the burden of collecting documents for social assistance registration and other public services from people to public servants. It became the genesis for far-reaching administrative reforms that contributed to the streamlining of the social assistance process, utilizing technology and the coordination of 24 different agencies to decrease the application from 15–20 days to minutes. In Ghana, a cash-for-work program saved 13 million person-hours of administrative work by registering, enrolling, and verifying beneficiaries through automated processes, reducing the time it takes to pay workers from four months to one week after work is completed. In Pakistan, participatory approaches to communications and program monitoring through "mother leaders" of beneficiary groups improved children's enrollment in primary schools. Chile has family counselors who work with vulnerable people, families in extreme poverty, seniors living alone, the homeless, and children with parents in prison to determine which social services and cash transfers they need and to ensure access.

The World Bank has supported governments with respect to implementation of their programs and policies for as long as it has been working in social protection. Over time, the attention and in-house skills devoted to implementation have grown. Five years ago, to deepen knowledge on the topic even more, the Social Protection and Jobs Global Practice made delivery systems the focus of a Global Solutions Group, including a stream of country engagements, knowledge products, and learning events. This focus on delivery systems in the absence of policy is somewhat artificial but enables heightened focus in the same way that converting a color painting to a black-and-white photo may help emphasize the shapes. Understanding the shapes contributes to a deeper understanding of the composition and effectiveness of the art.

The work of the Delivery Systems Global Solutions Group has covered many kinds of programs, including categorical programs, poverty-targeted transfers, labor market programs, unemployment assistance, disability assistance, and labor and social services and the linkages among them. It has yielded rich insights, including the fact that the same basic delivery chain applies across many programs, which makes it possible for individual programs to learn from a host of others, and also for some sharing or integration of functions across a wide range of programs.

This *Sourcebook* is a milestone in the journey of learning and codifying knowledge about delivery systems, fed by addressing practical problems with many client counterparts, programs, and countries. The work has involved an unusually large team of authors, and an even larger group of people contributed to the many brainstorming sessions, clinics, missions, and seminars that were the first proving grounds of the ideas contained here. The team put it forward to make the lessons and techniques widely accessible, to prompt discussion on some of the dilemmas common in delivery systems, and to inspire program managers to continue to raise standards in their work, possibly prompted by one of the examples cited within these pages.

The *Sourcebook* comes at a time of increasing demand for the delivery of shock-responsive social protection. In the wake of the COVID-19 pandemic, governments around the world are responding to the socioeconomic shocks with social safety nets for millions of households. Nearly 200 countries have introduced various forms of social protection to compensate workers for lost income as a result of the extensive lockdowns and the broader economic downturn and to mitigate adverse impacts on the poor and the vulnerable. End-to-end digital delivery of programs, with safety, security, and speed, is helping compliance with social distancing requirements.

Furthermore, as countries work toward universal social protection, a goal announced in many national social protection strategies and codified in the Sustainable Development Goals, the coverage and complexity of their programming will call even more on good delivery systems. They will face challenges of ensuring inclusion of the most excluded and of coordinating across many programs for the best client experience and for the most efficient set of programming. This policy surge can draw from and contribute to subsequent know-how with respect to delivery systems.

Michal Rutkowski
Global Director for Social Protection and Jobs
World Bank

Preface

This *Sourcebook* synthesizes practical knowledge and experience on social protection delivery systems from countries around the world, with a focus on social and labor benefits and services. It addresses questions relating to the "how." Specifically, how do countries deliver social protection benefits and services? How do they do so effectively and efficiently? How do they ensure dynamic inclusion, so that people can access them when in need? How do they promote better coordination and integration—not only among social protection programs, but also among programs in other parts of government? How can they meet the needs of their intended populations and provide a better client experience?

Social protection delivery systems address these crucial questions. What are delivery systems? The short answer is that delivery systems are implementation. The longer answer: delivery systems are the operating environment for implementing social protection benefits and services. That operating environment is anchored in core implementation phases along the delivery chain. These phases are common to most programs and include outreach, intake and registration, assessment of needs and conditions, eligibility and enrollment, payments of benefits and provision of services, and monitoring and management, including beneficiary exits. People and institutions interact all along the delivery chain. Those interactions are facilitated by communications, information systems, and technology, among other factors.

The *Sourcebook* takes a broad view of social protection. It covers various intended populations such as demographic groups, poor or low-income families, unemployed workers, persons with disabilities, and individuals facing social risks. It discusses many types of interventions that governments provide to individuals, families, or households. This includes benefits, such as categorical programs (for example, child allowances and social pensions), conditional and unconditional cash transfers for the poor, unemployment assistance and insurance, and disability assistance and insurance. It also includes labor and social services, such as employment services to help people find jobs, active labor market programs to help people boost their employability, and social services (including social work services, social care services, and specialized services), as well as services provided as accompanying measures of unconditional cash transfers (mainly on human development and productive inclusion).

The *Sourcebook* takes a global perspective on social protection delivery systems. Examples come from every region (Africa, East Asia and the Pacific, Europe and Central Asia, Latin America and the Caribbean, the Middle East and North Africa, and South Asia), including a range of lower-income, middle-income, and higher-income countries.

Although the *Sourcebook* gleans lessons from good practices and challenges, it is not meant to be prescriptive. Rather, the delivery systems framework is a practical way to organize the discussion about implementation of social protection programs. The *Sourcebook* highlights eight key principles that can frame the delivery systems mindset:

1. Delivery systems evolve over time, evolution is nonlinear, and the starting points matter.

2. Efforts should be made to "do simple well" before adding complex features to programs or systems.
3. Quality of implementation matters, and weaknesses in any of the core elements will affect the entire system.
4. The first mile for client interface matters (but is often the weakest link in delivery systems).
5. Delivery systems do not operate in a vacuum and should not be developed in silos.
6. Social protection delivery systems can contribute more broadly to a government's ability to deliver interventions in other sectors, such as health insurance subsidies, scholarships, social energy tariffs, housing benefits, and legal services.
7. There is no single blueprint for delivery systems, but there are commonalities, and those common elements constitute the core of the delivery systems framework.
8. The dual challenges of inclusion and coordination are pervasive and perennial and also contribute to the objectives of effectiveness and efficiency.

Acknowledgments

This *Sourcebook* is the product of a team led by Kathy Lindert, Tina George, and Inés Rodríguez Caillava and which included Kenichi Nishikawa Chávez, Lucía Solbes Castro, Estelle Raimondo, Briana Wilson, Phillippe Leite, Verónica Silva Villalobos, Sara Giannozzi, Surat Nsour, Vasumathi Anandan, Laura Rawlings, Luz Stella Rodríguez, Ana Verónica López Murillo, John Blomquist, Ahmet Fatih Ortakaya, Saki Kumagai, Alex Kamurase, Emil Tesliuc, Juul Pinxten, Conrad Daly, Anita Mittal, Karen Peffley, and Helena Makarenko. Elizabeth Schwinn and Nita Congress provided editorial assistance. Overall guidance was provided by Michal Rutkowski (Global Director), Margaret Grosh (Senior Advisor), Lynne Sherburne-Benz (Regional Director), and Anush Bezhanyan (Practice Manager), all from the Social Protection and Jobs Global Practice.

The *Sourcebook* synthesizes the experience, knowledge, and contributions on social protection delivery systems that the World Bank has accumulated over the past 20 years. The creation of the Delivery Systems Global Solutions Group (GSG) in the Social Protection and Jobs Global Practice in June 2015 provided the opportunity to systematize and connect decades of experience and engagement by the World Bank in this area. The contributions of GSG members build on direct engagements with government counterparts and other stakeholders who are at the frontlines of delivering social protection programs in countries around the world.

We would like to thank our peer reviewers and regional focal points for their insights and feedback at various stages of preparing the *Sourcebook*. Benedicte de la Briere (Africa Region), Changqing Sun (East Asia and the Pacific), Marina Petrovic (Europe and Central Asia), and Melis Guven (Africa) all served as both peer reviewers and regional focal points. Some regional focal points were also team members on the *Sourcebook*, including Kenichi Nishikawa Chávez (South Asia), Lucía Solbes Castro (Latin America and the Caribbean), Phillippe Leite (South Asia), Surat Nsour (Middle East and North Africa), and Verónica Silva Villalobos (Latin America and the Caribbean). Other regional focal point team members include Alessandra Marini (Europe and Central Asia), Elena Glinskaya (East Asia and the Pacific), and Khalid Ahmed Moheyddeen (Middle East and North Africa).

In addition, the team would like to extend sincere thanks to the many colleagues who provided inputs and feedback throughout the process, including Aleksandra Posarac, Amjad Zafar Khan, Anand Raman, Anita Kumari, Asha Williams, Ashiq Aziz, Aylin Isik-Dikmelik, Boban Varghese Paul, Bojana Naceva, Cem Mete, Chipo Msowoya, Christabel Dadzie, Claudia P. Rodríguez Alas, Colin Andrews, Craig Kilfoil, David Ian Walker, Dominik Koehler, Elena Bardasi, Emily Weedon Chapman, Gisela Garcia, Gregory Chen, Gustavo Demarco, Hana Brixi, Harish Natarajan, Heba Elgazzar, Iffath Sharif, Indhira Vanessa Santos, Jehan Arulpragasam, Jimena Garrote, Johannes Koettl, Josefina Posadas, Julieta Trias, Junko Onishi, Karol Karpinksi, Laura Ripani (IDB), Mahamane Maliki Amadou, Mariana Novikova, Matteo Morgandi, Mina Zamand, Mitchell Weiner, Muderis Abdulahi Mohammed, Nahla Zeitoun, Natalia Millan, Nina Rosas Raffo, Oleksiy Ivaschenko, Oleksiy Sluchynskyy, Pablo Ariel Acosta, Pablo Gottret, Philip O'Keefe, Quanita Khan, Raiden C. Dillard, Rashiel Velarde, Rasmus Heltberg, Rebecca Riso, Rene Antonio Leon Solano, Richon Mattis

Nembhard, Robert Chase, Rovane Battaglin Schwengber, Ruslan Yemtsov, Samira Ahmed Hillis, Samantha Zaldivar, Sandor Sipos, Stefano Paternostro, Sylvia Baur, Ubah Thomas Ubah, Ugo Gentilini, Vlad Alexandru Grigoras, Yasuhiko Matsuda, Yasuhiro Kawasoe, Yoonyoung Cho, Yuliya Smolyar, and Zachary Green.

We are also grateful for the partnership with the Independent Evaluation Group (IEG) of the World Bank, in the framework of an IEG learning engagement in support of chapter 9, "Assessing the Performance of Social Protection Delivery Systems." Finally, the team wishes to recognize the generous award of a grant from the Rapid Social Response Trust Fund Program, which is supported by Australia, Denmark, Norway, the Russian Federation, Sweden, and the United Kingdom, without which this work would not have been possible. This grant allowed us to systematize knowledge on integrated social information systems, which provided valuable inputs for several chapters. This *Sourcebook* is expected to contribute to further discussions with development partners under the Interagency Social Protection Assessment initiative.

About the Editors, Authors, and Contributors

Editors

Tina George Karippacheril is a Senior Social Protection Specialist in the Africa Region of the World Bank. She leads a regional operation in six countries (the West Africa Unique Identification for Regional Integration and Inclusion Program) that won the World Bank President's Award for Excellence. Previously she served as Global Co-Lead for the Delivery Systems Group. Her work spans digital governance, social protection delivery systems, social registries, foundational IDs, social protection payments, and platforms for the poor. Recent publications include *Investing in People: Social Protection for Indonesia's 2045 Vision* (2020) and "Social Registries for Social Assistance and Beyond" (2017). She holds a PhD in technology, policy, and management from Technische Universiteit Delft (the Netherlands).

Kathy Lindert served as the Global Lead for the Delivery Systems Group in the Social Protection and Jobs Global Practice of the World Bank. Kathy worked for five years in the World Bank's office in Brazil, where she managed the partnership with the Bolsa Família Program. She also served as Sector Manager for Social Protection for the Europe and Central Asia Region. She has written papers on social safety nets, poverty, social spending, redistribution and transfers, social registries, decentralized implementation of conditional cash transfers, and food subsidy reform. She has a BA in international economics from the American University of Paris and an MA and a PhD in economics from the University of California at Davis.

Kenichi Nishikawa Chávez is a Senior Social Protection Economist for the World Bank Social Protection and Jobs Global Practice in South Asia. He has worked extensively in program implementation design and on adaptive social protection in Latin America and South Asia. Before joining the World Bank, Kenichi was Director of Implementation in the Ministry of Social Development in Mexico. He holds an MA in public administration from Cornell University and an MA in international development from Nagoya University (Japan).

Inés Rodríguez Caillava is a Social Protection Specialist in the Social Protection and Jobs Global Practice at the World Bank. She is a core team member of the Delivery Systems Global Solutions Group, contributing to the global knowledge program on delivery systems. She has worked on social safety net programs and delivery systems in Angola, Burkina Faso, the Republic of Congo, Djibouti, Guinea-Bissau, and Mozambique. She holds a BA and an MA in international relations from the Universidad de San Andrés (Argentina) and an MA in international development from the George Washington University.

Authors

Vasumathi Anandan is a Policy Specialist and Sociologist with more than 10 years of experience in international development, public policy, research, and information and communication technologies. She has worked in the Social Protection and Jobs Global Practice at the World

Bank since 2014. Previously she worked at the Indian Institute of Technology Madras, India's leading research and technology institution. She has an MPH with a specialization in policy from the George Washington University and an MSc in medical sociology from Loyola College (India).

John Blomquist is the Global Lead for Social Protection and Jobs Delivery Systems Global Solutions Group at the World Bank. His work focuses on delivery systems and program design especially for the informal, unorganized sector. He has experience in the private sector, and over the past 25 years he has worked in most regions of the world. John holds a PhD in economics from the University of Pennsylvania.

María Cecilia Dedios is Assistant Professor at Universidad de Los Andes (Colombia) and a Research Officer at the London School of Economics and Political Science. Her work focuses on peer and family socialization processes among young people in contexts of disadvantage and on social cognition in relation to violence among the same population.

Sara Giannozzi is a Senior Social Protection Specialist in the East Asia and Pacific Unit of the Social Protection and Jobs Global Practice at the World Bank. She has worked extensively on delivery systems, intermediation services, safety nets, and economic inclusion in Africa, East Asia, and Latin America and the Caribbean. She holds a degree in economics from the University of Florence (Italy) and a master's in international development from the Johns Hopkins University School of Advanced International Studies.

Margaret Grosh is the Senior Adviser for the Social Protection and Jobs Global Practice at the World Bank. She has written, lectured, and advised extensively on social protection—and especially on social assistance—globally and for Latin America. She has extensive experience with social protection both for crisis response and for improving equality of opportunity. She holds a PhD in economics from Cornell University.

Alex Kamurase is a Senior Social Protection Specialist at the World Bank. He has several years of experience in operations, analytical work, and policy dialogue covering programs with strong poverty reduction objectives in Africa, the Caribbean, and the Middle East. He has coauthored papers and reports on safety nets, human development, and citizen engagement. Alex holds an MSc in public economic management and public finance from the University of Birmingham (UK) and a bachelor's of commerce from Makerere University (Uganda).

Saki Kumagai is a Governance Specialist at the World Bank. She specializes in supporting governments that are working toward more transparent, accountable, and participatory systems. Saki leads the Governance Global Practice's citizen engagement and civic technology work and supports multiple World Bank–financed service delivery operations in countries such as the Arab Republic of Egypt, Ethiopia, Malawi, and Somalia.

Phillippe Leite is a Senior Social Protection Economist in the South Asia Unit of the Social Protection and Jobs Global Practice at the World Bank. He has worked extensively on support design of social assistance programs in Africa and Latin America and at the World Bank's Development Research Group on determinants of poverty and inequality, poverty maps methodology, and microeconometric simulation models. He holds a BA and an MS in statistics (sampling and modeling) from ENCE/Brazil and an MS and a PhD in economics from École des Hautes Études en Sciences Sociales (Paris).

Ana Verónica López Murillo has been a Consultant in the Social Protection and Jobs Global Practice at the World Bank since 2012. She has coauthored and contributed to research on payment systems, social information systems, targeting, and youth employment, among other social protection and jobs topics. She holds an MA in development economics from American University.

Anita Mittal is a Senior IT Expert working at the World Bank with the Social Protection and Jobs Global Practice team on the Identification for Development (ID4D) Initiative. She works on technical practitioner notes and solution architectures and advises client countries on the implementation of digital ID and social protection systems. She has extensive experience in implementing e-governance projects, including India's Aadhaar project. She is a certified Project Management Professional and has a BA and an MA in computer science and engineering.

Surat Nsour is a Senior Social Protection Specialist in the Africa Human Development Department at the

World Bank. She joined the World Bank in 2002 and has been working extensively on social protection, focusing on a range of interventions, including social funds, social safety nets, and labor markets. She contributed to the Social Protection Strategy and led country engagements and regional work on social assistance in middle- and high-income, International Development Association, and postconflict countries. She has an MS in social and organizational development from George Mason University and a BS in architectural engineering from Jordan University of Science and Technology.

Ahmet Fatih Ortakaya is a Senior Social Protection Specialist at the World Bank, with more than 14 years of implementation, research, and policy development experience. Before joining the World Bank, he worked as a Consultant at the Organisation for Economic Co-operation and Development and also served as a Senior Official in the Turkish government. He led a project to reform the targeting approach for social safety net programs and the design and development of Turkey's Integrated Social Assistance System. Currently he leads the World Bank's social safety net reform efforts in Saudi Arabia. His main interests are program design and implementation, social protection delivery systems, job-matching algorithms, targeting approaches, and predictive analytics. He holds a PhD in statistics from Turkey's Middle East Technical University.

Juul Pinxten is a Social Protection Specialist for the World Bank, based in Jakarta, Indonesia. He has worked one year in the Poverty and Equity Global Practice and five years in the Social Protection and Jobs Global Practice, both while based in Indonesia. He has worked extensively in Indonesia and Timor-Leste on cash transfer design and implementation, social assistance delivery systems, and targeting methodologies.

Estelle Raimondo is a Senior Evaluation Officer in the World Bank's Independent Evaluation Group. With 10 years of experience in development evaluation, she is a faculty member of the International Program for Development Evaluation Training and serves on the board of the European Evaluation Society. Her research has been published in several internationally peer-reviewed journals and manuscripts. She received her PhD in evaluation research from the George Washington University.

Laura B. Rawlings is a Lead Economist at the World Bank. She has led research, operational, and advisory work on the design, implementation, and evaluation of human development programs. She was the Team Leader and coauthor for *Impact Evaluation in Practice* and for *Resilience, Equity, and Opportunity: The World Bank's Social Protection and Labor Strategy 2012–2022*. She is a member of the Human Capital Project team and an Adjunct Professor in Georgetown University's Global Human Development program.

Luz Stella Rodríguez is a Social Protection Specialist at the World Bank working with governments of Latin America and the Caribbean to strengthen the design and delivery of social protection systems. Luz also contributes to the global knowledge agenda to improve the efficiency and impact of human-centric government-to-person payments. Before joining the World Bank, Luz worked as a government official at the Ministry of Finance, the National Planning Department, and the President's Office in Colombia. She has also worked with international financial institutions and United Nations system organizations.

Verónica Silva Villalobos is a Senior Social Protection Specialist for the Social Protection and Jobs Global Practice at the World Bank. She has extensive experience with social assistance and social services interventions, both managing social policies and programs at the government level and advising governments globally and in Latin America and the Caribbean.

Lucía Solbes Castro is a Social Protection Specialist in the Europe and Central Asia Unit of the Social Protection and Jobs Global Practice at the World Bank. She joined the World Bank in 2010 as part of the team that produced the *World Development Report 2012: Gender Equality and Development*. She has since worked on social safety net programs and social protection delivery systems in Africa, Europe and Central Asia, and Latin America. She holds a BA in mathematics from Universidad Complutense (Spain) and an MS in economics from the European University Institute (Italy).

Emil Tesliuc is a Senior Economist at the World Bank. He coauthored two books on the design and implementation of social assistance programs, *For Protection and*

Promotion: The Design and Implementation of Effective Safety Nets (2008) and *Income Support for the Poorest: A Review of Experience in Eastern Europe and Central Asia* (2014), and ADePT SP, a tool for estimating the incidence of social protection programs. He holds a PhD in economics from the Bucharest University of Economic Studies and an MA in public policy from Princeton University.

Briana Wilson is a Senior Social Protection Specialist in the World Bank's Social Protection and Jobs Global Practice. She specializes in monitoring and evaluating social protection interventions and, since 2009, has contributed to designing and evaluating programs in Africa, Europe and Central Asia, and Latin America. Before 2009 she was working in advisory services for the International Finance Corporation. She holds a BA from Northwestern University and an MA from the Johns Hopkins University School of Advanced International Studies.

Contributors

Ashiq Aziz, Senior Social Protection Specialist, World Bank
Sylvia Baur-Yazbeck, Financial Sector Analyst, Consultative Group to Assist the Poor
Greg Chen, Lead Financial Sector Specialist, Consultative Group to Assist the Poor
Christabel Dadzie, Social Protection Specialist, World Bank
Conrad Daly, Senior Legal Consultant, World Bank
Gustavo Demarco, Lead Economist, World Bank
Heba Elgazzar, Program Leader, World Bank
Melis Guven, Senior Social Protection Economist, World Bank
Karol Karpinski, Financial Sector Specialist, World Bank
Amjad Zafar Khan, Senior Social Protection Specialist, World Bank
Quanita Khan, Former Consultant, World Bank
Craig Kilfoil, Consultant, World Bank
Yasuhiko Matsuda, Program Leader, World Bank
Harish Natarajan, Lead Financial Sector Specialist, World Bank
Karen Peffley, Operations Analyst, World Bank
Anand Raman, Consultant, World Bank
Nina Rosas Raffo, Senior Economist, World Bank
Ambrish Shahi, Social Protection Specialist, World Bank
Oleksiy A. Sluchynskyy, Senior Economist, World Bank
Cornelia Tesliuc, Senior Social Protection Specialist, World Bank
Ubah Thomas Ubah, Social Protection Specialist, World Bank
Nahla Zeitoun, Senior Social Protection Specialist, World Bank

Abbreviations

4Ps	Pantawid Pamilyang Pilipino Program (the Philippines)
ALMP	active labor market program
ASPIRE	Atlas of Social Protection Indicators of Resilience and Equity (World Bank)
ATM	automated teller machine
BBC	BISP Beneficiary Committee (Pakistan)
BFP	Bolsa Família Program (Brazil)
BISP	Benazir Income Support Programme (Pakistan)
BOMS	beneficiary operations management system(s)
BPC	Benefício de Prestação Continuada (Brazil)
BPR	business process review
BUS	Beneficiary Update System (the Philippines)
CBA	cost-benefit analyses
CBT	community-based targeting
CCT	conditional cash transfer (program)
CEA	cost-effectiveness analyses
CPU	central processing unit
CTR	cost-transfer ratio
CV	curriculum vitae
D2D	door-to-door
DA	disability assistance
DEA	data envelopment analysis
DHHS	Department of Health and Human Services
DHS	Department of Human Services
DI	disability insurance
DIPRES	Dirección de Presupuesto (Chile)
DLE	Department of Labor and Employment
DMI	differentiated minimum income
DSWD	Department for Social Welfare and Development (the Philippines)
DTT	District Training Team
ECEC	early childhood development, education, and care
EEZ	Exclusive Economic Zone
EFC	error(s), fraud, and corruption
e-GOV	electronic-governance (program)
ESO	Employment Service Office
FA	Familias en Acción Program (Colombia)
FCV	fragility, conflict, and violence
FED	Fondo de Estimulo al Desempeño y Logro de Resultados Sociales (Peru)
FMIS	Family Medicine Information System (Turkey)
G2P	government-to-person (payments)
GDP	gross domestic product
GDRP	General Data Protection Regulation (European Union)
GDSA	General Directorate of Social Assistance (Turkey)
GIS	geographic information system
GMI	guaranteed minimum income
GPS	Global Positioning System
GRM	grievance redress mechanism
HCD	human-centered design
HH	household
HMT	hybrid means testing
HTTP	hypertext transfer protocol
IAP	individualized action plan
IBGE	Brazilian Institute of Geography and Statistics
ID	identity/identification
IFMIS	integrated financial management information system(s)
ILO	International Labour Organization
ISAS	Integrated Social Assistance System (Turkey)
IT	information technology
JSCI	Job Seeker Classification Instrument (Australia)
LGBT	lesbian, gay, bisexual, and transgender
LTU	long-term unemployed/unemployment
MCC	Maryland Community Connection
MDS	Ministry of Social Development (Brazil)
MENA	Middle East and North Africa Region

MIDIS	Ministerio de Desarrollo e Inclusión Social (Peru)
MIS	management information system
MNO	mobile network operator
MoE	Ministry of Education
MoH	Ministry of Health
MoLFSP	Ministry of Labor and Social Protection (Romania)
MoLSAE	Ministry of Labor, Social Assistance, and Equal Opportunities (Albania)
MoSA	Ministry of Social Affairs (Indonesia)
MoU	memorandum of understanding
MT	means testing
NEET	not in education, employment, or training
NEIS	National Employment and Insurance System
NES	National Employment Service
NGO	nongovernmental organization
NPMO	National Program Management Office (the Philippines)
NQSF	National Quality Standards Framework (Ireland)
NSER	National Socioeconomic Registry (Pakistan)
NTB	National Trust Bank
OECD	Organisation for Economic Co-operation and Development
P2G	person-to-government (payments)
PATH	Programme for the Advancement of Health and Education (Jamaica)
PES	public employment service(s)
PIN	personal identification number
PKH	Program Keluarga Harapan (Indonesia's conditional cash transfer program)
PMED	Planning, Monitoring, and Evaluation Division
PMT	proxy means testing
POS	point(s) of sale
PSP	payment service provider
PSSN CCT	Productive Social Safety Net Conditional Cash Transfer (Tanzania)
PWD	people with disabilities
RAM	random-access memory
RSH	Registro Social de Hogares (Chile)
SAGI	General Secretariat for Evaluation and Information (Brazil)
SAR	special administrative region
SASF	Social Assistance and Solidarity Foundation (Turkey)
SCTP	Social Cash Transfer Program (Malawi)
SIBEC	benefits management system (Brazil)
SICEC	Electronic Certification System of Co-responsibilities (Mexico)
SIIOP	Prospera's information system (Mexico)
SIM	subscriber identity module
SISBEN	Sistema de Selección de Beneficiarios para Programas Sociales (Colombia's social registry)
SLA	service level agreement
SMS	short message service (text)
SP	social protection
SSI	Social Security Institute
SSIOs	Social Security Institute Offices
SSO	Social Service Office
TCTR	total cost-transfer ratio
TCV	time, costs, and visits
TSA	treasury single account
UA	unemployment assistance
UBR	Unified Beneficiary Registry (Malawi's social registry)
UCA	Universal Child Allowance
UCA-PLUS	Universal Child Allowance-PLUS (includes supplement for vulnerable children)
UCT	unconditional cash transfer
UDB	Unified Database (Indonesia)
UI	unemployment insurance
UWOI	unemployed without insurance
VUP	Vision 2020 Umurenge Program (Rwanda)
WeT	Waseela-e-Taleem Program (Pakistan)

Chapter 1

Objectives, Approach, and Road Map

The World Bank's Social Protection Delivery Systems Global Solutions Group

Most countries possess social protection systems that seek to build equity, opportunity, and resilience for their people. They provide support through a wide range of benefits and services that redistribute income to reduce poverty and inequality, support investments in human capital, and help insure against shocks and various risks, including poverty, loss of earnings from old age, economic crisis, natural disaster, climate change, conflict, and forced displacement. Those interventions are typically grouped into three "pillars" of social protection: social assistance (noncontributory benefits and social services), social insurance (contribution-based benefits), and labor (both contributory and noncontributory benefits, as well as employment services).[1]

While much attention is paid to the design of social protection interventions, this Sourcebook addresses another key question: the "how." Specifically, how do countries deliver social protection benefits and services? How do the various elements of delivery systems come together to implement programs as they were intended to function? How do they do so effectively and efficiently? How do they ensure dynamic inclusion, so that people can access them when in need? How can delivery systems be leveraged to promote better coordination and integration—not only among social protection programs but also programs in other parts of government? How can they meet the needs of their intended populations and provide a better client experience? Social protection delivery systems address these crucial questions.

The objectives of this Sourcebook are to synthesize practical knowledge and experience on social protection delivery systems from countries around the world, with a focus on social and labor benefits and services. The aim is to delve into "how-tos" of delivery systems, taking social protection financing, policy, and program design as givens while acknowledging interactions and potential tensions between implementation and policy objectives. The primary audience of the Sourcebook is practitioners, World Bank staff, and other development partners working on social protection programs and systems in countries around the world.

Delivery systems constitute the operating environment for implementing social protection benefits and services. The delivery systems framework elaborates on the key elements of that operating environment. The framework is anchored in core implementation phases along the delivery chain. These phases are common to most social protection programs and include outreach, intake and registration, assessment of needs and conditions, enrollment (the determination of eligibility, decisions on enrollment and the benefit-service package, and onboarding), provision (payments of benefits and provision of services, depending on the intervention), and beneficiary operations management including their compliance, data updates, grievances, exits, and case outcomes. Key actors interact all along that delivery chain, including people (applicants and beneficiaries) and institutions (central and local). Those interactions are facilitated by communications, information systems, and technology, among other factors. This framework can apply to the delivery of one or many programs, and to the delivery of adaptive social protection.

The Sourcebook takes a broad view of social protection, covering a wide range of intended populations and interventions. Intended populations include demographic groups, poor or low-income families, unemployed workers, persons with disabilities, and individuals facing social risks (table 1.1). The Sourcebook covers many types of social protection interventions that governments provide to individuals, families, or households. This includes benefits such as categorical programs (child allowances and social pensions), conditional and unconditional cash transfers for the poor, unemployment assistance and insurance, and disability assistance and insurance.[2] It also covers various labor and social services, including employment services to help people find jobs, active labor market programs to help people boost their employability (including training services), social services (including social work services, social care services, and specialized services) as well as services provided as accompanying measures of unconditional cash transfers (mainly on human development and productive inclusion).[3]

The advantages of this broad perspective of social protection are numerous. First, it is instructive to see how different types of benefits and services are implemented at each phase of the delivery chain. Second, interventions are often bundled together in benefit-service packages. For example, activation packages may combine cash assistance with job-finding services and require beneficiaries to show that they are also taking responsibility for finding work. Social services may also be combined with benefits, either through tailored individualized action plans or as a bundled intervention with accompanying measures delivered to a cohort of beneficiaries. Third, this broader view fits with the trend we see in many countries to move toward integrated social protection systems. While many of the Sourcebook's examples of delivery systems relate to a specific intervention, others relate to many programs because countries are increasingly leveraging their delivery systems to serve as interoperable platforms for multiple programs. The commonalities in the framework highlight concrete opportunities for integrating delivery systems, which can also help with coordination and efficiency—and get away from the siloed approach of building parallel systems, one for each program. In fact, delivery systems are often used as platforms for adaptive social protection as well as for interventions beyond social protection, including health insurance, scholarships and preschool vouchers, utility subsidies, housing assistance, and other forms of support.

Nonetheless, even with this broad view of social protection, the Sourcebook does not cover all types of interventions equally. The types of interventions mainstreamed across the chapters is indicated in table 1.1. That said, the balance of examples favors social assistance over labor benefits and services, and both of those over disability and social services.[4] Moreover, while the Sourcebook does address delivery of some types of social insurance (primarily, unemployment and disability insurance), it does not include many examples of social insurance pensions for the elderly—and it does not discuss the contributions side of any types of social insurance since our focus is on delivery, not financing.[5]

The Sourcebook takes a global perspective on social protection delivery systems. The primary knowledge base has been accumulated largely through direct engagements in countries around the world (by the authors or their colleagues). Through those engagements, we have developed and tested the delivery systems framework in various countries in all regions of the world, and that

Table 1.1 Typology of Intended Population Groups and Social Protection Programs Used in This Sourcebook

Intended population groups		Types of programs (examples)
	Demographic groups • Children • Elderly	Categorical programs • Birth/child allowances • Old-age pensions
	Socioeconomic status • Low-income families • Poor families	Poverty-targeted programs • Unconditional cash transfers such as guaranteed minimum income or other forms of cash assistance • Conditional cash transfers • Public works programs • Beyond social protection programs: health insurance subsidies, scholarships, housing benefits
	Labor force status • Unemployed • Discouraged/inactive • Job-seekers	Labor benefits and services • Unemployment insurance and assistance benefits • Employment services to help people find jobs: self-service, job search assistance, and so on • Active labor market programs to help people improve employability: training, start-up support, and so on
	Persons with disabilities • Disabled persons (moderate versus severe, short-term versus long-term, medical impairments versus functional limitations)	Disability benefits and services • Disability insurance and assistance benefits • Disability services, such as casework services, care services, specialized services
	Individuals facing social risks • Children • Youth • Adults • Elderly	Social services • Social work services: information and awareness; assessment and referrals; counseling and mediation • Social care services: home-based, community-based, institutional • Specialized and preventive services

Source: Original table for this publication.

framework has proved to be robust. We complement that direct knowledge base with existing literature, and each chapter includes a bibliography specific to that topic for handy reference. We deliberately sought to include examples from every region. Countries covered in the various chapters are listed below; those in bold are discussed in more depth in at least one chapter:

- **Africa: Benin**, **Burkina Faso**, the **Republic of Congo**, **Côte d'Ivoire**, Ethiopia, **Ghana**, **Kenya**, Madagascar, **Malawi**, Mali, Mauritius, Niger, **Nigeria**, Rwanda, Senegal, Sierra Leone, South Africa, South Sudan, **Tanzania**, Uganda, **Zambia**
- **East Asia and the Pacific:** China, **Indonesia**, Republic of Korea, **the Philippines**, Singapore, Thailand, Vietnam
- **Europe and Central Asia: Albania**, Armenia, Austria, **Bulgaria**, Croatia, **Denmark**, **Estonia**, **Finland**, France, Georgia, **Germany**, **Greece**, **Ireland**, **Italy**, Kosovo, the Kyrgyz Republic, Lithuania, **Moldova,** Mongolia, the Netherlands, **North Macedonia, Norway**, Portugal, Romania, the Russian Federation, **Serbia**, the Slovak Republic, Slovenia, Spain, Sweden, Switzerland, Tajikistan, **Turkey**, the **United Kingdom**, Uzbekistan
- **Latin America and the Caribbean:** Argentina, **Brazil**, **Chile**, **Colombia**, **Costa Rica**, the Dominican Republic, Honduras, **Jamaica**, **Mexico**, **Nicaragua**, **Peru**

- **Middle East and North Africa:** Bahrain, Djibouti, the **Arab Republic of Egypt**, the Islamic Republic of Iran, **Iraq**, Jordan, Kuwait, Lebanon, Morocco, Tunisia, West Bank and Gaza, the **Republic of Yemen**
- **South Asia: Bangladesh**, **India**, **Pakistan**, Sri Lanka
- **Other Organisation for Economic Co-operation and Development (OECD) countries: Australia**, **Canada**, New Zealand, the **United States**, other country mentions

In addition to regional diversity, we sought to include examples from lower-income countries, middle-income countries, higher-income countries and some from specific contexts, such as countries experiencing fragility, conflict, and violence.

The Sourcebook covers various operating models. In addition to taking perspectives on social protection programs and using diverse country examples, the Sourcebook considers a variety of operating models. While the delivery systems framework is common among all social protection interventions, we see variations in operating models across countries and programs. We discuss two pairs of variations throughout the Sourcebook:

- ***Delivery systems for one or many programs.*** Some operating systems are developed to deliver one program (single-program systems). However, countries typically offer multiple programs, not just one. In a growing number of countries, multiple programs may use a common delivery system or an interoperable platform to support certain functions (such as social registries).
- ***On-demand or administrator-driven models.*** An important distinction is whether the process of intake and registration is carried out on-demand or is administrator-driven. Three key features distinguish between these operating models: whether the process is initiated by people (on-demand) or by administrators (administrator-driven); whether people apply as individuals (on-demand) or whether they are registered as a group (administrator-driven); and whether the timing is adapted to people who can apply whenever they choose (on-demand), or whether they must follow a group calendar (administrator-driven). These distinct operating models affect not only intake and registration but influence the entire delivery chain.

These pairs of operating models illustrate two key challenges: coordination and inclusion. Those are two of the most common challenges facing social protection systems.

- ***The challenge of coordination.*** The distinction between creating separate delivery systems for each program or integrating many programs within a delivery system relates to the challenge of coordinating social protection efforts. Fragmentation can occur when numerous programs are implemented using their own program-specific delivery systems. It can be costly and inefficient for people to navigate each program separately, providing the same information and documentation over and over, and waiting in long lines at different offices. It can also be inefficient for administrators because it can result in duplications or gaps in coverage, overlapping processes, wasted resources, and an inability to keep track of which clients have received which services or how social protection money is spent. Many countries are integrating various aspects of delivery systems to avoid fragmentation and to promote synergies across programs. Such integration requires a great degree of coordination between institutions, which can be a challenge.
- ***The challenge of dynamic inclusion.*** Dynamic inclusion—the principle that anyone who needs assistance can access it at any time—is a core tenet of social protection. Regarding delivery systems, this raises the issue of whether they are static or dynamic, particularly their intake and registration phase. On-demand systems are more amenable to dynamic inclusion because people can apply or update their information at any time. In contrast, the administrator-driven approach is typically more static, with large groups of people registered only every few years or in response to covariate shocks, such as a natural disaster in a specific region. Another aspect of dynamic inclusion is portability of benefits, which is typically more feasible with on-demand approaches than administrator-driven approaches.

The task for this Sourcebook is somewhat daunting, given that it seeks to cover a diverse array of social protection programs in countries and regions around the world as well as various operating models and challenges. As such, the Sourcebook aims to cover the basic and intermediate principles, concepts, and practical steps of delivery systems, while selectively diving deeper into more advanced topics. There are many other topics that could be included that are not systematically covered here, simply because the scope of the book is already large. Some examples include humanitarian assistance for refugees and asylum seekers, and specialized programs targeted to very specific subgroups of a population. In addition, we do not specifically address the delivery of benefits and services in contexts of fragility, conflict, or violence. Nonetheless, we encourage readers with specialized interventions or other target groups to consider the likelihood that the delivery systems framework could be adapted to cover those programs and to explore how the lessons presented in this book might be relevant.

Moreover, the Sourcebook is not meant to be prescriptive. While we glean lessons from good practices and from the challenges facing countries around the world, we refrain from making prescriptive recommendations for the most part. Rather, the delivery systems framework is a practical way to organize discussion about implementation of social protection programs.

Following this introductory chapter, chapter 2 presents a conceptual overview of the delivery systems framework, including implementation phases, key actors (people and institutions), and enabling factors (communications, information systems and technology). Chapter 2 also discusses pairs of distinct operating models and their relation to the dual challenges of coordination and inclusion. Finally, it illustrates the whole delivery chain end-to-end, using a hypothetical composite example. In doing so, the chapter illustrates some fundamental principles to keep in mind for social protection delivery systems. They are not prescriptive conclusions but rather reflections that can help encourage a delivery systems mindset.

Subsequent chapters of the Sourcebook are organized around the delivery chain, which anchors the delivery systems framework (figure 1.1).

Figure 1.1 Anchoring the Chapters of the Sourcebook around the Social Protection Delivery Chain

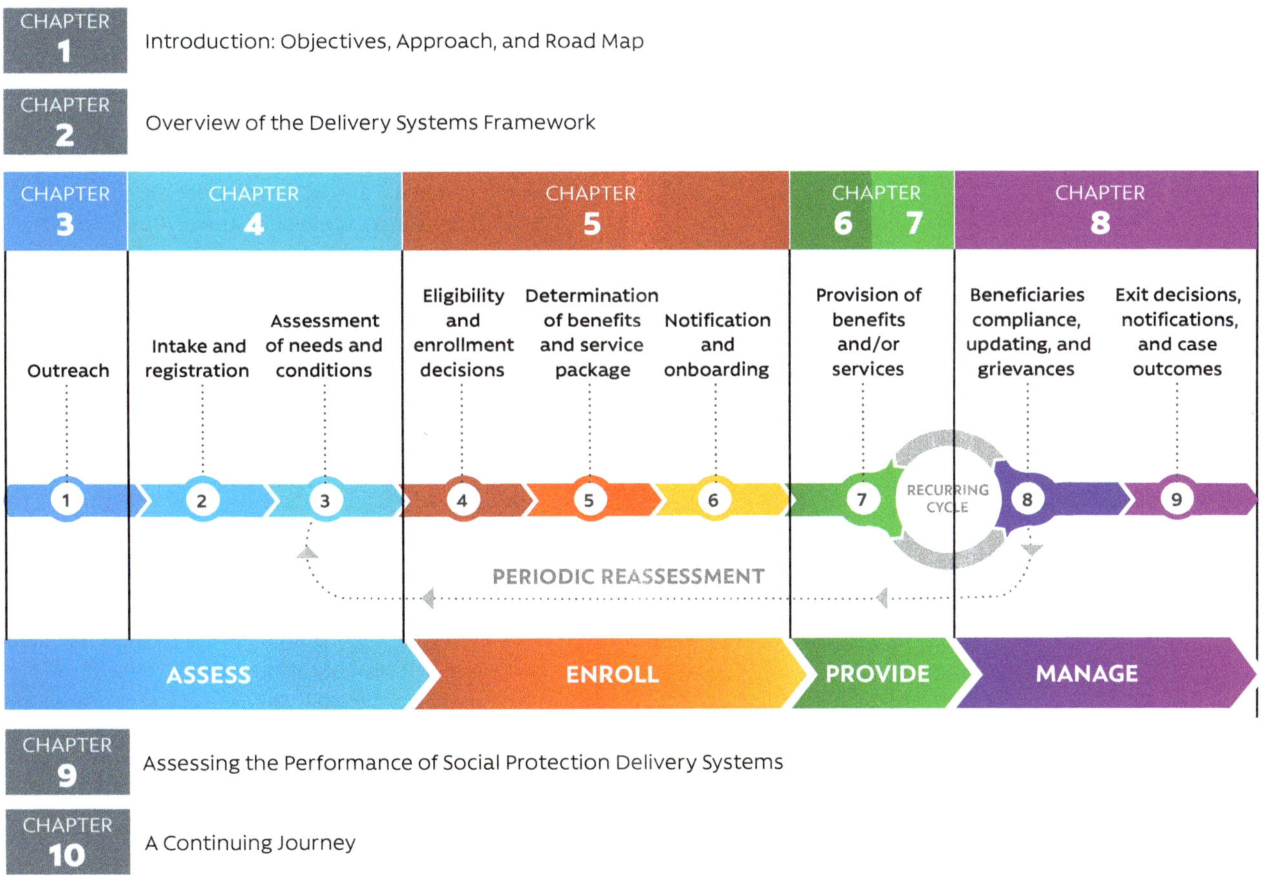

Source: Original figure for this publication.

- Chapter 3 reviews outreach, which is crucial but often neglected.
- Chapter 4 covers intake, registration, and the assessment of needs and conditions.
- Chapter 5 presents the enrollment phases, which include determining eligibility, making decisions about enrollment, choosing what combination of benefits and services to offer, notifying applicants, and onboarding beneficiaries. The next two chapters turn to the provision phases of the delivery chain.
- Chapter 6 covers the provision of benefits (social protection [SP] government to person [G2P] payments), while chapter 7 covers the provision of services, with a focus on integrated service models.
- Chapter 8 turns to the broad topic of beneficiary operations management including (1) beneficiary data management (including exit decisions); (2) monitoring of education and health conditionalities for conditional cash transfer programs; (3) monitoring of labor-related conditionalities such as job search requirements for activation packages; (4) grievance redress mechanisms; and (5) error, fraud, and corruption monitoring.
- Chapter 9 ties these topics together to cover performance measurement, including performance indicators along the delivery chain and a typology of tools that can be used to assess delivery systems.
- Finally, chapter 10 looks ahead to the future agenda for delivery systems.

Finally, the Sourcebook does not have to be read sequentially cover to cover. True, the chapters are tightly organized around the delivery systems framework, and each of the delivery chain chapters feeds into the next. However, as long as readers understand the framework, as presented in chapter 2, they can opt to read topics of interest in various chapters. In fact, this Sourcebook was written precisely because of the many requests we have received over the years for specific information on the "how-tos" presented in these chapters. We hope that the Sourcebook provides a useful reference on the many topics covered here.

Notes

1. In this Sourcebook, social protection is defined as systems, policies, and programs that help individuals and societies manage risk and volatility and protect them from poverty and destitution—through instruments that improve resilience, equity, and opportunity. See the World Bank's *Social Protection and Labor Strategy 2012–2022* report (World Bank 2012). The report focuses on social and labor benefits and services, including some types of social insurance (such as unemployment and disability insurance).
2. Benefits are defined as "something tangible that is given by social protection programs to individuals, families, or households." While this Sourcebook covers provision of cash benefits (chapter 6) and services (chapter 7), we do not delve deep into the provision of in-kind benefits. The other phases of the delivery chain covered in chapters 3, 4, 5, and 8 would all pertain to in-kind benefits, but it is beyond the scope of the Sourcebook to cover the actual provision of in-kind benefits (which, in addition to the delivery chain, also include an element of procurement of goods). Moreover, food-related benefits have recently been covered extensively in Alderman, Gentilini, and Yemtsov (2018). Similarly, while we touch upon public works programs in the Sourcebook, we do not cover the procurement aspect (of works projects); the topic has been treated extensively in Subbarao et al. (2013).
3. Services are defined as intangible acts, activities, or works provided to, or with the participation of, beneficiaries as a contribution to their well-being (such as to reduce poverty, provide opportunities, enhance employability, and reduce social risks).
4. The ample availability of examples in social assistance reflects the many country engagements that the World Bank's Social Protection and Jobs Global Practice has had in social assistance, both at present and over the past 20–30 years.
5. From a delivery systems perspective, the basic phases for delivering social insurance cash benefits are similar to those for other types of cash transfers. As discussed in chapters 4 and 5, with social insurance, contributions history is included in the assessment of needs and conditions used to determine eligibility and calculate benefit amounts. While we do cover some types of social insurance (such as unemployment and disability insurance), we do not get into the topic of social insurance pensions for the elderly for two reasons: (1) their tight link with contribution histories over long periods of time (working life) make it harder to disentangle contributions and financing aspects, which are beyond the scope of this Sourcebook; and (2) the World Bank and International Social Security Association are currently collaborating on a guidance note and toolkit on the administration of social insurance schemes (covering both financing and delivery) and we do not want to duplicate

those efforts (see "Social Insurance Administrative Diagnostic (SIAD): Guidance Note" [Sluchynsky 2019]). Where there are overlaps in topics (e.g., for grievance redress, detection of errors and fraud, and outreach and communications), we have largely aligned this delivery systems Sourcebook with the 2019 guidance note.

Bibliography

Alderman, Harold, Ugo Gentilini, and Ruslan Yemtsov, eds. 2018. *The 1.5 Billion People Question: Food, Vouchers, or Cash Transfers?* Washington, DC: World Bank.

Grosh, Margaret, Carlo del Ninno, Emil Tesliuc, and Azedine Ouerghi. 2008. *For Protection and Promotion: The Design and Implementation of Effective Safety Nets*. Washington, DC: World Bank.

Leite, Phillippe, Tina George, Changqing Sun, Theresa Jones, and Kathy Lindert. 2017. "Social Registries for Social Assistance and Beyond: A Guidance Note and Assessment Tool." Social Protection and Labor Discussion Paper 1704, World Bank, Washington, DC. http://documents.worldbank.org/curated/en/698441502095248081/Social-registries-for-social-assistance-and-beyond-a-guidance-note-and-assessment-tool.

Sluchynsky, Oleksiy. 2019. "Social Insurance Administrative Diagnostic (SIAD): Guidance Note." World Bank, Washington, DC; International Social Security Association, Geneva, Switzerland.

Subbarao, Kalanidhi, Carlo del Ninno, Colin Andrews, and Claudia Rodríguez-Alas. 2013. *Public Works as a Safety Net: Design, Evidence, and Implementation*. Directions in Development Series. Washington, DC: World Bank.

World Bank. 2012. *Resilience, Equity, and Opportunity*. Washington, DC: World Bank. https://openknowledge.worldbank.org/handle/10986/12648.

World Bank and ILO (International Labour Organization). 2016. "A Shared Mission for Universal Social Protection: Concept Note." World Bank, Washington, DC; ILO, Geneva, Switzerland.

Chapter 2

Overview of the Delivery Systems Framework

Kathy Lindert, Tina George Karippacheril, Kenichi Nishikawa Chávez, and Inés Rodríguez Caillava

With contributions from Sara Giannozzi, Surat Nsour, Vasumathi Anandan, Anita Mittal, and Yasuhiko Matsuda

This chapter provides an overview of the delivery systems framework for social protection programs. The framework was developed through direct experiences in diverse countries around the world. This overview presents principles and concepts, with some brief examples to illustrate specific points. More richly detailed examples of practices in specific countries are shared in subsequent chapters that examine the nuts and bolts of each of the implementation phases along the delivery chain.

The first section of this chapter defines the general concept and core elements of social protection delivery systems. This includes (1) the implementation phases of the delivery chain; (2) the key actors that interact along that delivery chain (institutions and people); and (3) the enabling factors that facilitate those interactions: communications, information systems, and technology.

The chapter's second section highlights two common challenges facing social protection delivery systems: the challenge of coordination and the challenge of inclusion. Countries have adapted different operating models in response to these dual challenges. Two pairs of contrasting models discussed in this chapter—and throughout the Sourcebook—include (1) whether delivery systems are developed separately for each program or whether multiple programs operate using an integrated delivery system (or integrated aspects of parts of the system), which relates to the challenge of coordination; and (2) whether operational models are built around on-demand systems or are administrator-driven. Although these distinctions most strongly influence intake and registration, they affect delivery systems all along the delivery chain.

The third section of the chapter presents a hypothetical example based on a composite of real cases. The example serves multiple objectives:

- It illustrates the framework and the phases of the delivery chain for both benefits and services, using an example of unemployment assistance that includes activation requirements and employment services. This end-to-end perspective is valuable because subsequent chapters will delve more deeply into the parts of the delivery chain.

- It demonstrates how these delivery systems can be used as integrative platforms to coordinate programs outside social protection (such as health insurance subsidies and social energy tariffs).
- It illustrates the value of using process maps, journey maps, performance management indicators, and other diagnostic tools to assess the effectiveness and efficiency of delivery systems from the perspectives of both administrators and clients.
- It touches on many of the overarching messages of this Sourcebook; these are further delineated in the fourth section of this chapter.

2.1 CONCEPTS AND CORE ELEMENTS OF THE DELIVERY SYSTEMS FRAMEWORK

While much attention is paid to the design of social protection interventions, this Sourcebook addresses another key question: How? Specifically, how do countries deliver social protection benefits and services? How do the various elements of delivery systems come together to implement programs as they were intended to function? How do they do so effectively and efficiently? How do they ensure dynamic inclusion, such that people can access them when in need? How can delivery systems be leveraged to promote better coordination and integration—not only within social protection but also in other areas? How can they meet the needs of their intended populations and provide a better client experience? Social protection delivery systems address these crucial questions.

What are delivery systems? The short answer is that delivery systems are implementation. The longer answer: delivery systems are the operating environment for implementing social protection benefits and services. That operating environment includes the implementation phases of the delivery chain, the main actors, and enabling factors. Another important component of the delivery systems framework is performance. Assessing the performance of delivery systems is essential to ensure that delivery systems contribute to an effective and efficient delivery of benefits and services. (For a detailed discussion on performance, see chapter 9.)

The Delivery Chain as the Anchor for the Framework

Virtually all social protection programs pass through similar implementation phases along the delivery chain. In developing the delivery systems framework, we reviewed how a broad spectrum of social protection programs are implemented in diverse contexts, including numerous types of social and labor benefits and services (see table 1.1 in chapter 1). Although benefits and services seem so different, virtually all were implemented in similar ways (figure 2.1). Delivery systems for all benefits and services

- need some sort of ***outreach*** to promote awareness and understanding among the intended population.
- involve some form of ***intake and registration***, to gather information on people's characteristics, needs, and conditions.
- undertake some type of ***assessment*** to profile those characteristics, needs, and conditions.
- use those profiles to determine potential ***eligibility***, assign the appropriate level of ***benefits and services***, take ***enrollment decisions***, and ***notify and onboard*** beneficiaries.
- ***provide*** enrolled beneficiaries with the intervention, which may involve ***payment of cash benefits*** and/or the ***provision of services***, which can vary depending on the nature of the specific service.
- ***manage*** data on beneficiaries to ensure that their information is accurate and up to date and that they comply with any co-responsibilities, grievances, and appeals, as well as reassessments and/or beneficiaries exiting the program(s).

Although these implementation phases are common among social protection delivery systems, the intensity and order of each phase may vary according to program specifics. Some phases may be more intensive, depending on the nature of the program. For example, services may be monitored more intensively than benefits, and monitoring of conditional cash transfers may be more complex than monitoring of unconditional cash transfers. Some programs may switch the

Figure 2.1 The Social Protection Delivery Chain

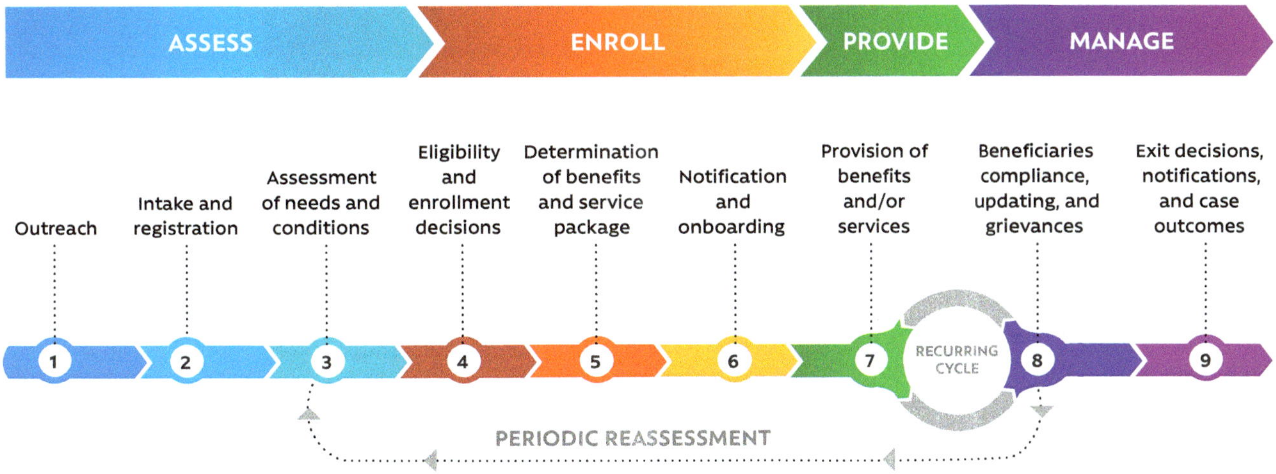

Source: Original figure for this publication.

order of some phases, combine some phases, or carry them out virtually simultaneously. For example, with social services, a caseworker may assess the individual for social risks during the intake interview. Similarly, for many programs, the determination of eligibility and the determination of the appropriate package of benefits and services may occur in a single step (for example, with benefit menus that are calculated depending on the applicant's income in relation to eligibility thresholds). In addition, the specific processes within each phase will vary by program type, the nature of institutional arrangements, and the technology and information systems that are available. Yet even when specific processes differ, social protection programs share common implementation phases.

The commonality of these phases along the delivery chain provides the functional anchor for the delivery systems framework. Clarity around these core functions serves as an organizing framework. It can also help avoid some of the pitfalls we commonly see with misused terminology (box 2.1). Finally, the harmonization of key functions across programs could provide the basis for an integrated delivery model. An awareness of these commonalities can help prevent fragmentation of social delivery systems and improve effectiveness and efficiency, which comes with coordination of administration and synergies in bundling interventions.

In tracing the delivery chain, the outputs of each implementation phase are inputs to the next. While the main chapters of this Sourcebook are devoted to individual phases of the delivery chain, it is helpful to recognize the linkages across those phases. Figure 2.2 shows the links between the phases with inputs and outputs color-coded to represent their location in the delivery chain.[1]

- ***Outreach (chapter 3).*** Most programs kick off with outreach, which typically involves communication and interaction to build awareness, inform people (the intended population and vulnerable groups) about the program(s), and encourage the intended population to engage and provide their information for potential inclusion. The key inputs to outreach include program information, core messages, and communications and "active search" tools. The core outputs of outreach would then be that the intended populations and vulnerable groups are informed and understand the interventions, and are willing to engage, apply, and provide information. That output becomes input in the next phase of the delivery chain.
- ***Intake and registration (chapter 4).*** The inputs to intake and registration are the intended population and vulnerable groups who were reached and informed during the outreach phase and would be willing to engage and provide information. Another source of input might be information from other administrative systems. The outputs of this phase would then include complete, validated, and verified information on those who have registered. Those outputs feed into the next phase of the delivery chain.

Box 2.1 Clarifying Some Commonly Misused Terms: Implementation and People along the Social Protection Delivery Chain

The development community uses a variety of terms to describe people and implementation phases along the social protection delivery chain, which unfortunately can cause confusion. Some examples of terminology that often can take on multiple or confusing meanings include the following:

- **"Beneficiaries" versus "registrants."** We often see practitioners referring to registrants as "beneficiaries," referring to people in social registries as "beneficiaries," or using the term "identification of beneficiaries" (as described below). Not all registrants will become beneficiaries. This miscommunication may even create a liability for programs because registrants may think they are beneficiaries, even though in the early phases of the delivery chain, people are not beneficiaries and there is no guarantee that they will become beneficiaries.[a]
- **"Identification of beneficiaries."** Development practitioners and program administrators often refer to the combined phases of intake and registration, assessment of needs and conditions, and determination of eligibility as the "identification of (potential) beneficiaries." That terminology can be convenient as shorthand, but it is important to avoid any confusion around the word "identification" (which could be misconstrued as "proof of identification," as in foundational or functional IDs). In addition, using the term "beneficiaries" to refer to applicants or registrants can hinder communication, as discussed above.
- **"Targeting."** Some practitioners refer to those same upstream phases as "targeting" (or to the social registry systems that support them as "targeting systems"). They also use the term "target criteria" to refer to eligibility criteria. In general, we try to avoid using the term "targeting" to refer to implementation for several reasons: (1) not all social protection benefits and services are "targeted," and even universal programs pass through similar phases along the delivery chain; (2) "targeting" can sound rather fierce to a layperson (as in, "we are here to target you for program x" versus "we are here to register you for potential inclusion in program x"); and (3) the term "targeting" is used to describe many concepts and its overuse can be confusing.[b] We do occasionally use the terms "target group" (to mean intended population) and "targeting mechanisms," as those are both design concepts that we take as given. Finally, we also use the terms "targeting accuracy" or "targeting outcomes" as those are evaluation concepts.
- **"Registration" versus "enrollment."** Some practitioners also interchange the terms "registration" and "enrollment." This is confusing for some audiences because all applicants register but only beneficiaries enroll in a program.
- **"Case management."** The term "case management" is particularly polemic as it is used differently by various professions (for example, by social workers, health care workers, and IT specialists).[c] Further, some may use the term "case management" to mean what we call the " beneficiary operations management" stage of the delivery chain. Some practitioners use the term to mean social work (covering awareness, intermediation, referrals, and counseling). Others use the term to refer to an integrated approach to managing clients all along the delivery chain (through the entire "life of the case," as some practitioners call it). To avoid confusion, we avoid the term.
- **"Service delivery" versus "delivery systems."** There is also a tendency for people to use the term "service delivery" to mean delivery systems. This stems from the common use of the term "service delivery indicators" in human development, or "public services" in governance. We avoid using "service delivery" to mean delivery systems for various reasons, including: (1) social protection delivers both benefits and services (as "products")—not just services; and (2) the "systems" part of delivery systems matters, with recognition of the simultaneous interaction of many moving parts in this operating environment for implementing social protection.
- **"MIS," or "management information system."** The term "MIS" has different definitions in the business community, the international development community, and the IT community. In the business world, "management information system" (MIS) is an academic discipline or a course of study that focuses on the art of managing information systems effectively, including people, organizations

continued

Box 2.1 *(continued)*

and technology. In the international development and nongovernmental organization communities, MIS is a catch-all term that has been used to refer to systems that manage information in specific sectoral contexts. For example, the Human Resource MIS, Education MIS, Health MIS. In social protection, development practitioners often use the term MIS to refer to systems (or software applications) that manage information for the functioning of registration and eligibility systems—or for the operation of specific programs to deliver benefits and services (e.g., payments transactions, conditionalities monitoring, etc.) Meanwhile, in the IT world, the definition of MIS is an information system that produces reports that management need for planning and control, by processing information captured by transaction processing systems, stored in databases. MIS is a dated turn of phrase in IT parlance. Contemporary terminology for information systems that produce reports and dashboards include terms such as "business intelligence" and "analytics." In contemporary IT terminology, the term MIS as it was intended in the development community refers to information systems; in particular, software applications and database management systems. Given the confusion around the term, we prefer to avoid using the term MIS in this book. Wherever possible, we refer to information systems, software applications, and database management systems as defined in IT parlance. If more specificity is needed to identify an information system, we are more explicit, such as "beneficiary operations management system" or "social registry" platform.

To minimize the confusion that occurs when people understand the same word differently, this Sourcebook seeks to adopt a clear and consistent terminology. The glossary for this book explains how particular terms are used. For the phases along the delivery chain, we anchor the terminology in the core functions that are being implemented. At the same time, we recognize that the terminology used here may need to be adapted for use in specific settings. For example, in some countries, the term "screening" may be used instead of "assessment of needs and conditions," while other countries may use the term for an initial screening (or prescreening) that will be followed by a more in-depth assessment (such as those sometimes conducted for a subset of applicants). Another example: while the term "social registries" is a common label for information systems that support outreach, intake and registration, and the assessment of needs and conditions, some countries may not use the term at all, instead referring to "targeting systems," "automated registration and eligibility systems," etc. While recognizing that individual users may need to adapt the terms used here, this book strives for consistent terminology within these pages.

a. For example, some practitioners use the term "beneficiary identification" to refer to the processes of outreach, intake and registration, assessment of needs and conditions, and eligibility and enrollment. Since we do not know the status of people before they apply, are assessed, and deemed eligible, we cannot call intended populations or applicants "beneficiaries." At the very least, that shorthand should be stated as "identification of potential beneficiaries," but that still runs the risk of implying people would become beneficiaries (and the term "identification" is also confusing). Along the same lines, some practitioners confuse the terms "social registries" and "beneficiary registries."

b. For example, there are targeting mechanisms (such as geographic, categorical, socioeconomic, etc.); target groups (intended populations); target criteria (eligibility criteria); the act of "targeting" (as a verb) to mean implementation (which we try to avoid as noted above); "targeting systems" to mean information systems (like social registries) that support the upstream phases of outreach, intake and registration, and assessment of needs and conditions; and targeting outcomes (such as coverage, absolute and relative incidence, and errors of inclusion and exclusion).

c. An example of the confusion around the term case management is illustrated in the following text: "There is no one standardized or nationally recognized and widely accepted definition of case management. An Internet search for the definition of the term case management will result in thousands of references . . . Despite the large search outcome, experts would agree that there are no more than twenty or so definitions of case management [that are] considered appropriate. These definitions are available in peer-reviewed professional case management literature or on websites of case management (or case management-related) organizations, societies, and agencies." https://www.cmbodyofknowledge.com/content/introduction-case-management-body-knowledge.

Figure 2.2 Inputs and Outputs along the Social Protection Delivery Chain

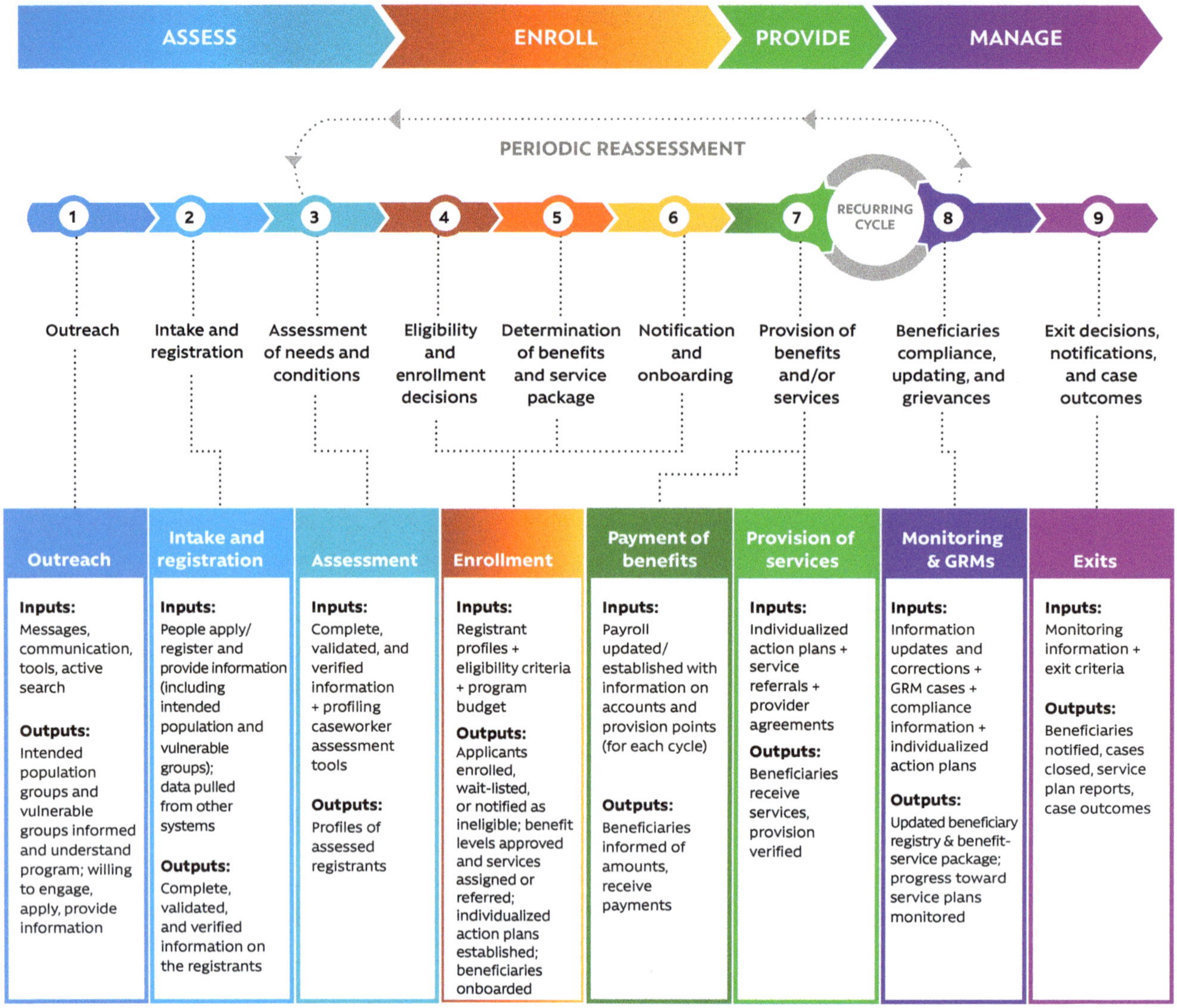

Source: Original figure for this publication.
Note: GRM = grievance redress mechanism.

- ***Assessment of needs and conditions (chapter 4).*** In addition to verified information, various assessment tools would constitute inputs to the assessment of needs and conditions. The outputs of this phase are the profiles of assessed registrants.
- ***Eligibility and enrollment (chapter 5).*** Registrants' profiles along with program-specific eligibility criteria are the inputs to the determination of eligibility. Enrollment decisions are further informed by available budget, as well as protocols for wait-listing eligible individuals if there are insufficient slots due to capacity or budget constraints. Registrants' profiles also inform ***decisions on the benefit/service package***, according to program rules (such as benefit menus) and caseworkers' discretion (to assign or refer eligible registrants to appropriate services). Applicants are ***notified*** of their status (eligible or ineligible and enrolled or wait-listed), and enrolled beneficiaries are ***onboarded***, including an explanation of rules, activities, expectations, and the rights and responsibilities of beneficiaries. Caseworkers also discuss individualized action plans (IAPs) with beneficiaries at this stage, if they are used. Additional information may be gathered during onboarding as needed (such as bank account information for payments). After beneficiaries are notified and onboarded, the output of enrollment is information about the specific beneficiaries (or a cohort of beneficiaries if being processed

as a group) that is added to the beneficiary operations management system, with associated information on benefits and services.

- ***Provision of benefits: Government-to-person (G2P) payments (chapter 6).*** The beneficiary operations management system provides input data to the payroll for provision of benefits. Other inputs include information on registrants' bank account, mobile money, digital wallet, or payment coordinates. For beneficiaries who are already in the program, additional inputs to the payroll for subsequent implementation cycles come from the beneficiary operations management stage, including any adjustments to beneficiary status or amounts. Additionally, other inputs come from reconciliation of payments from the last cycle. The outputs of the payments phase would then be the release of funds and the disbursement of benefits to beneficiaries for the current implementation cycle. This phase would then feed into the beneficiary operations management stage (chapter 8) as part of the recurring cycle of implementation.
- ***Provision of services (chapter 7).*** The main inputs to the provision of services are information on beneficiaries, IAPs, service referrals, and agreements with service providers (if service provision is outsourced). Inputs may also come from the beneficiary operations management stage of the previous implementation cycle, including any updates to the IAPs, service package, beneficiary status, or other changes. The primary output is verification that services are being provided. This phase would feed into the beneficiary operations management stage (chapter 8) as part of the recurring cycle of implementation. The actual provision of services is the most idiosyncratic of all phases along the delivery chain. This is because the "products" being provided tend to be quite specialized (labor and social services) and the modalities for provision vary significantly (e.g., public provision, private provision by contracted firms, or provision by partner foundations).
- ***Beneficiary operations management (chapter 8).*** Key inputs to beneficiary operations management are (1) the verified provision of benefits (from chapter 6) and services (from chapter 7), as well as (2) the outputs from the enrollment phase for newly added beneficiaries (from chapter 5). Key activities in the beneficiary operations management stage include updating and correcting information on beneficiaries and their benefit-service packages; monitoring any conditions imposed on beneficiaries related to education, health, or labor-related activities (depending on the specific program); and filing, investigating, and resolving grievance and appeals cases. The overall outputs of this phase are an updated beneficiary operations management system (including changes in information, beneficiary status as a result of reassessment, and decisions on exit), changes in the benefit-service packages, decisions on any penalties or sanctions for noncompliance with conditions, and resolution of grievances (in some cases leading to the addition of new beneficiaries or changes in benefit/service packages). This phase feeds back to the provision of benefits (chapter 6) and the provision of services (chapter 7).

Main Actors: People and Institutions

People

People are core actors in delivery systems. Ultimately, they are the most important element of social protection programs. But "they" are not easily described. In human terms, they may be individuals, families, or households. They may be young or old; male, female, or other gender-identifying. They may be poor, nonpoor, employed, unemployed, or inactive. They may be disabled or vulnerable to social risks. They may have faced a health or economic shock or catastrophic event, either on their own or as part of a group. They may be living in remote areas, dense urban slums, or areas plagued by fragility, conflict, and violence. Or they may have migrated from another country or region, either voluntarily or due to displacement. As discussed in chapter 1, this Sourcebook focuses on demographic groups (such as children or the elderly), poor or low-income people (individuals, families, or households), unemployed workers, persons with disabilities, and individuals facing social risks (see table 1.1).

Finding the right technical term to describe "people" once they are part of the social protection delivery system is a challenge. We confront the terminology challenge in three ways (and the glossary provides definitions of these and other terms used throughout the Sourcebook):

- ***The first challenge is that people's operational status changes throughout the delivery chain.*** That transition is depicted in figure 2.3. In the outreach phase, they are typically referred to as the "intended population." During intake and registration and the assessment of needs and conditions, people are technically either "applicants or registrants," depending on the type of operating model and whether people actively apply for programs via on-demand systems or whether they are registered during a mass registration wave with administrator-driven approaches. For simplicity, we refer to both applicants and registrants as "registrants" throughout the Sourcebook (unless the discussion is about only an on-demand system, in which case we also use applicants). Once eligibility is established and registrants are enrolled in a program, they become "beneficiaries." (See box 2.1 for the confusion that can arise with the misuse of the terms "registrants" and "beneficiaries.")
- ***Second, the distinction between the terms "assistance unit" and "designated recipient" is important.*** The assistance unit can be an individual, a family, or a household, depending on the focus of an intervention. When it comes to the designated recipient, in some instances an individual other than the intended beneficiary may be the designated recipient (such as a parent or guardian who collects a child allowance on behalf of a child). In other cases, even when the assistance unit is the family or household, an individual beneficiary within the household is selected as the designated recipient (the person who collects the benefits on behalf of the family).

Figure 2.3 Population Reference Groups along the Social Protection Delivery Chain

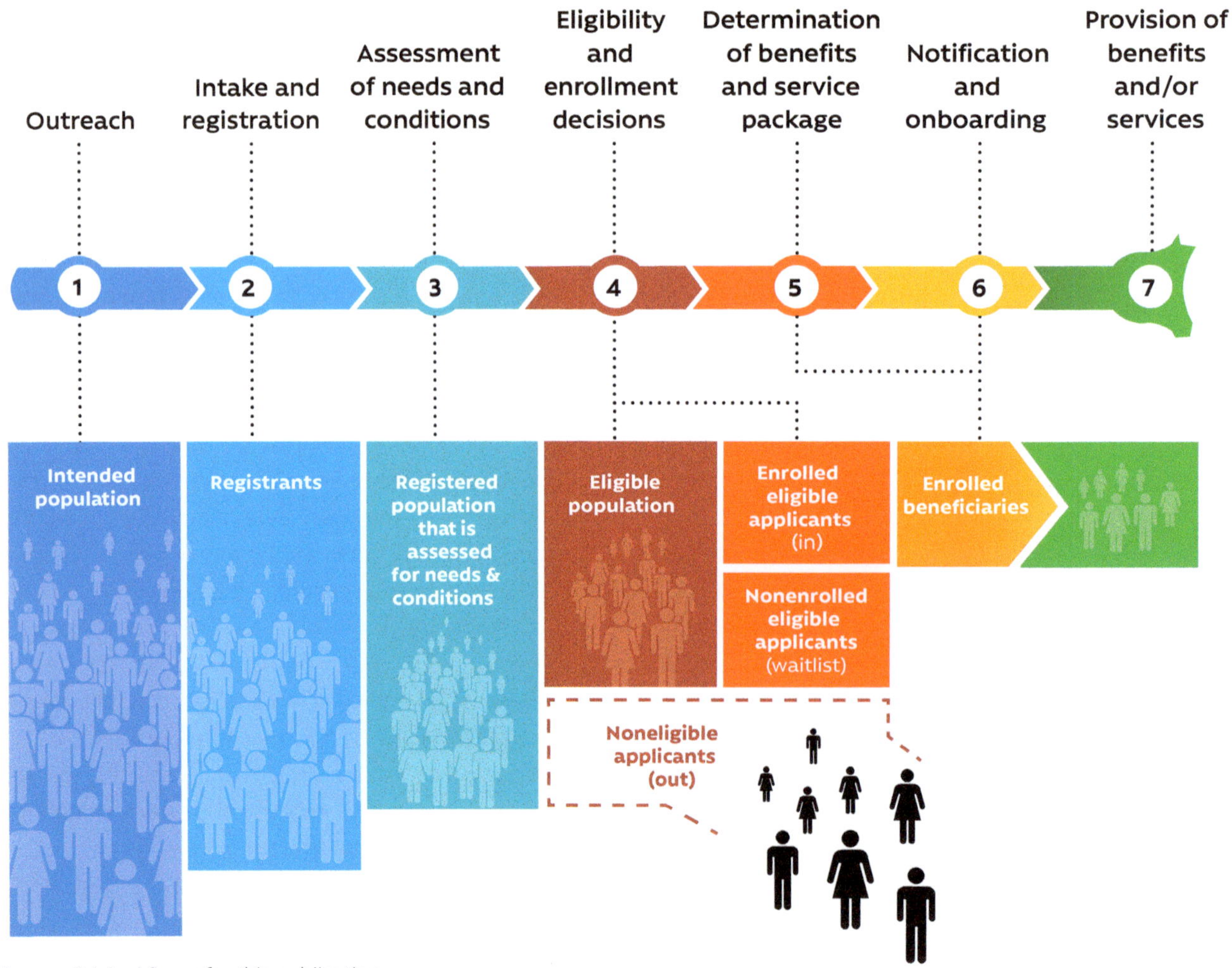

Source: Original figure for this publication.

- ***Third, there is no universal technical term that encompasses all of the following people: intended population, applicants, registrants, beneficiaries, individuals, families, households, assistance units, and designated recipients.*** In some countries, they are all referred to as "clients," in the sense that the programs seek to serve them. Other countries use the term "customers," again with a service-oriented intention. However, some practitioners object to the terms "clients" or "customers" because those terms may imply that people have to pay for public benefits or services. The term "citizens," which derives from the public administration concept of "citizen service" is similarly fraught because it could be misinterpreted to imply citizenship or legal residency is necessary to receive benefits or services. In this Sourcebook, we will use the term "people" as much as possible or refer to them in the appropriate technical categories (intended population, applicants, registrants, beneficiaries, individuals, families, households, assistance units, or designated recipients). In certain instances, this Sourcebook may use the term "client," for example with "client interface" (since "people interface" could imply that program administrators or staff are not people).

Institutions: Central, Local, and Providers

Social protection programs typically deliver a variety of benefits and services to improve and manage the welfare of poor and vulnerable individuals and families. Benefits and services are provided by different institutions, which can include government agencies, nongovernmental organizations, foundations, and/or private providers such as payment agents. These can cut across administrative levels (central, subnational, local) and sectors, since social protection programs often involve agencies and partners in other sectors.

There is no blueprint for the set of institutional arrangements supporting social protection delivery systems.[2] Usually, many actors are involved, and the definition of roles and responsibilities is context-specific. Moreover, institutional arrangements are dynamic. The starting point matters, and that starting point is typically not a blank slate. In addition, systems and arrangements tend to evolve, and the factors that affect them may be hard to control. Political economy shapes choices, as does the availability of financial, physical, and human resources, at least in the short run. In the long run, it is possible to reduce these constraints by investing in capacity-building and infrastructure, but the speed and scope of such investing is also conditioned by the starting point and prevailing institutional constraints.

Features of the overall country context such as the level of decentralization, the capacity of local governments, and the local and central political dynamics condition and constrain optimal, or even merely feasible, options for institutional arrangements for the delivery of benefits and services. Macro-level institutional arrangements are—by definition—a "given" from the perspective of the program implementer, and these include the following:

- ***Country-level administrative structure.*** The degree of autonomy of the subnational level has strong implications for how the institutional arrangements get shaped. Arrangements in highly centralized, unitary states and in highly decentralized states will necessarily vary, and even federal countries can have vastly different arrangements when it comes to division of responsibilities for social protection.[3] The constitution itself may assign responsibilities to a particular level of government. While social development is the responsibility of the central government in Mexico, in Brazil poverty reduction/social welfare is a concurrent responsibility of the different levels. Moreover, political, administrative, and financial decentralization can proceed at different speeds, and create tensions and trade-offs that are hard to manage.
- ***Local-central political dynamic.*** To the extent subnational governments that are not under direct hierarchical control of the implementing agency play a role in delivery, the task of inducing their cooperation and ensuring effective coordination during implementation will become a relevant consideration (and constraint).
- ***Assessment of local-level resources to support the existing arrangements.*** In addition to the ability of the central government to provide the right incentive structure, the quality of decentralized delivery depends on the capabilities of the subnational governments directly in charge of providing benefits and services. Assessing the existing human resources capacity, the current workload and distribution

of tasks, ratio of field staff to beneficiaries and to central-level staff, the use of technology, and so on, is critical for choosing the most appropriate institutional arrangements and incentive structures for final delivery outcomes. This must be done at the central and local (e.g., citizen interface) levels, as well as for contracted service providers if these are used (for example, as payment agents in the case of cash transfers) and consider which elements are "static" (e.g., given in the short run) and which are modifiable.

Various institutional roles influence social protection outcomes. At the policy-making level, institutions are responsible for the definition of social protection policies, budget allocation, program selection, and parameters for programs (for example, intended populations, benefit levels, and eligibility criteria). This policy-making role can be held by a single agency or shared across different institutions. The implementation role, which is the focus of this book, refers to the delivery of benefits and services. The actors involved in delivery systems typically include those responsible for overseeing and managing the program(s) and supporting systems and those responsible for day-to-day program operations, including the key elements of client interface.

The policy-making role refers to those responsible for the definition of social protection policies and programs. This role can be held by one agency or shared across different agencies. Unlike other social sectors such as health and education, social protection is relatively new as a "sector" and institutional arrangements vary significantly. Social protection programs are often organizationally complex, involving multiple government actors, systems, and processes. In many countries, programs have evolved and been added to over time, and as a result, social protection systems and programs frequently lack an overall strategic vision and a clear institutional structure. Social protection programs are often multisectoral and may fall under the responsibility of multiple ministries and government agencies.

In most instances, central actors fill the roles of financing, policy making, and managing delivery systems. Core central agencies commonly include ministries of labor and social protection (joint or separate) and social insurance institutes, though social protection programs can also be spread across many other central agencies (with some programs managed by the ministries of health, education, or agriculture, among others). Central (national) governments are often the principal financiers of social protection programs, due to their role in raising revenues (via general taxation for noncontributory programs or the contribution collection for social insurance programs) and their ability to redistribute funds to reduce interregional inequalities.[4] Central agencies also typically set policies and define the main parameters for nationwide programs. Central agencies often manage and oversee implementation of delivery systems. In addition, central agencies in many countries manage delivery platforms such as information systems. In many cases, numerous central actors are involved, which can require explicit mechanisms for horizontal coordination or integration (see the hypothetical example in the next section of the chapter).

Horizontal institutional arrangements play a key role for one of the two main challenges of social protection delivery systems: coordination. A key question is the extent to which roles and responsibilities are distributed horizontally among different ministries/agencies, requiring specific arrangements to support the coordination role. In some instances, there may be one central ministry with a mandate for policy making, delivery, and inter-institutional coordination. This is the case, for example, of the strong central ministries in Brazil, Indonesia, Peru, and the Philippines, but also of more recent ministries still in the process of consolidating capacity such as in Guatemala. Alternatively, social protection policy making may not have a dedicated body, but rather be the responsibility of a national multisectoral planning agency, as in Nepal. In this latter case, the delivery role is effectively separated from the policy-making role and program-level oversight tends to be weak, diluting the potential impact of the policy. And many cases lie in between these two, with multiple ministries/agencies assigned separate (though often overlapping) policy mandates and program portfolios, sometimes aided by inter-institutional coordination bodies and sometimes not.[5] Although it is still possible for an individual program to be delivered efficiently under a single ministry, weak horizontal coordination weakens aggregate impacts of disparate programs and reduces efficiency at the systemic level.

The implementation role refers to the delivery function. Unlike education or health which is often assigned to a particular level of government in its entirety (e.g., primary education for the municipal level, secondary for the provincial level, hospitals only at the provincial and/or national level, etc.), the most important social protection programs tend to be national in nature and yet dependent on subnational levels for their delivery.[6] The institutional arrangements put in place to deliver benefits and services to the public vary across programs,[7] and so do the roles of central and local levels of government.

Local governments are called upon to fulfill specific functions during implementation, such as outreach, and intake and registration.[8] The advantage of shifting responsibility for program implementation closer to clients comes from local governments' close proximity to the beneficiary communities, which in turn facilitates client-facing transactions and their presumably greater responsiveness/sensitivity to local needs and preferences, which can be instrumental in strengthening accountability. This is particularly true for social programs targeted to the poor or vulnerable groups, who suffer from greater risk of exclusion, due to cost and other barriers, to accessing benefits and services. However, separation of responsibilities for financing and implementation across government levels also implies the need to carefully think about the institutional incentives to ensure that service providers are held accountable for program outcomes. Vertical coordination can be complicated because of, among other things, lack of clarity in assigned roles and responsibilities, mismatch in roles and resources, absence of common information, inability of local governments to respond to the central government requirements due to weak capacity, and political discord.

Countries adopt various schemes in terms of the set of vertical institutional arrangements that support the central-local division of responsibilities for the delivery of social protection benefits and services, based on their institutional and administrative context. In many low- and middle-income countries, where social protection is a relatively nascent sector (compared to, for example, health and education), institutional setups are still evolving. A main difference between the delivery of cash benefits and that of social or labor services relates to the different degrees of administrative intensity required for the delivery. It may be possible to roll out large cash transfer or social assistance schemes with relatively centralized institutional arrangements, but as a country's social protection system matures and evolves into a more complex mix of interventions tailored to varied needs of the poor and the vulnerable, the institutional setup also tends to grow more complex, especially in terms of its ability to provide face-to-face support to people.[9] It is important to note that such arrangements can vary across programs within the same country (for example, there may be different arrangements for social insurance and social assistance) or for similar programs in different countries (there are diverse arrangements for conditional cash transfers around the world). Figure 2.4 summarizes some of the variations commonly found in vertical relationships for social protection delivery systems, which include the following:

- ***Centralized with deconcentrated local offices.*** An individual program can be fully centralized in a constitutional sense, with implementation by deconcentrated local offices that report directly to the central agency. Such arrangements are quite common for social insurance, for example, when local social security agencies report to the central social security institute. In social assistance programs, examples of such centralized-deconcentrated arrangements include Mexico's Prospera program (with deconcentrated local offices reporting to the central SEDESOL agency) and Indonesia's PKH conditional cash transfer program (with thousands of facilitators contracted by the central Ministry of Social Affairs [MoSA], although they are recruited in specific localities and deployed all over the country).
- ***Central-local partnerships in decentralized contexts.*** In countries where more administrative functions (especially those related to decision making) are decentralized to local governments (e.g., federal states, but also some nominally unitary states with relatively high political autonomy), the central ministry may enter into partnerships with autonomous local governments to ensure delivery of social protection programs. Such is the case in Brazil's Bolsa Família Program or Tanzania's Productive Social Safety Net, where program financing and overall management remain centralized while many client-facing functions are managed by municipalities. These arrangements have been formalized by intergovernmental collaboration agreements which,

Figure 2.4 Main Patterns of Vertical Institutional Arrangements for Social Protection

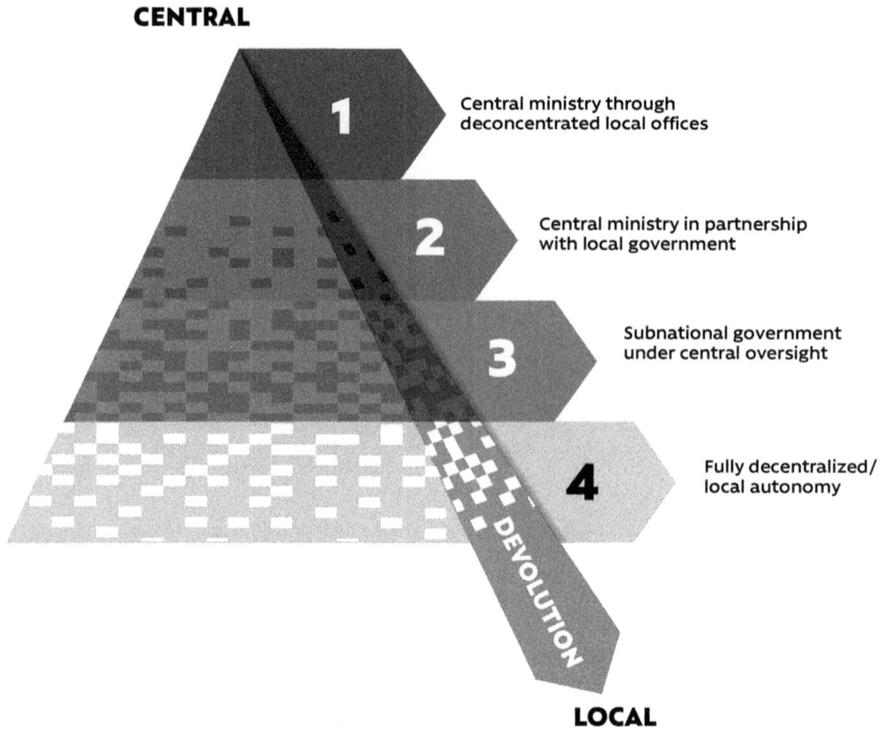

Source: Original figure for this publication.

in some cases, also include partial cost-sharing of administrative costs. In the case of Brazil, for example, the federal government provides administrative cost-sharing subsidies based on performance indicators to ensure more heterogeneous implementation across municipalities.

- ***Subnational management and implementation with central oversight.*** In some countries, management and implementation of certain programs may be fully decentralized to subnational actors, either with full central financing or with joint cofinancing between central and subnational governments, often through block or matching grants. One example is the Temporary Assistance for Needy Families (TANF) program in the United States, which is cofinanced by the federal and state governments through block grants and implemented by state and county administrators with limited federal government oversight. Another example is public employment services offices which operate at the local level in China and India, but regulations and guidelines are defined centrally (Auer et al. 2008).
- ***Fully decentralized.*** Some programs operate fully decentralized, with little or no involvement by the central government. This arrangement is common for social services, which can be "local" not only in their management and implementation, but also in their financing. Examples of such programs include childcare, child protective services, and homeless shelters. In some instances, the central body may have centrally mandated quality standards and regulations (sometimes including cofinancing from the central government).

In addition, many programs outsource some or all aspects of delivery to partner agencies, which can include other public agencies, foundations, nonprofits, and specialized for-profit firms. Outsourcing is particularly common for the provision stage of the delivery chain. For example, provision of benefits is commonly outsourced to payment agents (such as banks). Provision of social and labor services are also frequently outsourced. In these cases, governments have contractual relationships with providers. These can be output-based (contracts that pay for delivering a certain number of services) or outcome-based (contracts that pay by result). These latter types will transfer a larger share of the outcome risk onto the provider but are also complex to manage. In either case, outsourcing requires significant oversight. While it is at times used to compensate for lack of capacity, it requires significant management capacity both in establishing the contract and supervising it.

It is also crucial to define the respective roles of various actors along the delivery chain from a practical and functional perspective. As discussed below, process mapping tools can be useful in mapping out who does what along the delivery chain.

Delivery chain process maps are useful management tools for plotting the sequencing of implementation processes across actors (box 2.2). They identify who does what and when they do it for core processes

Box 2.2 Social Protection Delivery Chain Process Maps ("Swim Lane" Diagrams): Conceptualizing the Organization as a System

Delivery chain process maps are useful management tools for plotting the sequencing of processes across actors. These charts use the principles behind "swim lane" diagrams, which are common management tools that visually distinguish roles and responsibilities for business processes. Each actor is assigned a "swim lane," and then core implementation processes are mapped in sequence across those lanes. The term "swim lane" symbolizes the concept that "each actor stays in their own lane" without crossing lanes to avoid "collisions" or role confusion.

This mapping helps assess the robustness of the delivery chain by identifying "who does what" and "when" for core processes supporting the functions of the main implementation phases. Uniqueness of role assignments is crucial for the principles of clarity and accountability. Delivery chain process maps can be plotted end to end for the entire delivery chain, or for the processes of specific implementation phases within the delivery chain (such as plotting a process chart for the payments phase without all the other phases). These tools can help promote efficiency, transparency, and effectiveness of social programs and delivery systems.

Ideally, process mapping would be carried out in a participatory manner with the participation of core actors. In this manner, each actor understands their own role, how their role fits with the bigger system, and can help identify potential improvements and reforms. The participatory approach also helps build trust, consensus, ownership, and understanding of the key processes along the delivery chain. Common office software packages can be used to help plot and visualize these delivery chain process maps—and they can also be drawn in a participatory and initial way on flipcharts. The basic steps for delivery chain process mapping include the following:

- Identifying the actors: central agencies, other agencies or providers, local actors, and clients;
- Discussing the roles and responsibilities of each actor along the delivery chain;
- Assigning a "swim lane" to each actor (we usually use horizontal swim lanes with central actors on the top lane, then other agencies or providers, then subnational and local, then people);
- Identifying the steps for carrying out implementation phases along the delivery chain;
- Mapping the steps in sequence across the "swim lanes" for each actor;
- Reviewing processes for efficiency and effectiveness. Are all steps necessary? Which are "value-added" steps? Can some non-value-added steps be eliminated to reduce unnecessary bureaucracy? Can some steps be automated with information systems?

Delivery chain process mapping is integral to developing or assessing implementation of social protection programs. Swim lane delivery chain process mapping tools replace the usual "spaghetti diagrams" commonly seen in program operations manuals—the ones with numerous actors, many squiggly lines, and no clear start, sequence, or ending. Delivery chain process maps also help anchor and identify the processes and functions that could be automated with information and operating systems.

This chapter presents examples of delivery chain process maps for two hypothetical scenarios. Many real-world examples are presented elsewhere in this Sourcebook.

Sources: Rummler and Brache 1990; Hammer and Champy 2003; Karippacheril and Lindert 2016, 2017, 2018; Karippacheril, Nishikawa Chávez, and Rodríguez Caillava 2019.

supporting the functions of the main implementation phases, which helps avoid confusion. The uniqueness of role assignments is crucial for the principles of clarity and accountability.

Tools such as delivery chain process maps can help identify three main functions:

- ***Client-facing functions.*** Which actors carry out client-facing functions? Implementation of client-facing functions is typically carried out by local actors and/or outsourced providers. Subnational or local actors are typically better placed than central agencies to implement client-facing functions, because they may have greater knowledge of, or contact with, the client base for programs. Subnational actors may include the administrative branches of states, regions, or provinces. Local actors may include municipal administrative offices, local offices of the central agency, specialized local offices, and mobile teams. In some instances, client-facing functions are outsourced to specialized providers, such as foundations or nongovernmental organizations, private contractors, payment agents, specific service providers (such as training institutes, childcare providers, shelters or other protective services), and other actors. The network for client interface can involve a variety of formats. This interface is discussed in more depth below.
- ***Decision-making functions.*** Which actors make operational decisions along the delivery chain (for example, about eligibility, enrollment, benefit/service packages, sanctions, and exits)? In many programs, responsibility for such decisions remains centralized. The advantages of centralized decision making are that people in similar circumstances receive standard treatment all over the country; political and client pressures on local actors are reduced; and local discretion in decision making is limited. In other programs, such decisions are decentralized to local actors (to municipalities, local councils, communities, even to caseworkers or facilitators). This can have the advantage of incorporating local realities in decisions, but its disadvantage is that by enabling local discretion, it may also introduce potential bias.
- ***Managing operating systems.*** Who manages supporting delivery platforms, such as information systems? In many instances, such systems are managed centrally (even if the data are stored virtually). Among such systems are Turkey's Integrated Social Assistance System, Chile's Social Household Registry and integrated information system, and the social registries in the Philippines and Pakistan. In other instances, there are no national systems. For example, there is no national system for managing social assistance in the United States; each state is responsible for designing and building (or procuring) and maintaining its own system. In some cases, such systems are outsourced to operating agents, such as Brazil's Cadastro Único (social registry), which is managed by the social ministry but operated by a national federal bank (which also runs the program's payment system). Another example is Australia's Centrelink, which is the managing agent and operating system for all social protection benefits.

Client Interface: The Interaction between People and Institutions

People and institutions interact throughout the delivery chain. On the institutional side, local actors or outsourced providers are typically responsible for client-facing implementation. The key client-facing phases are outreach, intake and registration, notification and onboarding, payment, provision of services, and some aspects of beneficiary operations management. On the client side, people need to be able to (1) learn about a program and its processes, and who to contact; (2) understand how and where to register, and navigate the processes for doing so; (3) understand and be informed of decisions regarding their eligibility status, enrollment, and benefits-service package (if enrolled); (4) participate in onboarding activities (if enrolled); (5) interact with payment or service providers and receive timely delivery of benefits and quality services; and (6) update their information, be informed of any changes in their status (including for noncompliance of conditionalities), and file grievances.

There are many modalities or "touch points" for client interface. Many interactions occur in person with frontline workers, such as caseworkers, employment officers, social workers, promotors or facilitators, extension agents, and community health workers. The location of the interactions can be people's homes (via home visits by mobile teams), community sites, local offices, service centers, public employment services, or specific points of service (including payment providers). Or interactions may occur digitally, via mobile devices, tablets, laptops, personal computers, ATMs, self-service kiosks in public spaces, chatbots, etc.

The network for client interface can be a weak link in delivery systems—which can be a binding constraint on inclusion. An adequate network for citizen interface is crucial for the delivery system, and an efficient network is ideal. Many countries and programs, however, neglect what is often referred to as the "last mile" of delivery systems. In fact, given the centrality of people to the effectiveness and efficiency of social protection programs, this Sourcebook considers people to be the "first mile" of the system. An inadequate focus on the "first mile" hampers the ability of social protection programs to scale up, reach national scope, respond to shocks, and move toward dynamic inclusion so that anyone can apply for benefits and services at any time.

In many countries, the network for client interface is incomplete: offices operate only in a few districts and there is little or no outreach to remote areas; the number, training, or skills of frontline agents are insufficient to their tasks; or mobile teams visit local communities only every few years. Programs that rely on mobile teams may lack a permanent local presence. Or they may be hesitant to partner with autonomous local governments due to institutional constraints, lack of capacity, or mistrust. Technology has sometimes helped ease these gaps with online or mobile capabilities for some processes, but often the constraint still proves to be binding.

Even with an extensive network for client interface, first-mile interactions may be overly bureaucratic. Typically, scant attention is paid to people's actual experiences in navigating the network. Despite their good intentions, most social agencies adopt and visualize processes and systems from the administrator's point of view. They focus on organizational processes and institutional requirements, making general assumptions about their clients. As a result, people may find it frustrating to engage with government services. They find the client interface is bureaucratic and difficult to navigate, distant, or nonexistent, or so fragmented that they must apply for various benefits and services at multiple locations, waiting in line over and over, and incurring the costs of making numerous visits to seek aid. This results in excessive time, costs, and visits—an indicator of the amount of time people spend on the process, the amount of money they spend to participate (such as transport costs, childcare costs, missed work, and notary fees), and the number of visits they must make to the local office or other agencies. It also results in various "pain points" along the client journey through the system (as discussed in section 2.3 below).

Whether it is in person or digital, people's interactions can be improved by human-centered design techniques. Human-centered design (HCD) is the process of continually understanding and meeting users' needs. Various HCD tools can help assess the quality of interactions (or "user experiences") in social protection systems, including journey maps, which seek to trace clients' experiences throughout the delivery chain (see box 2.3 and section 2.3 below).

HCD is particularly important for the inclusion of specific vulnerable groups. Often, social agencies design interventions with an average applicant or beneficiary in mind. The intended user population for most programs, however, can be quite diverse, including those living in remote areas or zones with fragility, conflict, and violence (FCV); people with disabilities; people of different cultures and languages; women; children and youth; informal-sector workers; homeless people without a fixed address; and migrants and forcibly displaced people. They may require particular adaptations or accommodations to ensure that they are reached and served. HCD approaches can help ensure that the interventions are adapted to their specific needs and constraints through the development of personas and the testing of interventions and processes with these diverse groups.

Enabling Factors: Communication, Information Systems, and Technology

The interface between people and institutions is facilitated by enabling factors such as communication, information systems, and technology. These are the other core elements of the delivery systems framework. To some extent, communication and information systems help facilitate processes and the flow of information between these actors. They can both be technology-assisted, depending on the technologies available.

Box 2.3 Journey Maps: Understanding the Client Experience of Social Protection Delivery Systems

Journey maps are a compact visualization of an end-to-end client experience. They trace the client's experiences, expectations, behaviors, and emotions (highs, lows, and pain points) along that journey. A key aspect of journey mapping is empathy with the client's own experience and perspective, which can be quite distinct from the administrative process perspective.

Journey maps can be built by following ("shadowing") clients as they attempt to access social protection benefits and services or listening to their recount of the experience. They do not have to be complex, drawn-out exercises: even a quick description of client experiences from start to finish can be enlightening. Basic components of journey maps include the following:

- **"Doing":** Plotting the main activities, steps, actions that the client takes during various phases and understanding the different touch points or modalities through which clients interact with the system (in person, online, by phone, etc.)
- **"TCV":** Keeping track of their time, costs, and visits (TCV): (1) the amount of time each step takes (in minutes or hours for each activity plus total elapsed calendar days from their "trigger event"); (2) the amount of money or private costs required for the client to carry out the activities (bus fares, notary fees, missed work, childcare costs, etc.); and (3) the number of visits to the local office or other point of service plus other trips (such as to other agencies or former employers to gather documents)
- **"Feeling":** Understanding the feelings that the client may experience during the journey, both from the interactions with the processes, and the contextual feelings and pressures they may be experiencing due to their situation and any delays (such as worries about missed paychecks, paying bills, etc.)

The journey map can also assess how well performance metrics and quality standards meet client expectations. For example, quality standards may hold that an interview should occur within 7–10 business days of the client filing an application for a benefit, and that a benefit should be paid within 7–10 business days of the beneficiary filing a claim. Those may be perfectly reasonable quality standards from an administrator point of view. However, they do not consider the additional actions that may be needed for the client to prepare the application package or benefit claim—and the lapse in calendar days from their own trigger event (such as a job loss) that is a "ticking time bomb" for the client who has to pay bills and make it through the month.

Together with delivery chain process maps, journey maps can expose real bottlenecks in processes, inefficiencies, non-value-added or unnecessary steps, delays (and their root causes), tensions between expectations and realities, and so on. They may even uncover unnecessary bureaucratic processes that are inefficient not only for the clients but also for the caseworkers and the overall system—such as duplications in processes, documents that clients are expected to provide because they are part of the "traditional routine" even when no longer required, and so on. They can be a vital input to "business process redesign," and, of course, improvements in client services.

Sources: US Digital Services 2014; IDEO 2015; Solomon 2017; Karippacheril 2018.

Communication

Strategic and operational communication is critical for the effectiveness and efficiency of social protection policies, programs, and delivery systems. Strategic communication helps build awareness, understanding, support, and ownership among key stakeholders. Operational communication facilitates delivery processes and interactions among core actors. In doing so, it facilitates transparency, trust, and accountability. The risks of weak communication are significant. For policies and programs, misinformation can result in a negative spiral of perceptions, lack of credibility, and failure or reversal of reforms. For delivery systems, misinformation can cause havoc and confusion among actors, impede implementation, waste resources, generate inefficiencies and errors, and reduce the effectiveness of the interventions.

Social protection systems must communicate with many stakeholders. A communication assessment can help identify and map core stakeholders for social protection programs and systems. Obvious stakeholders are the core actors involved in delivery systems, such as clients (intended populations, registrants, and beneficiaries) and core institutional actors. Additional stakeholders can include other partner agencies (including donors); policy makers; politicians and opinion-makers; the media; and the general public. A communication plan should clarify the strategic and operational elements of communications with each stakeholder. Strategic elements include the communication's objectives, the behavior desired of the recipient, messages and information (content), as well as communication activities, risks, and expected outcomes. Operational elements include specific communication tools, channels, timing, and resource needs, as well as designation of those responsible for communications. Communication activities, channels, and tools consider the target audiences (stakeholders). With clients, this can involve adapting to preferred language or offering communications in diverse languages, overcoming potential access barriers (such as disabilities), and taking account of literacy levels, media preferences, location, and other challenges.

Operationally, communication facilitates all processes and interactions along the delivery chain. It is the "grease on the wheels" that ensures all actors understand all processes. At each phase of the delivery chain, it is important to identify the key stakeholders, as well as strategic and operational elements.

Communication is intrinsic to outreach. The core audience for outreach is the intended population and vulnerable groups. A key element of good outreach is that it reaches people in locations that are close to their environment, in ways that they will comprehend. Chapter 3 elaborates on outreach approaches, including special adaptations for specific groups who may face access barriers, such as older adults, persons with disabilities, linguistic and cultural minorities, and other marginalized groups. It also discusses the specific challenges of implementing outreach in FCV zones. Key messages at this phase focus on informing people about social protection programs and delivery processes. Outreach explains the intervention (objectives, intended population, program rules, eligibility criteria, scope, and content) as well as operational aspects such as processes, procedures, points of contact, timing and place of registration, and the rights and responsibilities of registrants and beneficiaries. The objective of such communication is to encourage the intended population to engage, apply, and provide their information as inputs into the intake and registration phase. The main risks of communication gaps at this phase is a target population that is missed, unaware of the programs, or that fails to understand the programs or how to register.

Communication tools also facilitate intake, registration, and the assessment of needs and conditions. Two-way communication is needed in client interface to (1) notify people about intake and registration procedures, locations, and points of contact; (2) support scheduling (of appointments, registration events, or community meetings); (3) conduct the interview (possibly with checklists, questionnaires, and technology-assisted tools); (4) gather accurate information and documentation; (5) respond to queries; and (6) facilitate corrections or updates as needed. The risks of miscommunication in these phases are many: that people will not know where to go, how and where to register, or what documents and information to provide. Such confusion contributes to process inefficiencies and inaccurate information. It can also create bureaucratic hurdles that deter the intended population from registering, with the result being low take-up rates among people who would likely be eligible for social protection programs (see chapter 4).

In the enrollment stage, communication is crucial for notification and onboarding. All registrants must be notified whether they are eligible or ineligible, and whether they are enrolled or wait-listed. Notifications should clearly explain the basis for such decisions as well as the enrollee or registrant's next steps. For enrolled beneficiaries, notifications and onboarding would clarify the benefit/service package, rights and responsibilities, expectations, points of contact, additional documentation needed, points of contact, the timing and location of subsequent activities, and so on. For those who have been wait-listed or deemed ineligible, notifications would include the basis for such decisions and clear instructions for grievances and appeals. The risks of miscommunication at this phase can include failure to deliver notifications (resulting in delays or eligible applicants not knowing whether they are enrolled), misunderstandings regarding benefit/service packages (such as when benefit calculations are complex), delays and inefficiencies in onboarding, and excessive grievances and appeals that can overwhelm the system. This chapter's hypothetical example illustrates some of these challenges (see chapter 5).

For payments, communications involve the beneficiaries, payment agent, and managing institutions. Communications typically include payment notifications and alerts and payment schedules. Beneficiaries need to know the amount of their benefits, the timing and frequency of payments, when and where to collect payments, how to withdraw money (including any passcodes or PINs), what documents they need to bring to make withdrawals, whom to contact with questions or grievances, and other information. Payment agents and managing institutions also need to know if payments are delayed or do not arrive, and whether the amount is wrong, or payment is not disbursed—and people need to be able to communicate such events and concerns. The risks of miscommunication at this phase are significant: delays or missed payments, unclaimed payments, payments made to the wrong people, inefficiencies in the payment process such as long lines or multiple visits, and the resulting large numbers of grievances and complaints. (See chapter 6.)

Multiple stakeholders may be involved in the provision of services, including beneficiaries, caseworkers, and service providers. Beneficiaries need to know who the service providers are, when and where to participate, and so on. An IAP established during onboarding may be used to set parameters and guide communications during the provision of services. Quality standards are also critical to communicate (see chapter 7).

Communication is also essential for the many actors and activities involved in beneficiary operations management. With beneficiary data management, the key stakeholders are the beneficiaries themselves plus local and central institutional actors. Key messages for beneficiary data management include alerts regarding errors, gaps or inconsistencies in information, notifications regarding the need for beneficiaries to update their information or be reassessed, and notifications regarding time limits and exits. When monitoring compliance with conditionalities (such as requirements related to the beneficiary's education, health, or labor), beneficiaries first need to know what is expected of them, and they should be alerted if the system detects noncompliance, issues warnings, or imposes sanctions. Communications play an instrumental role in grievance redress mechanisms. Grievances can involve beneficiaries—as well as people appealing their nonbeneficiary status. People need to know where and how to file grievances, appeals, and complaints. They need to be kept abreast of the status of their grievances and informed of resolution and subsequent steps (see chapter 8).

A wide range of technologies are used for communication in delivery systems. Communication between institutions and clients can occur via direct (in-person) interaction, word-of-mouth transmission, phone, email, SMS text, other mobile channels, and chatbots, among other avenues. Indirect communication tools include mass media, such as radio, TV, websites, social media, and printed media. As discussed in chapter 3, it is important to tailor communication tools to stakeholders. For example, younger people may be more inclined to use social media than the elderly, who may be better reached via print media, while isolated populations may be reached via mobile communications, radio programming, or TV. Communications may also need to be adapted for language differences, disability, or other access barriers.

Despite the risks of mis- or noncommunication, social protection programs typically do not pay enough attention to communication, which requires strategic planning, budgeting, and human resources. Instead, programs often delegate communication roles to nonspecialized staff, assume that frontline caseworkers are taking care of communicating with clients, or treat communication as a one-time activity carried out by consultants or nongovernmental organizations. Programs with successful communication strategies have regular communication diagnostics, plans, updates, and monitoring. They also rely on earmarked resources or budget lines that are dedicated for communications, and properly staffed teams. One example of a successful communication strategy is the 4Ps conditional cash transfer and social registry in the Department of Social Welfare and Development in the Philippines. Another example is the communications of Brazil's Bolsa Família Program and Cadastro Único. Both countries have dedicated communications staff and budgets as well as proactive outreach and communication strategies and activities.

Information Systems and Technology

Information systems and technology function as a bridge between people and institutions all along the delivery chain. They help transform the operations and administration of social protection programs, enabling the flow of information as well as the automation of some processes. Social protection delivery systems may be designed to support one program (a specific intervention) or multiple programs. As discussed below, countries are increasingly relying on integrated delivery systems to serve multiple programs, rather than continuing to build separate, disconnected information systems for each program. These systems may be designed using a modular services architecture approach, supporting discrete functions. See the glossary for definitions of information systems terminology used in the Sourcebook.

Integrated social information systems include social registries and beneficiary operations management systems (BOMS) or the so-called MIS, among other modules. Social registries support the process of the intake and registration of information on people and enable information processing to assess their needs and conditions. BOMS automate information processing for eligibility and enrollment decisions, decisions on the benefits and service package, the provision of benefits and services, beneficiary operations management (including beneficiary data management, monitoring of compliance with conditionalities, grievance redress, and decisions on exit, as discussed in chapter 8). Data from social registries and BOMS may be integrated or made interoperable to form an integrated data platform.[10] Figure 2.5 provides an overview of these core elements, with color-coding to match the phases along the delivery chain, as well as the opportunities for integrated social information systems to link with and contribute to whole-of-government systems.

The approach to building integrated social information systems incorporates a business-process orientation and a systems architecture approach. **A systemic process-oriented approach is not always adopted.** In several countries, information systems for managing and administering social programs tend to be limited in scope or nonexistent. In these countries, interventions are limited to developing "mere" databases and managing data as lists (socioeconomic classification registries, beneficiary registries, payments registries, etc.), rather than building full-fledged, automated information systems that will support the daily operations and administration of social programs. Associated software applications are limited to visual interfaces for applying to programs and providing basic reporting. Software applications that automate key functions and processes such as cross-checks, validation and verification, administration of benefits, administration of payments, beneficiary data management, or even grievance redress are semi-manual or manual. These software applications are not built as part of an information system or an overall integrated social information system. With limited capacity, building information systems from the traditional perspective of pulling together databases in the form of a spreadsheet or even a small-scale database management system may well be a worthy approach in the short term.[11] However, over the medium-to-long term, countries tend to develop a business process orientation when building information systems to ensure that the end-to-end processes of managing social programs are automated, as a by-product of which timely, accurate, complete, and high-quality transactions data are generated (Leite et al. 2017).

A business-process orientation is critical to building full-fledged information systems. This includes comprehensive process maps of the delivery chain, with clarity on roles and accountabilities of various institutions, who does what and when (box 2.2). The next important step is to conceptualize the overall integrated social protection systems architecture for the country, and how to sequence the implementation of those components, in tandem with legislative reforms, public administration reforms, and technology application within the local context. However, this is not to say that the building of information systems is incremental and that countries are entirely devoid of risk-taking. The policy agenda when building full-fledged information systems for social programs is not limited to that of cautious incrementalism, but that of learning from the experiences of other countries and leapfrogging, utilizing clever technology options where appropriate, especially where countries have the capacity and the ability to quickly develop "good-enough" business processes and systems designs. Governments develop integrated social information systems as part of their overall agenda to build trust with people through their day-to-day interactions and delivery of services and benefits to them.

Integrated social information systems are not developed in isolation separate from other systems.

Figure 2.5 Integrated Social Information Systems to Support Delivery of Social Programs: Overview of Core Elements and Links to Whole-of-Government Systems

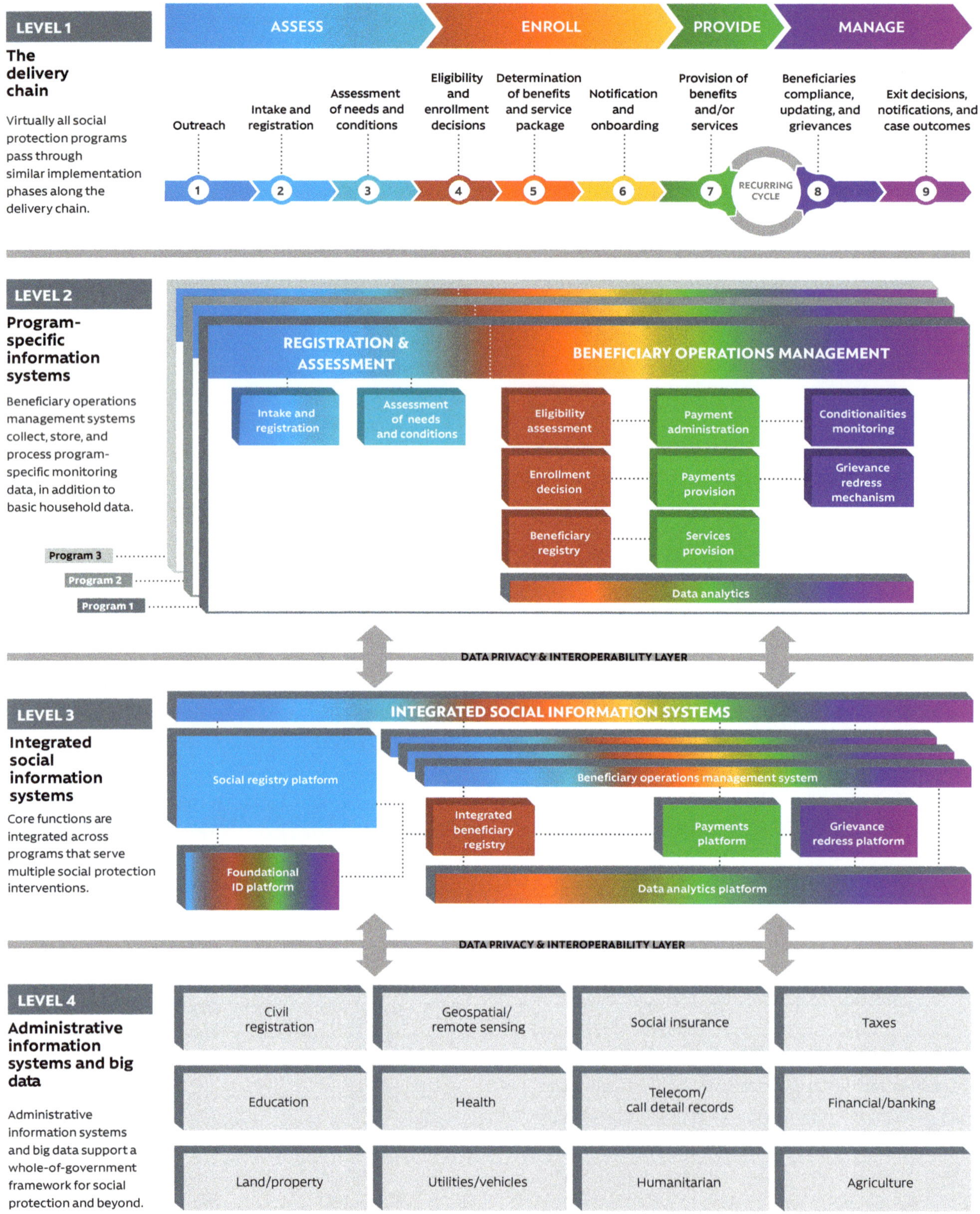

Sources: Tina George Karippacheril; Anita Mittal, consultant, Social Protection and Jobs, World Bank; Inés Rodríguez Caillava; and Kenichi Nishikawa Chávez; with inputs from Valentina Barca, consultant, GIZ and DFID.

Fragmentation of social protection programs often results in the proliferation of siloed information systems for each program. This creates inefficiencies and poses an administrative burden for end-users of these systems, including applicants, beneficiaries, administrators, and caseworkers, as well as the policy makers who work on finance and planning. It implies a duplication of functions and lack of interoperability across systems, as well as multiple parallel systems supporting similar functions. When each program conducts intake and registration separately, for users, this can imply providing the same type of information repeatedly to apply to more than one program. Likewise, when each program develops its own payment provision system, this can result in fragmented and uncoordinated methods of delivery to end-users or beneficiaries. Similarly, separate management of programs can impede intermediation and referrals for service provision as caseworkers lack information on available services and what other programs the beneficiary is receiving.

Integrating delivery functions across multiple programs reduces fragmentation, improves coordination, and promotes harmonization across protection programs and beyond. A seamless flow of information from the moment people express interest in a program until the moment they receive a benefit or service is realized through the interoperability of systems to support the various functions and processes along the delivery chain. This ensures that people can access programs, and that household needs are met in a timely manner.

Besides the integrated social information systems layer, foundational technology platforms support a whole-of-government framework for social assistance and beyond. Integrated social information systems draw on various foundational platforms for social protection and beyond. Figure 2.5 shows some of these interaction with whole-of-government platforms, and the use of interoperability and data protection frameworks. The social registry itself is a foundational platform that supports interventions in and beyond social protection. Other foundational platforms that can be used by social protection delivery systems include the following:

- **Civil registries** to maintain information on life events. Integration with civil registries keeps household data updated in the systems.
- **Geographic information systems (GIS) platforms** to link to geospatial information on households, service providers, and so forth. When data from social information systems are overlaid with GIS platforms, they can facilitate shock-responsive and adaptive social protection systems.
- **Foundational ID platforms** support the process of assigning a unique identifier to an individual that establishes "you are who you say you are." ID systems are important for social protection delivery systems in four ways: (1) to ensure uniqueness—ensuring one individual is registered and receives benefits from a program only once; (2) to meet KYC requirements, set by the financial services regulator and the payment service providers; (3) to authenticate the identity of a recipient during a payment transaction; and (4) to foster interoperability across different databases and thereby improve targeting accuracy and benefit and service delivery. In the absence of an ID system that establishes uniqueness, there could be repeated identity proofing; credential issuance for each functional system such as social assistance, social insurance, education, health, and so forth, leading to proliferation of functional ID credentials and biometric capture by each program. This could lead to an escalation of administrative costs due to identity proofing, credential issuance, and management.
- **Social protection G2P payment platforms** support payment administration and payments service provision, to make payments to beneficiaries. As discussed in chapter 6, countries are increasingly using multiprogram and multiprovider payment platforms rather than simple program arrangements.
- **Grievance redress mechanisms (GRMs)** support filing of eligibility appeals, complaint handling, feedback, and engagement of applicants, beneficiaries, and potential beneficiaries, of social programs. GRM systems are specific to a program, support many programs, or are part of a broader grievance handling system for the whole of government.
- **Data analytics platforms** allow the transformation, generation, aggregation, analysis, and visualization of data into meaningful and useful information for social policy analysis and strategic decision support for social programs. It includes techniques such as data visualization, data mining, reporting, time series analysis (including predictive techniques), online analytical processing (OLAP), statistical analysis, standardized reporting, ad hoc analysis, query and reporting, unstructured analytics, text analytics, and so on.

A whole-of-government architecture relies on data integration and interoperability frameworks to facilitate data exchange from other administrative information systems. Examples include linking social registries to administrative information systems such as civil registration databases, land or property cadasters, vehicle registration, the tax system, the social security contributions system, the pensions payments system, labor and unemployment, education and health, to create assessment profiles of individuals and households.

Interoperability frameworks are underpinned by a political, legal, organizational, semantic, and technical context. Politically, there must be a real need, endorsed by political decisions and having a legal basis. Participating organizations have a commonly held view and objective. Legally, they must comply with laws governing information such as personal data protection, digital signatures, information security, public information, and public procurement. Semantically, the framework must be based on different organizations understanding the meaning of information similarly. This entails building of common data dictionaries (with common definitions of variables, reference units, and time reference periods), metadata, thesaurus, taxonomies, ontologies, and service registers. Technically, the framework complies with service-oriented IT architecture standards. Interoperability also requires that some sort of unique identifier is included in information systems such that data on individuals can be matched up when appropriate and authorized.

Given the complexity of social protection programs involving large flows of data and transactions, data privacy and protection are paramount. Delivery agencies devote specific attention and resources to ensure that their IT systems and data repositories are properly governed and secure, and that they support social protection programs in achieving their core mandates. The data gathered and used in social protection delivery systems can be highly sensitive including (1) personal identity information; (2) sensitive personal data; (3) socioeconomic information; (4) information on employment or unemployment; (5) information on disability status; and (6) highly confidential information on various social risks to the individual and family. While integrated social information systems require that certain information be shared across actors, protections must be in place to ensure that personal information is kept accurate and secure, and not made available to unauthorized persons. See the Data Protection, Privacy, and Security section in chapter 4.

Finally, a number of governments are moving toward a shared data center approach to manage the time and cost of procurement, investment, and operations and to achieve economies of scale for government as a whole.[12] Fragmentation of programs has resulted in duplicate investments in software applications, databases, and information and communication technologies (ICT) infrastructure across and within government agencies. Increasingly, governments are opting for a cloud-based (infrastructure-as-a-service) approach,[13] to minimize procurement, investment, and operations costs, and to take advantage of potentially unlimited computing power, considering that this approach also entails a loss of control as well as additional security concerns.

2.2 ADAPTING OPERATING MODELS TO CONFRONT THE CHALLENGES OF COORDINATION AND INCLUSION

Coordination and inclusion are two common challenges facing social protection systems around the world. The challenge of coordination arises for many reasons, including the diversity of actors involved in social protection programs and systems, as well as the multiplicity of programs. The challenge of inclusion has many faces. The first is overall coverage: many countries are aiming to scale up programs and even to reach national coverage. The second is coverage of specific vulnerable groups, including those with potential access barriers that make them harder to reach. The third is the principle of dynamic inclusion, which holds that anyone who needs social protection can access it at any time. This is also closely related to adaptive social protection, in which coverage can expand or be redirected in a flexible manner to respond to shocks. Finally, the challenge of inclusion is tightly linked to constraints on administrative capacity and available financing.

Countries have adapted their operating models for social protection delivery systems to confront these dual challenges in various ways. While it is beyond the scope of this book to identify and describe all possible variations in delivery systems around the world, we point out four variations that we commonly see. They are in two contrasting pairs of operating models that touch upon these dual challenges:

- ***Separate versus integrated delivery systems.*** The first contrasting pair is the operation of separate delivery systems for each program versus shared delivery systems (or common elements) for multiple programs. This distinction relates to the challenge of coordination. Delivery systems are sometimes designed to support a single program (or each program separately). Yet with many programs operating in parallel, this can result in fragmentation. As such, many countries are moving toward integrating various aspects of their delivery systems to serve multiple programs.
- ***On-demand versus administrator-driven approaches.*** The second contrasting pair of operating models is the distinction between systems that are accessed by clients on demand versus administrator-driven approaches that carry out en masse registration waves infrequently, typically only every three to five years. These distinct operating models have emerged in diverse contexts to confront the challenge of inclusion given differences in administrative capacity and funding constraints.

The Challenge of Coordination: Separate versus Integrated Delivery Systems

Lack of coordination, or fragmentation, among social protection programs is a challenge facing programs and systems around the world. Given the number of actors involved in social protection, great effort is needed to effectively coordinate benefits and services among actors operating at different administrative levels (vertical coordination) or at the same administrative level (horizontal coordination).

Effective coordination of programs is important for many reasons. First, coordination at the policy-making level helps prioritize objectives, programs, and various population groups. Second, many individual programs are multidimensional or multisectoral in nature. For example, conditional cash transfers provide cash assistance to poor families, with incentives for their children to go to school and receive health care and incentives to ensure that they do so. Third, coordination enables benefits and services to be bundled. An example of the bundled approach is an activation package, in which the unemployed individual receives income support as well as various services to help them find a job, access active labor market programs (ALMPs) such as training, job readiness skills, or other services, or otherwise improve their employability. Many countries offer multiple benefits and services, and fragmentation is a greater risk when those programs are implemented through separate delivery systems. This section focuses on the challenges of this latter type of coordination.

Countries offer myriad benefits and services. While some countries offer fewer than a dozen programs, others offer many times that number. In many instances, separate delivery systems are developed for each of those programs (figure 2.6). Each system carries out the same or similar processes along the delivery chain, but for only one program. Those processes include outreach, intake, registration, and assessment of needs and conditions; enrollment; provision of benefits or services; and beneficiary operations management. Each delivery system has its own institutional arrangements (central, local, and service providers), makes its own communications, and operates its own information systems and technology platforms.

Although the various programs help meet the diverse needs of their populations, operating them through multiple delivery systems brings a greater risk of fragmentation. Separate systems are inefficient for people because they must go to multiple offices or service points for separate programs, incur travel costs and wait in long lines, provide the same documents over and over, and face the frustration of navigating a complicated bureaucracy. Moreover, people may miss opportunities to access some benefits and services because they are never informed that other programs exist. For program administrators, fragmentation means that processes are duplicated, the burden and cost of administration is greater, and information is lacking on what other benefits and services their client population may be receiving. Finally, for policy makers, fragmentation means that

Figure 2.6 The Risks of Fragmentation: Separate Delivery Systems for Numerous Social Protection Programs

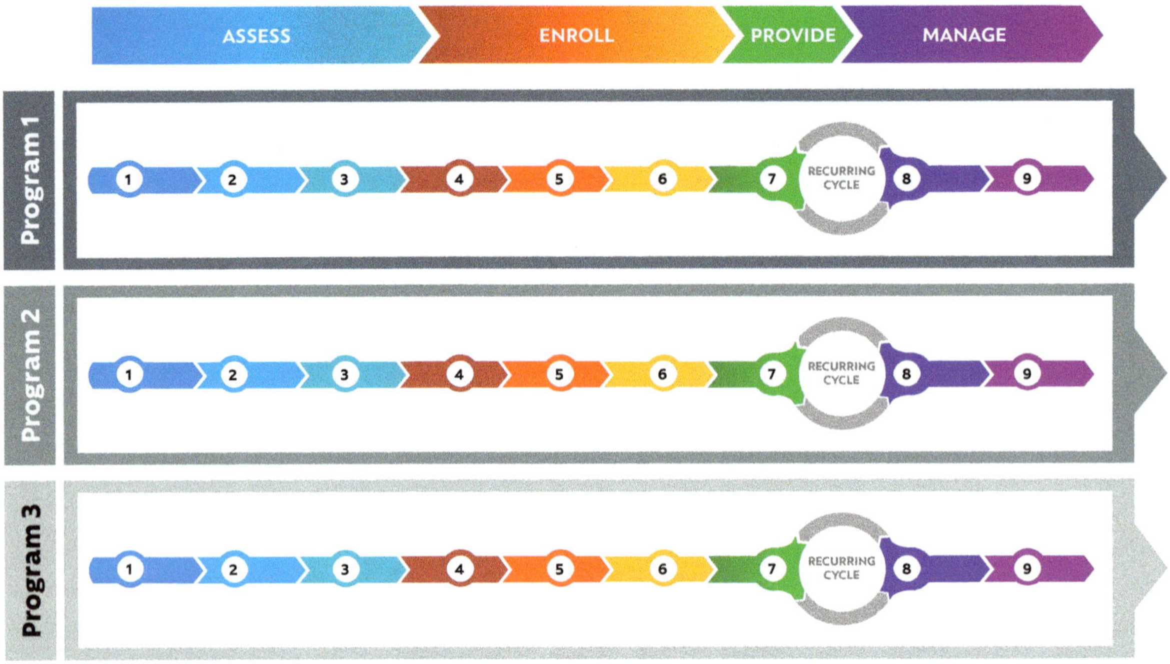

Source: Original figure for this publication.

they lack information on key policy questions, such as: Who benefits from which programs? Where does the money go? What are the gaps and duplications in coverage among programs? What are the opportunities for generating synergies from the provision of bundles of benefits and services?

Recognizing the benefits of coordination, a number of countries are moving toward integrated or coordinated systems for delivering multiple programs rather than operating separate systems for each program. Since most programs pass through similar implementation phases of the delivery chain (figures 2.1 and 2.6), these commonalities create opportunities to strengthen coordination, often through shared or coordinated processes. Some of the many ways that countries are integrating delivery systems across programs include the following:

- ***Coordination and integration along the delivery chain.*** Some processes are common (or can be made common) across multiple programs, such as outreach, intake and registration, assessment of needs and conditions, payments, and some aspects of beneficiary operations management. Delivery chain process mapping tools can help identify such opportunities for coordination as well as help the implementation of coordinated processes, as shown in the hypothetical example that follows.
- ***Shared client interface along the delivery chain.*** Many countries are combining resources for the first mile of delivery. Frontline integration can be physical, in terms of shared local offices or one-stop shops/service centers for numerous benefits and services. Such shared offices typically also entail shared human resources. In remote areas, mobile teams of facilitators reach out to dispersed communities about multiple programs rather than just one. Integrated digital self-service windows also support a coordinated approach in the virtual first mile of delivery.
- ***Inter-institutional coordination.*** Legal mandates, formal cooperation agreements, budget-sharing, or administrative-cost-sharing arrangements can also facilitate coordination for implementation.
- ***Integration/interoperability of information systems.*** Coordination across multiple programs typically involves information-sharing among agencies and actors, either through common information systems or through interoperability. While that sharing can facilitate efficiency and effectiveness, it also carries risks for personal data protection and privacy. The following are some examples of integrated social information systems:

- **Social registries.** Collecting information and documentation to support intake, registration, and assessment of needs and conditions is costly. Many countries are using shared tools (such as common application forms) and shared information systems that support those processes for multiple programs, rather than duplicating them for each program.
- **Data analytics platforms.** These are planning and coordination tools that link information on beneficiaries across programs, to help policy makers assess and coordinate who receives benefits from which programs.

- ***Common payment platforms*** facilitate payment of benefits for multiple programs, while offering convenience and choice in payment providers by channeling payments through the broader financial system.
- ***Integrated service approaches,*** sometimes called "integrated case management," helps caseworkers support clients end to end along the delivery chain. These approaches involve multidimensional assessments to identify an individual's complex needs, the provision of a bundle of services (and sometimes benefits as well), and intensive monitoring. The service bundle may include social work services (including information, awareness, referrals, counseling, and mediation), social care services (which may be home-based, community-based, or institutional), and specialized and preventive services.

Coordination and integration across multiple programs extends well beyond social protection. Social protection delivery systems are increasingly being used to support interventions in other sectors, linking clients to health insurance, scholarships, energy subsidies, housing benefits, and other programs.

The Challenge of Inclusion: On-Demand Systems versus Administrator-Driven Models

Two distinct operating models have emerged in diverse contexts to confront the challenge of inclusion given differences in administrative capacity and funding constraints. This variation derives from intake and registration processes, and whether people apply when they choose or whether they are registered only en masse during certain periods. We refer to these distinct models as on-demand and administrator-driven. The context and objectives of a program typically dictate the choice of models. Table 2.1 summarizes the models' key features, uses, and requirements. As it turns out, these approaches affect not only intake and registration, but also have implications for the entire delivery chain, as discussed below.

Worldwide, most social protection programs adopt the on-demand approach. This includes programs for demographic categories of individuals, many poverty-targeted programs, most labor-related benefits and services for the unemployed, disability programs, and social services for at-risk individuals.[14] The on-demand approach requires flexibility in design, implementation, and program budgets (to allow program outlays to expand or contract with changes in demand). The approach also requires an extensive permanent network for client interface (physical, mobile, or digital) supported by a continuous administrative budget. While many developing countries do operate on-demand systems for social protection programs, in other countries, this approach has not yet been feasible due to a lack of one or more of these key ingredients.

Given capacity and financing constraints, many developing countries use the administrator-driven approach, particularly for poverty-targeted programs. This approach is especially common when a country first sets up social protection programs. The administrator-driven approach makes sense as a practical solution to challenges associated with a high degree of asymmetric information (or lack of data), weak administrative capacity (or low confidence in government institutions), or remote populations with little access to institutions or government services. Financing also plays a role: we often see administrator-driven approaches in developing countries with a high reliance on donor financing, since the administrator-driven approach requires only occasional funding—often large sums—to cover en masse registration efforts in specific time periods.

The philosophy behind the two approaches is distinct. The on-demand approach envisions people approaching government for support. Clients initiate engagement and apply for benefits and services according to their own perceived needs and conditions, on their own timetable. The other approach sees government approaching the people. It initiates contact and registers groups of potential clients (usually households) on its own timeline.

Three key features distinguish between these approaches (table 2.1).

- ***Initiative.*** Who takes the initiative for engaging? The people or the government? With on-demand approaches, the impetus comes from the client who applies to be considered for potential eligibility in the program (or programs). With administrator-driven approaches, the program (or even social registry) initiates the process to register clients to be considered for potential eligibility.
- ***Individual or group registration.*** With the on-demand approach, specific clients (individuals, families, households) are served according to their

Table 2.1 Key Features, Uses, and Requirements of On-Demand Systems versus Administrator-Driven Approaches to Social Protection Programs

	On-demand approach	Administrator-driven approach
Distinguishing features	Initiative: people approach the state People: specific individuals, families, or households Timetable: the specific client's own timing	Initiative: the state approaches the people People: groups of clients (usually households) Timetable: determined by administrative factors such as capacity and financing
Intended populations and associated program types	Individuals in demographic categories (children, elderly) Categorical programs	
	Individuals, families, or households based on socioeconomic status Poverty-targeted programs	Families or households based on socioeconomic status: transient, chronic poverty, or low-income Poverty-targeted programs (Groups are typically more homogeneous in their situation)
	Unemployed, job seekers, inactive Labor benefits and services	
	Disabled persons Disability benefits and services	
	At-risk individuals Social services	
Responses to events or shocks	Used with idiosyncratic shocks or changes in the specific client's situation Used with covariate shocks to allow clients affected by the shock to apply for support	Used with covariate shocks to register groups of households affected by shock in an en masse registration wave—common starting point Not useful for idiosyncratic shocks facing specific clients
Delivery capacity and financing requirements	Requires permanent and extensive network for client interface (physical, mobile, or digital) Requires continuous administrative budget Requires flexibility in design and implementation	Temporarily requires large numbers of mobile teams, vehicles, and other inputs for en masse registration waves Requires large and lumpy administrative budget for registration waves

Source: Original table for this publication.

own circumstances. With the administrator-driven approach, clients (usually families or households) are registered and assessed together as a cohort. This personalized versus cohort distinction carries through the entire delivery chain, as discussed below.

- ***Timing.*** A major difference between the two approaches relates to timing. With the on-demand approach, the specific client's own timetable dictates, particularly for intake and registration. This means that people can apply to be considered for benefits and services at any time. With the administrator-driven approach, the timetable is not determined by idiosyncratic needs and conditions. Usually the timetable relates to administrative factors, such as capacity or availability of financing for registration efforts or for the program(s).

The timing feature drives the extent to which an approach can facilitate the principle of dynamic inclusion. This principle is closely related to a core tenet of social protection, whereby anyone who needs social protection can access it at any time. In practice, this raises the issue as to whether delivery systems are static or dynamic, particularly at the intake and registration phase. With on-demand systems, a permanent and extensive network for client interface facilitates dynamic inclusion because people can apply or update their information at any time. The en masse registration waves associated with administrator-driven approaches are typically more static in that they carry out registration infrequently (typically every three to five years) or in response to a specific event (such as a natural disaster). This means that, in the interim periods, registration is typically closed—and the system is static.

In static systems, the risks of errors of exclusion and inclusion at registration rise with the passage of time. With the administrator-driven approach, newly formed households or those whose situations have changed may have to wait long periods of time for the next wave of en masse registration. Those risks of exclusion multiply when static systems serve multiple programs because nonregistered households or those whose situations have changed risk being shut out of multiple programs, not just one. That does not necessarily mean that households would have accessed all of the programs separately, but it does suggest that as systems mature, they should explore the feasibility of moving to a dynamic on-demand system, or at least updating and opening registration more frequently.

Portability of benefits also relates to the principle of dynamic inclusion. If people move from one location to another, do their benefits move with them? At the very least, can they reapply in the new location when they get there? Such portability is typically more feasible with on-demand approaches rather than administrator-driven approaches (since registration is carried out only once every few years).

The ability of each type of operating model to respond to shocks also differs. Technically, both approaches can be (and are) used to respond to covariate shocks. In many countries, when a natural disaster or economic crisis hits, people can apply for benefits and services on demand at local offices (or online). Some programs even offer expedited benefit processing for such situations (such as expedited food stamps in the United States). En masse registration can be an effective way to respond to a shock, such as a natural disaster, that affects all or most households in a specific geographic area at the same point in time. However, if the registration sweep was conducted many years prior, the data may be quite outdated. One way around that challenge is to carry out high-frequency updates in shock-prone areas. With idiosyncratic events, however, only the on-demand approach is compatible with responding promptly. Such events could include the birth of a child, an individual reaching a certain age, loss of a job, the onset of disability, worsening of a family's socioeconomic situation, or the occurrence of vulnerabilities and social risks. With those events, people know their own situations and can apply on-demand for benefits and services when the need arises.

The differences in the two approaches extend beyond the intake and registration phase. Table 2.2 summarizes these differences at various points along the delivery chain, noting also where the two approaches diverge in relation to key design parameters, such as eligibility criteria or the definition of benefits and services to be provided.[15] Given the implications of these two models along the delivery chain, this Sourcebook delves deeper into these distinctions in chapters that follow.

The implications of the on-demand approach permeate many phases of the delivery chain. Outreach must be conducted for on-demand approaches because

Table 2.2 Distinct Design Parameters and Operational Models: On-Demand versus Administrator-Driven Approaches to Social Protection

	On-demand approach	Administrator-driven approach
Assistance unit (AU)	Individuals, families, or households	Usually families or households
General approach	Each AU enters and moves along the delivery chain on its own timeline Tailored package of interventions and referrals Extensive network of permanent client interface	Groups (or cohorts) of AUs move together across the delivery chain, from mass registration to provision of a common package of interventions
Outreach	Outreach is crucial to ensure people know about the programs, how and where to apply, and so on	Outreach often part of the initial mass registration
Intake and registration	AUs can apply any time on demand Different AUs enter system and start process at different times and at different localities Application (registration) is fluid (dynamic inclusion)	En masse registration sweeps on location All AUs are registered at similar point in time (during the registration wave) Community-based targeting is sometimes used to prioritize who gets registered Registration waves are often carried out only every 3–5 years
Assessment of needs and conditions	Each AU is assessed using assessment tools (MT, PMT, HMT, etc.) Assessment creates a profile of their specific situation at the time of intake and registration Relative rankings do not make sense because people apply at different times	Each AU is assessed using assessment tools (MT, PMT, HMT, etc.) The cohort group of AUs is "ranked" from richest to poorest (relative rankings) Community-based targeting is sometimes used to validate the relative rankings
Eligibility decisions	AUs are determined to be eligible or not according to program rules Usually use absolute eligibility thresholds (if their income or PMT score is below the threshold, they qualify—an entitlement approach) Relative rankings and eligibility thresholds do not make sense because people apply at different times and in different localities	AUs are determined to be eligible based on their ranking in relation to the rest of the group The programs often use relative eligibility thresholds applied to the ranking of AUs such that the poorest XX% are eligible, as a way to manage demand given limited budget and capacity constraints (though some also use absolute thresholds)
Benefits and service decisions	Benefit levels: determined according to program rules Service packages: may be tailored to individual needs Referrals: AU may be referred to other services or programs based on their specific situation or characteristics Individualized action plans may also be used to establish rights and responsibilities If limited capacity, may have to manage waiting lists for specific services (training, care services, etc.)	The cohort of eligible beneficiaries is assigned benefit and service package In some programs, the cohort will receive a calibrated sequence of interventions or accompanying measures

continued

Table 2.2 *(continued)*

	On-demand approach	Administrator-driven approach
Payments (benefits provision)	Adding specific clients to the payroll when they become eligible Using individualized payments calendars (e.g., paying benefits when their claims are processed rather than waiting for a group payroll or payment event)	Common payments calendar Group payments events (with manual payments)
Service provision	Beneficiaries receive tailored package of services according to their needs, conditions, and timetable	With some programs, the cohort may advance together through common sequenced phasing or set of interventions, such as with accompanying measures, family development sessions, and productive inclusion approaches
Beneficiary operations management	Updating: information is updated for each AU when their situation changes (e.g., birth, death, change of address/locality, change of school, etc.) Reassessment: each AU is reassessed according to established due date given their starting point (e.g., less than two years from entry) Portability: if AU moves to another locale, may continue as beneficiaries or reapply in the new locality Exits: each AU exits when own time limit is up, or when no longer meeting program eligibility requirements, or upon completing individualized action plan, and so forth	Updating: program may seek to update demographic information on AUs periodically Reassessment: whole cohort would be reregistered and reassessed jointly (along with other AUs that had not been registered in initial sweep) Portability: if AU moves to another locale, unlikely that they would be able to continue as beneficiaries or reapply given that registration occurs only in mass waves every 3–5 years Exits: mostly the group enters and exits (or recertifies) together; individual AUs may exit if demographic updates result in status changes, or when the time limit is up

Source: Original table for this publication.
Note: AU = assistance unit; HMT = hybrid means testing; MT = means testing; PMT = proxy means testing.

people need to be aware of a program and know where and how to apply for it. Without sufficient outreach, intended and vulnerable populations risk being excluded. For intake and registration, people can apply for benefits and services on demand at any time when their own situation suggests a need. The assessment of their needs and conditions must determine whether they meet absolute eligibility criteria. This means that their entitlement to benefits and services does not depend on their ranking relative to others. Eligible clients receive a specific benefit/service package that may or may not be tailored to their specific needs and conditions.[16] With services (or benefit/service packages), clients may be referred to a tailored set of programs depending on their circumstances—and this may be accompanied by an individualized action plan (IAP). Benefit claims may be paid on a timetable based on the specific date of clients' claims, or on a common timetable for everyone on the payroll. Services may be provided to clients according to their own timetable and IAP. When it comes to beneficiary operations management, clients update their information when their circumstances change. Beneficiaries can be reassessed according to a schedule established in relation to their entry date or their own changing circumstances. They may exit on their own timeline—when they complete the program or IAP, exceed time limits, or fail to meet ongoing eligibility requirements.

The administrator-driven approach also influences various phases of the delivery chain. Outreach is typically associated with en masse registration waves, which involve mobile teams going to communities to register and assess groups of households. The approach also determines eligibility standards: households are ranked from richest to poorest and their eligibility is determined by their position in the ranking. For example, the poorest one-third of households in the ranking might be eligible.[17] The benefit/service package is not individualized but common to all beneficiary households. Benefits are typically paid according to a common calendar, either through in-person group payment events or digitally. In some programs, the cohort of beneficiaries may proceed through different stages of sequenced interventions as a group. Such practices are common with certain measures (such as family development sessions that adopt a sequenced curriculum) or productive economic inclusion and graduation approaches. Households are all monitored, updated, and reassessed as a group on the same time frame.

Each approach also manages differently in the face of budget constraints. Regardless of the operating model, countries and programs around the world face the challenge of how to manage when the demand for social protection programs exceeds available resources, either due to financing or capacity constraints. At the human level, this dilemma can involve painful choices since so many people face so many needs, and resources cannot come close to meeting them.[18] At the policy and design stage, this can involve adjusting core program parameters to meet limited budgets, such as setting low benefit levels, establishing tighter eligibility criteria, or introducing and enforcing time limits. Although these design choices imply tough trade-offs, rules-based parameters have the advantage of being more transparent. When it comes to implementation, the distinct operating models employ various implicit and explicit strategies all along the delivery chain to contain budgetary outlays:

- ***Managing demand with on-demand systems.*** While on-demand approaches technically allow anyone to apply at any time, programs have a variety of ways to limit that demand from coming in—or from making it through to enrollment. Some are implicit, such as passive outreach: if fewer people know about a program, then fewer will apply. This can make sense from a practical efficiency standpoint: if a program is oversubscribed, why spend scarce administrative resources to promote it? Why keep raising expectations? On the other hand, passive outreach risks missing those most in need who may be less connected or aware of benefits and services. Inefficiencies and overly bureaucratized processes for intake and registration can deter people from applying. While these obstacles could result in lower errors of inclusion by deterring likely noneligible people from applying, they can also lower take-up rates for those who would likely be eligible—and are costly, inefficient, and nontransparent for administrators and clients alike. At the assessment and eligibility phases, caseworkers may "direct traffic" away from oversubscribed programs by applying rigid and discretionary assessments or enforcing tight eligibility criteria. This brings us to one of the main instruments for managing demand in on-demand systems: waitlists, which are discussed in more detail in chapter 5. Other cost-containment strategies further downstream on the delivery chain include sanctioning beneficiaries for noncompliance with program conditionalities and enforcing exit rules. The tension between the push for inclusion and the realities of limited capacity and financing makes for tough choices even in on-demand systems.
- ***Controlling entry doors in administrator-driven systems.*** With the administrator-driven approach, three tools are used to limit entry and manage expectations in the face of budget and capacity constraints. The first two relate to intake and registration, while the third relates to eligibility and enrollment for specific programs. First, with the administrator-driven approach, the doors for inclusion do not open often due to infrequent waves of en masse registration (usually every three to five years). Second, even when the doors are open, not everyone has the opportunity to register because many programs (or social registries) use registration quotas, as discussed in chapter 4. On the one hand this can make sense: why register large shares of households and raise expectations when programs can select only a small share to be enrolled in the program? On the other hand, the use of registration quotas can result in a perceived lack of transparency as to who is included or excluded from registering (particularly since there is usually limited recorded information on why households were or were not registered), as well as the potential to replicate existing local inequalities and exclude poorer households from registering. Moreover, errors of exclusion can multiply when limiting the people who can register in social registries that serve multiple programs. The third mechanism is the use of relative rankings and thresholds for assessment and determination of eligibility for social programs.

Since the number of households is known once en masse registration is complete, selecting a percentage for eligibility facilitates predictable budget planning. Although there is no official waitlist with this approach, latent demand remains, and biases can be introduced, as discussed in chapter 5.

The trade-offs between inclusion and limits on financing and capacity are tough. There are downsides to the various mechanisms used to manage demand in the face of constraints with both the on-demand and the administrator-driven approaches. However, as capacities improve, some countries are seeking to shift from administrator-driven to on-demand systems because of their dynamism—particularly with integrated approaches that serve multiple programs. This option has implications all along the delivery chain, as discussed above and shown in table 2.2.

Even if the on-demand and administrator-driven approaches constitute two distinct models, they operate in a spectrum. In practice, there are variations along the spectrum between the two models. Several countries that operate in administrator-driven models are starting to implement a few features of on-demand approaches (see chapter 4 for examples), and this can be the basis for a transition to an on-demand approach.

While the on-demand approach and the principle of dynamic inclusion are aspirational, it is important to recognize that there is a tension with what is feasible in practice. The choice of one model over the other is usually highly dependent on each country's local administrative capacity and availability of budget.

2.3 ILLUSTRATING THE DELIVERY SYSTEMS FRAMEWORK WITH A COMPOSITE EXAMPLE

This section illustrates the delivery systems framework with a hypothetical example of a program of unemployment assistance benefits combined with activation requirements. The example is a composite of actual practices in social protection benefits and services that we have observed in various countries. The example demonstrates (1) how the various elements of the delivery systems framework come together in implementing benefits and services with an end-to-end view of the delivery chain; (2) the value of using delivery chain process maps, journey maps, performance indicators, and other diagnostic tools to assess the effectiveness and efficiency of delivery systems from the perspectives of the administrators and clients; and (3) many of the overarching messages of this book.

Setting the Stage: Social Protection in the Republic of Morlandia

Setting: Republic of Morlandia. The composite example takes place in Morlandia, a dynamic middle-income country with a population of 28 million. The economy has experienced strong growth in the past decade, with a diversified economy based on seafood and agribusiness, sustainable tourism, textiles, electronics, renewable energy, financial services, and a small but growing tech and tech services industry that has attracted substantial domestic and foreign investment. The economy is a mix of private firms and state-owned enterprises. With a large coastline, Morlandia has also developed Exclusive Economic Zones to promote the marine economy. In addition to strong growth, Morlandia has been experiencing the adverse effects of climate change, especially in the coastal zones. It is also vulnerable to intense tropical storms and flooding.

Government: Morlandia's government is a unitary presidential constitutional democracy with 12 administrative regions. The Ministry of Local Government oversees local authorities, municipal councils, and townships. Relative to other countries in the region, Morlandia has invested a significant share of GDP in the social sectors: 4.3 percent on education, 3.9 percent on health, and 6 percent on social protection (mostly for pensions and social insurance, but also 1.3 percent for social assistance). However, social protection programs are spread across several agencies and require collaboration with even more parts of the government.

- ***The Ministry of Social Affairs (MoSA)*** is responsible for social programs aimed at empowering and protecting the poor and vulnerable. Key programs include (1) a small Universal Child Allowance (UCA) given to all children from birth until age 16, with a supplemental amount (UCA-PLUS) for orphans, children of poor or unemployed families, street children, and other vulnerable categories; (2) the Program for Needy Families, a cash transfer for the chronic poor; (3) means-tested Unemployment Assistance (UA) for working adults who have recently lost a job but do not have unemployment insurance; and (4) many other small benefits and social services tailored to specific vulnerable populations. MoSA operates deconcentrated ***Social Service Offices (SSOs)*** at the local level. MoSA also operates a social registry called UNISO, which supports registration and eligibility determination for various social programs, including UCA-PLUS, the Program for Needy Families, and UA.
- ***The Department of Labor and Employment (DLE)*** in the Ministry of Labor, Industry, and Economy oversees Morlandia's Unemployment Insurance Fund (UIF) for formal sector workers and provides employment services, such as information, registration, counseling, job placement, work permit inspections, and training services. DLE operates deconcentrated ***Employment Service Offices (ESOs)*** at the local level. DLE operates the National Employment and Insurance System (NEIS), which maintains information from both employers and employees on job contracts and monthly insurance contributions.
- ***The Social Security Institute (SSI)*** is a semi-autonomous agency under the general supervision of the Ministry of Labor, Industry, and Economy, which manages social security benefits for retiring formal sector workers, as well as a small social pension for the poor, elderly, and disabled. SSI operates its own deconcentrated offices (SSIOs) at the local level. SSI's benefits information system links to the tax authority (since mandatory social security contributions are collected with taxes).
- ***The Central Civil Registration Office (CCRO)*** manages the civil registry and the identification system. Morlandia is one of the few countries in the region with very high coverage of civil registration and identification. Morlandia previously had a paper ID card, but the card was phased out and replaced by the new biometric Morlandia ID Card (MIC), which serves to prove an individual's unique identity and allows secure and reliable e-service transactions. The MIC contains name, photograph, ID number, "SC" logo for senior citizens, machine-readable barcode, date of birth, residential address, four fingerprint templates, and a digital certificate that ensures the data on the card can be read only through the MIC Certificate Authority.
- ***Other agencies relevant to social protection*** include the ***Ministry of Innovation and Technology (MIT)***, which has been actively involved in promoting Morlandia's growing digital economy, and in spearheading a major e-Governance (e-GOV) Program to improve the provision of public services for greater convenience of the public. The e-GOV Program has been rolling out information systems projects across the line ministries, encouraging interoperability capabilities among ministries and supporting the development of UNISO in MoSA. The ***Ministry of Health (MoH)*** manages means-tested health insurance subsidies, while the ***Ministry of Education (MoE)*** manages the national school feeding program, scholarships (both need- and merit-based), and "JumpStart" vouchers for children from poor families to participate in early childhood programs.

Two scenarios and the evolution of social protection delivery systems: Our composite hypothetical example is split across two points in time: Scenario 1 takes place "a few years ago" and Scenario 2 takes place "a few years later." It would be tempting to tell a story of a bad bureaucracy and reforms that have led to improvements, but that is not typically the experience of delivery systems. Rather, the evolution of social protection delivery systems is continuous, but often nonlinear: mistakes, learning, midcourse corrections, adjustments, reversals, and so on, usually play a role in growth and improvement. Therefore, we present our two scenarios as points along a continuous evolutionary path, and each scenario is alive with previous reforms, improvements, and challenges that still need to be tackled.

- ***Scenario 1, which takes place several years in the past: Digitalization and MIC pave the way for interoperability of information systems.*** MIT's e-GOV Program has invested heavily in developing the biometric MIC to ensure identification and authentication of all residents of Morlandia. This has been a major improvement for public and private services, and in helping link various administrative systems via interoperability through the unique MIC number across systems. To facilitate these efforts, the government of Morlandia adopted legislation governing the use and protection of data, along with standardized protocols for personal data sharing and additional investments in security. The interoperability project is being rolled out across agencies and over time. After some initial systems glitches due to duplicate or inconsistent records across agencies, as well as incomplete and poor-quality data in some of the systems, most records for formal sector workers are now linked between the Ministry of Labor, Industry, and Economy and SSI, as well as with the Tax Authority and various other ministries and departments. More recently, MIT has also been working with MoSA, including supporting the development and operation of UNISO, MoSA's social registry and beneficiary operations management system. UNISO was a big step in harmonizing means testing for all social benefits. While UNISO supports household-level information, it also has some interoperability with other systems for individual-level data. Unfortunately, most of these interoperability improvements have been purely administrative, and many of the functions for frontline officers in the local ESOs, SSOs, and SSIOs still do not connect with each other.

- ***Scenario 2, which occurs a few years after Scenario 1: Systems continue to improve, including frontline systems.*** Morlandia has made significant systems improvements. Government-wide, MIT has pushed to rapidly digitize all social protection (SP) G2P payments, extend its interoperability project to additional agencies, and develop an interactive online service window called "MyMorlandia.gov." MoSA has also made continued systems improvements, including various "quick-win" reforms, process simplification, and other improvements. As part of the government's "Morlandia Cares" social policy strategy, MoSA has also entered into agreements with several ministries to allow them to use UNISO to facilitate access to other means-tested benefits (such as MoH's health insurance subsidies, MoE's JumpStart program, and the social energy tariff). The rollout of these reforms faced some glitches and challenges remain, but the effectiveness and efficiency of social protection programs has improved in many ways.

The clients: Anaïs and Naomi. Our scenarios involve two working mothers, Anaïs and Naomi. Their backgrounds are very different, but both have worked hard and manage to make it through each month on their earnings, plus the small child allowances for their children. Anaïs's disabled mother also lives with her and receives a small disability pension from SSI. For reasons beyond their control, both lose their jobs, which is a significant blow to their families' economic situations. Let us follow their journey as they navigate the process of seeking benefits and services to help them get by in the face of these setbacks, first Anaïs in Scenario 1 and then Naomi in Scenario 2.

Scenario 1: Anaïs's Journey, Several Years Ago

In Scenario 1, which occurs several years before the present day, we meet Anaïs, a single mother who lives with her aging mother and two children who are both in elementary school. Their home is a small concrete house with outdoor plumbing. It was constructed in the 1970s and is owned by Anaïs's mother following the untimely death of her husband in an accident. Anaïs's mother was disabled in the accident and receives a small disability and widow's pension from SSI. Anaïs dropped out of school before completing high school because she needed to help support her family. Anaïs works at one of the artisanal fisheries in the Exclusive Economic Zone (EEZ). Her company is a small female-led entrepreneurship that supplies fresh seafood to the nearby ecotourism resort and promotes sustainable fishing that does not deplete the coral reefs around their coastal town. Last week, a severe tropical storm swept through their coastal township. Small fishing companies, including those in the EEZ, were badly affected, with damaged equipment and fishing boats. This included the small enterprise that Anaïs works for. The manager is apologetic and assures everyone that they will rebuild. In the meantime, Anaïs is now facing the loss of her job. She is not eligible for unemployment insurance because she worked at the company for only a few years, and in any case, as a small firm, the company was not obliged to participate in the scheme. Anaïs is devastated by the loss of her job, and worried about how her family will get by without her income, despite her mother's pension and the child allowances. She hears MoSA's announcements on the radio directing people to apply for unemployment benefits at their local SSO. Various friends recount horror stories about how hard it was for them to get benefits. Although it is better now, they say, she should not have high expectations for getting support. Anaïs wonders whether she will be able to get unemployment benefits and services.

Delivery Chain Process Map with UNISO, Interoperability, and Manual Payment Systems

The "business" processes for all MoSA programs were mapped using delivery chain process maps to clarify roles and facilitate coordination. (See box 2.2.) These diagrams for unemployment assistance benefits are presented for Scenario 1 in figure 2.7. Although unemployment assistance is managed by MoSA and implemented by the SSOs, the clients also interact with the Labor Ministry's ESOs for two purposes: (1) they must register as unemployed at the ESOs and obtain a certified declaration that they are unemployed without insurance (UWOI); and (2) UA benefits have job-search and service requirements, and those functions are carried out by the ESOs. Although MoSA and DLE have established interoperability capabilities on the back end, these reforms have not reached their front offices, where many functions remain manual, without automated connections. Therefore, the main actors plotted in figure 2.7 include: MoSA (top row), the SSOs (which report to MoSA, second row), the ESOs (which report to DLE, third row), and the clients (bottom row).

Figure 2.7 Delivery Chain Process Map for Unemployment Assistance Benefits and Services in Morlandia: Scenario 1

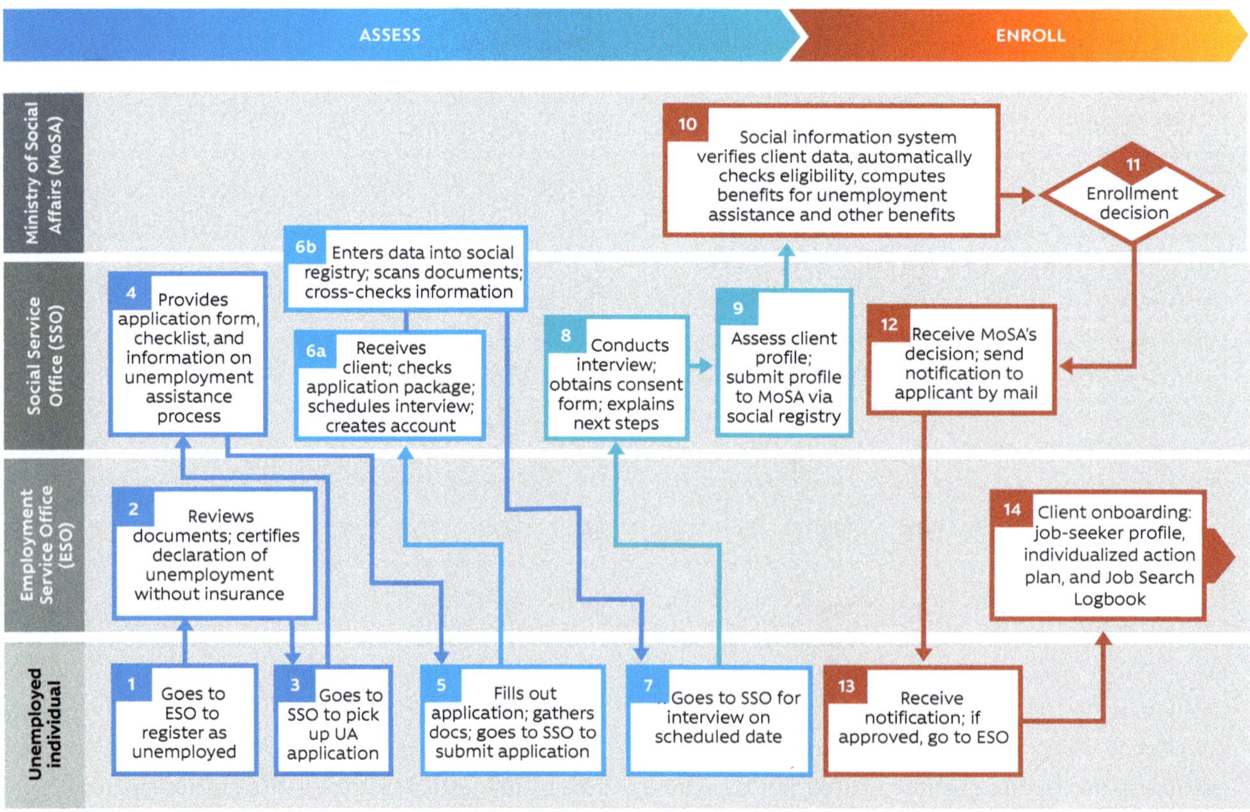

continued

Figure 2.7 plots basic steps for Scenario 1 for the processes of intake, registration, and assessment of needs and conditions in blue and the processes for enrollment in red. Those basic steps are as follows:

- ***ESO registration.*** When someone becomes unemployed and wants to apply for UA benefits, they must first go to the ESO to register as unemployed and certify their declaration of "unemployed without insurance," as shown in step 1 on figure 2.7. The unemployed person must show their MIC and provide proof that they were previously employed and a dismissal letter. The ESO intake officer reviews the client's documents and checks their employment and contributions history in the NEIS. If they do not qualify for unemployment insurance, the ESO then issues the UWOI declaration (step 2 on figure 2.7).
- ***Initial contact with the SSO.*** The unemployed individual then goes to the SSO to pick up the application form (step 3 on figure 2.7). The SSO provides the application form, a checklist of required documentation, and information about the process for applying, such as next steps, overview of process, rights, and responsibilities, including job search requirements (step 4 in figure 2.7).
- ***Application package.*** The unemployed individual fills out the application, gathers the required documentation, and returns to the SSO to submit the application package (step 5 in figure 2.7). Although the assistance unit for unemployment benefits is the individual, because unemployment assistance is means-tested, household-level information is required as well. The information and documentation requirements are listed in table 2.3. (Interoperability capabilities have reduced the number of forms and documents required, but only somewhat.)

Figure 2.7 *(continued)*

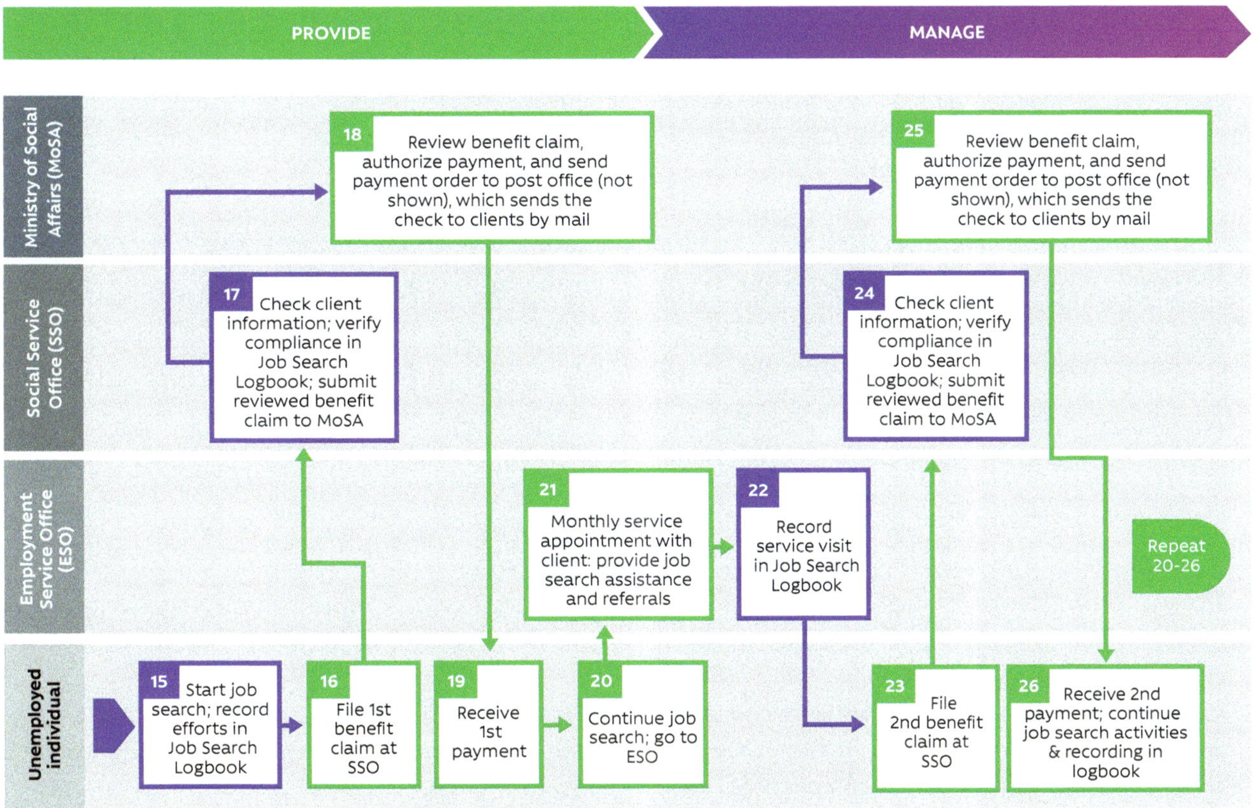

Source: Original figure for this publication, based on composite of observed cases.
Note: ESO = Employment Service Office; MoSA = Ministry of Social Affairs; SSO = Social Service Office; UA = unemployment assistance.

Table 2.3 Information and Documentation Requirements for Means-Tested Benefits in Morlandia: Scenarios 1 and 2

	Scenario 1: A few years ago: Anaïs	Scenario 2: A few years later: Naomi
Application form, with information consent	√ Signed by applicant and all working-age adults	√ E-signatures by applicant and all working-age adults
Morlandia ID Card (MIC) for identity, residence, and so on	√ All adults	√ All adults
Birth certificates for children under 18—from the CCRO	√	√
Educational attainment levels (for adults) and education status (for children)	√ Self-declared	√ Self-declared
Disability status (if applicable)	DX with SSI (disability registry), with consent	DX with SSI (disability registry), with consent
Certified Declaration of Unemployed Without Insurance (UWOI, issued by the ESO)	√	No longer needed
Proof of previous employment, dismissal, and reason for dismissal	√	√
Employment and income information for all working-age family members, such as • earning statements for past three months • tax returns for past year from tax authority • income from any social benefits	√ √ DX with UNISO, DLE, and SSI, with consent	√ DX with tax authority, with consent DX with UNISO, DLE, and SSI, with consent
House deed or lease from national land and property agency	√	DX with national land and property agency, with consent
Rental income if any (obtain certified documentation from municipal office)	√	√
Expenses for utilities (energy, water, and sanitation)	Applicant presents utility bills	DX with utility companies, with consent
Ownership of vehicles (DX possible, but low-quality data in Department of Transport)	√ (if applicable)	√ (if applicable)
Bank account statements for past three months plus a certification of current financial balances	√	√
Other information on recent changes in household socioeconomic status	√ (if any)	√ (if any)
Number of documents required (if applicable)	12 (down from 17 before DX)	9

Source: Original table for this publication, based on composite of observed cases.
Note: CCRO = Central Civil Registration Office; DLE = Department of Labor and Employment; DX = data exchange with other administrative systems; ESO = Employment Service Office; SSI = Social Security Institute. "UNISO" is the name of Morlandia's social registry.

- ***Registration of the application package and data entry.*** The intake officer at the SSO then receives the application package, reviews it for completeness, creates a client account, records receipt of the application in the system, and schedules an interview (step 6a in figure 2.7). This step triggers MoSA's performance tracking because the interview must be scheduled within 10 business days of receiving the application package. The data entry officer then enters information into UNISO, scans documents into the client's electronic folder, and runs internal and external cross-checks with other systems (step 6b).

- ***Interview.*** The intake officer meets with the client to discuss the client's recent hardship and review the client's situation based on the application package (steps 7 and 8). They also identify data gaps, errors, or inconsistencies. The intake officer explains that the interview and application do not guarantee eligibility for any benefits or services and reviews the client's rights and responsibilities including job search requirements. The intake officer also obtains the client's consent for use and sharing of their information and explains the next steps and likely timeline.
- ***Assessment of client's needs and conditions.*** The intake officer assesses the client's needs and conditions using means-testing tools in UNISO to aggregate income and asset information for the household. A needs profile is created and submitted for the applicant and household (step 9).
- ***Automated determination of eligibility and computation of benefits.*** UNISO automatically verifies the client's profile, checks for eligibility, and computes UA and other social assistance benefits (step 10). If the applicant meets the eligibility criteria, MoSA then authorizes enrollment and notifies the SSO of the decision. MoSA centralizes eligibility and enrollment decisions to ensure equitable and objective treatment of candidates across the country, promoting redistribution and reducing the potential for pressures and discretionary decisions by local officials.
- ***Notification of applicants.*** Subsequently, the SSOs notify all applicants of the decisions on their applications (step 12). Formal notifications are sent through the postal service. For approved beneficiaries, the notification letter also includes information on their benefit amounts, steps, and forms for filing benefit payment claims, and instructions for them to go to the ESO to register their job-seeker profiles and initiate job search activities, which are conditions for receiving UA benefits. The notification letter for nonapproved applicants includes instructions for filing grievances and appeals.
- ***Onboarding at the ESO.*** Enrolled beneficiaries go to the ESO (step 13), where caseworkers carry out onboarding (step 14), which includes creating their job-seeker profiles and picking up their Job Search Logbooks, since they must record job search activities as a condition for filing UA benefit claims. After enrollment, the beneficiary enters the recurring implementation cycles of "benefit and service provision" and beneficiary operations management. These steps are illustrated in green (provision) and purple (management) in figure 2.7 as follows:
- ***Filing first claim.*** There is an official seven-day waiting period before beneficiaries can file their first claim, and during that time they must initiate their job search activities and record them in their Job Search Logbooks (step 15). Such policies are common in countries to ensure a "work first" approach. Payment claims are filed at the local SSOs (step 16).
- ***Monitoring of compliance with conditionalities.*** When beneficiaries file their claims, the SSOs verify their identity with their MICs. They also review the Job Search Logbooks to verify compliance with the job search conditionalities. They enter the benefit claim and compliance information into the computer and print a claim receipt for the clients so that they can track their payments (step 17).
- ***Payments.*** MoSA's payments department reviews the information, adds the new beneficiary to the payroll, and authorizes payments with a payments order that is sent to the post office (step 18). The post office then prints and sends a check to the beneficiary by mail. According to MoSA quality standards, the payment order must be issued within five business days of receiving the claim, and the post office must send and postmark the check within five business days of receiving the payment order (for a total of 10 business days from receipt of the claim to disbursement of the payment).
- ***Service provision and monitoring of compliance with conditionalities.*** Beneficiaries must attend monthly service appointments at the ESO. Employment officers review the client's logbook, discuss job search strategies, and provide job search assistance and referrals.

The process continues with subsequent claims, monitoring, payments, service provision, and so forth. Beneficiaries can receive UA benefits for up to 12 months as long as they continue to meet the conditions of the program. To support incentives to work, if beneficiaries find a job during those 12 months, they can continue to receive gradually declining benefits for an additional three months during the transition (100 percent in first month on the job, 50 percent in the second month, and 30 percent in the third month). If they do not find a job, they can apply for a six-month extension, for up to 18 months, total UA benefits. (Clients who receive an extension revert to step 5 in figure 2.7.)

Journey Mapping: Anaïs's Experience Navigating Unemployment Benefits after the Loss of Her Job

Although systems investments have improved information flows in the back office, public criticism has been mounting due to long processing and wait times. Focus-group discussions with frontline staff, applicants, and beneficiaries confirm many of the challenges reported in the press. MoSA has commissioned a team to undertake a series of in-depth journey mapping exercises to track the actual experience of applicants and beneficiaries (see box 2.3 earlier in this chapter).

One of those journey maps traces Anaïs's experience (figure 2.8). The team's report tracks her experience every step of the way, with details on each activity, the number of visits she had to make, the time each step took, and any out-of-pocket costs. The team kept track of MoSA's quality standards, including turnaround times for key stages. It also calculated the total number of days end to end from the day she lost her job until the day she received her first payment; although this was not a performance indicator for MoSA, it reflects the applicant's journey and is ultimately what matters most to the client. Finally, the report details her feelings at each step in the process, including pain points as well as positive experiences.

The journey mapping exercise uncovered many bottlenecks and inefficiencies. Some of the main points in the summary report included the following:

- ***Excessive time, costs, and visits (TCV).***[19] Anaïs had to make nine visits to the SSO or ESO from the start of the process to the first benefit payment. There was no ESO in her township. Although the SSO had a satellite office in her town, she still walked long distances each time she went, going through a neighborhood that made her feel unsafe. Anaïs also had to make numerous trips to other agencies to gather documents (see below). These trips plus notary fees cost her a total M$34. Additionally, Anaïs spent a total of 53 hours navigating the process.
- ***Burdensome documentation.*** Anaïs spent several days and many visits gathering the required documents. In addition to the initial trip to the ESO to obtain the certified UWOI declaration, Anaïs had to visit her former employer (twice) to obtain the dismissal letter indicating the reason for her job loss (to prove it was not her own fault, which would have disqualified her for benefits), as well as her payroll statements for the past three months. She had to go to the Tax Authority to get her official tax statements. Since her mother owned their house, she and her disabled mother had to travel to the National Land and Property Agency (NLPA), which also meant arranging for a neighbor to watch her children. She also had to go to her bank (twice) to obtain her bank account statements for the past three months, as well as the certification of her financial balances as of the date she submitted her application. Finally, she had to go to a notary public to have all of the documents, plus the application form, notarized.
- ***Interview delay.*** Two weeks elapsed from the day Anaïs lost her job until the day she could finally submit the application package. Her interview was scheduled a further two weeks after that submission. While this was within MoSA's 10-business-day target, the additional weekend days added to Anaïs's wait time. Moreover, even though Anaïs arrived early for her interview, she waited a long time before the caseworker could see her, which meant that she had to walk back home in the dark through a potentially dangerous neighborhood.
- ***Missed notification.*** For some reason, even though MoSA sent the notification of her enrollment on time (within the seven business days after the interview), it did not arrive in the mail. Anaïs had to make two additional trips back to the SSO to inquire, and they finally asked MoSA to send another notification. A total of 18 calendar days elapsed from the date of the interview until the date Anaïs finally received the enrollment notification.
- ***Seven-day waiting period.*** Per MoSA's policy, Anaïs then faced the required seven-day waiting period, during which she had to visit the ESO for the second time, wait for a clerk to help her register her job-seeker profile in DLE's job bank, and wait in another line for the Job Search Logbook.

- ***Filing the claim and receiving payment.*** By the time Anaïs filed the benefits claim, 53 calendar days had elapsed since the day she lost her job. She had to go in person to the SSO's "cashier" to file the claim. In practice, the cashier does not make payments, but that is what the desk is called because at one time payments were made there. Now payments are sent by mail, and with processing times and a national holiday, another nine days elapsed before Anaïs finally received the benefit.
- ***Pain points and positives.*** The journey map traces Anaïs's feelings throughout the process. She felt distraught after the loss of her job, frustrated with bureaucracy, humiliated, discouraged, worried, hopeful, and eventually relieved. In addition to the obvious pain points of having to go to multiple offices, the daunting process of gathering documents, the TCV burden, the missed notifications and delays, Anaïs faced other hassles. Each time she visited the SSO or ESO, she waited in long lines, often with nowhere to sit. In two instances, she was misdirected to the wrong line, and then humiliated by the person at the desk. In another instance, a man pushed in front of her even though it was her turn, and the caseworker shrugged it off and made her wait. When she submitted her application form, she was loudly informed that she would face criminal penalties for false declarations. She also worried about her family's finances and her safety when walking to get to the SSO. As for positives, Anaïs

Figure 2.8 Journey Map for Unemployment Assistance Benefits and Services, Scenario 1: Anaïs's Experience

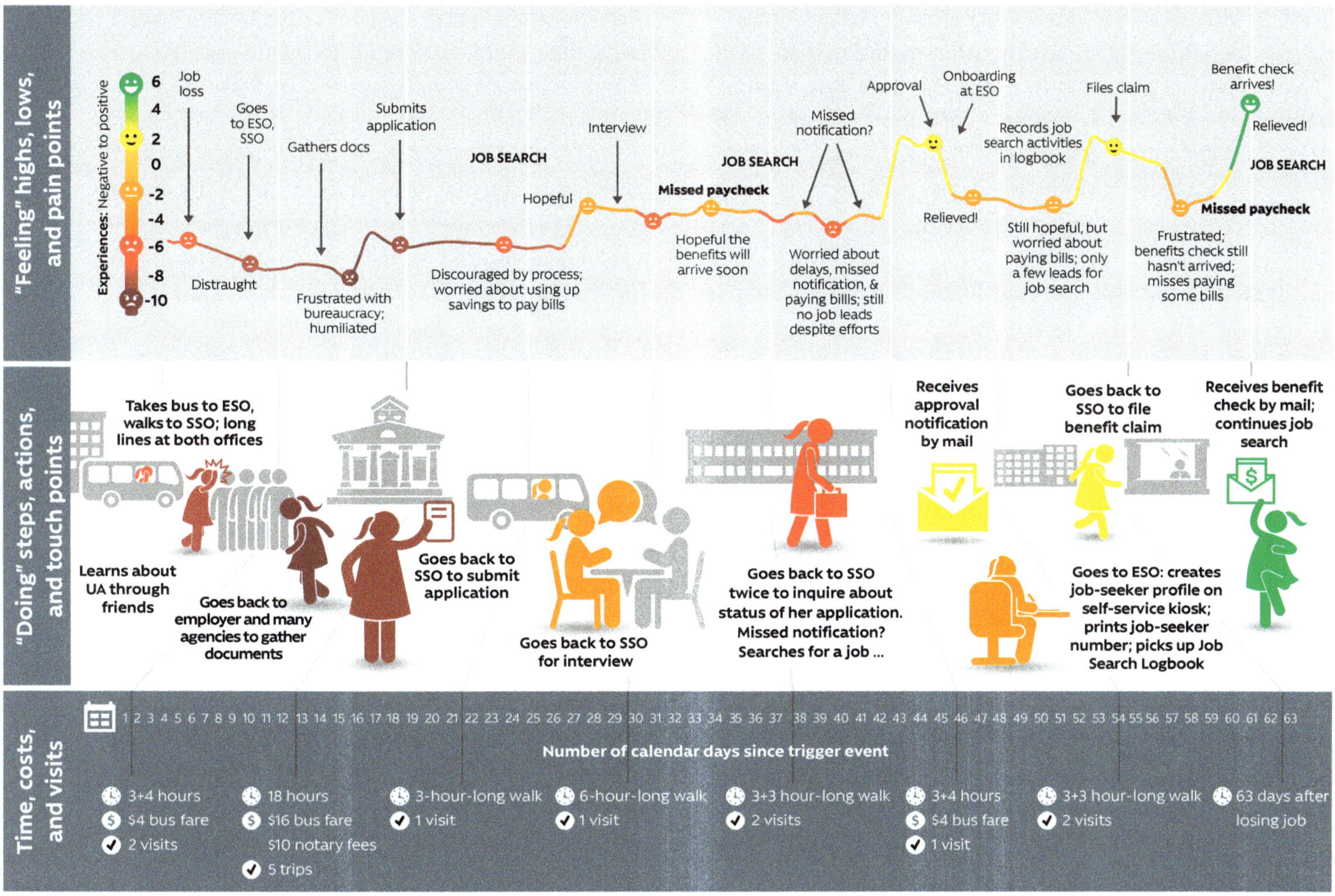

Source: Original figure for this publication, based on composite of observed cases.

Note: ESO = Employment Service Office; SSO = Social Service Office; UA = unemployment assistance.

appreciated the friendly and encouraging caseworker who conducted her interview and felt a huge sense of relief when the benefits arrived.

- ***Elapsed time and economic hardship.*** Sixty-three calendar days elapsed from the day Anaïs lost her job to the day she received her first payment. In the meantime, she missed two paychecks, and she and her family used up their savings during the two months without sufficient income. Meanwhile her children fell ill, possibly because of contaminated water after the tropical storm, and Anaïs faced medical bills. She applied for health insurance subsidies, but that was another process (with many of the same documents as those required by MoSA) and the response did not come in time to help her cover the medical bills for her children. Moreover, the extra time she spent caring for them and bringing them to the clinic meant less time she could devote to looking for a job. To make ends meet, Anaïs and her family also had to cut back on nutritious foods, "adding more water to the soup," and buying protein only every few days. Anaïs made most of the sacrifices herself to ensure that her children had enough to eat. Finally, the family was unable to make the needed repairs on their small house after it was damaged by the storm.

Interestingly, although Anaïs faced many challenges in navigating the process, MoSA achieved its performance indicators for each critical phase. First, the quality standard for the time lapse from submission of the application package to the scheduled interview was met (10 business days). Second, the notification of enrollment was postmarked less than 10 business days after the interview (service standard met), even though it did not reach Anaïs for nearly three weeks. Third, the benefit check was sent by the post office less than 10 business days after Anaïs filed the claim (service standard met). Other qualitative procedural aspects commonly considered good practice were also implemented: the application form requested consent for use of the applicant's information, and the SSO intake officer clearly explained that there would be no guarantee of benefits at the time Anaïs submitted her application (which is important for managing expectations). An important difference between MoSA's and the client's experience is that MoSA's quality standards were measured in business days and anchored in processes, but Anaïs, like other people in need, was racing against time to make ends meet, so for her, what mattered was the lapse in actual calendar days; the emotional and economic starting point for the client is the day of the actual job loss. As such, despite MoSA's positive performance measurement, the total number of calendar days from the time Anaïs lost her job to the time she received a benefit was 63 days (over two months), with a lapse of 50 calendar days from the date she submitted her application package.

Still, MoSA's systems in Scenario 1 had some good features. One huge structural advantage is that Anaïs was able to apply for UA benefits on demand. The fact that Morlandia even has a network for client interface that permits people to apply for benefits and services on demand is a major achievement—one not seen in many countries. Moreover, the interoperability investments by MIT and MoSA reduced the number of documents required for applications (see table 2.3), even though there is room for improvement. For example, Anaïs did not have to provide documentation of her mother's disability benefits because those were already picked up by UNISO via interoperability with SSI. She also did not have to provide documentation of expenses for utilities (such as their electricity bill) because data exchange allows UNISO to pull that information on a quarterly basis from the Morlandia Electric Company. Furthermore, Anaïs was able to qualify for the supplemental child allowance (UCA-PLUS) without having to apply separately for that benefit because of MoSA's previous efforts to harmonize its benefits system. Moreover, although UA and UCA-PLUS benefits do not fully replace the income Anaïs had earned on her job, when they are combined with the base UCA and disability pension for her mother, the family is able to make ends meet while Anaïs looks for a new job. Finally, while the lapse of 50 calendar days from the time of application to the time of first benefit payment is long for the client, it is not an outlier among actual programs around the world. In many countries, receiving benefits can take much longer. Still, there is significant room for improvement.

Scenario 2: Naomi's Journey, a Few Years Later

A few years after the events of Scenario 1, we meet Naomi, a tech worker and mother of two young children. Naomi is the first in her family to complete high school and receive a college degree. She and her two children rent a small concrete house on the outskirts of the city. When she can, Naomi sends money to her family, who live in another part of the country. Naomi has worked for the past several years as a data entry operator and occasionally as a customer service personnel worker, answering clients' questions at several of the offshore multinational businesses. Her jobs have been piecemeal, coming through a private tech firm that receives a cut of her pay. Recently, with advances in robotic process automation, low-tech jobs involving repetitive tasks such as data entry are being replaced. Similarly, with the onset of natural language processing, companies are starting to use virtual assistants that can answer client queries around the clock for less than half the cost of hiring human customer-service personnel. Naomi's contractor has been affected by the rapid automation in low-tech jobs and has informed her that Naomi must find employment elsewhere. Naomi worked hard to put herself through school and had been proud of her ability to sustain herself and her family. Moreover, Naomi's job had allowed her the flexibility to look after her children after school. After working so hard, she is devastated by the loss of her job and worried about how to pay the bills, especially the rent, because her landlord is strict about late payments. She sets out on her journey to apply for unemployment benefits—through her mobile phone. Let us see how that journey plays out.

In the previous few years, Morlandia continued to invest in improving its delivery system platforms. That has greatly improved the effectiveness and efficiency of social protection programs, and other programs as well. Some of the major changes include the following:

- ***Adopting quick reforms.*** After the journey mapping exercises, MoSA carried out a full business process and information systems review, an institutional and functional review, and an assessment of human resource workloads and capacity in the SSOs. These diagnostics identified a road map for reforms, including some "quick wins" such as (1) dropping the seven-day waiting period between enrollment and benefit claims, which had been the subject of fierce criticism by the press and opposition parties; and (2) simplifying some processes and eliminating "non-value-added" steps. One example was eliminating the requirement for unemployed applicants to register at the ESOs and obtain UWOI declaration. The diagnostic assessments found that the operations manual had not been updated to reflect interoperability and the SSOs required the UWOI declaration from the ESOs only because that was the way they had always done it. MoSA promptly issued an official bulletin to all SSOs, ending the unnecessary hurdle. MoSA also tightened its processing turnaround times and started monitoring calendar days rather than business days in its processes.
- ***Shifting from manual to digital payments.*** Payments are now managed and processed by National Trust Bank (NTB), the semi-public bank, which also handles other G2P payments for insurance, civil servant salaries, and so forth. Payments are now directly deposited in beneficiaries' bank accounts. MIT, MoSA, and other ministries are still looking at the option of working directly through the financial system via integrated payments to give people more convenience, choice, and options to use mobile money accounts. That reform, however, is at least a year or two away.
- ***Continuing systems improvements by MIT and MoSA.*** First, MIT continued to roll out its interoperability project to bring in additional agencies, such as the Tax Authority, the National Land and Property Agency, the Judicial Branch, and the Ministries of Health, Education, and Transportation (though data quality problems in the Ministry of Transportation continue to hamper use of information on vehicle ownership). Second, MoSA continued its efforts to improve its internal systems, including entering into data-exchange agreements with various ministries to reduce the number of required documents for UNISO, simplifying and automating various processes, and launching a new user-friendly web services platform for frontline offices with support from MIT.
- ***Expanding the use of UNISO as an integrated platform for social policy.*** Under the "Morlandia Cares" social policy strategy, many agencies have signed data-sharing agreements with MoSA. People can apply for all sorts of means-tested benefits and services through a common application linked to UNISO, both from MoSA and other agencies. For example, MoH can pull data directly from

UNISO to determine eligibility and calculate subsidy levels for health insurance rather than collecting applications and documentation separately. MoE uses data from UNISO to determine eligibility for its JumpStart program. Morlandia Electric Company uses data from UNISO to calculate social energy tariffs. UNISO can also send basic client profiles to the Judicial Branch to allow people to qualify for pro bono legal services and court fee waivers. This use of UNISO for whole-of-government social policy improves efficiency for people and administrators at these many agencies.

- ***Launching an interactive online service window for clients.*** MoSA's diagnostic assessments revealed that people made an excessive number of visits to the SSOs and ESOs. These visits were burdensome for clients and overwhelmed frontline staff, who had to carry out repetitive bureaucratic processing tasks rather than providing higher-end services to clients with complex needs. The Ministry of Labor and Social Protection (MLSP) had started developing an online service window, but when MIT launched a government-wide service platform called "MyMorlandia.org," MoSA shifted to working with that platform, which now connects to UNISO. Initially, MIT's online service window faced a lot of glitches, including system-maintenance time-outs, confusing drop-down menus, scheduling errors, and unclear navigation. The call centers were inundated with clients, who still had to come in to deliver printed applications and documents because of incompatibility with the software. Many clients skipped the online service window altogether and continued to apply in person, waiting in line just as they always had. The press and opposition jumped

Figure 2.9 Delivery Chain Process Map for Unemployment Assistance Benefits and Services in Morlandia: Scenario 2

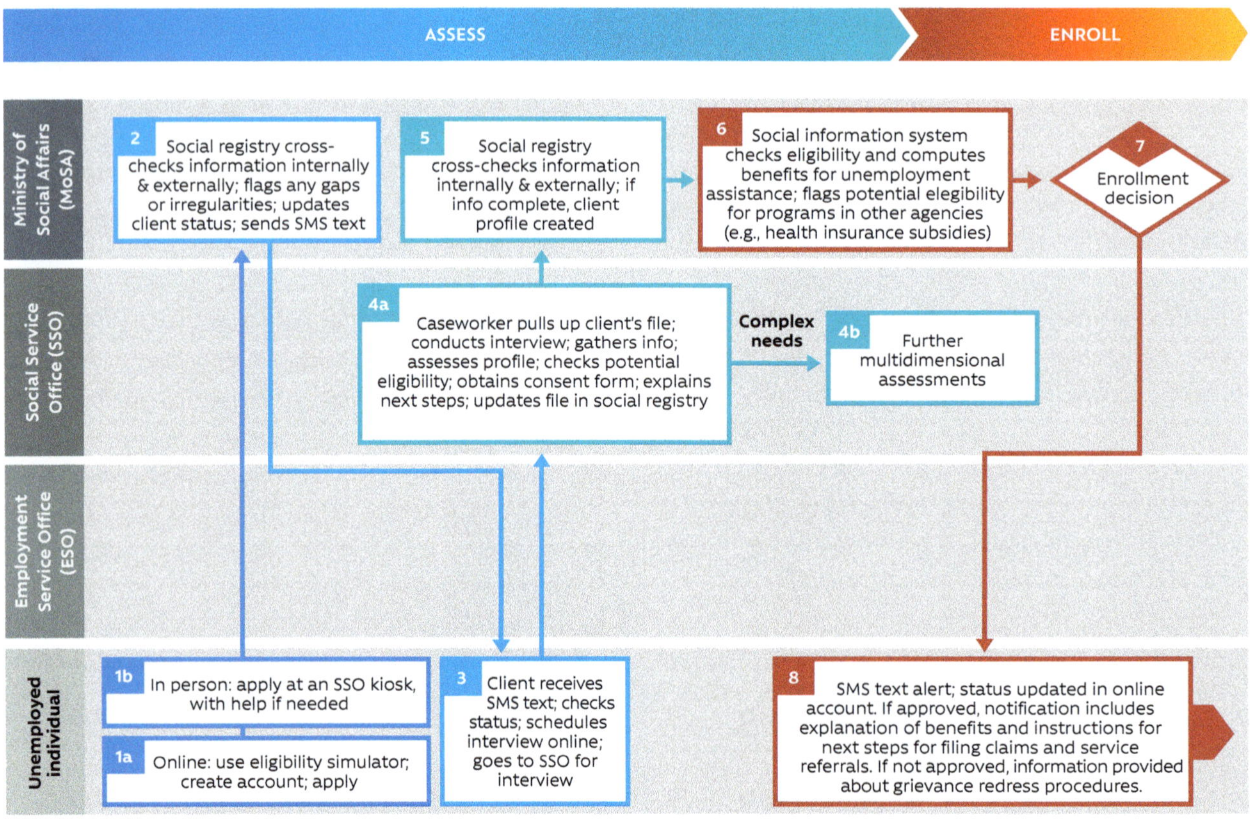

continued

on these malfunctions, which made news headlines multiple times. MIT then procured a new contractor for MyMorlandia.org, this time with the requirement that the developers involve at least 100 users in prototype design, development, and testing; that they employ human-centered design tools and techniques, and that the website should be able to operate on multiple devices, including with a mobile app. The costs of the new app were much less than the first time, since the contract stipulated that the app developers use open-source software and open standards for many aspects of the design. With the relaunch of the new app, an increasing share of clients is successfully switching to MyMorlandia.org.[20]

- ***Launching JobMatch.com.*** DLE also contracted a specialized private firm to partner with a nationwide job-matching platform called "JobMatch.com," which actively courts employers to advertise vacancies and workers to keep their profiles updated for job opportunities. JobMatch.com has been successful for many professions, including for firms and workers in Morlandia's booming tech and tourism industries. JobMatch.com is accessible through MyMorlandia.org.

Delivery Chain Process Map with Continued Systems Improvements, Digital Payments, and Service Windows

These reforms have streamlined the processing steps for MoSA's programs. Figure 2.9 shows the delivery chain process maps for unemployment assistance benefits and services under this scenario.

Figure 2.9 *(continued)*

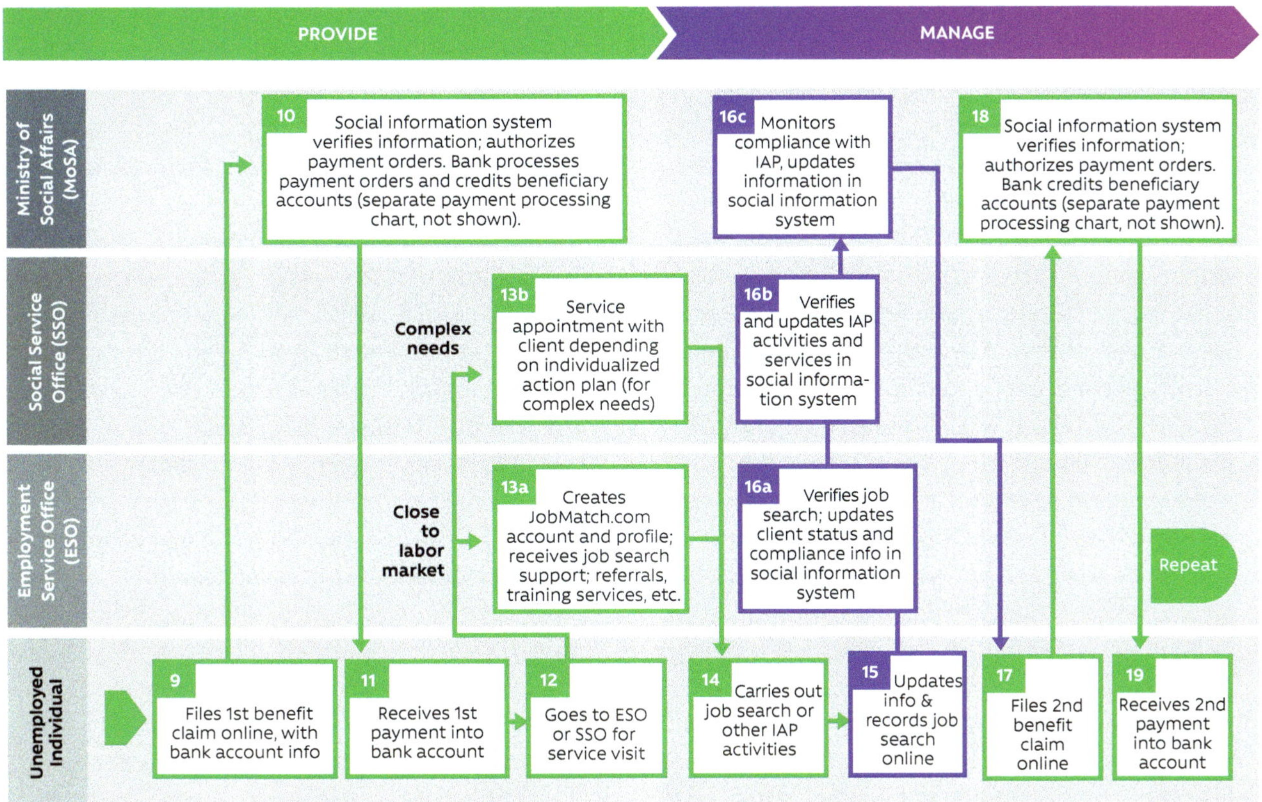

Source: Original figure for this publication, based on composite of observed cases.

Note: ESO = Employment Service Office; IAP = individualized action plan; NTB = National Trust Bank; SSO = Social Service Office; UA = unemployment insurance.

- ***Outreach, intake, registration, and assessment of needs and conditions.*** People can obtain information and apply either online or in person at kiosks in the SSOs. Information is also promoted in communities and public service areas such as hospitals, schools, and community centers. Prospective clients create a MyMorlandia account and enter their MIC and basic identifying information (steps 1a/1b in figure 2.9). UNISO pulls their information from various administrative systems (step 2). MoSA has established clear protocols for updating information and rectifying any errors, and the system then generates a list of required documentation and information to fill any gaps. The number of documents required has been reduced to a maximum of nine (see table 2.3), and clients can upload their documents electronically to their account. The system is programmed to automatically send status updates both to the clients' accounts and their mobile devices via SMS text (step 3). It also allows them to schedule their intake interview using the online calendar system. Caseworkers conduct interviews within seven calendar days of receiving the client's application (step 4). A questionnaire helps caseworkers guide the interview, so they get a more complete understanding of their clients' needs and conditions. Clients are profiled to assess their closeness to the labor market and whether they face complex needs. Their responses may automatically trigger additional multidimensional assessments (step 4b) and possibly individualized service supports. In the back office, UNISO automatically verifies the client's information with internal and external cross-checks (step 5). If information is complete, the client's full profile is generated, including aggregate welfare measures (for means testing) and the caseworker's assessment (step 5).
- ***Determination of eligibility, benefits and services, enrollment and onboarding.*** UNISO automatically checks for eligibility and computes benefit levels for UA and other benefits (step 6). With the reforms, UNISO now automatically flags potential eligibility for benefits and services from other agencies, such as subsidized health insurance from MoH, JumpStart preschool vouchers from MoE, social energy tariffs, and so forth.[21] MLSP then authorizes enrollment decisions for MoSA's benefits (step 7), and applicants receive a notification by SMS text to check their online client accounts in MyMorlandia (step 8). If the application was approved, the online notification includes an explanation of benefits and instructions for next steps, as well as service referrals. If the application was not approved, the notification includes procedures for filing appeals and grievances. Quality standards hold that enrollment decisions and notifications must be issued within seven calendar days of the individual applicant's interview, and within 15 days of the application's receipt.
- ***Benefits provision.*** With the elimination of the seven-day waiting period, beneficiaries can immediately file claims online with NTB (step 9 in figure 2.9). MoSA then verifies the information and authorizes and processes payment orders (step 10). NTB then processes the payment orders and credits the beneficiaries' bank accounts (see step 11). MoSA has tightened its quality standards for turnaround time (see table 2.4), as reflected in the performance contract with NTB.
- ***Service provision.*** Beneficiaries who are profiled as "closer to the labor market" are referred to go to the ESO (step 12) for their service visits (step 13a). They can create their profiles on JobMatch.com, or the ESO employment coaches can help them with it. Beneficiaries must report their job search activities at each visit and participate in a series of "Strategies for Success" training video sessions at the ESOs. The coaches also provide job search assistance and other service referrals, as well as vouchers for specialized training programs depending on their profiles. Beneficiaries who are profiled as having complex needs instead go to the SSO (or other specialized service agencies) for additional risk assessments (step 13b) and an individualized action plan (IAP) with tailored services and required actions for their specific situations.
- ***Data updates and monitoring of compliance with conditionalities.*** Clients must keep their information up to date in their online account (step 15), and there are protocols for updating and correcting information. They also log their job search activities (step 14) via their MyMorlandia account, which also links to their JobMatch.com profiles. ESO employment coaches and SSO caseworkers also verify compliance with job search requirements and/or IAPs and maintain notes in UNISO (steps 16a-c).

The process continues with subsequent claims, monitoring, payments, service provision, and so on. Beneficiaries can receive UA benefits for up to 12 months as long as they continue to meet the conditions of the program. To support incentives to work, if beneficiaries find a job during the 12 months, they can continue to receive gradually declining benefits for an additional three months during the transition (100 percent in first month on the job, 50 percent in the second month, and 30 percent in the third month). If they do not find a job, they can apply for a six-month extension, for up to 18 months total UA benefits (clients who receive an extension revert to step 3 in figure 2.9), but then they also move to a "complex needs" classification and must work with SSO caseworkers for an IAP.

Journey Mapping: Naomi's Experience Navigating Unemployment Benefits after Losing Her Job in the Changing World of Work

The reforms have transformed MoSA's business processes, but how has this played out for clients? MoSA continues to gather feedback, tracking the experience of clients through focus groups and journey maps, including the case of Naomi, who lost her data-entry and call-center jobs (see Naomi's journey map in figure 2.10). The summary report for Naomi's experience included the following points:

Figure 2.10 Journey Map for Unemployment Assistance Benefits and Services, Scenario 2: Naomi's Experience

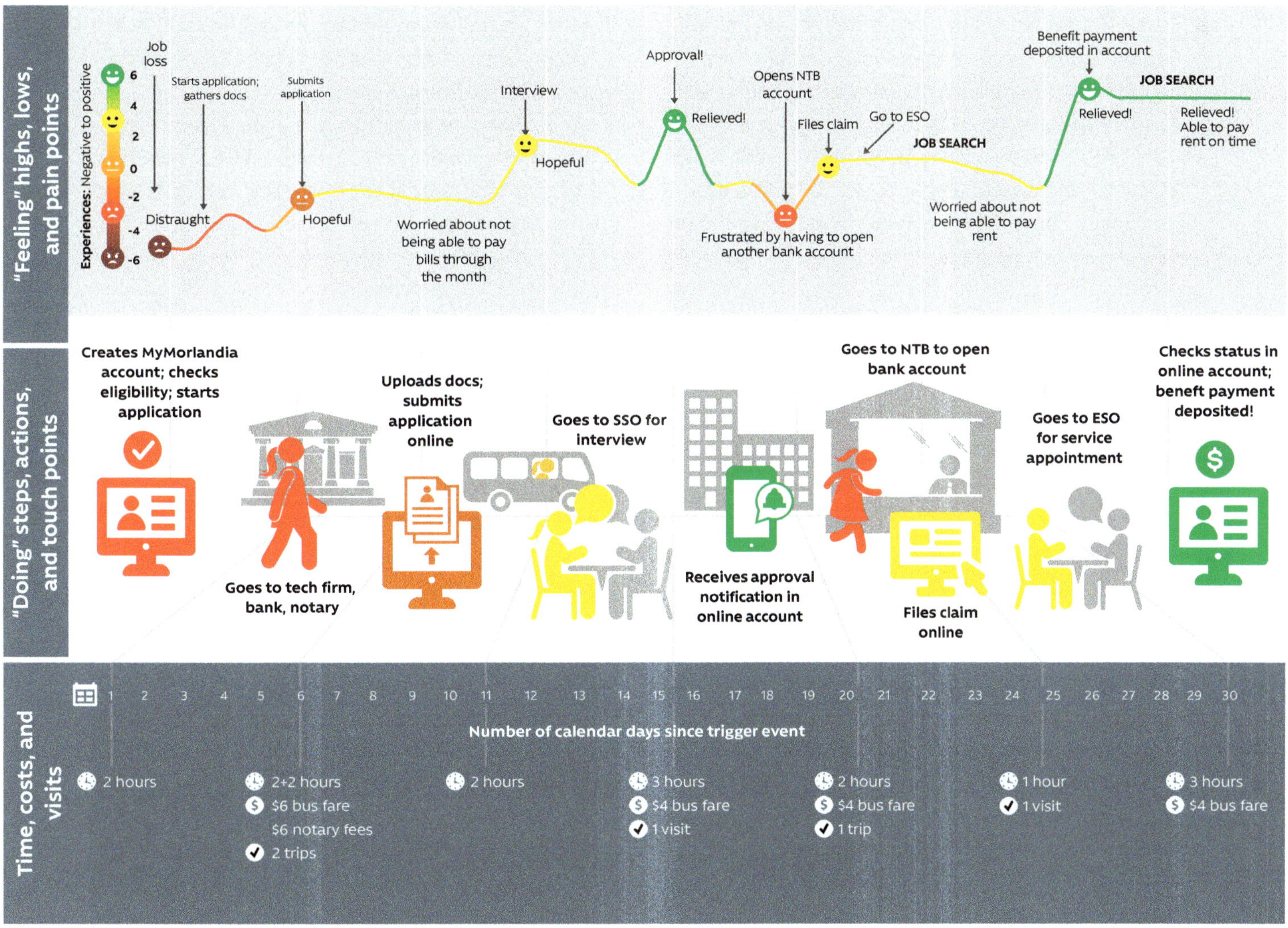

Source: Original figure for this publication, based on composite of observed cases.

- ***The transition to digital processes.*** This was mostly successful. Although Naomi had been receiving universal child allowances, she had not previously migrated them to a digital account. She had to learn about the process and create a new account on MyMorlandia.org. The online process was easy, but her UCA benefits did not appear immediately in her account, so she had to call the helpline. She was on hold for about 30 minutes, but eventually got her problem resolved. The next time she logged in, the UCA benefits appeared with her information. Naomi also noticed that some of the personal information pulled up in the system was incorrect, so she had to follow various protocols to make the corrections. Again, it was easy, but took time for the system to reflect the changes, which prompted Naomi to call the helpline again. Naomi made use of the "Check My Eligibility" button,[22] which allowed her to simulate her potential eligibility for various benefits and services with just minimal information. Within just a few minutes, she learned she was potentially eligible not only for unemployment assistance benefits, but also for the UCA-PLUS supplement, as well as subsidized health insurance and electricity subsidies. What a relief! Naomi was then prompted to start an application but had to save it in a draft while she gathered the required documents. Once she had uploaded all the documents, submitting the application package was easy. Naomi immediately received an SMS text message alert confirming her submission, and her MyMorlandia.org account is regularly updated to keep her abreast of her status and the process.
- ***Document collection.*** Despite MoSA and MIT's push for interoperability, there were still some documents to gather, including (1) the official dismissal letter from the tech firm explaining her previous contracting status and the reason for her dismissal; (2) the past three months of pay statements from her former employer; and (3) her bank statements and current balances (for privacy reasons, that information is not available via data exchange). After gathering those documents, Naomi had to take them to the notary public to get them notarized.
- ***TCV burden.*** In total, from the point of initiating the process to the date of first payment, Naomi spent M$24 out of pocket (on transport and notary fees) and 17 hours on the process. This included one visit to the SSO for the interview, trips to gather documents, and a service appointment at the ESO. Because she did not previously have an account with NTB, she also had to make the trip to the bank to open an account and put in a minimum deposit of M$50, as discussed below.
- ***Eligibility for UA, UCA-PLUS, and various other benefits.*** Naomi was thrilled to learn that, once she qualified for UA and UCA-PLUS with just a few extra actions on MyMorlandia.org, she also qualified for subsidized health insurance and social energy tariffs on her electric bill.
- ***Claims and payments.*** One source of frustration and inconvenience for Naomi was the requirement that she open a bank account with NTB, which did not have any branches or ATMs near her house. Naomi already had an account in a commercial bank and had been receiving her UCA payments by mail. However, she now had to add a new bank to receive a combined payment for her unemployment benefits plus the UCA and UCA-PLUS supplement, requiring that Naomi take several buses and put down a minimum deposit of M$50. This also meant a delay in filing her benefit claim so that she could get the account information.
- ***Pain points and positives.*** Like Anaïs, Naomi experienced many feelings during the process. At various points, she felt distraught, frustrated, worried, hopeful, and relieved. Her main pain points included (1) clarifying some initial glitches in information on her MyMorlandia.org account; (2) gathering the required documents from her commercial bank and employer (though the document burden was not as demanding as in the past); and especially (3) having to open another account at NTB. In addition, an intangible pain point was expectations, which are always higher with digital services, so delays are often met with frustration. There were many positives, however, including that (1) she carried out much of the process on her mobile device; (2) the caseworkers were friendly; (3) she qualified for multiple benefits both from MoSA and from other agencies; and (4) on the service side, she got some leads from JobMatch.com, learned some tips from the career coach, and was able to enroll in some training courses with the help of the training vouchers from the ESO.
- ***Elapsed time.*** In total, it took 26 calendar days from the date Naomi lost her job to the date of her first payment, including 20 calendar days from the date she submitted her application. This meant that Naomi was able to receive her benefit before the following month's rent was due, thus avoiding significant

hardship for her family. She still had to cut back on expenses but was able to make it through the month with benefits while looking for a job.

The reforms clearly improved the process for administrators and clients. Comparing the experiences of Anaïs and Naomi, we find significant improvements in TCV, elapsed time, and performance indicators between the two cases (table 2.4). In fact, both scenarios performed better than many systems we have seen around the world, and the turnaround time for Naomi's case was exceptionally fast (even for mature systems).

Table 2.4 Comparison of Anaïs's and Naomi's Experiences

Performance from client perspective		
	Anaïs (several years ago)	**Naomi (a few years later)**
Main pain points	Having to go to multiple agencies many times Gathering documents Missed notifications in mail Must apply for health insurance subsidies separately and does not know about other benefits and services she may qualify for	Expectations higher with digital services so any delays (even due to holidays) can be met with frustration Gathering documents Had to open another bank account at NTB with a $50 minimum, which also delayed filing claim Some initial glitches with her MyMorlandia.org account
Positives	Benefits were calculated accurately Caseworker at SSO was friendly Waiting periods shorter than in past Fewer documents required than in the past due to MoSA internal interoperability Qualified for UA benefit and UCA-PLUS supplement all with one application	Able to carry out much of the process from home on her mobile device Caseworkers friendly Waiting periods shorter than for Anaïs Far fewer documents required than for Anaïs Qualified for UA benefit, UCA-PLUS supplement, health insurance subsidies, and social energy tariff plus received vouchers and referrals to training courses
Elapsed time	63 calendar days from job loss to benefit payment 53 calendar days from application to benefit payment	26 calendar days from job loss to benefit payment 20 calendar days from application to benefit payment
Time, costs, and visits	53 hours spent on the process $34 in out-of-pocket costs 9 visits to SSO/ESO + 5 trips to other agencies for documents	17 hours spent on the process $24 in out-of-pocket costs + had to make minimum deposit of $50 for NTB account 1 visit to SSO, and then 1 service visit to ESO + 2 trips to gather documents + 1 trip to open bank account
Official performance quality standards (modified with reforms)		
Application to interview	≤10 business days (met)	≤7 calendar days (met)
Interview to notification	≤10 business days (met)	≤7 calendar days (met)
Benefit claim to payment	≤10 business days (met)	≤8 calendar days (met)
Application to payment	(Not a service standard, but it took 53 calendar days)	≤30 calendar days (met)

Source: Original table for this publication.
Note: ESO = Employment Service Office; NTB = National Trust Bank; SSO = Social Service Office; UA = unemployment assistance; UCA-PLUS = Universal Child Allowance (plus supplement for vulnerable children).

The systems agenda is never complete, and challenges remain. People have grown used to near-instantaneous responses in the digital world, which translates into higher expectations—including for public services. Even with relatively fast turnaround, delays can cause frustrations. However, the automated SMS text communications and account-status updates helped manage expectations by keeping clients posted. They are good practice and can be replicated elsewhere. For the future, MoSA could make one simple reform: offer free notary services in the SSOs. Alternatively, the MyMorlandia system could avoid notary requirements altogether by moving entirely to electronic signatures and certification. Finally, the main pain point for Naomi was the fact that she had to open another bank account (at NTB) and put in a minimum deposit just to file a claim and receive benefits. MIT is developing plans to improve digital payments further by enabling clients to select payment modalities with an integrated payments gateway for all G2P transactions and mobile money accounts—but that reform is still at least a year or two off. MIT also needs to continue investing in data protection, and in protecting the confidentiality of users' information.

2.4 SOME CONCLUDING POINTS: FUNDAMENTAL PRINCIPLES

The hypothetical composite example above and the examples presented elsewhere in this Sourcebook illustrate some fundamental principles to keep in mind for social protection delivery systems. These seven principles are not prescriptive; rather, they are reflections that can help build a delivery systems mindset.

1. Delivery systems evolve over time, and their starting points matter. That evolution is nonlinear: systems may go in one direction, face challenges, and then make new investments or corrections to continue evolving. Sometimes those investments and corrections are marginal improvements on the existing system. Sometimes corrections require a quantum leap or a systems overhaul. Or they need to rebuild capacity where it was lost (for example, in FCV situations or after disasters). Even when system implementation is smooth, policies and programs change, context and circumstances change, or technology changes. There will always be room for improvements. Delivery systems must always evolve to keep up.
2. When it comes to designing delivery systems and the programs they support, a key principle should be to "keep it simple." Efforts should be made to "do simple well" before adding complex features to programs or systems. This is especially true when designing or reforming programs: get the basic functions working well before adding complex features that could complicate implementation and compromise the overall effort. For example, a cash transfer program should be able to register and enroll people and pay out benefits properly before too many additional features are added on. Similarly, implementation processes should be kept as simple as possible with deliberate efforts to reduce or prevent "non-value-added steps," excessive paperwork, or confusing navigation. Delivery chain process maps can be used to plot implementation steps across actors, to clarify sequencing and handoffs, and to ensure uniqueness of roles.
3. Quality of implementation matters and weaknesses in any of the core elements will affect the entire system. There are downsides to low quality of implementation, as this can lead to a lower overall impact, errors of inclusion and exclusion, wasted resources, and a higher number of grievances. Delivery systems are only as good as their weakest link. That is because they involve the simultaneous interaction of many moving parts.
4. The first mile for client interface matters—but it is often the weakest link in the delivery chain. Ideally, people can apply for social protection benefits and services whenever they need them. However, such dynamic inclusion requires an extensive, permanent network for client interface, which is often lacking in developing countries. Even with permanent client interface, bureaucratic hurdles can make navigating the system challenging. In some instances, systems improvements on the back end can make it harder for clients to navigate the system on the front end. Or, while such improvements result in

greater efficiency for the mainstream client, they fail to consider challenges for specific subgroups (such as people in remote areas). When client interface is weak, people will suffer, inefficiencies will permeate the system, and even the best technically designed program will fail to meet its objectives. Moreover, such weaknesses or failures on the frontlines are highly visible and can be attacked by the press and political parties.

5. Social protection delivery systems do not operate in a vacuum and should not be developed in silos. Rather, they are part of a much broader government system and should be designed as such. This wider view can be particularly helpful in creating efficient information systems with interoperability links to other systems, personal data privacy and protection standards, as well as payment systems that take advantage of G2P payment systems and a country's financial system. It can also encourage efficient institutional arrangements that build on existing capacities at the central and local levels rather than setting up parallel systems.
6. Social protection delivery systems can potentially contribute more broadly to a government's ability to deliver. Social registries, for example, can help people access benefits or services outside social protection (such as health insurance subsidies, scholarships, social energy tariffs, and legal services). Similarly, caseworker referral systems can link people to a wide range of benefits and services. Since social protection benefits are often a mark of a government's first transfer of funds to the poor, they can also spawn the development of broader G2P payment gateways and financial inclusion of the poor.
7. There is no single blueprint for delivery systems, but there are commonalities. Although the contexts, programs, people, institutions, and operating models of delivery systems are diverse, they share many features in common. Those commonalities are the core elements of the delivery systems framework, particularly the common implementation phases in the delivery chain. The framework described in this Sourcebook does not aim to be prescriptive, but to provide a useful and practical way of organizing our understanding of how social protection programs are implemented.
8. The dual challenges of inclusion and coordination are pervasive and perennial, and also contribute to the objectives of effectiveness and efficiency. Effective delivery systems are by their essence inclusive, as they not only reach the intended population, but also include vulnerable populations, and clients who have specific access barriers. Efficient delivery systems necessarily operate in contexts of high coordination, as they exploit synergies within and across programs to minimize costs for administrators and promote integration across programs to minimize costs for clients.

Notes

1. We differentiate between various levels of implementation: (1) "Stage" refers to the higher levels of "assess," "enroll," "provide," and "manage"; (2) within the stages, there are various implementation phases (outreach; intake and registration; assessment of needs and conditions; determination of eligibility; decisions on enrollment; decisions on the benefit-service package; notification and on-boarding; provision of benefits; provision of services; beneficiaries' compliance with conditionalities, data updates, and grievances; exit decisions; notifications; and case outcomes); (3) within each implementation phase, there can be more detailed levels, such as processes, steps, and so forth.
2. Institutional arrangements include formal organizational structures (actors), rules, and informal norms.
3. Discussing here only noncontributory programs/services. See Matsuda (2017) for some illustrations of these variations.
4. There are exceptions, of course, with various examples of states or subnational governments financing (or cofinancing) social protection programs, particularly in large and/or federal countries such as Canada, India, the Russian Federation, and the United States.
5. In all of the above-mentioned situations, understanding the policy-making body's formal (de jure) responsibilities is not enough. Its actual (de facto) capacity, level of technical capability, and financial/political clout is what makes the difference in practice.
6. In highly decentralized states, subnational governments often take on some residual responsibilities in social protection. However, it is rare for social protection to be a primary responsibility of subnational governments.

7. That is, formal organizational structures, rules, and informal norms.
8. In an effort to more closely align incentives and increase accountability, some countries have attempted to transfer to the local level the responsibility for program implementation as well as program financing. However, results on the latter have been mixed at best, particularly in ECA. See Bassett, Giannozzi, Pop, and Ringold (2012) and Grosh et al. (2008).
9. For a full discussion of this point in the context of Pakistan, see Matsuda (2017).
10. See glossary on the distinction between Integration and Interoperability, which are often conflated.
11. Some so-called social registries are developed as "mere databases," but these do not fulfill the functions of social registries as inclusion and information systems.
12. The Republic of Korea built a whole-of-government integrated data center in 2005 with more than 20,000 pieces of hardware and a 30 percent reduction in data center costs.
13. Parts of the U.S. government use cloud-based Amazon Web Services.
14. Public works programs are an exception: they tend to adopt administrator-driven cohort approaches but are targeted to unemployed or underemployed individuals.
15. Design parameters can differ between the on-demand approach and the administrator-driven approach. Certain types of design parameters are consistent with the cohort approach, but not with the on-demand approach. The most obvious example is the use of relative rankings and eligibility thresholds. Under the on-demand approach, clients apply and enter at different times, so the relative rankings approach cannot be used. Another design difference between the two approaches is the calibration of sequencing of accompanying measures or productive economic inclusion interventions for a group of beneficiaries, which assumes that a cohort of beneficiaries would move through the stages of the intervention together and on a common timetable. Thus, if program administrators want to transition from mass registration to an on-demand approach to promote dynamic inclusion, design parameters may also need to change, such as eligibility criteria and the sequencing of interventions.
16. Guaranteed minimum income schemes epitomize the tailored approach because they calculate the difference between the specific client's incomes and an established minimum level.
17. Not all programs adopting an administrator-driven cohort approach use relative rankings and thresholds to determine eligibility. Some use absolute thresholds applied to welfare measures for each household within the cohort.
18. While this discussion focuses on benefits, such limits can be equally heart-wrenching for services, for example when a program for developmentally disabled children does not have enough slots to meet demand due to limited capacity and financing.
19. See box 2.3 for a discussion of the TCV indicator.
20. Clients without digital access or knowledge can still apply in person at the SSOs, where clerks help them carry out the process on digital self-service kiosks in the lobby. So far just under 60 percent of MoSA's clients have switched to digital applications from their own devices, and that percentage continues to grow.
21. While UNISO can prequalify people for potential eligibility for these other programs, the institutional mandate and jurisdiction for actual eligibility, enrollment, and benefit decisions lies with the other agencies (such as MoH for health insurance subsidies). When someone prequalifies through MoSA's common application, UNISO sends a flag to MoH, which then notifies the clients of eligibility status via their MyMorlandia.org accounts.
22. These kinds of "check my eligibility" simulators are quite useful and can be used in online service windows even if the program/country does not yet have full online applications. They help avoid clogging on-demand systems with ineligible applicants, unnecessary creation of accounts, and/or unneeded interview appointments in the offices. This can save on TCV for people who would be unlikely to qualify for benefits and services and for frontline staff. When used, the simulators clearly need to state that they do not guarantee eligibility but are just an indication of potential eligibility.

Bibliography

Alderman, Harold, Ugo Gentilini, and Ruslan Yemtsov, eds. 2018. *The 1.5 Billion People Question: Food, Vouchers, or Cash Transfers?* Washington, DC: World Bank.

Auer, Peter, Ümit Efendioglu, and Janine Leschke. 2008. *Active Labour Market Policies around the World: Coping with the Consequences of Globalization*. 2nd ed. Geneva: International Labour Office.

Barca, Valentina, and Richard Chirchir. 2019. "Building an Integrated and Digital Social Protection Information System." Deutsche Gesellschaft für Internationale Zusammenarbeit (GIZ) GmbH, Bonn, Germany. https://www.giz.de/de/downloads/giz2019-en-integrated-digital-social-protection-information-system.pdf.

Bassett, Lucy, Sara Giannozzi, Lucian Pop, and Dena Ringold. 2012. "Rules, Roles, and Controls: Governance in Social Protection with an Application to Social Assistance." Social Protection and Labor Discussion Paper no. SP1206, World Bank, Washington, DC. http://documents.worldbank.org/curated/en/301371468151778608/Rules-roles-and-controls-governance-in-social-protection-with-an-application-to-social-assistance.

Cavoukian, Ann. 2011. "Privacy by Design: The 7 Foundational Principles—Implementation and Mapping of Fair Information Practices." Information and Privacy Commissioner of Ontario, Canada. https://lab.org/wp-content/IAB-uploads/2011/03/fred_carter.pdf.

Grosh, Margaret, Carlo del Ninno, Emil Tesliuc, and Azedine Ouerghi. 2008. *For Protection and Promotion: The Design and Implementation of Effective Safety Nets*. Washington, DC: World Bank.

Hammer, Michael, and James Champy. 2003. *Reengineering the Corporation: A Manifesto for Business Revolution*. New York: Harper Business Essentials.

IDEO.org. 2015. *The Field Guide to Human-Centered Design*. IDEO.org, San Francisco.

Karippacheril, Tina George. 2018. "The First Mile in Delivering Social Protection and Jobs (SPJ): Human-Centered Design." Presentation at the World Bank's Social Safety Nets and Delivery Systems Core Course, Washington, DC.

Karippacheril, Tina George, and Kathy Lindert. 2016. "Delivery Chain Process Mapping and End-to-End Implementation Planning for Social Safety Net Programs." Social Protection and Labor Delivery Systems Global Solutions Group. Presentation at the World Bank's Social Safety Nets and Delivery Systems Core Course, Washington, DC.

Karippacheril, Tina George, and Kathy Lindert. 2017. "Delivery Chain Process Mapping and End-to-End Implementation Planning for Social Safety Net Programs." Social Protection and Labor Delivery Systems Global Solutions Group. Presentation at the World Bank's Social Safety Nets and Delivery Systems Core Course, Washington, DC.

Karippacheril, Tina George, and Kathy Lindert. 2018. "Delivery Chain Process Mapping and End-to-End Implementation Planning for Social Safety Net Programs." Social Protection and Jobs Delivery Systems Global Solutions Group. Presentation at the World Bank's Social Safety Nets and Delivery Systems Core Course, Washington, DC.

Karippacheril, Tina George, Kenichi Nishikawa Chávez, and Inés Rodríguez Caillava. 2019. "Delivery Chain Process Mapping for Social Programs." Presentation at SPJ Learning Days, Human Development Week, Washington, DC.

Karippacheril, Tina George, and Inés Rodríguez Caillava. 2019. "Institutions and Coordination: Delivery Chain Process Mapping for Social Programs." Presentation at the World Bank's Social Safety Nets and Delivery Systems Core Course, Washington, DC.

Leite, Phillippe, Tina George, Changqing Sun, Theresa Jones, and Kathy Lindert. 2017. "Social Registries for Social Assistance and Beyond: A Guidance Note and Assessment Tool." Social Protection and Labor Discussion Paper 1704, World Bank, Washington, DC. http://documents.worldbank.org/curated/en/698441502095248081/Social-registries-for-social-assistance-and-beyond-a-guidance-note-and-assessment-tool.

Lindert, Kathy, and Tina George Karippacheril. 2017. "A Framework for Social Safety Net Delivery Systems." Social Protection and Labor Delivery Systems Global Solutions Group. Presentation at the World Bank's Social Safety Nets and Delivery Systems Core Course, Washington, DC.

Lindert, Kathy, and Tina George Karippacheril. 2018. "Social Protection Delivery Systems and the Dual Challenges of Inclusion and Coordination." Presentation at the World Bank's Social Safety Nets and Delivery Systems Core Course, Washington, DC.

Matsuda, Yasuhiko. 2017. *Organizing Social Protection in Federal States: International Examples of Federalism and Social Protection and Implications for Pakistan*. Washington, DC: World Bank. http://documents.worldbank.org/curated/en/525311532077545572/Organizing-social-protection-in-federal-states-international-examples-of-federalism-and-social-protection-and-implications-for-Pakistan.

Rummler, Geary A., and Alan P. Brache. 1990. *Improving Performance: How to Manage the White Space on the Organization Chart*. 2nd ed. Jossey-Bass Management Series. San Francisco: Jossey-Bass.

Sluchynsky, Oleksiy. 2019. "Social Insurance Administrative Diagnostic (SIAD): Guidance Note." World Bank, Washington, DC; International Social Security Association, Geneva, Switzerland.

Solomon, Jake. 2017. "Human Centered Design in Social Programs: Direct Experience from the US." Presentation at the World Bank, Washington, DC.

Subbarao, Kalanidhi, Carlo del Ninno, Colin Andrews, and Claudia Rodríguez-Alas. 2013. *Public Works as a Safety Net: Design, Evidence, and Implementation*. Directions in Development Series. Washington, DC: World Bank.

US Digital Services. 2014. "Digital Services Playbook." https://playbook.cio.gov/.

World Bank and ILO (International Labour Organization). 2016. "A Shared Mission for Universal Social Protection: Concept Note." World Bank, Washington, DC; ILO, Geneva, Switzerland.

Chapter 3

Outreach

Surat Nsour, Vasumathi Anandan, Kathy Lindert, and Tina George Karippacheril

How do people become aware of social protection programs? How do they learn about program objectives and rules, as well as delivery processes such as intake and registration? How do administrators ensure that intended populations and vulnerable groups are reached? Those are the tasks of the outreach phase of social protection delivery systems.

Outreach involves interactions to inform people about social protection programs and delivery processes and to create adaptations to encourage them to engage.[1] Outreach aims to reach intended populations who may include, among others, (1) children, youth, the elderly, or other demographic groups; (2) the poor or other groups defined according to their socioeconomic status; (3) the unemployed or other job seekers; (4) persons with disabilities; (5) vulnerable individuals and families facing social risks. Active outreach should also make adaptations to ensure that vulnerable groups are informed and reached, such as those with cultural or linguistic differences, the disabled, or people with other potential access barriers. Adaptations may also be needed to reach marginalized populations such as the homeless; lesbian, gay, bisexual, and transgender (LGBT) youth; and those living in remote areas or in situations of fragility, conflict, or violence (FCV). In addition to the intended population, outreach efforts should involve other stakeholders who often have characteristics that may influence, directly or indirectly, those who are hard to reach. Beyond the intended population, the program needs outreach to others, including the following:

- At the household level, key members who influence behaviors and increase the level of motivation and participation; for example, in Djibouti, outreach efforts emphasize the involvement of grandmothers to promote child nutrition, health, and women participation
- At the community level, professionals and relevant service providers who help facilitate referrals as well as staff of other programs who might be in a position to inform about the program, such as community

leaders, teachers, doctors, and others who can influence changes through interactions with parents and caregivers, as well as one-on-one interaction with hard-to-reach populations of children and youth
- At the level of intermediaries, or those who are able to influence changes in the community, who then do outreach to the intended population, such as social workers and civil society
- At the local and national levels, other key stakeholders, including media, politicians, donors, and local bodies or leaders who are able to influence the atmosphere and attitudes, generating relevant knowledge about the intended population and available programs and services.

Outreach is the first phase of the delivery chain (figure 3.1) and is critical to determining the effectiveness of delivery systems for any social protection program. While communications and outreach are needed across the delivery chain, this section focuses on initial outreach, which aims to inform the intended and wider population about program(s) so that they are aware, informed, able, and encouraged to engage. The key inputs to outreach include information about program(s) and delivery processes, core messages, and tools for communication and active search. The core outputs would be that the intended population is informed, understands the intervention(s), and are willing to engage, register, and provide their information. Those outputs then feed into the next phase on the delivery chain: intake and registration (see chapter 4).

This chapter is organized as follows:

- Sections 3.1 and 3.2 define the concept and core elements of outreach. and discuss its challenges as well
- Sections 3.3 and 3.4 provide an overview of outreach strategies, modalities, and instruments, including tailoring them to specific groups and contexts.
- Section 3.5 highlights some institutional aspects.
- Section 3.6 summarizes and concludes

Various country examples are discussed in this chapter, including some from each region:

- **Africa:** Benin, Kenya, Rwanda
- **East Asia and the Pacific:** the Philippines
- **Europe and Central Asia:** Bulgaria, Denmark, Estonia, Finland, Germany, Portugal, Romania, the Slovak Republic, Slovenia, Sweden, the United Kingdom
- **Latin America and the Caribbean:** Brazil
- **Middle East and North Africa:** Iraq, the Republic of Yemen
- **South Asia:** Pakistan
- **Other Organisation for Economic Co-operation and Development (OECD) countries:** the United States

3.1 CORE CONCEPTS AND ELEMENTS

Although most social protection practitioners agree that outreach is vital, there is no single definition of what it means. We combine many of the elements used in the literature and in practice to define outreach in social protection delivery systems as "deliberate efforts to reach and inform intended populations and vulnerable groups about social protection programs and delivery systems in ways that they will comprehend so that they are aware, informed, able, and encouraged to engage." This definition has several elements: (1) purpose: to inform people about

Figure 3.1 The Outreach Phase of the Social Protection Delivery Chain

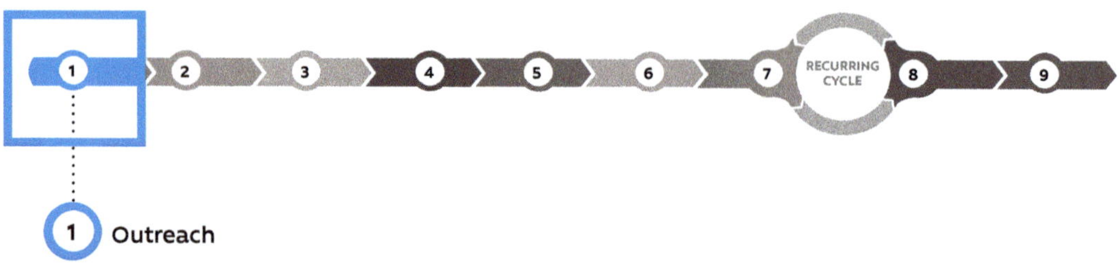

Source: Original figure for this publication.

social protection programs and delivery systems; (2) people: the focus is on the intended population, including ensuring that the underserved or vulnerable groups are reached; and (3) proactive approach: the efforts are deliberate and tailored to ensure that the intended population is reached and that they promote understanding, awareness, and ability to engage.

The purpose of outreach is to inform people about social protection programs and delivery systems so that they understand and are able and encouraged to engage. That means: first, ensuring that people understand various aspects of social protection program(s), such as their objectives, intended population, program rules, eligibility criteria, scope and content; second, facilitating their understanding of delivery systems, including processes; institutional actors; points of contact and how to contact them; timing and place of registration; rights and responsibilities of registrants and eventual beneficiaries; channels for filing grievances, complaints and appeals, etc.; third, facilitating understanding, awareness, and access to specific components of delivery systems, such as social registries, or other related systems, such as payment systems, civil registration, and foundational ID systems.

Active outreach is critical for promoting potential inclusion of "hard to reach" and marginalized groups—for consideration of eligibility for social programs. If the social registry is to serve its "inclusion" role, it is important that it covers as many potential recipients of social programs (or other "user programs") as possible. Active outreach efforts are important for dynamic and on-demand intake and registration. Vulnerable populations may not be aware of social program benefits they could be eligible to receive.

Evidence shows that in the absence of a well-thought-through outreach strategy, social protection programs may run the risk of exacerbating exclusion errors for lack of information and skepticism that the programs may not yield an immediate or longer-term benefit, particularly for people living in remote and isolated locations. A proactive outreach effort can help in managing expectations, minimizing grievances, and developing better mutual understanding to avoid risk of negative spiral, program failure, external manipulation, loss of credibility, and politicization.

3.2 OUTREACH CHALLENGES

This Sourcebook focuses on challenges faced by intended populations. These include (1) children, youth, the elderly, or other demographic groups; (2) the poor or other groups defined according to their socioeconomic status; (3) the unemployed or other job seekers; (4) persons with disabilities; (5) vulnerable individuals and families facing social risks. Table 3.1 highlights some of the outreach challenges that could be faced by these groups. The ensuing chapters of the Sourcebook use the construct of this table to highlight adaptations that are needed to encourage people to engage with the different phases of the delivery chain.

Within those populations, several vulnerable marginalized groups require some proactivity and tailored efforts. While groups may lack awareness of social protection programs or be deterred by complex or confusing procedures, some groups face additional challenges.

Proactive effort is a core element of outreach. Human-centered, deliberate, and tailored approaches ensure that the intended population is reached and that the outreach promotes understanding, awareness, and the ability to engage. Outreach uses communication tools, instruments, and platforms to reach people in locations that are close to their environment and in ways that they can comprehend. Examples of proactive outreach strategies, modalities, and instruments are included in the next section.

3.3 OUTREACH STRATEGIES, MODALITIES, AND INSTRUMENTS

Outreach strategies for social protection programs include messages aimed at the intended population and those who have an influence on and play a role in their lives. There is no one-size-fits-all approach. Outreach strategies vary according to context, objectives, and the characteristics of the intended populations. Adapting outreach

Table 3.1 Common Intended Populations for Social Protection Programs and Associated Outreach Challenges

Demographic groups along the life cycle	
Children	Dependent on parents and guardians for access.
Elderly	May have limited literacy, digital access, mobility, or challenges relating to aging.
Women	May face mobility issues, domestic violence, or stigma.
Groups constrained by socioeconomic status	
People living below the poverty line	May lack awareness or have misconceptions about programs; may be deterred by complex procedures; may lack trust in institutions. May have limited literacy or digital access. May face family challenges or stigma or shame for their economic situation.
Homeless	May be "invisible" to the programs or system; may lack awareness of programs; may face stigma or shame; may lack a fixed address, hampering their efforts to connect to programs or apply.
People living in isolated and remote areas	May lack transport, mobility, or physical access. May be widely dispersed, with difficult physical access; may be without electricity or internet access. Remoteness can complicate outreach efforts (and delivery more generally) given the dispersion of people, difficult physical access, lack of electricity and internet connections, and so on. May have no permanent address, and poor or no identification credentials or official government papers. (People in remote areas can easily be overlooked by social protection programs as they are less visible.)
Pastoralist, nomadic, and semi-nomadic groups	May have no permanent address and poor or no identification credentials or official government papers.
Indigenous groups	May have challenges associated with living conditions, income levels, employment rates, access to safe water, sanitation, health services, and food availability; may be facing destruction to their lands, territories, and resources essential to their survival; may be dealing with adverse consequences of climate change and environmental contamination (heavy metals, industrial gases, and effluent wastes); may be living in geographic isolation and poverty, not having the means to pay the high cost for transport; challenges may be compounded by discrimination, racism, a lack of cultural understanding and sensitivity, and language barriers.[a]
Refugees, stateless, immigrants, internally displaced populations (IDPs), and people living in areas affected by fragility, conflict, and violence	May be physically and socially isolated, presenting obstacles to direct contact; may be faced with a variety of dangers and risks.
Ethnic, religious, linguistic, and visible minorities	May face violence, attacks, stigma, or fear. May have poor or no identification credentials or official government papers. May face language and cultural barriers, discrimination, lack of awareness of programs or their rights, and fears (particularly if residence status is not formalized).

continued

Table 3.1 *(continued)*

Group	Barriers
Labor and work conditions	
Unemployed	May lack awareness or have misconceptions about programs; may be deterred by complex procedures; may face other barriers such as stigma, shame, perceived lack of need, or lack of trust in institutions.
Discouraged/inactive workers	May have given up on finding employment or support. Could be invisible to the program(s) or system (because they are not registered at employment services). (Subgroups could include inactive women, inactive older workers, and migrant or refugee workers.).
Informal sector workers	May have poor social insurance, health, worker's compensation, or savings for old age.
Forced or child laborers	Child laborers may face violence, fear, malnutrition, poor working conditions, abuse, neglect, or lack of parental care. (Remains a prevalent problem in many industries, particularly informal garment manufacturing and stitching and leather processing, as well as some agriculture such as tea and cocoa harvesting.)
Disability	
Persons with disabilities	May have access barriers related to mobility, physical status, cognition, or language or reading challenges. May face stigma or discriminatory attitudes.
Vulnerable individuals facing specific social risks	
Children at-risk	Children are dependent and may face challenges advocating for themselves and are likely uninformed about their rights and social services that could help them (especially if they are facing abuse, neglect, or lack of parental care).
Youth at-risk	Adolescents who are not in education, employment, or training (NEETs) may not be visible to the program(s) or the system; they may also be unaware or skeptical of programs, caseworkers, or other professionals.
Adults at-risk	May be in abusive relationships and unable to advocate for themselves; may lack information about protective services; may face stigma or shame; may face a multitude of complex needs and not know where to go for help—or even that such help would be available.
LGBT	May face stigma, shame, or fears; discrimination; homelessness and rejection by their families; lack of support from the community; physical risks; violence; challenges in securing identity documents or credentials; challenges accessing health insurance coverage or health care.

Source: Original table for this publication.

Note: LGBT = lesbian, gay, bisexual, and transgender.

a. See the United Nations' *State of the World's Indigenous Peoples* at https://www.un.org/esa/socdev/unpfii/documents/2016/Docs-updates/SOWIP_Health.pdf.

modalities for the specific intended populations and vulnerable groups enhances the likelihood of their effectiveness. This chapter is not intended to be prescriptive, but rather documents various types of strategies, modalities, and instruments used in diverse country contexts and for a variety of social protection programs.

Outreach Strategies and Diagnostics

Ideally, outreach strategies are shaped and informed by diagnostics. While these may be carried out in advance, they can also be helpful during implementation to help provide feedback and support mid-course corrections to improve understanding, verify that intended population groups are being reached, and clarify myths and misperceptions. The approach and ambition are to be tailored according to the size and characteristics of the intended population. Diagnostic tools can include situational analyses, communication needs assessments, and stakeholder assessments. Stakeholder assessments can make deliberate efforts to identify and understand various aspects of the intended populations, including: their characteristics (socioeconomic aspects, language, literacy, access to computers or other systems, proximity to the program and to delivery systems' frontlines, etc.), their communications habits (for example, do they rely on social media or newspapers), and their precise location (aided by GPS if needed).

Outreach strategies are tailored to the program's objectives and its intended populations. Once core stakeholders or intended populations are identified, proactive and tailored strategies are developed to reach them. Such strategies are inclusive by design, making adaptations for specific vulnerable groups. Kenya's Outreach Strategy for the Inua Jamii National Safety Net Program is one such example (box 3.1).

Diverse Modalities and Instruments for Outreach

Social protection programs and delivery systems use a variety of modalities for outreach, often in combination. Surveying the terrain, we find numerous modalities for conducting outreach in social protection programs. Four broad categories emerge: (1) direct modalities; (2) community-based outreach; (3) outreach via intermediaries; and (4) outreach via information campaigns and technology (summarized in table 3.2).

Direct outreach modalities seek to communicate directly with people—either one-on-one or in groups. Communication and outreach efforts are carried out by program or delivery systems administrators and directly reach intended populations. These direct interactions can take place in the office or in the environment of the intended population. The administrators may be specialized outreach officers or caseworkers and the interaction may occur on demand, when people come to local offices, satellite offices, or kiosks to seek information. (The latter requires that the intended population already knows enough about the existence of the program(s) and/or local offices to seek support.) Alternatively, mobile teams may go to households, neighborhoods, or communities directly, which has the advantage of proactively bringing outreach efforts to the intended populations in their own environment, but such efforts can be costly. Mobile employment service officers are used in Bulgaria, Estonia, Germany, and Romania (Mosely, Scharle, and Stefanik 2018). They typically visit local communities once or twice a month to raise awareness of available job vacancies, specific labor market programs, and sometimes also deliver counseling, mediation, or training services on the spot.

Community-based outreach modalities rely on local actors to reach out to intended populations and disseminate information. Such methods can involve trained peers who both come from the intended population and reach out to them on behalf of the program. They can be quite effective with youths, who may be more likely to trust their own peers. Community-based methods can also involve local leaders, mother groups, faith-based leaders, community organizations, etc. Such methods can be effective with people living in remote areas or representatives of culturally or linguistically distinct communities, since the peers or community leaders are one of their own, can speak their language, and understand their situation (though efforts are made to ensure that existing inequities or biases are not reinforced within the community). A community-based outreach model in the Republic of Yemen's Social Development Fund focuses on using existing networks in the community for outreach. Box 3.2 provides an example of community-based outreach in Pakistan's Benazir Income Support Programme (BISP), which was tailored on the basis of communications diagnostics

Box 3.1 Outreach Strategy: Kenya's Inua Jamii National Safety Net Program

Inua Jamii is Kenya's national flagship Social Safety Net Program, covering four main cash transfer programs: (1) the Older Persons Cash Transfer; (2) Persons with Severe Disability Cash Transfer; (3) Cash Transfer for Orphans and Vulnerable Children; and (4) the Hunger Safety Net Programme. The government developed a proactive Outreach Strategy as a subcomponent of the existing Communications Strategy to reach out to current and potential cash transfer beneficiaries, stakeholders, and implementing partners at county and subcounty levels. The main intent of the Outreach Strategy was to improve awareness of key features of the Inua Jamii program, including the program's objectives, eligibility criteria, registration and enrollment processes, payments, and grievance redress mechanisms. In addition, the strategy sought to empower intended populations to effectively engage with the program with adequate knowledge and understanding of their rights, responsibilities, and entitlements.

The Outreach Strategy was built around three key pillars. First, the program sought to promote branding and awareness building of the Inua Jamii program to communicate a coherent, credible, and recognizable brand identity for the intended audience. This was realized through a visibility campaign that aimed to engage local actors and program staff for their proactive support in active outreach. Stakeholders' forums accompanied with dissemination of program information through materials, such as brochures and leaflets, helped develop a shared understanding of the program, mobilizing local actors from the civil society, community, and local media. Second, internal communication mechanisms were strengthened to sensitize staff and implementation partners toward ensuring efficiency in engagement and program communication with the intended population. This was achieved through training of the implementing officers at the county and subcounty levels to develop a motivated and well-informed team. Finally, outreach efforts aimed at informing the intended populations about the key features of the Inua Jamii's delivery processes and their potential rights, entitlements, and responsibilities. A mix of tailored approaches were central to the outreach strategy, including the following:

- **Context-specific, inclusive, and human-centered approach.** The human-centered approach led to a strategically and tactically coherent design that employed the use of field diagnostics to understand local context, communication barriers, and information consumption habits of the intended population. As a result, messages embedded in local language and visual vocabulary delivered an outreach campaign, which was easy to recollect and identify with. A visual storytelling and messaging framework tailored to local realities promoted ease of information delivery, resulting in enhanced understanding of the program.
- **Bilingual messaging in Swahili-English.** This was designed and introduced in addition to the visual aids for the semi-literate population and the monolingual population that did not speak or read English.
- **Simple, relevant, and practical design.** Program information was presented in a simple, concise manner to reach the intended population. The messaging included simple and clear calls to action delivered through beneficiary mobilization, interpersonal communication, and outreach tools such as leaflets, posters, and flash cards.
- **Collaborative and complementary approach.** Efforts were made to facilitate two-way communication channels (face-to-face, opportunities to express feedback, satisfaction, grievances, etc., via toll-free helplines). Collaboration with local partners helped ensure accountability, coverage, and low-cost methodology through multipurpose service points (e.g., use of beneficiary welfare committees, health clinics, faith-based organizations, and Huduma Centre one-stop shops).
- **Phased and manageable implementation.** A phased program of context-specific, time-sensitive, and manageable activities was designed to inform, educate, and engage intended populations and other key stakeholders. Feedback mechanisms were set up to collect continuous feedback from stakeholders.

Source: Kenya, Ministry of Labour and Social Protection 2018.

Table 3.2 Typology of Outreach Modalities Used in Social Protection Programs

Direct outreach modalities	On-demand with outreach officers (in local offices, satellite offices, kiosks) Mobile teams going door-to-door in neighborhoods or communities
Community-based outreach	Peer-to-peer outreach and mentoring Community-based, relying on local capacities for disseminating information and connecting people, including community leaders, mother groups, and faith-based leaders
Outreach via intermediaries	Personal referrals from other professionals or programs Disseminating information and promoting awareness via other services: schools, health clinics, shelters, jails Disseminating information via other groups and organizations such as employer or trade associations, foundations and community organizations
Indirect outreach	Printed media: brochures, bulletins, posters Mass media: TV, radio, newspapers, social media Websites, online self-service windows; hotlines

Sources: Based on Dewson, Davis, and Casebourne (2006); Mosley, Scharle, and Stefanik (2018); and Scoppetta and Buckenleib (2018).

Box 3.2 Community-Based Outreach in Pakistan's Benazir Income Support Programme

Pakistan's Benazir Income Support Programme (BISP) is the national flagship social safety net program that provides eligible families with an unconditional cash transfer of between PRe 5,000 and PRe 5,500 (approximately US$36) every quarter of the year. When the BISP communication team studied their beneficiaries, they found that most of the beneficiaries (96.43 percent) were not literate, and 68 percent were below the poverty line, were vulnerable, and lacked mobility, in addition to the prevailing cultural and language barriers.

The media habits of the beneficiaries were closely observed before designing the outreach plan for BISP. A closer look at the beneficiaries revealed that most of them relied on word-of-mouth, but more than 52 percent of them had access to a phone; they were acquainted with vernacular informal outreach tools (e.g., mosque announcements); and had minimum use of radio. The beneficiaries also displayed low recall of information, education, and communications material. While literacy was low, they did recall nonverbal visual material. Beneficiaries also displayed a limited level of financial literacy and knowledge of the operation of electronic payment systems.

Given these setbacks and challenges, Pakistan designed a participatory outreach model that engaged the beneficiaries with local leadership and leveraged informal communication channels. Local BISP Beneficiary Committees (BBCs) were formed with group mother leaders, and traditional communication channels such as town hall meetings, mosque announcements, automated voice calls for the illiterate and semi-literate populations, and street theater ensured a high level of success.

Source: Sagheer and Khan 2018.

and involves an extensive network of mother groups and mother leaders as outreach agents.

Outreach can also be promoted via intermediaries. Information on social protection programs and client interface points can be promoted or posted through other services, such as schools, health clinics, shelters, jails, housing offices, and so on. Health workers, school counselors, or caseworkers from other programs may make personalized referrals for individuals or families to the social programs based on risk flags or other factors. Other intermediaries can include foundations, faith-based organizations, charities, and employee or trade associations (see box 3.3 for an example in Benin). In Montgomery County, Maryland (U.S.), the Department of Health and Human Services reached out to faith-based institutions, charities, and other foundations to notify impoverished families of social assistance and services.

Finally, outreach can take place less directly, with information tools. Such tools can include traditional approaches, such as physical distribution of printed matter and information. Mass media, such as TV, radio, and newspapers, may also be used to disseminate information. Box 3.4 illustrates the use of mass communication channels to promote outreach in Rwanda's Vision 2020 Umurenge Program. Online technologies are increasingly being used to promote outreach for social protection programs and delivery systems, including websites, online self-service windows, mobile apps, and online notices via social media to raise awareness. These technologies rely on a certain degree of proactivity by the intended population to seek out the sites and apps, gather the information, and use the digital self-service windows. Hotlines are also used and can be critical channels for people facing social risks.

Box 3.3 Building Awareness and Trust with Informal Sector Workers: Partnering with Associations in Benin

Social insurance pensions for the elderly rely on having public confidence and support, through the collection of contribution revenues and the dispensing of benefits. Trust is also important given the significant amounts of personal data that are collected and stored. Communications and outreach are critical to help build awareness, understanding, and trust in the social insurance pension system both for (1) contributors—to incite people and firms to join and contribute and to keep them informed across their lifetime of contributions; and (2) beneficiaries—to ensure that they know their potential benefit amounts, to understand payment processes, and so on.

Such outreach and communication challenges are common to all social insurance pension schemes—but take on additional significance when such programs are trying to reach informal sector workers who are traditionally outside of any formal social security regime.

In Benin, a pilot pension insurance scheme for informal sector workers is being developed and the possibility of working with associations (e.g., federations of informal sector workers) is being explored. Outreach is critical for reaching out to informal workers, explaining clearly the voluntary old-age savings scheme, encouraging participation, and managing expectations. The advantages of partnering with associations could include their reach among informal workers and their representation at all levels of the administrative structure of the country. Survey and focus group results suggest that informal workers would be more willing to participate in the scheme if their associations were also involved.

Sources: Guven 2019; Sluchynsky 2019.

Box 3.4 Mass Communication Channels: Rwanda's Vision 2020 Umurenge Program

Rwanda's Vision 2020 Umurenge Program is an integrated local development program to accelerate poverty eradication, rural growth, and social protection. The Ministry of Local Government (MINALOC), through the Local Administrative Entities Development Agency, is responsible for sharing and explaining Rwanda's Vision 2020 Umurenge Program (VUP) with all the communities under their mandate, including nonrecipient households. For this purpose, the MINALOC prepared a communication strategy to share information on VUP including objectives, policy, and procedures. The mass communication strategies used are listed below:

- **Radio and television shows.** Representatives of local government, central government, and beneficiaries regularly appear on live radio and television shows to explain the program. Further, these radio and television programs offer toll-free numbers for listeners to call with their questions.
- **Program workshops.** Workshop and training events target mayors, vice mayors, and district and sector executive secretaries. Participants learn how to present VUP and provide guidance on how to communicate about VUP effectively and accurately to community members.
- **Program information brochures.** Brochures containing key information about the program are distributed to communities, using local language (Kinyarwanda) and simple illustrations.
- **Program website.** The VUP program information is periodically posted on the Ministry of Local Government's website.
- **Newspaper and newsletter.** Articles are periodically published in national newspapers discussing VUP progress. An electronic newsletter has been published biweekly since November 2009.

Source: Rwanda, Ministry of Local Development 2010.

3.4 TAILORING MODALITIES TO SPECIFIC INTENDED POPULATIONS AND VULNERABLE GROUPS

Outreach modalities are tailored to specific population groups to encourage poor and vulnerable groups to engage with social programs by building in adaptations. Diagnostics clarify the communication habits and capabilities of the intended population groups to better tailor the channels that would reach specific stakeholders. Table 3.3 highlights various modalities to use with intended populations that are common for social protection programs.

Additionally, this chapter takes a closer look at tailored outreach modalities for some of these groups, including (1) disabled persons, (2) at-risk youth, (3) remote or vulnerable populations, (4) ethnically and linguistically diverse groups (including migrants and refugees), and (5) people living in FCV situations.

Tailored Outreach Modalities for Persons with Disabilities

Over a billion people live with some form of disability that affects their daily lives. That constitutes 15 percent of the world's population, with the majority living in developing countries.[2] Outreach for people with disabilities needs to consider their specific access barriers. Inaccessible environments create barriers to participation and inclusion, such as a deaf individual without a sign language interpreter, an individual in a wheelchair at an outreach office without a ramp, or a blind person using a computer without screen-reading software. These scenarios can be directly applied to designing inclusive outreach strategies for individuals with disabilities.

Table 3.3 Common Intended Populations for Social Protection Programs and Associated Outreach Strategies

Demographic groups along the life cycle	
Children	Outreach strategy needs to include parents or guardians who would be the designated beneficiaries.
Elderly	May rely more on direct communications or mass media, less on internet-based tools; door-to-door outreach can also facilitate outreach to those who face mobility challenges.
Women	Outreach through direct communications, advocacy, counseling, or mass media; working with women's self-help groups and organizations, other community-based efforts, intermediaries, and media.
Groups constrained by socioeconomic status	
People living below the poverty line	Many modalities could work, such as direct outreach, community-based efforts, and via intermediaries such as schools, health clinics, foundations, shelters, and so on. (Those in rural or remote areas may have less access to internet, social media, and so on; illiteracy could constrain the use of printed matter.)
Homeless	Outreach through direct communications, counseling, and community-based efforts, and through nongovernmental and faith-based organizations.
People living in isolated and remote areas	Specialized outreach through direct communications, integration with remote communities, door-to-door outreach, and a robust network of local offices for client interface; radio-based communications and mobile devices.
Pastoralist, nomadic, and semi-nomadic groups	Typically raise livestock and move to places with water and pasture seasonally. Outreach may include direct communications, counseling, and advocacy by mobile teams and social workers; radio-based communications; and mobile devices.
Indigenous groups	Specialized outreach through direct communications, culturally appropriate messaging, communication through intermediaries and community leaders. Special considerations include cultural adaptation and sensitivity as well as mobile outreach.
Refugees, stateless, immigrants, internally displaced populations (IDPs), and people living in areas affected by fragility, conflict, and violence	Technology-enabled modalities; partnerships with communities and humanitarian organizations, the United Nations, NGOs, and civil society actors.[a]
Ethnic, religious, linguistic, and visible minorities	Specialized outreach through direct communications and community-based efforts.

continued

Table 3.3 *(continued)*

	Labor and work conditions	
	Unemployed	Many modalities could work, such as direct outreach, community-based efforts, or via intermediaries such as trade associations and unions. For skilled workers and those with internet access, online tools can be helpful; former employers may provide information upon dismissal, and employment offices may provide information to unemployed workers on-demand.
	Discouraged/ inactive workers	Proactive efforts needed since they do not register at employment services; tailored efforts needed for subgroups such as inactive women, inactive older workers, and migrant or refugee workers.[b] Outreach to women through family and welfare agencies, NGOs, and civil society groups. National policies to increase female labor force participation. For ethnic minorities, outreach may be aimed at social inclusion. Outreach through print and mass media; the internet; data exchange with social programs; and community outreach services in shopping centers, job fairs, and schools.
	Informal sector workers	Worker boards set up through the Ministry of Labor: Labor Welfare Board (often organized sector firms but may hire informal workers), Agricultural Workers Board, Construction Workers Board, Kretek Workers Board (Indonesia), and so on; outreach through associations of informal sector workers and community-based efforts (such as self-help groups in Bangladesh or India); outreach through NGOs and other organizations working in rural communities; outreach through local government/village heads; outreach via traditional media campaigns through newspapers, radio/TV, and street theater; and outreach via mobile phone.
	Forced or child laborers	The general outreach options are similar, but may need to be more discreet so that forced or child labor is reported and acted upon. Outreach would include companies and manufacturers, making them aware of laws and consequences, to support standards and to help enforce them with other companies in the supply chain (e.g., large companies in cocoa value chains and clothing brands). Outreach could also include waste or ragpickers associations. Community groups, NGOs, and CSOs; education campaigns; and multiple access points for complaints and action.
	Disability	
	Persons with disabilities Workers with disabilities	Door-to-door outreach for individuals with mobility challenges or other disabilities. Increased accessibility to offices and service centers, such as wheelchair accessibility, specialized waiting and parking areas, sign language translators, and braille. Assistive technologies for online, mobile, and other technology-based outreach.

continued

Table 3.3 *(continued)*

Vulnerable individuals facing specific social risks	
Children at risk	Proactive efforts via schools, health clinics, hotlines, door-to-door, and community approaches (to reach both children and parents).
Youth at risk	Peer-to-peer outreach and mentoring, canvasing door-to-door and in neighborhoods, and other efforts to bring outreach to youths in their environment; technology-based outreach such as social media, websites, and so forth.
Adults at risk	Hotlines, community-based approaches via intermediaries such as health clinics and hospitals, faith-based organizations, and so forth.
LGBT	Outreach through community fairs, college campuses, local social establishments, and LGBT events; social media; postcards; and strategic partnerships with organizations that work closely with LGBT groups.[c]

Source: Original table for this publication.

Note: CSO = civil society organization; LGBT = lesbian, gay, bisexual, and transgender; NGO = nongovernmental organization.

a. https://www.unhcr.org/516d658c9.pdf.

b. https://publications.europa.eu/en/publication-detail/-/publication/ce86219d-2d84-11e8-b5fe-01aa75ed71a1/language-en.

c. https://aspe.hhs.gov/basic-report/outreach-and-enrollment-lgbt-individuals-promising-practices-field

Tailored outreach modalities can help overcome challenges faced by persons with disabilities. Requiring the disabled to come to the office is less effective than, say, door-to-door approaches or community-based approaches. Inclusive orientation is also helpful in breaking down the barriers of stigma, for example, adopting inclusive language that focuses on the person rather than the disability (such as "a woman who uses a wheelchair" rather than "a woman in a wheelchair"). Assistive technologies can also help. Outreach modalities and communication channels like websites are designed to be inclusive. Adaption to simple assistive techniques like sending a user with visual impairment an automated voice message about program details rather than an automated text message can improve the user experience. Similarly, making program websites more inclusive by introducing a video with sign language illustrating the program details or adding subtitles to the program video can help individuals with hearing impairment. Introducing screen reader software that can read out the text displayed on the monitor and magnify type can help individuals with learning disabilities as well as individuals with visual disabilities.

Reaching Out to At-Risk Youth

Tailored outreach modalities are more effective with at-risk youth, such as those who are not in education, employment, or training (NEETs). Youth may not participate in social protection programs (such as employment and training) due to a lack of information, inaccessible locations, and skepticism that the programs will yield immediate or longer-term benefits. Program administrators may face challenges in reaching out to youth due to a disconnect between their outreach strategies and modalities compared to young people's interests, needs, and behaviors. Tailored outreach methods can help connect with teens, build awareness, overcome teen skepticism, and make them likely to engage. Such modalities can include peer-to-peer outreach and mentoring (with trained peer youth recruiters), canvassing door to door and in neighborhoods, and other efforts to bring outreach to youths in their environment, such as youth centers, shopping malls, parks, health clinics, clubs, movie theaters, community-based and faith-based organizations, shelters, and so on. Internet, social media, and other technology-based outreach can also be effective.

Active Search with Remote and Marginalized Populations

Geographically remote and vulnerable populations risk being excluded if proactive and tailored outreach strategies are not adopted. Remoteness can complicate outreach efforts (and delivery more generally), given the dispersion of people, difficult physical access, and lack of electricity and internet connections. People in remote areas can easily be overlooked by social protection programs as they are less visible. Some countries adopt "active search" (or active outreach) methods whereby program administrators, local officials, foundation representatives, or others deliberately and proactively reach out to people living in remote areas or vulnerable populations who may otherwise be overlooked or are unaware of social protection programs. Two such examples were carried out for multiprogram social registries in Brazil and the Philippines (box 3.5).

Diverse Approaches to Reach Out to Ethnic Minorities and Migrants

Ethnic minorities and migrants may face a variety of access barriers to social protection programs and delivery systems. Such barriers can include language and cultural barriers, discrimination, fears (particularly if residence status is not formalized), geographic and social isolation, lack of trust in public institutions, lack of awareness of programs, and low self-confidence in navigating bureaucratic processes. A recent review surveyed several approaches to outreach that were being used to encourage Roma, other ethnic minorities, and migrants to promote labor-market integration and participation in employment services in various European countries:

- ***Peer-to-peer outreach and mentoring.*** In this approach, the employment office trains and works through members of the target group. Such methods can increase effectiveness of communication with potential clients, due to language and cultural adaptations, trust, and motivation. In Bulgaria, for example, some labor offices successfully employed Roma mediators for outreach. Similar approaches have been used in the Slovak Republic (for Roma), Portugal (for migrants), and Denmark (for other ethnic minorities).
- ***Other community-based outreach modalities.*** In this approach, labor programs relied on local capacities to disseminate information on employment services. Examples include outreach efforts in Roma communities in Finland, Germany, and the United Kingdom.
- ***Mobile PES teams.*** Mobile public employment services (PES) teams or temporary remote PES offices can facilitate outreach, for example, with frequent visits to raise awareness about job vacancies or employment services. Examples of mobile teams include "employment caravans" to reach out to inactive workers in Roma communities in Romania and mobile offices in Bulgaria, Estonia, and Germany.
- ***Online information and printed information.*** Integration packages were distributed to unemployed migrants, refugees, and asylum seekers in Slovenia, and the PES website in Sweden promotes its services for refugees in their native languages.

Leveraging Technology to Help Overcome the Challenges of Outreach in Fragile-Conflict-Violent Situations

Outreach is particularly challenging—and critical—in countries emerging from decades of economic uncertainty, fragility, violence, and conflict. The right use of outreach can build trust and bolster confidence in the program being launched. Information on critical program details such as criteria for participation, program selection, employment duration, gender composition, benefits, and packages can be disseminated clearly, consistently, and comprehensively. Outreach is a part of program planning prior to the launch, or programs can be set on the wrong path before they even begin (Subbarao et al. 2013). This is particularly important when new interventions are being introduced in response to emerging and urgent needs after conflict and violence. With the emergence of new affordable technologies, outreach activities can reach remote areas more readily. Box 3. 6 illustrates the results from a technology and landscape assessment done for Iraq and the Republic of Yemen, with suitable technologies

Box 3.5 Active Search to Promote Outreach for Social Registries in Brazil and the Philippines

Many countries operate social registries to carry out intake and registration for multiple social programs, as discussed in chapter 4. Social registries can be cost-effective tools for providing potential access to multiple programs, but depend on the ability of deliberate and active outreach efforts to ensure that the intended populations are reached and informed. That can be challenging with remote and marginalized populations. Social registries in Brazil and the Philippines have adopted proactive, deliberate, and tailored approaches to reach out to such groups and ensure they are registered.

Brazil's Busca Ativa. Brazil's social registry—the Cadastro Único (Cadúnico) has operated on an on-demand basis since 2007. Anyone can register and apply for benefits from the Bolsa Família Program and many other benefits and services that use the Cadúnico as an integrated gateway at any time—this process is known as dynamic inclusion. By 2012, over 22 million families had registered into the Cadúnico (about 40 percent of the population). However, the Ministry of Social Development was concerned that the program was missing some extremely poor families, particularly hard-to-reach groups such as indigenous and other ethnic communities, the disabled, the homeless, those living and working in trash dumps, people working in extractive industries, fishermen, people living in remote areas, and so on.

The government of Brazil developed an Active Outreach strategy under its Brasil Sem Miséria (Brazil Without Poverty) initiative with the goal of finding and registering all extremely poor families that had not yet been included in the Cadúnico. This new "active search" (busca ativa) strategy was developed and implemented at the municipal level, with financing of a specific plan from the federal government. The strategy followed an active search process based on the philosophy that it was the responsibility of the state to go to high-poverty areas to find the poor who may otherwise be missed in the social registry, rather than waiting for them to register on demand. The efforts targeted specific populations—whose underregistration in social programs had been identified through statistical analysis that combined poverty maps and administrative data from the Cadúnico. The active outreach strategy included door-to-door visits by social workers, visits of mobile "social assistance" vans to remote localities, as well as partnerships with government and civil society agencies, following a snowball approach that first visited a household registered in the Cadúnico to inquire about friends or families not registered, to find those excluded families. Partners included health community agents and even electric power concessionaires.

Active outreach in the Philippines. Listahanan is the Philippines's social registry, and registration into Listahanan is carried out using en masse data collection efforts once every few years. Even with these "census-sweep" approaches, there is always the risk of missing marginalized, remote, or otherwise hard-to-serve populations. During the recent nationwide data collection effort in 2015, the Department for Social Welfare and Development (DSWD) developed an active outreach strategy that involved close cooperation with local governments to assist enumerators in penetrating remote and hard-to-reach populations, including with mobile teams on small boats, canoes, and other forms of adaptive transportation. Special efforts were also made to reach people living in trash dumps without a fixed address.

Sources: Leite et al. 2017; the Philippines Department for Social Welfare and Development; the Brazil Learning Initiative for a World Without Poverty at http://wwp.org.br/.

Box 3.6 Technologies to Promote Outreach and Communications in FCV Contexts: Iraq and the Republic of Yemen

Iraq has long-running armed conflict that began in 2003, with continuous insurgency adding a lot of strain on the country's institutional capacity to plan social programs. The Republic of Yemen's civil war began in 2015 and has created a rapid onset of humanitarian crisis in the country. Both these countries have resource constraints, field challenges, and setbacks in institutional capacity and require urgent interventions. The traditional methods and approaches to communications and outreach might be unrealistic in the given contexts. However, the recent technological advancements have created an opportunity to provide real-time solutions in these fragile, conflict-affected, and violent regions. Following a technology landscape assessment, the technology solutions recommended for Iraq and the Republic of Yemen are listed below.

- Mobile technologies and Computer Assisted Personal Interviewing (CAPI) facilitate the outreach, intake, and registration phases. They have proved to be remarkable technologies for improving inclusion, transparency, and accountability in resource-poor and low-budget contexts. The ubiquity of mobile devices and increasing tele-density make mobile solutions work effectively in urban and rural areas—and increasingly in FCV areas as well.
- Finding the intended populations is challenging. Satellite imagery, geospatial technologies, geotagging the location of intended populations, and program sites help create realistic poverty maps to plan accurate outreach activities for specific vulnerable populations. Geotagging the location of intended populations can be carried out with GPS and other diverse media such as photographs, videos, and location of SMS text messages. This helps locate intended populations, and to find them again during subsequent phases. Farther along the delivery chain, geo-referenced apps link eventual beneficiaries to distributors, payment points, retailers, and other services. They also help with oversight of vendors and third-party auditors.
- The inability to access areas physically presents an informational challenge, which hampers outreach efforts. Technologies such as remote sensing—the acquisition of information about an object or phenomenon without making physical contact with the object (the "internet of things")—uses a sensor device to capture and transmit data about the physical environment, and unmanned aerial vehicles (UAV) or drones to observe, scan, and document the state of the program sites, all help inform outreach efforts.
- Social media-based grievance redress/complaints may be monitored through interactive chatbots. Social media feedback mechanisms engage with beneficiaries to verify work done, confirm payments made, and report any grievances issues.
- Social media big data analysis may be used to track highly visible works that attract a lot of attention, dialogue, and discussion. Social media can also be used to gather feedback on trainings done and handle any grievances and complaints.

While planning technology interventions for FCV regions, it is important to acknowledge the resource constraints, and that not all technical solutions can work in all scenarios. The outreach team can use the technological landscape to identify specific features and capabilities of potential technologies and assess and articulate the cost-benefit of implementing potential technologies. A primary qualitative analysis can be used to determine the needs and appropriateness of the selected technologies.

Source: Vital Wave 2017.
Note: FCV = fragility, conflict, and violence.

that were recommended for outreach, intake, and registration in these countries.

Measuring the performance of outreach is critical. Well-performing delivery systems ensure effectiveness and efficiency throughout the delivery chain, from outreach to routine oversight, and are supported by effective and efficient information systems, client interfaces, and institutions. To measure the performance of the outreach plan and activities, key performance indicators that are monitored regularly to help diagnose bottlenecks in the delivery chain early on help identify alternatives to correct or prevent further challenges. The following indicators can be used as guidance to assess the effectiveness of the outreach phase: (1) percentage of intended population who understand the program, (2) percentage of intended population who apply to the program, (3) percentage of vulnerable groups or populations facing access barriers who applied to the program, and (4) number of grievance-redress cases decreasing over time as a result of better understanding and engagement. Indicators selection may vary across countries and the objectives and nature of the program and can be tailored as needed.[3]

3.5 INSTITUTIONAL ASPECTS

Institutional arrangements for outreach can be diverse because so many modalities are used. Some of the variations include the following:

- ***Direct versus community actors or intermediaries.*** Program administrators may conduct outreach efforts directly, or they may work through communities, peers, or other intermediaries to implement outreach for a specific program or multiple programs. These arrangements can be informal or formal.
- ***Single program versus multiprogram outreach.*** In some modalities, program-specific actors (caseworkers, outreach officers, mobile teams) implement outreach efforts on behalf of the program. In other modalities, outreach agents will implement outreach on behalf of multiple programs or social registries. Multiprogram approaches require harmonization of outreach messaging, information on all programs, clarity on the rules of each program, and so on.
- ***On-demand versus administrator-driven approaches.*** As discussed in chapter 2 and throughout the Sourcebook, there are two distinct operating models for delivery systems. One involves on-demand systems, and the other involves administrator-driven approaches. On-demand systems depend extensively on people being informed enough to take the initiative to apply for programs (either in person or digitally). However, the approach cannot be passive. If outreach efforts are inadequate, intended populations or vulnerable groups may lack the awareness or ability to seek aid, and may be missed. All of the modalities for outreach can be used with on-demand methods. Administrator-driven approaches bring intake and registration to communities and even to households directly. As such, outreach is implicit—but still proactive and includes reaching out to communities, disseminating information, taking measures to adapt to linguistic or cultural differences, and so on.
- ***Budgets and administrative considerations.*** Outreach is often neglected, particularly when it comes to assigning resources, supplying qualified staff, and making logistical inputs. Costs of outreach can include hiring and training of outreach staff or other agents (mobile teams, peer mentors, or community agents), providing necessary logistical inputs (which can become dated and unusable over time), communications materials, website development and maintenance, transportation, and so on.
- ***On the institutional side, local actors, including central or local government actors, or outsourced providers are typically responsible for client-facing implementation at the outreach phase.*** Many programs outsource some or all aspects of delivery to partner agencies, which can include other public agencies, foundations, youth professionals, nonprofits, and specialized for-profit firms. In outreach, service providers/outreach officers will identify their target group and will be close to the intended population. Outreach can be done in different environments: streets and other outdoor locations, homes, homeless communities, youth centers, village community centers, clinics, or schools. Regardless of

the environment, outreach workers listen actively and find out the needs of the intended population. They determine the appropriate benefit and service options and explain them such that the intended populations understand and are willing to engage in the application process.

3.6 SOME CONCLUDING POINTS

Outreach is essential for social protection programs and delivery systems to be effective and efficient. Outreach involves the deliberate effort to reach and inform intended populations and vulnerable groups about social protection programs and delivery systems in ways that they will comprehend so that they are aware, informed, able, and encouraged to engage. It seeks to ensure that people understand both the program(s) and the delivery systems. Outreach goes beyond disseminating information and creating awareness. It also humanizes the intended population, builds trust, actively engages stakeholders to build consensus, and promotes inclusion. The main practical risk of inadequate outreach is an uninformed intended population, who is either missed, unaware, or fails to understand the program(s) or how to register. Broader risks include missing intended populations or vulnerable groups, errors of exclusion and inclusion, confusion, inefficiencies and lack of transparency.

Outreach involves purpose, people, and proactivity. There is no one-size-fits-all strategy. Tailored approaches are needed, particularly given the diversity of contexts, social protection programs, and population groups. Various modalities include (1) direct outreach; (2) community-based outreach; (3) outreach via intermediaries; and (4) outreach via information tools and technology. Such modalities should be adapted to the communications habits and contexts of specific population groups, as well as operating models for delivery systems (one-program or multiprogram systems, and on-demand versus administrator-driven approaches).

Notes

1. Intended populations are not yet registrants or beneficiaries. Some people use the terms "potential beneficiaries" or "identifying (potential) beneficiaries." Since we do not know the circumstances of people before they register, are assessed, or deemed eligible, we cannot call them "beneficiaries." We also prefer to avoid calling them "potential beneficiaries" to avoid the risk of implying that they would become beneficiaries—and to avoid raising expectations of entitlements that may not be met.
2. https://www.who.int/disabilities/world_report/2011/report.pdf.
3. More details in chapter 9: Assessing the Performance of Social Protection Delivery Systems.

Bibliography

Andersson, Björn. 2013. "Finding Ways to the Hard to Reach—Considerations on the Content and Concept of Outreach Work." *European Journal of Social Work* 16 (2): 171–86.

Andersson, Bjorn. 2018. "Fringe Work—Street-Level Divergence in Swedish Youth Work." In *The Sage Handbook of Youth Work Practice*, edited by Pam Alldred, Fin Cullen, Kathy Edwards, and Dana Fusco, chapter 21. London: SAGE.

Dewson, Sara, Sara Davis, and Jo Casebourne. 2006. "Maximising the Role of Outreach in Client Engagement." Research Report 326, Department for Work and Pensions, London.

EURoma (European Network on Roma Inclusion under ESI Funds). 2009. "Study Visit to the ACCEDER Programme in Spain." Final report, EURoma, Madrid.

Fox, Charles, and Benjamin Stewart. 2018. "Need Better Maps? Take It to the Crowd!" World Bank Blogs, June 26, 2018. https://blogs.worldbank.org/digital-development/need-better-maps-take-it-crowd.

Guerreo Gamez, Sofia, Ana Rodriguez Coteron, and Guillermo Romero Rodriguez. 2018. "Accessibility and Inclusion: Two Key Factors for Individuals with Disabilities." World Bank Blogs, December 4, 2018. https://blogs.worldbank.org/latinamerica/accessibility-and-inclusion-two-key-factors-individuals-disabilities.

Guven, Melis. 2019. "Extending Pension Coverage to the Informal Sector in Africa." Social Protection and Jobs Discussion Paper 1933, World Bank, Washington, DC.

Iraq, Ministry of Labor and Social Affairs. 2018. "Emergency Social Stabilization and Resilience Project." Paper presented at the knowledge exchange event between South Sudan and Iraq, July 25, 2018.

Kenya, Ministry of Labour and Social Protection. 2018. "Beneficiary Outreach Strategy and Action Plan." State Department of Social Protection, Pensions and Senior

Citizens Affairs. Working Paper, Pensions and Senior Citizens Affairs, State Department of Social Protection, Kenya.

Leite, Phillippe, Tina George, Changqing Sun, Theresa Jones, and Kathy Lindert. 2017. "Social Registries for Social Assistance and Beyond: A Guidance Note and Assessment Tool." Social Protection and Labor Discussion Paper 1704, World Bank, Washington, DC. http://documents.worldbank.org/curated/en/698441502095248081/Social-registries-for-social-assistance-and-beyond-a-guidance-note-and-assessment-tool.

Lindert, Kathy A. 2016. "Communication and Outreach in Social Safety Nets." Slide presentation, World Bank, Washington, DC.

Mikkonen, Mika, Jaana Kauppinen, Minna Huovinen, and Erja Aalto, eds. 2007. "Outreach Work among Marginalised Populations in Europe: Guidelines on Providing Integrated Outreach Services." Foundation Regenboog AMOC, Amsterdam.

Morse, Gary. 1987. "Conceptual Overview of Mobile Outreach for Persons Who Are Homeless and Mentally Ill." Paper presented at the American Public Health Association Annual Convention, New Orleans, October.

Mosley, Hugh, Agota Scharle, and Miroslav Stefanik. 2018. "The Role of PES in Outreach to the Inactive Population." European Commission, Brussels, Belgium; ICON-INSTITUTE, Germany.

Paynter, Ben. 2017. "How Blockchain Could Transform the Way International Aid Is Distributed." *Fast Company*, September 18, 2017. https://www.fastcompany.com/40457354/how-blockchain-could-transform-the-way-international-aid-is-distributed.

Rhodes, Tim. 1996. "Outreach Work with Drug Users: Principles and Practice." Council of Europe, Strasbourg, France.

Rwanda, Ministry of Local Development. 2010. "VUP Public Awareness Program Summary."

Sagheer, Sumaira, and Quanita Ali Khan. 2018. "Pakistan: Reaching the Poor through the National Social Safety Net System—Role of Communication and Outreach in Stimulating Inclusive Participation." Presentation at the World Bank's Social Safety Nets and Delivery Systems Core Course, Washington, DC.

Scoppetta, Anette, and Arthur Buckenleib. 2018. "Tackling Long-Term Unemployment through Risk Profiling and Outreach." Technical Dossier 6, ESF Transnational Platform, European Commission, Brussels, Belgium.

Sluchynsky, Oleksiy. 2019. "Social Insurance Administrative Diagnostic (SIAD): Guidance Note." World Bank, Washington, DC; International Social Security Association, Geneva, Switzerland.

Subbarao, Kalanidhi, Carlo del Ninno, Colin Andrews, and Claudia Rodríguez-Alas. 2013. *Public Works as a Safety Net: Design, Evidence, and Implementation*. Directions in Development Series. Washington, DC: World Bank.

Sudan. 2018. "The Safety Net and Skills Development Project (SNSDP)." Slide presentation at the knowledge exchange event between South Sudan and Iraq, July 25, 2018.

United States, National Council on Disability. 2012. "Guiding Principles: Successfully Enrolling People with Disabilities in Managed Care Plans." National Council on Disability, Washington, DC.

Villarreal, Fernando. 2013. "ACCEDER: Programme for the Employment of Roma through the Operational Programme Fight against Discrimination under the European Social Fund: Assessment Report." Fresno Consulting, Madrid. https://www.fresnoconsulting.es/upload/79/47/2013_assessment_report_acceder_fresno-osi.pdf.

Vital Wave. 2017. "Utilizing Technology for Smart Fiduciary Oversight in Fragile, Conflict Affected, and Violent Contexts." Slide presentation, Vital Wave, Palo Alto, CA.

WFP (World Food Programme). 2018. "Blockchain for Zero Hunger." Innovation Accelerator. WFP, Munich, Germany.

WHO (World Health Organization) and World Bank. 2011. *World Report on Disability*. Geneva, Switzerland: WHO; Washington, DC: World Bank.

WWP (Brazil Learning Initiative for a World Without Poverty). 2015. "Active Search and Targeting: The Importance of the Unified Registry for Brazil without Extreme Poverty Plan." Series No. 4. WWP.

Chapter 4

Intake, Registration, and Assessment of Needs and Conditions

Kathy Lindert, Phillippe Leite, Tina George Karippacheril, and Inés Rodríguez Caillava

With contributions from Nina Rosas Raffo, Gustavo Demarco, Nahla Zeitoun, Ahmet Fatih Ortakaya, Anita Mittal, Conrad Daly, Vasumathi Anandan, and Karen Peffley

How do people apply to social protection programs? How are their needs and conditions assessed to determine whether they are eligible for benefits and services? These are the questions that are answered during the processes of intake and registration and assessment of needs and conditions. This chapter elaborates on these gateway phases in the delivery chain (figure 4.1).

Intake and registration and assessment of needs and conditions are the second and third phases of the delivery chain, and their objectives are that the intended populations are registered efficiently, their information is recorded accurately, and they are accurately profiled. Intake is the process of initiating contact, engaging clients, and gathering information, while registration consists of recording and verifying that information. In some systems, information reported by registrants is complemented by additional data from other administrative systems. Intake and registration are usually simultaneous. Following outreach efforts (discussed in chapter 3), the inputs to intake and registration involve people (individuals, families, or households) who apply for assistance, engage with an agency, and provide information and documentation. The primary output from intake and registration is complete information on the applicant that is verified and validated for use as an input to the assessment of needs and conditions. The assessment of needs and conditions is the process of profiling registered individuals, families, or households according to various assessment tools (such as socioeconomic welfare measures, risk profiles, and labor profiles). That profiling is the main output of this phase and informs the determination of potential eligibility for specific programs and the benefits or services that may be awarded (see chapter 5). On a broader level, an outcome of this phase is measure of the need for social protection programs, which can help agencies in planning, budgeting, and coordination.

The focus of these two phases is on people: individuals, families, or households. They may belong

Figure 4.1 The Assessment Phases of the Social Protection Delivery Chain

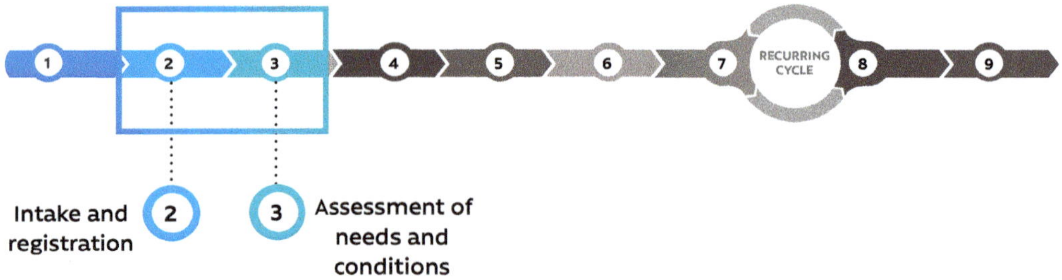

Source: Original figure for this publication.

to various intended populations (or "target groups") such as (1) categories of demographic groups at a certain stage of life (such as children or the elderly); (2) groups defined according to their socioeconomic status; (3) people with disabilities; (4) people with a particular labor status (job seekers and the unemployed); (5) vulnerable individuals classified by social risks; or (6) a combination of these categories. At this stage of the delivery chain, we refer to people as applicants or registrants (not beneficiaries) since they have not been deemed eligible for any programs. It is important to collect and maintain information on all applicants or registrants, not just those who eventually become beneficiaries of programs (as discussed in chapter 5).

This chapter is organized as follows:

- Section 4.1 gives an overview of intake and registration including intake modalities, registration modalities, instruments and techniques, and a discussion of how the principle of dynamic inclusion relates to intake and registration.
- Section 4.2 reviews the types of information collected during the intake and registration process for intended populations. It also considers opportunities for using integrated approaches in intake and registration.
- Section 4.3 reviews the tools used to assess the needs and conditions of those various groups (demographic, socioeconomic, disabilities, labor, social risks), as well as discussing opportunities for leveraging integrated approaches.
- Section 4.4 presents some process maps to illustrate the sequencing of steps and institutional roles for the phases of intake, registration, and assessment of needs and conditions.
- Section 4.5 reviews the structural aspects of those processes, such as institutional arrangements and information systems that support them.
- Finally, section 4.6 summarizes key features of intake, registration, and assessment of needs and conditions that can be used to support dynamic inclusion and coordination.

Various country examples are discussed in this chapter, including some from each region:

- **Africa:** Burkina Faso, the Republic of Congo, Malawi, Mali, Mauritius, Senegal, Sierra Leone, Tanzania
- **East Asia and the Pacific:** China, Indonesia, the Philippines
- **Europe and Central Asia:** Albania, Denmark, Finland, France, Georgia, Greece, Italy, Kosovo, the Kyrgyz Republic, the Netherlands, North Macedonia, Romania, the Russian Federation, Serbia, Sweden, Turkey, the United Kingdom
- **Latin America and the Caribbean:** Brazil, Chile, Colombia, the Dominican Republic, Mexico
- **Middle East and North Africa:** Djibouti, the Arab Republic of Egypt, Jordan, Lebanon, Morocco
- **South Asia:** Pakistan
- **Other Organisation for Economic Co-operation and Development (OECD) countries:** Australia, Canada, the United States, other country mentions

4.1 INTAKE AND REGISTRATION

Intake and registration require structures and processes for interfacing with people, who are the "first mile" rather than the "last mile" (see chapter 2 on the client interface and human-centered design). The client interface is the point of contact for registrants and applicants. Modalities for intake and registration should have clear points of contact, ideally with multiple channels such as (1) local office, service window, or kiosk; (2) via mobile teams; (3) via social workers, frontline staff or enumerators; and (4) via digital service windows (figure 4.2). They can be managed by central agencies (e.g., staff or contractors) or by local governments.

The client interface also has an important "time dimension": Is the point of contact for people available to them on a permanent or infrequent basis? Another related aspect is whether this "contact" (e.g., intake and registration) is initiated by the applicants themselves (e.g., on demand) or by the administrators (e.g., via administrator-driven, en masse data collection). Finally, an important aspect of the client interface is the "user experience" of the people themselves—and if the point of contact and associated processes are people-centered and service-oriented. A key feature is whether they allow for dynamic inclusion, such that anyone can apply for social programs at any time. In other words, dynamic inclusion means that access to intake and registration is open and continuous—usually with an on-demand application window for the client interface. People should be able to register for consideration of potential eligibility for social programs when in need or update their information if their situations change. The client interface is particularly important when developing "adaptive social protection systems" (Leite et al. 2017).

Intake Modalities: On-Demand and Administrator-Driven Approaches

When it comes to intake, whether the on-demand approach or the administrator-driven approach is used affects other decisions in the delivery chain.[1] Three key features distinguish these approaches: (1) whether the client takes the initiative to apply (on demand) or the program or

Figure 4.2 Client Interface: Modalities for Intake and Registration

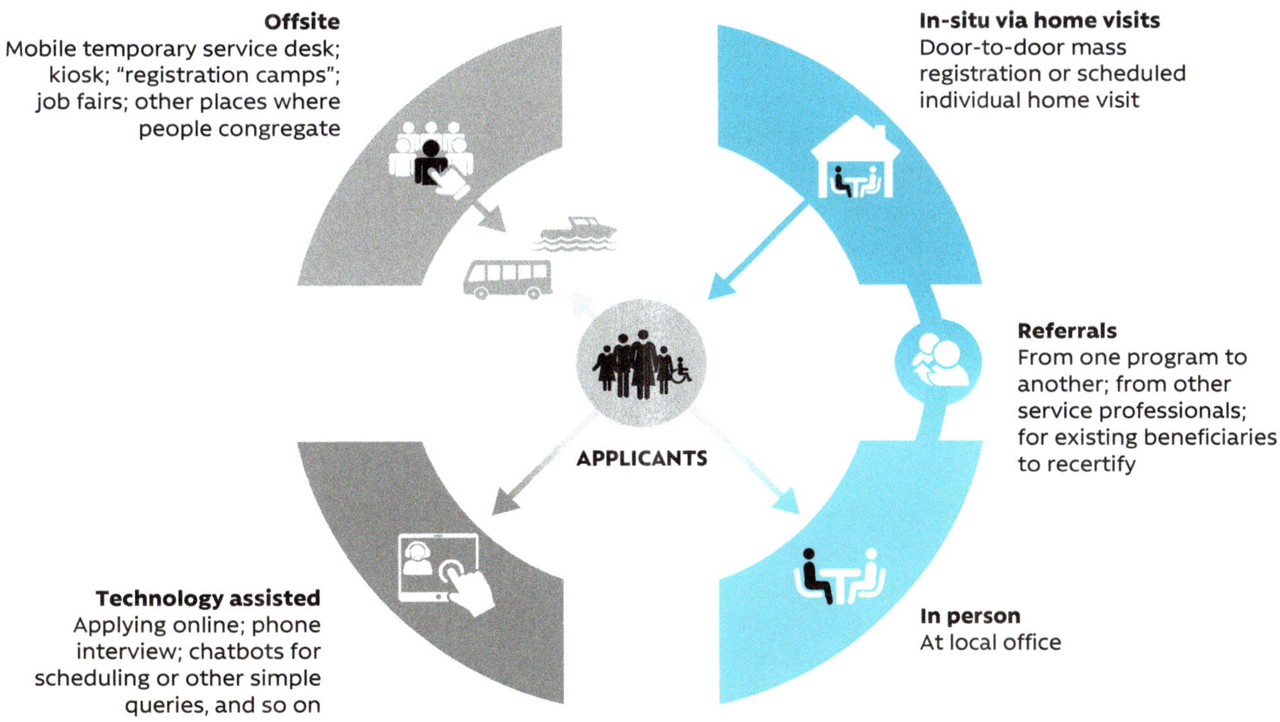

Source: Original figure for this publication.

social registry initiates registration (administrator-driven); (2) whether clients engage separately (on demand), or are registered together as a group (administrator-driven); and (3) whether clients apply at a time of their own choosing (on demand), or the timetable is a function of financing and capacity (administrator-driven).

While the administrator-driven and on-demand approaches are two distinct models, they operate in a spectrum. Some countries have a full on-demand approach, such as Brazil's Cadastro Único, and others have a full administrator approach, such as Burkina Faso, Malawi, and Tanzania. There are other cases, such as Pakistan's National Socioeconomic Registry (NSER), the Republic of Congo's social registry, and Sierra Leone's SPRINT, that use administrator-driven approaches and include some on-demand elements.

The range of programs that use on-demand and administrator-driven approaches differs. On-demand approaches are used for all types of social protection programs (see chapter 2). They can be used for one or many programs at a time, and in situations of idiosyncratic or covariate shocks. Administrator-driven approaches are more common for poverty-targeted programs and in response to covariate shocks where everyone in the group intended to be registered faces the same shock. Some social protection programs tend to be more on-demand than others. For example, health insurance and pensions allow for dynamic intake and registration, as well as labor and social services. Social assistance programs, on the other hand, tend to be more administrator-driven and carried out through periodic census sweeps. Nevertheless, in higher-income countries, better administrative information systems allow for dynamic inclusion with regard to social assistance.

Whether the intake process satisfies the principle of dynamic inclusion depends on whether the approach is on demand or administrator-driven. The timetable for intake matters. Can people apply at any time (on demand) according to their own situation? That facilitates dynamic inclusion. Or do people have to wait several years for the next en masse registration wave, as is the case with administrator-driven approaches? That means many people will not be able to apply at a time of need, but instead will have to wait for the next registration drive.

Defining the approach for intake depends on country context and administrative capacity. While the on-demand approach and guaranteeing dynamic inclusion are aspirational, for many countries they are feasible in contexts of high capacity and availability of a permanent network for client interface. When administrative capacity is low and the network for client interface is limited, the administrator-driven approach might be more appropriate.

On-Demand Intake

With on-demand approaches, people proactively apply for one or more benefits and services. The assistance unit may be individuals, families, or households. The impetus for that application comes from the specific clients, though it may also be stimulated by outreach efforts and/or referrals from other programs or professionals.[2] The timing of their application is largely dictated by their own circumstances. For example, an individual may reach a certain age (such as 65), a family may have a child or suffer chronic poverty or an idiosyncratic shock specific to their own situation, a worker may be dismissed from their job, a person may face the onset of a disability, or an individual may confront complex social risks. The timing of the application triggers the timing of the other phases along the delivery chain.

Intake can take place at the household or at a government office, it can rely on paper or digital forms (both offline and online), and the process can be carried out by the administrator (such as a social worker or caseworker) or it can be a self-service process. In practice, most countries use a combination of these modalities. For example, the process can start with the client visiting a government office followed by a household visit by a social worker, or an online application done at the applicant's home followed by a visit to a government office for an interview or to submit additional documents or information.

Probably the most common on-demand modality is for people to apply in person at local offices or kiosks. In many countries, people go to a local office to apply for social protection programs. On-demand applications can be made at local social welfare offices, employment agencies, or local government offices.[3]

Often, local offices conduct intake and registration in an integrated manner, so that people can use one application form for many benefits and services. One example is Georgia, where regional and local Social Service agencies serve as one-stop shops/service centers where people can file a common application to be considered for multiple benefits and services. In Brazil and Chile, people apply and are interviewed and registered in social registries. The registrants are assessed for numerous social programs. In Turkey, people apply for a variety of social and health benefits and services at 1,000 local autonomous Social Assistance and Solidarity Foundations (SASFs).[4] In Germany, municipal job centers are the point of entry for both employment services and income support (box 4.1).

In some counties in the United States, health and social assistance (often referred to as health and human services) have been integrated at the county level. For example, in Montgomery County, Maryland, people can access 134 health and social programs at the county's local offices and satellite offices. An innovative real-time lobby management system helps minimize wait times and optimizes staff allocation to various general or specialized desks (box 4.2).

Digital applications are also quite common. Some steps in the intake process may be facilitated by technology, such as applying online (either initial or full applications), interviewing by phone, and scheduling in-person appointments or answering simple queries via chatbots. Online applications for unemployment benefits are common in OECD countries, though use of the online option varies from 1 or 2 percent of applicants in Spain to 30 percent in New Zealand, 58 percent in the United States, 88 percent in the United Kingdom, 95 percent in the Netherlands, and 100 percent in Iceland and Italy (with the option of requesting assistance to help file their applications) (OECD 2015). Some countries have also introduced initial online self-service applications for social programs, sometimes with simulators to help people decide whether to fill out a complete application by determining whether they are likely to be eligible for benefits. Box 4.3 reviews some examples of online registration in Greece, Chile, and the United States (state of California).

Even though they do not involve humans, digital self-service windows are the "face" of the agency or program for the public. Therefore, online systems must be user-friendly. Difficulty navigating the online process may deter clients from applying—even if they are potentially eligible. In the United States, for example, a large share of eligible families in many states does not apply for food stamps. A recent review of low take-up rates in the state of California found that bureaucratic hurdles—including a complicated and confusing online interface—deterred people from applying.

Administrator-Driven Intake

Intake for administrator-driven approaches is primarily carried out at the household, usually via door-to-door registration campaigns. En masse registration drives, also known as census sweeps, are often used in areas with a high concentration of the intended population, or in countries with limited data or administrative capacity. Field teams typically go door to door with registration questionnaires for all or most families in a specific region. Such is the case in Burkina Faso, where all households in selected regions, provinces, and villages are interviewed and registered. In some countries, communities prioritize which households are interviewed and registered (as in Malawi, discussed below). When en masse registration approaches are used at a national level, a large share of the population may be registered, as seen in the case of Listahanan in the Philippines (box 4.4).

The administrator-driven approach tends to be periodic and typically does not capture the entire population, particularly in contexts with limited financing and capacity. With the administrator-driven approach, the doors for inclusion open on a periodic basis (usually every three to five years) rather than allowing continuous inclusion. The decision to conduct registration less frequently tends to be driven by limited resources for program budgets to finance benefits and services using the information gathered during registration. It can also reflect capacity constraints for carrying out the registration waves, especially the existence of adequate structures or institutional capacity at the local levels to carry out more frequent recurrent processes. But even when the doors open for all at a specific point in time, it is still challenging to capture everyone: to date, no en masse registration wave has covered 100 percent of households. Several countries have registered upwards of 70 percent of the population **at the point in time** when they were carried out.[5]

In such resource- and capacity-constrained environments, where exclusion is to an extent beyond the control of the actors involved in registration efforts, registration quotas are sometimes used. Many countries use quotas to limit the number of households that can be registered. These quotas are typically set as a

Box 4.1 Front-Office Setup for Triaging Clients for Employment and Social Assistance: Mannheim's Job Center

In Mannheim, Germany, the joint municipal job centers manage both employment and social benefits and services. While people may come into the local offices seeking income support benefits, they are also assessed for employment-related services. The signs in the office windows emphasize that work is a primary objective. The offices are set up to triage people to various stations for intake, registration, and assessment for the various benefits and services (see figure B4.1.1 below).

1. The Welcome Area receives both drop-in clients and those with appointments. There are stations for quick placement and self-service in the front, and a "30-second rule" for service standards at the initial reception area.
2. Clients are then directed to the Initial Application Zone, where they receive personalized support for intake and registration.
3. Based on the initial intake interview and the information provided, they are then triaged according to their profiles and steered to "Protected Zones": (1) employment services for advising, assistance with CVs/job readiness, and job placement with job counselors; and/or to (2) income and social support services where they will be assessed for eligibility for cash assistance, and if relevant, support by other social services that are located in the same building, such as psychosocial supports, substance abuse experts, medical teams, personal debt consultants, immigration law consultations, child maintenance specialists, and so on.
4. Youth (<25 years old) are also directed to specialized services for immediate placement in training, employment, or "jump plus" (a cooperative scheme with local training social enterprise agencies). They receive individual support and intensive assistance if needed, as well as close support by case managers. They are also loaned bicycles for transportation to jobs/training centers as needed.
5. Nearby, there are Job-Marts in every neighborhood, which helps reduce the stigma that could arise if they were located only in poor areas. Each Job-Mart has a local business leader/politician (patron). The Job-Marts support job seekers with identifying vacancies in the area, canvassing for jobs, and so on.

Figure B4.1.1 Office Setup for Triaging Clients

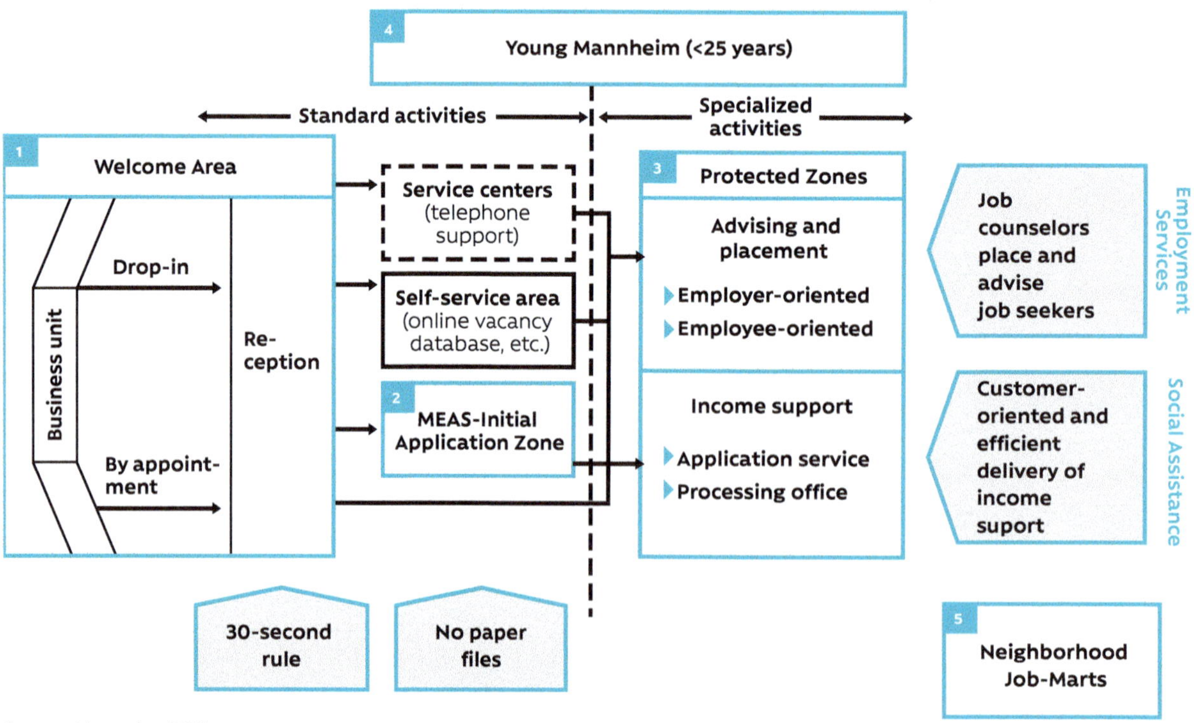

Source: Hoerning 2011.

Box 4.2 Innovative Tools for Optimizing Lobby Management in Montgomery County, Maryland (US)

Montgomery County's Department of Health and Human Services (DHHS) has been innovating to provide an integrated approach across service areas. This is critical given that DHHS must manage, administer, and implement some 134 federal, state, and county programs across six core service areas: children-youth-family programs (including food stamps, TANF cash assistance, social services, etc.), aging and disability, behavioral health crisis services, public health services (including Medicaid and Affordable Care Act health insurance), homeless services, and community affairs. Integration efforts have occurred at the policy and institutional levels, in the practice of integrated casework, in personnel management, and through IT infrastructure. Some of these innovative tools include "QLess," a system for managing, triaging, and monitoring client flows in the front office, and "eICM," an integrated case management system which supports the functions of prescreening, intake and registration, assessment of needs and conditions, eligibility, enrollment, benefits/service management, and case dispensation.

QLess is a lobby management system that seeks to improve customer service, eliminate long lines, reduce walk-aways and customer complaints, boost staff productivity and operational efficiencies, gain valuable insights with tracking and reporting, and enhance communication and customer engagement. Since an office may serve 200–500+ clients per day for numerous benefits and services plus administrative appointments (recertification, document drop-offs, questions, and complaints), effective lobby time and resource management is critical.

- **For clients.** When clients arrive, they sign in at conveniently placed kiosks, which offer multilingual options. The preferred language indicators not only help the clients navigate, but they also help the office allocate multilingual staff to the various stations. The clients enter their names and cell phone numbers and select the buttons for the types of services that correspond with the main reasons for their visit. Once a customer has signed into the QLess kiosk, an avatar will be assigned to their case and displayed on the monitors in the selected queue for that customer, to indicate their place in line. The avatars change colors according to status and move on the screen with the customers through the phases (waiting, summoning, servicing, concluding, departing). The customer will receive a text message alert when they are next in line, and to direct them to the station or window where they will be served when it is their turn.
- **For office administration.** Operationally, the site manager is always aware of the lobby size at any point of the day with a live dashboard and able to react to customer influx. The site manager can monitor wait times, click on specific avatars for client details, or reallocate staff to the various desks for better optimization of resources (including assigning specialized staff or language-resource staff according to client needs). They can also use the system to schedule appointments and manage the calendar while avoiding peak flow times.

Customer avatars transition through colors indicating status in QLess:

Green: wait time ≤ original forecast
Yellow: wait time 25% > original
Red: wait time 50% > original
Gray: "call ahead" client who has not yet checked in
Purple: flex-appointment client automatically advancing in virtual queue

Sources: QLess Training Guide Version 6.0: 2018 version, Department of Health and Human Services, Montgomery County, Maryland; notes from field visit and discussions with DHHS staff.
Note: TANF = Temporary Assistance for Needy Families.

Box 4.3 Online Applications in Greece, Chile, and California (US)

Although digital self-service windows are becoming increasingly common, they still are not widespread for social protection programs in developing countries. Examples from Greece, Chile, and the US (state of California) illustrate some of the uses of online applications for social assistance programs, as well as the importance of human-centered design.

Greece's Social Solidarity Income (SSI) program uses online applications on the SSI website. Initially, the online applications faced some challenges in the pilot phase (unclear aspects, insufficient clarifying information, lack of a PDF version for viewing offline, etc.). However, those glitches were resolved, and the current version was extensively pretested and designed to be user friendly, with explanatory notes that appear as the applicants move the cursor to every field, a Frequently Asked Questions section, and a link to an online training module. The application form can also be filled out with the help of municipal staff, which helps promote inclusion for people who are uncomfortable with online services, such as the elderly, foreigners, Roma, or persons with disabilities or limited education. Participants in focus groups of individuals and municipal officials reported that the online application was generally user-friendly (Marini et al. 2016). Two key features make Greece's online application particularly efficient: (1) the application form leverages interoperability with other administrative systems to prefill various questions (data fields); and (2) automation allows for an indication of the eligibility outcome immediately upon submission of the application, for those applicants who do not need to submit additional information at municipalities.

In Chile, people can apply and be registered into the Registro Social de Hogares (RSH), the country's social registry, to be assessed and considered for eligibility for numerous social programs. There are three intake modalities, two of which are online, and a third which is in person at the municipality. The first online intake modality requires the use of the applicant's civil registry password and allows the applicant to submit all required data and supporting documents through the RSH website. The municipality later validates this information, with no need for the applicant to go to the municipality in person, and this is followed by a household visit conducted by a municipality enumerator. The second online intake modality requires the use of the applicant's unique identification number and allows the applicant to apply and submit required documents. This modality requires an in-person visit to the municipality so that the applicant can show proof of their identity, validate the information, and hand in any pending documents.

Experiences with online applications for food stamps in the United States demonstrate the importance of human-centered design, and the pitfalls that can occur if digital self-service windows are not user-friendly. In the state of California, take-up rates for food stamps are quite low: less than two-thirds apply.[a] A review by the civic-tech firm CodeForAmerica .org found that a key reason for low take-up is bureaucracy—even though people can apply online. Journey mapping exercises (like those discussed in chapter 2) found that the online service windows were incredibly difficult to navigate: the site was down ("closed") for scheduled maintenance every day from midnight to 6 a.m., navigation on the site was confusing, the online application was more than 50 web pages long with more than 100 questions (many redundant and/or confusing), the process took up to an hour to complete, and it did not work on mobile devices despite the fact that most low-income people rely on smartphones.[b] The state of California has been teaming up with civic-tech specialists to design a user-friendly app to facilitate these processes based on human-centered design principles.

Sources: Greece: Marini et al. 2016; Chile: Chile, Ministry of Social Development 2017; California: Solomon 2017.

a. Primary source: CalFresh stats at http://www.calfresh.ca.gov/PG844.htm.

b. Solomon 2017 and https://www.codeforamerica.org/featured-stories/california-counties-make-it-easier-to-apply-for-calfresh.

Box 4.4 Census Sweep Modality for Intake and Registration: The Philippines's Listahanan 2015

The Philippines's Listahanan (formally known as the National Household Targeting System for Poverty Reduction [NHTS-PR]) is a social registry that gathers information on the socioeconomic characteristics of households/families nationwide. The Listahanan 2015 family assessment form (FAF) contains 45 question fields as well as a community questionnaire with 11 question fields. Data from the Listahanan are used by numerous social programs, including the 4Ps conditional cash transfer, social pension for poor elderly, and the PhilHealth subsidized health insurance, as well as 1,095 local government units and various other users. Following the 2015 registration wave, the Listahanan contains records of 15 million households nationwide (about 75 percent of the population), of which 5.2 million have been classified as poor and prioritized for government programs. The 2015 registration wave was carried out in just six months using the following modalities, instruments, and techniques:

- Primary modality for intake and registration was the **door-to-door census sweep approach**, in situ at the homes of those registered. On-demand applications were also used during the community validation phase to allow households to be registered if they were missed by the registration wave.
- **Paper-based questionnaires** were complemented by **computer-aided data collection**. Some 13,000 android tablets and 4,500 laptops were purchased to aid data collection and supervision. The tablets were deployed mainly in urban areas where internet connections were more reliable for data submission. Laptops were equipped with specialized applications, such as the data management system for area supervisors and coordinators. This application allowed supervisors to monitor enumerators' daily completion of household assessments and keep track of the enumeration schedule. They also facilitated faster re-reviews and spot checks by area supervisors, as well as automated validation routines to check for inconsistencies. Paper questionnaires were deployed mainly in rural areas where electricity for charging and internet connectivity are problematic. On average, it took 30 minutes to complete each electronic questionnaire, as compared with 33 minutes for interviewing and another 19 minutes for data entry using paper-based questionnaires.
- Extensive **training, communications, and outreach** were also used. The 2015 wave made extensive use of videos for training across the country (including the 39,000 field workers). These video training materials helped a lot for consistency of messages, concepts, and protocols, as well as for quality controls. The Philippines's Department for Social Welfare and Development is also recognized for its extensive use of strategic and operational communications, and the Listahanan 2015 made extensive use of such tools. The Listahanan teams also used proactive outreach techniques to involve local authorities and communities, and to reach marginalized populations, such as those in geographically dispersed areas and the homeless.

Source: Velarde 2018.
Note: 4Ps = Pantawid Pamilyang Pilipino Program.

percentage of households in a particular locality (district or municipality), sometimes the same percentage for each locality for political reasons. In some instances, communities themselves prioritize which households are registered, either through local leaders or through community meetings. Such approaches can leverage local knowledge to help prioritize the poorest. In some cases, quotas are used with the objective of minimizing further exclusion. For example, in Tanzania's Productive Social Safety Net scale-up in 2014, registration quotas were set because the program, which is composed of multiple interventions, could cover only the bottom 15 percent of population living in or vulnerable to extreme poverty rather than everyone in basic-needs poverty (World Bank 2016). Higher operational targets in terms of number of registration questionnaires were set in poorer communities to increase the chances of inclusion of the poorest, and communities prioritized which households would be registered. Quotas can also help manage expectation in resource-constrained contexts. Why register large shares (or even 100 percent) of the households and raise expectations when programs can select only a small percentage or number of households to be eligible and enrolled in the program(s)? However, efforts are needed to mitigate risks associated with these partial openings, including (1) strong communication to help manage perceptions around fairness and transparency about the reasons why some are excluded; (2) a systematic process to validate community decisions to minimize the potential to replicate existing local inequalities (e.g., certain disadvantaged segments are excluded because they are less informed or less connected); and (3) channels (such as a grievance redress mechanism [GRM]) to address issues of incorrect exclusion or inclusion.

A few countries that have been operating an administrator-driven approach have started incorporating features of the on-demand approach. For example, mobile teams can set up temporary registration desks in remote locations. Although the temporary desk resembles the on-demand approach in that clients have to self-select into the process and bear the costs of the physical displacement, it is primarily administrator-driven in terms of the impetus for and timing of registration, as temporary desks are open only for the duration of the en masse registration campaign. Pakistan has been experimenting with temporary desks in addition to door-to-door methods in its 2018–19 en masse registration wave (box 4.5). Similarly, in other countries, to a certain extent, the client takes the initiative to attend an initial registration event to be prescreened prior to registration, as in Sierra Leone, or a government office, as in the Republic of Congo (box 4.6). Even if these examples

Box 4.5 Experimenting with Different Modalities for En Masse Registration: Pakistan's NSER

In 2017, Pakistan began the process of updating its National Socioeconomic Registry (NSER), which contains data on household and socioeconomic characteristics for more than 25 million households (>85 percent of the population). Updating the registry regularly would improve equitable and efficient distribution of benefits, reduce errors and misreporting, and better serve its intended population/potential beneficiaries. For the 2017 registration wave, Pakistan decided to experiment with two methods to compare their effectiveness and efficiency: the traditional door-to-door approach and a pilot temporary desk approach. With the traditional approach, mobile teams visit all or most households at their homes, conduct interviews with the household members, and visually take stock of the housing and other conditions of the family. With the desk approach, the teams set up temporary desks at the Union Council level, conduct outreach to ensure people are aware of the registration efforts, and encourage them to come to the temporary desk to provide their information and be registered. While this temporary desk approach has some degree of self-selection and demand, it does not possess all features of the on-demand methods discussed in this Sourcebook because it is still part of an en masse registration wave with the state going to the communities; it still involves registering households as a group or cohort; and most important, the timing is still driven by the administrators and is temporary (such that people could not come apply to be registered at any time but rather during a defined period).[a]

Source: Rosas, Jamy, and Khan 2017.

a. See chapter 2 and the glossary for definitions of on-demand versus administrator-driven approaches.

Box 4.6 Administrator-Driven Approaches with Elements of the On-Demand Approach: The Republic of Congo and Sierra Leone

The Republic of Congo's RSU is a social registry that gathers information on the socioeconomic characteristics of households. These data are mainly used by the Lisungi cash transfer programs (cash transfer to children and the elderly and income-generating activities) and to offer free health care for the poor and vulnerable, and soon will be used to support the provision of vocational training for the poor and vulnerable youth. Previously, the RSU used a census-sweep approach in which only households preselected by the community social workers were registered and the questionnaire was administered by the National Statistical Institute. Currently the country is transitioning to an approach in which the household has to apply at the local social assistance office (Circonscription d'Action Sociale [CAS]), and intake and registration are conducted by social workers or temporary hired enumerators. This approach has been tested for the subsidized health care program.

Similarly, Sierra Leone's Social Protection Registry for Integrated National Targeting (SPRINT) is a social registry whose data are used by four programs, including the Social Safety Nets Program, the Rapid Ebola Response Social Safety Nets Program, the Labor-Intensive Public Works, and the Ministry of Agriculture's seed distribution program. In order to register, the households come to the administrator. Intake and registration are done in two stages. First, poorest households are preselected by the Community Identification Committee (CIC) through a structured participatory exercise, and then representatives of preselected households attend a registration event during which a short questionnaire based on "light" proxy means test (LPMT) is applied. The questionnaire is based on a reduced version of the PMT formula (including a few key variables that are the highest predictors) and is administered by mobile phone or tablet by the implementing agency at a central location for the community or cluster of communities that have been selected through the geographical targeting. Second, for those passing the LPMT calculated at the central level, the statistical agency then visits the households to administer a longer questionnaire based on the full PMT formula.

While these two cases show some features of the on-demand approach, notably that the client takes the initiative to apply (at a social assistance office in the case of the Republic of Congo and at a registration event in the case of Sierra Leone), they do not show the three features that define the on-demand approach. In particular, clients do not get registered at a time of their own choosing but rather on a timetable defined by the administrator, as registration is not open at any time. Even if they apply at their own initiative, clients are somehow being registered as a group, as they belong to a cohort corresponding to a specific registration wave.

Sources: The Republic of Congo's Lisungi program mid-term review report, 2017; Sierra Leone's "Simplified Community-Based Targeting Processes for Rapid Ebola Social Safety Nets," 2014.

have some features of the on-demand approach, they do not classify as on-demand as clients cannot apply at a time of their own choosing.

Registration Modalities

While the specifics vary, registration processes typically include recording applicants' information, collecting additional data on them, applying quality controls to the data, and consolidating and storing the revised data set. After information gathered from an applicant during intake is recorded, agencies may collect additional information from other administrative systems, as discussed below. Quality controls may include validating data to ensure that the information is complete and consistent, verifying data to confirm that they match information that was provided to other government agencies or programs (this step involves cross-checking the applicant's information with other data sources), and supervisor reviews and spot checks. Data are consolidated and stored, often with further steps to improve quality such as de-duplication of records.

Figure 4.3 Registration Modalities

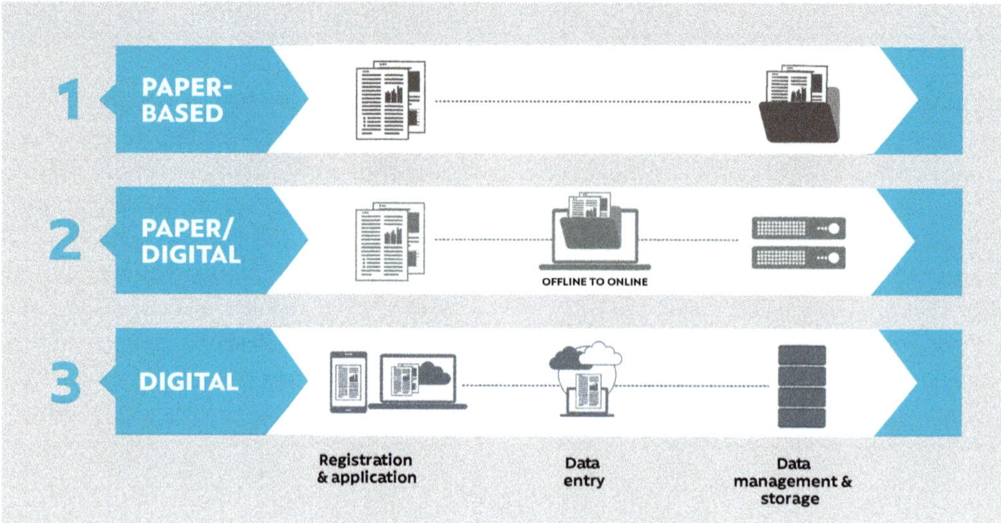

Source: Original figure for this publication.

Technology and information systems capabilities typically determine to what extent registration will be automated. Until recent decades, registration was paper-to-paper: it was recorded on paper by the intake officer or enumerator, who then relied on paper-based files (modality 1 in figure 4.3). With the expansion of technology, some social welfare offices and public employment offices started managing information with spreadsheets and digitized records. Today, many countries still use paper-based registration or application forms to collect data during the intake process, and then enter that data into computers (modality 2 in figure 4.3). Others use portable devices to record information digitally (online or offline) during intake and registration, and then transmit the information to an information system (modality 3 in figure 4.3). The process is similar for online applicants.

Instruments and Techniques for Intake and Registration

Ideally, intake and registration processes are based on human-centered design principles. Those principles apply to all aspects of intake and registration: interview techniques; questionnaire design; documentation requirements; digital service windows; process complexity; the amount of time, cost, or visits required of applicants or registrants; forms and instructions; and so on.[6] Journey mapping can reveal bottlenecks, pain points, and inefficiencies by tracing applicants' experience in navigating intake and registration.[7] Difficulties in applying or registering for assistance could deter clients from applying even if they are potentially eligible, resulting in low take-up.

One aspect of human-centered design is ensuring that people with access barriers can apply and register for assistance. People with disabilities, non-native language speakers, the homeless or those without fixed addresses, people living in remote areas, refugees, and others may struggle to complete the process. Barriers to access may not be only physical, but may also include conditions, policies, or attitudes that hamper or prevent access to benefits and services. For instance, an applicant with a print disability may not be able to complete application forms (paper or electronic) without assistance. Similarly, an applicant with a motor disability may be prevented from accessing local offices because they do not have specialized transportation, or because the offices are difficult for them to enter (such as entry doors not at grade or doors that are too heavy or narrow to allow passage). Accommodations for those who might otherwise not be able to apply or register include personal assistance in completing forms, translation, mobile teams who can visit potential applicants, or other help. Such accommodations may also benefit nondisabled users. For instance, the use of plain language can benefit not only persons whose comprehension is limited but also non-native speakers. Similarly, physical accessibility can also help parents using strollers, persons using walkers, and delivery personnel.

Interviews are central to the intake process.[8] They should cover basic introductions; objectives (including the clients' reasons for applying if they initiated the process); information needed to assess needs and conditions (see below); any questions registrants may have; information confidentiality, use, disclosures, and consent; and so on. The interviewer also needs to clearly communicate that there is no guarantee that registrants will be eligible for any specific benefits or services. While the intake interview may follow a certain sequence or questionnaire (see below), it is not a survey. Rather, it is a conversation between interviewers and individuals, usually about many aspects of their lives (see information content section below), and often at a time of critical need. Conversations may need to go beyond the questionnaire. The dignity of the individual or family members must also be preserved. Therefore, interview protocols and training are critical. It is also important to get people's consent of use of information, which becomes particularly important in social services that deal with very delicate situations (minors, domestic violence, etc.). Interviewers should be trained in effective interviewing techniques. The interviewer may adopt interpersonal tactics that build trust and avoid a formulaic application of the questionnaire. Efforts should be made to accommodate diverse populations. Those efforts may include culturally sensitive adaptations of questionnaires or interview styles, language translation (via multilingual intake officers or remote translators who can be reached by phone during the conversation), and accommodations for people with disabilities (such as for the blind or hearing-impaired).[9]

The questionnaire or application form is another core instrument for intake and registration. Applicants may fill out an application form or questionnaire themselves (on paper or digitally), or an interviewer or enumerator may do so (on paper or digitally). Either way, the form collects enough information to enable an agency to assess the needs and conditions of the applicants. A key principle is to collect minimal information—that is, the form should collect only the necessary information, and no more. If any information is already available to the agency, it should not be required again. All forms may be pretested in a variety of contexts by program personnel, interviewers, and people outside the agency or process. Pretesting can include role-playing situations (box 4.7). Human-centered design principles mean that the form or questionnaire should be user-friendly: it should not take too long to fill out or administer, and it should be easy to comprehend and navigate. These principles are pertinent for digital applications as well because complex online applications can deter people from applying for social protection programs.

In addition to completing a form, applicants may be required to supply documentation. Depending on the information needed (which is discussed below), required documents may include (1) identification and residence information (for an individual or for all family members), such as ID credentials, marriage and birth certificates, or proof of residence; (2) documentation pertaining to labor status (certificates from employment offices); (3) income statements (from employers or the social security administration); (4) ownership certificates of land, property, automobiles, and so on; and (5) certificates of disability, pregnancy, and other health status. Obtaining documents can impose costs on applicants, including the time and expense of traveling to various agencies to collect the documents, and the cost of gathering them (such as notarization and photocopying). An extensive review of income-support programs in Europe and Central Asia calculated the time and monetary cost of gathering documentation in support of applications (Tesliuc et al. 2014). That study found that in Romania it took applicants a median of five days to gather documents, and it cost them about 10 percent of one average monthly benefit per family. The average time to gather documents in the Kyrgyz Republic was two days, and cost between 15 percent of the average monthly benefit per family in rural areas and 80 percent of that average benefit in urban areas (because transportation costs were higher and documentation requirements were more expansive in the cities). Turkey is a notable example in this regard: It succeeded in reducing documentation requirements from 17 certificates or official documents to one: the ID credential of individuals or family members, though a home visit is still required (see box 4.15 later in this chapter).

High-quality data are also essential. Since information is both the key input and an output of intake and

Box 4.7 Role-Playing and Live-Case Simulations in Albania's Ndihma Ekonomike Program

In Albania, the Ministry of Labor, Social Assistance, and Equal Opportunities (MoLSAE) made extensive use of role-playing to pretest the questionnaire and train staff in the interview processes for the Ndihma Ekonomike Program. The training and pretesting activities were very innovative and included the following:

- **Training and role-playing simulations.** Training was provided to the MoLSAE team and social administrators from the two local government offices where the pretest was held. The objective of the training was to prepare for the field pretest that followed in the second week of the mission. The training included an overview of the objectives of the reforms, a detailed review of the draft questionnaire and instructions prepared for different roles in the field pretest: general observer, questionnaire observer, guidelines for interviewers, time taker, home visit form, and so on. The training included role-playing simulations with the help of two fictitious case studies which gave the participants the opportunity to practice the interview process using the new questionnaire in advance of the actual field pretest.
- **Field pretest with real "live cases" of families in different settings.** The field pretest was conducted in two sites—Tirana (urban) and Berzhite (rural)—with two interview/observer teams at each site. In total, 32 applicants were interviewed in two days by four teams that included members from MoLSAE, local governments (social administrators), and the World Bank, all of which actively participated in the pretest. The applicants included a mix of families that are currently beneficiaries as well as those who were previously rejected to receive Ndihma Ekonomike benefits.
- **Debriefing day.** All four teams presented their reflections/experience/observations from the field pretest on the debriefing day. According to the observations, (1) interviews took progressively less time as the social administrators became more familiar with the questionnaire; (2) some of the questions in the questionnaire needed to be further clarified or simplified; (3) local knowledge of the social administrators was valuable to the interview process; (4) home visits helped verify/correct the responses provided by the applicants during the interview; and (5) relative scores produced particularly for the families for which home visits were conducted by each team were consistent with the observed relative poverty of these applicant households during the home visits.

The process greatly improved the questionnaire and interview methods and was successful in building ownership and understanding at all levels.

Source: World Bank, Government of Albania 2011. Social Assistance Modernization Project—Technical Assistance Mission. Field Pre-Test for Scoring Formula and Intake Questionnaire. Aide Memoire, June 6–17.

registration, it is vital to ensure that data are accurate and complete. Many tools enhance data quality. Field supervision, double-data entry, and automated error checks help ensure the quality of data at the time of capture. Random re-reviews and independent spot checks of newly acquired data are also useful. Automated internal cross-checks help validate information by checking and correcting for data consistency and completeness. Some countries include additional variables to be collected during intake and registration to cross-check the consistency of information provided (Brazil, for example, includes additional proxy variables on its questionnaire to check answers related to self-reported incomes). Home visits are used to gather and verify information. They can help caseworkers formulate a better qualitative understanding of an applicant's overall situation. External cross-checks verify and validate information. They may draw on information in other agencies via interoperable systems (as discussed in the Social Registries and Interoperability with Other Administrative Information Systems section later in this chapter). Or external validation can come from communities as a third-party check, especially to validate the list of preselected households. Malawi and Burkina Faso are examples of this approach.

Intake can be a labor-intensive process. Staffing is a central element of intake. Staff may include enumerators, interviewers, intake officers, social workers, employment service officers, supervisors, and spot-checkers. Many factors determine the configuration and numbers of personnel that would be needed to carry out intake and registration: (1) the characteristics of the intended population, such as the number of individuals, families, or households to be registered; their geographic concentration; and language or other access barriers; (2) the modalities of intake and registration; (3) the complexity and amount of information to be collected; (4) the number of applicants or registrants that will be processed per day; and (5) other factors such as logistics, administrative capacity, and so on.

- Staffing for administrator-driven en masse registration drives can take many forms. Some countries hire contracted field teams to carry out en masse registration drives for their social registries. In the Philippines, 39,000 field workers, including enumerators, area supervisors, encoders, and verifiers, registered 15 million households nationwide over a period of six months in 2015 (see box 4.4) (Velarde 2018). Others, such as Malawi, have taken advantage of existing district and community staff to roll out en masse registration across entire districts, as discussed below (Lindert et al. 2018). Both approaches have advantages. Contracting teams can be an efficient way to register large numbers of people rapidly. Using existing institutions and staff can boost local ownership and understanding of a registry, and the know-how staff gain from the experience could subsequently be used to update the registry.
- With on-demand modalities, frontline staff may perform a variety of functions in addition to intake and registration, or some may be specialized intake officers, leaving guidance functions such as social work and employment service counseling to more highly skilled staff. Technology can reduce the amount of staff time spent on intake and registration. For example, with digital self-service windows, applicants can register much of their information directly (sometimes followed up by an in-person interview). If there is interoperability between agencies, many data fields on a form can be prefilled (see box 4.3 and the Social Registries and Interoperability with Other Administrative Information Systems section later in this chapter). With less time spent registering and processing information, more time can be spent providing other services to clients—or serving more clients in an efficient manner. Technology also helps optimize the use of frontline staff in Montgomery County, Maryland (US) (see box 4.2).

Training of intake personnel is fundamental. Training should be carried out at all levels and for all types of personnel (enumerators, interviewers, supervisors, etc.). In the case of social services, the need for continuous training becomes particularly important. Different modalities can be used for training intake personnel. For example, video training sessions can standardize training and ensure consistency in the lessons and practices that are passed along, especially when training large numbers of field workers. The 2015 registration wave in the Philippines made great use of training videos, which were produced and distributed to all field offices and helped make sure that standard practices were adopted with quality controls and reference materials. That contrasts with the approach in 2011, when training was carried out in a cascaded "training of trainers" manner: central staff trained regional staff, who then trained area coordinators and supervisors, who then trained enumerators. Loss of key concepts occurred at each stage, resulting in additional time spent on supervision and correction of errors (Velarde 2018). Brazil's Cadastro Único also makes use of video training materials, with professional telenovela-style actors who act out various intake and registration scenarios. Ongoing learning and knowledge-sharing is also important to pass on new information, share good practice approaches, and communicate lessons learned. During the rollout of Greece's guaranteed minimum income (GMI) program, municipal staff were able to exchange information, respond to queries, and troubleshoot with the support of a call center and an email list of all staff in the municipalities. In Albania, innovative pretesting and role-playing simulations were used to train ministry staff and local field workers in a new questionnaire and scoring formula (box 4.7).

4.2 INFORMATION TO BE GATHERED DURING INTAKE AND REGISTRATION

The content of the information gathered during intake and registration will vary significantly depending on the characteristics of the intended population and the nature of the program(s) that will use the information. The examples in table 4.1 outline the content that would be sought depending on the characteristics of the intended populations. A key concept related to information content is the definition of the "assistance unit," which may be the individual, the family, or the household. Even when the application is for an individual, however, in some instances, information may also be needed for a designated guardian or caregiver if the individual is a dependent (such as a child or an adult with a severe disability).

Target Groups Defined by Demographic Status

Many countries operate benefits programs targeted to specific demographic groups. Examples include pregnancy benefits, parental leave, one-time birth or adoption allowances, child allowances, single-parent benefits, family benefits, and old-age pensions. These are particularly common in Europe, Central Asia, and OECD countries.

Applications for old-age benefits require basic information. That information includes the following:

- Basic identifying information: name, date of birth, place of birth, sex at birth, marital status, address (residential and mailing if different), ID number, with proof of age (usually a birth certificate)
- Residence status, as well as residence history (with documentation for those with minimum residence requirements or for citizens living outside the country at time of application)

Additional information is needed if the pensions are means-tested or if eligibility and benefit levels depend on an individual's prior contributions. Many social pensions for the elderly have both categorical eligibility criteria, such as age, and need-based eligibility criteria, such as means testing (World Bank 2018 b). In those cases, additional information is needed not only for an individual pensioner but also for the household. (See discussion of socioeconomic information below.) For social insurance pensions, eligibility and benefits levels depend on the individual's insurance contributions. As such, information on employment and contributions histories would be needed. (See chapter 5.)

With child-related benefits, information must be provided for both the child and the guardian. While the assistance unit is the individual, the benefit is paid to a designated recipient. As such, information is required for both the child and the guardian, and typically includes the following:

- Basic identifying information for the child and the guardian: name, date of birth, place of birth, sex at birth, marital status of guardian, address (residential and mailing if different, ID number), with proof of age for the child (usually a birth certificate)
- Residence status for the child and the guardian (with documentation for those with minimum residence requirements or for citizens living outside the country at time of application)
- Proof of guardianship, custody (legal, financial, residence situation), and relation to the child. Most child-related benefits are paid to only one designated recipient, who must establish the relation to the child, which can be complicated in cases of divorce.

When child allowances are also need-based, further information would be needed, such as information on household incomes or other socioeconomic measures or disability, as discussed below.

Target Groups Defined by Socioeconomic Status

Many benefits and services are directed at specific population groups according to their socioeconomic status. Examples of benefits provided for particular groups include: means-tested demographic benefits (such as child benefits and social pensions for the elderly), GMI programs, cash transfers, need-based scholarships, and so on.

Table 4.1 Various Target Groups and Associated Types of Information to Be Collected

Target groups	Information to be collected
Demographic groups along the life cycle (assistance unit = individuals)	
• Children • Elderly • Women	• Basic identifying information (for individual + designated guardian if relevant) • Residence/citizenship status (for individual + designated guardian if relevant)
Groups constrained by socioeconomic status (assistance unit = individuals, families, households)	
• People living below the poverty line • Homeless • People living in isolated and remote areas • Pastoralist, nomadic, and semi-nomadic groups • Indigenous groups • Refugees, stateless, immigrants, internally displaced populations (IDPs) and/or people living in areas affected by fragility, conflict, and violence • Ethnic, religious, linguistic, and visible minorities	• Basic identifying information (for individual + designated guardian if relevant) • Residence/citizenship status (for individual + designated guardian if relevant) • Characteristics of household members • Employment status of household head and/or working-age adults • Income information for all household members • Assets of the household • Household expenses • Other info (proxies, catastrophic events, etc.) • Geospatial information on the location of the household, including address and other contact information, as well as GPS geo-coding information (where possible)
Labor and work conditions (assistance unit = individuals)	
• Unemployed • Discouraged/inactive workers • Informal sector workers • Forced or child laborers	• Basic identifying information • Residence/citizenship status and proof of residency • Current labor-force status (employed, unemployed, inactive); work history • Distance to labor market and barriers to work
Disability (assistance unit = individuals)	
• Persons with disabilities • Workers with disabilities	• Basic identifying information (for individual + designated guardian/caregiver if relevant) • Residence/citizenship status (for individual + designated guardian/caregiver if relevant) • Medical information: nature, type, severity and duration of the disability, as well as any secondary or comorbid conditions that may require prevention or treatment • Functional limitations: functions that are impaired due to the disability; care needs • Nonmedical socioeconomic considerations (see above) that may or may not be directly related to the experience of disability • Support sought: the types of benefits and services that the individual is seeking (which can also be informative in assessing their needs and conditions)
Vulnerable individuals facing specific social risks (assistance unit = individuals, families)	
• Children at-risk • Youth at-risk • Adults at-risk • LGBT	• Basic identifying information • Residence/citizenship status and proof of residency • Socioeconomic status • Labor-related information • Key risk factors: family, social, substances, violence, health, homelessness, legal, and so on • Self-assessment, aspirations, goals, perceptions, attitudes, concerns, and so on
Integrated approaches for intake and registration	
	• Multiple programs could use shared intake and registration

Source: Original table for this publication.

Note: LGBT = lesbian, gay, bisexual, and transgender.

Some services (including some outside of social protection) may also be targeted to individuals or households according to their socioeconomic profile, such as subsidized health care or health insurance, free/subsidized transportation, subsidized childcare, labor and employment services, social services, and pro bono legal services. Most countries use socioeconomic assessments to prioritize aid for the poor or other vulnerable populations. However, in some countries, socioeconomic status is used to exclude high-income families from aid (or reduce their level of benefits), such as with child benefits in Denmark, France, and the United Kingdom.[10] The practice is sometimes called "targeting from the top."

Information on socioeconomic status is collected at the household level. Because socioeconomic status typically relates to a household's economics, the assistance unit for this target group is the family or household. The information an agency collects depends on context as well as on profiling tools for assessing needs and conditions. (Those tools are discussed in detail below.) Questionnaires typically seek the following:

- Basic identifying information for the individual applicant and all family/household members as well as their relation to the household head or applicant (see listing above)
- Residence status for all members of the household (see listing above)
- Characteristics of household members, such as literacy, educational attainment, current education status and school, disability, and chronic illness
- The employment status of household head and/or working-age adults (discussed below for labor programs)
- Income information for all household members
- A household's financial and physical assets
- Household expenses
- Recent catastrophic events (for example, a death in family, catastrophic health event, loss of job or property, theft, or natural disaster)
- Other proxies such as number of meals per day or types and diversity of foods consumed
- Geospatial information on the location of the household, including address and other contact information, as well as GPS geo-coding information (where possible)

Income information can cover a range of activities, requiring various types of documentation.[11] Income information may be in cash or in kind, with imputations for in-kind values. All household members with formal employment or informal jobs are usually required to report their income from work. Income information typically includes the type and place of work, the employer's name and address (if the employment is formal), the wages earned over a specific period (before taxes), the frequency of wage payments, and the duration of employment. This information may be self-reported, possibly with supporting documentation, and verified by cross-checking with information in other government administrative systems. Household members with self-employment income are also required to report that income, both for nonfarm self-employment (earnings from sales) and for agricultural income (earnings from sales of crops, processed crop products, animal products, and consumption of self-produced food). Information is usually also required for other types of income such as the receipt of social assistance benefits, social security benefits, unemployment benefits, income from nonresidential parents, scholarships, rental income, interest income, other help with expenses, donations or private transfers, remittance income, lottery income, etc.

Assets can include both financial and physical possessions. The definition of these depends on contextual factors and the type of information required to carry out the assessment of needs and conditions. Financial assets may include holdings in cash, bank accounts, stocks or bonds, life insurance, and so on. Physical assets may include housing (and occupancy status, such as owning, renting, rent-free, or squatting), land property (size, location), livestock, vehicles, and other substantial durable goods. Information on housing quality may also be gathered, such as the number of rooms or bedrooms; number and type of windows; the foundation; the material of roof, walls, or floor; plumbing and source of drinking water; main fuel used for cooking, lighting, and heating; garbage collection; and the presence of a paved access road.[12] Other types of physical assets that may also be considered include mobile phones, televisions, radios, refrigerators, freezers, washers, dryers, stoves, irons, bicycles, and sewing machines, to name some examples.

Information on household expenses may also be collected. The specific expenses depend on context (the type of aid sought) and information that will be needed for the assessment of needs and conditions. Some examples include rent, mortgage, property or other taxes, homeowner fees, utility bills (electric, gas, fuel oil, water and sewage, phone, and internet or cable), transportation, child or elder care, school expenses, food, hygiene, medical bills, and health insurance premiums.

Target Groups Defined by Employment Status

Many benefits and services are directed to individuals based on their labor or employment status. Examples include unemployment benefits (in the form of insurance or assistance), employment services to help people find jobs, employability-enhancing services to boost people's chances of finding a job, and activation benefit-service packages that may combine all of the above (see chapter 7 for a typology of labor benefits and services).

Information requirements range from simple to more complex, depending on the type of assessment. Basic information would include

- Basic identifying information for the individual applicant, as outlined above
- Residence status (see listing above)
- Current labor-force status: If **employed**, the job title, activity, duration, wages, contributions history (for unemployment insurance), and employer information (name, address, and tax ID). If **unemployed**, the duration of unemployment, previous employment (type, duration, reason for departure, wages). If **inactive**, the duration of inactivity, reason for inactivity, previous job-search efforts, previous employment (type, duration, reason for departure, and wages).
- References (especially for first-time job seekers)
- Information about expectations on the type of job and labor status to be achieved

More elaborate information may also be sought to facilitate the assessment of barriers to work and activation readiness. Such information may include the following:

- Readiness to work: aspirations and goals; education, skills, literacy, and numeracy; work experience and history; and job preferences (type, working hours, geographic area, willingness to move)
- Potential barriers to work: self-identified obstacles; attitudinal factors (self-perceptions, motivation and openness to work); disability or functional impairment (previously outlined); mental or physical health conditions; transportation limitations; family responsibilities, such as child or elder care; language skills or limitations; homelessness or the lack of a fixed address; contacts with the law or prison system; or other social risks (discussed below).

Target Groups Defined by Disability

For disability benefits and services, applicants are usually asked to provide some certification of disability in addition to the basic demographic and identifying information described above. That certification is usually based on a disability assessment. There are different methodologies for assessing and certifying disability, including the medical impairment approach, the functional limitation approach, and the disability approach based on the International Classification of Functioning, Disability and Health. Intake and registration would thus gather information on the following:

- The medical nature of the disability (its type, severity, and likely duration)[13]
- Functional limitations (as reported by professionals or self-reported by the individual)[14]
- Nonmedical socioeconomic considerations that may or may not be directly linked to the experience of the disability
- The types of benefits and services that the individual is seeking (which can also be informative in assessing needs and conditions) (Bickenback et al. 2015)

Disability information can be gathered in various ways.[15] A disability assessment may be based on a self-assessment or on an independent assessment. The self-assessment may be a simple declaration of disability by the applicant, or it might involve responses to a more in-depth questionnaire about condition and limitations.[16] Independent assessors may be nurses, doctors, psychologists, therapists, physical therapists, rehabilitation specialists, other professionals, or even a multidisciplinary team. Assessors may be appointed or contracted by the individual, public agency, or insurance agency. The assessment may involve an interview (in-person, by phone, or online) using a standardized questionnaire, or it may be a performance test or medical examination. The latter may include a physical examination and medical history, provided that the individual has consented to the use of such information subject to data protection legislation and regulations. The language choices used in soliciting disability information may greatly affect the information provided. Inquiring about an individual's assessment of their abilities and functional limitations rather than their disability status can be effective. For example, elderly people may have functional limitations and would benefit from disability services but may not consider themselves people with disabilities. In addition, it may be impossible to identify nonvisible disabilities without probing for functional limitations (such as chronic or episodic conditions, such as diabetes or epilepsy). When the focus is on children with disabilities, it is important to assess not only a child's current circumstances, but also risk factors for acquiring a disability, such as emerging developmental delays, nutrition, health care, and socialization (for more information, see the discussion of social risk assessments below).

Socioeconomic information may also be needed. When a program requires means testing to determine eligibility, socioeconomic information may be required. In addition, the socioeconomic situation may be critical to assessing the needs and conditions of an individual, particularly since people with disabilities may face constraints on income-generating activities.[17] As discussed above, socioeconomic status is generally assessed for the entire family or household, so the assessment would go beyond the individual with a disability. Finally, it is important to note that the reason someone applies for aid may be unconnected to their medical condition or disability. The priority should be to gather information on the stated needs and conditions for which someone is seeking support.

Vulnerable Individuals Facing Social Risks

Social services seek to address risks faced by vulnerable individuals (children, youths, adults, or the elderly). Such services are typically organized around individuals as the assistance unit, but they may also involve other family members. Examples of social services include social work (which includes building awareness or providing information about such services, providing referrals to them, and providing counseling and mediation), social care (home-based, community-based, and institutionalized), and specialized services for specific groups and situations (such as child or adult protective services, adoption, and foster care). A typology of social services is discussed in chapter 7.

The information that may be gathered during intake and registration for social services could include the following:

- Basic identifying information (see listing above)
- Residence status (see listing above)
- Socioeconomic status (see listing above)
- Labor-related information (see listing above)
- Information pertaining to key risk factors, such as family dynamics, social challenges, relationships, substance abuse, domestic violence, health issues (mental or physical), homelessness; and recent or previous contacts with the law or prison system
- Individual's own self-assessment, aspirations, goals, perceptions, attitudes, and concerns

Beyond the content of the information, the process for collecting it matters because the individual, couple, or family may face serious risks. A mix of formal and informal approaches is typically used, facilitated by both a standardized questionnaire and qualitative open-ended questions. The intake process for social services is usually more effective when it is handled by a trained social worker rather than a clerical aide, in order to start building trust between the beneficiary and the service provider, since they will be interacting often. Moreover, this first interview to gather information is already part of the diagnosis or assessment and can even represent a service in itself depending on the degree of counseling provided.

Integrated Approaches for Intake and Registration

Both intake and registration can be costly, so integrating intake and registration among different social protection programs is an efficient way to reduce costs. When different programs require common information from similar population groups, it can be efficient to share intake and registration processes rather than collecting the same information multiple times. One example of such sharing is a social registry, which supports intake and registration and the assessment of socioeconomic needs and conditions for multiple programs. This enables program administrators to share resources for intake and registration and reduce duplication of work and administrative costs. It can also simplify intake and registration procedures for people, allowing them to apply for multiple benefits and services with a common application form so that they do not have to provide the same information over and over at different offices. A social registry requires the programs that use it to agree on key units of analysis, variables, geographic location codes, classifications, and so on. A social registry can also facilitate access by needy individuals, families, and households to a package of multiple benefits and services, even those outside social protection.

4.3 ASSESSMENT OF NEEDS AND CONDITIONS

The assessment of needs and conditions involves systematic processes for profiling registered individuals, families or households according to various assessment tools (such as socioeconomic welfare measures, risk profiles, labor profiles, etc.). The information gathered during intake and registration is a key input that feeds into the assessment of needs and conditions of registered individuals, families, or households. The primary output from this phase is the classification or profiling of the applicant, which informs the determination of potential eligibility for specific programs or the mix of benefits and services that may be awarded (discussed in chapter 5). On a broader level, an outcome of this phase is its measurement of the potential demand for social protection programs. That measurement can help in planning, budgeting, and coordination.

The instruments and techniques for assessing needs and conditions vary depending on the characteristics of the target group (table 4.2). One method is simply to classify applicants according to demographic characteristics, such as gender or age (in the case of demographic categorical programs). Another approach relies on caseworker assessments (common in employment and social service assessments). A third method involves the use of automated tools to aggregate key assessment indicators (typically used for aggregating socioeconomic welfare measures). Finally, statistical tools, such as predictive analytics and data integration and analytics, can generate profiles of individuals or families (these are sometimes used for labor profiling or for predicting social risks).

Often, agencies use a combination of instruments and techniques. The remainder of this section reviews the approaches used for the following types of assessments: socioeconomic assessment of needs and conditions; disability assessments; assessments of job seekers and the unemployed; and social risk assessments for vulnerable individuals and families. Finally, the section ends with a discussion of opportunities for integrated use of instruments and techniques.

Socioeconomic Assessment of Needs and Conditions

Many tools for assessing socioeconomic status construct aggregated welfare measures or indexes using the information gathered during intake and registration. These tools essentially generate a variable as an indicator of aggregate welfare. The variables are calculated by automated algorithms that are built into information systems. These algorithms (1) calculate the total amount of income (self-declared or obtained from other agencies); (2) estimate income through a combination of estimated parameters and observable sociodemographic and socioeconomic characteristics; and (3) generate an aggregate measure that combines total income and estimated income, when most of the aggregated income can be verified by independent sources and a small part is estimated.[18] The assistance unit for a socioeconomic assessment is typically the household or family, even if the program itself supports individuals as the assistance unit. Examples of automated socioeconomic assessment tools include the following:

- ***Means testing (MT),*** which can include income testing, asset testing, or both. **Income tests** aggregate information on all sources of revenue for all members of the family or household (depending on the assistance unit) with a common reference period (such as total household income for the past month, 60 days, six months, etc.). As discussed above, incomes can

Table 4.2 Intended Population Groups and Associated Tools for Assessing Needs and Conditions

Intended population groups	Tools for assessing needs and conditions
Categorical assessments of demographic groups along the life cycle (individuals)	
• Children • Elderly • Women	Rules-based classification of people according to group characteristics (May combine with other factors in categories below, such as means testing. May assess worker-contribution histories as "conditions" for qualifying for social insurance pensions.)
Assessing socioeconomic status (assess for families and households)	
• People living below the poverty line • Homeless • People living in isolated and remote areas • Pastoralist, nomadic, and semi-nomadic groups • Indigenous groups • Refugees, stateless, immigrants, internally displaced populations (IDPs), and/or people living in areas affected by fragility, conflict, and violence • Ethnic, religious, linguistic, and visible minorities	• Means testing (MT), including income tests and/or asset tests • Proxy means testing (PMT) • Hybrid means testing (HMT) • Multidimensional indicators of poverty (MDIP) • Community-based targeting (CBT)
Assessing job-seekers and the unemployed (individuals)	
• Unemployed • Discouraged/inactive workers • Informal sector workers	• Caseworker assessments • Labor profiling tools
Disability assessments (individuals)	
• Persons with disabilities • Workers with disabilities	• Medical assessments of disabilities as impairments or conditions • Functional assessments of disabilities, taking into account capacities, care needs, and contextual factors
Social risk assessments (individuals and families)	
• Children at-risk • Youth at-risk • Adults at-risk • Lesbian, gay, bisexual, and transgender	• Caseworker assessments with formal and informal tools • Some experimental use of predictive modeling
Integrated approaches for assessment of needs and conditions	
	• Multidimensional assessment of needs and conditions: An example could include screening job seekers for social risks as well as typical work-related factors determining their distance to the labor market • Multiple programs using common assessment tools and information, for example, with socioeconomic assessments from social registries

Source: Original table for this publication.

include earned incomes from work, rental incomes, receipt of some types of cash benefits, incomes from agriculture or self-employment, and so on. **Asset tests** consider the value or possession of various financial and physical assets (as discussed above). Income and asset information can be self-reported or obtained from other systems via systems interoperability (see the Social Registries and Interoperability with Other Administrative Information Systems section later in this chapter) by verifying assessments against independent sources for robustness. Verified means tests are commonly used in OECD countries, and rely on a high degree of labor market formality and interoperability of information systems (World Bank, forthcoming). In a simple test, the means test is based on self-reported incomes, though sometimes self-reported income data are cross-checked with additional information or proxies (as in Brazil).

- ***Proxy means testing (PMT),*** which estimates a family's socioeconomic welfare using a composite measure that estimates welfare or an index as a weighted score based on observable household characteristics, such as demographic structures, education levels, location and quality of the household's dwelling, ownership of durable goods and other assets, and respective weights for each characteristic that has been estimated using other information sources, such as income and expenditure household surveys. The word "proxy" reflects the fact that observable characteristics are considered proxies for actual incomes or consumption.[19] PMT is used when actual income or consumption is difficult to measure or observe, such as in situations of high informality, or when asset values are not obtained directly.[20] All data for these proxy variables are collected during the intake and registration process, while the weights are obtained from modeling. The score is then automatically calculated using an algorithm that assigns weights to the variables. Countries that use PMTs include Albania, Pakistan, the Philippines, Malawi, Burkina Faso and Turkey.[21]
- ***Hybrid means testing (HMT),*** which combines MT and PMT by gathering information on a household's observable income that can be verified against independent sources, as well as collecting information on certain household assets with the purpose of estimating the income or consumption that cannot be verified, as in PMT. HMT depends on the availability and quality of administrative data, as well as the frequency of updates. HMT combines all the sources of household income that can be found in administrative data with an estimation of income from informal activities. Thus, the HMT score is the sum of the individual's formal income and imputed income, based on certain characteristics from self-declared information or from other administrative records. This method is recommended when formal income represents a large share of a household's income and is more often used in Eastern Europe and Central Asia (Tesliuc et al. 2014). The addition of imputed income to verifiable income makes this method a hybrid. It can be considered an intermediate targeting method between MT and the PMT.

Another tool for socioeconomic assessment is community-based targeting (CBT). CBT can be used to prioritize which households will be registered (input to intake and registration). CBT can also help validate income and consumption scores or estimates. Malawi uses CBT both to prioritize which households are registered and to validate PMT scores. Burkina Faso uses CBT to validate the list of households eligible based on their PMT score. Finally, CBT can be a tool for directly assessing the needs and conditions of families in a community and ranking them from richest to poorest. In those cases, that CBT qualitative ranking would feed directly into eligibility decisions (see chapter 5). CBT uses community members' or leaders' local knowledge to identify program participants according to those leaders' subjective view of household needs. The rationale for using CBT is that local knowledge may be more accurate than any outsider's determination.

Socioeconomic assessments may be conducted on demand (at the time people apply for aid) or administrator-driven (done in batches). With an on-demand approach, the absolute measure of registrants' well-being is computed (for example, in terms of their aggregate income, the value of their assets, or their absolute PMT score). With an administrator-driven approach, the measure used is often a ranking of households from poorest to richest. (The measure of well-being is thus relative to the other households in the group.) While absolute measures are also possible with the administrator-driven approach, relative rankings can be used only with the administrator-driven cohort approach, and then only when households are all registered and assessed as a group in a common time frame. Relative rankings cannot be used with the on-demand approach because it is not feasible to rerank all households whenever a new household is registered (nor is it meaningful to compare rankings of households that are registered at different points in time). As we shall see in chapter 5, this distinction has important implications for how eligibility is determined for social programs.

Assessing and Profiling Job Seekers and the Unemployed

When job seekers or unemployed individuals apply for benefits and services, it is important to differentiate them according to their needs, conditions, and employability. An accurate assessment can match people with packages of benefits and services that are tailored to their needs (see chapter 5). It can focus intensive interventions on those who need them most, and optimize the allocation of staff, benefits, and services. Accurate assessments help people get jobs, improve their employability, and avoid long periods of unemployment. An inaccurate assessment can waste resources by assigning intensive interventions to those who do not need them. Poor assessments result in missed opportunities to intervene early and appropriately to prevent long-term unemployment, and can result in overwhelming caseworkers, employment services, and active labor market programs (ALMPs) by spreading their resources too thinly across too many cases, reducing the quality of services for all.

Various profiling instruments are used to differentiate unemployed individuals. Such instruments typically involve caseworker assessments, statistical profiling tools, or some combination of the two. The relative influence of assessments and profiling tools depends on an agency's capacity to manage human resources and information. Caseworkers' capacity depends on their training, their ability to leverage information effectively, and their caseloads (which determine how much time they can devote to each case). The type and sophistication of information that is available also influences the assessment. As discussed above, such information can include basic identifying and legal data, information on employment status and work history, and more complex information on employability and barriers to work. Such information is usually gathered by the caseworker during the interview process but may also be supplemented by or cross-checked with other agencies. Depending on these capacities of the caseworker and the agency, four approaches may be used to assess the needs and conditions of job seekers and the unemployed (figure 4.4):[22]

- ***Rules-based categorization.*** When the caseworker's capacity and the information available are limited, the caseworker may simply categorize applicants according to group characteristics, such as the duration of unemployment, their age (for example, youth seeking their first job or workers over 50), or any disabilities. The caseworker is the main actor, but their degree of discretion is limited. The advantage of this approach is that categorical rules are relatively simple to administer. The disadvantage is that it does not allow for assessment of each individual's needs and conditions.
- ***Statistical profiling.*** Some countries use statistical profiling tools to predict the likely duration of unemployment for job seekers and distinguish between those who are easy to place from those who are harder to place (Loxha and Morgandi 2014). (See box 4.8.) These tools use econometric modeling to analyze data on job seekers and predict their likelihood of returning to work (as a measure of their employability) according to a statistical model. By generating a spectrum of statistical scores related to unemployment risk, the models enable employment agencies to segment job seekers by risk group on a sliding scale from low- to high-risk. Those results inform decisions on eligibility and packages of benefits and services. The advantages of statistical labor profiling tools include providing an objective, standardized assessment of job seekers' reemployment prospects while generating individualized risk scores. Disadvantages arise with poor-quality or outdated data, which can result in high errors. Even with high-quality data, statistical modeling cannot capture some of the information that caseworkers can obtain through in-depth interviews and other methods, including information on applicants' motivations, attitudes to work, and behavioral traits (Loxha and Morgandi 2014).
- ***Caseworker assessments.*** Caseworkers often rely primarily on information collected during interviews,

Figure 4.4 Instruments and Approaches for Assessing and Profiling Job Seekers and the Unemployed

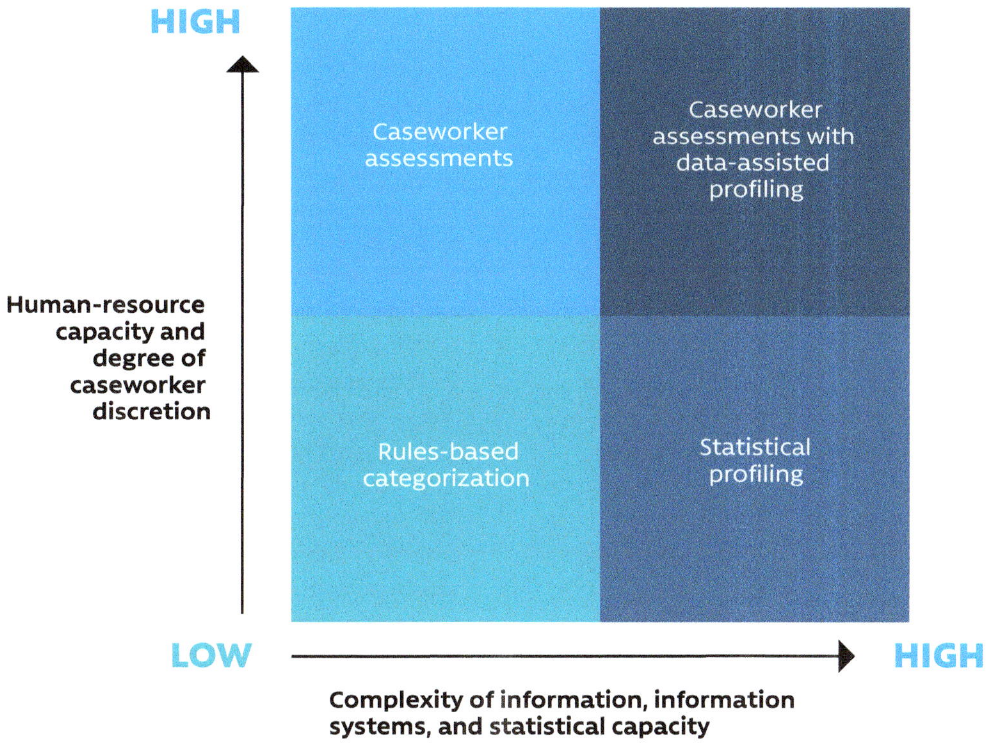

Source: Original figure for this publication.

qualitative tools, and their own clinical assessment of the applicants (Kuddo 2012). The main advantage of this approach is that caseworkers can assess the job seeker's individual needs and conditions through close interactions with them. A commonly cited disadvantage is that caseworker assessments are subjective, meaning that different caseworkers may evaluate the same job seeker differently or that biases may creep into their judgments. Another disadvantage is that they are typically labor-intensive requiring significant time and effort from the caseworkers themselves. These requirements can be prohibitive in countries with limited human resources and high caseloads. For example, the International Labour Organization recommends caseloads of 100 registrants for each public employment services (PES) staff member. While caseloads in the European Union are close to that (150:1), caseloads are much higher in developing countries such as Albania, Jordan, and Serbia (all just under 500:1); Egypt, North Macedonia, and Turkey (all over 500:1); Lebanon and Morocco (both over 1,000:1); and Kosovo (nearly 2,000:1).[23] With such high caseloads, there can be little assessment of individual needs and conditions. In such situations, rules-based categorization is more common and administratively feasible, but statistical profiling tools could prove useful as well, depending on the agency's information systems capability.

- ***Caseworker assessments with data-assisted profiling.*** This approach incorporates statistical profiling tools into caseworker assessments. Caseworkers collect information through interviews and questionnaires, and also apply statistical profiling tools to the data they have collected. Caseworkers thus retain their central role in assessing applicants, but they use data more intensively for diagnostics. Additional tools may also be used, such as psychometric or attitudinal screening and soft-skills profiling. These profiling tools are often embedded into client workflows and online questionnaires. Countries using this combined approach include Ireland, the Netherlands, and Sweden (Loxha and Morgandi 2014). This approach combines the individual tailoring that can emerge from close interactions between the counselor and applicant with the objectivity that can come from statistical profiling.

Box 4.8 Statistical Profiling Tools to Differentiate between Job Seekers and the Unemployed

Statistical profiling tools can predict likely duration of unemployment and differentiate between easy-to-place job seekers from those that are more hard to place (Loxha and Morgandi 2014). These tools exploit data on job seekers to predict their likelihood of resuming work (as a measure of their distance to the labor market) according to a statistical model. This type of profiling method is typically based on the econometric analysis of demographic, socioeconomic, and labor-related data on job seekers. By generating a spectrum of statistical scores related to unemployment risk, the models enable employment agencies to segment job seekers by risk group on a sliding scale from low to high risk. The results then inform decisions on eligibility and benefit-services packages (see chapter 5).

Australia has used a statistical profiling system since 1998 to help identify those at risk of becoming long-term unemployed. The **Job Seeker Classification Instrument (JSCI)** is conducted via a questionnaire that job seekers answer upon registration with Centrelink.[a] Based on the job seekers' answers, a JSCI score is calculated and used to categorize job seekers into three different streams: (1) job-ready; (2) those who receive some caseworker support and service provision; and (3) those who receive intensive caseworker support and service provision. If the JSCI identifies serious barriers, clients may be further assessed through an **Employment Services Assessment** to determine whether they should be referred to stream "3" or to a specific Disability Employment Services Provider. Job seekers are also reassessed and may be upgraded to a higher stream if they remain unemployed longer than 12 months. The JSCI has proved effective, with Centrelink reporting a 95 percent accuracy rate (Finn 2011).

Other statistical profiling systems have also proved successful in their predictions.[b] For example, the statistical model in **Finland** was evaluated for its predictive power using a 60,000-person representative sample. The model correctly predicted employment outcomes for 89 percent of cases. In **Ireland**, the statistical model correctly predicted outcomes in 69 percent of cases among those with a 50 percent chance of finding a job.

The advantages of statistical labor profiling tools for assessing needs and conditions include (1) providing objective and standardized assessments of job seekers' reemployment prospects; and (2) generating applicant-specific risk scores that can deepen the individualized assessment of each job seeker. These approaches have potential in situations where caseloads are prohibitively high for employment officers.

Disadvantages arise with poor quality or outdated data, which can result in high errors. Even with high-quality data, statistical modeling cannot capture the type of information that caseworkers can obtain through in-depth interviews and other qualitative assessment methods, including information on applicants' motivations, attitudes to work, and behavioral traits (Loxha and Morgandi 2014). Finally, caseworker resistance to the use of statistical profiling tools has been documented as a barrier to their adoption, with employment officers perceiving that it did not add value relative to their own judgments. As such, some countries have experimented with statistical modeling, but have not formally mandated or incorporated it into the processes for assessing needs and conditions of job seekers (and some have even abandoned its use).[c]

Sources: Finn 2011; Kurekova 2014; Loxha and Morgandi 2014; Scoppetta and Buckenleib 2018; Ortakaya 2018b.

a. Australia's JSCI has evolved since its introduction, following continuous reviews. The model described here has been in place since 2015 and the description comes from Scoppetta and Buckenleib (2018).

b. Predictive modeling results as summarized in Loxha and Morgandi (2014).

c. Loxha and Morgandi (2014) note that statistical modeling was piloted but never institutionalized in Denmark, Germany, and Switzerland.

Disability Assessments

Disability assessments are not only used for social protection programs, but for other programs as well. They can be used to determine an individual's eligibility for specific benefits (such as disability assistance or insurance), their need for accommodations and support (e.g., to help them at school or in the workplace), or for specialized care services (in the home, community, or institution).

Disability determinations or assessments are meant to certify that a person meets the legal definition of disability and qualifies them to receive benefits or services. Other eligibility criteria may also be considered such as age, residence, or level of income. In light of the limitations of the impairment or medical assessment, many countries are now shifting toward combining this with the functional approach, with elements of disability assessments that more accurately reflect people's difficulties, while other countries are ambitiously moving toward a comprehensive disability assessment which requires a lot more information and is necessary for the provision of services. The optimum scenario is to strive to combine a three-tiered system:[24]

- ***Medical assessments*** documenting health-related reasons for difficulties and where disability is seen as a medical problem located in an individual's body
- ***Functional assessments*** to qualify as "having a disability" and determining degree of disability and the nature of support needed. They move away from the premise that disability is fundamentally a condition of a person's body, but rather biomedical features of a person's body/mind, and the impact of these within the overall physical and social environmental context in which the person carries out his or her life.
- ***Comprehensive disability assessments*** for the design and delivery of benefits and services promoting full participation where disability is not just about how a person's body functions or just the environmental or social disadvantages, but rather the interactional, or bio-psycho-social, view of disability which is at the heart of the World Health Organization's (WHO's) International Classification of Functioning, Disability, and Health (ICF), formally endorsed by the World Health Assembly in 2001. Hence the focus is not on what the person has, but what the person can do.

Disability Assessment Process

It is important for any given assessment to be valid, reliable, transparent, and standardized so that the criteria for disability determination are clear and fair. The legitimacy of the disability assessment process depends on it being objective, fair, impartial, and based on evidence. Assessments should also be structured to meet the purpose of the policies or programs they necessitate.

The process of disability assessment usually starts with a medical assessment, administered by physicians or medical doctors and believed to be scientific and objective. There are two main methods for medical assessments. The first defines disability in terms of having a specific impairment or illness, and the assessment is based on the existence of a medical diagnosis which identifies an individual as having that impairment or illness. The second is the Barema method, which ranks the disability on "a fixed scale set out in a table according to which a certain percentage of disability is attached to specific impairments. The Barema list or table is divided into sections covering physical or mental components of the body or the body system, and guidance is set out regarding medical benchmarks against which assessments should be made" (Waddington et al. 2018). However, the day-to-day practice has shown that this process, if not standardized and monitored, can lead to a great deal of malingering and fraud. Moreover, this impairment approach has been strongly criticized in terms of its reliability and underlying assumption.

The medical assessment can be complemented by the functional assessment, which goes beyond a medical diagnosis to consider the impact that a disability has on an individual's capacity and need for care. A functional assessment seeks to establish limitations on specific activities, such as the ability to work, study, or care for oneself. Alternatively, the functional assessment may establish care or support needs, including evaluating the types of activities the individual can carry out for themselves or for which they would require support. Functional assessments may also evaluate the individual's capacity or need for care by taking into account contextual and external circumstances such as workplace accommodations or other environmental supports. To assess these capacities, a range of Functional Capacity

Evaluation (FCE) tools were developed based on the ICF which provides a comprehensive and standardized framework and language for the description of functioning and disability. The functional tool can be applied by a trained assessor who could be a social worker, nurse, or occupational therapist—different countries have different approaches. The different set of questions covering the different domains of disability have weighted scores and can be used to specify the degree of disability (profound, moderate, low). The functional approach has its own limitations as well because it assesses work capacity based on subjective proxies (box 4.9).

Box 4.9 Karama Program: Transitioning from a Purely Medical Approach to a Functional Approach in the Arab Republic of Egypt

The government of Egypt launched the Takaful and Karama Programme (TKP) in 2015 to provide income support and expand social inclusion to poor families with young children, as well as the elderly and persons with severe disabilities. The main goals of the program include protecting vulnerable households from severe poverty; investing in human capital by ensuring that children grow up healthy and well educated; as well as empowering women through cash transfer. Takaful (solidarity) is a family income support with co-responsibility (conditional) cash transfer (CT) program aimed at reducing poverty and producing human development improvements (in health and education), while Karama (dignity) is an unconditional income support and social inclusion subprogram that aims at the protection and inclusion of the poor elderly (above age 65) and persons with disability.

Karama had initially undertaken a stocktaking and benchmarking exercise to pinpoint challenges and bottlenecks in the existing disability assessment process prior to developing a new solution. This exercise identified challenges and gaps within the current application process, including lengthy and costly procedures with unclear requirements, as well as some defects in the assessment that were subjective and relied only on a medical assessment. The gap analysis led to the following:

- Rollout of a new functional disability assessment tool for adults and children used by a trained cadre of medical commissions to certify eligible Karama cash transfer beneficiaries. The new tool aimed at determining the functional and social impact of disability on the applicant and guaranteed simplicity and, ease of use, as well as objectivity and fairness.
- Development of a new, efficient, and automated application process using a website/call center to guarantee transparency and fairness in accessing information to all citizens, increasing efficiency, and reducing waiting time for booking an appointment. The old system suffered from long waiting times and multiple visits. All beneficiary data was also entered using tablets, enabling the setup of a disability beneficiary operations management system in place.
- Putting in place a grievance and redress system to receive citizen feedback and improve service delivery
- Putting in place a disability task force to ensure proper governance and to oversee the transition from medical to functional approach, including lobbying with the medical doctors regarding the rationale for combining the medical approach with the functional approach.

Today, the Karama program has standards and tools aligned with ICF and the United Nations Convention on the Rights of Persons with Disabilities (UN CRPD). Eligibility is based on a functional assessment tool combined with a proxy means test. The data collected so far is also providing insights on types and prevalence of disability across the different governates. Moving forward, Karama aims to go beyond just a functional approach for offering cash transfers to a comprehensive disability approach where employment opportunities and services are directed to eligible beneficiaries through a referral system.

Source: Nahla Zeitoun, senior social protection specialist, World Bank.

Finally, the comprehensive disability approach attempts to give equal consideration to all determinants of disability—medical, functional, environmental, and personal. Several countries are now making the gradual shift in their disability assessment procedures toward a more rights-based disability assessment approach based on ICF and WHO Disability Assessment Schedule 2.0 (WHODAS 2.0). The world has witnessed a movement from impairment to functional to comprehensive disability approaches with more and more countries embracing ICF and WHODAS 2.0, including high-income countries (Canada, France, Germany, Sweden, the United Kingdom, the United States, Saudi Arabia) as well as middle-income countries (Argentina, Brazil, Cyprus, Greece, and Egypt). The process needs to be gradual, culturally sensitive, and driven by what type of objective or policy the country is aiming at—giving cash, rehabilitation, employment, and so on.

There is no simple one-size-fits-all approach that can transform a country's disability assessment and evaluation procedures. Each country needs to develop its own culturally sensitive and adapted assessment tool guided by international benchmarks and standards. It is very important to reiterate regardless of which approach any country adopts, the first entry point for any disability assessment must always start with a medical exam administered by an authorized body. This part needs to be standardized to guarantee rigor and accuracy. This is then followed by a disability assessment including a functional assessment to assess work capacity or work ability. This is sometimes also combined with a proxy means test to determine eligibility for poverty-targeted programs. For any country that wishes to gradually adopt a rights-based disability assessment approach, the key aspects to take into account are the following:

- A legal framework defining disability (disability law)
- A governance structure composed of a multidisciplinary disability task force which includes all the relevant stakeholders including government, people living with disability (PWDs), and disabled peoples organizations (DPOs)
- A practical, transparent, and feasible application process (including a website or hotline) and a disability assessment tool and training manual
- Technical requirements including automation of the application process, data gathering, data comparability and validation, measurement tools, monitoring and evaluation, a grievance and redress mechanism, and training of a new cadre of disability assessors
- Clear referral processes to direct eligible beneficiaries to the correct package of benefits and services including rehabilitation, assistive devices, cash benefits, or employment opportunities
- Clear procedures for assessment

Social Risk Assessments for Vulnerable Individuals

Caseworker assessments are the most common tool for diagnosing the risk factors facing vulnerable individuals. Risk assessments may be conducted in multiple phases, for example, with caseworkers conducting an initial screening to identify possible vulnerabilities, followed by a more in-depth assessment of risk factors. Recognizing that individuals operate within a family and community, these risk factors are commonly assessed at three levels. **Individual risks** include mental and physical health, disability, adverse childhood experiences, self-esteem and self-image, social skills, communications challenges, substance abuse or addiction, and behavioral disorders. **Family risks** include parental depression/mental health, poor parenting or lack of parental supervision, neglect, child abuse, sexual abuse, domestic violence, marital conflict/divorce, family conflict, teen pregnancy, parental substance abuse, loss of a parent or relative, socioeconomic status, and unemployment. **Community-level risks** include unsafe neighborhoods or community violence (including violence at school), stressful or traumatic events in the community (including at school), bullying or peer rejection, association with peers who use drugs, and the loss of a friend or mentor, among others. Risk factors tend to be interrelated, and people may face multiple risks simultaneously.

Social workers typically combine formal and informal methods in their assessments. Formal assessment tools often include interviews, questionnaires, and checklists. Questionnaires may be of particular help in classifying an individual or family into key risk categories. Such is the case in North Macedonia, where caseworkers screen people for 22 risk categories, such as orphans; children with no parental care; children of divorced parents; pregnant teens; children whose parents are divorcing or are single parents; victims and perpetrators of domestic violence; victims of sexual abuse, human trafficking, or prostitution; the homeless; ex-convicts or those in conflict with the law; asylum seekers; the elderly, and the disabled; among other categories.[25] Once the risk categories are identified, social workers use risk-specific questionnaires for a deeper assessment. Formal assessment approaches also use multidisciplinary teams, specialized staff, or partner agencies to conduct specific assessments using specialized tools, such as education and skills assessments, disability assessments, substance-abuse assessments, and psycho-social assessments. The latter may cover a registrant's medical history, family history of physical/psychiatric illness, chemical (alcohol/drug) history, gambling history, sexual history, domestic violence history, education/learning, social history, measures of functioning (for example, ability to carry out activities of daily living), employment history, legal involvement, interactions with family/household members, history of previous treatment, recent stressful life situations, mental status, client's strengths, and clinical impression (Thompson, Van Ness, and O'Brien 2001). **Informal assessment approaches** rely heavily on the caseworker's interpersonal soft skills to build trust, observe behavioral patterns, and entice the individual or family members to divulge often-private information that would help assess their needs, conditions, and vulnerabilities (sometimes even information that the individuals themselves may not recognize as relevant). The output of these assessments is typically a social worker's assessment report that describes the client's situation, needs, and conditions, including key risks and vulnerabilities and the social worker's overall impressions. The assessment report informs the intervention and service plan (see chapter 5).

Although predictive analytics and statistical profiling tools are not yet a mainstay in social work, some countries are experimenting with them as an input to social risk assessments. The Department of Human Services (DHS) in Allegheny County, Pennsylvania (US), has been using integrated data and analytics to support an integrated practice model for social services. One tool they have developed is a Screening Score to supplement caseworkers' clinical assessments of reported child abuse cases, using integrated data from internal and external sources. The Screening Score has proved to be quite accurate in predicting the likelihood that a child will face out-of-home placement due to future abuse. The county has adapted its business practices, policies, and decision making to incorporate the Screening Score into caseworker assessments of child abuse (box 4.10). That said, some of the critiques of the approach are the design flaws that limit the accuracy of predictive models and their impact on the poor and vulnerable (Eubanks 2018).

Box 4.10 Using Integrated Data and Predictive Analytics to Support Screening and Decision Making: Allegheny County, Pennsylvania (US)

The Department of Human Services (DHS) in Allegheny County, Pennsylvania (US), is actively experimenting with various uses of integrated data and analytics to support an integrated practice model for social services. One way they have been using such approaches is to improve decision making in child abuse assessments and prevention.

Objectives. The goal was to develop a tool that would help child welfare caseworkers decide whether to refer a reported case of child abuse for further investigation. The aim was to **supplement** (not replace) caseworkers own clinical assessment with a Scoring Tool that would integrate data on the individuals involved in the case to reflect past patterns and predictions on the likelihood that the child was in danger.

Problem statement. Prior to the development of the Scoring Tool, historical data showed that 48 percent of the lowest-risk cases were erroneously assessed as high risk, and thus screened **in** for further investigation (errors of inclusion), and 27 percent of the highest-risk cases were erroneously assessed and screened **out** without further investigation (errors of exclusion). The challenge is that the information accessible to child welfare caseworkers is typically limited to the details of the specific allegations of the alleged child abuse event, and that information is asymmetric

continued

Box 4.10 *(continued)*

(with the potential abuser having incentives to hide their behaviors and many factors potentially clouding the assessment of the situation). Even with interoperable information systems, caseworkers may have access to other data, but no systematic way to factor in that information

Predictive analytics modeling with integrated data. A research team working with DHS developed a predictive analytics model to predict the likelihood that a judge would order the child to be removed from the home after a child abuse hotline report.[a] This dependent variable (the likelihood of out-of-home placement) reflects extreme situations of child abuse, and the model sought to identify risk factors associated with such outcomes. They identified more than 100 factors that predict future referral or out-of-home placements using administrative data that were already "in the system" from both internal and external data sources. Internal information systems include those from various DHS units covering aging, child welfare, drug and alcohol services, early intervention, family support centers, HeadStart (an early childhood development program), the homeless, housing supports, mental health services, and intellectual disabilities services. External data sources came from other administrative systems, including birth records, autopsy records, public social assistance benefits, public housing, physical health (Medicaid), the school system, juvenile probation, the county jail, adult/family court system, emergency 911 dispatches, and labor and industry (private sector sources). With these data and predictive analytics models, they developed a Screening Score from 1 to 20 whereby the higher the score, the higher the chance of a future event (child abuse, out-of-home placement, re-referral). To test if the model could improve the accuracy of child-abuse assessment decisions, they scored thousands of historical child abuse reports and then traced the children's cases in subsequent referrals to see how often the model was correct.

Results. They found that their model accurately predicted future out-of-home placements to a high degree. Specifically, for children with a predicted score of 1 (predicted low risk), 1 in 100 were later placed out-of-home within two years of the call. For children with a predicted score of 20 (predicted highest risk), 1 in 2 were later removed from the home within 2 years of the call. External validation showed that the relative risk of a child whose placement score at referral is 20 versus a child whose score is 1 is 21 times more likely to have a self-inflicted injury, 17 times more likely to be physically assaulted, and 1.4 times more likely to be seen for an accidental fall

Subsequent changes in business processes, policies, and decision making. The tool resulted in changes to policies and business processes. First, the county developed a frontline user-interface that would allow caseworkers to essentially "push a button" and calculate the Family Screening Score. They also incorporated the calculation of the score into their standard business processes. Second, faced with some caseworker skepticism, they had to work on some cultural changes to encourage the caseworkers to actually use the tool—including emphasizing that the tool does not replace their clinical assessment, it merely gives them additional information to use in making that assessment. Third, the county then passed measures that required caseworkers to use the Screening Tool and calculate the Family Screening Score for all reported cases of child abuse. Finally, the county passed a measure that mandated that all reported cases of child abuse that receive a Screening Score of 20 must be referred for additional investigations. See Eubanks (2018) for a critique of using such predictive models.

Source: Dalton 2018.

a. The research team included Rhema Vaithianathan, Auckland University of Technology; Emily Putnam-Hornstein, University of Southern California; Irene de Haan, University of Auckland; Marianne Bitler, University of California Irvine; Tim Maloney, Auckland University of Technology; and Nan Jiang, Auckland University of Technology. The team also included ethics experts, including Tim Dare, University of Auckland; and Eileen Gambrill, UC Berkeley, as well as evaluators: Hornby-Zellar Associates (to evaluate process aspects) and Stanford University (to evaluate impacts).

Integrated Approaches for Assessing Needs and Conditions

People often face multiple needs and risk factors. Working in silos, agencies or offices can miss that complexity, resulting in ineffective or mismatched interventions. Integrated approaches that pool the skills and knowledge of different bureaucracies can better assess complex needs and conditions, resulting in packages of benefits and services that are more closely tailored to individual needs and conditions.

Such multidimensional approaches can comprehensively assess people's needs and conditions across various characteristics. One example of such an approach is to screen individuals for social risks as part of a profile of a job seeker's employability. Figure 4.5 plots both employability and complexity of social risks to illustrate that challenge. Employment counselors typically profile job seekers and the unemployed to determine their employability, focusing on groups 1 and 2 in figure 4.5. However, such profiling might miss social barriers that affect the ability to work. Some people may be relatively employable—and willing to work—but face other social barriers that would be helped by interventions other than employment services and ALMPs (group 3 in figure 4.5). Examples of such barriers include: (1) disabled workers who can be easily matched with jobs provided they can access key accommodations (service dogs, apps that can transcribe for the blind and deaf, etc.); and (2) able-bodied single parents with young children who can work provided they have adequate childcare services. Other job seekers may face complex social risks and may not be immediately employable (group 4 in figure 4.5). If labor profiling and assessments miss those social risk factors, resources could be wasted matching these individuals with regular employment services and ALMPs.

Common assessments of specific factors may also be shared across programs. As with intake and registration, multiple programs may require similar information for assessing needs and conditions. This is common with

Figure 4.5 Value of Integrated Approaches for Assessing Needs and Conditions: Labor and Social Barriers to Work

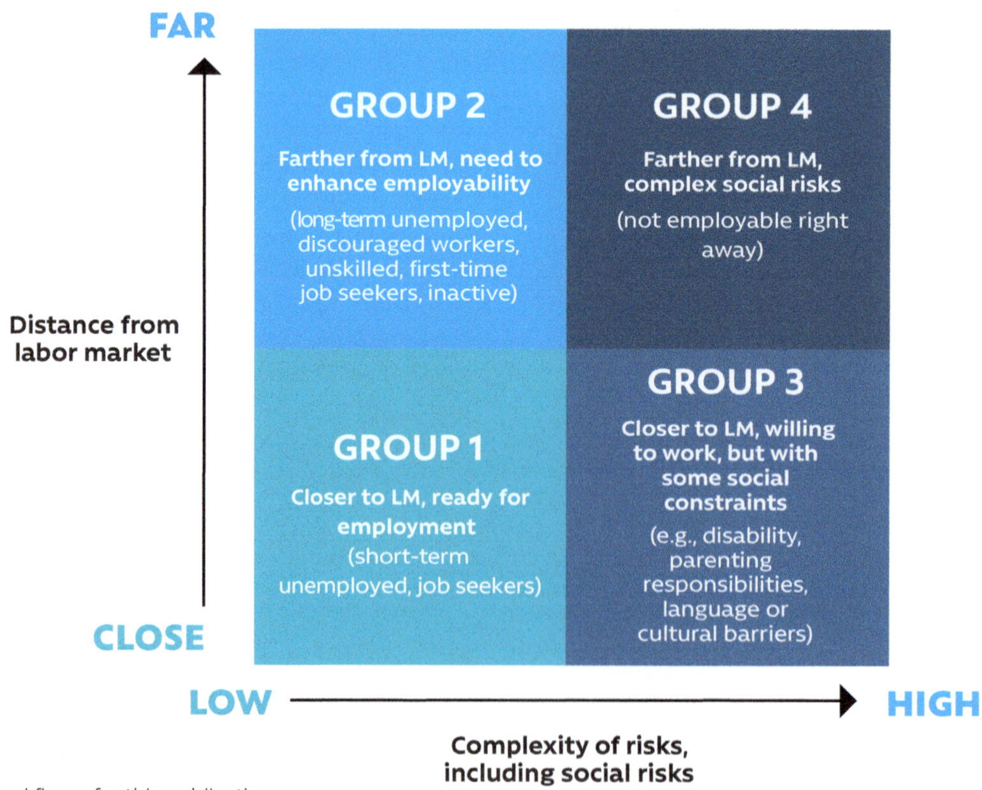

Source: Original figure for this publication.
Note: LM = labor market.

assessments of socioeconomic status, which may be needed for many programs, such as means-tested social pensions for the elderly poor or disabled; activation benefits and service packages for low-income workers; social services for low-income families; and need-based scholarships and means-tested health insurance subsidies. While there may be program-specific requirements, these programs all also require some sort of socioeconomic assessment of needs and conditions. Social registries support integrated approaches to assessments by providing integrated information on socioeconomic status to multiple programs.

Reassessment

In addition to the initial assessment of needs and conditions, most programs or social registries have "recertification requirements." While that is the conventional term for it, we prefer to use the term "reassessment requirements" as it links back to the assessment phase along the delivery chain and because there is no guarantee that anyone would be certified or recertified, which essentially means being deemed eligible for a benefit or service.

Reassessment and time limits are related but are not the same thing. They can coincide—but they do not always. Within a certain time limit, there can be multiple reassessment periods. Not all programs have time limits, but most programs have reassessment requirements.

The periodicity of reassessment varies across programs and countries, and even within programs across types of beneficiaries. Several factors influence the periodicity of reassessment: (1) objectives of the program; (2) characteristics of the intended population; (3) administrative capacity; (4) whether the original intake and registration was on demand or administrator-driven; and (5) (usually implicit) attitudes toward the intended populations.

With respect to objectives and characteristics of the intended population, programs for the chronic poor may have longer periodicity for reassessment than those supporting groups with more "transient" conditions, such as the unemployed. Some unemployment benefits require monthly or quarterly proof of continued unemployment (along with evidence of compliance with job search conditions—which is a distinct concept). Even though social assistance programs are commonly targeted to the chronic poor, some GMI programs have very frequent reassessment requirements (see box 4.11), such as every three months in Latvia and Lithuania. Periodicity of reassessments for disability benefits and services usually relates to the expected severity duration of the disability established at the time of the initial assessment.

There are also variations in the periodicity of reassessments within programs by type of beneficiary. For example, in the food stamps program (SNAP) in the United States, the length of the "certification period" depends on the characteristics of the household: most households are certified for 6–12 months, but for the elderly poor and persons with disabilities, the period is 24+ months. With social services, which typically involve a high-degree of caseworker involvement, reassessment may be a continuous part of the individualized action plan (and in fact, part of the intervention itself).

Periodicity of reassessments is also dependent on administrative capacity. A short periodicity of reassessments increases the workload of staff and thus the administrative cost. Therefore, the decision on a program's or social registry's reassessment requirements will depend on the country's capacity to implement them. In fact, a number of social registries and programs in practice implement reassessments less frequently than what their rules of operation establish (for examples, see box 4.11).

With on-demand models, reassessments typically range from a more frequent periodic requirement (every 1–3 months) to a less frequent one (every 6, 12, or 24 months). Many programs aim for the 12–24 month range. With on-demand approaches, beneficiaries are typically notified in advance to alert them that their certification period will be ending. This gives them a chance to gather the required documentation to reapply (or apply to be reassessed) before their benefits expire. If they fail to do so, however, benefits can be terminated—and these alerts and risk of termination serve as incentives or prompts to nudge them to reapply.

With administrator-driven models, en masse registration waves are carried out less frequently, typically every 3–8 years. These registration waves cover both existing beneficiaries, whose needs and conditions are reassessed, and new registrants, who are assessed for the first time. For examples on reassessments in administrator-driven models, see box 4.12.

Box 4.11 Reassessments in the On-Demand Model: The Case of LRIS and GMI Programs in ECA

In the context of last-resort income support (LRIS) and guaranteed minimum income (GMI) programs in Eastern Europe and Central Asia (ECA), a regular reassessment of needs and conditions is performed for each beneficiary at given time intervals. The approach to reassessment and the time intervals vary from country to country.

Process. Usually the reassessment process consists of a visit by the beneficiary to the social assistance office during which an abridged application form or a declaration is completed stating whether there have been any changes in the welfare status or family composition. This application or declaration must be accompanied by updated documents and certificates, but in most cases not all the documents submitted with the initial application are required. In case of changes in household composition or welfare status, the beneficiaries are asked to fill out a full application form, and their eligibility status and benefit level are reassessed. The reassessment process can include mandatory home visits, home visits only if the beneficiary declares a change in the eligibility criteria, or no home visits at all.

Beneficiary-driven reassessment. Reassessment is the responsibility of beneficiaries. If they fail to submit the application and accompanying forms, they are suspended from the program for a short period (a grace period of up to four months), and then excluded. By design, in some countries (for example, the Kyrgyz Republic) beneficiaries should receive a notification before the recertification deadline in order to prepare their documents. In practice, however, this rule is not enforced, and notifications are rather random.

Frequency. In general, the frequency of reassessment may vary from three months to one year (see table B4.11.1 below for examples). Albania is one exception to this rule, requiring a monthly visit by

Table B4.11.1 Frequency of Reassessment and Updates of Beneficiary Information

Country	Reassessment cycle	Cross-checks	Mandatory update of (selected) documents	Home visits required for updates or reassessment
Albania Ndihma Ekonomike (NE)	Monthly	Monthly	Annually	Yes; every 6–12 months (less frequent if income is unlikely to change)
Armenia Family Benefit Program (FBP)	Annually (can be semestrial, quarterly in specific cases)	Monthly	Annually	Yes; annually (but not for all cases, because of staff shortages)
Bulgaria guaranteed minimum income (GMI)	Annually	Annually	Annually	Yes; annually
Kyrgyz Republic Unified Monthly Benefit (UMB)	Annually (can be semestrial, quarterly in some cases—especially in urban areas)	No	Annually	No; only at the initiative of the implementation unit
Lithuania social benefit (SB)	Quarterly (less frequent if incomes are not likely to change)	Quarterly	Quarterly (less frequent if incomes are not likely to change)	No; only at the initiative of the implementation unit
Romania GMI	Annually (quarterly for proof of registration with employment offices)	No	Annually	Yes; every 6 months (or at the initiative of the implementation unit)
Uzbekistan BLIF (benefit for low-income families)	Quarterly	Quarterly	Quarterly	Yes; quarterly

Source: Tesliuc et al. 2014.

continued

Box 4.11 *(continued)*

beneficiaries to Ndihma Ekonomike (NE) offices—more as a mechanism of increasing the opportunity cost for beneficiaries and reducing the risk of paying benefits to those who migrate abroad. In practice, in some countries the frequency of reassessment varies by groups of beneficiaries. In the Kyrgyz Republic, reassessment is done more often (every three to six months) in urban areas, where the opportunities of employment are higher. In Lithuania, municipalities are entitled to allow for a reassessment period longer than three months but less than a year. The social workers may decide on the frequency of reassessment based on profiling of the beneficiary (for example, in cases where the social worker estimates that the family composition or income is likely to remain unchanged, or in the case of the disabled and the elderly).

Source: Tesliuc et al. 2014.

Box 4.12 Reassessments in the Administrator-Driven Model: Mexico, Colombia, and the Philippines

In the administrator-driven model, reassessments are usually conducted every three to eight years. This is mainly due to the fact that this model relies on the census-sweep approach, which can be costly and time-consuming, and that the intended population for these programs is usually the chronic poor.

There are several examples of this approach to conducting reassessments, which vary in their frequency. In **Mexico**, families that were in Prospera's beneficiary registry needed to be reassessed every eight years. The reassessment process consisted of the following stages: (1) the beneficiary families were informed about the reassessment process; (2) the socioeconomic and demographic information of each household subject to this process was collected through a home visit; and (3) families were informed of the result of the reassessment process.[a]

Colombia's SISBEN, the country's social registry, has to be updated every three years according to national legislation. However, in practice the updates have been less frequent. SISBEN, in its first version (SISBEN I), started being implemented in 1995. The implementation of SISBEN II started in 2005 (10 years later than SISBEN I), and SISBEN III started being applied in 2011. SISBEN is currently going through the fourth round of updates.

In the **Philippines**, the social registry, Listahanan, has to be updated every four years. The first wave of Listahanan, was implemented in 2011, and the second in 2015 (see box 4.4). An additional registration was ongoing in 2019.

Sources: Colombia, Departamento Nacional de Planeación 2016; Mexico, Secretaría de Desarrollo Social 2018; Velarde 2018.
a. The program has recently been transformed and no longer exists as a conditional cash transfer program due to shifts in the social policy in Mexico.

Attitudes toward the intended population can also influence the periodicity of reassessment. In some countries, there is an implicit (but often pervasive) mistrust of the poor or concern that they will become "lazy" or "dependent" on benefits. As such, in some countries, beneficiaries are expected to provide documentation to prove their eligibility quite frequently. In other countries, there is an explicit policy against reassessing too often. For example, even if someone gets a job or their earned income increases, some programs may not want their eligibility status to change too frequently because there are other service-related objectives that require longer-term beneficiary participation objectives beyond the payment of benefits.

4.4 PROCESSES INVOLVED IN INTAKE AND REGISTRATION

Specific processes for the implementation of intake and registration can vary substantially. A process can be as simple as submitting information online for review. Some countries may even skip intake and registration altogether, as Canada does in awarding its Old Age Security Pension (see box 4.13). Other processes may involve transactions at local offices, supported by back-office processing in central information systems. Still others involve field teams, communities, and central information systems. To give a flavor of that variety and some of the basic steps involved, this section presents some sample process maps for various modalities and target groups.

Box 4.13 Skipping the Intake and Registration Process Entirely? Automated Intake with Canada's Old Age Security Pension

In principle, the concept of skipping the intake process altogether could be enticing. What if "the system" would know in advance that someone qualified for benefits? Or what if "the system" could predict that someone's situation was suddenly changing and could anticipate those changes to provide support automatically?

Canada's Old Age Security Pension already implements a simple version of automatic intake for some citizens: if their information is up-to-date and they meet all eligibility requirements, they are automatically enrolled in the pension a month after their 65th birthday. This does not apply to all potential beneficiaries, however: if there are any "gray areas" on eligibility (such as residing outside the country for significant periods of time), they still need to apply directly for the benefit and provide the additional documentation.

Australia's Centrelink is also exploring the potential for using predictive analytics with integrated information systems to immediately anticipate when someone faces a change in circumstances that could trigger a need for assistance. For example, the system could detect that a person loses a job and immediately connect the individual with job services or unemployment services (see box 4.8).

Sources: Employment and Social Development Canada; Australia Centrelink.

Malawi's UBR: En Masse Registration and Socioeconomic Assessment Based on CBT and PMT

Malawi's UBR presents a good example of district-level en masse registration and socioeconomic assessment based on community-based targeting (CBT) and proxy means testing (PMT).[26] The UBR was designed to support both intake and registration and the assessment of needs and conditions for multiple social programs. It is considered a social registry.

A major strength of the UBR is its use of existing local structures. These include District Social Support Committees (DSSCs) and District Training Teams (DTTs), as well as Area Executive Committee Members (AECs), Community Social Support Committees (CSSCs), and community leaders. The advantages of implementing a social registry within existing local structures cannot be overstated. First, local arrangements put a known "face" on the social registry for communities, and are a point of contact (for queries, grievances, and appeals). Second, reliance on known local organizations helps build understanding, ownership, and credibility for the UBR at the district level (rather than engendering suspicion by having an outside unit conduct registration, as has happened in other countries). Third, these arrangements avoid the costly, confusing, and inefficient duplication associated with the use of parallel structures. Fourth, they strengthen ties and interaction between central and local actors. Fifth, the use of local structures effectively recognizes the permanent and core function of social registries and positions the registry for sustained operations, including for future updates and a possible future shift toward an on-demand model (Lindert et al. 2018).

The core steps in implementing the UBR can be grouped into three phases along the delivery chain (figure 4.6). These are outreach, sensitization, and training (steps 1–4); intake and registration (or data collection, steps 5–6); and assessment of needs and conditions to determine potential eligibility for social programs (steps 7–9).

After initial outreach and training, intake and registration included three key steps and involved both

Figure 4.6 Process Map for Malawi's UBR: Registration, PMT, and CBT

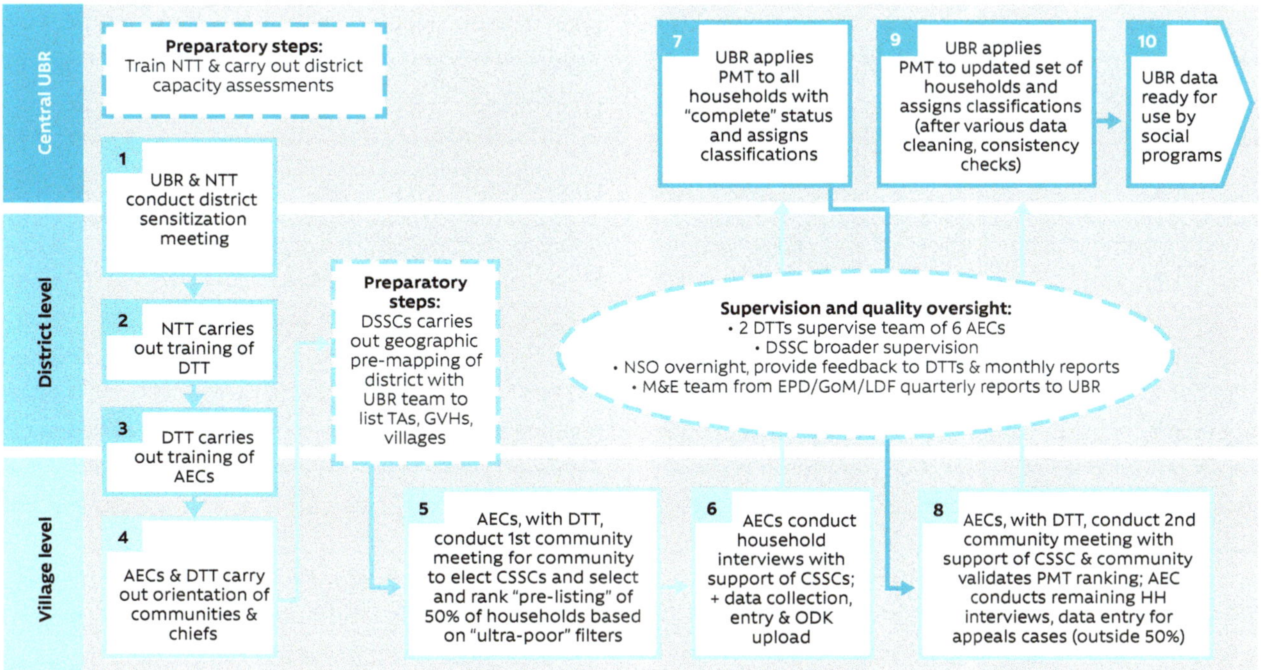

Source: Lindert et al. (2018) building on the operations guidelines for Malawi's UBR ("unified beneficiary registry," though actually a social registry).

Note: AEC = Area Executive Committee Member; CBT = community-based targeting; CSSC = Community Social Support Committees; DSSC = District Social Support Committee; DTT = District Training Team; EPD = Department of Economic Planning and Development; GoM = Government of Malawi; GVH = Gazetted Village Heads; HH = household; LDF = Local Development Fund Mechanism; M&E = monitoring and evaluation; NSO = National Statistics Office; NTT = National Training Team; ODK = Open Data Kit; PMT = proxy means testing; TA = Traditional Authority.

district and community actors. First, a preparatory step mapped all the communities and households in the district. Second, each community selects which households will be registered during the first community meeting (step 5 in figure 4.6). For the first phase of the UBR rollout, they were instructed to prioritize the poorest 50 percent of households to be registered using participatory CBT methods.[27] Third, intake and registration was carried out, with the AECs conducting household interviews and home visits, and entering the data on tablets, using open-source Open Data Kit (ODK) software (step 6 in figure 4.6).

The socioeconomic assessment of needs and conditions involved both the calculation of PMT scores and community validation using CBT participatory approaches. Specifically, the UBR information system applied PMT scoring algorithms to the data that was collected and entered during intake and registration (step 7 in figure 4.6). A second community meeting was held so that the community could discuss and validate the PMT rankings (step 8 in figure 4.6). Additional households were interviewed and registered during this phase based on appeals or the community discussions. The PMT algorithm was applied to the revised set of households/data (step 9 in figure 4.6). Once the process was complete, the UBR data, including the PMT scores, were ready for social programs to use in making eligibility and enrollment decisions.

Turkey's ISAS: On-Demand Registration with Information Interoperability and Socioeconomic Assessment Based on PMT Scores

Turkey's Integrated Social Assistance System (ISAS) provides a good example of on-demand registration with interoperable information systems and district-level socioeconomic assessments based on PMT. ISAS is an integrated social protection information system that includes a social registry component (which supports intake and registration and assessment of needs and conditions), a multiprogram beneficiary registry, and systems for payments and beneficiary operations management. ISAS electronically facilitates all steps needed to manage several social protection programs including intake and registration, assessments of needs and conditions, eligibility and enrollment decisions, selection of a benefits package, notification and onboarding, the provision of benefits and services, disbursement of funds, and monitoring and auditing (Turkey, Ministry of Family and Social Policy 2018).

The system's key strengths include its extensive interoperability, coordination between institutions, and effective use of local offices. ISAS is managed by the General Directorate of Social Assistance (GDSA) and implemented locally through 1,000 autonomous social assistance and solidarity funds (SASFs) located in each district. Based on established data-sharing and implementation protocols across multiple ministries, ISAS is linked with 24 different public authorities, such as the population and citizenship registry, social security, tax authority, vehicle registration, land registry, farmer registration, health control information, education (school attendance, grade transition, etc.), and the employment agency, among others. As a result, ISAS can collect data in real time from those entities' databases using a unique identifier in the national ID. In addition, the system uses the local knowledge of social workers (who conduct household visits) and the Board of Trustees of each SASF. Each Board of Trustees includes representatives of several local entities, such as the highest district-level officials from the ministries of education, health, finance, and agriculture; village leaders; representatives of nongovernmental organizations; and charitable organizations enabling the inclusion of different perspectives, coordination among stakeholders, and consensus-based decision making. These arrangements increase the efficiency of service delivery through the highly dynamic and interoperable information system, frequent community and household visits, and participative and transparent decision making.

The core steps in implementing ISAS can be grouped into four phases along the delivery chain (figure 4.7). These are: (1) initial intake and registration; (2) interoperability to collect administrative information and prefill in-depth intake questionnaire; (3) home visits to collect remaining information using the in-depth questionnaire; and (4) automated generation of the household's socioeconomic profile using PMT/HMT scores as the main measure of the assessment of needs and conditions. The household's PMT profile information is then used by the Board of Trustees in each SASF for eligibility and enrollment decisions.

Initial intake and registration include three key steps and mainly involve district actors. The process initiates with an adult household member (usually a woman) applying to the SASF in his or her district. The only document required of the applicant is the National ID (step 1 in figure 4.7). To complete the application, all adult household members sign a written consent form to allow the SASF to access their personal data from all of the administrative systems listed on the form (step 2 in figure 4.7). Finally, an SASF employee creates a household file in the ISAS by entering the ID of the applicant (step 3 in figure 4.7).

Collecting administrative information through ISAS involves two steps, which are carried out at the central level. First, ISAS collects administrative data about the household from 24 interlinked public authorities and more than 112 web services (which only takes a few seconds) and creates a household profile (step 4 in figure 4.7). Second, the household file is updated with the collected information. These steps allow ISAS to automatically complete most fields of the questionnaire (step 5 in figure 4.7). (The introduction of ISAS greatly improved the efficiency of these processes.)

The remaining household information is gathered via a community and home visit. Social assistance workers print out the partially completed questionnaires from ISAS for use in community and household visits (step 6 in figure 4.7). SASF workers then conduct home and community visits to gather the remaining information from households using the prefilled questionnaires (steps 7 and 8 in figure 4.7). The workers enter the remainder of the information into ISAS (step 9 in figure 4.7).

The information gathered during intake and registration is used in the assessment of needs and conditions. That assessment incorporates the social worker's own professional assessment and the automated calculation of PMT/HMT scores (step 10 in figure 4.7). The socioeconomic profile generated by this assessment is then forwarded to the Board of Trustees of the local SASF for eligibility and enrollment decisions for specific programs.

Figure 4.7 Process Map for Intake, Registration, and Assessment of Needs and Conditions in Turkey's ISAS

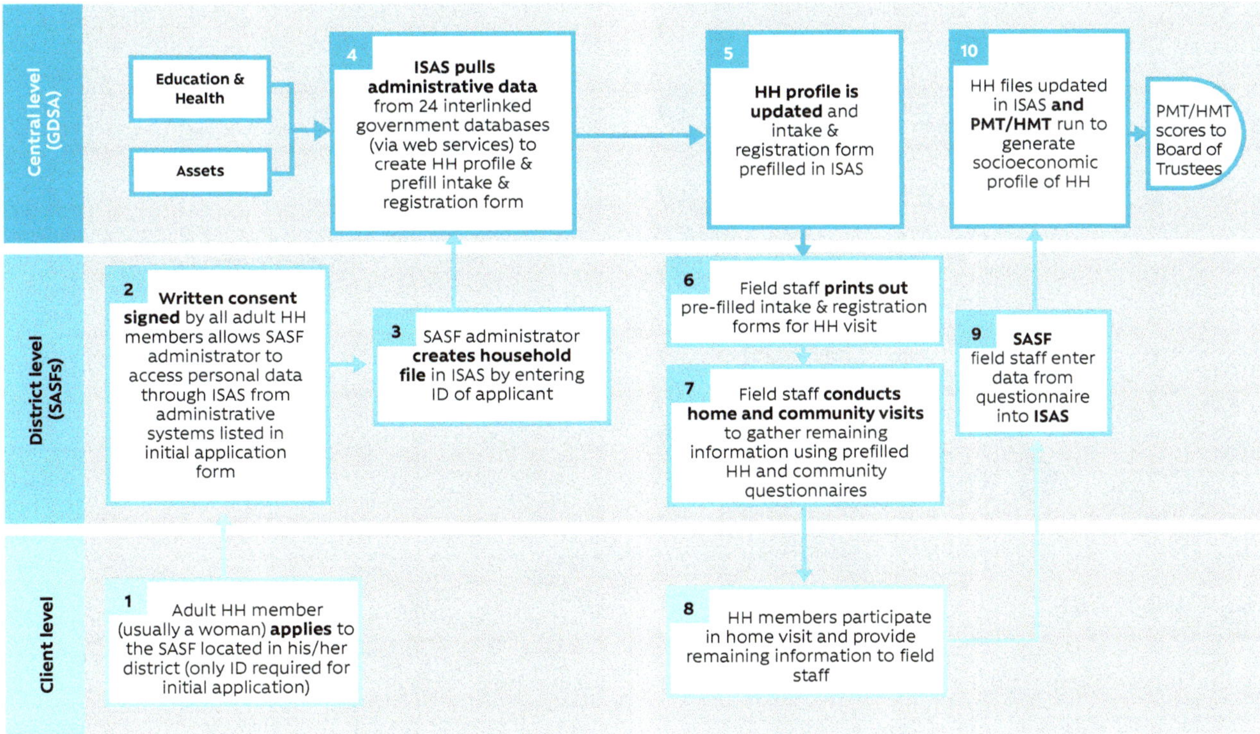

Source: Ortakaya 2018a.

Note: GDSA = General Directorate of Social Assistance; HH = household; HMT = hybrid means testing; ISAS = Integrated Social Assistance System; PMT = proxy means testing; SASF = Social Assistance and Solidarity Foundation.

Italy's RdC Program: On-Demand Registration and Multitiered Assessment of Needs and Conditions

Italy's Citizenship Income (Reddito di Cittadinanza [RdC]) Program illustrates a multitiered assessment of needs and conditions for a package that includes cash assistance and individually tailored labor and social service intervention plans.[28] Intake and registration are carried out mainly at centers for tax assistance (Centri di Assistenza Fiscale [CAF]) and local post offices, where people fill out application forms (shown in step 2 in figure 4.8). The data are transmitted to the central information system of Italy's National Institute of Social Security (INPS). INPS then checks the information against its social and fiscal registries and other administrative systems (such as the civil registry and national registry of vehicles).

Several tiers of assessment follow intake and registration. First, means-testing algorithms are applied to the data as the basis for the socioeconomic assessment (step 3, figure 4.8), which is an input into determining conditional eligibility for the GMI program (to be eligible, beneficiaries must agree to comply with individualized action plans). Second, beneficiaries are split in three main categories depending on their vulnerability situation. A first group of beneficiaries (mainly youth, elderly, people with disability, or employed who are not working poor)[29] is exempted from any conditionality, and will be receiving the cash transfer monthly based solely on the eligibility criteria (see step 9 of figure 4.8). A second group of beneficiaries, identified as "closer to the labor market,"[30] is directed to employment services where beneficiaries will be asked to sign an activation pact (step 12L of figure 4.8). Remaining beneficiaries are sent to social services where they will sign a social inclusion pact to be negotiated with social workers (step 12S of figure 4.8). The splitting of beneficiaries between social and labor services can be revisited during the assessment phase by social workers or officials of public employment services.

When beneficiaries are directed to social services, a mandatory multidimensional assessment of needs and conditions is carried out. If that initial assessment suggests that the family's needs are complex, a

Figure 4.8 Process Map with Multiphased Assessments of Needs and Conditions for GMI + Labor and Social Services in Italy

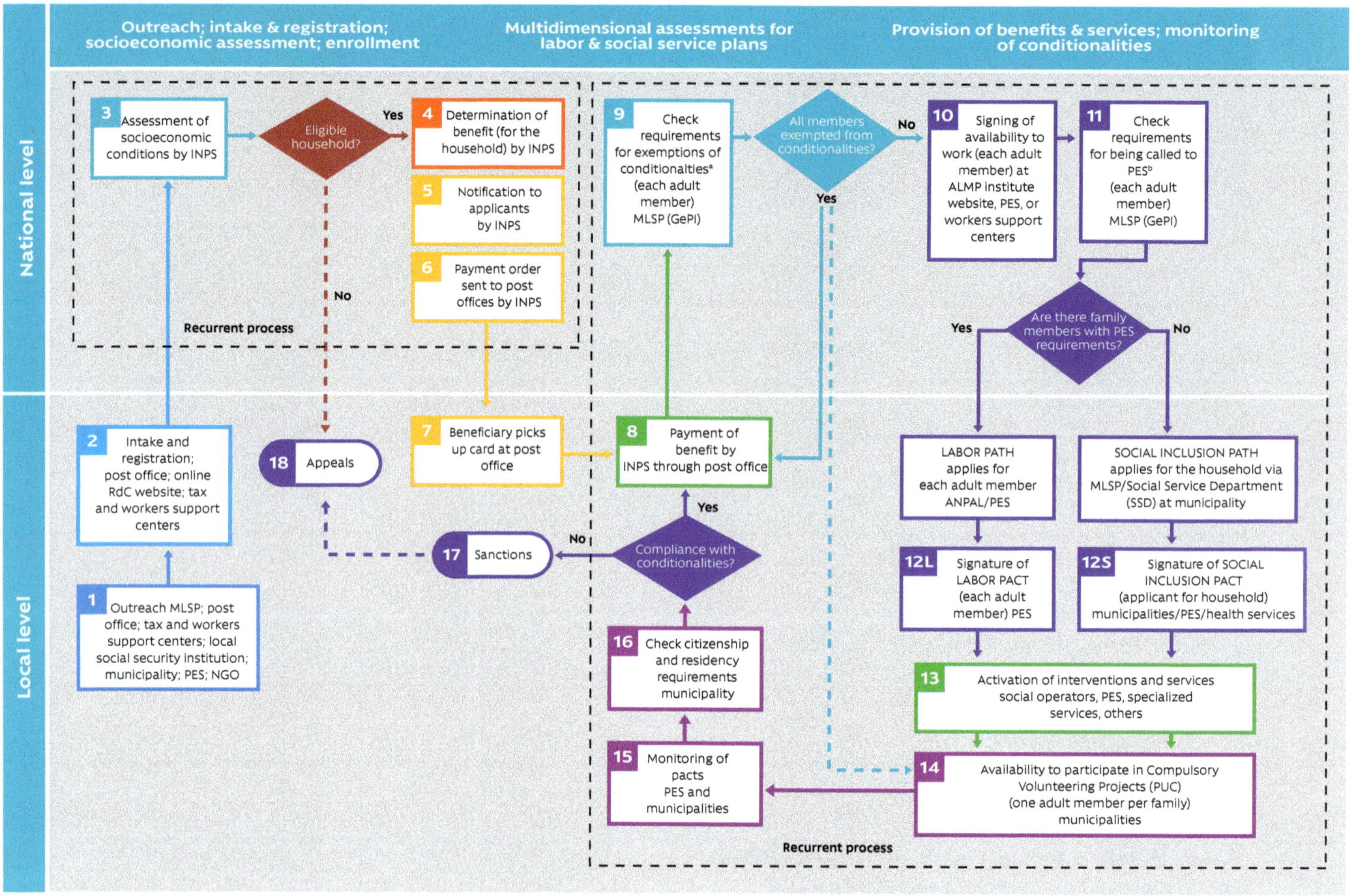

Source: Adapted from a presentation by the Ministry of Labor and Social Policies of Italy, March 18, 2020.

Note: ALMP = Active Labor Market Program; ANPAL = National Agency for ALMPs; GePI = case management information system; INPS = National Institute of Social Security; MLSP = Ministry of Labor and Social Protection; NGO = nongovernmental organization; PES = Public Employment Service(s); RdC = Reddito di Cittadinanza (Citizenship Income Program).

a. Excluded from RdC conditionality (single household member): (1) <18 years old; (2) employed (income >8,145€ dependent work and >4,800€ self-employed); (3) attend regular studies; (4) retired or 65 years old; or (5) member with disabilities (unless voluntary request to join a personalized path).

b. Requirements to be called to PES (the individual household member required to fulfill obligations with at least one of the following requirements and with the condition of not having subscribed to an REI Personalized Project at Social Services): (1) no employment for more than two years, (2) NASPI beneficiary or other social safety net for involuntary unemployment or termination of use for no more than a year, and (3) active service agreement with PES signed in the last two years.

follow-up comprehensive assessment is carried out by multidisciplinary teams using assessment tools chosen by the Ministry of Labor in agreement with representatives from the regions and other stakeholders. For families without complex needs, a caseworker determines whether household poverty is primarily related to health or other factors. This series of assessments influences the decision on the household's service package: complex and personalized for those with complex needs, a more basic personalized service package for those whose poverty is determined by other factors in addition to unemployment, and a service package focused on activation measures for those whose poverty is mostly associated with unemployment. This approach optimizes resources and staff and client time in the way it uses assessments on a tiered basis, such that (1) multidimensional risk assessments are carried out only for those whose means-tested socioeconomic assessment shows that they need it; and (2) the more comprehensive multidisciplinary risk assessments are carried out only for those who have been prescreened and found to present complex needs.

4.5 INFORMATION SYSTEMS AND INSTITUTIONAL ARRANGEMENTS

Information Systems Supporting Intake, Registration, and Assessment of Needs and Conditions[31]

Information is a core input and output of intake and registration and the assessment of needs and conditions. Information systems thus play an important role in supporting those processes: recording, transforming, and using that information and helping to automate the processes themselves. Although most countries develop separate systems for socioeconomic characteristics, labor force status and assessments, and social risk assessments, those systems have many commonalities in terms of information management. They all need to record information gathered during intake, collect additional data, validate and verify data, and then use the information to support an assessment of needs and conditions. Some of that information, such as income data, may be structured data; some, such as social worker assessment notes and reports, may be unstructured data.

Information systems can support intake, registration, and assessment for a single program or for multiple programs. When they contain socioeconomic information, these systems are typically called social registries, though social registries can contain specialized information as well, such as disability status. Indeed, social registries are defined as information systems that support the processes of intake, registration, and the assessment of needs and conditions to determine potential eligibility for one or more programs.

Social registries gather information on all applicants, supporting the processes of intake and registration and determination of eligibility based on socioeconomic data, among other characteristics. A social registry gathers and assesses information as part of a broader operations management system for a specific program. It may also run as a multiprogram social registry that supports common intake and registration processes and a common approach to assessing needs and conditions (for example, with harmonized variables and welfare measures for socioeconomic status). As discussed above, social registries are efficient for program administrators (who then do not have to collect the same information from the same people) and for clients (who do not have to provide the same information separately to multiple programs). Figure 4.9 illustrates the role of social registries in supporting common processes for intake and registration and assessment of needs and conditions for multiple programs. The programs that use the social registry each retrieve that common socioeconomic information to make their own eligibility and

Figure 4.9 Social Registries for Multiple Programs

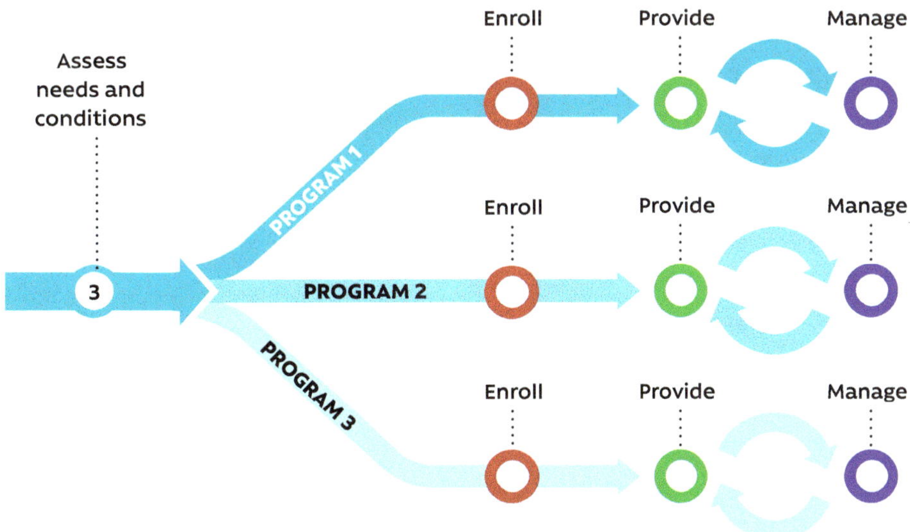

Source: Adapted from Leite et al. 2017.

Figure 4.10 Social Registries as Integrated Platforms for Social Protection and Beyond

a. Social protection programs

b. Usage in selected countries

	Legal services	Cash transfers	Social pension & other	Labor & employment	Social services	Emergency assistance	In-kind programs	Housing benefits	Energy & other subsidies	Education & training	Health benefits	Productive inclusion
Brazil		●					●	●	●	●		●
Chile	●	●	●	●	●	●	●	●	●	●	●	●
China		●		●	●	●		●		●	●	
Colombia		●	●	●	●			●			●	●
Djibouti		●			●	●		●			●	
Dominican Republic		●			●	●			●	●	●	
Georgia	●	●	●		●	●	●		●	●	●	●
Indonesia		●					●		●	●		
Mali		●			●						●	
Mauritius		●	●					●				●
Mexico		●	●			●	●					●
North Macedonia		●							●			
Pakistan		●			●	●	●	●			●	●
Philippines		●	●	●	●	●	●	●		●	●	●
Senegal		●			●						●	
Sierra Leone		●		●		●						●
Turkey		●	●		●	●	●	●	●	●	●	

Source: Original figure for this publication.

enrollment decisions, in some instances also supplementing the data with other program-specific information and assessments.

Countries around the world are using social registries to support numerous programs in social protection and expanding their use to other sectors as well (figure 4.10). A recent review by Leite et al. (2017) found that countries are using social registries for numerous government programs, many of which go well beyond social protection. Examples within social protection include cash transfers, social pensions, labor and employment benefits and services, social services, emergency assistance, and in-kind assistance programs. Examples outside social protection illustrate the power of these platforms in supporting a whole-of-government approach. They include housing benefits, utilities subsidies, education and training programs (such as need-based scholarships or training vouchers), subsidized health insurance, productive inclusion programs, and legal services (such as court waivers or pro bono legal support).

Social Registries as Multisided Service Platforms

From Guinea to Chile, Turkey, Djibouti, Pakistan, and Indonesia, social registries are helping connect people to a range of public services. These include social protection, health, and financial inclusion, based on the principle of "progressive universalism," expanding coverage, and in the process, prioritizing the poorest people. This improves coordination of programs and creates savings. When linked to a unique ID number, these platforms can reduce costs associated with inclusion errors. In Pakistan, the social registry, which includes about 85 percent of the population and has provided access to data to 70 institutions and programs both for eligibility and analytical purposes, contributed to savings of US$248 million. In South Africa and Guinea, a similar process saved US$157 million and US$13 million, respectively. In Argentina, linking 34 social program databases to the unique ID number of beneficiaries revealed inclusion errors in eligibility for various social programs. This led to US$143 million in savings over an eight-year period. Social registries serve as multisided service platforms serving a range of government programs (box 4.14).

Social Registries and Interoperability with Other Administrative Information Systems

Social registries may draw on data from other information systems. Data can be collected from other administrative systems to prefill application forms or supplement self-reported information provided by registrants. Integration with other systems verifies the information captured from the client by making sure that it matches information contained in other authoritative administrative systems (external cross-checks). Finally, data resulting from the assessment of needs and conditions can be delivered through the registry to other programs to help them make eligibility and enrollment decisions. Turkey's ISAS presents an example of a system that has greatly improved its efficiency with such interoperability (box 4.15).

Box 4.14 Multisided Social Protection Platforms Are Connecting People to Social Benefits and Beyond

Social registries and foundational ID platforms, shopping malls, and AirBnB—all are multisided service platforms that provide a common meeting ground where one side can provide services to the other side (Evans, Hagiu, and Schmalense 2006; Gawer 2009; Karippacheril, Nikayin, De Reuver, and Bouwman 2013; Rochet and Tirole 2003). Shopping malls are multisided platforms. Their developers create platforms that attract both merchants and customers. They make their money from the merchants, while customers visit the mall for free. The more enticing the mall to customers (more services provided, more user friendly, etc.), the more incentive for merchants to want to sell through that mall. AirBnB, the online marketplace for vacation rentals, is an even more comparable analogy. It operates an information systems platform as an "invisible engine" which, combined with information, trust, and human connections, brings both sides to the platform at the same time (the potential renters and landlords). Social registries are also "invisible engines" that serve to intermediate between people and governments (programs, providers) to determine potential eligibility for one or more social programs. When they serve multiple programs, they are essentially acting as a multisided service platform. The more programs that are signed on, the more people will likely register or be willing to provide their information to social registries. Foundational ID platforms serve to intermediate between people and public and private service providers to determine that "you are who you say you are." When they serve multiple service programs, they are also acting as multisided service platforms. The more service programs that are signed on, the more people will likely register or be willing to provide their information to obtain a foundational ID credential.

Social protection platforms. Social inclusion is both the means to transitioning to the digital economy, and the goal of successful technological innovations. These three key platforms—identification, social registries, and social protection (P2G/G2P) payment platforms—support inclusive access to the digital economy (see figure B4.14.1). They highlight the importance of building a digital ecosystem to enable access to social assistance, insurance, labor, jobs and youth employment. An ID platform unfolds its true potential only when the poor and vulnerable are the first mile (and not the last mile) for receiving IDs. The almost billion people without government-recognized proof of identity tend to be those excluded from society. Building an ID platform without prioritizing the most vulnerable therefore risks reinforcing exclusion and is bound to fall short in having a truly transformational impact. When everyone, regardless of legal, economic, or social status has a government-recognized proof of identity through a foundational ID platform, social registry platforms can reach universal coverage and reliably assess eligibility for social assistance, health, pro bono legal services, and water sanitation programs. SP payment platforms can then not only transfer benefits, but also contribute to digital financial inclusion of the poorest and women.

continued

Box 4.14 *(continued)*

Figure B4.14.1 Social Protection Platforms in the Digital Economy

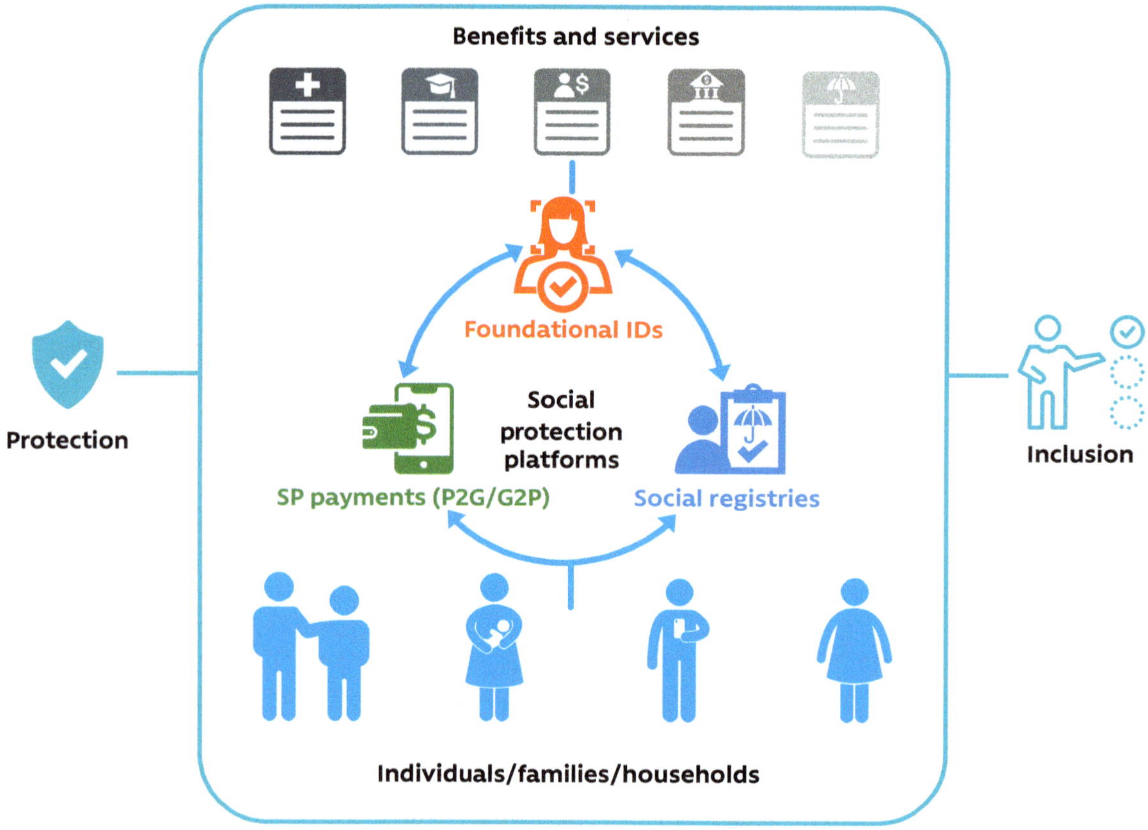

Sources: Tina George Karippacheril's presentation "Social Protection in the Digital Economy," World Bank, 2019; and presentation "Digital Social Protection" at Bonn, September 2016.
Note: Social protection (SP) payments include person-to-government (P2G) and government-to-person (G2P) payments.

With the rapid penetration of mobile devices and mobile coverage, mobile applications are being used for intake and registration, cross-checks, and eligibility assessment. In a number of countries, front-office software applications may be available to caseworkers at their offices (or in tablets/mobile devices) or to data entry operators to input that data into the system. Despite the availability of such software applications, caseworkers may still end up using paper forms for speed and efficiency when they are face-to-face with registrants (applicants) in the office or in the field. They may use the software application to input data in their spare time. Such scenarios more likely than not suggest that those software applications need to be designed with human-centered design principles in mind so as not to impose an undue administrative burden on clients or caseworkers.

Information sourced from clients is housed and managed in database management systems. The architecture for data management varies significantly across countries, and there is no one single model for this. Information systems are developed over time using different database management technologies and approaches and may be owned by different parts of an organization. As a result, data are fragmented across a number of hardware, software, organizational, and geographic boundaries.

Box 4.15 Improving Efficiency with Turkey's Integrated Social Assistance System

In 2010, Turkey's Integrated Social Assistance System (ISAS) was launched by the General Directorate of Social Assistance (GDSA) to help address the following identified weaknesses in Turkey's social assistance system: (1) limited integration across the local Social Assistance and Solidarity Foundations (SASFs), which meant that households could apply for similar programs at more than one office with the risk of double-dipping, (2) bureaucratic inefficiencies affecting both applicants and beneficiaries, (3) lengthy processing times, and (4) poor quality of information.

ISAS builds on earlier attempts to improve the situation—including the introduction of one-stop shops/service centers in 2005 to shift the administrative burden from applicants who were responsible for providing supporting documents to frontline agents—and in the launch in 2009 of a Social Assistance Information System (SAIS), which automated the process of web-service-based data collection from various administrative information systems such as Mernis (IDs), social security, and employment. These efforts paved the way for an Integrated Social Assistance System (ISAS) in 2010 that links information from 24 different public authorities to facilitate the management of social protection programs, including for applications, determination of eligibility, enrollment decisions, payments, beneficiary operations management, automated accounting, and auditing.

Since its introduction, ISAS has made a major impact on the delivery of social protection programs in Turkey. It has enabled the General Directorate of Social Assistance (GDSA) to move forward with a household approach and ensure standardization of application, eligibility assessment, payments, and beneficiary operations management. Further, it has significantly reduced the time, cost, and effort of social protection program administration and has improved client experience of interacting with frontline agents. Examples of efficiencies realized through ISAS include the following:

- **Improved efficiency in the intake and registration process.** Before ISAS, the overall application process for any social protection program was entirely paper-based. For application of a single program, at least 17 different documents—in hard copy—were required to be collected from relevant government entities and organizations, including, but not limited to, information and records on identification, social security (from three institutions), employment, assets, vehicles, land registry, taxes, tuition fees and scholarships, education, and health. The application process alone used to take from 15 days to a month. With ISAS, the application process has been decreased to minutes. Individuals can apply to the SASF in their district without providing any valid documents except their ID. ISAS then creates a household file and gathers the required information from interlinked public authorities' databases for every individual in the household within seconds. After initial prescreening, social workers conduct a home visit to complete and verify the information.
- **Decreased fragmentation across programs and fewer staff allocated.** Before ISAS, social protection was fragmented across many programs and institutions. For instance, old-age and disability pensions were administered by the more than 250 staff members of the Directorate General for Non-Contributory Payments. The pension program, initiated in 1976, had more than 1.2 million active beneficiaries. It was completely paper-based, and it took an average of 1.5 years for an individual to become eligible. With the launch of ISAS and a major legislative and regulatory update, the previous directorate general was shut down and the old-age and disabled pension program transferred to the GDSA. Now administered by a department composed of five to seven staff members, the program's application and eligibility period has decreased to less than a month.
- **Other achievements.** Before ISAS, public authorities had been more wary of sharing data across institutions and line ministries. With ISAS, the relevant authorities have come to realize the benefits of such sharing in terms of improved targeting efficiency, decreased administrative cost, greater transparency in eligibility assessment, and more effective use of public funds.

ISAS has also had a significant impact on improving the efficiency of program implementation, as with conditionalities monitoring for conditional cash transfers; this is discussed in chapter 8.

Source: Turkey, Ministry of Family and Social Policy 2018.

Several kinds of architectural models are possible for managing data to improve the performance of the system.

- For some countries, the social registry operates a self-contained database management system without links to other administrative systems across government agencies or levels of government. It is programmed to answer requests from client computers connected to a database server. Self-contained social registries rely largely on self-reported information from clients, sourced through en masse census survey sweeps or intake and registration forms.
- In countries where the social registry operates as part of a whole-of-government architecture for managing information systems across agencies, it may use either a centralized or a virtual/federated model. In a centralized model, data are sourced from other systems, replicated, and stored locally. A federated or virtual model allows data exchange with other systems that store data in incompatible database management systems or storage models and that may have been developed at different times by different entities. A federated or virtual database pulls from multiple sources as if it were a single entity. These databases are connected via a computer network and are then accessed as if they are from a single database. The goal is to be able to view and access data in a unified way without needing to copy and duplicate it in several databases or manually combine the results from many queries.

Interoperability of systems is necessary for social registries to communicate with other administrative systems. Technical standards, data standards, and process standards need to be laid down for ensuring interoperability. The client needs to be uniquely identified across systems to enable data to be linked. The ID credential also plays a key role in uniquely identifying the client at the time of registration. Examples of the types of administrative systems that social registries link to include foundational ID platforms (key for identification and interoperability), civil registries for birth and death information, tax systems, housing and property registries, and systems related to social security contributions, pension benefits, health insurance, education, and vehicle administration, among others.

Protocols can address issues arising from data conflicts between the social registry and other information systems. In some countries, the software application displays red flags or warning messages signaling the need for verification, updating, or rectification, which are then cross-checked with the clients orally when they come into contact with the social worker, mobile teams, the service center, or other frontline staff. Pakistan, for example, has piloted this approach. In other countries such as Chile, there are protocols for data updates and rectification. The data point with the most recent time stamp is given precedence and is then cross-checked with the clients to verify orally at the point of intake and registration, or when they come into contact with the frontline staff. In Turkey, the system alerts administrators when there are data conflicts, using a task list with action items.

Social registries may interoperate with beneficiary operations management systems to provide data on potentially eligible applicants/registrants for further program-specific eligibility determination (see also chapter 5). In Malawi, the Social Cash Transfer Program (SCTP) and the Public Works Program (PWP) access data in the social registry (called UBR) on households, and their PMT scores, to create potential beneficiary lists, which are then validated through community meetings, following which a final set of beneficiaries are enrolled in the program (figure 4.11).

Social registries may also interoperate with other systems through a whole-of-government approach, allowing people to apply and be considered for programs through digital self-service windows in real time. A whole-of-government approach for sharing data across agencies allows for dynamic inclusion, data quality, efficiency, and integrity. Such an approach requires a robust data exchange protocol that can facilitate cross-agency sharing of the most current information updates captured from clients through frontline agencies such as health facilities, schools, citizen service centers for registering property, land, vehicles, businesses, and so on. Real-time integration between the social registry and other administrative systems can help detect data with the most current time stamp, because some types of data are dynamic and transactional. Dynamic data have a time dimension, or a numerical value, and refer to one or more reference data objects.[32] They change as a result

Figure 4.11 Social Registry Is Used by Multiple Social Protection Programs in Malawi

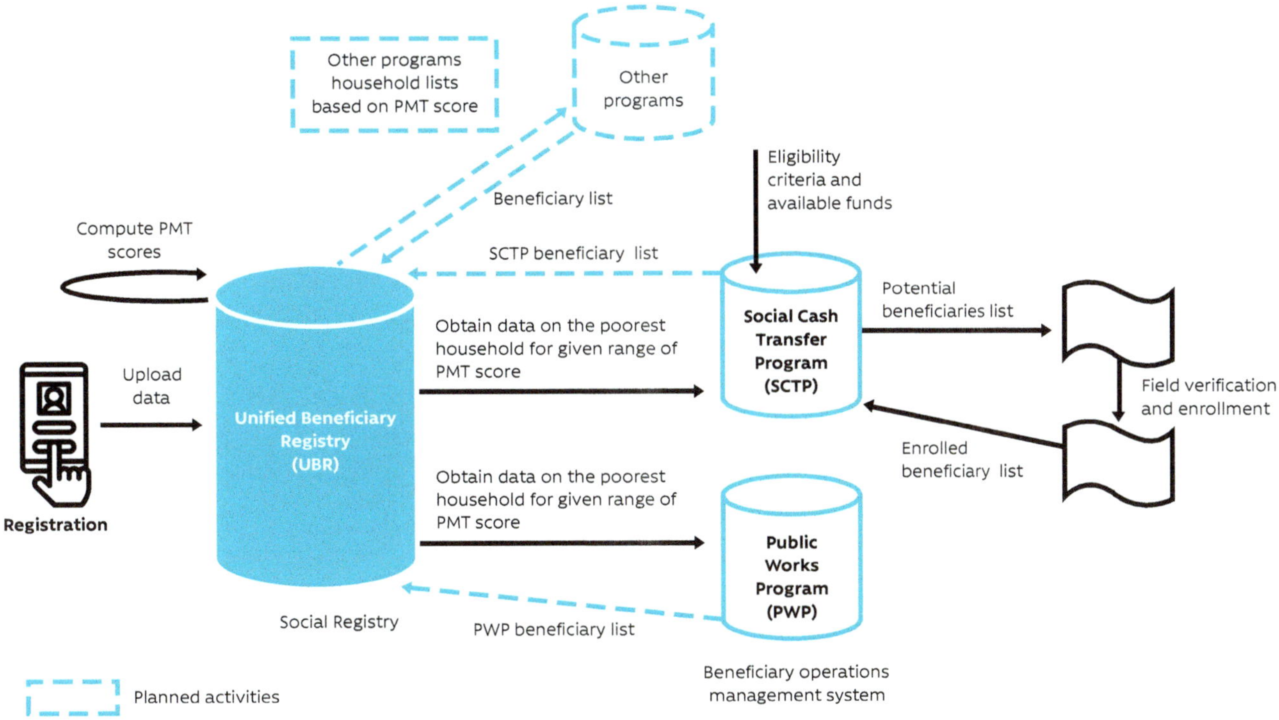

Source: Lindert, Andrews, et al. 2018.
Note: PMT = proxy means testing.

of an event (or a transaction), and therefore the individual or the families' needs and conditions change. Examples include life events such as birth, marriage, and death, or health conditions, or employment status. However, it may not always be feasible to develop real-time connections between the social registry and other administrative systems due to issues of performance and latency. Some data are static or fixed and rarely change after they are recorded. Examples are name, gender, date of birth, and so on. Other kinds of data change infrequently (for instance tax data, which changes once a year) and do not need to be updated using real-time integration between the social registry and other administrative systems. Accordingly, institutions agree on a periodic schedule for data exchange, and data are sourced through a bulk data transfer.

Inter-organizational data exchange protocols are typically based on an interoperability framework defined at the country or broader regional level. Estonia, designed a whole-of-government data exchange layer called X-Road.[33] The objective is to allow citizens, businesses, and government entities to securely exchange data and access information maintained in various agencies' databases over the internet, based on the Once-Only Principle, which states that "The State shall not request from citizens and businesses any data that are already in its possession" (European Commission 2016). For example, applying for a categorical parental benefit is through e-services (a distributed software) and does not require submission of any supporting documents. The different certificates and documents required are generated automatically by e-services by using different agencies' databases to collect data about the applicant (see Kalja, Reitsakas, and Saard 2005) (figure 4.12). Nonetheless, data exchange protocols do not negate the need for self-reported information from clients registering for social benefits and services, at least in the form of an application or claim to express need. Even in Estonia, minimum income guarantee benefits require submission of an application, along with documentation of property and movable assets and demonstration that, after paying housing expenses, families or individuals would not be able to cover basic subsistence needs.

Figure 4.12 Estonia's X-Road for Interoperability and Secure Data Exchange for Social Programs

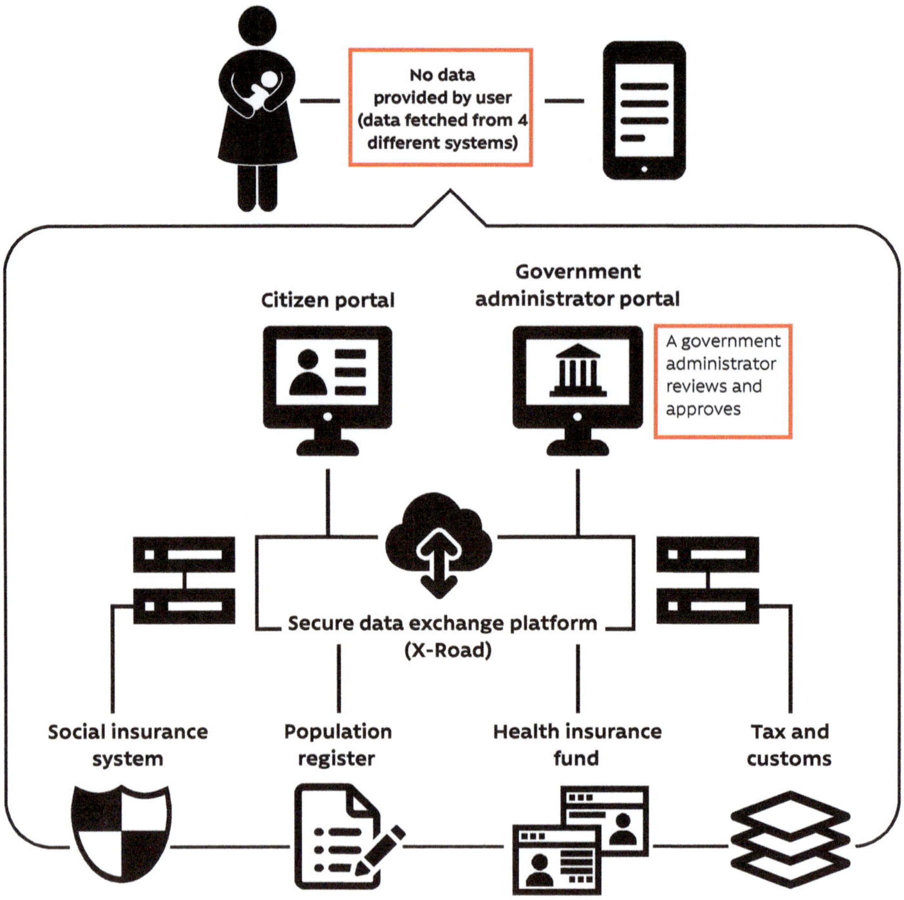

Source: Anita Mittal, consultant, Social Protection and Jobs, World Bank; adapted from Kalja, Reitsakas, and Saard 2005.

Data Protection, Privacy, and Security[34]

Data privacy risks can arise from any activity that collects, stores, or processes personal data. These risks include exposure of personal data, data and identity theft, discrimination or persecution, exclusion, unjust treatment, and surveillance. Social registries work with socioeconomic data, as well as data sourced from multiple government systems to run assessments of needs and conditions for individuals, families, and households for social protection programs. Furthermore, the data collected in a social registry is not only of a personal nature, but it necessarily cuts across systems in order to assess needs and conditions.

Given that social registries involve significant amounts of personal identifying and socioeconomic information, it is critical that legal instruments be implemented to support information security and protection of this information (Leite et al. 2017). Such protections—which include legislation, policy measures, protocols, and the like—are critical not only to the good functioning of the system, but also to the credibility and trust of the system—and without trust, individuals will be reluctant to either engage with it or to provide the necessary information. As such, the development of a social registry should be articulated around the concept of digital governance, including access to information, cybersecurity, data security, data confidentiality, privacy standards, and personal data protection.

Box 4.16 Data Protection and Privacy in the GDPR Era

Data are a powerful tool that help to grow understanding and improve delivery. In light of the increased recognition of the value of data and the increased need to process it, there has been a steady evolution in global understandings of what good practice for protecting both data and individuals should look like. The European Union's General Data Protection Regulation (GDPR) ushers in a new era of data protection and privacy standards. While more of an evolution than a revolution, and with many of the underlying principles remaining the same, the GDPR is considerably more comprehensive and far-reaching, preserving many of the same basic principles while progressively implementing stricter and more extensive rules. Shifting the approach from one of "do's and don'ts," the GDPR looks to place data subjects at the center by giving them control and knowledge of how their data are being used. To understand the obligations created for social registries, it is important to understand a few notions, as follows.

While there is no theoretical or legal universally applicable umbrella concept for the right to privacy,[a] it can perhaps most basically be understood as the "right to be let alone."[b] **Data privacy**, by contrast, is a more nuanced and narrowed concept that might be best understood as **the appropriate and permissioned use and governance of personal data**. The differentiation is noteworthy as the personal data collected in social registries is typically collected and used for certain ends—to determine eligibility, assess needs and conditions, or the sort; it is in the interim space—where that information is not being accessed by authorized users for permissioned ends—that the data should be kept private and the notion of data privacy emerges. **Data protection**—that is, the securing of collected information—is fundamental to ensuring data privacy. Data privacy, a process and legal matter, focuses on who has authorized access, while data protection is more of a technical one.

Not all data merit the same level of protection. **Personal data** refers to "any information relating to an identified or identifiable natural person" (GDPR, Article 4). An **identifiable natural person** (or "data subject") is defined as a natural person "who can be identified, directly or indirectly, in particular by reference to an identifier such as a name, an identification number, location data, an online identifier, or to one or more factors specific to the physical, physiological, genetic, mental, economic, cultural, or social identity of that natural person" (GDPR, Article 4). **Sensitive personal data** (or "special categories of data") refers to "personal data that, by its nature, are particularly sensitive in relation to fundamental rights and freedoms and merits specific protection as the context of their processing could create significant risks to a person's fundamental rights and freedoms." It includes data consisting of racial or ethnic origin, political opinions, religious or philosophical beliefs, genetic, biometric, health, life, or sexual orientation (GDPR, Recital 51).

Source: Conrad Daly, senior legal consultant, Legal-Operations, World Bank.

a. See "Right to Privacy" article by Anna Jonsson Cornell in *Max Planck Encyclopædia of Comparative Constitutional Law*, 2016.

b. See "The Right to Privacy" by Samuel Warren and Louis Brandeis in *Harvard Law Review*, vol. 4, p.193, December 15, 1890.

Social registries are important sources of personal data, but little has been written about the data protection and privacy risks that need to be taken into account when building social registries. At the same time, however, international good practices are increasingly raising the bar as recognition grows of the importance of the right to privacy generally speaking and of data privacy in particular. Indeed, several national courts have recognized the right to privacy, even where not explicit in their constitutional instruments.[35] Of particular note is the European Union's General Data Protection Regulation (GDPR), which sets a new international good-practice standard for data protection and privacy; that instrument provides useful—and, depending on the context, possibly binding—guidance for those building social registries (box 4.16).

The GDPR speaks to the data protection and privacy, setting obligations squarely upon those collecting and processing data; however, effective implementation requires additional elements. To that end, other instruments supplement the space—for instance, the United Nations Personal Data Protection and Privacy

Box 4.17 Principles for Processing Personal Data

Although developed within the context of the United Nations organizations, the UN Personal Data Protection and Privacy Principles[a] build upon prior international good practice; according to these principles, personal data should be

- **processed in a fair and legitimate manner**, taking into account the person's consent and best interests, as well as larger legal bases.
- processed and retained **consistent with specified purposes**, taking into account the balancing of relevant rights, freedoms, and interests.
- **proportional to the need**, by being relevant, limited, and adequate to what is necessary to the specified purposes.
- **retained only for the time necessary** for the specified purposes.
- **kept accurate** and up-to-date in order to fulfill the specified purposes.
- processed with due regard to **confidentiality.**
- secured by **appropriate safeguards** (organizational, administrative, physical, and technical), and procedures should be implemented to protect the security of personal data, including against or from unauthorized or accidental access, damage, loss, or other risks presented by data processing.
- processed with **transparency to the data subjects**, as appropriate and whenever possible.
- transferred to a third party only when given **appropriate protections.**
- **processed accountably**, with adequate policies and mechanisms in place to adhere to these principles.

a. From the UN High-Level Committee on Management, 2018.

Principles, the OECD Guidelines for Fair Information Practices and Protection of Privacy and Trans-border Flows of Personal Data, and the U.S. Federal Information Processing Standards—often by providing guidance as to how data should be handled or governed to assure that good international standards and expectations are met (box 4.17).

Consent Framework and Consent Architecture

Consent is at the heart of putting power over collected personal data back in the hands of the individual. The personal data collected belongs to the individual—the "data subject," as the GDPR puts it. For that reason, good international practice not only looks to assure strong data protection guarantees, but also to put control of the use of that collected data back into the hands of the individual. A key element in that regard is requiring those processing or controlling data to acquire user consent. This consent is at the heart of the notion of data privacy: it conditions the collection of personal data on the exclusive use for particular purposes. When the data are not being used for such permissioned ends, they are by and large to be kept secure and unused (see box 4.16).[36] Informed consent requires certain, specific elements: it must be freely given, specific, informed, and unambiguous (box 4.18).

Data sharing requires consent. The appropriate, permissioned use and governance of personal data that makes for data privacy requires that data sharing between entities also requires the individual's consent. This aspect is particularly important where there are multiple providers but only one data collector, and thus particularly important for social registries.

The National Unique Registry (Registre National Unique [RNU]) in Senegal has applied the principles of data protection to key processes enabled by the registry. The principles are applied to the processes of (1) data collection, (2) analysis and storage, and (3) data transmission and use. For the data collection phase, the recommendations are to inform households about the purpose of social registry, potential users, right to not respond (would prevent inclusion), and duration, and to obtain households' consent, collect only data that are needed for this phase, and ensure the secure uploading of data.[37]

The adoption of data-sharing protocols, legal agreements, and a memorandum of understanding (MoU)

Box 4.18 The Elements of Consent

Consent requires certain, specific elements: in order to be valid, consent must be given by a clear, affirmative act showing that it was freely given, specific, informed, and unambiguous agreement to the processing of personal data.[a]

- **Freely** given consent implies not only that it is given voluntarily, but that it is a genuine choice made by the individual. As such, any inappropriate pressure or influence that could affect the outcome of that choice renders the consent invalid. This standard is the same used in the medical community, with due concern for power imbalances between collector and controller of the data and the individual. It bears noting that performance of a contract may not be conditioned upon the consent to process further personal data that is not necessary for performance.
- **Specific** consent aims to limit "function creep," meaning that all activities and processing to be carried shall be identified; and where the processing has multiple purposes, consent should be specifically given for all of those purposes. Similarly, any use of automated decision making should be identified.
- **Informed** means that the individual has been notified at the least about (1) the controller's identity, (2) the kind of data to be processed, and (3) the purpose(s) for processing the data.
- **Unambiguous** consent means that the act of consent must be clear and affirmative and must be given through an active declaration of opting-in (e.g., statement, website checkbox, choice of technical settings, or clear, contextualized conduct). Consent may be withdrawn at any time, and with the same ease with which it was given.

a. See Art. 7 and Recital 32 of the European Union's General Data Protection Regulation (GDPR).

between social programs and the custodian of social registries data are vital. Doing so helps to assure the appropriate and permissioned use of personal data between the collecting entity and the processing entity. Those MoUs serve to institutionalize the individual's consent and would ensure that not only the entity collecting the data but also that all "downstream" entities subsequently processing the individual's data adhere to the terms of that consent of the individual. Generally speaking, MoUs should assure good governance of data, adhering to good international practices (see box 4.16). That said, data-sharing agreements should be clear on the agreed and specific use of the information to be shared, exact types of information to be shared (e.g., specific variables, time periods), specification of confidentiality and security principles and safeguards, specification on specific users and their access levels, and so on.

A core principle governing these agreements is that social registries should share only specific information needed for the agreed purposes with legitimate user programs in order to protect information security and confidentiality (that is, just the agreed minimum set of variables needed for user programs to make their decisions). Thus, where possible, data should not be shared "wholesale" but only the data necessary to the activity at hand shared in a variable fashion. In this regard, Estonia serves as an excellent example. In addition to assuring the appropriate and permissioned use of personal data, MoUs should assure good data governance, both in data processing and in data protection and security.

Designing a System that Assures Data Protection and Privacy

Good international practices espouse an integrative, life-cycle vision of data protection and data privacy. Of particular note is the privacy-by-design (PbD) approach (Cavoukian 2011), which requires complementary controls at each stage of the life cycle. The PbD approach can be applied to social registries and foundational ID systems, to offer valuable guidance for meeting the requirements set by the GDPR (see box 4.19). Although speaking to many of the elements discussed, the PbD approach takes a larger view, moving beyond the legal framework and the principles or guidelines governing data processing to speak to system design and implementation, with a particular eye to the fashion in which individuals are engaged.

Box 4.19 Building a Privacy-by-Design Approach into Social Registries

The privacy-by-design (PbD) approach offers valuable guidance to meet the data protection and data privacy needs laid down by the European Union's General Data Protection Regulation (GDPR), to include

- **Developing proactive not reactive systems** that take a preventive and not remedial approach
- **Making privacy the default setting**, rather than requiring affirmative action
    - **Purpose specification:** The purposes for which personal information is collected, used, retained, and disclosed shall be communicated to the individual at or before the time the information is collected. Specified purposes should be clear, limited, and relevant to the circumstances.
    - **Collection limitation:** The collection of personal information must be fair, lawful, and limited to that which is necessary for the specified purposes.
    - **Data minimization:** The collection of personally identifiable information should be kept to a strict minimum. The design of programs, information and communications technologies, and systems should begin with non-identifiable interactions and transactions, as the default. Wherever possible, identifiability, observability, and linkability of personal information should be minimized.
    - **Use, retention, and disclosure limitation:** The use, retention, and disclosure of personal information shall be limited to the relevant purposes identified to the individual, for which he or she has consented, except where otherwise required by law. Personal information shall be retained only as long as necessary to fulfill the stated purposes, and then securely destroyed.
- **Embedding privacy into the technical design** from the start rather than retrofitting it
- **Construing privacy in a positive-sum manner** ("win-win"), and not as a zero-sum ("either/or")
- **Developing end-to-end security** with a view to full-lifecycle protection
    - **Security:** Entities must assume responsibility for the security of personal information (generally commensurate with the degree of sensitivity) throughout its entire life cycle, consistent with standards that have been developed by recognized standards development bodies.
    - **Applied security standards:** Entities must assure the confidentiality, integrity, and availability of personal data throughout its life cycle including methods of secure destruction, appropriate encryption, and strong access control and logging methods.
- **Building-in visibility and transparency** and keeping systems open and accountable
    - **Accountability.** The collection of personal information entails a duty of care for its protection. Responsibility for all privacy-related policies and procedures shall be documented and communicated as appropriate and assigned to a specified individual. When transferring personal information to third parties, equivalent privacy protection through contractual or other means shall be secured.
    - **Openness.** Openness and transparency are key to accountability. Information about the policies and practices relating to the management of personal information shall be made readily available to individuals.
    - **Compliance.** Complaint and redress mechanisms should be established, and information communicated about them to individuals, including how to access the next level of appeal. Necessary steps to monitor, evaluate, and verify compliance with privacy policies and procedures should be taken.
- **Keeping the system user-centric**, with an eye to respecting user data privacy
    - **Consent.** The individual's free and specific consent is required for the collection, use, or disclosure of personal information, except where otherwise permitted by law. The greater the sensitivity of the data, the clearer and more specific the quality of the consent required. Consent may be withdrawn at a later date.
    - **Accuracy.** Personal information shall be as accurate, complete, and up-to-date as is necessary to fulfill the specified purposes.
    - **Access.** Individuals shall be provided access to their personal information and informed of its uses and disclosures. Individuals shall be able to challenge the accuracy and completeness of the information and have it amended as appropriate.

Source: Adapted from "Privacy by Design" (Cavoukian 2011).

Institutional Arrangements

The institutional arrangements for intake and registration and assessment of needs and conditions involve a variety of actors. These can include local actors, central agencies, and partner agencies. Depending on the target populations involved, intake and registration require a direct client interface. The assessment of needs and conditions is also often carried out locally—especially caseworker assessments. With socioeconomic assessments, however, central information systems may automate the aggregation of measures of income and consumption. The institutional arrangements for intake and registration depend greatly on whether the client interaction is in person or online, and whether intake and registration is on demand or administrator-driven.

With on-demand approaches, client interaction typically relies on local institutional actors. For social benefits and services, the local entry points in some countries are deconcentrated offices of the central ministry, such as Georgia's regional and local Social Service Agencies (SSAs), which serve as one-stop shops/service centers where people can file a common application for numerous benefits and services. In other countries, the local offices are managed by municipalities, as in Brazil, where people can apply, be interviewed, and be registered in the social registry (Cadastro Único). From that registry, they will be assessed and considered for eligibility for numerous social programs. The roles and responsibilities of municipal offices are closely monitored for implementation quality, which also determines the amount of administrative cost subsidies they receive (box 4.20). In Turkey, people can apply for numerous

Box 4.20 Vertical Collaboration Tools for Implementing the Cadastro Único in Brazil

Vertical collaboration can be a challenge, often requiring formal agreements, quality oversight, and administrative cost-sharing. Brazil's Ministry of Social Development (MDS) leverages three key tools to support implementation in a decentralized context in partnership with 5,570 autonomous municipalities.

- First, it maintains **formal joint management agreements** with each of the 5,570 municipalities. Those agreements detail key roles and responsibilities and minimum institutional standards for program implementation.
- Second, it has developed an **index for monitoring the quality of decentralized implementation** known as the IGD (decentralized management index). This tool tracks numerous indicators of implementation, including (1) indicators of quality of data in the social registry, such as the share of families registered with a "valid" registry (complete and consistent information); (2) the share of families with registry information updated at least within the past two years. It also tracks other indicators of implementation of the Bolsa Família Program's conditional cash transfer program (such as conditionalities monitoring) and provision of social services.
- Third, it uses the IGD to calculate **performance-based incentives for quality of decentralized implementation**. These incentives provide administrative cost support to municipalities to (partially) reimburse them for the costs of implementing the Bolsa Família Program. Payment of these financial incentives is conditional on having signed the joint management agreements and on the scores received under the (performance-based) IGD. The administrative cost subsidy is determined by multiplying a financial coefficient by the municipalities' scores on the IGD. To encourage quality implementation in smaller municipalities (which may have less capacity), municipalities receive twice the amount for the first 200 families in their quota. MDS has also established a minimum quality floor for the IGD, such that municipalities with lower than certain threshold score on the IGD receive no administrative cost subsidies. In such cases, MDS would take additional actions to help strengthen implementation quality in these municipalities. MDS transfers the administrative cost subsidies to municipalities using block grants.

Sources: MDS-IGD Operational Manual at http://www.mds.gov.br/webarquivos/publicacao/bolsa_familia/Guias_Manuais/ManualIGD.pdf and Lindert et al. 2007.

social benefits and services at 1,000 autonomous local Social Assistance and Solidarity Foundations (SASFs). For labor benefits and services, public employment agencies typically function as independent implementing agencies that operate autonomously within the established legal and policy framework and operating budgets of the line ministry, though some countries (such as Australia and the United Kingdom, and many counties in the United States) have outsourced those functions to private contractors.

With administrator-driven approaches, client interface is temporary, since intake and registration are carried out through infrequent en masse registration waves. With administrator-driven approaches, most countries rely on contracted teams or community agents to register households.[38] These arrangements are particularly common for en masse registration modalities. Some social registries (such as the Philippines's Listahanan, Colombia's SISBEN, and the Dominican Republic's SIUBEN) hire contracted field teams to register local populations. Others use a combination of contracted field teams plus communities, such as Djibouti's RSU, Mali's RSU, Senegal's RNU, and Sierra Leone's SPRINT. Indonesia's Unified Database (UDB) relied on teams from the Statistics Office to carry out its en masse registration efforts in 2015.

Central actors may take on various roles, such as managing information systems. Those systems can be used to automate socioeconomic assessments. This is the case with multiprogram social registries (such as Brazil's Cadastro Único) or integrated social information systems (such as Turkey's ISAS or Chile's RSH). Those central actors may be the social or labor ministries. When information systems serve multiple programs (such as with social registries), the institutional arrangements for those systems may be distinct from the programs that use them. Such is the case for Malawi's UBR (which is managed centrally by a multiagency working group). Even when the social registry is housed in the central social ministry, it often serves user programs outside that ministry (as in Brazil, Chile, the Philippines, and Turkey).

4.6 SOME CONCLUDING POINTS

This chapter has reviewed the modalities, instruments, and techniques used in intake and registration and the assessment of needs and conditions. The focus of those tools is on the people who apply, register, and are assessed according to specific characteristics, including demographic categories, socioeconomic status, labor status, disability, and social risks. Both intake and registration and assessment of needs and conditions are affected by two key challenges faced by countries around the globe: dynamic inclusion and coordination.

Dynamic inclusion depends greatly on whether delivery systems use on-demand or administrator-driven approaches for intake and registration.

- **With on-demand systems**, people (individuals, families, households) can apply to be assessed and considered for potential inclusion in social programs at any time. Worldwide, on-demand systems are the most common method of intake for a broad range of social protection programs, including demographic categorical programs, poverty-targeted programs, labor programs (such as unemployment benefits, employment services, and ALMPs), disability benefits and services, and social services. On-demand systems have the advantage of facilitating dynamic inclusion because people can apply at any time according to their own situations. However, on-demand approaches have the drawback of demanding substantial administrative capacity. They depend on the existence of a permanent and extensive network for client interface (in person or digital), as well as continuous financing of fixed administrative costs (such as staffing local offices).
- **With the administrator-driven approach**, cohorts of households are registered en masse on a timetable that depends primarily on capacity and financing. Administrator-driven processes are primarily used for social assistance programs targeted to poor or vulnerable households in developing countries. They are typically used in situations with limited local administrative capacity. They tend to be more static (meaning that their information is often out of date) because they open registration only infrequently, usually every

three to five years. Such one-time rapid en masse registration waves may also be used to support disaster response in specific areas. However, administrator-driven cohort approaches do not enable agencies to respond to idiosyncratic circumstances or shocks that are specific to individual client situations (such as birth of a child, aging, job loss, disability, an individual family's socioeconomic situation, or client-specific vulnerabilities). Administrator-driven approaches typically rely on contracted teams. Their financing needs are "lumpy"—meaning that large sums are required to fund en masse registration waves, with less financing needed in the interim years.

Shared processes and systems for intake and registration and the assessment of needs and conditions offer opportunities for coordination by multiple programs. Two aspects of integration have been discussed in this chapter:

- The use of common processes for intake and registration and assessment of needs and conditions by multiple programs. When programs require common information from similar population groups, it can be efficient to share intake and registration processes rather than collecting similar information separately. This requires harmonized questionnaires for intake and registration. Multiple programs may also use common assessment tools, such as means testing or proxy means testing, which can be used to determine eligibility for benefits such as social pensions for the poor, elderly, or disabled; activation benefits and service packages for low-income workers; social services for low-income families; need-based scholarships; and means-tested health insurance subsidies. While these programs may have specific individual requirements, they all also require some sort of socioeconomic assessment of needs and conditions. Social registries support common processes of intake and registration and assessment of needs and conditions for multiple programs.
- Multidimensional assessment of needs and conditions. Since people are multifaceted, these processes could gather information and assess people's profiles based on various characteristics. One example is screening job seekers for social risks in addition to work-related factors. Other examples include means-testing categorical, unemployment, or disability benefits.

In sum, several factors promote accurate and efficient intake and registration and assessment of needs and conditions:

- Simple, human-centered processes (whether digital or in person)
- Well-trained intake officers or caseworkers with interpersonal soft skills
- Accommodations for people with access barriers (disability adaptations, language translation, etc.)
- Short, easily understood intake questionnaires and application forms based on the principle of minimum information collection
- Use of information already in the system to avoid collecting it again
- Strategically located intake points that are close to the individuals in their communities
- Adequate and ideally permanent network of client interface that would allow for dynamic inclusion, such that anyone can register at any time
- Integrated approaches to intake and registration that can potentially enable people to be considered simultaneously for multiple programs

Notes

1. See chapter 2 for a discussion of these two approaches plus the glossary for definitions.
2. Referrals are particularly common for labor and social services, as discussed in chapter 7. Other service providers typically making referrals include a social worker, an employment officer, personnel from another program, school officials, health care workers, and the court system. Some referrals involve legally mandated services (such as a referral to child protective services by a teacher or health care worker). Others will be based on program participation requirements (such as referrals to labor intermediation services as required under a mutual-responsibilities contract for activation benefits). Many referrals are made as recommendations to the client(s) to benefits and services that could help them improve their situations (such as referrals to disability benefits and services by a social worker or public employment services officer). When someone is referred, sometimes his/her intake information will be transferred by the sending agency. Usually the receiving agency or program will have at least some additional information requirements of their own, and thus the intake process proceeds to gather remaining information at the referred agency.

3. In Montgomery County, Maryland (US), the Department of Health and Human Services (DHHS) has an "all doors open" policy and promotes outreach to allow for intake and registration in many locations in addition to its field offices. For example, intake officers are regularly stationed with laptops to be able to register people at other public services, such as hospitals, jails (where visiting families may need support), and nonprofit agencies.
4. Turkey's Social Assistance and Solidarity Foundation (SASF) offices are founded as private legal entities according to Law No. 3294 under the chairmanship of the provincial and subprovincial governors. They are located in each district (highly decentralized). There is no hierarchy among SASFs and they all have separate decision bodies (boards of trustees). They are autonomous in their decisions, but they must comply with Law No. 3294, decisions of the Board of Social Assistance Solidarity Fund, and any relevant regulations and decisions of the General Directorate of Social Assistance. Boards of trustees usually meet once a week.
5. Leite et al. (2017). Colombia's SISBEN covers approximately 73 percent of the population, the Philippines's Listahanan covers 75 percent, the SIUBEN in the Dominican Republic covers 85 percent, and Pakistan's NSER covers 87 percent.
6. As discussed in chapter 9, private costs of participating in processes can be measured as "time costs," "money costs, "or "number of visits" that citizens must make to complete the processes (in this case, referring to the processes of intake and registration).
7. Journey maps are a compact visualization of an end-to-end client experience along the delivery chain. They trace the client's experiences, expectations, behaviors, and emotions along that journey. See chapter 2.
8. Except with digital-only applications.
9. Brazil's Cadastro Único, for example, has specialized modules to adapt for cultural practices of distinct population groups, such as for the indigenous or quilombolo communities.
10. MISSOC comparative tables, January 2018, at https://www.missoc.org/missoc-database/comparative-tables/.
11. See Tesliuc et al. (2014) for a comprehensive review of income information used to assess needs and conditions and determine eligibility for income-support programs in Europe and Central Asia.
12. Such information sometimes includes (geo-coded) photographs of dwellings and assets, which can help with verification and quality of data. Consent should be obtained to take and use photographs in this way.
13. Information on the cause of the disability may or may not be needed. On the one hand, the cause of the disability is often irrelevant for determining needs and gathering such information may introduce the opportunity for stigmatization. On the other hand, some programs may have priority access depending on the circumstances that caused the disability (veteran, work injury, etc.).
14. Including identifying what functions are impaired due to the disability (activities of daily living such as driving, maintaining a household, holding a job, etc.) as well as the unmet need and extra costs associated with the disability (for instance need for nondurable goods such as medical supplies, and health facilities fees for intake paperwork requests).
15. This section draws significantly on a recent report by Waddington et al. (2018), which provides an overview of disability assessment methodologies for social protection and other programs.
16. It must be reiterated that disability often appears to be the most salient characteristic of a person, which may not be consistent with the lived experience of disability. People that may benefit from disability interventions and accommodations may not identify as a person with a disability and may not be aware of the opportunities or may fear stigmatization and restrictions that may accompany being labeled as a person with a disability. Rarely, and understandably, do disability assessments address positive aspects of disability, such as strengths that are developed as a consequence of, or in no relation to, a disability.
17. Persons with disabilities often face additional costs due to their disability (Mitra, Posarac, and Vick. 2011). In addition to financial costs, there may be strains on time, energy, and health to consider.
18. Unidimensional and multidimensional models are mainly estimated using predefined weights to observable characteristics. Weights are estimated based on statistical models as principal components, fuzzy models, linear regression, binary regression, quantile regression, regression trees, and correlation analysis.
19. This proxy estimation tool is also applied to other welfare measures, such as asset indexes and multidimension indexes, since the core objective is to use statistical models and information about the target group from past surveys to have a better representation of the importance of each variable to the actual welfare or index.
20. Algorithms may be used to estimate the value of those assets, or the asset tests may adopt yes-no filters for possession of assets in the determination of eligibility. For example, often for land values we multiply the land size by the average land value obtained from land taxes; for livestock value we multiply the number of heads by the estimated production/sale value of the animals.

21. PMT is often combined with other approaches such as community-based targeting or geographical targeting.
22. Much of this section is based on framework presented in a paper by Loxha and Morgandi (2014).
23. Caseload data for 2009 (Kuddo 2012).
24. Much of this section draws on materials from a recent paper by Waddington et al. (2018), which provides a review of the conceptual and practical aspects of conducting disability assessments, with examples from Europe, as well as on Bickenbach et al. (2015).
25. From a presentation by officials at the North Macedonia Ministry of Labor and Social Policy.
26. This section draws heavily on the recent rapid social registry assessment of Malawi's UBR by Lindert et al. (2018). Although UBR stands for "Unified Beneficiary Registry," we use the acronym since the name is a bit of a misnomer. The UBR is actually a social registry (not a beneficiary registry) and the households registered into the UBR are not guaranteed any form of benefit.
27. This practice of prioritizing and registering the 50 percent poorest households is being replaced by a 100 percent registration principle for phase 2 of the UBR (in other districts). Lindert et al. (2018).
28. The RdC was launched nationally on January 28, 2019, to replace the Inclusion Income, or Reddito di Inclusione (REI), while incorporating some of its features. The REI was launched nationally on December 1, 2017.
29. Beneficiaries working with income greater than €8,145/year or greater than €4,800/year if self-employed.
30. Beneficiaries who have not exempted from the conditionality, who have not been sent to social services in the past, and who have been unemployed for less than two years, received unemployment support, or have signed a labor pact recently.
31. This section builds on more extensive discussion of information systems in the recent social registries paper by Leite et al. (2017) and a forthcoming Interagency Social Protection Assessments (ISPA) tool on integrated social assistance systems.
32. In the context of data management, reference data are a list of permissible values used by master data or transactions data. They are often defined by standards organizations such as ISO. Examples include units of measure, country codes, and so on. Master data are a single source of common business data that are agreed on and shared across an organization, and are used across multiple systems, applications, and processes. For social programs, examples of master data include data on citizens (individuals, families, households), social programs (cash transfers, food), and so on.
33. "Interoperability of the State Information System: Framework: Version 3.0," 2011, Ministry of Economic Affairs and Communication, Estonia.
34. This section is based on "Data Protection, Privacy, and Security for Social Protection Programs" (forthcoming) by Conrad Daly, Tina George Karippacheril, et al., World Bank, Washington, DC.
35. See, e.g., Justice KS Puttaswamy (Retd.) v. Union of India, August 24, 2017. The Court overruled precedent in its unanimous, nine-justice decision: "The right to privacy is protected as an intrinsic part of the right to life and personal liberty ... of the Constitution."
36. In addition to consent, data may be processed for the following reasons: contract, legal obligations, vital interests of the data subject, public interest, and legitimate interest (European Union's GDPR, Article 6[1]).
37. From Solene Rogeaux's presentation on data protection and social registries in Senegal, World Bank, Washington, DC, December 2017.
38. See Leite et al. (2017) for a more extensive review of the institutional arrangements for social registries.

Bibliography

Almeida, Rita, Juliana Arbelaez, Maddalena Honorati, Arvo Kuddo, Tanja Lohmann, Mirey Ovadiya, Lucian Pop, Maria Laura Sanchez Puerta, and Michael Weber. 2012. "Improving Access to Jobs and Earnings Opportunities: The Role of Activation and Graduation Policies in Developing Countries." Social Protection and Labor Discussion Paper 1204, World Bank, Washington, DC.

ANED (Academic Network of European Disability Experts). 2018. "Disability Assessment in European States: ANED Synthesis Report." https://www.disability-europe.net/.

Barca, Valentina, and Richard Chirchir. 2014 and revised draft 2016. "Single Registries and Integrated MISs: De-mystifying Data and Information Management Concepts." Department of Foreign Affairs and Trade, Australia.

Baum, Tinatin, Anastasia Mshvidobadze, and Josefina Posadas. 2016. *Continuous Improvement: Strengthening Georgia's Targeted Social Assistance Program*. Directions in Development Series. Washington, DC: World Bank.

Beegle, Kathleen, Aline Coudouel, and Emma Monsalve, eds. 2018. *Realizing the Full Potential of Social Safety Nets in Africa*. Africa Development Forum Series. Washington, DC: World Bank.

Bickenbach, Jerome, Aleksandra Posarac, Alarcos Cieza, and Nenad Kostanjsek. 2015. "Assessing Disability in Working Age Population: A Paradigm Shift: From Impairment and Functional Limitation to the

Disability Approach." Report No. ACS14124, World Bank, Washington, DC.

Cavoukian, Ann. 2011. "Privacy by Design: The 7 Foundational Principles—Implementation and Mapping of Fair Information Practices." Information and Privacy Commissioner of Ontario, Canada. https://lab.org/wp-content/IAB-uploads/2011/03/fred_carter.pdf.

Center for Community Health and Development. 2018. Community Tool Box, University of Kansas. https://ctb.ku.edu/en/table-of-contents/implement/access-barriers-opportunities/overview/main.

Chile, Ministry of Social Development and Family. 2017. "Household Social Registry: System that Supports the Selection of Users of Social Benefits." Undersecretary of Social Evaluation, Ministry of Social Development and Family, Santiago.

Coady, David, Margaret Grosh, and John Hoddinott. 2004. *Targeting of Transfers in Developing Countries: Review of Lessons and Experience*. Washington, DC: World Bank.

Colombia, Departamento Nacional de Planeación. 2016. "Declaración de Importancia Estratégica del Sistema de Identificación de Potenciales Beneficiarios (Sisbén IV)." Documento CONPES 3877, Departamento Nacional de Planeación, Bogotá. https://colaboracion.dnp.gov.co/CDT/Conpes/Econ%C3%B3micos/3877.pdf.

Dalton, Erin. 2018. "Data and Analytics to Support an Integrated Case Practice Model." Allegheny County Department of Human Services, Pennsylvania.

Dewson, Sara, Sara Davis, and Jo Casebourne. 2006. "Maximising the Role of Outreach in Client Engagement." Research Report 326, Department for Work and Pensions, London.

Eubanks, Virginia. 2018. *Automating Inequality: How High-Tech Tools Profile, Police, and Punish the Poor*. New York: St. Martin's Press.

European Commission. 2016. "European eGovernment Action Plan 2016–2020." https://ec.europa.eu/digital-single-market/en/european-egovernment-action-plan-2016-2020.

Evans, D. A., A. Hagiu, and R. Schmalense. 2006. *Invisible Engines: How Software Platforms Drive Innovation and Transform Industries*. Cambridge, MA: MIT Press

Finn, Dan. 2011. "Job Services Australia: Design and Implementation Lessons for the British Context." Research Report 752, Department for Work and Pensions, Sheffield, UK.

Gawer, A. 2009. "Platform Dynamics and Strategies: From Products to Services." In *Platforms, Markets, and Innovation*, edited by A. Gawer. Cheltenham, U.K.: Edward Elgar Publishing.

Grosh, Margaret. 1994. "Administering Targeted Social Programs in Latin America: From Platitudes to Practice." World Bank, Washington, DC.

Grosh, Margaret, Carlo del Ninno, Emil Tesliuc, and Azedine Ouerghi. 2008. *For Protection and Promotion: The Design and Implementation of Effective Safety Nets*. Washington, DC: World Bank.

Grosh, Margaret, and Phillippe Leite. Forthcoming. "An Updated Take on Targeting Methods and Concepts." World Bank, Washington, DC.

Hoerning, Ulrich. 2011. "Activation-Safety Net Links in Germany: Hartz Reforms Six Years On." Slide presentation, Astana, Kazakhstan, February 26.

InclusionNL. 2019. "Accommodations in Service Delivery." InclusionNL, St. John's, Newfoundland and Labrador, Canada.

Indonesia, Office of the Vice President. 2015. "Indonesia's Unified Database for Social Protection Programmes: Management Standards." National Team for the Acceleration of Poverty Reduction, Secretariat of the Vice President of the Republic of Indonesia, Jakarta.

JAN (Job Accommodation Network). 2019. Searchable Online Accommodation Resource (SOAR). https://askjan.org/a-to-z.cfm.

Kalja, A., A. Reitsakas, and N. Saard. 2005. "eGovernment in Estonia: Best Practices." In *Technology Management: A Unifying Discipline for Melting the Boundaries*, edited by T. R. Anderson, T. U. Daim, and D. F. Kucaoglu, 500–506. Portland, OR: Portland International Conference on Management of Engineering and Technology (PICMET) and IEEE.

Karippacheril, Tina George, and Phillippe Leite. 2019. "Integrated Social Information Systems and Social Registries." Social Safety Nets and Delivery Systems Core Course, October, World Bank, Washington, DC.

Karippacheril, T. G., F. Nikayin, M. De Reuver, and H. Bouwman. 2013. "Serving the Poor: Multisided Mobile Service Platforms, Openness, Competition, Collaboration and the Struggle for Leadership." *Telecommunications Policy* 37 (1): 24–34.

Konle-Seidl, Regina. 2011. "Profiling Systems for Effective Labour Market Integration: Use of Profiling for Resource Allocation, Action Planning, and Matching." European Commission Mutual Learning Programme for Public Employment Services: DG Employment, Social Affairs, and Inclusion, Brussels, Belgium.

Kuddo, Arvo. 2009. "Employment Services and Active Labor Market Programs in Eastern European and Central Asian Countries." Social Protection and Labor Discussion Paper 0918, Human Development Network, World Bank, Washington, DC.

Kuddo, Arvo. 2012. "Public Employment Services and Activation Policies." Social Protection and Labor Discussion Paper 1215, World Bank, Washington, DC.

Kurekova, Lucia Mytna. 2014. "Review of Profiling Systems, Categorization of Jobseekers and Calculation of Unit Service Costs in Employment Services: Implications and Applications for

Slovakia." Central European Labour Studies Institute, Bratislava, Slovak Republic.

Leite, Phillippe, Tina George, Changqing Sun, Theresa Jones, and Kathy Lindert. 2017. "Social Registries for Social Assistance and Beyond: A Guidance Note and Assessment Tool." Social Protection and Labor Discussion Paper 1704, World Bank, Washington, DC. http://documents.worldbank.org/curated/en/698441502095248081/Social-registries-for-social-assistance-and-beyond-a-guidance-note-and-assessment-tool.

Leite, Phillippe, and Tina George Karippacheril. 2017. "Social Registry Information Systems for Social Assistance (and Beyond): Framework, Definition, Typology, and Trajectories." Presentation at Social Safety Nets Core Course, March 9, World Bank, Washington, DC.

Lindert, Kathy. 2005. "Implementing Means-Tested Welfare Systems in the United States." Social Protection Discussion Paper 0532, World Bank, Washington, DC.

Lindert, Kathy. 2017a. "Georgia's Social Registry Information Systems: Overview and Strategic Directions." Informal Technical Note, World Bank, Washington, DC.

Lindert, Kathy. 2017b. "Social Registries as Integrated Gateways for Social Safety Nets and Beyond." Lightning Talk at Human Development Week 2017, World Bank, Washington, DC.

Lindert, Kathy, Colin Andrews, Chipo Msowoya, Boban Varghese Paul, Elijah Chirwa, and Anita Mittal. 2018. "Rapid Social Registry Assessment: Malawi's Unified Beneficiary Registry (UBR)." Social Protection and Jobs Discussion Paper 1803, World Bank, Washington, DC.

Lindert, Kathy, Tina George Karippacheril, and Phillippe Leite. 2018. "Social Registries, Beneficiary Registries, and Integrated Social Information Systems." Social Safety Nets and Delivery Systems Core Course, May, World Bank, Washington, DC.

Lindert, Kathy, Anja Linder, Jason Hobbs, and Benedicte de la Briere. 2007. "The Nuts and Bolts of Brazil's Bolsa Família Program: Implementing Conditional Cash Transfers in a Decentralized Context." Social Protection Discussion Paper 0709, World Bank, Washington, DC.

Loxha, Artan, and Matteo Morgandi. 2014. "Profiling the Unemployed: A Review of OECD Experiences and Implications for Emerging Economies." Social Protection and Labor Discussion Paper 1424, World Bank, Washington, DC.

Marini, Alessandra, Michele Zini, Eleni Kanavitsa, and Alexandro Karakitsios. 2016. "Greece: Initial Support to the Guaranteed Minimum Income Rollout: Process Evaluation of the First Phase of the GMI Rollout." Social Protection and Labor Global Practice, World Bank, Washington, DC.

Mazza, Jacqueline. 2017. *Labor Intermediation Services in Developing Economies: Adapting Employment Services for a Global Age*. Cham, Switzerland: Palgrave Macmillan.

Mexico, Secretaría de Desarrollo Social. 2018. Reglas de Operación de Prospera Programa de Inclusión Social para el ejercicio.

Mikkonen, Mika, Jaana Kauppinen, Minna Huovinen, and Erja Aalto, eds. 2007. "Outreach Work among Marginalised Populations in Europe: Guidelines on Providing Integrated Outreach Services." Foundation Regenboog AMOC, Amsterdam.

Mitra, Sophie, Aleksandra Posarac, and Brandon Vick. 2011. "Disability and Poverty in Developing Countries: A Snapshot from the World Health Survey." Social Protection Discussion Paper 1109, World Bank, Washington, DC.

Mostafa, Joana, and Natália G. D. Sátyro. 2014. "Cadastro Único: A Registry Supported by a National Public Bank." Working Paper 126, International Policy Centre for Inclusive Growth, Brasilia, Brazil.

OECD (Organisation for Economic Co-operation and Development). 2014. *Connecting People with Jobs: Activation Policies in the United Kingdom*. Paris: OECD Publishing. https://doi.org/10.1787/9789264217188-en.

OECD (Organisation for Economic Co-operation and Development). 2015. *OECD Employment Outlook 2015*. Paris: OECD Publishing. https://doi.org/10.1787/empl_outlook-2015-en.

Ortakaya, Ahmet Fatih. 2018a. "Monitoring Conditionalities in Turkey's CCT Program: Background Note." Delivery Systems Global Solutions Group, Social Protection and Jobs Global Practice, World Bank, Washington, DC.

Ortakaya, Ahmet Fatih. 2018b. "Improving Decision-Making in Delivery Systems by Predictive Analytics." Internal note, World Bank, Washington, DC.

Ortakaya, Ahmet Fatih. 2018c. "Improving Efficiency with Turkey's Integrated Social Assistance System: Before and After." Internal note, World Bank, Washington, DC.

Rochet, J.-C., and J. Tirole. 2003. "Platform Competition in Two-Sided Markets." *Journal of the European Economic Association* 1 (4): 990–1029.

Rosas, Nina, Gul Najam Jamy, and Amjad Zafar Khan. 2017. "Value for Money of Different Registration Approaches—Preliminary Findings: Pakistan's National Socioeconomic Registry Update." Slide presentation, December 2017.

Scoppetta, Anette, and Arthur Buckenleib. 2018. "Tackling Long-Term Unemployment through Risk Profiling and Outreach." Technical Dossier 6, ESF Transnational Platform, European Commission, Brussels, Belgium.

Silva Villalobos, Verónica. 2016. "Integrating Social Protection Programs and Delivery Systems: Chile's

Evolving Trajectory. Presentation, Washington DC, October 4, 2016.

Silva Villalobos, Verónica, Gaston Blanco, and Lucy Bassett. 2010. "Management Information Systems for Conditional Cash Transfers and Social Protection Systems in Latin America: A Tool for Improved Program Management and Evidence-Based Decision-Making." Social Protection Unit, Human Development Network, World Bank, Washington, DC.

Silva Villalobos, Verónica, et al. 2015. "Avanzando hacia sistemas de protección social y trabajo en América Latina y el Caribe." Social Protection and Labor Global Practice, World Bank, Washington, DC.

Sluchynsky, Oleksiy. 2017. "Better Data for Better Programs and Policies in Social Protection Enabled by e-Government Solutions: Case Studies." Presentation at Human Development Week 2017, World Bank, Washington, DC.

Solomon, Jake. 2017. "Human Centered Design in Social Programs: Direct Experience from the US." Presentation at the World Bank, Washington, DC.

Sundaram, Ramya, and Nithin Umapathi. 2016. "Greece Social Welfare Review: Institutional Mapping." Social Protection and Labor Global Practice, World Bank, Washington, DC.

Tesliuc, Emil, Lucian Pop, Margaret Grosh, and Ruslan Yemtsov. 2014. *Income Support for the Poorest: A Review of Experience in Eastern Europe and Central Asia.* Directions in Development Series. Washington, DC: World Bank.

Thompson, Terri S., Asheley Van Ness, and Carolyn T. O'Brien. 2001. *Screening and Assessment in TANF/Welfare-to-Work: Local Answers to Difficult Questions.* Washington, DC: U.S. Department of Health and Human Services; Washington, DC: Urban Institute.

Turkey, Ministry of Family and Social Policy. 2017a. "ISAS Butunlesik: Turkey's Integrated Social Assistance System." Presentation by the Government of the Republic of Turkey, Washington, DC, April 21, 2017.

Turkey, Ministry of Family and Social Policy. 2017b. "Turkey's Integrated Social Assistance System." Ministry of Family and Social Policy, Ankara; World Bank, Washington, DC.

Turkey, Ministry of Family and Social Policy. 2018. "Turkey's Integrated Social Assistance System." Ministry of Family and Social Policy, Ankara; World Bank, Washington, DC. http://documents.worldbank.org/curated/en/515231530005107572/Turkey-s-integrated-social-assistance-system.

Velarde, Rashiel B. 2018. "The Philippines' Targeting System for the Poor: Successes, Lessons, and Ways Forward." Social Protection Policy Note 16, World Bank and Australian Aid, Washington, DC.

Villalobos, Verónica Silva. 2017. "Integrated Social Information System (SIIS): The Case of Chile." Presentation at Human Development Week 2017, World Bank, Washington, DC.

Waddington, Lisa, et al. 2018. "Disability Assessment in European States: ANED Synthesis Report." Academic Network of European Disability Experts (ANED).

WHO (World Health Organization) and World Bank. 2011. *World Report on Disability.* Geneva, Switzerland: WHO; Washington, DC: World Bank.

Wiseman, William. 2015. "Turkey's Integrated Social Assistance Service System: Case Study." Presentation, World Bank, Washington, DC.

World Bank. 2016. *Evaluating Tanzania's Productive Social Safety Net: Targeting Performance, Beneficiary Profile, and Other Baseline Findings.* Washington, DC: World Bank. http://documents.worldbank.org/curated/en/273011479390056768/Evaluating-Tanzanias-productive-social-safety-net-targeting-performance-beneficiary-profile-and-other-baseline-findings.

World Bank. 2018a. *Guidelines for ID4D Diagnostics.* Washington, DC: World Bank. http://documents.worldbank.org/curated/en/370121518449921710/Guidelines-for-ID4D-Diagnostics.pdf.

World Bank. 2018b. *The State of Social Safety Nets 2018.* Washington, DC: World Bank.

World Bank. Forthcoming. *An Updated Take on Targeting Concepts and Methods.* Washington, DC: World Bank.

World Bank and ILO (International Labour Organization). 2016. "A Shared Mission for Universal Social Protection: Concept Note." World Bank, Washington, DC; ILO, Geneva, Switzerland.

Zini, Michele, Alessandra Marini, Eleni Kanavitsa, Chrysa Leventi, Natalia Millan, and Nithin Umapathi. 2018. "Greece: Initial Support to the Guaranteed Minimum Income Rollout: Quantitative Evaluation of the GMI Rollout." Social Protection and Labor Global Practice, World Bank, Washington, DC.

Chapter 5

Eligibility and Enrollment

Kathy Lindert, Phillippe Leite, Tina George Karippacheril, Kenichi Nishikawa Chávez, Inés Rodríguez Caillava, and Anita Mittal

With contributions from Gustavo Demarco, Karen Peffley, and Nina Rosas Raffo

The enrollment stage involves determining which registrants qualify for programs and what benefits and services they will receive. Its objective is that eligibility is effectively determined according to specific criteria, that the benefit and service packages are accurately determined, and that eligible registrants are enrolled and onboarded efficiently with minimal leakage to ineligible populations. This stage of the delivery chain involves several phases: (1) determining eligibility and making enrollment decisions; (2) establishing each beneficiary's package of benefits and services; (3) notifying all registrants of their eligibility and enrollment status; and (4) onboarding beneficiaries by introducing them to program(s) and gathering additional operating information if necessary.[1] The primary inputs to this stage derive from the assessment of needs and conditions, which characterizes applicants according to various assessment tools (chapter 4), program eligibility criteria, and available budget. The primary output is the updated beneficiary roster, which feeds into the provision phase for actual delivery of benefits (chapter 6) and services (chapter 7).

This chapter focuses on programs and beneficiaries. Programs can include categorical benefits (such as child allowances or old-age pensions); programs for the poor or people of a particular socioeconomic status; benefits and services for the disabled; labor benefits and services (such as employment services, employability-enhancing services, and activation packages of benefits and services); and various social services to support individuals and families vulnerable to social risks. In this stage of the delivery chain, the people in question may be individuals, families, or households. *They enter this stage as registrants and become beneficiaries if they are deemed eligible, enrolled, and onboarded* (figure 5.1). Once eligibility decisions have been made, the focus is on beneficiaries.

This chapter is organized as follows:

- Section 5.1 reviews the factors involved in determining eligibility as they apply to the various types of programs that we are covering in this book, including categorical programs, poverty-targeted programs,

Figure 5.1 The Enrollment Stage of the Social Protection Delivery Chain

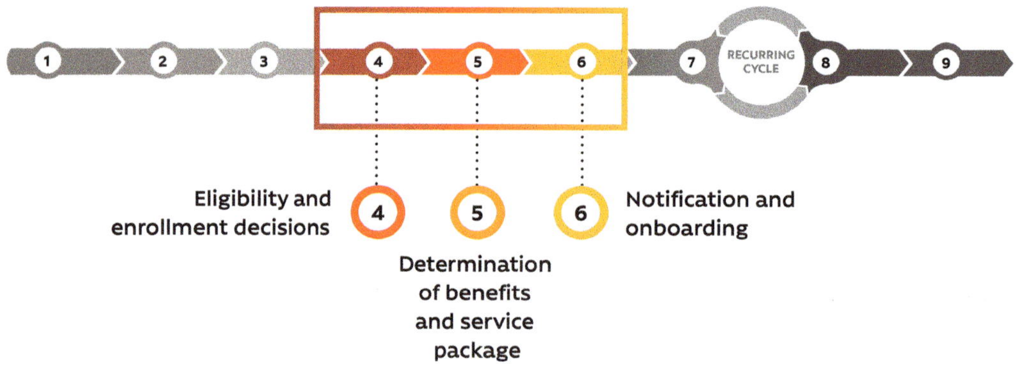

Source: Original figure for this publication.

labor benefits and services, programs for the disabled, and social services.

- Section 5.2 discusses enrollment decisions, which can diverge from eligibility decisions when there are not enough funds to enroll all eligible recipients.
- Section 5.3 looks at the factors involved in determining the package beneficiaries will receive, distinguishing between (1) benefit menus and decisions; and (2) service packages.
- Section 5.4 gives an overview of the final phases in the enrollment stage: notification and onboarding.
- Section 5.5 reviews the institutional arrangements and information systems that may be used to support the various functions in this stage.
- Finally, section 5.6 provides a summary checklist of implementation considerations for the enrollment stage of the delivery chain, including highlighting some of the tensions between designing for program objectives versus designing for implementation.

Various country examples are discussed in this chapter, including some from each region:

- **Africa:** Burkina Faso, Kenya, Malawi, Mauritius, South Africa, Tanzania
- **East Asia and the Pacific:** Indonesia, the Republic of Korea, the Philippines, Thailand
- **Europe and Central Asia:** Albania, Armenia, Bulgaria, Croatia, Denmark, Estonia, Finland, France, Georgia, Germany, Greece, Ireland, Italy, Kosovo, the Kyrgyz Republic, Lithuania, Moldova, the Netherlands, North Macedonia, Norway, Portugal, Romania, the Russian Federation, Serbia, Slovenia, Sweden, Turkey, the United Kingdom, Uzbekistan
- **Latin America and the Caribbean:** Argentina, Brazil, Colombia, Jamaica, Mexico
- **Middle East and North Africa:** Bahrain, the Arab Republic of Egypt, Kuwait
- **South Asia:** Pakistan
- **Other Organisation for Economic Co-operation and Development (OECD) countries:** the United States

Reflected in this listing are the countries included in annex 5A, which provides an overview of design parameters (eligibility criteria and benefit structures) for various types of benefits (categorical, socioeconomic, unemployment, and disability).

5.1 DETERMINING ELIGIBILITY

Once people's needs and conditions have been assessed, their profiles are compared to eligibility criteria for specific program(s). Three key elements help determine eligibility for social protection programs: eligibility criteria, profiles of registrants based on the assessment of their needs and conditions (chapter 4), and the definition of the assistance unit (individual, family, or household). It is beyond the scope of this Sourcebook to comment on the relative merits of different eligibility criteria. Instead, this chapter provides an overview of the implementation considerations that are associated with different types of criteria. Tables 5A.1–5A.4 in annex 5A provide an overview of the eligibility criteria used for various programs in a number of countries.

Most programs use a combination of criteria to determine eligibility. Table 5.1 summarizes the features of programs that are discussed throughout the Sourcebook. However, most programs use more than one factor to determine eligibility. For example, socioeconomic criteria are often used in addition to demographic criteria to determine eligibility for social pensions and child allowances. Socioeconomic criteria are used in addition to labor force status to determine eligibility for unemployment assistance, and socioeconomic criteria are weighed with disability status to determine disability assistance. While recognizing that programs often use a mix of criteria, we focus on the implementation aspects of three types: (1) eligibility based on socioeconomic criteria; (2) eligibility based on unemployment status, employment history, and insurance contributions; and (3) eligibility based on disability status.

Eligibility Based on Socioeconomic Criteria: Absolute Thresholds, Relative Thresholds, and Filters

Many benefits and services rely on socioeconomic criteria with eligibility thresholds pertaining to income, assets, and other measures of welfare. Examples include (1) social assistance benefits, including both conditional cash transfers (CCTs) and unconditional cash transfers (such as guaranteed minimum income [GMI] programs, some child and family allowances and social pensions, and disability benefits); (2) labor benefits and services, such as means-tested unemployment assistance benefits and activation packages that combine benefits and services; (3) various social services targeted to low-income individuals; (4) benefits and services outside social protection, such as health insurance subsidies, need- and merit-based scholarships, and housing and utilities subsidies.

Three types of socioeconomic eligibility criteria are common: absolute thresholds, relative thresholds, and filters. We first focus on the implementation of absolute and relative thresholds, and then turn to the use of filters.

Before getting into details, it is important to flag the differences in use of these criteria between on-demand versus administrator-driven models for intake and registration. Relative eligibility thresholds require registration to be carried out for a group of households. Since every household's eligibility depends on its standing compared to other households with relative eligibility thresholds, they are incompatible with on-demand systems.

Absolute Thresholds

With absolute thresholds, a household is eligible if its welfare measure falls below a certain level. Estimated "welfare" would come from intake, registration, and assessment of needs and conditions (see chapter 4).[2] With means testing, absolute thresholds are usually set either as a specific level of income or income ranges. Examples include Brazil's social pensions and Bolsa Família Program; GMI programs in Bulgaria, Croatia, Greece, and Romania; and social pensions, social assistance for vulnerable children, and disability benefits in South Africa (see annex 5A for additional examples). Some programs that rely on proxy means testing (PMT) also use absolute cutoffs. Examples include Burkina Faso's Burkin-Naong-Sa Ya unconditional cash transfer (UCT) program (box 5.1), Colombia's Familias en Acción CCT program, Jamaica's Programme for the Advancement of Health and Education (PATH) CCT Program, Mexico's Prospera,[3] Pakistan's Benazir Income Support Programme (BISP) UCT and Waseela-e-Taleem (WeT) CCT, and Tanzania's Productive Social Safety Net Program (box 5.1).

The left panel of figure 5.2 illustrates how absolute thresholds work. In this simplified example, Household 1 (HH1) is assessed and deemed eligible because its estimated welfare (aggregate income, PMT score, etc.) is 110, which is less than the absolute eligibility threshold of 150. HH2 is not eligible when it first applies because its estimated welfare is 160, which is above the threshold. If circumstances change, however, and HH2's welfare falls to 90 (say, due to loss of a job), HH2 could update its information and become eligible. Importantly, with absolute thresholds, the eligibility status of HH1 and HH2 are independent of each other.

In many countries, complex rules govern welfare measures and the application of absolute thresholds. Many criteria may be introduced, and program

Table 5.1 Inputs to Eligibility Determination for Various Types of Social Protection Programs

	Eligibility criteria (many programs use combination)	Assessed profile and assistance unit
Demographic-categorical programs	Demographic rules, such as children under 5, elderly persons over 65 (gender may also be a program eligibility criteria) Citizenship and/or residence requirements Employment and contributions history for social insurance pensions Socioeconomic criteria also often used to determine eligibility for social pensions and various types of child/family allowances	Assessed profile: verified information on demographic status Assistance unit: individual; designated recipient may differ from beneficiary in dependency situations (parent, caregiver, guardian, etc.) Base for assessment would be family or household with socioeconomic criteria
Poverty-targeted programs	Absolute thresholds Relative thresholds Exclusionary filters (yes-no) Various other types of criteria	Assessed profile: MT, PMT, HMT Assistance unit: usually family or household
Programs for the unemployed (UI, UA, services)	Unemployment status Duration of unemployment Employment history Minimum contributions history for UI Socioeconomic thresholds also often used to determine eligibility for UA	Assessed profile: labor profile from caseworker assessment and/or statistical profiling Assistance unit: individual Base for assessment would be family or household with socioeconomic criteria
Disability programs (DI, DA, services)	Thresholds or categories based on severity, type, duration of disability Percent functional loss in work capacity Unemployment status and minimum contributions history for DI Socioeconomic thresholds also often used to determine eligibility for UA	Assessed profile: disability status Assistance unit: individual; designated recipient may differ from beneficiary in dependency situations (e.g., caregiver) Base for assessment would be family or household with socioeconomic criteria
Social services	Some services: no eligibility criteria (available on demand for local residents) Some services: demographic criteria, category of social need or risks, socioeconomic criteria, or other specialized criteria Eligibility based on caseworker discretion and/or referrals Some services may be legally mandated	Assessed profile: social needs or risk profile Assistance unit: individual, family

Source: Original table for this publication.
Note: DA = disability assistance; DI = disability insurance; HMT = hybrid means testing; MT = means testing; PMT = proxy means testing; UA = unemployment assistance; UI = unemployment insurance.

Box 5.1 Use of Absolute Thresholds to Determine Eligibility for Burkina Faso and Tanzania

Burkina Faso's Burkin-Naong-Sa Ya unconditional cash transfer program uses a combination of geographical targeting, proxy means testing (PMT), and community validation. The first wave of the program was implemented in 2015 in the North region of the country. The planned coverage target for this region was 15,000 households. After PMT scores were calculated, the threshold was defined based on the PMT score selection up to the 15,000 household target. The second wave of the program was implemented in 2016, covering the East and Center-East regions. Once PMT scores were calculated, the number of households that were eligible surpassed the planned targets for those two regions, which had been estimated based on available poverty data. Even if this implied a larger budget than originally planned, the government decided to use the same threshold that had been used in the North, in order to guarantee that households with equivalent levels of poverty in different regions would have the same opportunities of becoming beneficiaries of the program. In late 2018, the program started expanding to the Sahel region, with a target of 20,000 households. When PMT scores were calculated, about 29,000 households were eligible for the program. Due to budget constraints and increasing insecurity across the country, the government decided to keep the original target by enrolling the poorest 20,000 households, while prioritizing expansion to other regions during the second half of 2019. While not all eligible households in the Sahel were enrolled, beneficiary households were still below the same threshold used in the rest of the regions, while eligible households that were not enrolled become a latent waitlist which could be covered in future program expansions.

Tanzania's Productive Social Safety Net (PSSN) program uses a combination of geographic targeting, community-based targeting, and verification of welfare status using a PMT. Quotas or targets are defined at the subnational level—for districts, wards, and communities (i.e., villages, *mitaa*, or *shehia*)—using a resource allocation formula that prioritizes coverage in the poorest areas. Within the selected areas, the selected community representatives assess and shortlist households through a census-sweep approach. The PMT is applied to the shortlisted households to assign each one a welfare score. Households whose welfare score falls below the threshold would capture those living under or close to the extreme poverty line and are considered eligible for the program, even if this means that the resulting number of beneficiaries for the district differs somewhat from the initial targets. There is a single threshold applied to all areas to minimize implementation complexity and communities' understanding of the process, although the PMT formula also includes location components to prioritize the poorest households. Households are then provided different components of the PSSN based on their needs. While all households are eligible for the basic transfer, only households with children are eligible for the conditional transfers, and only households with able-bodied members are eligible to participate in public works.

Sources: Burkina Faso's Burkin-Naong-Sa Ya program documents; Tanzania's PSSN Operational Manual; World Bank 2016.

rules are often multifaceted, reflecting multiple program objectives. Differentiated thresholds may be set to determine eligibility for varied benefit levels or benefit-service packages. Some programs use earnings disregards, whereby a certain amount or type of income may be exempted from eligibility calculations to provide positive work incentives. Some programs may also exempt certain assets (primary housing of a particular size, agricultural or forest land, or a vehicle used to transport children or the disabled).

Considerations in implementing absolute thresholds include information requirements, the complexity of computations, clarity in communications, and the potential for grievances. With absolute thresholds, once welfare profiles are assessed (chapter 4), the main steps include computing algorithms to determine eligibility (which can be automated) and approving eligibility decisions (depending on institutional roles). In using absolute thresholds, one consideration is whether to use a single cutoff versus multiple cutoffs, for example, cutoffs

Figure 5.2 Absolute versus Relative Thresholds for Social Protection Program Eligibility

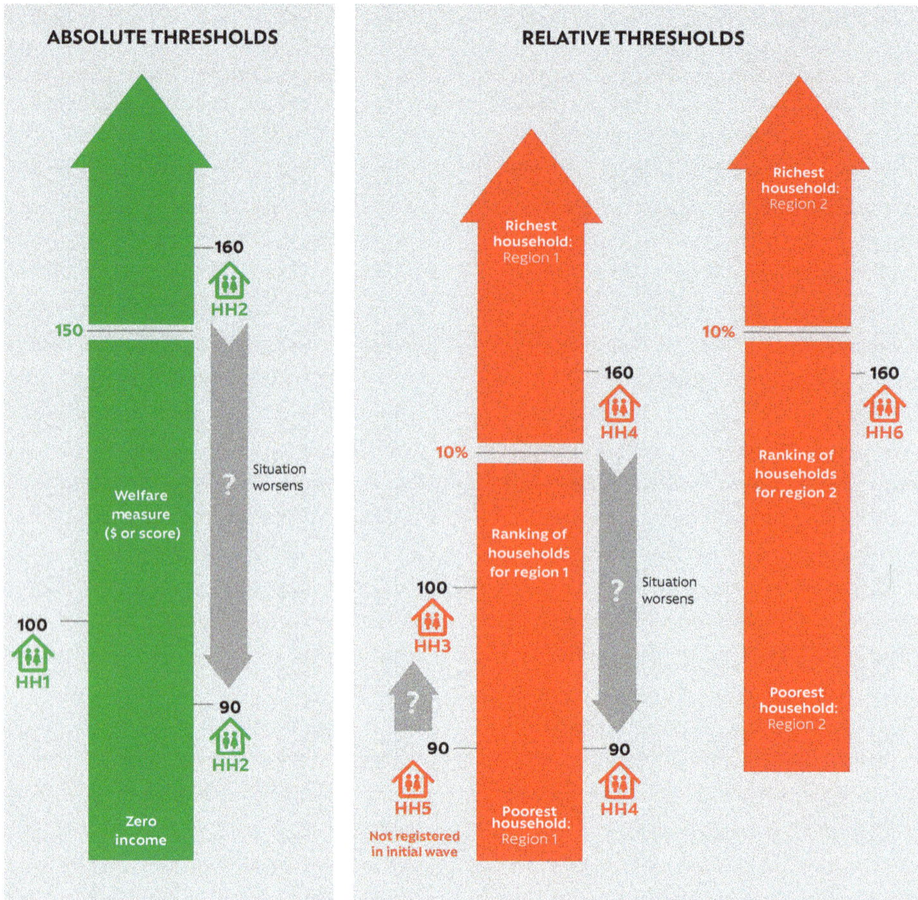

Source: Original figure for this publication.
Note: HH = household.

that vary by geographical areas. A single threshold is often applied in contexts where additional algorithm complexity does not bring improved precision in the prediction of the welfare status or there are other data limitations. It can also increase the clarity with which a decision can be communicated to all applicants. If eligibility rules are abstract or complex, it may be difficult for people to understand such decisions, thus causing higher rates of grievances and appeals. A single threshold can also help reduce the number of computations that must be carried out, which can reduce errors especially in capacity-constrained environments where processes have not been fully automated.

Relative Thresholds

In contrast, with relative thresholds, each household's eligibility is determined in relation to the eligibility of others. The registered population is assessed and ranked from poorest to richest according to a specific welfare measure such as PMT (chapter 4). Eligibility thresholds are then applied to that relative ranking as a percentage. The right side of figure 5.2 illustrates the basic functioning of relative thresholds. In this panel, the "welfare yardstick" is not a quantitative value such as currency or scores. Rather, it is the ranking of households from poorest to richest. HH3 is part of the 10 percent of eligible households. HH4 was not included because other households (not shown) were poorer than HH4 and filled the program eligibility quota of 10 percent.

Two challenges can arise with the use of relative rankings and thresholds. The first relates to dynamism over time. *The use of relative rankings and thresholds is inherently static because it requires registering, assessing, and ranking families as a group at a specific point in time.* Thus, if the situation of HH4 worsens, it would not be enrolled even it has become poorer than HH3 because the program eligibility quota of 10 percent is already filled.

Moreover, if HH5 is inadvertently missed during the initial registration wave, or if HH5 is a newly formed household, it too would not be able to enroll despite being worse off than HH3. The only way for HH4 or HH5 to enroll would be if another household exits (such as HH3). Yet that could mean that HH3 would be removed from the program even if its socioeconomic situation has not changed. This inflexibility inhibits the principle of dynamic inclusion, whereby anyone can register or update their information and be considered for potential eligibility at any time. Second, with relative thresholds, the treatment of families with comparable circumstances may not be equal across the country.[4] A common practice with relative thresholds is to make the same percentage of households eligible in each region because this is often viewed as more politically viable. However, if poverty in one region is significantly higher than in another, low-income families in the poorer region may be excluded, while better-off families in the wealthier region may be included. In figure 5.2, for example, both HH6 and HH4 have similar welfare measures. However, because HH6 is in region 2 (with fewer poor families), it is included in that region's 10 percent eligibility quota, while HH4 is not included in region 1's quota because so many households are poorer than HH4.

Relative eligibility thresholds are sometimes used with administrator-driven models for intake and registration. The ability to rank and prioritize families' needs and conditions in relation to each other depends on their being registered as a group. En masse registration allows families to be ranked from poorest to richest so that programs can then select the poorest share of the group that will be eligible. Such welfare rankings are sometimes used with PMT scoring approaches, and also often incorporate community-based targeting methods to prioritize households to be registered or to validate the resulting rankings. For example, Kenya's National Safety Net Program uses a targeting approach based on an expansion plan adopted in 2014 for the four cash transfer programs. Geographic expansion is guided by poverty where 30 percent of new beneficiaries is allocated equally to all constituencies and 70 percent is prioritized on the basis of their poverty profiles. A common intake and registration form has also been developed for all of the four programs. Poor and vulnerable households are prioritized to be registered as well as validated by community members, and households are registered, assessed, and ranked according to their categorical vulnerability and relative PMT scores. Similarly, relative rankings and thresholds determine eligibility for various programs in Malawi (box 5.2) and Indonesia (box 5.3).

The main rationale for using relative thresholds is to ensure that the poorest households are given priority under tight budget limitations. Unfortunately, resources are constrained in most countries, especially in the lower-income countries where relative rankings, relative thresholds, and the administrator-driven model tend to be used. Since there are insufficient funds to cover everyone in need, those countries need a way to focus scarce resources on the poorest. Relative rankings facilitate this principled objective. Relative thresholds also facilitate budget management and predictability. Planning and budgeting are simplified when a program's eligibility threshold is calculated as a percentage of a fixed number of registered and ranked households. Moreover, the relative threshold can be set according to the available budget.

As countries switch to on-demand registration to support more dynamic systems, they will likely need to shift from relative to absolute thresholds to determine eligibility. Because relative thresholds require mass registration to determine the relative ranking of households to each other, they are not compatible with on-demand approaches. As systems mature, many countries are considering shifting to on-demand systems. As they move in that direction, the use of relative rankings and thresholds, if used, needs to be abandoned.

Exclusionary Filters

In addition to eligibility thresholds, some countries also use "yes-no" exclusionary filters. Such filters are often used to exclude households based on their apparent wealth. Examples include the possession of certain assets: a vehicle, a second home, luxury durable goods, electronics, rental income, and savings or financial assets over a certain amount. If the household possessed any of these assets, the yes-no filter would exclude them from eligibility regardless of other criteria. Such filters are common for income-support programs in Europe and Central Asia, for example in the GMI programs in Bulgaria and Greece (see annex 5A). In Malawi, extremely poor households with an able-bodied adult are excluded from the Social Cash Transfer Program (SCTP) but are still eligible for public works programs (box 5.2).

Box 5.2 Determining Eligibility for Programs Targeted to Various Categories of the Poor Using Malawi's UBR

In Malawi, eligibility for packages of social programs is determined using a social registry known as the UBR (see also chapter 4). Communities prioritize households to be registered, and then validate the relative ranking of registered households based on their proxy means testing scores. Based on that relative ranking, they are grouped into three poverty groups, each with their own bundle of benefits and services. First, the poorest 10 percent are considered ultra-poor and incapacitated (with no able-bodied adults, which is an additional exclusionary filter). That poorest 10 percent is eligible for the Social Cash Transfer Program (SCTP) and school feeding. Second, the next poorest 15.5 percent are classified as ultra-poor with labor capacity who are eligible for public works and school feeding. Finally, 26.2 percent are classified as moderately poor, with potential eligibility for various programs, including productive inclusion programs (see figure B5.2.1).

Figure B5.2.1 Poverty Categories and Respective Social Protection Interventions in Malawi

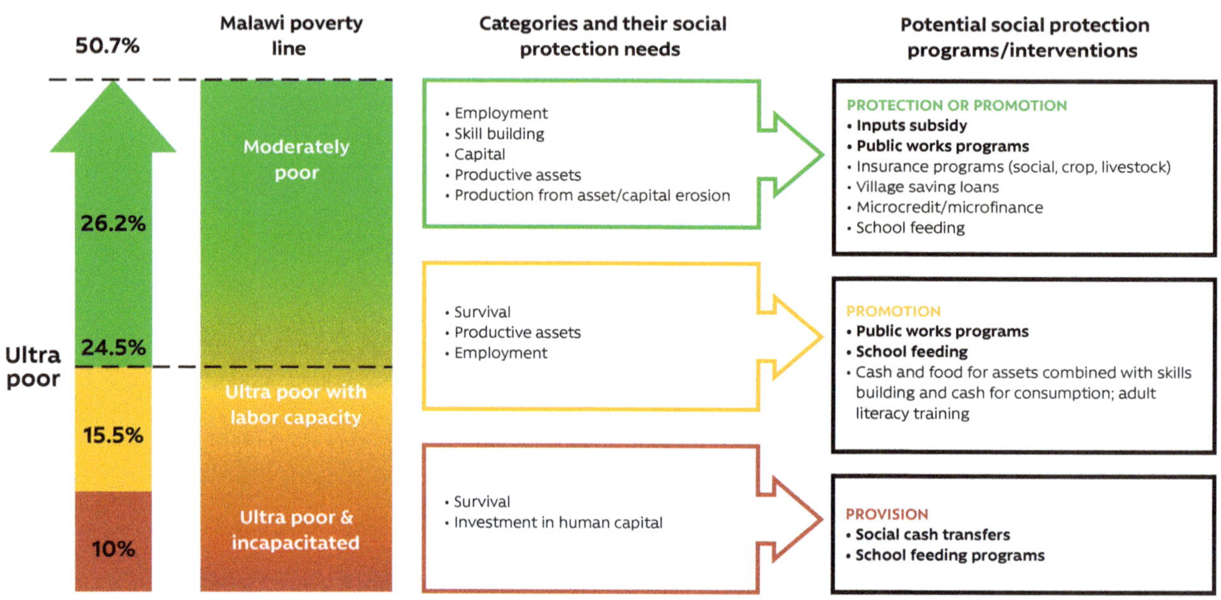

Sources: Lindert et al. 2018; Malawi's Ministry of Finance, Economic Planning and Development.

From an implementation standpoint, filters are not particularly complex. The information required would be collected during intake and registration, and then assessed in a checklist that could be used to filter applicants for specific programs. Information on many filters may already be recorded in administrative systems, such as records of beneficiaries in other programs, or registries of immovable property, movable assets, financial assets, and passports. Communication to excluded applicants about the reason for their exclusion is necessary, and applicants may contest their classifications through the grievance system. From a design perspective, however, excessive use of filters can result in high rates of exclusion errors for poor households that might otherwise be eligible for support. Tesliuc et al. (2014) demonstrate the effects of filters in excluding the poor from social assistance programs in Albania, Croatia, and Romania.

Box 5.3 Determining Eligibility for Multiple Human Development Programs Using Indonesia's UDB

Indonesia's social registry, the Unified Database (UDB), is used to determine potential eligibility for multiple social programs. Intake and registration was carried out in 2015 using the census sweep approach. About 40 percent of households were registered and assessed using proxy means testing models. The registered households were then ranked from poorest to richest. Relative eligibility thresholds were then applied to that household ranking to select beneficiaries for a range of human development programs, including: 16 percent for the conditional cash transfer program ("PKH"), 25 percent for the scholarships for the poor ("BPNT"), and 38 percent for the health insurance subsidy (see figure B5.3.1).

Figure B5.3.1 Poverty Categories and Social Protection Interventions in Indonesia

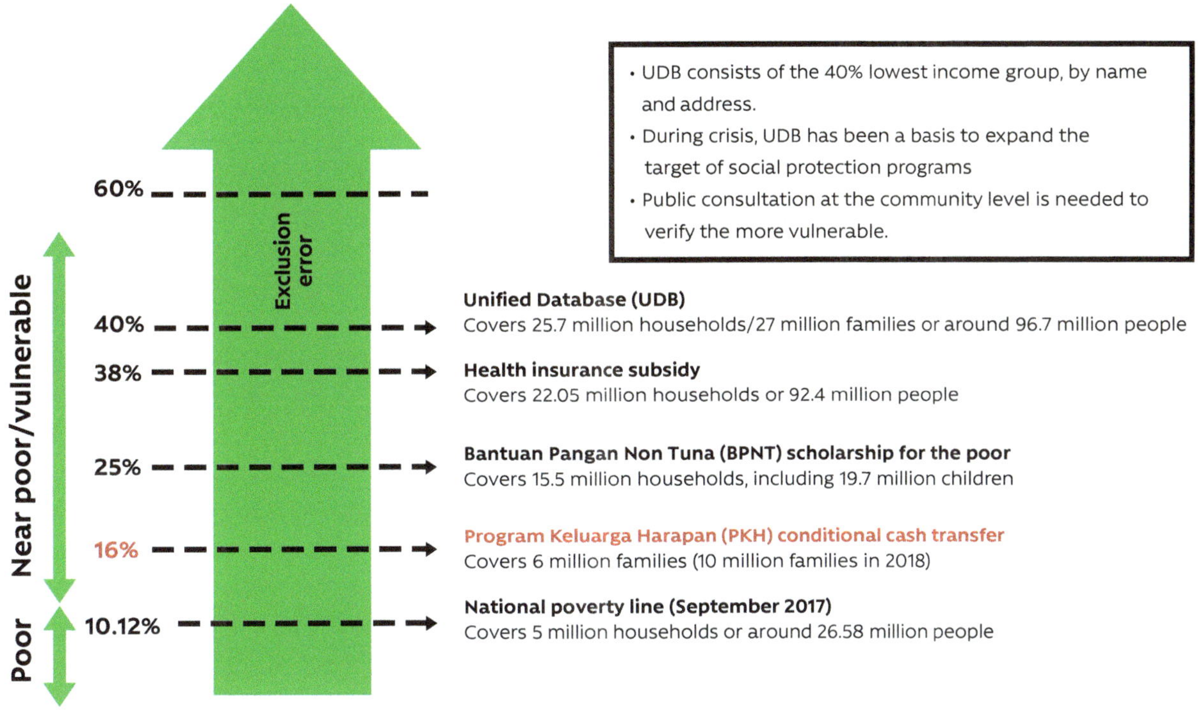

Source: Indonesia 2015.

Eligibility Based on Unemployment Status, Employment History, and Insurance Contributions

Many social protection benefits depend on unemployment status, employment history, and insurance contributions. Such benefits include unemployment insurance (UI) benefits, disability insurance benefits, and old-age social security, among others. Annex 5A includes examples of unemployment and disability insurance programs that rely on such criteria.

- ***Requirements to formally register as unemployed*** at local employment offices are often required for eligibility for unemployment benefits, as well as to gain access to employment services and ALMPs. It may also be a prerequisite for other entitlements, such as eligibility for health insurance benefits (Kuddo 2012).

Such registration is required in most countries in Europe and Central Asia, for example.

- ***Unemployment status*** filters typically require that the person became unemployed involuntarily (not because of misconduct or because he or she quit). Some countries elaborate on specific eligible and ineligible reasons for dismissal. In Armenia's UI scheme, for example, the employee's separation must be the result of enterprise reorganization, staff reduction, or cancellation of collective agreements. In the UI program in Mauritius, the individual must have been laid off for economic, technological, or structural reasons affecting the firm or because the firm's employment agreement was illegally violated. In Thailand, the UI program bars specific reasons for unemployment: dishonest performing of duties, intentionally committing a criminal offense, seriously violating work rules, and so on.
- ***Employment history*** filters typically require a minimum number of years of employment preceding unemployment. Filters can also apply to the worker's last job category. UI benefits are typically reserved for formal sector workers. Some countries have extended coverage to the self-employed and informal sector workers. For example, in Korea, coverage is offered to the self-employed and to firms with fewer than five employees.
- ***Insurance contribution requirements*** dictate the minimum number of months of contributions that must immediately precede unemployment. In our sample of countries, these range from six months in Korea, Mauritius, and Thailand to 24 months in Moldova (see table 5A.3 in annex 5A). Others differentiate based on first versus subsequent claims, such as Bahrain's UI scheme which requires 12 months for first claim, 12 out of 18 months for second claim, 18 out of 24 months for third claim, and so on. Others distinguish by type of worker, such as Argentina's UI program, which requires six months in past three years for regular workers, three months in past 12 for temporary workers, and eight months in past 24 for construction workers.

Implementation of these types of filters requires formal documentation and information. Information is gathered during the intake and registration phase, as discussed in chapter 4. Implementation requires proof of previous employment and contributions history, which is usually available from the firm, the employee, or the insurance firm and can thus be cross-checked. Evidence of the reason for unemployment may be more challenging to document. The unemployed worker must obtain documentation from the former employer with the explanation for dismissal. This can be a problem if the firm and the former employee disagree on the reasons underlying the separation. Additional challenges can arise if an individual has had more than one spell of unemployment in the period leading up to the benefit application.

Eligibility Based on Disability Status

Many programs are aimed at supporting people with disabilities. Benefits include disability assistance (DA) benefits (noncontributory) and disability insurance (DI) benefits (contributory benefits, typically for workers who become temporarily or permanently disabled). Services support disabled individuals (children, adults) and their families in many ways, including (1) social work services, which offer advocacy, screening, referrals, and coordinated care services; (2) care services, including in-home care, accessibility adaptations, support for independent living, community and medical day-care services, and institutionalized services; and (3) a range of specialized services. Employment-related disability services also include rehabilitation support services and on-the-job accommodations.

Eligibility criteria typically classify individuals by the type or degree of their disability. Given tight budget constraints, the aim is often to ensure that benefits are provided only to those who meet tightly defined eligibility criteria (Waddington 2018). In many programs, eligibility is based on a scale relating to the degree or duration of disability. For example, eligibility for Argentina's DA benefit requires that the individual must have at least a 76 percent assessed loss of earning capacity to qualify for benefits. The corresponding eligibility coefficient for degree of disability is 71 percent for Bulgaria's DA program, 60 percent for DA in Mauritius and DI in Turkey, and 50 percent for DI in Kuwait (see table 5A.4 in annex 5A). In other programs, eligibility relates to specific types of disability. In Albania, for example, DA benefits are reserved for those with "physical, sensory, mental, or psychological disability resulting from birth, an accident, or illness."

Implementation can be challenging because of information requirements and because disability criteria can be contested. The information requirements relate to the medical, functional, or comprehensive disability assessments, as discussed in chapter 4. Subjectivity can enter the process when program officials apply eligibility criteria to those assessments. The program's eligibility criteria may not align or be completely defined by the medical or functional assessment, necessitating a degree of caseworker discretion or self-declaration. This can lead to challenges in communicating eligibility decisions to applicants, as well as a high rate of grievances and appeals. Those appeals can even reach the judicial system. One such example is Brazil's Benefício de Prestação Continuada (BPC) Social Pension, which is a constitutionally guaranteed right for the poor elderly and poor persons with disabilities. Given that right and some room to interpret eligibility criteria, applicants who were initially denied benefits have appealed to the courts, leading to a significant number of beneficiaries who have been deemed eligible by the judiciary (box 5.4).

Box 5.4 Invoking the Court System When Benefits Are a Constitutional Right: Brazil's BPC Social Pension

In terms of public outlays, the Benefício de Prestação Continuada (BPC) social pension is the largest social assistance program in Brazil. The BPC provides income support to the poor elderly and poor disabled.[a] Outlays on the BPC have increased from 0.3 percent to 0.69 percent of GDP over the period from 2000 to 2015. This is in comparison with outlays on the well-known Bolsa Família conditional cash transfer program, which represented 0.45 percent of GDP (in 2015).

Rising coverage has been one of the key factors driving the increase in outlays on the BPC. Specifically, coverage has risen from 1.6 million individuals in 2002 to a total of 4.2 million by 2015. The disabled represent the larger beneficiary group, accounting for 55 percent of BPC beneficiaries in 2015, with the elderly representing the other 45 percent. Aging and demographic change account for some, but not all, of the upward pressures on coverage of the BPC.

One factor explaining the rise in coverage is an increase in the prevalence of court-awarded eligibility for BPC benefits. This relates to the legal underpinnings of the BPC, which is tied to constitutional rights. As such, many applicants have turned to the court system to obtain these benefits when their applications via regular channels in local social security offices were denied. Numerous studies have documented the role of the judiciary in awarding benefits, highlighting tensions between the citizens' rights agenda, practical challenges of implementation, and fiscal pressures. Indeed, a significant and growing share of benefits have been awarded via the court system, reaching 18.7 percent of all BPC benefits by 2015, up from 2.6 percent in 2004. The two most frequently contested issues in court cases have involved (1) disability status, and (2) income criteria, with judges allowing for the determination of sustenance via factors other than income. Indeed, the share of BPC disability benefits awarded through the court system reached nearly 30 percent by 2015 and, as discussed above, overall coverage of disability benefits grew particularly fast in recent years, rising an average of 5 percent per annum from 2010 to 2015. The Supreme Court has subsequently deemed the framing legislation guiding eligibility and the definitions of "social vulnerability" to be unconstitutional but not nullified, and the situation remains as yet unresolved.

Sources: Brito leal Ivo and Silva 2011; Meneguetti Pereira 2012; Louback da Silva 2012; World Bank 2017.

a. The program was formally regulated by the Organic Law of Social Assistance (Lei Organica de Asistencia Social [LOAS]) No. 8.742/1993—Article 20 to fulfill constitutional obligations set forth in Article 203, V of the 1988 Constitution. Specifically, the BPC makes a cash payment equivalent to one monthly minimum wage (R$937 in 2017) to people with disabilities and the elderly who prove they are unable to support themselves or be supported by their families. This threshold is defined as household income per capita below ¼ of the minimum wage (or less than R$220 in 2016). Although it is overseen by MDSA and appears as a line item in the MDSA budget, the BPC is administered and implemented by the Social Security Institute (INSS). Potential beneficiaries apply for BPC benefits at local social security offices (APS) operated by the INSS, and the program is means-tested based on self-reported incomes.

5.2 ENROLLMENT DECISIONS

Once people have been deemed eligible, program administrators decide whom to enroll. As shown in figure 5.3, several steps are required to becoming a beneficiary once applicants have been registered, assessed to establish a profile of their needs and conditions, and deemed eligible. The next step is to decide whether eligible people should be enrolled or wait-listed for a program when space is limited.

Waiting lists are one of many tactics that countries use to manage demand in the face of resource constraints, as discussed in chapter 2. The rationale behind waiting lists should be to give highest priority to the neediest with the available resources. Waiting lists are primarily used with on-demand approaches. While people who apply on demand for a program may be deemed eligible, there may be insufficient slots for everyone (unless the program is an entitlement, in which case additional slots must be created). Hence the use of waiting lists or other rationing mechanisms. The transfer of eligible applicants to a waiting list rather than to the program's enrolled roster of beneficiaries is illustrated in figure 5.3. While waiting lists may be visible, the way they are managed may not be transparent. Many programs use a first-come, first-served approach, which is easy to administer, and to audit if applications and enrollment decisions are date-stamped. However, that approach unfairly biases enrollment decisions in favor of those with connections and awareness of the

Figure 5.3 Becoming a Beneficiary of Social Protection Programs

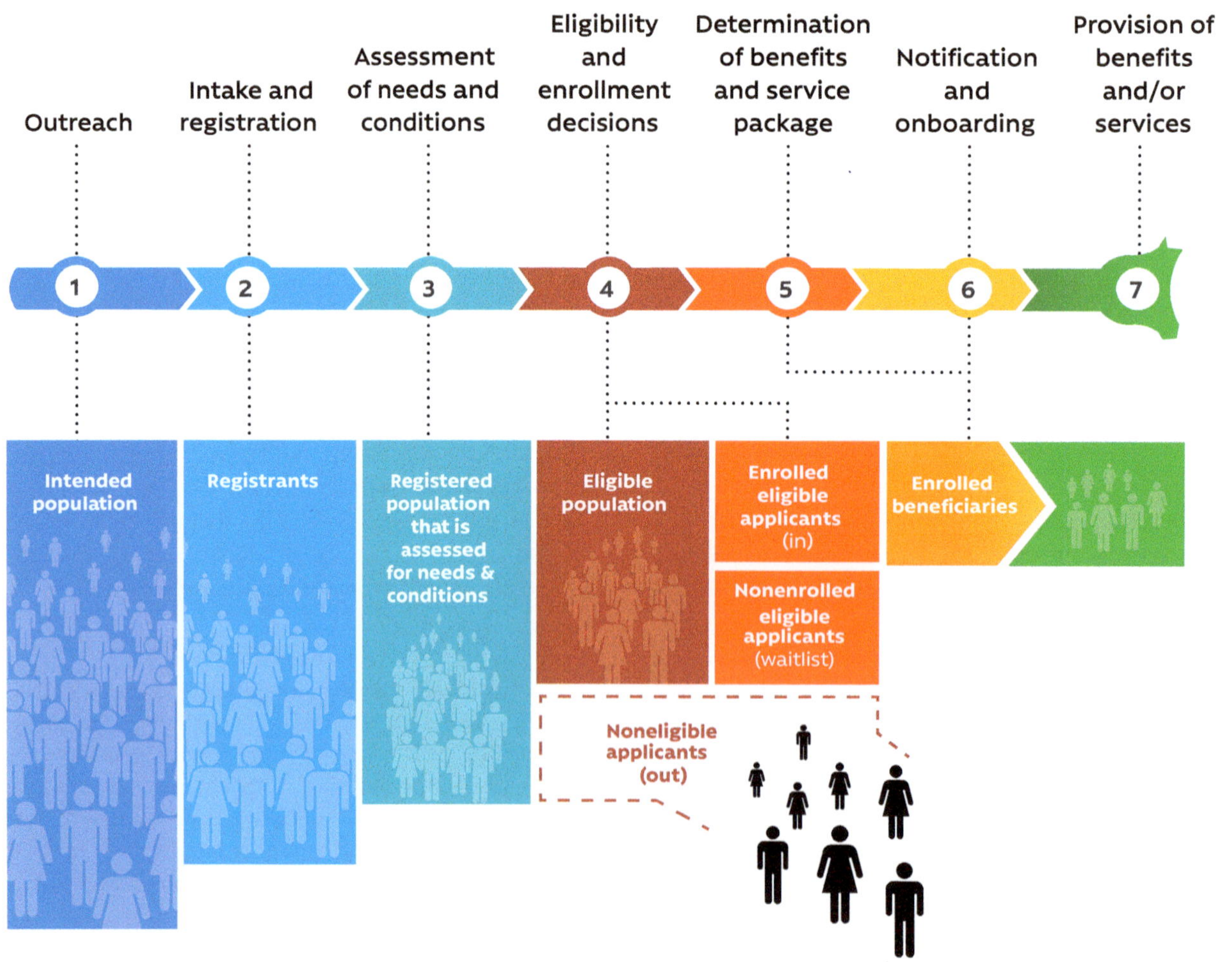

Source: Original figure for this publication.

program (who would be quicker to apply) and against marginalized populations with access barriers. It also may not prioritize those most in need, just those at the front of the line. In addition, the first-come, first-served approach opens the door to caseworker discretion and possible favoritism. *Some programs use a completely opaque approach: there are no protocols or rules guiding it*, no records of how or why decisions were made, and no clear explanation or discernible pattern in those chosen for enrollment. *Such a secretive approach can open the door to unidentified interference, political manipulation, and corruption.* In contrast, some programs select a random sample of eligible applicants for enrollment, as is the case for disability services in the State of Maryland (US, see box 5.5). This is probably the most transparent system because the rules of the game are clear, the system automatically selects applicants, and all eligible applicants have an equal opportunity to get into the program. It is also attractive because it is fairly easy to administer and audit; the only variables are the timing of the selection and the grouping of applications (for example, selecting from all eligible applicants in the past month or other specified period, or from all applicants within a geographic area). However, protocols are needed for selecting among the remaining eligible applicants when someone leaves the program.

5.3 DETERMINING THE PACKAGE OF BENEFITS AND SERVICES

Once eligibility and enrollment decisions have been made, the next step involves determining what benefits or services beneficiaries will receive. This can include benefits, services, or a benefit/service package (as with activation packages and social benefit/service combinations).

From a process perspective, this is a decision phase. Once information is available from the assessment of needs and conditions and the determination of eligibility, this phase essentially involves making decisions on benefits or services that the beneficiaries will be granted by applying program rules or caseworker discretion. We first look at benefits menus, and then at services (including packages that combine labor and social benefits or services).

Benefits Menus and the Selection of Benefits

From a design perspective, benefit levels and structures are typically set to achieve program objectives, taking into consideration the inherent trade-offs between generosity and existing budget constraints (Grosh et al. 2008). Those objectives may include supplementing income for poor or low-income households, replacing income for those who are not working (because they are unemployed, disabled, or elderly), replacing children's incomes to reduce child labor and support schooling, supporting investments in human capital, and so on (Grosh et al. 2008; Grosh and Lindert 2018). Objectives need to be weighed against the potential for inducing disincentives for adults to work. Both the level and structure of benefits can affect such disincentives. Annex 5A presents select countries' benefit structures including (1) those targeted to demographic categories of individuals; (2) those targeted to families or households based on their socioeconomic status (poverty-targeted programs); (3) social assistance and insurance benefits for the disabled; and (4) unemployment assistance and insurance programs.

Social protection literature has long recognized the tensions between complex program objectives and simplicity of benefit structures for implementation (Grosh et al. 2008). Benefits may be flat, that is, all beneficiaries receive the same amount of money (per person or per family). Alternatively, depending on program objectives, benefit amounts may vary depending on beneficiaries' characteristics. For example, benefits may vary based on the size and composition of households in order to favor larger households or specific categories of individual family members (such as pregnant women, young children, school children, or the elderly). Benefit structures may vary by socioeconomic groups to favor poorer households. Or they may be differentiated by the specific income level of each household to ensure that the poorest households receive a minimum level of income. With social insurance benefits, benefits menus may vary according to past earnings and contributions history in order to support some degree of income replacement for unemployed, disabled, or retired workers.

Box 5.5 Managing Waiting Lists When Funding Is Insufficient: Random Process Selection in Maryland (US)

The state of Maryland's Low Intensity Support Services program (LISS) supports children and adults with developmental disabilities (DD) and is designed to support persons with DD living at home with their family or in their own home in the community. The program provides up to $2,000 to assist persons with DD and their families to purchase approved services or support items to address their needs. Examples of the types of services/items that may be purchased with LISS funds include assistive technology; attendant care; barrier removal; camp (youth and adult); childcare; day care; employment-related services; health services; housing adaptations; identification services; individual and family counseling; medical equipment purchase, rental, and repair; personal care; respite support for caregivers; specialized equipment; therapeutic services; training and support for self-advocacy; transportation assistance; adaptive equipment; and tuition for postsecondary academic/vocational training.

The number of eligible applicants exceeds available slots for the program due to funding limitations. As such, the program uses random process selection (RPS) to ensure equal opportunity access among eligible applicants. How does that work?

- **Institutional arrangements.** The program is overseen by Maryland's Developmental Disabilities Administration which outsources program implementation to foundations that are contracted by region (groupings of counties in the state), such as Maryland Community Connection (MCC).
- **Outreach.** Outreach is carried out by MCC as well as county coordinators and other professionals. Since the application and documentation are complex, MCC staff also provide information sessions and assistance with application forms.
- **Intake and registration.**
  - On-demand, but applications must be submitted by certain dates (two rounds per year)
  - People must fill out an application form, gather required documentation, and file the application either in person or by mail to MCC.
  - Required documentation includes proof of identity, proof of residence in the state of Maryland, proof of disability (certification by medical professional or individualized education plan with disability diagnosis), proof of medical assistance (such as Medicaid subsidized health care).
- **Assessment.** MCC staff carry out the assessment of the individual's disability status. The staff also screen out applicants who receive support from other specified programs to avoid duplication of benefits/services.
- **Eligibility criteria.** The staff screens for children or adults living in the home and having a developmental disability that is attributable to a physical or mental impairment, other than the sole diagnosis of a mental illness, or to a combination of physical and mental impairments, and which is likely to continue indefinitely.
- **Enrollment with random process selection.** Because more people qualify as eligible than there are available slots, the Developmental Disabilities Administration uses random process selection, which is an automated system of selecting among eligible applicants to ensure equal opportunity access. RPS is applied to each round of applicants (round 1 in July and round 2 in November).
- **Notification and onboarding.** LISS providers then notify applicants of their status by mail. For those who are selected, their notification will include the LISS Program Services Eligibility Guide and Form. With this form, selected applicants indicate a detailed list of the services and items they are requesting funding for (up to US$2,000) with documentation for each service/item (invoice or quote from a service provider, information on the service provider, etc.).
- **Provision.** LISS providers will pay service providers directly, purchase eligible items online, and have them shipped to the beneficiary, for a total up to US$2,000.
- **Management.** MCC monitors beneficiaries and the services/items requested, as well as the payments to the vendors.

Sources: Maryland Community Connection (https://marylandcommunityconnection.org); Maryland Developmental Disabilities Administration 2018.

Finally, benefit structures may vary by degree of disability to favor those with more severe disabilities. While such variations may be central to a program's objectives, they have implications for implementation.

How do different benefit structures affect implementation? The delivery chain framework helps unpack the many aspects of implementing various types of benefit structures, such as the following:

- ***Information to be gathered during intake and registration.*** Although automation can facilitate the computation of any algorithm for benefit calculations regardless of how complex they are, information requirements can vary depending on the type of benefit. Flat benefits rely on minimal information—a determination that the individual, family, or household is eligible as well as the name and identifying information of the designated recipient. Some variable benefits also rely on minimal information, as the differentiation in benefit levels can be done by household size or composition, ages of household members or socioeconomic group, which are data that have been gathered at intake and registration. In other cases, as benefit calculations grow more complex, they sometimes require more information. In such cases, the information needed for calculating benefits is not necessarily the same as for determining eligibility. For example, eligibility for a program may be universal, but benefits might be set according to household incomes so that higher-income families do not receive as much money. An example is Denmark's child and youth allowance, which is universal but means-tested for benefit calculations (box 5.6). Another example is the UI scheme in Korea: eligibility relates to unemployment status and contributions history, but benefit amounts are calculated according to the insured's recent earnings history (see table 5A.3 in annex 5A). For implementation, the result is that more information must be collected, not only for eligibility purposes, but also to support benefit calculations. The additional information may be collected from all applicants during intake and registration (chapter 4) or during the onboarding process for those deemed eligible (as discussed below).
- ***Notification and ease of beneficiary understanding.*** Beneficiaries need to receive communications that explain benefit levels in a way that is easy to understand. The more complex the calculations, the more difficult they could become to communicate and comprehend. Beneficiaries need to understand how much they are entitled to, and, ideally the basis for calculating the benefits. They also need to understand any subsequent changes in benefits and the reasons for those changes. When benefits are complex, additional communication efforts need to be

Box 5.6 "Targeting from the Top" with Universal Benefits: Denmark's Child and Youth Allowances

There has been much discussion in the literature on universal income support benefits. One option that has been discussed is the notion of "tapered universal basic income" (TUBI). With this option, *eligibility* would be universal, but *benefit levels* would taper down for higher-income individuals. Although not used for *eligibility*, information on household incomes and assets would be means-tested to accommodate this tapering of *benefit levels*.

One example of such tapering or "targeting from the top" is Denmark's Child and Youth Benefit. The scheme is universally available to all children and youth under age 18 (citizens and residents). Benefit levels are then calculated with: (1) higher benefits for younger children (with differential benefits for ages 0–2, 3–6, 7–14, and 15–17); and (2) lower benefits for those with higher incomes. For this latter factor, the Child and Youth Benefit is reduced for families with a high income. The reduction of the benefit starts when the income exceeds DKr 765,800 (€102,854) and equals 2 percent of the income exceeding DKr 765,800 (€102,854). For married couples the reduction is 2 percent of each spouse's income exceeding DKr 749,000 (€100,598). As such, even though family income information is not needed for determining eligibility for this universal child and youth benefit, such information would be needed for this "targeting from the top" to taper benefits for higher-income families.

Sources: World Bank 2018c; MISSOC database for Denmark's Child and Youth Benefit.

made so that the justification for the differentiation in benefit levels can be easily understood.

- ***Payments.*** Complex benefit formulas can also have implications on the payments process, both for administrators and for beneficiaries. For beneficiaries, an often-overlooked problem is the practical importance of getting a benefit in an amount they can withdraw from an automated teller machine (ATM). Unusual benefit amounts can make disbursements particularly complex. For example, when one beneficiary is to receive $100 and the other beneficiary is to receive $118.50, in practice both can withdraw only $100 if the ATM used for the payment disburses only $20 bills. True, they could seek alternative payment points (such as bank offices), but that would add to their time and travel costs and be seriously inconvenient. Benefits that must be paid by bills or coins of various denominations also complicate manual delivery of payments because the payment service providers must carry exact change, count out individual benefit amounts for each family, and record the specific amounts disbursed. More generally, flat or simple benefit formulas might be easier for administrators in terms of processing, cashing out, reconciliation and auditing.
- ***Beneficiary operations management: Updates, corrections, and grievances.*** Uniform benefit amounts can facilitate beneficiary operations management, including updating records. With fewer benefit categories or simpler benefit calculations, there will be fewer updates or changes to benefit amounts and thus fewer changes to the payroll for the subsequent cycle. With more complex benefits, small changes can affect benefit amounts, resulting in more frequent updates and changes to payroll. Similarly, more complex benefit formulas can spawn more grievance cases and corrections because beneficiaries were confused, or administrators made errors in benefit calculations. Finally, while we focus primarily on benefit structures, it is also important to note some implementation challenges relating to benefit levels. Namely, the larger the benefit is, the greater the risk for fraud, and the greater the need for extensive and intensive oversight and control mechanisms (see chapter 8).

Implementing flat benefits is relatively straightforward. Flat benefits are used with all types of social protection programs: social pensions, child allowances, conditional and unconditional cash transfers, and disability benefits (see annex 5A). Most flat benefits are set as a fixed amount for each beneficiary (per individual, family, or household). Some, however, are calculated as a percent of a reference value, such as the minimum wage. Examples include Armenia's unemployment assistance benefit and Brazil's social pension. Flat benefits have minimal information requirements, are easy to communicate, and require less frequent updates, corrections, and grievances. Flat benefits also simplify payment processing, reconciliation, and audits.

Some programs calculate benefits based on household size, and some consider both household size and composition. Design objectives can include favoring larger households (or at least not disfavoring them on a per capita basis); favoring those with specific types of individual members who may be more vulnerable (such as pregnant or lactating women, young children, the elderly, or disabled); and promoting specific incentives, such as higher benefit levels for adolescents who would face higher opportunity costs for attending school than would their younger siblings. Malawi's Social Cash Transfer Program differentiates benefit levels by household size. Similarly, Burkina Faso's Burkin-Naong-Sa Ya cash transfer program differentiates benefit levels by number of children; households with fewer than five children under the age of 15 receive a transfer of CFAF 30,000 (US$51) every three months, and for households with five or more children the transfer is of CFAF 40,000 (US$68) every three months. Mexico's Prospera differentiates benefit levels by school grade and sex, and Tanzania, by education level of children in beneficiary households (see table 5.2). Other examples of poverty-targeted programs that differentiate by household size and composition include conditional or unconditional cash transfers in Croatia, Jamaica, the Philippines, and Tanzania. Those benefit structures do not add much complexity to implementation. Information requirements for calculating benefits based on household size and composition rely largely on the information already collected for eligibility. They can sometimes add more complexity for the beneficiary operations management stage. Since the assistance unit is the household (rather than the individual), and household size and composition are dynamic, data requirements for benefit calculations include tracking and linking information for each household member, not just for the designated recipient. Such information needs to be kept up-to-date, which adds to the task of beneficiary operations management.

Table 5.2 Benefit Structure of Tanzania's PSSN Program

PSSN component	Transfer type	Transfer name	Co-responsibility	Benefit (T Sh)	Monthly cap (T Sh)	Annual maximum (T Sh)
CCT	Fixed	Basic transfer	Extreme poverty	10,000	10,000	120,000
	Fixed	Household child benefit	Household with children under 18	4,000	4,000	48,000
	Variable	Infant benefit	Infants 0–5 health compliance	4,000	4,000	48,000
	Variable	Individual primary benefit	Child in primary education compliance	2,000	8,000	96,000
	Variable	Individual lower secondary benefit	Child in lower secondary education compliance	4,000	12,000	144,000
	Variable	Individual upper secondary benefit	Child in upper secondary education compliance	6,000		
PW	Variable	Public works benefit	Extreme poverty and older than 18, able to work	2,500	37,500	150,000

Source: World Bank 2016.
Note: CCT = conditional cash transfer; PSSN = Productive Social Safety Net; PW = public works.

Some programs also differentiate benefit calculations by socioeconomic group, with the objective of providing greater benefits to households in the poorer groups. An example is Brazil's Bolsa Família Program, which pays higher benefits to households classified as extremely poor than to those classified as moderately poor (the program also differentiates benefits based on household size and composition). From an implementation perspective, once eligibility has been established, there is little additional information needed to calculate benefits because the household has already been established as poor. It is similar in complexity to benefits based solely on household size and composition. To be sure, it may be slightly harder for people to understand their benefit levels (or how they differ from their neighbors' benefit levels), which may cause some additional number of grievances (see chapter 8 section on grievances). Payment processing and reconciliation is not overly challenging with this benefit structure, though audits may be more complex if they verify household size and composition as well as poverty classifications. Other than periodic reassessments, requirements at the management stage are comparable to programs where household benefits are calculated based solely on household size and composition.

The most complex benefit structures differentiate benefits according to how much money a household would need to receive for its income to reach a certain minimum level. Bulgaria's GMI program typifies this approach (box 5.7), setting levels for existing family income in addition to household size and composition. Benefits are calculated for each family member according to their characteristics and the difference between their family's income and the differentiated minimum income (DMI) in order to bring their income up to this tailored minimum level. The examples in box 5.7 are shown for just two hypothetical income levels (Lev 50 and Lev 20), but such calculations are tailored to every household according to its size, composition, and income levels. Other examples are included in annex 5A. From an implementation standpoint, these GMI programs are the most complex of benefit structures. Although software programs could compute the algorithms needed to calculate benefits, the information requirements for such calculations are not small—and there can be significant measurement errors in the incomes and asset values of each household. Moreover, the complexity of these calculations is quite challenging for an institution to explain and for beneficiaries to understand, which can result in

Box 5.7 Benefits Menu Example: Calculating Guaranteed Minimum Income Benefits in Bulgaria

Bulgaria's guaranteed minimum income (GMI) benefit aims to ensure a minimum level of income for extremely poor families and vulnerable individuals. Eligibility depends on means testing with an absolute threshold, as well as the application of various filters. The benefit structure aims to differentiate by type of individual (demographic characteristics) and pay the difference between the differentiated monthly income (DMI) for each individual and the actual monthly family income (benefit is paid monthly). The DMI is calculated as a social coefficient (percentage) multiplied by the fixed GMI level (Lev 75 as of 2017). The specific social coefficients (percentages) are assigned to individuals or individual family members according to demographic categories. Benefits are calculated for each individual in the family; those meeting the criteria for more than one category are entitled to the most favorable percentages. The amount of the monthly benefit = DMI − income from the previous month, as illustrated by table B5.7.1 and the examples that follow.

Example 1: Mariana (lone parent) with son Peter (age 13) and daughter Katia (age 7, with permanent disabilities); family income = 20 per capita. Mariana's benefit = 75 − 20 = 55; Peter's benefit = 68.25 − 20 = 48.25; Katia's benefit = 75 − 20 = 55. Total benefits for family = 55 + 48.25 + 55 = 158.25 Lev/month.

Example 2: Sofia (lone parent) with son Ivan (age 13) and daughter Boryana (age 7, with permanent disabilities); family income = 50 per capita. Sofia's benefit = 75 − 50 = 25; Ivan's benefit = 68.25 − 50 = 18.25; Boryana's benefit = 75 − 50 = 25. Total benefits for family = 25 + 18.25 + 25 = 68.25 Lev/month.

Example 3: Georgi, elderly man living alone, age 78, income = 50. Benefit = 123.75 − 50 = 73.75 Lev/month.

Example 4: Ana, adult living alone, age 50, income = 20. Benefit = 54.75 − 20 = 34.75 Lev/month.

Table B5.7.1 Amount of Minimum Allowance, by Category

Category of individual	Social payment coefficient (K1, %)	Differentiated minimum income = K1*GMI, where GMI = 75	Benefit varies by income (Y) of each family	
			If Y = 50, then benefit =	If Y = 20, then benefit =
Elderly >75 living alone	165	123.75	73.75	103.75
Elderly >65 living alone	140	105.00	55.00	85.00
Elderly >65	100	75.00	25.00	55.00
Adult <65 living alone	73	54.75	4.75	34.75
Adults cohabiting (each)	66	49.50	0.00	29.50
Person with reduced working capacity of >50%	100	75.00	25.00	55.00
Person with reduced working capacity of 70%	125	93.75	43.75	73.75
Child aged 0–16 (up to 20 when studying)	91	68.25	18.25	48.25
Child aged 7–16 with >5 unexcused absences	30	22.50	0	2.50
Child aged 7–16 not in school	20	15.00	0	0
Child without certificate of required vaccines	30	22.50	0	2.50
Orphan or child in foster family	100	75.00	25.00	55.00
Child with permanent disabilities	100	75.00	25.00	55.00
Lone parent taking care of child <3	120	90.00	40.00	70.00
Lone parent with child < 16 (< 20 if studying)	100	75.00	25.00	55.00
Pregnant woman 45 days before due date and taking care of child <3	100	75.00	25.00	55.00

Source: Jeliazkova and Minev 2014.

a higher rate of grievances or appeals (see chapter 8). In focus group interviews in Greece, for example, beneficiaries of the first pilot of the GMI program said they expected to receive the full threshold amount (rather than the difference between their measured incomes and the threshold). If payment reconciliation processes or audits are required to match the amounts paid to the entitled amounts, they must link to the date-stamped information on household size, composition, and income levels at the time benefits are authorized. Finally, beneficiary operations management would require maintaining accurate, updated information on household size, composition, and income.

Most unemployment insurance benefits are variable, calculated based on earnings history, often with minimum floors and maximum caps. From a design perspective, the rationale for earnings-based benefits structures is to smooth incomes in the face of unemployment, with at least a minimum replacement rate for earnings lost. At the same time, since most UI benefits are calculated as a percentage of recent earnings up to a cap, the system is designed to "make work pay," so that people will earn more from working than from being unemployed. Many examples of such UI systems are inventoried in table 5A.3 of annex 5A, including Albania, Argentina, Armenia, Bahrain, Greece, Kuwait, Korea, Mauritius, Moldova, South Africa, Thailand, and Turkey. From an implementation standpoint, variable benefit calculations based on earnings and contributions history can be complex. Although earnings records may not be required for eligibility, the individual or the administrative system must be able to track and verify earnings history for the reference time period (for example, average earnings or highest wages in past six months). Such tracking would be less complex than computing household income and asset values, since labor earnings are for the individual. The complexity of the system could be challenging for beneficiaries to understand, so these cases would require clear communication on the benefits received, in order to avoid grievances. Payment processing and reconciliation are not overly difficult for this benefit structure, though audits may be more complex if they verify earnings history to match the amount of benefits paid with the amount the beneficiary is entitled to. Monitoring an individual's unemployment status is generally more dynamic than monitoring a household's longer-term socioeconomic situation; as such, monitoring requirements for unemployment benefits (eligibility and benefit calculations) can be more demanding and increase the workload for program administrators.

Some benefit structures differentiate by the degree of disability. In Albania, for example, the disability assistance scheme pays different amounts for various categories of disability, such as non-work-related, paraplegic, tetraplegic, or blind. Moldova's disability assistance scheme likewise distinguishes between medical classifications of disability for both children and adults. In Bulgaria, benefit levels are calculated according to the functional assessment of disability, paying 120 percent of the base social pension to those with an assessed loss of capacity greater than 90 percent; 110 percent for those assessed to have lost 71 to 90 percent of their working capacity, and so on (see table 5A.4 in annex 5A). The challenge of implementing benefit schemes that distinguish by degree of disability is comparable to the challenges of implementing programs that distinguish by poverty group: once eligibility has been established, one doesn't need to collect a lot of additional data. If the benefits are paid to a designated recipient (such as a guardian), the information for that person is also linked to the beneficiary. Communication of benefit levels and classifications to beneficiaries is important because they need to understand what they are entitled to and why. Other than periodic reassessments of disability status, beneficiary operations management requirements are to be comparable to other types of benefits paid to individuals, though verification of support via designated recipients can be challenging.

Determining the Service Package

The profiling carried out during the assessment phase typically informs the service package that beneficiaries will receive. Another factor is the availability of services: When slots are limited, people may be wait-listed or caseworkers may try to steer people away from oversubscribed services. Assuming availability exists, the aim is to match people with appropriate services given their needs and conditions.

Many countries use an integrated approach to services: they bundle multiple services together, sometimes including benefits. Or services may be delivered as a single intervention, whereby an individual applies for a specific service, is assessed, determined eligible, enrolls, and is then awarded that service. When they are bundled, services are assigned depending on the profile and needs of the individual or family. Chapter 7 delves more deeply into this integrated service approach. Some benefit/service packages include: (1) activation packages; and (2) combined social services and assistance. Sometimes the benefit is the base intervention, and the services are added on, such as social assistance programs that include accompanying measures that link people to services such as parenting classes, nutrition, early childhood interventions, and productive inclusion services.

Employment Services and Activation Packages

For labor services, many countries assign activation benefit/service packages to the unemployed according to their employability, or "distance" from the labor market. Figure 5.4 illustrates this triaging approach based on a composite of various countries. After intake and registration, the unemployed individual is profiled, using the caseworker's assessment and statistical labor profiling tools (see chapter 4). Based on that assessment, the individual is classified according to their distance from the labor market. Those who are "closer" to the labor market (easy to place) might get a package of unemployment benefits (insurance or assistance) plus employment services to help them find a job (such as job search, job assistance, referrals, career counseling, etc.). Those who are further from the labor market (for example, unemployed for a longer period or employed only periodically, discouraged workers, etc.) may be assigned a package that would combine unemployment benefits (insurance or assistance), some counseling, ALMPs to help boost their employability (such as training), and employment services. Finally, the long-term unemployed, inactive or discouraged workers, and those with more complex social needs and risks may be assigned a package that includes intensive counseling, longer-term social assistance benefits, referrals to specialized labor or social services, and possibly ALMPs (such as training) to help them boost their employability if they are believed to be employable. Box 5.8 shows Ireland's approach to such triaging of beneficiaries and benefit/service packages.

Figure 5.4 Triaging Activation of Benefit-Service Packages According to Labor Profile

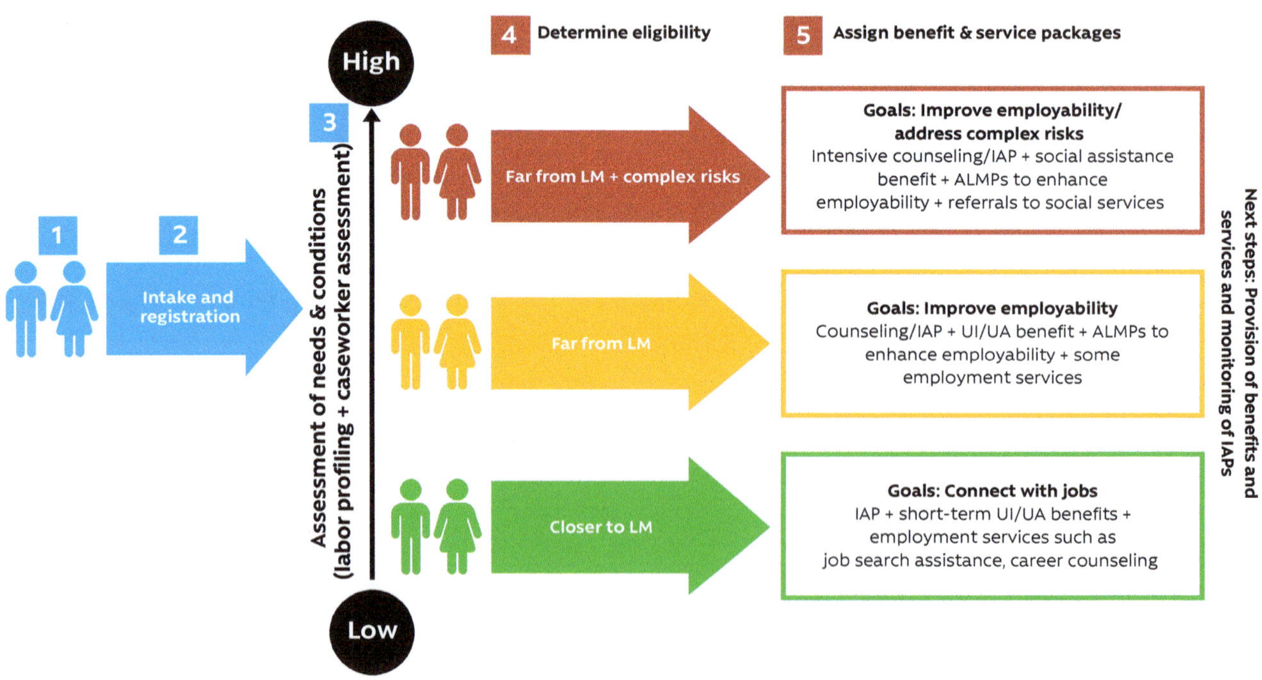

Source: Adaptation as a composite of examples presented in Loxha and Morgandi (2014).

Note: ALMP = active labor market program; IAP = individualized action plan; LM = labor market; UA = unemployment assistance; UI = unemployment insurance.

Box 5.8 Triaging Activation Benefit-Service Packages in Ireland Using Labor Profiling Tools

Many countries triage unemployed beneficiaries according to their labor profiles and likelihood of remaining long-term unemployed to assign tailored benefit-service packages. This can help optimize the allocation of public resources across beneficiaries for better effectiveness and efficiency. In Ireland, statistical labor profiling has become a critical tool for prioritizing individuals for appropriate services based on their risk of remaining unemployed over the long term. The statistical profiling generates three risk groups of unemployed in the Live Registry of the Department of Social Protection (DSP).

- The first category is low-risk clients, who are expected to remain unemployed and in the Live Registry for less than three months. People in this group would receive caseworker-led planning and job search guidance.
- The second group is medium-risk clients, who are expected to remain unemployed and in the Live Registry for more than three months. Unemployed individuals in this group would be prioritized for group counseling sessions and training sessions to enhance their skills and boost their employability.
- The third group consists of high-risk clients, who are at risk of long-term unemployment (remaining in the Live Registry longer than 12 months). They would be deemed to have immediate needs and be prioritized for one-on-one intensive support and activated for work-placement measures (such as public works projects).

Source: Loxha and Morgandi 2014.

Participation in labor services may be voluntary or mandated. For some job seekers, participation in employment services is voluntary. They go to the local employment offices or to online service windows and use a variety of self-service options (such as job banks). Or they may even use services, such as training courses, career coaching, and other employment services, as they choose. For those receiving unemployment or social assistance benefits, however, the activation package may mandate participation in the assigned services. In fact, beneficiaries may even face sanctions if they do not actively participate in the required services. The aim of such activation benefit/service packages is to provide income support and employment services while incentivizing able-bodied adults to return to work and limiting dependence on benefits.

Individualized action plans (IAPs) are often used to fine-tune the activation benefit/service package, along with rights, responsibilities, and other activities. IAPs may have different names in different countries such as personal progression plans, or mutual responsibilities contracts. Regardless of the name, an IAP is often used to document the service agreement for the beneficiary (IAPs are also used for social services, as discussed below). With the unemployed, IAPs are used to plan and carry out activities to help the job seeker find work. IAPs are typically prepared during the assessment or enrollment stages of implementation, usually with the participation of the caseworker and the client, and then monitored via regular check-ins. Key components of the IAP include a summary of the individual assessment including profiling results; goals and agreed steps toward the goals; benefits (if any); the list of services assigned (employment services, ALMPs, and other activities available to the job seeker); required actions and commitments of both parties (the job seeker and the caseworker or employment counselor); rules and procedures regarding sanctions for noncompliance with required actions; the rights of the job seeker; and information on grievance redress mechanism (GRM) procedures. During the onboarding phase (discussed below), the IAP is signed by both the beneficiary and the caseworker.[5] The actions required may be different depending on the category of the client. For clients closer to the labor market, the requirements may include reporting on weekly job search activities, committing to respond to job vacancies, participating in assigned employment services, and the timing of subsequent meetings. For those further from the labor market, the required actions may include participating in orientation, specialized screening, and job readiness supports; taking part in other training, work practice, and job coaching; using specialized services; and so on.

Social Services

A triaging approach similar to those used to match services to needs for the unemployed may also be used for social services. This usually involves caseworker discretion, though some services are mandated while others have formalized eligibility criteria. Italy's GMI program with tailored service packages, which was presented in chapter 4, illustrates such triaging for a mix of labor and social services, depending on the profile of the individual or family.

With social services, triaging depends on the social risks and type of services. While some services may be requested (by applicants) or recommended (by caseworkers) on a voluntary basis, others may be legally mandated or required as part of an IAP. Whether services are voluntary or required depends on the type of service and social-risk profile of the individual. For example, parenting classes, teen-parent support services, early childhood services, substance-abuse screening, and social services may be available to anyone on demand, but they may also be required activities in an IAP. Certain social services are legally mandated: either the individual must participate in them, the state must provide them, or both. Examples include some types of child or adult protective services and some programs for at-risk youth. In some instances, the legal mandate is a general statute for anyone facing a specific social risk; in others it is a court order for an individual case. Some services may be referred by social caseworkers or other professionals. For example, some types of parenting, child, and youth support services may be offered when a health professional or school official observes potential risk flags. Community outreach workers may also refer youth for gang prevention or other programs for at-risk youth.

Disability Services

For disability services, eligibility depends on caseworkers' assessments, the severity and duration of disability, and specific needs. Even if eligibility for benefits is not used as a gateway for disability services, the criteria and assessment used to determine eligibility may be similar. Alternatively, the assessment and criteria may be more qualitative, taking into consideration the specific disability and activities the individual may need help with to determine the appropriate level of care (for example, if the individual needs help with self-care or transportation assistance). With services, eligibility criteria may have two objectives: to restrict eligibility in order to ration scarce resources and to ensure that the needs of the disabled person are met by finding the best match with available services (Waddington 2018).

An integrated approach to the provision of adequate social services and assistance to persons with disabilities (PWD) would entail a package of benefits and services, including income support, rehabilitation, skills development, and social-productive inclusion. The main shortcoming observed in most countries is program fragmentation. Social insurance and social assistance are typically responsible to provide income support. There are usually weak links to rehabilitation programs, which tend to be limited in size in middle- to low-income countries and delivered by different agencies. Similarly, programs to develop skills and support people with disabilities getting into jobs are also frequently in parallel through separate interventions, again with weak links to income support and rehabilitation programs. Ideally, countries should develop an integrated approach for an entire array of programs such as the ones described in table 5.3.

Table 5.3 Integrated Approach for Determining Benefit and Service Packages for People with Disabilities

Objective	Description	Expected outcomes
Income support	Social insurance programs provide income replacement to insured workers who become disabled, and social assistance or social pensions provide categorical income support to poorer PWD.	Adequate income support Well targeted (minimize exclusion and inclusion errors) Sustainable (adequate funding provision, clear determination of costs)
Rehabilitation	Rehabilitation is sometimes linked to income support programs, eventually supporting social inclusion and labor market reinsertion. Too often narrowly focused on physical rehabilitation and medical aid devices.	From physical to functional rehabilitation in order to access jobs
Skills development	These programs should be a natural complement to inclusive education, supporting access to education and jobs for children and youth with disabilities to improve their life and work opportunities.	Increased number of PWD with skills to perform jobs according to their functional abilities
Employment opportunities	Access to jobs is provided and the employment of PWD is encouraged through enforcement of quotas or incentives.	Increased number of PWD in jobs
Social services	Programs go beyond income support, providing, for example, day care centers, sport and cultural programs, and social activities in general to promote social inclusion.	Full integration of PWD in society Provide support for participation in activities of daily living, and particularly to aid life-cycle transitions (e.g., infant to school-age; primary into tertiary education; school to employment; post-acute disability return to employment; elder care)

Source: Original table for this publication.
Note: PWD = people with disabilities.

5.4 NOTIFICATION AND ONBOARDING

Although much of the enrollment stage of the delivery chain relates to decisions, there are some process steps, including notification and onboarding. Both involve client-facing actions (in person, by mail, or online) and are enabled by communication.

Notification is straightforward but often neglected. The basic principle is that everyone should be notified of enrollment decisions, regardless of whether they are beneficiaries, wait-listed, or deemed ineligible. This step is often skipped in administrator-driven systems, since households are registered but do not officially apply (and since there is often a significant lapse in time between the time of registration and the time of eligibility and enrollment decisions). *In many countries, only beneficiaries are formally notified. That leaves people wondering about their status and undermines credibility and transparency.* The content of notifications will vary depending on whether someone is enrolled, wait-listed, or ineligible. For those who are wait-listed or deemed ineligible, the notification should include the basis for the decision as well as instructions for filing grievances and appeals. At a minimum, notifications should indicate the decision; what the beneficiary will receive; when, where, and how they will receive it; rights and responsibilities; contact points and information; and next steps. Additional information for onboarding is discussed below. Other aspects of notification steps include (1) institutional responsibilities for executing the notification; (2) communication channels to be used (in person, formal letter, email, updating of status on online account, etc.); and (3) quality standards.

Onboarding can be conducted via various modalities, depending on the program and operating model. The objectives of onboarding are to orient, integrate, and prepare new beneficiaries for participation in program(s). At this point, beneficiaries need to have a more detailed and operational understanding of how the program works; who to contact; where and how to get benefits and services (payment points, payment providers, and channels, or service providers); payment and service provision schedules; the timing and location of any monitoring meetings; their rights, roles, and responsibilities; where and how to file grievances; and so on. There are various modalities for onboarding, and some are used in combination, including the following:

- ***Printed communications***, including onboarding kits and materials, in addition to the notification itself. The beneficiary kit may also include distribution of electronic benefit cards, passbooks or logbooks for monitoring, and other program materials. They may also include the printed version of the signed IAP. Simple distribution of printed media and beneficiary kits without in-person onboarding involves less effort but relies on the beneficiaries being literate in the language of the printed matter.
- ***In-person one-on-one meetings*** to explain how the program operates, its expectations, the beneficiary's rights and responsibilities, and so on. Meetings sometimes also involve finalizing and signing IAPs. One-on-one meetings are mainly used for on-demand programs because beneficiaries enter the system at different times.
- ***Group orientation sessions*** are commonly used with programs that use administrator-driven approaches to intake and registration because beneficiaries are enrolled as a cohort at the same starting point. Examples of group onboarding sessions are discussed in box 5.9 for Malawi's Social Cash Transfer Program and Indonesia's CCT program.

In addition to orienting beneficiaries about the program, onboarding also typically includes collecting additional information that is needed for program operations. Such information may include a photo (for program or functional ID), cell phone number, bank account or e-wallet information, consent forms signed by the beneficiaries (or designated recipient), and so on. With CCTs, the program would also collect information on health care facilities as well as school assignments for each relevant family member, which is critical for monitoring compliance with conditionalities, as discussed in chapter 8.

In conclusion, the outputs of the enrollment stage result in updating the beneficiary operations management system. The enrollment stage encompasses many decisions (eligibility, enrollment, and benefit/service package) and some processes (notification and onboarding). The outputs of this phase include notifying all registrants, onboarding all beneficiaries, and establishing or updating the roster of beneficiaries in the beneficiary registry. This roster then feeds into either the payroll (for benefits) or the listing of beneficiaries and their assigned services.

Box 5.9 Group Onboarding Sessions for Social Assistance Programs: Examples from Malawi and Indonesia

Social assistance programs often carry out group onboarding sessions when beneficiaries are enrolled (or recertified) as a cohort at the same starting point. These are sometimes carried out simultaneously with enrollment. They are critical to ensure that beneficiaries understand their rights, roles, responsibilities, and so on. Two examples follow:

- **Malawi's Social Cash Transfer Program (SCTP).** Community meetings are held to enroll, announce, and onboard the final list of selected beneficiaries (within the 10 percent eligible threshold). The community social agents organize the community meeting. They remind the community of the processes that were used for registration and selection, including the community's role in prioritizing who would be registered and validating results of the assessment. They also explain that the program only has budget to accept those families ranked within the poorest 10 percent (relative threshold) who do not have able-bodied adults (filter). They then call out the names of those who were selected and proceed with the enrollment and onboarding activities which include confirming the designated recipient, verifying their IDs, taking their photos for a program ID, and explaining how the process will work for payments, and so on.
- **Indonesia's Conditional Cash Transfer Program (PKH).** After the beneficiaries are selected (those in the poorest 16 percent of the ranking of registered households) the district coordinators work with the facilitators and operators to determine the distribution of beneficiaries based on the facilitators' work area (to distribute the caseload). The facilitators then coordinate with the subdistrict and village officers to organize an initial onboarding meeting. The objectives of that meeting include (1) explaining the objectives and rules of the program; (2) disseminating information on the program, data validation, and PKH participation requirements; (3) explaining conditionalities (called "commitments") under the program (education, health, and participation in Family Development Sessions); (4) explaining the consequences for noncompliance; (5) explaining grievance redress mechanism procedures and listening to complaints; (6) explaining the rights and obligations of the designated recipients (women); (7) asking designated recipients to sign a letter of willingness to honor the conditionalities; (8) explaining the payments schedule, the schedule for health care visits, and school enrollment. If beneficiary families cannot attend the meeting, the facilitator must visit their house after the meeting and explain the same information.

Sources: Malawi's SCTP; Indonesia's PKH operational manual; observations and field visits by Kathy Lindert.

5.5 INSTITUTIONAL ARRANGEMENTS AND INFORMATION SYSTEMS

Institutional Arrangements

Institutional arrangements for the enrollment stage vary greatly across countries, programs, and operating models. Across countries, key influences on the arrangement include the degree and type of decentralization, administrative capacity, and the assigning of roles and responsibilities to central and local actors (as discussed in chapter 2). Variations among programs center around the type of program (benefit, service, or integrated), the target group (demographic, socioeconomic, unemployed, disabled, or those with social needs and risks), and other program-specific factors. Finally, the operating models may vary, for example between single-program and integrated approaches, and between on-demand and administrator-driven approaches.

It is important to identify the actor who will have decision-making power. In many programs, particularly for benefits, decisions regarding eligibility and enrollment are centralized, even if intake, registration, assessment, and onboarding are local. This has the advantage of relieving local actors of the pressures inherent in making such decisions and ensuring that eligibility criteria are applied evenly across the population. In other programs, such decision making is local, particularly for services. Another factor for services is whether the decision lies with the referring or the referred service. The referring caseworker may seek to offer a service to beneficiaries, but the referred service may not have available slots. Finally, another aspect of the decision-making point is the associated point for grievances and appeals, as discussed in chapter 8.

Institutional arrangements for the enrollment stage may differ from those for the assessment stage. This is the case with social registries; one agency may implement intake, registration, and assessment for many programs, and then those programs—which may be managed by the same agency or by other agencies—have their own institutional mandate and jurisdiction over eligibility and enrollment decisions.

Information Systems

Information systems act as an invisible engine, intermediating between people on the one hand and institutions on the other hand, interacting all along the delivery chain. Beneficiary operations management systems and the databases underpinning those systems, the so-called "beneficiary registries," are a core component of integrated social information systems, as described in chapter 2.

Many countries develop stand-alone systems for each social program, to automate processes for managing the operations of social programs. Ideally these information systems are designed and operated as cohesive, dynamic, and modular systems with feedback loops. The systems that automate these processes are sometimes referred to as "Program MIS." In the Sourcebook, we use the term "beneficiary operations management systems (BOMS)" to refer to information systems that automate functional processes and support decisions on eligibility determination, enrollment, level of benefits/service package, and underpin program administration. We also use the term "integrated beneficiary registries" to refer to the underlying databases of information on beneficiaries managed by each social program. Integrated beneficiary registries are data analytics platforms that provide information on "who receives what" benefits, and help pinpoint duplications, gaps, and overlaps across social programs (figure 5.5).

Beneficiary operations management systems support several processes along the delivery chain, focusing on the enrollment, provision, and management stages. They are built to support the implementation of a single

Figure 5.5 Functional Modules of Beneficiary Operations Management Systems

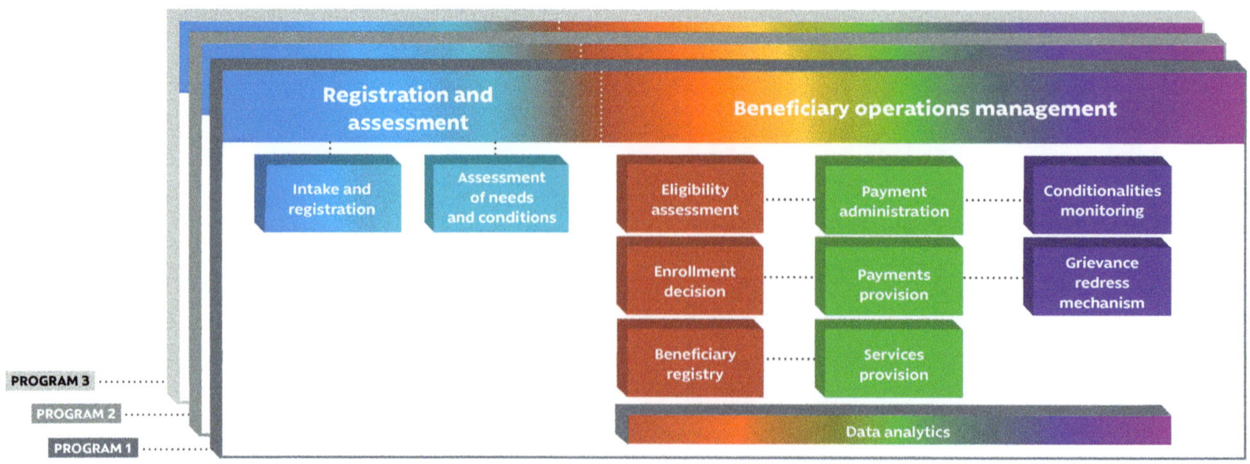

Source: World Bank, forthcoming: "Interagency Social Protection Assessment (ISPA) Tool on Integrated Social Information Systems," World Bank, Washington, DC. See also figure 2.5 in chapter 2.

program, though they can sometimes support multiple programs. They may be designed as a modular, micro-services architecture focusing on different processes or functions. In addition to the decision processes for eligibility determination and enrollment, these systems also underpin the functions of payments administration (covered in chapter 6), and the functions of beneficiary operations management (covered in chapter 8), as well as performance measurement (covered in chapter 9). These downstream functions are also covered below, given the inherent challenge of splitting systems up into component parts and distributing them across various chapters corresponding to the delivery chain.

- ***Decision processes on eligibility determination, enrollment, and determination of benefit levels and/or service packages.*** Through enrollment, eligible applicants become beneficiaries, based on eligibility criteria established by each program. The beneficiary operations management system supports the generation of a list of beneficiaries as well of beneficiary ID cards (see chapter 8 discussion of beneficiary data management). It also supports the decision on benefit levels and/or service packages according to program rules.
- ***Payments administration processes including reconciliation.*** The beneficiary operations management system generates lists of beneficiaries to be paid with their respective benefit amounts. After a payment session is finalized, the system also supports the process of reconciliation by receiving data on actual payments made and actual amounts disbursed. (See chapter 6.)
- ***Beneficiary data management processes.*** This includes: updating and rectification of information, such as changes in household composition (births, deaths, or members entering or leaving the household), monitoring the delivery of benefits and services, and managing grievances, as well as managing exit decisions.
- ***Monitoring of conditionalities or of participation in accompanying measures.*** If the program includes conditionalities (usually related to health and education), the beneficiary operations management system stores data on compliance with those conditionalities. BOMS also support the processes related to the consequences of lack of compliance, which could result in the household receiving a notification or warning, or in the reduction or termination of benefits being received by the household. If the program includes accompanying measures (such as sessions on nutrition and early childhood development, or household visits), the system will store data on participation in these sessions. (See chapter 8.)
- ***Dashboard for data analytics.*** Beneficiary operations management systems are also able to generate, aggregate, and analyze data which is useful for the overall monitoring of a program, as well as for general policy analysis and strategic vision support for social programs. These systems can generate basic monitoring indicators. (See chapter 9.)

Data in Beneficiary Operations Management Systems

Beneficiary operations management systems collect, store, and process program-specific monitoring data, in addition to basic household data. This can include data on the designated recipient of benefits and services within the household, the level of benefits, delivery of benefits and services, schedule of payments, monitoring of compliance with conditionalities or participation in accompanying measures, household visits, and grievances.

Integration of Data from Various Social Programs

As different social protection programs are created or scaled up, operating separate information systems for each program creates inefficiencies due to fragmentation. These can cause a burden for people who try to access them, administrators, and caseworkers, as well as social, planning, and finance agencies. When these systems operate in parallel, they support several of the functions listed above, including modules that support eligibility determination, enrollment, determination of the package of benefits and services, and payments administration. This implies duplication of functions and lack of integration across systems, with multiple parallel systems supporting the same functions.

Fragmentation can be frustrating, costly, and inefficient. Integrating data from various beneficiary operations management systems that support individual social programs within integrated beneficiary registries can help address many of these challenges for people, program administrators, and social programs (table 5.4).

Integrated beneficiary registries provide a useful "back-office" tool for coordination, monitoring, planning, analytics, and efficiency of benefits administration. Integrated beneficiary registries allow for monitoring and coordination of "who receives what benefits," and for identifying intended or unintended duplications across programs. Since integrated beneficiary registries link information on beneficiaries of social programs, they can be a signal of the potential "supply" of social programs. An integrated beneficiary registry operates as a data warehouse that collects information from different social programs and their benefits administration systems, such as the number and characteristics of beneficiaries, value, expenditure on social programs, and performance of programs, such as the frequency of payments/transfers, speed or cycle-time of key processes, and number of complaints received and resolved.[6] It allows for cross-checks using interoperability mechanisms between separate stand-alone benefits administration systems and other administrative information systems such as income tax, and civil registration, as well as the social registry. It allows for monitoring and reporting on that information, and disaggregation by geographic location. Such analytics on the various programs would not only be useful to the government, but also to

Table 5.4 Integrating Data from Social Programs in Light of Challenges of Fragmentation

	Challenges of fragmentation of social programs	Benefits of integrated beneficiary registries
For people	• Have to go to multiple offices for separate social programs • Long wait times • Provide the same documents over and over • Face the frustration of complicated bureaucracy • May miss opportunities, benefits, and services • Time and travel costs for service provision and payments	If maintained in real time: • Allowing people to check their benefit status and service referrals
For program administrators	• Complex myriad of program rules • Heavy administrative burden and high costs • Duplications in processes • Lack information on what other benefits and services are being provided • Not knowing which cases to prioritize	If maintained in real time: • Providing administrators information about what other benefits and services their client populations are receiving • Facilitating intermediation and referrals
For social planning and finance agencies	• Fragmented and uncoordinated programs in different institutions • Programs do not share information—risks duplication and wastes public resources • Inadequate administrative capacity • Inadequate financing versus demand for social assistance • Poor infrastructure and insecurity in some areas hinder delivery (eligibility assessment, payments, monitoring) • Programs are short lived and have limited reach • Lack information on - Profile of needs and conditions of population - Who benefits from which programs - Gaps and duplications in coverage - Potential synergies in bundles of benefits and services - Where does the money go? - How to leverage programs in times of crisis	• Coordination • Monitoring who receives which programs • Identifying complementary bundles of benefits and services • Identifying unintended duplications across programs • Analyzing and tracking the "supply" of programs • Monitoring, analytics, budgeting, and planning

Sources: Lindert and Karippacheril, SP Delivery Systems Presentation, Core Course 2016–18 and presentation on SP systems at Bonn Symposium, 2016.

clients for better transparency on the performance and management of social assistance programs. One example is Kenya's Single Registry system. The country disposes of several social safety net programs, including (1) the Cash Transfer Program for Orphans and Vulnerable Children, (2) the Older Persons Cash Transfer Program, (3) the Persons with Severe Disability Cash Transfer, (4) the Hunger Safety Net Program, and (5) the World Food Programme's Cash for Assets program. Kenya has consolidated these programs by creating an integrated beneficiary registry for social protection with a view to reducing overlap across programs and providing accurate analytical reports on the social protection sector. An integrated information system has also been developed for three of the four cash transfer programs. Prior to developing that system, three cash transfer programs managed under the same ministry had developed parallel software applications, databases, and information and communications technology (ICT) infrastructure for management of information on beneficiaries, benefits administration, and payments. Frontline social workers responsible for these programs relied on separate software applications. A gradual process of consolidation of those programs entailed the harmonization of the front-office software applications to have a similar look and feel, although their database components are all still separate. Eventually, those databases were consolidated by means of a data warehouse that serves as an integrated beneficiary registry, which is now called the Single Registry. The Single Registry has allowed efficient program monitoring, reduced double registration, increased transparency and accountability, promoted the efficient transfer of data, and enhanced the quality of operations.

Interestingly, many countries operate *either* a social registry *or* an integrated beneficiary registry.

- ***Some countries with social registries lack integrated beneficiary registries.*** Many countries have focused their efforts on developing social registries as tools for managing the "gateway" for consideration of eligibility of social programs. However, they do not link information on actual beneficiaries across social programs, particularly when those programs are managed by multiple agencies. In other words, they have not developed integrated beneficiary registry systems—and thus lack the ability to monitor and coordinate "who receives what benefits," and to identify intended or unintended duplications across programs. One example is Brazil. While the Cadastro Único social registry serves as a common gateway for some 30 social programs aimed at serving the poor and low-income groups, Brazil does not operate an integrated beneficiary registry that would allow it to coordinate and monitor benefits across these programs, particularly across the programs that are outside the Ministry of Social and Agrarian Development (MDSA). It thus has no way of tracking "who gets what" across programs managed by different agencies, even if they all use the common gateway of the Cadastro Único.
- ***Other countries have developed integrated beneficiary registries (figure 5.6), but do not operate social registries.*** Other countries have focused their efforts on the creation and integration of beneficiary registries to support benefits administration and coordination, but without developing social registries. As discussed earlier, Kenya has developed its Single Registry to consolidate beneficiary registries, as discussed above. Some countries (or programs) do not record information on all potential beneficiaries (registrants or applicants) of a social program. Rather, programs gather information only on beneficiaries, on the basis of enrollment decisions

Figure 5.6 Integrated Beneficiary Registries

Source: Original figure for this publication.

that are taken "outside the system." For example, with community-based targeting mechanisms, communities or local councils frequently make enrollment decisions without recording information on all potential beneficiaries. Instead, once these enrollment decisions are made, information on beneficiaries is recorded in beneficiary operations management systems. Efforts have then focused on consolidating these beneficiary registries into integrated beneficiary registries for greater coordination across programs. However, without social registries—which support intake and registration and determination of potential eligibility for all applicants—these systems lack social accountability mechanisms such as grievance redress systems to handle appeals for those individuals or households who are excluded from social programs (potentially eligible non-beneficiaries). Another example of countries with integrated beneficiary registries but not social registries is Vietnam, which has developed POSASOFT, an integrated beneficiary registry.

5.6 SOME CONCLUDING POINTS

This chapter has reviewed the enrollment stage of the delivery chain, which involves the different criteria used for determining which registrants qualify for programs, enrollment decisions based on eligibility criteria and available budget, and determining the benefit and services package as well as notifying and onboarding beneficiaries.

The challenges of coordination and inclusion become particularly relevant in the eligibility and enrollment stage. Coordination across different agencies and programs is key in order to determine the right benefit and service package for each individual, family, or household. The use of an integrated approach that bundles multiple benefits and services together offers opportunities for coordination. The challenge of inclusion is related to the types of eligibility criteria used (for example, the use of relative thresholds and rankings inhibit the principle of dynamic inclusion) and to enrollment decisions which, in the context of limited budget, can lead to the enrollment of only a fraction of the eligible population, resulting in the creation of waitlists.

The eligibility and enrollment stage also involves certain tensions and implementation challenges:

- Eligibility criteria and benefits menus affect implementation not only for these decision phases of the delivery chain but also for other parts of the chain:
  - Eligibility criteria and benefit structures influence the information that needs to be collected at the intake and registration phase. Some types of information may be hard to gather and document, such as the reason an unemployed worker was dismissed, or to what degree someone is affected by a disability.
  - Criteria may also affect the choice of operating model. For example, relative rankings and eligibility thresholds are commonly used in administrator-driven models but are not compatible with on-demand systems.
- There can be tensions between the design and implementation of eligibility criteria and benefits menus. A multiplicity of program objectives can require more complex design, but simplicity can facilitate the implementation of the program.
  - On one end of the spectrum, flat benefits are simpler to administer but are not as well tailored to various program objectives.
  - On the other end of the spectrum, complex eligibility criteria and benefits menus in GMI programs are used with the objectives of ensuring a minimum level of income for everyone and giving priority to the poorest households. However, the design features associated with those objectives can add complexity to some aspects of implementation.
- When programs have insufficient slots due to lack of capacity or funding, not everyone who is eligible may be enrolled. Programs use a variety of methods to manage demand in the face of budget constraints. Examples include waiting lists, random selection among eligible participants, enrollment in programs based on the order in which candidates applied, and caseworker's discretion based on profiling (for example, for services).
- Notification and onboarding are sometimes a neglected phase in the enrollment stage of the delivery chain. All registrants should be informed in a timely manner whether they are eligible or ineligible, and enrolled or wait-listed for programs as appropriate.

Beneficiaries (those who are eligible and enrolled) should also receive orientation and onboarding to prepare them to participate in programs.

In sum, several factors promote the effective and efficient implementation of eligibility criteria, enrollment decisions, determination of the benefit and service package, and notification and onboarding:

- Determining eligibility by applying program-specific criteria
- Clear rules for determining enrollment and establishing wait-lists in resource-constrained contexts
- Determining the right benefit and service package based on clear benefits menus, as well as available services
- Notifying registrants of their status within a reasonable period after application
- Providing a comprehensive onboarding program, including general information about the program and beneficiaries' rights and responsibilities

ANNEX 5A: EXAMPLES OF ELIGIBILITY CRITERIA AND BENEFIT STRUCTURES FOR VARIOUS TYPES OF PROGRAMS

Table 5A.1 Benefit Structures for Demographic-Categorical Programs: Old-Age Social Pensions and Family/Child Allowances

Program and agency	Eligibility criteria	Benefit structures per individual	
		Benefit calculation	Duration/time limit

Argentina Old Age Social Pension Current law 2016; Ministry of Social Development oversees the social assistance programs. National Pension Commission administers the social assistance pension programs.	**Demographic criteria:** Age 70+. Naturalized citizens must have at least five years of residence immediately before claiming the pension; foreign residents, at least 40 years. **Means-tested:** Income and assets below a subsistence level and not receiving any social security benefits or nutritional support from family members.	**Flat benefit:** 70% of the minimum monthly old-age pension (basic old-age pension, compensatory pension, and additional pension) is paid. **Benefit adjustment:** Benefits are adjusted when the minimum old-age pension is adjusted.	Death of beneficiary.
Brazil Old-Age Social Pension (Benefício de Prestação Continuada—BPC) Since 1993; National Social Security Institute administers benefits.	**Demographic criteria:** Age 65+. **Employment status:** Not gainfully employed. **Means-tested:** With monthly household income of less than 25% of the legal monthly minimum wage per person.	**Flat benefit = MW:** The monthly benefit is the legal monthly minimum wage. **Benefit adjustment:** Benefits are adjusted annually according to changes in the minimum wage.	Death; eligibility is reviewed every two years.
Bulgaria Old Age Social Pension Since 1924, current laws in 2000s; Ministry of Labor and Social Policy.	**Demographic criteria:** Age 70+ (age 65+ if living alone). **Income test:** Family income in the last 12 months must not exceed 12 times the guaranteed monthly minimum income for each family member.	**Flat benefit:** Fixed amount per month.	Death of beneficiary.

continued

Table 5A.1 *(continued)*

<table>
<tr><th rowspan="2">Program and agency</th><th rowspan="2">Eligibility criteria</th><th colspan="2">Benefit structures per individual</th></tr>
<tr><th>Benefit calculation</th><th>Duration/time limit</th></tr>
<tr><td>Bulgaria Various Family, Child Allowances

Since 1942, current law 2002; Social Assistance Agency of the Ministry of Labor and Social Assistance administers the program.</td><td>Birth grant (universal): Paid for each live birth regardless of family income.

Pregnancy grant (income tested with absolute threshold): Paid to non-insured women 45 days before the expected birth, provided the monthly income for each family member is not greater than absolute threshold.

Family allowance (demographic and income tested with absolute threshold): Paid for children attending school (from age 7 to age 20) who are not in specialized childcare institutions. Income test: Monthly income for each family member must not exceed absolute threshold (except if the child is permanently disabled).

Disability supplement: Paid for a child with a disability who is not in a specialized childcare institution.

Child-raising allowance (demographic and income tested with absolute threshold): Paid to a person caring for a child younger than age 1 (age 2 if disabled) who is not receiving maternity benefits. The child must not be in a specialized childcare institution. Income test: Monthly income for each family member must not exceed absolute threshold (except if the child is disabled).</td><td>Birth grant, varies by birth order: Fixed amount for birth of first, second, third child and each additional child. Additional amount for birth of child with disability.

Pregnancy grant,flat benefit: Flat lump sum payment.

Family allowance, varies by birth order: Fixed amount for first, second, third, fourth, additional children.

Benefits are doubled for children with disabilities.

Disability supplement, variable benefits: Specific amounts within a range for each eligible child, depending on the degree of disability.

Child-raising allowance, flat Benefit: Fixed amount per child.</td><td>Aging-out of eligible children.</td></tr>
<tr><td>Georgia Old-Age Social Pension

Since 1956; Ministry of Labor, Health, and Social Affairs oversees the program. Social Services Agency administers the program, with regional and local SSA offices (one-stop shops/service centers).</td><td>Demographic criteria: Age 70+ (men) or age 65+ (women). The pension is paid to an individual or to a family without other means of support.</td><td>Flat benefit: Social pension (old-age), fixed amount per month.

Benefit adjustment: Benefits are adjusted on an ad hoc basis.</td><td>Death of beneficiary.</td></tr>
</table>

continued

Table 5A.1 *(continued)*

Program and agency	Eligibility criteria	Benefit structures per individual	
		Benefit calculation	Duration/time limit
Greece Child Allowances (child-support benefits) First and current laws: 1958, 1999, 2012, 2013, 2014, and 2018; Ministry of Labor and Social Security oversees. Organization of Welfare Benefits and Social Solidarity (OPEKA) administers the program.	**Demographic/legal criteria:** Children <18 (<24 if student or disabled); must be unmarried residents of Greece. **Income test with absolute thresholds depending on HH size:** Annual family income for families with one child <€26,500; <€30,000 with two children; <€33,750 with three children; plus €1,500 added to threshold for each additional child.	**Variable benefits:** Up to €70 a month is paid for the first and second child, up to €140 for the third and any dependent child beyond the third one, depending on income and family situation.	Aging out of eligible children.
Kenya National Safety Net Program Since 2013; Ministry of Labor and Social Protection.	**Demographic categorization and prioritization:** HHs with OVCs; child-headed HHs. Older people and people with severe disability are prioritized. **Socioeconomic with PMT/relative rankings:** Extremely poor HHs. Three-stage targeting: geographic (prevalence of poverty); community prioritization; PMT rankings with community validation. **Receipt of other benefits:** HH must not be enrolled in other cash transfer programs.	**Flat benefit:** Per month, paid on bi-monthly basis.	When child no longer resides with the family, or ages out (turns 18); death of beneficiary.
Kyrgyz Republic Old-Age Social Allowance Since 1922; Social Fund administers pensions.	**Demographic criteria:** Age 65+ (men) and 60+ (women), 2 years above the normal retirement age. **No other coverage**: Persons who are not eligible for an old-age insurance pension.	**Flat benefit:** Fixed monthly amount.	Death of beneficiary.
Mauritius Basic Universal Old-Age Social Pension Since 1976; Ministry of Social Security, National Solidarity, and Reform Institutions.	**Demographic/legal criteria:** Age 60+; Mauritian nationals must have resided in Mauritius for >12 years after age 18. There is no residence requirement if aged 70 or older. Noncitizens must have resided in the country for >15 years since age 40, including the three years immediately before the claim is made. **Employment status:** Retirement is not necessary. **Specialized criteria/disability status:** Constant-attendance allowance: Paid to beneficiaries of the basic old-age pension who are assessed with at least a 60% disability and require the constant attendance of others to perform daily functions.	**Variable benefits by age category:** Fixed amount for those ages 60–89; higher for those ages 90–99; higher for those ages 100+. **Flat benefit:** For constant-attendance allowance (caregiver allowance).	Death of beneficiary.

continued

Table 5A.1 *(continued)*

Program and agency	Eligibility criteria	Benefit structures per individual	
		Benefit calculation	Duration/time limit
Moldova Old-Age Social Pension Since 1956, current law 1999; Ministry of Health, Labor, and Social Protection is responsible for social security policy. National Office of Social Insurance administers the programs.	**Demographic criteria:** Age 62 years and 4 months (men, gradually rising to age 63 by 2019) or age 57 years and 6 months (women, gradually rising to age 63 by 2028). **No other coverage:** Individuals who do not meet the coverage requirements for a social insurance old-age pension.	**Flat benefit:** Per month. **Benefit adjustment**: Benefits are adjusted in April based on changes in consumer prices in the previous year.	Death of beneficiary.
Moldova, Birth and Child Allowances First law 1977; current laws 1992 (children), 1993 (children and family protection), and 2002 (family allowances); Ministry of Health, Labor, and Social Protection coordinates and supervises the program. National Office of Social Insurance administers the program.	**Birth grant (universal):** Paid for each live birth, regardless of family income. **Childcare allowance:** Paid to a person caring for a child younger than age 2 who does not meet the contribution requirements for the social insurance childcare allowance.	**Birth grant**: Lump sum for each child. An additional grant is paid for multiple births or the adoption of two children at the same time. **Childcare allowance**: Per month.	Aging out of child (after age 2).
South Africa Old-Age Social Pension Since 2004; South African Social Security Agency administers the program.	**Demographic criteria:** Age 60+. **Means test (income and assets) with absolute eligibility thresholds:** Annual income must be <R 73,800 for single person or <R 147,600 for couple; and assets must be <R 1,056,000 for single person or <R 2,112,000 for couple. **Specialized criteria:** Eligibility for constant-attendance allowance: Person requires constant attendance of others to perform daily functions. **Receipt of other benefits:** Beneficiaries may receive only one social grant at a time.	**Variable benefits by age category:** Fixed amount/month for those ages 60–74; higher for those ages 75+. Benefit is reduced for those in institutional care >3 months. **Flat benefit:** For constant-attendance allowance (caregiver allowance).	Death of beneficiary.

continued

Table 5A.1 *(continued)*

Program and agency	Eligibility criteria	Benefit structures per individual: Benefit calculation	Benefit structures per individual: Duration/time limit
South Africa Social Assistance for Vulnerable Children Since 2004; South African Social Security Agency administers the program.	**Categorical and legal, foster child grant:** Paid to person caring for a foster child age 18 or younger (age 21 if a student). There must be a court order indicating the foster care status of the child. **Categorical + means-tested, child support grant:** Paid to the primary caregiver of a child age 18 or younger for up to six biologically unrelated children (no limit for biologically related children). The primary caregiver must be age 16 or older. Means test: Annual income must be less than 45,600 rand for single person; less than 91,200 rand for a couple. **Categorical + means-tested + disability, care dependency grant:** Paid to a parent, foster parent, or primary caregiver of a child age 18 or younger who requires permanent care or support services as the result of a severe mental or physical disability. The child must be cared for at home and the disability confirmed by a medical assessment. Means test: Annual income must be less than 192,000 rand for a single person; 384,000 rand for a couple. The foster child grant is not considered income in the means test.	**Flat benefits:** Per eligible child.	Aging out of the foster child.

Sources: Social Security Administration with the International Social Security Administration (ISSA), https://www.ssa.gov/policy/docs/progdesc/ssptw/2016, 2017, 2018, depending on country and region. Some information also derived from socialprotection.org program inventory, http://socialprotection.org/discover/programme/search, supplemented by country-specific government sources in some instances.

Note: HH = household; MW = minimum wage; OVC = orphans and vulnerable children; PMT = proxy means testing; SSA = Social Service Agency.

Table 5A.2 Benefit Structures for Poverty-Targeted Programs

Program and agency	Eligibility criteria	Conditionalities	Benefit structures per family or household	
			Benefit calculation	Duration/ time limit

Brazil Bolsa Família Program (CCT) Since 2003; managed by Ministry of Social Development and Agrarian Development (MDSA) with decentralized responsibilities implemented by municipal offices.	**Absolute thresholds applied to means test:** Extreme poor (XP) = those with per capita incomes less than R$89; moderate poor (MP) = those with per capita incomes less than R$178. **Other criteria:** Age, gender, pregnancy of family members.	School attendance >85% time for ages 6-15. School attendance >75% time for ages 16-17. Health: Schedule of health visits and vaccines as per MoH for pregnant/ lactating women and for children ages 0-6. (See chapter 8.)	**Benefit menu:** Differentiated in various ways according to household size, composition, and poverty group. **Flat base benefit for extreme poor:** R$89 for the XP (with incomes less than R$89). **Variable benefits based on HH composition:** For MP and XP: Children ages 6-15, R$41; ages 0-6, R$41; ages 16-17 (maximum of two family members in this category), R$48. Pregnant/lactating women: R$41. **Variable GMI-style benefit for the extreme poor:** Variable GMI benefit = value of R$89 - their reported incomes.	None; must be reassessed every two years.

continued

Table 5A.2 *(continued)*

Program and agency	Eligibility criteria	Conditionalities	Benefit structures per family or household	
			Benefit calculation	Duration/ time limit
Bulgaria Guaranteed Minimum Income (GMI) Since 1942, current law 2002; Social Assistance Agency of the Ministry of Labor and Social Assistance administers the program.	**Legal criteria:** Bulgarian citizens and permanent residents or those with asylum/refugee status. **Income test with absolute thresholds:** Monthly per capita family net income must not exceed the differentiated minimum income DMI, which is set as a social coefficient (%) of GMI. The social coefficient (%) varies depending on characteristics of each HH member. GMI = fixed level of monthly income Lev 75 (as of 2017). *Income* is defined as all the money from pensions, wages, rents, leases, child benefits, maintenance payments, and so on. **Asset filters:** Maximum one residence; maximum 1 room/person; no movable and immovable property that can generate income beyond usual needs of family (e.g., land, farm equipment, etc.); should not be registered as sole traders/owners of a company; certain financial assets; should not have sold a summer house or second property in past five years, and so on. **Exclusion filters for categories of people:** Such as adults up to age 30 cohabiting with parents, some categories of students, and so on.	Working-age able-bodied adults:[a] must be registered with the Labor Directorate at least 6 months before applying for social assistance; must not refuse proposed work or involvement in literacy training, vocational qualification or keyword competencies, or other employment services. Education: School attendance for beneficiary children. Health: Vaccine records for school-age children.	**Variable-GMI based on income, HH size, and composition:** The GMI allowance equals the difference between the differentiated monthly income (DMI) and the actual monthly family income (benefit is paid monthly). The DMI is calculated as a social coefficient (%) multiplied by the fixed GMI level (Lev 75 as of 2017). The specific social coefficients (%) are assigned to individuals or individual family members according to demographic categories. Benefits are calculated for each individual in the family; those meeting criteria for more than one category are entitled to the most favorable percentages. The amount of the monthly benefit = DMI – income from previous month.	Unlimited duration but must be reassessed periodically.

continued

Table 5A.2 *(continued)*

Program and agency	Eligibility criteria	Conditionalities	Benefit structures per family or household: Benefit calculation	Benefit structures per family or household: Duration/ time limit
Colombia Familias en Acción (FA-CCT) Since 2000; Social Prosperity Department.	**Absolute thresholds applied to PMT scores:** Eligible depending on PMT score within specific cut-off ranges for each region—based on SISBEN (social registry) and determined by the program in coordination with the Planning Department (DNP). **Demographic:** Must have children <18.	School attendance >80% for ages 5–18. Health visits for children under age 6. (See chapter 8.)	**Variable benefit depending on HH size,composition, and geographic location:** Benefit varies depending on region and school grade.	No time limit; periodic recertification.
Croatia Guaranteed Minimum Income (GMI) Since 1949 (first law), current law since 2015; Ministry for Demography, Family, Youth, and Social Policy provides general legal supervision. Social Welfare Centers administers the guaranteed minimum income program through regional offices.	**Legal:** Citizens and permanent residents of Croatia; and certain foreign citizens with temporary residence. **Means/asset-tested with absolute thresholds:** Paid to families and persons with low or no income. The income test is based on individual or family income and property.	Unemployed persons must be registered at an employment office, and be capable of, and available for, work. Must accept work offers, regardless of qualifications or experience (including seasonal or temporary jobs)—if refuse job offer, benefits are suspended.[b]	**Variable benefits depending on HH size and composition:** Calculated as a percentage of the guaranteed monthly income level (800 kunas in 2017). The benefit is calculated as 60% of the GMI level for an adult; 115% for a disabled single person; 100% for a non-disabled single parent; 40% for a child; and 55% for a child living in a single-parent family. **Maximum cap:** The maximum monthly benefit is the gross monthly minimum wage. The gross monthly minimum wage is 3,275 kunas (2017).	No time limit, except for those capable of work who may claim for only 24 months and are not allowed to reapply for a period of three months (but entitlement for other family members is maintained).

continued

Table 5A.2 *(continued)*

Program and agency	Eligibility criteria	Conditionalities	Benefit structures per family or household	
			Benefit calculation	Duration/ time limit
Greece Guaranteed Minimum Income (GMI) Since 2015; Ministry of Labour, Social Insurance, and Social Solidarity monitors the implementation and evaluation. The Electronic Governance of the Social Insurance (I.DI.K.A) supports information systems. OAED (employment office) supports labor links.	**Legal:** Resident of Greece. **Income testing with absolute threshold:** Income for 6 months prior to application cannot exceed the maximum-support threshold depending on HH size: €200/month for one-person HH, €100/month for each additional adult; €50/month for each minor child. Incomes = total gross income of all types, all benefits and other support received. Not counted as income: 20% of net income from salaried services; all noncontributory disability benefits. Earnings disregards: When adult beneficiaries find a job, the following income is disregarded: 100% of salary for first month; 40% of salary for next 2 months. **Asset values and filters:** Value of immovable property, movable property, and financial assets over specified thresholds; possession of specific assets (private recreational boats, aircraft, helicopters, gliders, swimming pools). (If any criteria are not met, applicant is deemed ineligible.)	School attendance by beneficiary children of school age. Unemployed adults able to work must register with employment offices (OAED), must accept any employment offer in line with their skills and abilities, and must participate in employment programs or vocational training if offered. Individual inclusion and integration plan established by social workers (not strictly enforced yet).	**Variable benefit depending on HH size and income:** Difference between guaranteed support level minus the average monthly income for past six months. **Maximum cap:** €900. **Links to other benefits and services:** Free access to public health care system; referrals to psycho-social services; social pricing for electricity, water supply, taxes; prioritization for training and educational services; links with other anti-poverty programs.	None, but must report any changes within 15 days and must submit tax information annually.

continued

Table 5A.2 *(continued)*

Program and agency	Eligibility criteria	Conditionalities	Benefit structures per family or household: Benefit calculation	Benefit structures per family or household: Duration/ time limit
Indonesia PKH (CCT) Since 2007; Ministry of Social Affairs (MoSA).	**Relative thresholds applied to PMT:** To be eligible for PKH, households must be included in the poorest 16% of households that were registered in the UDB (last mass registration wave was in 2015) and are reconfirmed through validation conducted by facilitators.	School attendance >85% for ages 6–21 until school fully completed. Health visits for P/L women and young children. Attendance to family development sessions (soft, so far). (See chapter 8.)	**Flat benefit:** Per HH in 2018. **Variable and differentiated benefits depending on HH composition:** For different categories of family members pre-2017 and starting again in 2019: P/L women, young children, school children, elderly, disabled, etc. For 2019: benefits provided in payment phase 1 of the calendar year. Fixed benefit per area: 550k rupiah per family in regular areas; 1,000k per family in remote areas. Variable benefits per household member: 2,400 rupiah for pregnant women and children under five, 900k for primary school, 1,500k for junior secondary school, 2,000k for senior high school, 2,400 for elderly and severely disabled. Maximum 4 variable benefits per family (chosen to maximize the value of the variable benefit), but all family members must comply with relevant conditionalities and will be monitored.	6 years, recertification, then 3 additional years if still poor, or exit if not. Recertification has not been implemented but is planned for 2019.
Jamaica PATH (CCT) Since 2001; Ministry of Labor and Social Security (PATH under the Public Assistance Division), with Parish Offices.	**Absolute thresholds applied to PMT scores:** Provisional eligibility until HH verification for those under threshold; HHs on borderline with 5 points above threshold. **Demographic criteria:** HHs must have members in following categories: children 0–6, children 6–18, P/L, elderly, disabled, adult poor.	School attendance >85% for children ages 6–18. Health visits for P/L women, young children, elderly, and disabled. (See chapter 8.)	**Flat minimum benefit:** J$800 (unconditional). **Variable benefits depending on HH composition (by category of family member):** children grades 1–6 (J$1,600); grades 7–9 (J$2,050); grades 10–13 (J$2,400); P/L women (J$ 1,850); elderly (2,250); disabled (J$1,850); adult poor (J$1,850).	No time limit; individual HH members may age out; reassessment every 4 years.

continued

Table 5A.2 *(continued)*

Program and agency	Eligibility criteria	Conditionalities	Benefit structures per family or household	
			Benefit calculation	Duration/ time limit
Malawi Social Cash Transfer Program [UCT, as part of broader social protection umbrella program with public works (PW), school feeding (SF), and other programs] Since 2015; Ministry of Gender, Children, Disability, and Social Welfare.	**Relative % thresholds applied to PMT:** 10% ultra-poor for SCTP and SF; 15.5% ultra-poor with labor capacity for PW and SF; 26.2% moderate poor for PW, input subsidy, village saving loans, other productive economic inclusion programs. **Exclusionary filter**: No able-bodied adults (i.e., without labor capacity).	None.	**Variable benefit per HH with adjustment for HH size:** 1 person = MK 2,600; 2 persons = MK 3,300; 3 persons = MK 4,400; 4+ persons = MK 5,600). **School bonuses:** Primary (MK 800); secondary (MK 1,500).	None mentioned but notional 4 years for reassessment.
Mexico Prospera Since 1997; managed by the Prospera National Coordination Office, a decentralized body of the Department of Social Development (SEDESOL).	**Absolute thresholds applied to PMT scores:** A household is eligible if its PMT score is below the adjusted minimum well-being line, as determined by the National Council for the Evaluation of Social Development Policy (CONEVAL).	School enrollment and fewer than 4 absences per month for primary and lower secondary, and certification of school permanence in high school. Registration in designated health center, attendance of all household members to scheduled health visits and participation in health self-care workshops.	**Variable benefit depending on HH size and composition:** Benefits vary according to the number of children under 9 years (child support), number of children in school and their school grade (scholarships), as well as to the number of older adults (elder support). A household can receive scholarships and child support for a maximum of 3 members.	No time limit; periodic recertification (every 8 years).
Pakistan BISP (UCT) and WeT (CCT) Since 2008, WeT since 2012; BISP agency, which operates autonomously under Ministry of Finance.	**Demographic/legal:** Families must have a female applicant holding a valid Computerized National Identity Card (CNIC). Individual applicants must be a widowed or divorced female without male relatives; for CCT, families with school-age children. **Absolute thresholds for PMT poverty scores:** Those with scores below cutoff (and meeting other criteria).	School attendance >70% for children ages 4–12 in WeT CCT. (See chapter 8.)	**BISP-UCT:** Flat benefit amount per HH. **WeT-CCT:** Additional benefit per child.	No explicit time limit; children age-out and/or complete primary schooling.

continued

Table 5A.2 *(continued)*

Program and agency	Eligibility criteria	Conditionalities	Benefit structures per family or household: Benefit calculation	Benefit structures per family or household: Duration/ time limit
Philippines's Pantawid Pamilyang Pilipino Program (4Ps, CCT) Since 2007; Department of Social Welfare and Development (DSWD).	**Absolute threshold:** Households classified as "poor" by Listahanan social registry according to "estimated income" predicted by PMT models. Thresholds established at provincial level. **Demographic:** HH must have children 0–18 years old and/or a pregnant family member (as of time of Listahanan registration). **Community-based verification:** Through community assembly (CBT).	School attendance >85% for children ages 3–18. Health visits for P/L women, children. (See chapter 8.)	**Health grant, variable dependent on HH size and composition:** P500/household/month for 12 months for families with P/L woman (at time of registration). **Education grant, variable by age of children, up to a maximum number of children:** of P300/child/month for those in day care/school, or P500/child/month for those in high school for 10 months, maximum cap of 3 child benefits/HH.	No time limit; individual HH members may age out; periodic recertification with census sweeps.
Romania Guaranteed Minimum Income (GMI) Since 1950, various laws and reforms in the 2000s-2010s; Ministry of Labor and Social Justice is responsible for general supervision and policy development; National Agency for Payments and Social Inspection administers all social benefits. Local offices, local councils, and other institutions pay the benefits.	**Legal:** All Romanian or foreign citizens (residents) and homeless people. **Means-tested with absolute thresholds:** Families and persons with income below a legally defined threshold for guaranteed minimum income (GMI). The means test is based on family income and property (nonmonetary assets such as livestock, land, etc.) that are quantitatively over the limits set for each category of assets considered strictly necessary.	Participation in active employment programs. Accept suitable work. Provide specified number of hours of community service.	**Variable benefits according to income and HH size:** The difference between family income and the differentiated level of GMI is paid. The level of GMI is calculated as a social coefficient (for HH size) multiplied by the Index of Social Insertion (set at 500 lei since January 2014). For a one-person HH, the GMI = 28.3% × 500 = 142 lei; for a two-person HH, the GMI = 51% × 500 = 255 lei; for a three-person HH, the GMI = 71.4% × 500 lei = 357 lei; for a four-person HH the GMI = 88.4% × 500 = 442 lei; for a five-person HH the GMI = 105.4% × 500 = 527 lei, etc. The benefit then equals the difference between the differentiated GMI and the income levels. **Top-up work incentive benefit:** Families with at least one member in employment get a top-up benefit of 15% to encourage work effort.	No time limit (may be paid indefinitely if eligibility and conditions met). Must provide an affidavit on family composition and income every three months, plus evidence of conditions.

continued

Table 5A.2 *(continued)*

Program and agency	Eligibility criteria	Conditionalities	Benefit structures per family or household	
			Benefit calculation	Duration/ time limit
Tanzania UCT, CCT, and other programs under PSSN umbrella program Since 2014; Tanzania Social Action Fund (TASAF).	**Absolute thresholds applied to PMT:** If welfare scores fall below thresholds, HH is considered eligible for programs associated with those thresholds (even if that means that resulting number of beneficiaries is greater than budget planning allocations for that district). **Demographic:** HH size and composition.	School attendance >80% for children ages 5–18. Health visits for pregnant women and children. (See chapter 8.)	**UCT, flat amount per HH:** T Sh 10,000 per month. **CCT: Additional variable amount per HH** depending on HH size and composition: additional T Sh 4,000 per month for HHs with pregnant women, children.	None, though family members may age out.
Turkey CCT Since 2003; managed by General Directorate of Social Assistances under Ministry of Family, Labor, and Social Services and implemented by 1,000 district-based Social Assistance and Solidarity Foundations.	**Absolute thresholds applied to means-test:** No income from formal employment among all HH members, and welfare scores that fall below thresholds. **Demographic eligibility criteria:** Education component: Age and enrollment in formal education. Health component: Pregnancy of family members.	School attendance >80% for children ages 6–25. Health visits for pregnant women and young children (0–6). (See chapter 8.)	**Variable based on HH size and composition, further based on the component (education or health):** For Education component (per month): Boys at primary and secondary school 35 TRY ($22.43), girls at primary and secondary school 40 TRY ($25.64), boys at high school 50 TRY ($32.05), and girls at high school 60 TRY ($38.46). For Health component (per month): Flat benefit for each child (0–6) 35 TRY ($22.43), prenatal and postpartum benefit 35 TRY ($22.43), and delivery benefit 75 TRY one-time benefit ($48.07). (Based on purchasing power parity [PPP] for 2017, $1 makes 1.56 TRY, per IMF.)	No time limit (may be paid as the eligibility and conditions met). HH profiles are updated by administrative data sources (at least once every 45 days) and HH visits (once or twice a year).

Sources: Socialprotection.org program inventory, http://socialprotection.org/discover/programme/search; Social Security Administration with the International Social Security Administration (ISSA), https://www.ssa.gov/policy/docs/progdesc/ssptw/. Brazil: Bolsa Família Operations Manual. Bulgaria: Jeliazkova and Minev 2014; IME 2015; European Commission website; Social Security Administration 2018b. Colombia: FA Operations Manual. Croatia: Stubbs and Zrinscak 2015. Greece: Marini et al. 2016; Vardaramatou and Pertsinidou 2018; Zini et al. 2018. Indonesia's Ministry of Social Affairs; PKH Operational Documents. Jamaica: PATH Operations Manual. Malawi: ICBS 2018; Lindert et al. 2018. Mexico: Prospera operational rules 2018. Romania: European Commission 2014; World Bank 2015. Turkey: Operations Manual on Centered Regular Assistance Programs of Turkey (General Directorate of Social Assistance, October 2014); Ortakaya 2018.

Note: BISP = Benazir Income Support Programme; CBT = community-based targeting; CCT = conditional cash transfer (program); DMI = differentiated monthly income; GMI = guaranteed minimum income; HH = household; MoH = Ministry of Health; MP = moderate poor; PATH = Programme for the Advancement of Health and Education; PKH = Program Keluarga Harapan; P/L = pregnant/lactating; PMT = proxy means testing; PSSN = Productive Social Safety Net; SCTP = Social Cash Transfer Program; UCT = unconditional cash transfer (program); UDB = Unified Database; WeT = Waseela-e-Taleem; XP = extreme poor.

a. "This condition does not apply to: (1) a parent raising a child up to 3 years of age; (2) a disabled person with permanent disability or type and degree of disability of 50% or above; (3) a person taking care of a seriously ill family member or cohabitant; (4) persons with mental illness certified by a document from the competent authorities; (5) persons over 18 years of age who are trained in a daily form of schooling from the system of public education and secondary special schools; (6) pregnant women after the third month of pregnancy (Jeliazkova and Minev 2014).

b. Some are exempted from these conditionalities, including those <5 years from retirement age; parents caring for a child under 1, twins under 3 or severely disabled child; children under 15 (or older if in full-time education); elderly 65+; disabled persons; pregnant/nursing moms (up to six months after giving birth), and so on (Stubbs and Zrinscak 2015).

Table 5A.3 Benefit Structures for Unemployment Insurance and Unemployment Assistance Benefits

Program and agency	Eligibility criteria	Conditionalities	Benefit structures per individual	
			Benefit calculation	Duration
Albania UI Since 1993; Ministry of Finance and Economics oversees; Social Security Institute administers; National Employment Service pays benefits; General Directorate of Taxes collects contributions.	**Unemployment status:** Must be involuntarily unemployed. **Contributions history:** >1 year of contributions preceding unemployment. **No other benefits:** (except partial disability).	Must register at employment office. Must be willing to undergo training.	**Flat benefit:** Per person.	3–12 months depending on length of contribution period.
Argentina UI Since 1967, current law since 1991; Ministry of Labor, Employment, and Social Security (MLESS) oversees; National Social Security Administration administers; separate administration for agricultural and construction workers.	**Unemployment status and contributions history:** Minimum period of contributions preceding unemployment (6 months in past 3 years; 3 months in past 12 months for temporary workers; 8 months in past 24 for construction). **Specialized criteria:** Extended benefit for unemployed person >45 years old with children. **No other benefits.**	Must register as unemployed. Must be available for suitable employment.	**Variable benefits:** Set at 50% of individual's highest wages in preceding 6-month period. **Minimum floor, maximum cap.** **Additional benefits:** For unemployed and dependents, social assistance medical benefits, family allowances, and may continue health insurance. **Lump sum benefit:** For unemployed person who plans to set up a business and presents a business plan to MLESS for approval.	2–12 months depending on length of contribution period. Extended benefit allowed for additional 6 months at a declining percentage.
Armenia UI Since 1992; State Social Security Services provides financing; State Employment Service administers the program through regional centers.	**Unemployment status:** Must be unemployed as a result of enterprise reorganization, staff reduction, or cancellation of collective agreement. **Employment category:** Employed and self-employed. **Contributions history:** >12 months of contributions.	Must register at employment office. Must be able and willing to work. Must be actively seeking work.	**Flat benefit:** Calculated as 60% of the minimum wage.	Up to 12 months.

continued

Table 5A.3 *(continued)*

Program and agency	Eligibility criteria	Conditionalities	Benefit structures per individual: Benefit calculation	Benefit structures per individual: Duration
Bahrain UI Since 2006; Ministry of Labor registers unemployed; makes decisions on eligibility, enrollment, and benefit entitlement; provides training; Social Insurance Organization administers program (contributions and payments).	**Demographic/legal:** Under retirement age; legal resident of Bahrain. **Unemployment status:** Must not be due to voluntary leaving, misconduct, or refusal of suitable job offer. **Employment category:** Formal public and private-sector employment (self-employed excluded). **Contributions history:** Minimum period of consecutive employment 12 months, 12/18 months, 18/24 months, 36/48 months for subsequent claims.	Must register at employment office. Must be capable of and available for work.	**Variable benefits:** Set at 60% of individual's highest wages in preceding 12-month period. **Minimum floor, maximum cap.**	Up to 6 months.
Bahrain UA Same as above.	**Demographic/legal:** Over age 17 and under retirement age; Bahraini citizen. **Employment category:** First-time job seekers or insured persons who do not qualify for UI. **Economic filter:** Must not be engaged in gainful activity or own a business.	Must register at employment office. Must be capable of and available for work.	**Flat benefit:** Two categories: higher amount for those with academic qualifications, lower amount for other unemployed persons.	Up to 6 months.
Greece UI Since 1954, current law since 1985; Ministry of Labor and Social Security oversees; Manpower Employment Organization (OAED) administers benefits and employment services through local employment offices; Unified Social Security Fund collects contributions.	**Demographic:** Under age 65. **Unemployment status:** Must be involuntary. **Contributions history:** Minimum contribution periods preceding unemployment (depending on categories of employed); eligibility for seasonal workers' benefit: >125 days of contributions in last 14 months. **Means-tested threshold:** Maximum income for self-employed. **Other benefits:** Not receiving disability pension.	Must be registered at employment office. Must be capable and available to work.	**Flat benefit amount.** **Additional means-tested dependency allowance:** 10% of insured's earnings for each dependent, up to 70%. **Lump-sum benefit:** For seasonal allowance.	Up to 12 months depending on prior contributions history.

continued

Table 5A.3 *(continued)*

Program and agency	Eligibility criteria	Conditionalities	Benefit structures per individual: Benefit calculation	Benefit structures per individual: Duration
Greece UA Same as above.	**Young person's benefit:** Unemployed ages 20–29. **Special unemployment assistance for LTU:** Unemployed persons ages 20–66 if no longer eligible for UI (unemployed >1 year); means-tested: annual income up to threshold (adjusted for each child).	Same as above.	**Flat benefit amounts.**	Up to 5 months for young person's benefit; up to 12 months for special UA benefit for LTU.
Korea, Rep. UI Since 1995; Ministry of Employment and Labor (MoEL) oversees program; Employment Security Offices under MoEL administers program and pays benefits; Korea Worker's Compensation and Welfare Service collects contributions.	**Demographic:** Under age 65. **Employment categories:** All employees; volunteer coverage for self-employed or those with <5 employees. **Exclusionary filters:** Persons working less than 60 hours a month or less than 15 hours a week, and family labor. **Contributions history:** Over 6 months of contributions coverage during past 18 months.	Must be registered at an employment security office. Must be capable of and available for work. Additional "conditional" allowances are paid to unemployed persons to encourage retraining or job search. Employment services are provided through the Employment Stabilization Program and the Vocational Competency Development Program.	**Variable benefit:** Set at 50% of the insured's average daily earnings during the 3 months preceding unemployment. **Minimum floor, maximum cap.** Additional conditional allowances include the early reemployment allowance, vocational ability development allowance, and transportation and home moving allowance.	The benefit is paid after a 7-day waiting period, and for up to 90 days to those with 6–12 months of coverage; for up to 240 days with >10 years of coverage or aged 50 or older or disabled.
Kuwait UI Since 2013; Public Institution for Social Security (board chaired by Minister of Finance) administers the program.	**Demographic/legal:** Ages 18–60 and Kuwaiti nationals. **Other benefits:** Ineligible for old-age pension. **Contributions history:** Minimum period of contributions preceding unemployment claims.	Must apply to Labor Force Restructuring Program within 6 months of termination. Required to undertake work or training that becomes available through that program.	**Variable benefit:** Set at 60% of individual's last monthly earnings plus old-age pension that the insured person would be entitled to receive under that supplementary system. **Maximum cap.**	Up to 6 months.

continued

Table 5A.3 *(continued)*

Program and agency	Eligibility criteria	Conditionalities	Benefit structures per individual: Benefit calculation	Benefit structures per individual: Duration
Mauritius UI Since 1983; Ministry of Labor, Industrial Relations, and Employment (MoLIRE), and Ministry of Social Security, National Solidarity, and Reform Institutions.	**Unemployment status:** Must have been laid off for economic, technological, or structural reasons affecting the firm, or illegal termination of employment agreement. **Employment categories:** Formal sector workers (excluded: civil servants, employees of SOEs, self-employed, part-time workers, migrant workers). **Contributions history:** Must have >6 months of continuous employment with employer at time of dismissal.	Must register with and participate in the Workfare Programme at the MoLIRE within 7 days of dismissal.	**Variable benefit:** Set at 90% of the insured's basic earnings. **Minimum floor.**	3–12 months.
Mauritius UA Since 1983; Ministry of Social Security, National Solidarity, and Reform Institutions administers the UA program.	**Unemployed status and family members:** Unemployed, head of household, dependents. **Means-tested:** Income tested to determine benefit amounts.	Must be willing and able to work. Must be actively seeking employment. Must be registered as unemployed at the unemployment exchange for at least 30 days.	**Variable benefit:** Means-tested up to a **maximum cap.** **Variable benefit:** For rental allowance (% of rent up to a **maximum cap**). **Flat benefits:** For spouse, children of varying age categories. **Minimum floor, maximum caps.**	Up to 12 months.
Moldova UI Since 1992; Ministry of Health, Labor, and Social Protection and National Employment Agency administer the program.	**Legal status:** Residents of Moldova. **Contributions history:** More than 9 months of covered employment in the 24 months before the date of registration. **Economic filter/means-tested:** Must have no taxable income.	Must be registered at an employment office. Must be willing and able to work. Benefits may be reduced, postponed, suspended, or terminated if the insured is discharged for violating work discipline rules, leaving employment without good cause, violating conditions for a job placement or vocational training, or filing fraudulent claims.	**Variable benefit:** Calculated as % of insured's average wage in last place of work; % varies by cause and circumstances of unemployment (30%, 40%, or 50%). **Minimum floor:** Minimum wage. **Maximum cap:** National average monthly wage.	Up to 6, 9, or 12 months, depending on preceding number of years of employment.

continued

Table 5A.3 *(continued)*

Program and agency	Eligibility criteria	Conditionalities	Benefit structures per individual	
			Benefit calculation	Duration
South Africa UI Since 1996; Department of Labor oversees; Unemployment Insurance Fund administers program (local benefit committees and claims officers).	**Unemployment status:** Must be result of termination of insured's contract, ending of a FT contract, dismissal of insured (except for disciplinary reasons), insolvency of employer, or death of employer (for household worker). **Unemployment time frame:** Must be unable to find work within 14 days of becoming unemployed. **Time frame:** Must apply for benefits within 6 months of first becoming unemployed. **Contributions history:** At least one accumulated credit before becoming unemployed.	Must register with and report to public employment exchange (unless unemployment is result of illness or pregnancy). Must be capable of and available for work.	**Variable benefit:** Set at % of daily earnings over past year (targeted with higher % for people with lower earnings). **Maximum cap:** On monthly earnings (as basis for calculation) and on daily benefit amount.	Up to 238 days minus any credits used for sickness, adoption, or survivor benefits.
Thailand UI Since 2004; Ministry of Labor oversees; Social Security Office collects contributions and pays benefits; Department of Employment under MoL registers the unemployed for job placement and training through the Government Employment Service Office. Department of Skills Development under MoL trains unemployed for new jobs.	**Demographic.** Ages 15–60. **Unemployment status:** Specific reasons for unemployment barred (dishonest performing of duties, intentionally committing criminal offence, seriously violating work rules, etc.). **Employment categories:** Employees included; self-employed excluded. **Contributions history:** More than 6 months of contributions coverage during past 15 months preceding unemployment.	Must register with Government Employment Service Office. Must be ready and able to accept any suitable job offer. Must report at least once/month to the Government Employment Service. Social Security Office may suspend benefit payments for failure to comply with conditions.	**Variable benefits:** Set at 50% of insured's wages (highest 3 months in the past 9 months) for involuntarily unemployed; 30% for voluntary unemployed. **Maximum cap.**	Up to 180 days for involuntarily unemployed. Up to 90 days for voluntary unemployed.
Turkey UI Since 1999 with most recent reforms in 2008; Ministry of Labor and Social Security oversees; Social Security Institution is responsible for collecting contributions; Employment Agency (IKSUR) administers program.	**Demographic:** 18 or older. **Employment category:** Employees with private or public contracts and certain other groups. **Contributions history:** More than 600 days of contributions in the 3 years preceding unemployment including the last 120 days of employment.	Must be registered and available for suitable employment.	**Variable benefits:** Set at 50% of average daily earnings based on last 4 months of earnings. **Maximum cap:** Depending on industry in which the insured worked.	Up to 180 days, 240 days, 300 days depending on number of days of contributions.

Sources: Social Security Administration with the International Social Security Administration (ISSA); https://www.ssa.gov/policy/docs/progdesc/ssptw/2016, 2017, 2018 depending on country and region. Some information also derived from socialprotection.org program inventory, http://socialprotection.org/discover/programme/search, supplemented by country-specific government sources in some instances.

Note: FT = fixed term; LTU = long-term unemployed; MoL = Ministry of Labor; SOE = state-owned enterprise; UA = unemployment assistance; UI = unemployment insurance.

Table 5A.4 Benefit Structures for Disability Assistance and Disability Insurance Benefits

Program and agency	Eligibility criteria	Benefit structures per individual	
		Benefit calculation	Duration/time limit
Albania Disability Insurance Benefits Since 1993; Ministry of Finance and Economics; Social Insurance Institute; General Directorate of Taxes.	**Functional assessment of disability:** Must be assessed with a total disability (blind, severely disabled, or incapable of any work); or partial disability (incapable of usual work but capable of work under certain conditions). For partial disability: Must be assessed with a 33% to 67% loss of work capacity. The Medical Commission assesses the degree of disability. **Employment and contributions history:** Must have coverage in at least 75% of the years since age 20, including at least one year in the five years before the disability began. **Specialized criteria:** Constant-attendance supplement: Paid if the insured requires the constant attendance of others to perform daily functions.	**Variable benefit depending on contribution and earning history:** Monthly pension is the ratio of the insured's coverage period to the coverage period required by law multiplied by the amount of the old-age social pension, plus 1% of the insured's average covered earnings for each year of coverage. Partial disability pension: 50% of the full disability pension is paid. Flat additional supplement for full disability. Constant-attendance supplement: 15% the insured's average covered earnings is paid. **Minimum floor:** The minimum monthly disability pension is 75% of the legal monthly minimum wage. **Benefit adjustment:** Benefits are adjusted annually.	None mentioned.
Albania Disability Assistance Benefits Since 1993; Ministry of Finance and Economics; Social Insurance Institute.	**Demographic/legal:** Must be a citizen of Albania. **Disability status:** Must be assessed with a physical, sensory, mental, or psychological disability resulting from birth, an accident, or illness. **No contributions history:** Does not meet the contribution requirements for the social insurance disability pension.	**Variable benefits by category of disability:** Specified amounts for various categories: non-work-related disabilities; paraplegic or tetraplegic (due to work-related or non-work-related causes); blind. **Benefit adjustment:** Benefits are adjusted annually based on the Council of Ministers Decisions (CMD).	None mentioned.

continued

Table 5A.4 *(continued)*

Program and agency	Eligibility criteria	Benefit structures per individual: Benefit calculation	Benefit structures per individual: Duration/time limit
Argentina Disability Assistance Benefit Current laws: 1971 and 2016; Ministry of Social Development oversees the social assistance programs. National Pension Commission administers the social assistance pension programs.	**Demographic/legal:** Must be younger than the normal retirement age. Naturalized citizens must have at least five years of residence immediately before claiming the pension; foreign residents must have at least 20 years of residence. **Functional disability status:** Must have at least a 76% assessed loss of earning capacity. **No other support:** Must not be receiving any other pension or nutritional support from family members. Doctors at public health care facilities assess the degree of disability.	**Benefit per person as % of MW:** 70% of the minimum old-age pension (basic old-age pension, compensatory pension, and additional pension) is paid. Additional benefits may be paid for dependents under Family Allowances. **Benefit adjustment:** Benefits are adjusted when the minimum pension is adjusted.	The disability pension ceases at the normal retirement age and is replaced by a universal old-age pension.
Bahrain Disability Insurance Benefits Since 1976; Ministry of Finance provides general supervision. Social Insurance Organization, managed by a board of directors, administers the program.	**Demographic/legal:** Bahraini citizen working in Bahrain/Gulf Cooperation Council. The insured must be younger than age 60 (men) or age 55 (women) when the disability began. **Contributions history:** The insured must have had at least 6 consecutive months of contributions immediately before the disability began or 12 nonconsecutive months of contributions with 3 months immediately before the disability began. The pension is also paid if the disability began within 1 year of the cessation of contributions.	**Variable benefit based on earning and contributions history:** The pension is 44% of the insured's average monthly earnings in the last year of contributions before the disability began or 2% of the insured's average earnings during the last year of contributions multiplied by the number of years of contributions, whichever is higher. **Minimum floor:** The minimum pension is 44% of the insured's average monthly earnings in the last year of contributions or 180 dinars, whichever is higher; an insured person with income less than 180 dinars receives a pension of 100% of his or her average contributory wage in the last year. **Maximum cap:** The maximum pension is 80% of the insured's average earnings plus an additional 10% of the pension. Instead of an additional 10%, the beneficiary can opt for a lump sum of 3% of the monthly average earnings in the last 2 years multiplied by 12 times the number of years of coverage.	None mentioned.

continued

Table 5A.4 *(continued)*

Program and agency	Eligibility criteria	Benefit structures per individual	
		Benefit calculation	Duration/time limit
Brazil Disability Social Pension (Benefício de Prestação Continuada [BPC]) Since 1993; National Social Security Institute administers benefits.	**Disability status:** Must be assessed with a disability. **Means tested:** Must have a monthly household income of less than 25% of the legal monthly minimum wage per person.	**Flat benefit = MW.** The monthly benefit is the legal monthly minimum wage. **Benefit adjustment:** Benefits are adjusted annually according to changes in the minimum wage.	None, but eligibility is reviewed every two years.
Bulgaria Disability Assistance Benefit Since 1924, current laws in 2000s; Ministry of Labor and Social Policy.	**Demographic criteria:** Must be age 16 or older. **Functional disability:** Must have at least a 71% assessed loss of working capacity. Ministry of Health Medical Expert Commissions assess the loss of working capacity.	**Variable benefit depending on degree of disability:** 120% of the monthly old-age social pension amount is paid for an assessed loss of working capacity greater than 90%; 110% for an assessed loss of working capacity of 71% to 90%.	None mentioned.
Georgia Disability Assistance Benefit (social pension for disabled) Since 1956; Ministry of Labor, Health, and Social Affairs oversees the program. Social Services Agency administers the program, with regional and local SSA offices (one-stop shops/ service centers).	**Disability status:** Must be assessed with a disability. **No other support:** The pension is paid to an individual or family without other means of support.	**Flat benefit per person:** Per month. **Benefit adjustment:** Benefits are adjusted on an ad hoc basis.	None mentioned.

continued

Table 5A.4 *(continued)*

Program and agency	Eligibility criteria	Benefit structures per individual	
		Benefit calculation	**Duration/time limit**
Jamaica Disability Benefit Since 1965; Ministry of Labour and Social Security administers the benefit through its National Insurance Division and local offices. Tax Administration Jamaica collects contributions.	**Functional disability:** Must be assessed with a permanent incapacity for work of at least 10%. An independent medical adviser appointed by the Ministry of Labor and Social Security assesses the disability. **Contributions history:** Must have >156 weeks of paid contributions.	**Variable benefit depending on degree of disability:** Weekly benefit is established within benefit range depending on assessed degree of disability of 10% to 100%. **Flat benefits:** Spouse's supplement per week; additional disability grant is paid as a lump sum.	None mentioned.
Kuwait Disability Insurance Pension Since 1995; Public Institution for Social Security managed by a board of directors and chaired by the Minister of Finance administers the program.	**Functional disability status:** An assessed degree of incapacity for work of more than 50%. The general medical council assesses the degree of disability.	**Variable benefit depending on contributions and earnings:** The benefit is 65% (75% for military personnel) of the insured's last monthly earnings, plus 2% for each year of contributions exceeding 15 years, up to 95% of earnings (100% for military personnel). The insured is credited with contribution years from the date the disability began until age 60. **Benefit adjustment:** Flat-rate adjustments are made to benefits every 3 years.	Until age 60.
Mauritius Basic Universal Disability Assistance Benefits Since 1976; Ministry of Social Security, National Solidarity, and Reform Institutions.	**Demographic/legal criteria:** Ages 15–59; no residence requirement for Mauritian nationals; noncitizens must have resided in Mauritius for at least five of the last 10 years, including one year immediately before the claim is made. **Disability status:** Assessed with >60% disability that is expected to last for at least 12 months; a medical board must assess the disability. **Specialized criteria:** Constant-attendance allowance: Paid to beneficiaries of the basic disability pension who require the constant attendance of others to perform daily functions.	**Flat benefits:** Per person.	None mentioned.

continued

Table 5A.4 *(continued)*

Program and agency	Eligibility criteria	Benefit structures per individual	
		Benefit calculation	Duration/time limit
Mauritius Disability Insurance Benefits Since 1976; Ministry of Social Security, National Solidarity, and Reform Institutions.	**Disability status:** Must be assessed with at least a 60% disability that is expected to last for at least 12 months. A medical board must assess the disability.	**Variable benefits:** According to contributions history and actuarial projections.	None mentioned.
Moldova Disability Assistance Benefit (Social Pension) Since 1956, current law 1999; Ministry of Health, Labor, and Social Protection is responsible for social security policy. National Office of Social Insurance administers the programs.	**Disability status (medical classifications):** Persons with a severe, significant, or medium disability that began in childhood; children younger than age 18 with a severe, significant, or medium disability; and adults assessed with a Group I, II, or III disability. **No other coverage:** For those who do not meet the coverage requirements for a social insurance disability pension. **Caregiver's allowance:** Paid to persons caring for a child younger than age 18 with a severe disability, a person with a severe disability that began in childhood, or a blind person with a severe disability.	**Variable benefit depending on degree of disability:** Highest monthly disability social pension is paid to a person with a severe disability that began in childhood or who is younger than age 18; slightly lower for a significant disability; and lower monthly amount for a medium disability. Benefit levels also vary for adults assessed with a Group I, II, or III disability who do not meet the coverage requirements for a social insurance disability pension (highest for Group I, moderate for Group II, lower for Group III). **Flat amount:** For caregiver's allowance. **Benefit adjustment:** Benefits are adjusted in April based on changes in consumer prices in the previous year.	None mentioned.
South Africa Disability Assistance Benefits Since 2004; Department of Social Development oversees program; South African Social Security Agency administers program.	**Demographic criteria:** Ages 18–59. **Disability status:** Assessed as temporarily disabled for more than six months. The disability must be confirmed by a medical assessment. **Means test (income and assets) with absolute eligibility thresholds:** Annual income must be <R 73,800 for single person or <R 147,600 for couple; assets must be <R 1,056,000 for single person or <R 2,112,000 for couple. **Specialized criteria:** Eligibility for constant-attendance allowance: Disabled person requires constant attendance of others to perform daily functions. **No other benefits:** Beneficiaries may receive only one social grant at a time.	**Flat benefit amounts:** For disability social assistance grant and for caregiver grant (lower).	None mentioned.

continued

Table 5A.4 *(continued)*

Program and agency	Eligibility criteria	Benefit structures per individual	
		Benefit calculation	Duration/time limit
South Africa Disability Insurance for Workers Since 1993; Department of Labor oversees program; Compensation Commissioner administers the program, including claims decisions and the management of funds from which benefits are paid.	**Disability assessment:** Temporary or permanent and partial or full (degree of disability). Must be confirmed by medical assessment. **Employment category:** Employed persons working more than 24 hours a month, including household and seasonal workers. **Exclusionary filters**: Civil servants, trainees, foreigners working under a contract, and persons receiving a work injury or occupational disease benefit from the compensation fund.	**Variable benefits for total disability, depending on earnings history:** If assessed with total disability (100%), benefit is set at 75% of insured's last monthly earnings. **Variable benefits for partial disability, depending on degree of disability and earnings history**: If assessed with partial disability, the % of earnings is determined by the Compensation Commissioner's office. If the assessed degree of disability is 31% to 99%, a percentage of the full pension is paid according to the assessed degree of disability. For an assessed degree of disability of up to 30%, a lump sum of up to 15 times the insured's last monthly earnings is paid. **Minimum floor and maximum cap:** For earnings and benefits.	For temporary disability: up to 12 months, may be extended for up to 24 months after further assessment of the disability.
Thailand Disability Insurance Since 1990; Ministry of Labor provides general supervision. Social Security Office collects contributions and pays benefits.	**Disability status:** Must be incapable of work; medical officers assigned by the Social Security Office assess the degree of disability annually. **Contributions history:** Must have at least 3 months of contributions in the 15 months before the total physical or mental disability began. The benefit is paid after entitlement to the cash sickness benefit ceases.	**Variable benefit based on earnings history:** 50% of the insured's average daily wage in the highest paid 3 months of the 9 months before the disability began. **Minimum floor and maximum cap:** For earnings. **Benefit adjustment:** Benefits are adjusted on an ad hoc basis according to changes in the cost of living.	The benefit is paid until death or until pensioner is rehabilitated. Annual reassessment.
Turkey Disability Insurance Since 1957, current laws since 2000s; Ministry of Labor and Social Security oversees; Social Security Institution collects contributions and administers the program.	**Functional disability:** Must be assessed with at least a 60% loss of working capacity. **Employment and contributions history:** Must have been employed and have at least 10 years of coverage, including at least 1,800 days of paid contributions. The requirement for the years of coverage is waived if the insured requires constant attendance. **Specialized criteria:** Constant-attendance allowance: The insured requires the constant attendance of others to perform daily functions.	**Variable benefit based on earnings history:** The pension is the insured's average monthly earnings multiplied by the accrual rate. Average monthly earnings are the insured's total lifetime earnings divided by the total days of paid contributions before the disability began, multiplied by 30. Additional 10% for constant-attendance allowance (caregiver allowance). Benefit adjustment: Benefits are adjusted in January and July of each year based on changes in the consumer price index.	None mentioned.

Sources: Social Security Administration with the International Social Security Administration (ISSA), https://www.ssa.gov/policy/docs/progdesc/ssptw/2016, 2017, 2018 depending on country and region. Some information also derived from socialprotection.org program inventory, http://socialprotection.org/discover/programme/search, supplemented by country-specific government sources in some instances.

Notes

1. These phases may or may not be carried out in this order, and some may be combined.
2. These phases may or may not be carried out in this order, and some may be combined. With multiprogram intake, registration, and assessments, the institutional arrangements for the assessment phase may be managed by an agency other than the program (such as with a social registry), whereas eligibility decisions are typically under the institutional jurisdiction of the specific program.
3. The program has recently been transformed and no longer exists as a CCT due to shifts in the social policy in Mexico.
4. Relative thresholds operate in a manner akin to "grading on a curve" where each student's grade depends on the others' performance. This would mean that if student 1 scored an 85 percent in a low-performing class, she might receive an A grade, whereas if student 2 scored an 85 percent on the same exam, he might receive a B grade despite his comparable performance because he was part of a relatively higher performing class.
5. A resource for IAPs is included in Tubb (2012).
6. In some instances, donors or other agencies operate digital platforms for integrated beneficiary and benefits management. For example, the World Food Programme's SCOPE is an in-house digital platform for beneficiary and transfer management that imports data on beneficiaries of a program, uses biometric capabilities to capture and store identity data to authenticate them at the point of registration, deduplicates data on beneficiaries, manages entitlements to beneficiaries, administers the delivery of benefits through commercial payment service providers (cash or mobile) with multifactor authentication (SCOPE card, barcoded household ID card, PIN, biometrics), and provides analytics on program operations. (Derived from discussions with UN World Food Programme staff in Washington, DC, March 2017, and from a presentation on SCOPE in Beirut, August 2016.)

Bibliography

Almeida, Rita, Juliana Arbelaez, Maddalena Honorati, Arvo Kuddo, Tanja Lohmann, Mirey Ovadiya, Lucian Pop, Maria Laura Sanchez Puerta, and Michael Weber. 2012. "Improving Access to Jobs and Earnings Opportunities: The Role of Activation and Graduation Policies in Developing Countries." Social Protection and Labor Discussion Paper 1204, World Bank, Washington, DC.

Beegle, Kathleen, Aline Coudouel, and Emma Monsalve, eds. 2018. *Realizing the Full Potential of Social Safety Nets in Africa*. Africa Development Forum Series. Washington, DC: World Bank.

Brito Leal Ivo, Anete, and Alessandra Buarque de A. Silva. 2011. "O hiato do direito dentro do direito: Os excluídos do BPC." *Revista Katálysis* 14 (1): 32–40.

Brown, Alessio JG, and Johannes Koettl. 2015. "Active Labor Market Programs—Employment Gain or Fiscal Drain?" *IZA Journal of Labor Economics* 4 (12): 1–36. https://doi.org/10.1186/s40172-015-0025-5.

Chile, Ministry of Social Development and Family. 2017. "Household Social Registry: System That Supports the Selection of Users of Social Benefits." Undersecretary of Social Evaluation, Ministry of Social Development and Family, Santiago.

Coady, David, Margaret Grosh, and John Hoddinott. 2004. *Targeting of Transfers in Developing Countries: Review of Lessons and Experience*. Regional and Sectoral Studies. Washington, DC: World Bank.

del Ninno, Carlo, and Bradford Mills, eds. 2015. *Safety Nets in Africa: Effective Mechanisms to Reach the Poor and Most Vulnerable*. Africa Development Forum Series. Washington, DC: World Bank and Agence Française de Développement.

European Commission. 2014. "European Minimum Income Network Country Report: Romania." European Commission, Brussels, Belgium.

Grosh, Margaret E. 1994. "Administering Targeted Social Programs in Latin America: From Platitudes to Practice." World Bank, Washington, DC.

Grosh, Margaret, Carlo del Ninno, Emil Tesliuc, and Azedine Ouerghi. 2008. *For Protection and Promotion: The Design and Implementation of Effective Safety Nets*. Washington, DC: World Bank.

Grosh, Margaret, and Kathy Lindert. 2018. "Design Choices for Cash Transfer Programs." Slide presentation at the World Bank's Social Safety Nets and Delivery Systems Core Course, Washington, DC.

Handa, Sudhanshu, Carolyn Huang, Nicola Hypher, Clarissa Teixeira, Fabio V. Soares, and Benjamin Davis. 2012. "Targeting Effectiveness of Social Cash Transfer Programmes in Three African Countries." *Journal of Development Effectiveness* 4 (1): 78–108.

ICBS (Ideal Consulting and Business Services). 2018. "Beneficiary Verification and Technical Audit of the Social Cash Transfer Programme in New World Bank Funded Districts." Final consultant report on Malawi's Social Cash Transfer Programme.

IME (Institute for Market Economics). 2015. "Challenges Faced by Social Assistance in Bulgaria." IME, Sofia, Bulgaria.

Immervoll, Herwig, and Carlo Knotz. 2018. "How Demanding Are Activation Requirements for Jobseekers?" IZA Discussion Paper 11704, Institute of Labor Economics, Bonn, Germany.

Indonesia, Office of the Vice President. 2015. "Indonesia's Unified Database for Social Protection Programmes: Management Standards." National Team for the Acceleration of Poverty Reduction, Secretariat of the Vice President of the Republic of Indonesia, Jakarta.

Jeliazkova, Maria, and Douhomir Minev. 2014. "European Minimum Income Network Country Report: Bulgaria." European Commission, Brussels, Belgium.

Karippacheril, Tina George. 2019. "Integrated Social Information Systems." Webinar to conference at ADB Manila, September 12, 2019. World Bank, Washington, DC.

Karippacheril, Tina George. 2019. "Integrated Social Information Systems and Social Registries." Webinar to Socialprotection.org, October 3, 2019. World Bank, Washington, DC.

Karippacheril, Tina George, and Phillippe Leite. 2019. "Integrated Social Information Systems and Social Registries." Social Safety Nets and Delivery Systems Core Course, October 2019. World Bank, Washington, DC

Karippacheril, Tina George, and Anita Mittal. Forthcoming. "IPSA Toolkit on Integrated Social Information Systems." World Bank, Washington, DC.

Konle-Seidl, Regina. 2011. "Profiling Systems for Effective Labour Market Integration: Use of Profiling for Resource Allocation, Action Planning, and Matching." European Commission Mutual Learning Programme for Public Employment Services: DG Employment, Social Affairs, and Inclusion, Brussels, Belgium.

Kuddo, Arvo. 2009. "Employment Services and Active Labor Market Programs in Eastern European and Central Asian Countries." Social Protection and Labor Discussion Paper 0918, Human Development Network, World Bank, Washington, DC.

Kuddo, Arvo. 2012. "Public Employment Services and Activation Policies." Social Protection and Labor Discussion Paper 1215, World Bank, Washington, DC.

Kurekova, Lucia Mytna. 2014. "Review of Profiling Systems, Categorization of Jobseekers and Calculation of Unit Service Costs in Employment Services: Implications and Applications for Slovakia." Central European Labour Studies Institute, Bratislava, Slovak Republic.

Leite, Phillippe, Tina George, Changqing Sun, Theresa Jones, and Kathy Lindert. 2017. "Social Registries for Social Assistance and Beyond: A Guidance Note and Assessment Tool." Social Protection and Labor Discussion Paper 1704, World Bank, Washington, DC. http://documents.worldbank.org/curated/en/698441502095248081/Social-registries-for-social-assistance-and-beyond-a-guidance-note-and-assessment-tool.

Lindert, Kathy. 2005. "Implementing Means-Tested Welfare Systems in the United States." Social Protection Discussion Paper 0532, World Bank, Washington, DC.

Lindert, Kathy, Colin Andrews, Chipo Msowoya, Boban Varghese Paul, Elijah Chirwa, and Anita Mittal. 2018. "Rapid Social Registry Assessment: Malawi's Unified Beneficiary Registry (UBR)." Social Protection and Jobs Discussion Paper 1803, World Bank, Washington, DC. http://documents.worldbank.org/curated/en/363391542398737774/Rapid-Social-Registry-Assessment-Malawis-Unified-Beneficiary-Registry-UBR.

Lindert, Kathy, Tina George Karippacheril, and Phillippe Leite. 2018. "Social Registries, Beneficiary Registries, and Integrated Social Information Systems." Social Safety Nets and Delivery Systems Core Course, May. World Bank, Washington, DC.

Lindert, Kathy, Anja Linder, Jason Hobbs, and Benedicte de la Briere. 2007. "The Nuts and Bolts of Brazil's Bolsa Família Program: Implementing Conditional Cash Transfers in a Decentralized Context." Social Protection Discussion Paper 0709, World Bank, Washington, DC.

Louback da Silva, Naiane. 2012. "A judicialização do Benefício de Prestação Continuada da assistencia social." *Serviço Social e Sociedade* 111 (July/September): 555–75.

Loxha, Artan, and Matteo Morgandi. 2014. "Profiling the Unemployed: A Review of OECD Experiences and Implications for Emerging Economies." Social Protection and Labor Discussion Paper 1424, World Bank, Washington, DC.

Marini, Alessandra, Michele Zini, Eleni Kanavitsa, and Alexandro Karakitsios. 2016. "Greece: Initial Support to the Guaranteed Minimum Income Rollout: Process Evaluation of the First Phase of the GMI Rollout." Social Protection and Labor Global Practice, World Bank, Washington, DC.

Maryland Developmental Disabilities Administration. 2018. Low-Intensity Support Services Program (eligibility guide, application form, frequently asked questions). https://dda.health.maryland.gov/Pages/liss.aspx.

Mazza, Jacqueline. 2017. *Labor Intermediation Services in Developing Economies: Adapting Employment Services for a Global Age*. Cham, Switzerland: Palgrave Macmillan.

Meneguetti Pereira, Luciano. 2012. "Análise crítica do Benefício de Prestação Continuada e sua efetivação pelo judiciário." *Revista CEJ* 56 (January/April): 15–27.

Mostafa, Joana, and Natália G. D. Sátyro. 2014. "Cadastro Único: A Registry Supported by a National Public Bank." Working Paper 126, International Policy Centre for Inclusive Growth, Brasilia, Brazil.

OECD (Organisation for Economic Co-operation and Development). 2014. *Connecting People with Jobs: Activation Policies in the United Kingdom*. Paris: OECD Publishing. https://doi.org/10.1787/9789264217188-en.

OECD (Organisation for Economic Co-operation and Development). 2015. *OECD Employment Outlook 2015*. Paris: OECD Publishing. https://doi.org/10.1787/empl_outlook-2015-en.

Ortakaya, Ahmet Fatih. 2018. "Improving Efficiency with Turkey's Integrated Social Assistance System: Before and After." Internal note, World Bank, Washington, DC.

Scoppetta, Anette, and Arthur Buckenleib. 2018. "Tackling Long-Term Unemployment through Risk Profiling and Outreach." Technical Dossier 6, ESF Transnational Platform, European Commission, Brussels, Belgium.

Social Security Administration. 2017a. "Social Security Programs throughout the World: Africa, 2017." Social Security Administration, Washington, DC. https://www.ssa.gov/policy/docs/progdesc/ssptw/2016-2017/africa/index.html.

Social Security Administration. 2017b. "Social Security Programs throughout the World: Asia and the Pacific, 2016." Social Security Administration, Washington, DC. https://www.ssa.gov/policy/docs/progdesc/ssptw/2016-2017/asia/ssptw16asia.pdf.

Social Security Administration. 2018a. "Social Security Programs throughout the World: The Americas, 2017." Social Security Administration, Washington, DC. https://www.ssa.gov/policy/docs/progdesc/ssptw/2016-2017/americas/index.html.

Social Security Administration. 2018b. "Social Security Programs throughout the World: Europe, 2018." Social Security Administration, Washington, DC. https://www.ssa.gov/policy/docs/progdesc/ssptw/2018-2019/europe/index.html.

Stubbs, Paul, and Sinisa Zrinscak. 2015. "ESPN Thematic Report on Minimum Income Schemes: Croatia." European Commission, Brussels, Belgium.

Sundaram, Ramya, and Nithin Umapathi. 2016. "Greece Social Welfare Review: Institutional Mapping." Social Protection and Labor Global Practice, World Bank, Washington, DC

Tesliuc, Emil, Lucian Pop, Margaret Grosh, and Ruslan Yemtsov. 2014. *Income Support for the Poorest: A Review of Experience in Eastern Europe and Central Asia.* Directions in Development Series. Washington, DC: World Bank.

Thompson, Terri S., Asheley Van Ness, and Carolyn T. O'Brien. 2001. *Screening and Assessment in TANF/Welfare-to-Work: Local Answers to Difficult Questions.* Washington, DC: U.S. Department of Health and Human Services; Washington, DC: Urban Institute.

Tubb, Helen. 2012. "Activation and Integration: Working with Individual Action Plans: Toolkit for Public Employment Services." European Commission Mutual Learning Programme for Public Employment Services: DG Employment, Social Affairs, and Inclusion, Brussels, Belgium.

Turkey, Ministry of Family and Social Policy. 2017a. "ISAS Butunlesik: Turkey's Integrated Social Assistance System." Presentation to the government of Turkey.

Turkey, Ministry of Family and Social Policy. 2017b. "Turkey's Integrated Social Assistance System." Ministry of Family and Social Policy, Ankara; World Bank, Washington, DC.

Vardaramatou, Dina, and Ioanna Pertsinidou. 2018. "EMIN Context Report: Greece." European Commission, Brussels, Belgium.

Velarde, Rashiel B. 2018. "The Philippines' Targeting System for the Poor: Successes, Lessons, and Ways Forward." Social Protection Policy Note 16, World Bank and Australian Aid, Washington, DC.

Waddington, Lisa, et al. 2018. "Disability Assessment in European States: ANED Synthesis Report." Academic Network of European Disability Experts (ANED).

Wiseman, William. 2015. "Turkey's Integrated Social Assistance Service System: Case Study." Mimeo. World Bank, Washington DC.

World Bank. 2015. "Romania: Major Social Assistance Benefits." Informal note, World Bank, Washington, DC.

World Bank. 2016. *Evaluating Tanzania's Productive Social Safety Net: Targeting Performance, Beneficiary Profile, and Other Baseline Findings.* Washington, DC: World Bank. http://documents.worldbank.org/curated/en/273011479390056768/Evaluating-Tanzanias-productive-social-safety-net-targeting-performance-beneficiary-profile-and-other-baseline-findings.

World Bank. 2017. *A Fair Adjustment: Efficiency and Equity of Public Spending in Brazil: Volume 1—Overview (English).* Washington, DC: World Bank. http://documents.worldbank.org/curated/en/643471520429223428/Volume-1-Overview.

World Bank. 2018a. *Guidelines for ID4D Diagnostics.* Washington, DC: World Bank. http://documents.worldbank.org/curated/en/370121518449921710/Guidelines-for-ID4D-Diagnostics.pdf.

World Bank. 2018b. "Risk-Sharing for a Diverse and Diversifying World of Work." Review draft, Social Protection and Jobs Global Practice, World Bank, Washington, DC.

World Bank. 2018c. *The State of Social Safety Nets 2018.* Washington, DC: World Bank.

World Bank. Forthcoming. "Interagency Social Protection Assessment (ISPA) Tool on Integrated Social Information Systems," World Bank, Washington, DC.

World Bank and ILO (International Labour Organization). 2016. "A Shared Mission for Universal Social Protection: Concept Note." World Bank, Washington, DC; ILO, Geneva, Switzerland.

Zini, Michele, Alessandra Marini, Eleni Kanavitsa, Chrysa Leventi, Natalia Millan, and Nithin Umapathi. 2018. "Greece: Initial Support to the Guaranteed Minimum Income Rollout: Quantitative Evaluation of the GMI Rollout." Social Protection and Labor Global Practice, World Bank, Washington, DC.

Chapter 6

Payments of Cash Benefits

Tina George Karippacheril, Luz Stella Rodríguez, Ana Verónica López Murillo, and Laura B. Rawlings

With contributions from Karol Karpinski, Ubah Thomas Ubah, Sylvia Baur-Yazbeck, Christabel Dadzie, Craig Kilfoil, Melis Guven, Amjad Zafar Khan, Quanita Khan, Harish Natarajan, Greg Chen, Ashiq Aziz, Kenichi Nishikawa Chávez, Cornelia Tesliuc, Heba Elgazzar, Ahmet Fatih Ortakaya, Anita Mittal, Ambrish Shahi, and Anand Raman

Provision of benefits and services is a key stage of the delivery chain. This chapter focuses on provision of cash benefits, in other words, on payments, while chapter 7 delves into the provision of services.[1] The process for payments provision is intimately linked to the enrollment process, as well as to verification of clients' compliance with conditions when required by the specific program. Payments is a core phase in the recurring implementation cycle and often is one of the main points of contact between a program and people (figure 6.1).

Cash benefits are widely used for social protection, and there is increasingly an emphasis on digitization to deliver safe, secure, swift, and convenient payments in the context of the COVID-19 pandemic. In social assistance, cash transfers account for 0.7 percent of GDP and represent well over half (55 percent) of all spending on social safety nets in the World Bank's ASPIRE database. In addition, in Organisation for Economic Co-operation and Development (OECD) countries, spending on unemployment benefits (insurance or assistance) accounts for 0.7 percent of GDP on average, public spending on disability- or incapacity-related benefits accounts for 1.5 percent of GDP,[2] and spending on pensions (insurance and assistance) averages 7.5 percent of benefits. In sum, significant spending is channeled from governments to people in the form of social protection cash benefits.

Globally, nearly a quarter of adults receive payments from the government—whether public sector wages, a public sector pension, or government transfers (social benefits such as subsidies, unemployment benefits, or payments for educational or medical expenses), according to the World Bank's 2017 Global Findex surveys.[3] In high-income economies, 43 percent of adults receive such payments, compared to 19 percent of adults in developing countries. In low-income countries, these payments are received mostly in cash or near-cash methods.

This chapter is organized as follows:

- Section 6.1 provides a brief overview of how social protection (SP) payments, specifically government-to-person (G2P), have evolved over time.[4] Changes in technology, urbanization, financial infrastructure,

Figure 6.1 Provision of Payments Phase on the Social Protection Delivery Chain

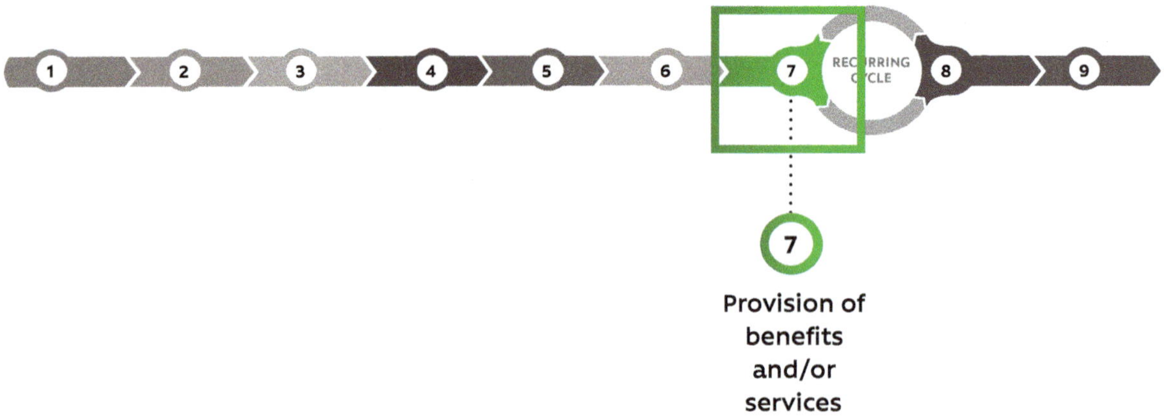

Source: Original figure for this publication.

and covariate shocks such as the COVID-19 crisis are introducing an array of new actors and instruments that have the potential of improving payments services for recipients and therefore have positive effects on financial inclusion and empowerment.

- Section 6.2 discerns what digitization can mean throughout an end-to-end payment process and details each generation in the evolution of SP payments from G2P 1.0 to 4.0.
- Section 6.3 describes key elements to consider in each stage of designing SP payments, from establishing a payments system to managing the recurring payments cycle, including the steps under payments administration and provision.
- Section 6.4 illustrates payment processes for the different generations (G2P 1.0 to 4.0) discerned through process maps of country examples (São Tomé and Príncipe, Nigeria, and Pakistan) reflecting these approaches.
- Section 6.5 has details about technologies supporting payments administration, as well as newer digital and mobile payments mechanisms and platforms that enable a more human-centered design approach to serve the poor and vulnerable.
- Finally, section 6.6 offers some concluding points on the unmet opportunity of improving financial inclusion and using new technologies and in employing a human-centered design approach to adapt payments provision to serve the needs of people.

The country examples discussed in this chapter follow:

- **Africa:** Côte d'Ivoire, Ghana, Kenya, Nigeria, Zambia
- **East Asia and the Pacific:** Indonesia
- **Europe and Central Asia:** Turkey
- **Latin America and the Caribbean:** Brazil, Colombia
- **Middle East and North Africa:** Islamic Republic of Iran, Iraq
- **South Asia:** Bangladesh, India, Pakistan
- **Other OECD countries:** Australia, United States

6.1 EVOLUTION OF G2P PAYMENTS FOR SOCIAL PROTECTION: FINANCIAL INCLUSION OF THE "FIRST MILE"

The digitization of government-to-person (G2P) payments is on the rise. According to the World Bank's Global Payment Systems Survey (2016) and Snapshot of Payment Systems Worldwide (2018), electronic instruments are by far the most widely used methods for G2P payments (including public sector salaries, pension and transfer payments, cash transfers and social benefits).[5] Of the 103 responding central banks, 55 percent indicated electronic instruments are used for cash transfers and social benefits, compared to 70 percent for pensions and transfer benefits and 81 percent for public sector salaries. Although more than a fifth of developing economies use cash for social protection, some countries are leapfrogging traditional payment approaches by adopting rapidly evolving financial and technological services to enhance access and minimize costs of administration and provision.

The impetus for digitizing SP payments arguably has been largely aimed at creating efficiency gains for government. Changes in technology, urbanization, financial infrastructure, and shocks such as the COVID-19 crisis are introducing a new array of instruments and actors in the development and delivery of cash transfers, focusing squarely on the people receiving those transfers. Transfers that a couple of decades ago used to be delivered in cash by line ministries are evolving to digital payments delivered by payment service providers, often into bank or mobile money accounts. The efficiency gains from digitizing payments have a significant fiscal impact for countries, as they offer cost saving options for governments by reducing leakages, improving transparency, and preventing errors, fraud, and corruption. When appropriately designed and implemented, digitizing SP payments can have a significant impact for recipients. Payments without manual intervention can improve safety, speed, security, convenience, choice, predictability, capillarity of liquidity points, increased privacy, and control over use of funds (Bold, Porteous, and Rotman 2012). However, provision of benefits using digital payments can be challenging to some individuals and households, particularly those in remote areas, and those with low levels of financial literacy, awareness, and readiness.

G2P payments to beneficiaries of social protection programs present an unmet opportunity for improving financial inclusion as well as women's economic empowerment for the "first mile." Being able to access transaction accounts or electronic instruments to store money and send and receive payments is the first step toward broader financial inclusion, where individuals can safely use a range of appropriate financial services, including savings, payments, credit, and insurance.[6] The Global Findex surveys find that while account ownership (through a financial institution or a mobile money provider) has increased worldwide, there is a strong access divide between gender, income groups, and rural and urban sectors. This is particularly prevalent in developing countries. Social protection beneficiaries tend to be poor, are often women, and carry a legacy of financial exclusion.[7] Reaching these "first mile" populations and ensuring their financial inclusion holds the promise of being transformational given the large numbers of people involved: while the civil service wage bill accounts for the greater share of GDP for G2P payments, the quantity of social protection beneficiaries receiving G2P payments outnumbers civil servants 5:1. This indicates that digitization of payments for social protection programs has the potential of substantially increasing financial inclusion, particularly among the poor and vulnerable.

There are different levels of digitization of social protection program payments. Figure 6.2 charts the evolution of government-to-person payment systems, and section 6.2 constructs a typology for digitization of payment systems. While most social protection programs tend to offer G2P 1.0, 1.5, and 2.0 payments, countries such as Zambia and Bangladesh are making the leap to G2P 3.0 and G2P 4.0.

The evolution from G2P 1.0 to 4.0 and beyond is not linear and many programs and countries have coexisting modalities. The choice of payment modality is circumscribed by both the digital infrastructure in a country (which is often more limited in poorer rural areas where social protection programs operate) as well as the financial regulatory environment, among other things. Whereas G2P 3.0 and 4.0 are considered more desirable models, they require not only supportive digital infrastructure and financial regulations, but also the ability to work across payment providers and potentially across programs. Although G2P 1.0, 1.5, and 2.0 are generally more prevalent in developing countries, advances in payment systems and infrastructure are evolving rapidly.

Figure 6.2 Evolution of Government-to-Person Payments for Social Protection

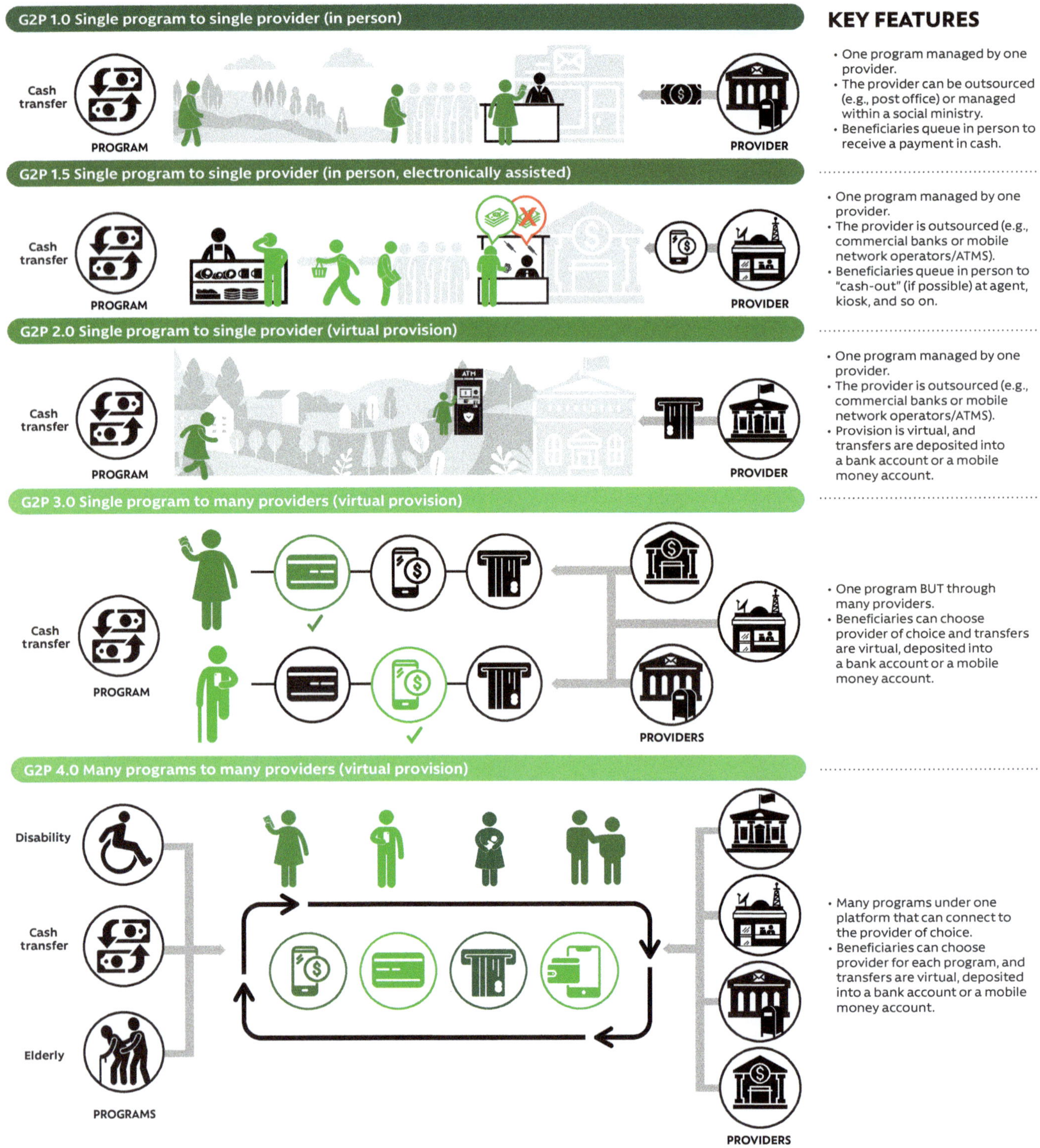

Source: Original figure for this publication, with input from Craig Kilfoil, consultant, Social Protection and Jobs, World Bank, and adapted from a presentation by Silvia Baur-Yazbeck and Gregory Chen of CGAP (Consultative Group to Assist the Poor) on G2P 3.0, "Future of Government Payments," World Bank, February 2019.

6.2 TYPOLOGY AND PURPOSE OF SOCIAL PROTECTION PAYMENTS DIGITIZATION

The simple construct of manual versus digital payments comes up short in helping to understand the spectrum and evolution of social protection (SP) payments. When an end-to-end payments process is digitized but at the very last step, people must turn up, stand in line, and receive cash or a smart card loaded with e-money from a field administrator or a payment service provider, would this be considered a manual or a digitized payment? The notion of payments digitization goes beyond the biometric authentication of beneficiaries or virtual provisioning of payments, both front-end processes visible to individuals, families, and households. Payments digitization extends backward to the automation of payments administration, the back-end processes that are visible only to program administrators. Furthermore, digitization extends forward, beyond administration and provision, to use (by individuals, families, and households) through interoperable systems and acceptance of digital transactions (by service providers and merchants). Where G2P payments are transferred through "closed-loop" systems, the funds might have flowed virtually or digitally end-to-end, but people eventually must cash those out as currency and fail to make use of cashless transactions or operate digital wallets, mobile money accounts, or bank accounts. Provisioning payments through interoperable "open-loop" systems ensures people are not obliged to cash out their transfers, but they can store them and use accounts easily and conveniently for everyday transactions, such as buying food from a merchant or paying for health visits, using point-of-sale (POS) systems.

This begs the question of whether digitization is an end unto itself or a means to an end. From a human-centered design perspective, SP payments digitization is a means to an end, by way of

- ***automating payments administration.*** Back-end payments processes are automated for efficiency, but payments may still be provided in person at the front end.
- ***virtualizing payments provision.*** Payments are made virtually to people at the front end, at times through human-centered design approaches to adapt to their context, providing financial inclusion and empowerment of the "first mile."

See figure 6.3 for a 2x2 matrix that scaffolds opposing characteristics on each end of the spectrum to provide insight into the typology of SP payments by automating back-end administrative processes and virtualizing the provision of front-end processes. Using this typology of payments digitization in figure 6.3, we explain how G2P 1.0 to 4.0 approaches for social protection (in figure 6.2) have evolved, using country case examples.

G2P 1.0, 1.5: Single Program to Single Provider

Payments administration processes are typically automated. Few countries if any manage the back-end payments administration process manually or through Excel spreadsheets (lower left quadrant of figure 6.3: G2P payments manual end to end). The main objective of automating payments administration is to increase the efficiency of public financial management, to prevent leakage, and to reduce operational costs.

G2P 1.0 refers to direct distribution of benefits, from a single program to a single provider, where provision is in person (lower right quadrant in figure 6.3: G2P administration digitized for government efficiency aims), a common modality in developing countries (see also figure 6.2). Provision of benefits in person continues to be offered by many programs even in cases where other methods are available. Payments may be made through instruments such as cash. In some instances, biometric authentication may be used for proof of identification and for proof of life.

Several developing countries use in-person cash provision as a means of disbursing pensions, transfer payments, and social benefits, much more often than high-income economies. More than a fifth (21 percent) of developing countries use cash for social benefits payments.[8] The usual motive is that the financial ecosystem is not developed enough to allow the high volume of low-value transactions at a reasonable transaction cost (to government, to people, or both). The traditional method of delivering benefits in cash does present a range of challenges, especially in the context of the COVID-19 crisis. For the program, challenges are

Figure 6.3 Typology for Digitizing Social Protection Payments Administration and Provision

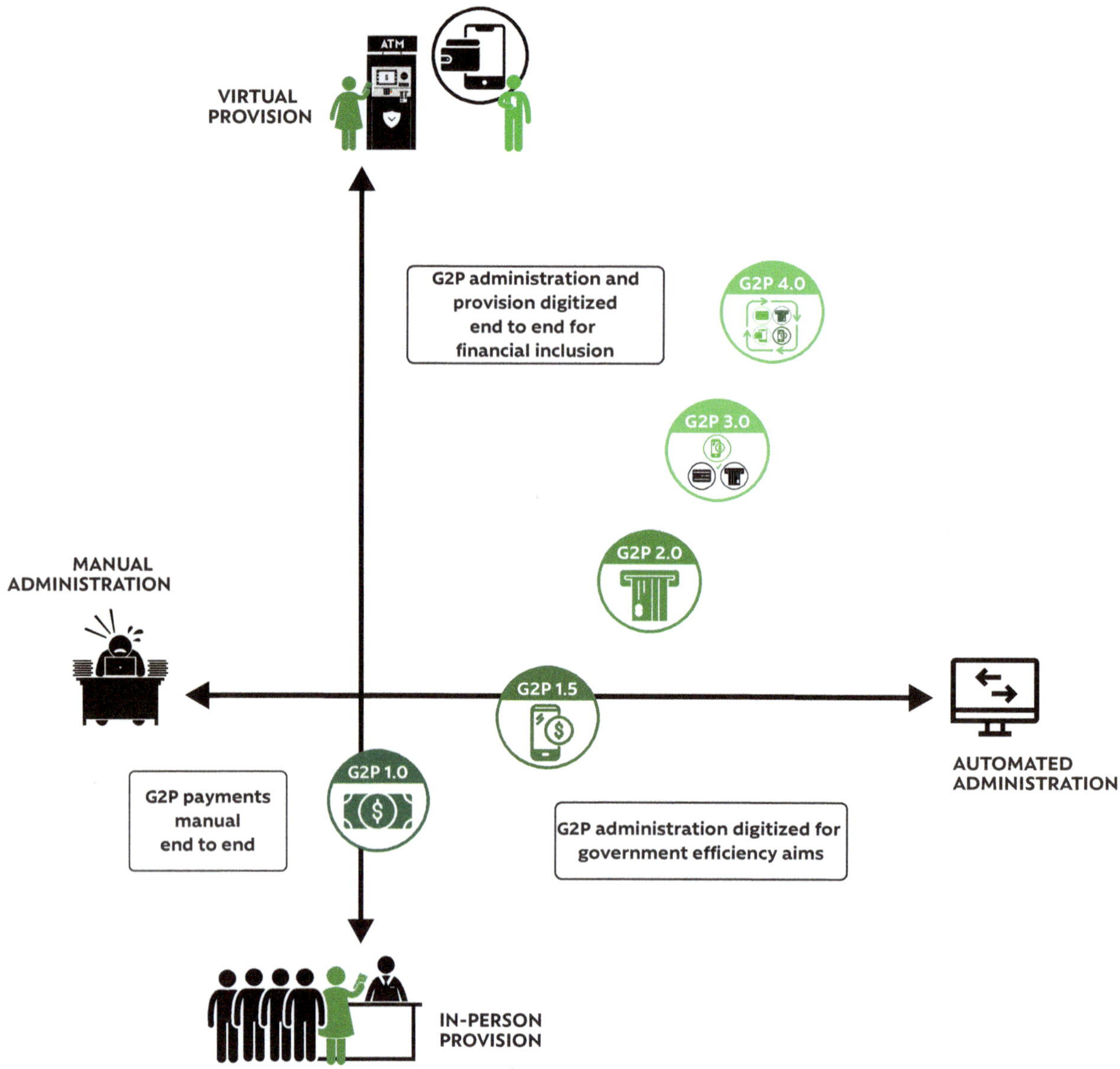

Sources: Original figure for this publication, with Craig P. Kilfoil, consultant, Social Protection and Jobs, World Bank, and inputs from the Consultative Group to Assist the Poor on the evolution of government-to-person payments for social protection.
Note: G2P = government-to-person.

centered on the logistics of distribution such as arranging payment dates, contacting beneficiaries and ensuring security in the transportation and delivery of cash. Beneficiaries often must travel long distances to receive payments at a scheduled time and place. In Niger, program recipients receiving cash had to travel approximately 2 km (one way), approximately half an hour, to get the transfer, while the group receiving transfers via mobile money had to travel less than 0.5 km (less than 10 minutes), and they were able to spread out their cash on different days (Aker et al. 2016). G2P 1.0 presents a missed opportunity for financial inclusion. However, these methods offer advantages as well in terms of beneficiaries' familiarity with the payment method, the use of payment days and points for setting up markets and providing training, and the direct contact provided between the program and the beneficiaries.

G2P 1.5 refers to a distribution of benefits from a single program to a single provider, where provision is in person and electronically assisted (see figure 6.2).

Box 6.1 Automated Payments Administration: Single Program to Single Provider in Ghana's LIPW

Ghana's Cash for Work program—LIPW—assigns beneficiaries to project activities. Beneficiaries clock-in and clock-out attendance on-site using biometrics. Attendance data are synchronized with the beneficiary operations management system (BOMS) for the program. Attendance data are validated and the BOMS generates a payroll schedule and pushes it through three rounds of administrative reviews before the final payroll is approved and financing is committed.

Previously, Excel-based daily attendance sheets (DASH) were printed and distributed on-site after 14 days of work and delivered physically to the local implementing authority. Once the authority cleared the files, the District Finance Office would generate a payroll using Excel to record beneficiary details and days worked. A manual payment list would be calculated and taken to the field as printed copies. Beneficiaries would stand in line and be called by name to offer a thumbprint against calculated earnings to receive cash. It would take up to four months to reconcile payroll and to transmit payments to beneficiaries. The payments administration module of Ghana's BOMS, called GHIPSS, was automated by building a software application, and by introducing a functional biometric application for automated attendance recording. As a result, the entire end-to-end payment administration process is carried out in real time. Once payments instructions are approved, the system loads up to 500,000 smart cards per hour with wage payments.

While payments administration is automated, payments provision is carried out physically, in person. Beneficiaries are biometrically authenticated in person to confirm they are the true owners of the cards before loading wage payments onto smart cards. People line up to cash out their payments. The smart cards allow storage of value in case a beneficiary does not want to withdraw all earnings or misses a payout date. Funds can be accessed at ATMs. The card can be used to make transactions at selected merchants, where these cards are accepted.

Source: Christabel Dadzie, social protection specialist, Social Protection and Jobs (SPJ), World Bank, SPJ Core Course, 2018.

Countries such as Ghana have made the leap from an Excel-based administrative process to a fully automated payment administration process (lower right quadrant in figure 6.3: G2P administration digitized for government efficiency aims), resulting in considerable administrative time and cost efficiencies for the government (box 6.1). **Nevertheless, payments are still provisioned in person, although electronically assisted.** This is primarily because rural bank branches are not close enough to beneficiaries, so payment service providers come to the work site to provide payments. The instrument used in this case is not cash, but a smart card. The government of Ghana is working to identify other options such as payments at gas stations and/or stores where ATM withdrawals can take place.

G2P 2.0: Single Program to Single Provider

G2P 2.0 refers to the initial stage in the digitization of payments provision, often through a single channel (see figure 6.2). Under the G2P 2.0 approach, the back-end payments administration processes between social programs and payment service providers is digitized. However, the aims of digitizing provision are only partially realized as the client experience of travel and wait times may be the same as in a G2P 1.0 or 1.5 model. Payments may be provisioned directly to a (limited purpose or mainstream) bank account or a mobile money account offering flexibility as to when people can access or withdraw their money. Nevertheless, recipients can incur significant private costs to withdraw cash as they may live farther away from a bank branch, ATM, or cash in/cash out (CICO) agent. The G2P 2.0 model can improve the efficiency of payments provision and, if structured properly, can extend some elements of financial inclusion to beneficiaries.

One challenge of the G2P 2.0 model is that different social protection programs in the same country tend to follow uncoordinated approaches to digitization. Individual programs may contract independently with a single payment service provider, or even multiple payment service providers, depending on geographic coverage, nature of payment, type of beneficiary, budget cycle, and so on. Nevertheless, when beneficiaries are not afforded their choice of provider, it is considered a "single channel" approach. When payments are distributed through an outsourced intermediary, a payment service provider, costs may be higher, as a percentage of the transfer.[9] Technical challenges can cause delays in payments. Technology tends to be bespoke and locked-in by vendors, and systems are closed loop, while procurement tends to be lengthy and opaque. Consequently, institutional coordination of payments digitization among social programs and interoperability between institutions and providers prove to be a challenge, although not impossible. Typically, less developed financial ecosystems with rigid (or outdated) payment regulations require multiple transfers between actors before reaching the final beneficiary, which generally translates into higher transaction costs.

Countries with a more robust and integrated payments infrastructure—systems that have adopted the treasury single account model—allow direct transfers from the Ministry of Finance (National Treasury) or the Central Bank to beneficiaries' accounts. Payment instructions are processed by the central bank, which debits the single treasury account and credits the beneficiary's account. Direct transfers from the government to individual bank accounts require banking institutions to confirm proof of identification and unique ownership of an account through KYC (know your customer) and CDD (customer due diligence) processes. Payments directly to mobile money or digital wallet accounts may require legal, regulatory, and technological reforms to public financial management systems.

Indonesia made a rapid shift from in-person delivery of cash payments to payments provided through bank accounts with considerable gains in efficiency and transparency. The government made an important step toward the development of a single payment distribution channel for social assistance cash and in-kind transfers for PKH (conditional cash transfer), PIP (education assistance), BPNT (food assistance), and some selected subsidies. Transfers are made directly from a treasury single account to beneficiary bank accounts. To do so, Indonesia opened up bank accounts for 10 million households served under the PKH conditional cash transfer program (upper right quadrant in figure 6.3: G2P administration and provision digitized end to end for financial inclusion) (box 6.2). Iran undertook an ambitious fuel subsidy reform in 2010–11, replacing subsidies with universal cash transfers. The government worked with banks to open 16 million new bank accounts—a 36 percent expansion in a year. The ATM network was expanded in rural areas. A total of 92 percent of G2P SP payments were delivered digitally into an account (Atansah et al. 2017).

Box 6.2 Enabling Electronic Payments to Bank Accounts: Single Program to Single Provider in Indonesia

The Ministry of Social Affairs (MoSA) defines which families are to be paid for Indonesia's conditional cash transfer program (PKH). A payment instruction is sent to the Ministry of Finance treasury for approval and then to the relevant HIMBARA (state-owned bank) for processing and delivering payments. When PKH implementers and HIMBARA started the initial transformation to digital payments, the accounts were opened at bank headquarters using beneficiary data sourced from the Unified Database (UDB) initially and then validated by facilitators. The facilitators collected the necessary know-your-customer (KYC) data and sent this to MoSA, who forwarded it to the banks.

PKH uses the public financial management information system, OMSPAN, to directly transfer payments from the treasury to individuals' bank accounts using the treasury single account (TSA). CSPAN is the government's mechanism to render payroll for civil servants directly from the treasury. By 2019, all PKH families in the first and second payment phase received

continued

Box 6.2 *(continued)*

payments directly to their accounts from the treasury, monitored via OMSPAN with delivery managed by HIMBARA.

These processes have significantly improved efficiencies for government and contributed to financial inclusion outcomes. They are being realized through the development of an integrated social assistance payments authority, and a collection of five state-owned banks (HIMBARA) with benefits and payments unified under a family welfare card (KKS—Kartu Keluarga Sejahtera). By the end of 2018, 10 million households received BPNT benefits (food assistance) managed under the KKS/HIMBARA platform and 10 million households received payments under the PKH program. Payments for PIP (education assistance) shifted to the banking system earlier than PKH but are not yet integrated under the same payment platform as PKH and BPNT. Other social assistance programs are not linked to this payments platform.

Knowing that the switch from cash to digitized payments would include some challenges, the government of Indonesia had an eye on field experiences in different places. Field visits revealed a number of insights from the perspective of the payment service provider (state-owned bank, Mandiri, one of the HIMBARA banks) and beneficiaries. Interviews with clients in Buru island, part of the Maluku province, in the East, reveal a not atypical range of issues:

- **Identification.** Many people still do not have NIK-ID cards (especially in mountainous areas). A marriage certificate is needed to get a Family ID Card (Kartu Keluarga, KK), but people can get marriage certificates only if they had an official religious ceremony; traditional/informal marriages are not recognized.
- **Access.** ATM machines are in town, over five kilometers from their village. They have to walk many hours to get to the subdistrict to then wait in line to get the cash from the bank (at cash distribution events).
- **Technical literacy.** Some had never used an ATM card and had to learn to punch in the PINs.

Digitization of payments is beneficial in improving administrative efficiencies for government, but remains operationally challenging, particularly in serving people in remote areas. Nevertheless, further adjustments need to be made to get the most benefit from G2P 2.0 systems.

Providing choice and convenience to beneficiaries through multiple channels (a G2P 3.0 or 4.0 approach) can help advance Indonesia's goals of social protection and financial inclusion for the poorest even further.

Sources: Kathy Lindert; Juul Pinxten, social protection specialist, Social Protection and Jobs, World Bank; Changqing Sun, senior economist, Social Protection and Jobs, World Bank; Tina George Karippacheril.

G2P 3.0: Single Program to Many Providers

G2P 3.0 refers to the digitization of payments, from a single program to multiple providers, offering choice and convenience to end-users (see figure 6.2). G2P 3.0 allows for recipients to access payments from one or many programs through accounts and service providers of their choice. It allows them to switch service providers, and transfer accounts based on their own analysis of cost and convenience. Governments can work with multiple service providers and offer larger transfer volumes, thus decreasing costs of provision and increasing the attractiveness of the business case to potential payment providers. The model offers incentives for greater interoperability among government institutions and service providers, thereby also allowing for a shift in the focus of service delivery to a more human-centered approach in contrast to the traditional approach of serving government agencies as the end-user. Human-centered design may allow for different solutions in remote areas or for clients with particular barriers, including sometimes cash payments where these are the most convenient. The G2P 3.0 model for SP is somewhat aspirational for a number of countries. Beyond the efficiencies introduced in this model, the approach has also signaled the viability and desirability of providing choice and convenience to the poor through digitizing payments. See the later section 6.5, Technologies Supporting Digital Payments, for more details.

Zambia has multiple social protection programs, of which the Social Cash Transfer is central. However, only the Girl's Education and Women's Empowerment and Livelihoods Project (GEWEL) program provides payments in a coordinated approach through multiple channels (see upper right quadrant in figure 6.3: G2P administration and provision digitized end to end). GEWEL is a productive inclusion and bursary program for women and girls and uses a national payments system to provide productive grants virtually over multiple channels to beneficiaries. GEWEL empowers beneficiaries to choose how they are paid. By the end of 2020, 75,000 women in rural and remote areas will have received transfers through a bank, mobile wallet account, or a prepaid card (box 6.3).

G2P 4.0: Many Programs to Many Providers

G2P 4.0 refers to the digitization of payments enabling multiple programs to link to multiple providers, through an interoperability approach (see figure 6.2). Bangladesh has multiple, fragmented social programs that strive to offer payments through a coordinated approach through multiple channels and seeks to build a multiprogram to multiprovider model. It is based on the premise that people should have the option to choose different payment service providers for different programs, or the same provider for different programs. A payments gateway approach can help with interoperability of payment methods for different programs to the same individual/family/household. Bangladesh, under the Social Protection Budget Management Unit (SPBMU) of the Finance Division, is building an interoperable payments management system to coordinate payments with various public and private service providers, where a mapper directory matches unique ID numbers to financial addresses. The objective is to provide the beneficiaries with the option to collect their payments anywhere at

Box 6.3 Enabling a Coordinated Approach to Provision: Single Program to Many Providers in Zambia's GEWEL Program

The Girl's Education and Women's Empowerment and Livelihoods Project (GEWEL) in Zambia, through its Support Women's Livelihoods component, provides a cash transfer of US$225 split into two payments. Analysis of financial sector providers showed that no single private sector provider had the capacity to make the GEWEL payments nationally. The government thus decided to allow families to choose among several options, rather than contract one or more PSPs. The GEWEL program developed a payments platform and established procedures for payments authorization, where five providers are participating: (1) Zoona, a person-to-person (P2P) transfer service and mobile wallet; (2) ZamPost, the Zambian national postal service, which offers transfer services, accounts, and loans; (3) United Bank for Africa, a commercial bank that offers a traditional account with an ATM Visa card; (4) National Savings and Credit Bank (NatSave), a state nonbank financial institution that offers traditional accounts; and (5) MTN, a mobile network operator that offers a mobile wallet. The platform offering these different providers is serving 30 districts in the program, and by the end of 2020 it will have expanded to all 51 districts in the program.

A national payments/electronic funds transfer (EFT) system manages transmittal from multiple programs to multiple payment service providers. When beneficiary payment instructions are received from multiple government agencies for social assistance programs, the National Payments System transmits to various payment service providers. They allow payment service providers to provide greater choice and convenience for beneficiaries to receive payments. Figure B6.3.1 illustrates the payment systems in Zambia where ZECHL, an interbank switch, connects to MTN, Airtel, and Zoona's mobile network operators, as well as banks (IndoZambia, Barclays, Stanbic, UBA, NatSave, Zenaco, Investrust, and Cavmont).

continued

Box 6.3 *(continued)*

Figure B6.3.1 Payment Systems Provision: The GEWEL Program in Zambia

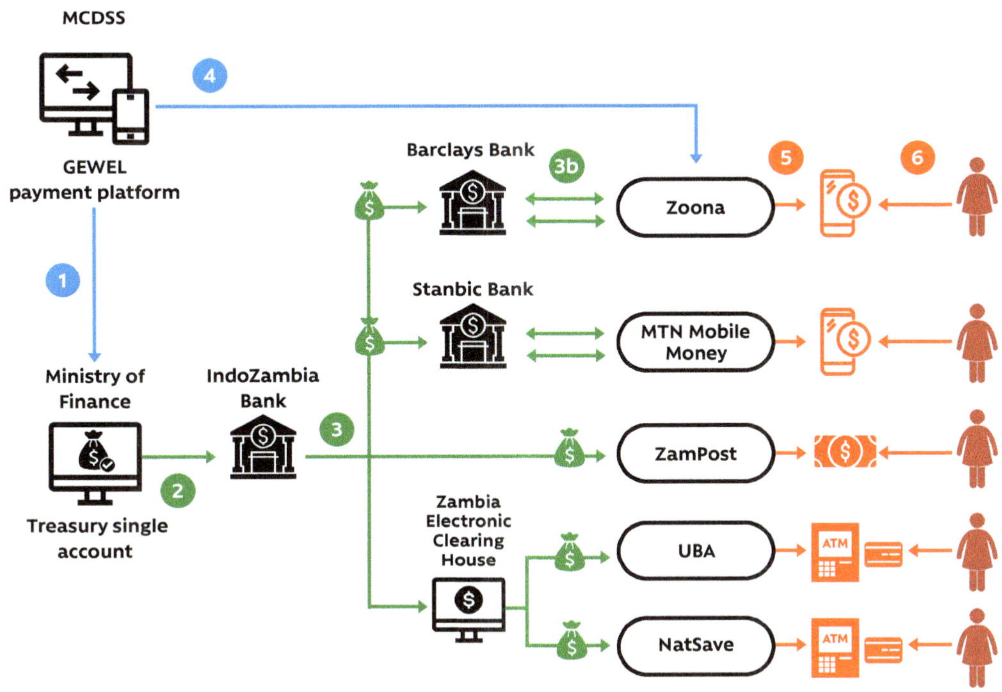

1 **The Ministry of Community Development and Social Services (MCDSS)** requests payment through the payments platform, providing aggregated transfer amount for each provider.

2 **Accountant General** at Ministry of Finance approves payment request and initiates payment from the treasury to IndoZambia Bank.

3 **IndoZambia Bank** transfers aggregated payments to providers through Zambia Electronic Clearing House Ltd. (ZECHL) or bilateral agreements.

3b **Barclay's and Stanbic Banks** credit Zoona's and MTN's (a mobile network operator) pooled accounts.

4 **The MCDSS** initiates a second payment request to each provider through the platform, providing transfer amount for each participant.

5 **Providers** credit participants' accounts with their entitlements.

6 **Participant** goes to her preferred access point for cash-out.

Sources: Craig Kilfoil, World Bank's SPJ (Social Protection and Jobs) Core Course, 2018; Baur-Yazbeck, Kilfoil, and Botea 2019.
Note: GEWEL = Girl's Education and Women's Empowerment and Livelihoods Project; UBA = United Bank for Africa.

any time. This contrasts with the closed-loop electronic payment modalities that have proliferated across several countries, where beneficiaries need to collect their payment at a temporary payment desk during a specific date or dates. The idea is to enhance the beneficiary experience by using the national identification (NID) for authentication (avoiding redundant debit cards and authentication mechanisms), through the mapper, to connect the beneficiary ID information to their respective accounts at the back end, allowing beneficiaries to withdraw their benefits at any commercial bank branch or mobile payment service provider agent, or a government-owned post office; this also allows them to easily switch providers and accounts (box 6.4).

Box 6.4 Building an Interoperable Payments Management System: Many Programs to Many Providers in Bangladesh

Bangladesh is building a payments mapper for interoperability. The mapper is interoperable with the national ID system (under the Election Commission) for verification of IDs, and with banks and mobile payment service providers for account verification and to exchange information on ID verification (see figure B6.4.1).

Figure B6.4.1 Payments Systems in Bangladesh

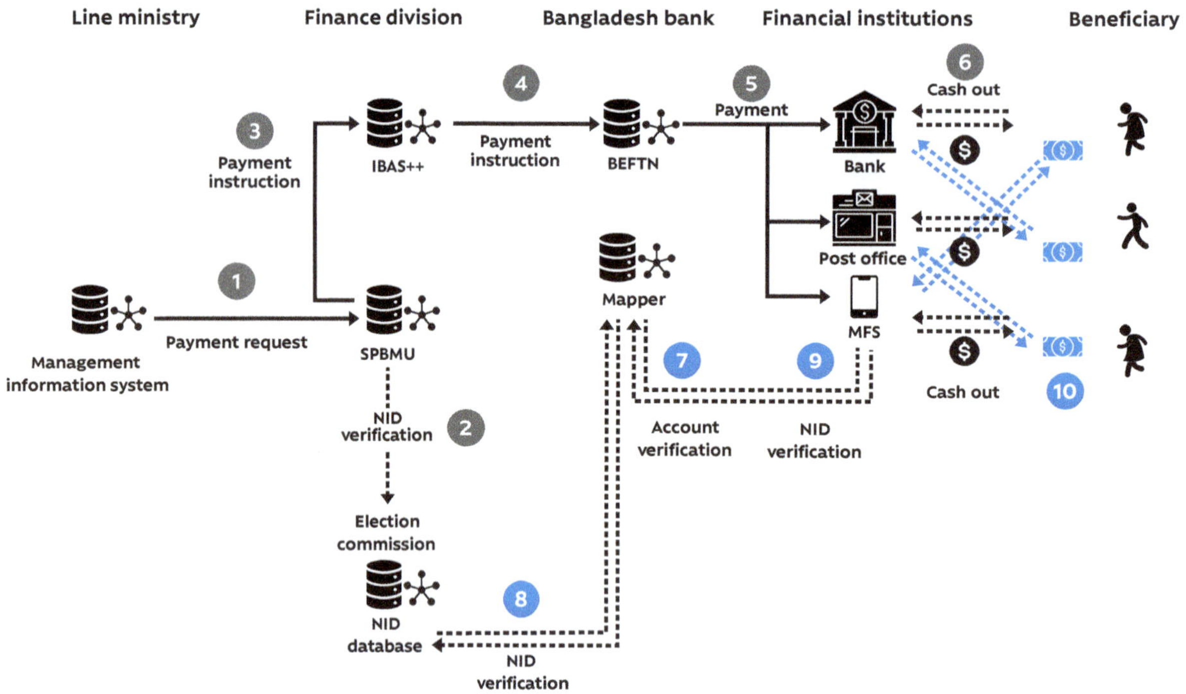

Sources: Ashiq Aziz, senior social protection specialist, Social Protection and Jobs, South Asia, World Bank; Yoonyoung Cho, senior economist, Social Protection and Jobs, East Asia and Pacific, World Bank; Kenichi Nishikawa Chávez, 2018.

Note: BEFTN = Bangladesh Electronic Funds Transfer Network; MFS= mobile financial service; NID = national identification; SPBMU = Social Protection Budget Management Unit.

6.3 HOW TO'S: DELIVERING G2P PAYMENTS FOR SOCIAL PROTECTION

Given the prominence of cash transfers in social protection spending, it is crucial to understand how G2P payments are designed, administered, and provided for SP programs. Payments are multiactor, multistep processes that require establishing a payment system, followed by the management of recurring payments cycles. We examine these steps in greater detail, paying specific attention to trends, innovations, and human-centered design considerations for designing, administering, and provisioning G2P payments in social protection, to advance the goals of financial inclusion and women's economic empowerment.

The implementation of payments involves **(1) payments administration processes** and **(2) payment provision and payment reconciliation.**

Figure 6.4 Payment of Government-to-Person SP Cash Transfers: Phases of Implementation

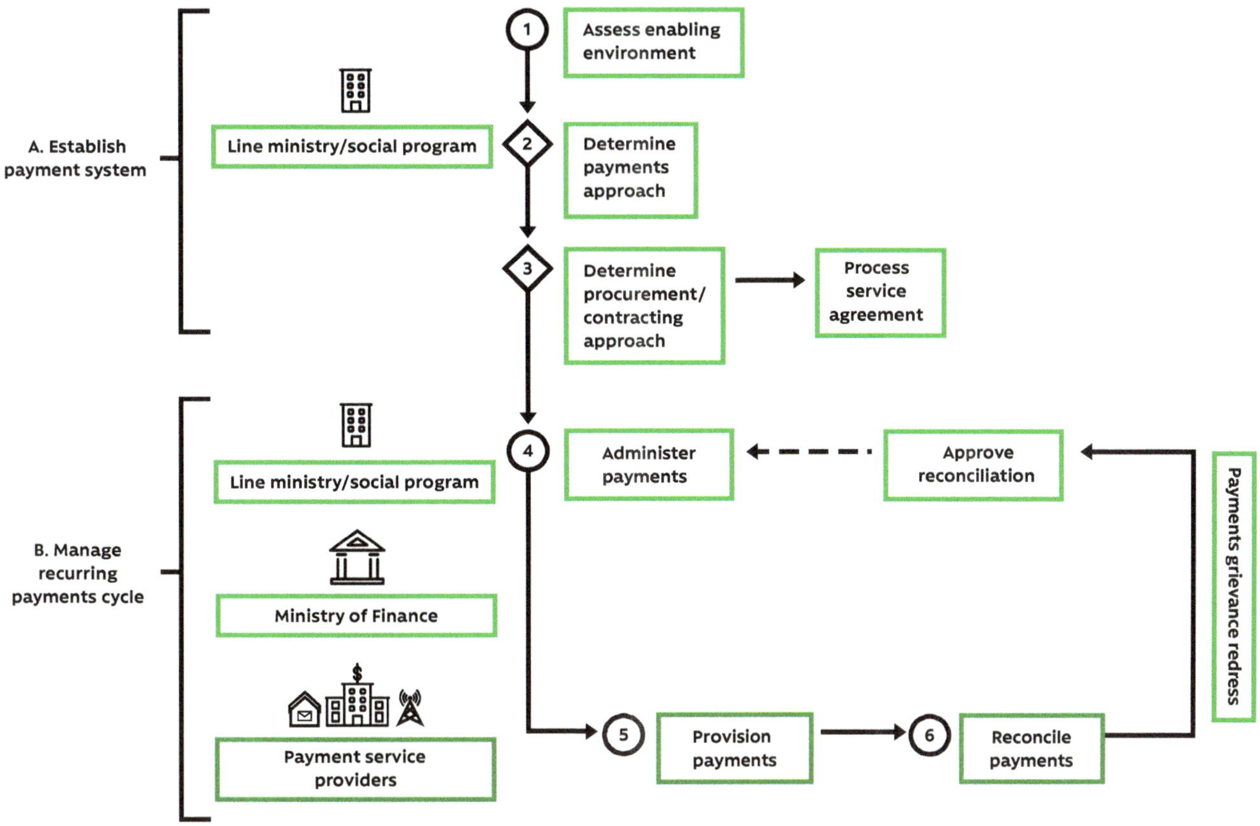

Source: Original figure for this publication.
Note: SP = social protection.

Figure 6.4 provides a step-by-step overview of the processes illustrated above, beginning with assessing the enabling environment (step 1), determining the payments approach (step 2), determining a procurement/contracting approach (step 3), administering payments (step 4), provisioning payments (step 5), and reconciling payments (step 6).[10]

Establishing the Payment System[11]

There are several decisions and factors behind setting up a payment system. Some are determined by external and country-specific realities, while others emphasize a human-centered design approach. An assessment of the enabling environment in a country provides key information to determine appropriate payment instruments (digital or in-person options), and the best suited approach, be it direct transfers from central bank to beneficiary's personal account at a bank of choice versus intermediating through a single or multiple payment service providers.[12] Ensuring a human-centered design in the payment system through onboarding and other design elements will support the payments experience of social protection beneficiaries.

Assess Enabling Environment

Decisions about payment mechanisms should be informed by a comprehensive assessment of the supporting payments environment. This includes gaining an understanding of the institutions that manage payments administration processes as well as the payments ecosystem, potential payment service providers, and physical infrastructure for distribution of transfers—potential cash-out access points—such as community centers, bank branches, ATMs, point-of-sale (POS) terminals, and other channels, including CICO agent networks. It requires an evaluation of geographical coverage as well as knowledge about the existing structure of costs. We examine in further detail the institutional arrangements for payments, regulatory aspects, interoperability, and coverage. Further detail on the overall enabling environment and a guide to assessing the payments environment are available in the Inter-Agency Social Protection Assessments (ISPA) Social Protection Payments tool (ISPA 2016).

Institutional Arrangements

SP G2P payments is intrinsically a multiactor and multisector agenda. Different actors play diverse roles in the delivery of SP G2P payments: policy makers, implementers, funders, regulators, aggregators, and payment service providers, among others. Often, an underdeveloped payments environment has fewer players, which translates to fewer payment options for recipients. Countries with a more evolved payments environment tend to offer a wider set of options, enabling regulations and a clearer distribution of roles and responsibilities (see table 6A.1 in annex 6A). Actors involved in social protection payments delivery include beneficiaries (or designated recipients), line ministries in charge of the delivery of social programs, ministries of finance, central banks, ID agencies, civil registration authorities, communications authorities, regulators, payment service providers, donors, and humanitarian agencies.

The ministry of finance plays a key role in the process. In countries that have adopted the treasury single account (TSA) model, the treasury department is responsible for authorizing payments out of government accounts. When the payment process is outsourced, the treasury transfers money to the PSPs responsible for the "first mile" account credits and withdrawals. For direct benefit payment schemes, the treasury directly makes the batch payment to beneficiaries' accounts (provided that all beneficiaries have a bank account). Interoperable payment switches enable the transfer of funds in a single transaction, from the account of the specific government program to the account or wallet of the social protection program recipient (see later section 6.5, Technologies Supporting Digital Payments).

Line ministries responsible for SP policies and programs oversee the design and implementation of programs and the administration of corresponding benefits. While the delivery of social services clearly corresponds to the line ministry's core activities, often the process of delivering cash tends to be new or outside of their expertise, and therefore ministries usually opt to involve external actors to take care of or participate in the delivery of payments. For in-person delivery of payments, line ministries may rely on local governments, community organizations, or nongovernmental organizations (NGOs).

Line ministries tend to outsource payments provision to payment service providers such as state banks, post offices, commercial banks, mobile money operators, and other money service businesses. The outsourcing of the end-to-end process may include account opening, crediting of beneficiaries' accounts or wallets, or cash-out through third-party providers. Payment service providers may have different motivations. While some stakeholders are involved in social protection payments for corporate social responsibility reasons, some are motivated by genuine expectation of a profitable business opportunity.

One of the challenges in the design and implementation of payments is in understanding the rationale of each stakeholder for participating in the provision of payments. When possible, multiple providers can be beneficial in terms of cost and convenience. Increased competition can bring down costs for programs and provide additional options for beneficiaries. Having single or multiple payment service providers is a practical choice that is circumscribed, for example, by geographical coverage or financial sector regulations. There are cases where some geographical areas are covered by only a single bank, or where availability of broadband or payment points are limited. Regulations can govern which types of entities are legally allowed to operate as payment service providers for G2P payments, and/or prohibit nonbank entities from processing monetary transfers. The participation of state banks could be explained by factors such as lack of geographic coverage by commercial financial institutions, costs related to service provision, or costs associated with reaching populations in remote areas.

Regulatory Framework and Infrastructure

Understanding the payments environment entails understanding the countries' legal and regulatory framework governing the financial sector, and financial infrastructure. Globally, the basic legal reference for payments is set by the central bank. Other relevant laws include the banking law, securities market laws (which explicitly refer to payment system issues), central bank regulations and payment systems laws, e-money laws (with explicit references to payments). Payment systems laws are usually seen in regions which tend to have a weaker legal infrastructure for financial transactions. The legal framework includes aspects of coverage of settlement finality, netting, and the electronic processing of payments.[13] Other legal aspects of payments include electronic money, individuals' access to accounts, regulation to allow nonbank provision of payment services, branchless banking regulations, KYC regulations, data protection and privacy, and consumer protection regulations, among others (Staschen and Meagher 2018).

Assessing financial infrastructure entails determining entities that are licensed and registered for operation in the country. These may include specialized service providers such as clearinghouses, entities operating mobile money platforms, payment card networks, switches, electronic fund transfer networks, and payment aggregators. In addition to financial institutions such as commercial and state banks, payment service providers (PSPs) include nonbank payment service providers, such as money transfer operators (MTOs), mobile network operators (MNOs), supervised and unsupervised nonbank financial institutions, and other nonfinancial institutions. Typically, central banks regulate and supervise payment systems operators, sharing responsibility with banking supervisory authorities.

In terms of the regulatory framework, assessments determine entities that can offer transaction accounts and payment services, particularly since G2P transfers for social protection tend to be large volumes of low-value transfers. Existing regulations may not authorize nonbanking institutions (such as telecom companies) to deliver G2P payments to avoid fiduciary risks. Other aspects of the regulatory framework include the Anti-Money Laundering/Combating the Financing of Terrorism (AML/CFT) Act, Financial Action Task Force (FATF) standards, and KYC and CDD laws and standards for opening accounts and wallets. These are standard controls and policies financial institutions use to verify identity and ensure payment service providers are doing business with legitimate entities. Regulations pertaining to fund transfer and cash-out fees, consumer protection standards, and existence of regulation-mandated products such as "no-frills" or basic bank accounts are also important.[14]

Payment instruments for cashless transactions include credit transfers, direct debits, payments with debit cards and credit cards, and e-money. Access points and channels include branches, agents, ATMs, POS terminals, and internet-enabled mobile devices. POS terminals may include magnetic stripe, biometric, or chip-enabled access. Underlying these transactions are clearing and settlement arrangements such as automated clearinghouses (ACHs) and real-time gross settlement systems.

Consider all fees, fixed and varied, that may be charged to programs and to beneficiaries, particularly when programs are preparing to scale up. Administrative and operational fees may include charges for identifying and opening bank accounts; fees associated to issuing banking cards, recurring fees for ATM use, POS, e-transfers, and individual transfers; and additional fees or charges for carrying out financial literacy trainings; among others. To mitigate costs, governments can allow PSPs to earn on float, by paying providers a fee, or by paying a top-up to recipients. (See annex 6B on payment service contracting models and table 6C.1 in annex 6C for fee distribution options.)

Interoperability and Coverage

Interoperability makes it possible for individuals to use their accounts/wallets/cards seamlessly (though probably at a cost) at any acceptance point. ATMs are more often part of an interoperable network than POS terminals, although in East Asia and Pacific, Sub-Saharan Africa, and South Asia, poor interoperability of access points is more likely.[15] A payment switch connects various institutions allowing interchange of payment transactions through routing authorization and authentication-related messages between participating institutions, and generation and distribution of clearing and settlement files. While switches originated in processing ATM and POS transactions, they have grown to include internet transactions, mobile devices, and smart payment cards (chip cards that store data on integrated circuit chips as well as magnetic stripes for backward compatibility). Payment switches can also host platforms for e-money. Interoperability increases positive network externalities to beneficiaries and effectively, the size of the access channel network.

To be accessible to SP beneficiaries, PSPs should have a large distribution network, including their own branches and third-party agents, without which the cost of access may be high. Coverage of infrastructure and quality of the network of agents are important, particularly their ability to offer sufficient liquidity and willingness to offer services to SP recipients. Many PSPs use agents to provision payments to recipients. Agents verify identity, enable transactions, and act as the client interface (ISPA 2017). For example, with 228 mobile money agents per 100,000 people and with large differences by country in Sub-Saharan Africa, mobile money agents have seven times more reach than ATMs and 20 times more reach than bank branches (Aker 2020).

An assessment of the coverage of foundational unique identification systems and social registries is essential. Government-recognized, foundational unique identity credentials enable recipients to open accounts and to authenticate their identity to receive transfers. ID systems are also integral to carrying out CDD for KYC requirements. Social registries enable the assessment of the needs and conditions of applicants/registrants to social programs. Data collected from applicants in social registries or beneficiary operations management systems (see chapters 4, 5, and 8) may include choice of payment methods as well as the existence of financial addresses for payments.

Determine Payments Approach

Careful choices need to be made regarding payments implementation and design, as these will have implications for accessibility of social protection benefits and the wider financial inclusion of the poor. The first set of choices are whether to automate the back-end payments administration processes to facilitate delivery, and accordingly either design for a single program (a common approach, but not necessarily ideal) or follow a coordinated approach with other social programs.

Digitizing Payments

Governments typically invest in digitizing back-end payments administration systems to build in efficiencies, but this is a partial digitization approach, as indicated in the earlier section on the evolution of SP G2P payments. With regard to digitizing the front-end payments service provision processes, a second set of choices need to be made: provision payments to individuals in person, or virtually using a variety of digital approaches, including to bank accounts. Depending on a combination of these choices, there are implications for financial inclusion and payments accessibility, particularly for the poor and vulnerable. For more details, see later section 6.5, Technologies Supporting Digital Payments including human-centered design adaptations (see box 6.8 and table 6.2).

Direct Transfer

In countries that have a TSA model of public financial management, the treasury department is responsible for authorizing payments out of government accounts as "direct transfers." One-third of countries in the World Bank's Global Payment Systems Survey (GPSS) indicated that ministries of finance (through national treasuries or equivalent institutions) make all payments directly to the beneficiary upon request by the executing agency.[16] Direct transfers can disintermediate payment service providers and other go-betweens that are typically responsible for distributing the transfers. Direct G2P transfers have the advantage of eliminating intermediaries and costs and improving security and discretion, while encouraging financial inclusion. Direct transfers are possible when beneficiaries all have bank accounts and can be uniquely identified. Nevertheless, some costs—that are typically covered by social programs—are transferred to beneficiaries.[17] In contrast, nearly half of all GPSS respondents reported that ministries of finance (through national treasuries or equivalent institutions) deposit funds to the accounts of the various government agencies, which in turn make the payment to the intended beneficiary.

Payment Service Provider

Depending on the understanding of the payments' environment, the line ministry or the program's administrator determines whether to distribute cash to beneficiaries (through local offices, post offices, bank branches, and cashiers or temporary/"pop-up" pay points), or to transfer directly to recipients' accounts. In both cases, the line ministry assesses the most appropriate channel to deliver payments, and if the process could be managed in-house within the government (without the intervention of external actors), or if it is necessary to contract out a payment service provider to assume that responsibility. The government may opt to have more than one modality and PSP involved. If the decision involves delivering all (or part) of payments into bank accounts, the line ministry is responsible for ensuring that:

- designated recipients from beneficiary families have accounts with financial institutions, know how to access their money, and that recourse and customer support mechanisms are available (**account opening**);

- accounts are credited with the funds—the amount of the benefit—and the beneficiaries know when the funds are available (**funds transfer**); and
- beneficiaries have the means to use the funds on the account to meet their needs without facing undue burdens or excessive transaction fees (**funds use**). This can be further divided into cash out (withdrawal of paper cash) and the use of funds for cashless payments (e.g., at shops, electronic instant payments).

Decisions on authentication methods should fit the context and need. Through different factors of authentication, it can be ensured that the intended recipient receives a payment. AML/CFT standards govern authentication for financial institutions. If payments are distributed in person by line ministries or subcontracted, single or two-factor authentication methods should be available. Technologies can support authentication, like biometric readers, but special care and calculations on ease of use and convenience to recipients, as well as returns on investment need to be determined beforehand, as they are typically costly endeavors.

Transitioning from in-person cash payments to virtual provision approaches may come at a cost to beneficiaries. In-person cash provision of transfers may be brought close to beneficiaries, while account-based payments rely on the existing financial infrastructure (branches, ATMs, POS), which may require that beneficiaries travel farther to payment points, although this varies. Therefore, considerations for private costs, such as travel costs, can be addressed in the cost structure, for example by topping up payments to compensate beneficiaries (see annex 6C). Similarly, interaction and experience with new interfaces require that beneficiaries adopt new skills. Financial education and customer service aspects should also be prioritized and planned as part of transitioning between approaches in payments provision.

Payment Frequency

Program design-related factors include (1) **the objective of the transfer,** considering that more frequent transfers are common for programs aimed at stabilizing income versus less frequent transfers for those with productive inclusion aims; (2) **the type of program**, for example, conditional cash transfers tend to have a different payment schedule than a social pension or a public works program, as conditionalities monitoring or number of days worked may have implications on frequency; and (3) **the size of the benefit** (in relation to private costs incurred by recipients). Provision-related factors include availability of funds, financial infrastructure (the availability and accessibility of payment points), and capacity of payment service providers (Rodríguez et al., forthcoming).

Financial factors, as well as administrative and regulatory constraints, may play a role in decisions to modify the frequency of payments, including efforts to reduce program costs. Typically, there are fees associated with individual payments (in addition to the cost incurred in having a lump sum of money "floating" in a payment service provider's account).[18] Reducing the number of payments in a year can translate into a significant reduction in transaction fees. Costs in terms of time and capacity can also determine the need for adjusting the payment frequency of a program. Constraints can arise from administrative processes related to conditionalities monitoring and/or in the reconciliation of payments. Technological changes, such as automation of processes or changes in payment modalities, can also affect the frequency of payments (i.e., moving from manual distribution of payments to direct deposits into recipients' account). Similarly, changes in the regulatory environment that restrict or allow changes in the delivery of payments (e.g., new modalities or providers) can have the same effect. The COVID-19 context and social distancing also play a role in the frequency and staggering of payments.

Payments frequency may also depend on recipients needs and preferences. For example, if private or program costs are too high (compared to the size of the actual benefit), the frequency may be reduced. See box 6.5 on the management, frequency, and timing of payments for Brazil's Bolsa Família Program.

Determine Procurement/Contracting Approach

Agreements for opening recipients' accounts and delivering payments are forged with payment service providers. The options include (1) a regulation whereby a payment service provider such as a state bank or post office is mandated to provide the payments for a fixed

Box 6.5 Payments for Brazil's Bolsa Família Program: Management, Frequency, and Timing

The Bolsa Família Program (BFP) pays a monthly conditional cash transfer to beneficiary families according to their per capita income, number of family members, and number of children or adolescents ages 0–17 or pregnant/lactating women in the household. Families can apply to be included in the program on-demand at municipal offices via the Cadastro Único (social registry). The program covers around 14 million families.

Payments are made each month and managed by the Caixa Econômica Federal (Caixa) through its management of the Cadastro Único and SIBEC (the benefits management system), under the supervision of the Ministry of Social Development (MDS). The Caixa is responsible for distributing BFP Social Cards to all families and crediting their accounts with payments each month.[a]

An innovative feature of the BFP is the staggered payments calendar**.** Not all beneficiaries are paid on the same day of the month. The date of payment is made according to the last digit of each beneficiary's Social Identification Number (NIS).[b] This staggering of payment days has many advantages: (1) it avoids clashing with days when other banking transactions are highest to avoid overloading the system with excess cash withdrawals on any single day; (2) it can contribute to the multiplier effect by smoothing the influx of cash into small local economies—and to avoid price spikes or gaps in supply (which can happen if everyone goes to market on the same "payday"); and (3) it can help protect the safety of beneficiaries because others do not know the day of their payments. The payments calendar is publicized widely so people know when their accounts will be credited. Key steps in the payments process include:

- ***Approving benefits.*** Any changes detected in the Cadastro Único, together with the outcomes of conditionalities monitoring, are reflected in the BFP monthly payments to families. New beneficiaries may be incorporated each month, and benefit amounts may be adjusted based on monitoring of conditionalities and beneficiary information. The benefit award depends exclusively on the MDS, which issues instructions to the Caixa to include the entitled and selected families on the BFP payroll. This process, undertaken by SIBEC (the benefits management system) and operated by the Caixa, is impersonal, which is a significant advantage of the system.
- ***Establishing the payroll.*** Once the benefit is approved, family data are entered in the BFP Payroll, which is updated monthly. It contains all beneficiary families identified by the NIS of the designated recipient, as well as the amount of the benefit approved and other information. The BFP Social Card contains the name and NIS of the designated recipient for each family. The Caixa processes the payroll at the beginning of each month.
- ***Cashing out.*** Payment is made during the last 10 working days of each month depending on the NIS of the designated recipient. The Social Card is the most common way to withdraw BFP cash. In May 2017, 73 percent of withdrawals were done this way. Other payment methods include (1) through a basic simplified bank checking account; (2) through off-line payment by means of a bank money order, upon presentation of ID by designated recipient (very rare); or (3) through a special withdrawal procedure used by Caixa mobile teams in remote areas where there are no functioning ATMs. Printed payment receipts include information on the date and amount of the payment. They are also used by MDS to convey messages to beneficiaries, such as information on upcoming deadlines for updating their information, reminders of conditionalities, updates on their compliance status, and so on. Beneficiaries can also download a smartphone app where they can consult the payment calendar, check their benefit status, find the nearest place where funds can be accessed.

Source: Kathy Lindert, based on WWP 2017.

continued

Box 6.5 *(continued)*

a. Beneficiary cards (functional IDs) are delivered to beneficiaries by the post and managed by a postal tracking number. Beneficiary families also receive information and guidance about the program and instructions for activating the cards by calling the Caixa Call Center and registering an electronic password in one of the bank branches or Caixa lottery points of service (lotéricas). At that stage, the designated recipient is required to sign a consent form. The entire process, from a beneficiary's name being added to the payroll to the activation of the card, can take up to 45 days. The card must be activated within 180 days, otherwise it expires.

b. For example, in January 2017, for beneficiaries with last digit of NIS = 1, payments were made on January 18; for those with NIS = 2, payments on January 19; NIS = 3, payments on January 20; NIS = 4, payments on January 23; NIS = 5, payments on January 24; NIS = 6, payments on January 25; NIS = 7, payments on January 26; NIS = 8, payments on January 27; NIS = 9, payments on January 30; NIS = 0, payments on January 31. Such calendars are posted for each year well in advance and publicized widely.

cost; (2) a contract in return for remuneration to reach the cash transfer recipients; (3) competitive bidding without subsidies or additional regulations; or (4) market provision without a contract nor special pricing. These contract options (or lack thereof) can exist in combination (see table 6.1).

Contracting of PSPs may be carried out through direct appointment or through national or international procurement processes. A common method to contract an external payment provider is by direct appointment (often used to select state banks and post offices through a contract or regulation).

In addition to the selection of the PSP, an agreement must be reached on the payment instrument to be used to distribute payments. The default instrument is cash,[19] and for virtual payments provision, the instrument could be vouchers, a card (debit, smart, prepaid), mobile wallet, mobile money, and so on (see later section 6.5).

It is advisable to sign a detailed and well-structured service level agreement between the government and the PSP(s). The agreement(s) should clearly describe modalities, instruments, fees, types and number of payment points, timelines, and other provisions for the delivery of SP payments. While some countries opt for annual agreements (that generally match the budgetary cycle), multiannual agreements (or automatic renewal based on performance) affords options to mitigate the risk of disrupting transfer schedules in between contracts and encourage PSPs to invest in technology and infrastructure to better serve clients. Agreements should be flexible enough to allow room for innovative payment mechanisms developed by PSPs.

The program ensures that PSPs provide their services responsibly, following consumer protection standards. The program should agree with PSPs on mechanisms for grievance redress and those used to inform and educate beneficiaries about payments. Contracts should specify data privacy, protection, and security, as well as the technical features of databases and information flows.

There are also alternatives to procurement of the payment service provider by the government. In G2P 3.0 and 4.0 models, individuals are free to use a payment service provider of their choice. In this model, competition and market choices are left to the individual rather than the institution. Such an approach can benefit recipients by shortening lengthy institutional procedures and administrative costs, as well as private costs incurred by people in remote and hard-to-reach areas.

Managing a Recurring Payments Cycle

Administer Payments

Payments administration in this context describes the processes underlying the disbursement of government payments. Payments administration involves a number of subprocesses for cash transfers, including establishing and verifying the payroll and setting up the payment schedule, requesting the inter-account transfer (by the overseeing ministry to the treasury), issuing the inter-account payment order (by the treasury to the payment service provider), issuing the payment instruction (by the overseeing ministry to the payment service provider),

Table 6.1 Types of Contracts with Payment Service Providers

Type of agreement with payment service providers	Characteristics of payments services			
	Customer service and training: Ensuring recipient has access to assistance and knows how to access transfer or other services if available	**Account opening:** Ensuring that the recipient of the social assistance program has access to an account or a wallet	**Funds transfer:** Debiting the account of the program and crediting accounts of beneficiaries	**Instruments:** Use of cashless instruments (card, mobile wallets) to make payments or cash withdrawal from branches or ATMs
Regulations: The government or the financial sector regulator mandates a financial institution to provide service at a prescribed cost.	Regulatory requirements to provide financial educations	Basic account regulations, which mandate that each citizen meeting certain criteria must be provided with an account, either free of charge, or at a low cost (Brazil, Costa Rica, India, Indonesia, Malaysia, Mexico) Government subsidies to financial institutions for opening accounts for eligible citizens (enshrined in law acts or secondary legislation)	Regulatory caps on transfer fees—either applying to all transfers, or specifically to social assistance benefits (Bangladesh, Ecuador, India, Malaysia)	Regulatory requirements to open branches in remote areas (Ethiopia; Payment Service Banks in Nigeria) Caps on interchange fees and ATM withdrawal charges (Bangladesh, India)
Bilateral agreements: The social protection program signs a contract with a financial institution, paying a fee in return for performing the service.	Contract may specify which institution provides financial education tailored to the needs of recipients.	Contract specifies a fee for opening of an agreed number of accounts.	Contract may specify fee per each transfer, percentage of transfer value, or tiered fee based on location of access point (might be different from the prevailing market rate) (Colombia, Dominican Republic)	Payments offered to establish agent presence in underserved areas (Bangladesh, Ethiopia, Nigeria)
Competitive bidding: Competitive pricing and conditions of the service	Financial institution provides information and customer service. No special facilitation for beneficiaries.	Variety of accounts according to market options (High-income economies: most OECD countries; Hong Kong SAR, China; Singapore)	Market-based fees. (High-income economies: most OECD countries; Hong Kong SAR, China; Singapore)	Use of instruments available in the market. No special facilitation for beneficiaries.
Market-based: No contract	Financial institution provides information and customer service. No special facilitation for beneficiaries.	Use recipients' existing account	Market-based fees (High-income economies: most OECD countries; Hong Kong SAR, China; Singapore)	Use of instruments available in the market. No special facilitation for beneficiaries.

Source: Karol Karpinski, financial sector specialist, Finance, Competitiveness, and Innovation, World Bank.
Note: OECD = Organisation for Economic Co-operation and Development.

and by providing the payments to the beneficiaries (by the payment service provider).

The objectives of this process are to produce the payroll, including calculating, validating, and approving the right amount for the right beneficiaries (see chapters 5 and 8). The payroll schedule is communicated to the payment service provider. The funds are transferred to the payment service provider. In the case of electronic payments, transactions should ensure the amounts are credited to the financial address of the beneficiary (bank account, mobile money account, mobile wallet, mobile number, or foundational/unique identification number).

Inputs to the payment administration process include an updated beneficiary list or roster. The list comprises information on the amount to be paid to each beneficiary, updated information on the benefits and service package, information on payment reconciliation from the previous cycle of payments, as well as information on the financial address. Payments administration is carried out through payroll calculation algorithms (through software applications, Excel spreadsheets, or manual calculations) and a validation and approval process, based on the authorizing environment for these transactions. Integrated financial management information systems (IFMIS), account accreditation systems (banks' internal transferring system, mobile financial services transferring systems), and service contracts or agreements are all instrumental to payment administration processes. Outputs of payments administration include payroll, beneficiary accounts credited (in the case of electronic transfers), and distribution of payments (in the case of manual payments). The outcome of these processes is the right amount of benefits administered to the right beneficiary, at the right time, through an established payment service provision channel.

There are two distinct activities in payments administration: establishing payroll and managing payments.

Establish Payroll

Establishing payroll involves the periodic administrative activities to produce a payroll schedule, thereby verifying and certifying beneficiaries and their payments. The payments administration module of a beneficiary operations management system (BOMS) establishes payroll based on enrollment data (with links to conditionalities monitoring when applicable). Payments are also linked to social registry and foundational or functional ID systems. Payroll information includes personal information on beneficiaries, such as a name, account, location, entitlement amount, and unique ID number. The central agency, usually the Ministry of Social Affairs, verifies the payroll and certifies the quality and accuracy of the data. These cross-checks can be conducted through interoperability with the social registry, BOMS, and unique ID systems. They may link to other administrative information systems such as property, vehicle, and civil registries.

Some aspects that are necessary to know for establishing payroll include the following:

- Agencies responsible for establishing, verifying, and certifying payroll
- Information systems supporting payments administration
- Agency that manages the BOMS
- Information needed to verify payroll
- Process steps for establishing payroll and cycle time for each step

Manage Payments

Managing payments involves periodically sending payroll transactions and payment instructions to the treasury and through approval workflows for funds transfer and release. The treasury schedules payment instructions and distributes funds to one or more PSPs for the delivery of funds. The payment instruction file is sent to the national treasury, which reviews the transaction, enters the payment request, and releases funds subject to budget availability (box 6.6). In many countries, there is a TSA that controls all transactions, transferring funds to the payment service provider from the spending agency. In some countries, the treasury transfers funds, allocated to a particular government agency, to bank accounts. The government agencies then instruct the bank to transfer funds to particular beneficiaries. Or, the treasury maintains control of funds, sweeps idle balances from bank accounts, and consolidates the government's cash position at the end of each day. The TSA sends a payment instruction file and requisite funds electronically to the PSP. PSPs include commercial and state banks, MNOs, NGOs, post offices, credit unions, microfinance institutions, and savings and credit cooperative organizations (SACCOs).

Box 6.6 Payments Administration in Turkey

Turkey has a sophisticated Integrated Social Assistance System (ISAS) that automates the payments administration process. A list of households to be paid is prepared through ISAS. The system allows the administrator to choose the program from the list (conditional cash transfer, widow support, disability and old-age pension, etc.). The administrator selects the relevant payment service provider. Then payment information is added (payment cycle, date, etc.). The payment data are written to a payment file and transmitted to service providers. The authorized department in the social assistance ministry prepares the payment list for transmittal. The payment file is a customized text file where payment information is consolidated into a single file with information on all beneficiaries, generating a separate one for each payment service provider. Payment data on the file includes the beneficiary's ID, name, surname, father's name, international bank account number (IBAN), branch code, payment-at-home option (if selected), address, benefit amount, and payment date. The payment files may be transmitted through a variety of methods including File Transfer Protocol (FTP), web services, and payment gateways, among others to the payment service provider.

Banks update payment/withdrawal information to ISAS every night. They also update the withdrawal status of benefits to the General Directorate of Social Assistance (GDSA) designated FTP address. Each bank sends a status update using a customized text file registered to GDSA's FTP address. When beneficiaries successfully withdraw their payments, the withdrawal time is processed to the text file by the relevant bank. When payments are unsuccessful, due to death, time-out, six months of inactivity, or cancellation of the payment by GDSA, information on the cancellation and the benefit amount returned to the GDSA account is recorded to the withdrawal status file. Once the withdrawal status files are transmitted through designated FTP, ISAS analyzes the withdrawal status files. Each file is interpreted depending on the bank's format automatically, depending on the agreement between banks and ISAS. The result of each payment is recorded to the respective social assistance benefit in the corresponding household profile in ISAS. Benefits payments are not always canceled due to death or time-out. Sometimes GDSA cancels benefits when they update the payment amounts or add new benefit types. In such a situation, GDSA sends a cancellation file to the relevant bank or PTT (Turkish post office). The cancellation file is also sent to the related bank using a predefined text file through a designated FTP address.

Source: Ahmet Fatih Ortakaya, senior social protection specialist, Social Protection and Jobs, World Bank, 2019.

Some aspects for managing payments include the following:

- Budget transfers management, through a TSA or other
- Payment transfers management to payment points and local or subnational payment service providers, especially important when scaling up remote and underserved areas

Provision Payments

Payments service provision in this context describes the process of disbursement of payments to beneficiaries, once line ministries transfer payments to PSPs. Payments are made either in person (cash) or virtually/electronically (cashless).

Cash payments for social programs often see program staff physically delivering cash to beneficiaries. Funds are transferred electronically to a series of accounts at the district or subnational levels where local officials, program staff, or local community leaders visit a bank branch or a government office to collect cash. The cash is physically transported to payment points (post offices, government offices, or community facilities) where recipients collect cash at a predetermined time. To complete the transfer, program staff must authenticate the recipient's identity. Some countries outsource these processes to national post offices or state banks to deliver cash to beneficiaries at specific payment points. Beneficiaries are notified where payments will be made (payment points), when (payment schedule), and how (what to bring) to collect transfers. However, physical delivery of cash is becoming a constraint in the wake of the COVID-19 crisis.

Electronic payments are typically outsourced to a third-party PSP, such as a bank (state bank or private), a mobile network operator (MNO), or a payment aggregator. The process entails electronic transfer of the total value of all beneficiary transfers for a payment period to the PSP. The PSP then makes electronic credits to the individual beneficiary accounts. While normally a single PSP handles all aspects of payment delivery, a consortium of providers may be responsible for different aspects in some cases (ISPA 2016). Similarly, countries may opt to choose or contract out to different PSPs according to their coverage and regional presence. PSPs are responsible for organizing the process of distributing payments to respective recipients. They communicate payment dates and payment points and authenticate ID credentials. For banks, this process will correspond to the banking system's CDD/KYC standards. When payments are delivered through a network of agents, beneficiaries' identities are verified at the payment points (box 6.7).

When recipients collect payments in person, they may incur significant personal costs, traveling to payment points and waiting for distribution of transfers into their hands. Without social distancing guidelines, that process becomes fraught for beneficiaries. When residing in remote areas, travel costs may represent a significant portion of the transfer. When collecting payments, recipients need to authenticate their identity using ID credentials and sometimes biometrics. For in-person payments, program staff and field administrators physically check beneficiaries off a printed payroll or muster roll. They may verify identity credentials by visually comparing a picture and demographic details on a government recognized ID credential for offline authentication. Online authentication is done through POS terminals, internet-enabled devices, and mobile devices. Together with the transfer, beneficiaries may also receive a proof of payment (e.g., a receipt, checkbook, passbook, etc.) (see box 6.7).

With electronic payments, beneficiaries may access multiple channels to cash out transfers provided systems are interoperable; nevertheless, these modalities could incur private costs for recipients in remote areas (see box 6.8 on human-centered design). When recipients are issued a card (e.g., prepaid card, smart card, or debit card) or a mobile device-operated account (e-wallet), it usually requires a PIN for authentication to

Box 6.7 Onboarding Beneficiaries of Social Protection Programs for Payments Provision

For payments transferred directly from the treasury to individuals, bank accounts need to be opened for beneficiaries of social protection programs. The number and details of the newly opened account need to be transmitted to the line ministry/agency. At times, recipients may already have access to an account with a bank or a nonfinancial institution. Nevertheless, programs that do not collect bank account information upfront, during intake and registration (chapter 4) or enrollment (chapter 5), tend to open brand new bank accounts for beneficiaries, resulting in fragmentation of accounts and cards for different social protection programs.

When payment service providers are responsible for payments provision, they must open accounts, provide instructions regarding the payment instruments (cards and mobile devices), methods of authentication of identification credentials at payment points, and grievance redress mechanisms to voice complaints. Account opening is facilitated by e-KYC ("know your customer") if these are connected to foundational identification platforms in the country. Authentication of identification credentials at the time of account opening minimizes anti-money laundering (AML) and counter-financing of terrorism (CFT) risks. India and Pakistan use biometric ID verification technology to allow agents to capture and verify identification credentials to meet KYC requirements and open accounts.[a] Depending on the enabling environment, digital self-service applications may be provided to allow beneficiaries to open accounts from their homes, schools, or social program offices. In this case, the marginal cost of onboarding new beneficiaries will be close to zero.

a. In India, the use of the Aadhaar ID is not mandatory. However, financial institutions may accept Aadhaar as one of the valid KYC documents.

Box 6.8 A Human-Centered Approach to Government-to-Person Digitization

Digitizing payments has the potential to increase both the ownership and use of accounts. Yet efforts to digitize government-to-person (G2P) payments have suffered from shortcomings. A common complaint among those receiving government transfers as digital payments is that the payment products are difficult to use. Recipients have reported long lines at bank agents and said that they struggle to get help when they have a question or a problem with their payments. Others have reported being targeted for fraud. Not only is it important to ensure one receives reliable and regular payments, but also to guarantee that transactions are simple and accessible and fraudulent practices avoided.

For an example of a journey mapping exercise conducted for humanitarian payments, see figure B6.8.1.

Figure B6.8.1 Mapping User Journeys for Cash Transfers

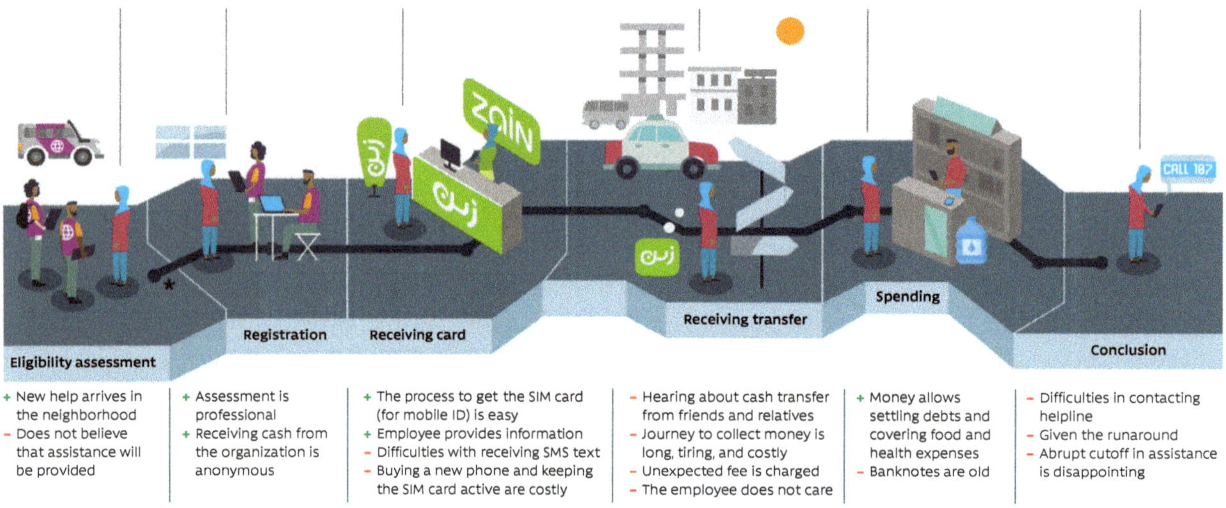

Source: From "Iraq Case Study: Improving User Journeys for Humanitarian Cash Transfers" by Ground Truth Solutions and the Humanitarian Policy Group, DFID, December 2018. Used with permission; permission required for reuse.

withdraw cash from bank and PSP branches, ATMs, and agent locations. Two-factor authentication is the minimum standard for electronic payments, corresponding to something you are (biometrics), something you have (card or token), and/or something you know (PIN or password). Depending on the existing regulatory, commercial, and interoperability framework, recipients should be able to use access points belonging to different providers. However, this may be associated with additional fees.

Human-Centered Design, Gender, and Payments Digitization

A human-centered design (HCD) approach is helpful to make adaptations to payments provision for common intended populations. For example, low mobile phone ownership among women and poor digital and financial literacy can all complicate women's adoption of digital payment methods over manual cash transfers. Explicit design choices through an HCD approach can address various challenges and adaptations to social protection payments for vulnerable groups (see table 6.2).

G2P payments digitization presents an opportunity to accelerate the closure of the gender gap in digital financial inclusion, and to amplify women's economic empowerment outcomes through active usage of digital financial services. As explained in the Bill & Melinda Gates Foundation's D3 Criteria (Chamberlin et al. 2019), women's economic empowerment can lead to better outcomes for children and the community, greater investment in women's human capital, and greater women's social capital. Increasing women's ownership

Table 6.2 Social Protection Government-to-Person Payments Challenges for Vulnerable Groups

Demographic groups along the life cycle	
Children	Depend on parents, guardians for payments.
Elderly	May have limited literacy, mobility, or other challenges relating to aging. They may find it difficult to remember passwords and PINs. They may rely heavily on a trusted nominee to cash out.
Women	Lack of bargaining power, low mobile phone ownership, poor digital and financial literacy, and limited mobility due to social or cultural norms; exposed to domestic violence and potentially cyber-violence; lack of time due to unpaid domestic work. Lack of female payment agents, which may inhibit uptake of payment systems (garment industry worker payments), and so on.
Groups constrained by socioeconomic status	
People living below the poverty line	May lack awareness or have misconceptions about programs; may be deterred by complex procedures; may lack trust in institutions. Payment-specific issues may include low literacy, difficulty remembering PIN numbers; may not be aware of the payment; poor neighborhoods and rural villages may lack financial infrastructure for payments.
People living in isolated and remote areas	May lack transport, mobility, physical access; setting up payment points may be costly (e.g., in some cases, payment delivery may include expensive air or sea transportation); payment points may be far, increasing beneficiary cost to access them; travel increases security risks; and so on. "Mobile banks" with "payment points" and precommunicated schedules are used in these settings, which requires preparedness. Approach suffers from issues such as physical insecurity to beneficiaries. These approaches remain a working solution until viable alternative arrangements are made for provisioning.
Pastoralist, nomadic, semi-nomadic groups	For pastoralist, nomadic, semi-nomadic, and migrant farm worker groups, constant mobility makes it difficult to assure accessible cash-out points; interoperable payment systems are preferable but may increase transaction costs, and so on.
Refugees, stateless, immigrants, internally displaced populations (IDPs) and/or those living in fragile-conflict-violent (FCV) areas	May lack formal identification (Rohingya camps in Bangladesh, etc.); use of cash and financial services may be restricted in the refugee camps.
Disability	
Persons with disabilities	May face access barriers: mobility, physical, cognitive, language or reading (blind, deaf), and other barriers such as stigma, attitudes, discrimination.

Source: Original table for this publication.

and usage of accounts through G2P programs could be transformational.

> Digital transfers of social protection payments can be a powerful tool to enhance women's empowerment. It can provide women with independent access to predictable income streams, and the arrival of a digital payment can give women greater control over how the money will be used, particularly if linked to a stored-value product such as an e-wallet.[20]

Identification and SP Payments

ID platforms are integral to authenticate identity, ensuring payments are made to the right person and for payment service providers to carry out CDD/KYC requirements. Authentication services offered by ID platforms may rely upon a minimal, challenge-response approach that asks "yes or no: is this person who they say they are?" thereby privileging the protection of the individual's personal data. Such a minimalistic approach to data sharing helps to support data protection and privacy. In the absence of a foundational ID platform, programs tend to authenticate individuals either through an offline check by visually comparing a name or a face to a paper or plastic card, or by electronically storing identification data on individuals in beneficiary operations management systems, which results in the sharing and exposing of personal data.

Authentication levels for different social programs must be determined appropriately based on the level of risk rather than a one-size-fits-all approach. Levels of authentication are the degree of confidence a relying party (the service provider) can have in the identity authentication, based on the risk, authentication method, and identity proofing. For low levels of risk, just one authentication factor may be required. For substantial levels of risk, at least two different factors may be required. For high levels of risk, there must be at least two different factors and added prevention against duplication and tampering. For a financial transaction, at least two different authentication factors may be required. Authentication factors include something you know (password or PIN), something you are (biometrics such as fingerprint and iris), and something you have (card, mobile phone, one-time password). Some of the factors that influence the choice of authentication systems and credential design are the level of assurance needed for authentication (high, substantial, low), internet coverage, mobile penetration, and additional equipment required for authentication (smart card readers, biometric readers, and the smart cards themselves).

Risk Mitigation and Controls

In some countries, beneficiaries receive a check or voucher that can be cashed out at a future time or used in exchange for food or services. While checks and vouchers may be a reasonable option due to ease of transport and reduced security risks in comparison to cash, they require both a system of bank branches and other establishments to withdraw or redeem money, as well as an audit system to make sure that vendors are not overcharging transfer recipients for their products and/or forcing them to acquire unwanted items. See box 6.9 on risk mitigation and controls for error, fraud, and corruption.

Reconcile Payments

Reconciliation allows line ministries to determine whether the transfer has been successful by means of being delivered to recipients or by means of accounts of recipients being credited. In SP programs utilizing direct benefit transfers and interoperable payments infrastructure, the process can be entirely automatic, and the funds that have not been credited are returned to sender.

In account-based systems, the funds are the property of the account holder upon the final settlement of the credit transfer. When benefits are disbursed to individual accounts of recipients, social protection agencies have only a limited scope to oversee their use. In traditional (cash-based) disbursement processes, it is usually assumed that funds that are not collected in cash by the beneficiary within a prescribed time are foregone. In account-based systems, it is ordinarily not legal to attempt to seize the funds back if the beneficiary has not made use of them by a certain date. Moreover, banking secrecy laws may prevent the agency from monitoring the transactions and obtaining personal details of individuals who have not cashed out their benefit. While most jurisdictions have account dormancy rules that ensure the forfeiture of balances on inactive accounts (and their return to the national treasury), they tend to require that the period of inactivity exceeds one year or more. If the social assistance program is dependent on exercising stricter control over fund use, its implementation may therefore require issuance of additional regulations or changes in law. Alternatively, the use of other payment modalities (such as prepaid cards) may be evaluated (Rodríguez et al., forthcoming).

In any form of payment, it is important to mitigate fiduciary risks that may emerge when the funds are not used for their intended purposes, or when funds are not properly accounted for. Fiduciary risk is not limited to the risk of fraud or corruption taking place, but includes risks such as funds being diverted into other areas of government spending. Poor program design, for example, risks transfers not reaching their intended recipients. There should be a reconciliation of the transfer with actual payments made to beneficiaries to identify any mistakes and abuse (DFID 2006).

Box 6.9 Risk Mitigation and Controls for Error, Fraud, and Corruption

Introduction of digital payments requires attention to new consumer risks. Because social protection government-to-person (G2P) recipients are often new to formal financial services and "virtual" money in particular, they are more likely to have a negative experience when accessing or using their digitized payments. There are at least five common consumer risks in digital payments that can impede their chances at financial inclusion:

- Inability to transact due to network downtime or service unreliability
- Insufficient agent or ATM liquidity
- Complex user interfaces and payment processes
- Poor or no recourse mechanism
- Fraud that targets the recipient

These risks need to be mitigated to build people's trust, confidence, and value in the use of digital payments and basic financial services.[a]

Controls should be in place to prevent fraud and leakage. Payments must be secure such that the full amount of money intended for beneficiaries reaches them. The process must be transparent and easy to audit. Transmission of payroll instructions should be made through secure channels, with measures in place to prevent any modifications to the final list of recipients and amounts. Data on proof of life, as well as authentication of biometric identity credentials, can curb leakages through ghost beneficiaries. Interoperability of data between key registries such as identification civil registration, beneficiary operations management systems, social registries, and payment systems can help reduce human error, fraud, and corruption in this regard.

Authentication of identity is key to ensure payments are made to the right person. There must be a secure authentication process in place using a variety of measures.[b] The choice of authentication approach should balance identification security requirements and the needs and conditions of end-users. For example, the use of a PIN may be hard to remember, requiring training and practice in creating PINs and passwords, changing them, memorizing them, and using them effectively. There is also literature on the appropriateness of biometrics in certain contexts, such as with the elderly, manual laborers, and persons with disabilities, compromising authentication and payments.

Agent-based payments provision require beneficiary protections against agent fraud. These include unauthorized deductions from beneficiary bank accounts or e-money wallets, charging unauthorized fees, or charging higher than normal prices for beneficiary purchases of goods. Appropriate measures could include ensuring trustworthy individuals are hired as agents, monitoring agent performance through payment service providers, and maintaining a grievance redress and appeals mechanism independent of the agents themselves, such as a toll-free phone helpline.

Distribution of cash in person raises significant security risks that require mitigation. The large quantities of cash on the way to and sitting at pay points require significant security, so armed guards, police, or soldiers are used to provide security. In insecure locations, cash-in-transit services may be unwilling to operate, or it may be expensive to implement—meaning that other payment delivery alternatives may need to be explored. When it is known when and where people are being paid en masse, recipients may also be at risk of thievery or extortion as they transit home or until they have spent their cash. Usually governments find it difficult to provide security for such dispersed targets.

A focus on security should be balanced between program objectives and people-centeredness. It is important to bear in mind that introducing security measures may increase the cost of access for recipients and ultimately for the government. While cash-based payments provision tends to be more vulnerable to fraud and theft, a digital system does not guarantee error-, fraud-, and corruption-free operations. Nevertheless, digital delivery has the potential to significantly cut down the incidence and volume of fraud, particularly where recipients are well-informed and trained to protect themselves. For a more detailed review of mechanisms to prevent error and fraud, refer to the ISPA Social Protection Payments tool (ISPA 2017).

a. Baur and Zimmerman 2016.

b. The Inter-Agency Social Protection Assessments (ISPA) tool on identification for social protection provides detailed guidance on how to assess the performance of identification and authentication processes in a social protection program (ISPA 2017).

6.4 PROCESS MAPPING FOR PAYMENTS ADMINISTRATION AND PROVISION

In this section, we examine how payments processes function in a few countries using delivery chain process mapping (described in chapter 2) with some analysis of process steps and activities that might be improved. Our objective here is to examine delivery processes that involve single provider payments provisioning (G2P 1.0, G2P 1.5, and G2P 2.0) and draw out process improvements that could help impel these systems toward a multiprogram and multiprovider, virtual payments provisioning approach (G2P 3.0 and G2P 4.0), where appropriate.

São Tomé and Príncipe (G2P 1.0—Single Program to Single Provider, In Person)

São Tomé and Príncipe is a small island nation and a lower-middle-income country, with a population of less than a quarter of a million. Payments are made through cash distributed in person for social programs. The Maes Carenciadas (Needy Mothers) provides a cash transfer to poor mothers with three or more children, and two old-age noncontributory pensions targeted to the poor. In terms of institutional arrangements, the Department of Social Protection (DPSS) has one team at the national level that is responsible for the coordination of the delivery of the social assistance program. DPSS also has district coordinators that, among other activities, support the delivery of payments in the seven districts of the country.

Step-by-Step Process

The Department of Social Protection at the Ministry of Employment and Social Affairs (MEAS) produces a payroll instruction, which is approved by the Ministry of Finance (see step 1 in figure 6.5). The MoF releases funds

Figure 6.5 Manual Payment Delivery in the Maes Carenciadas Program in São Tomé and Príncipe

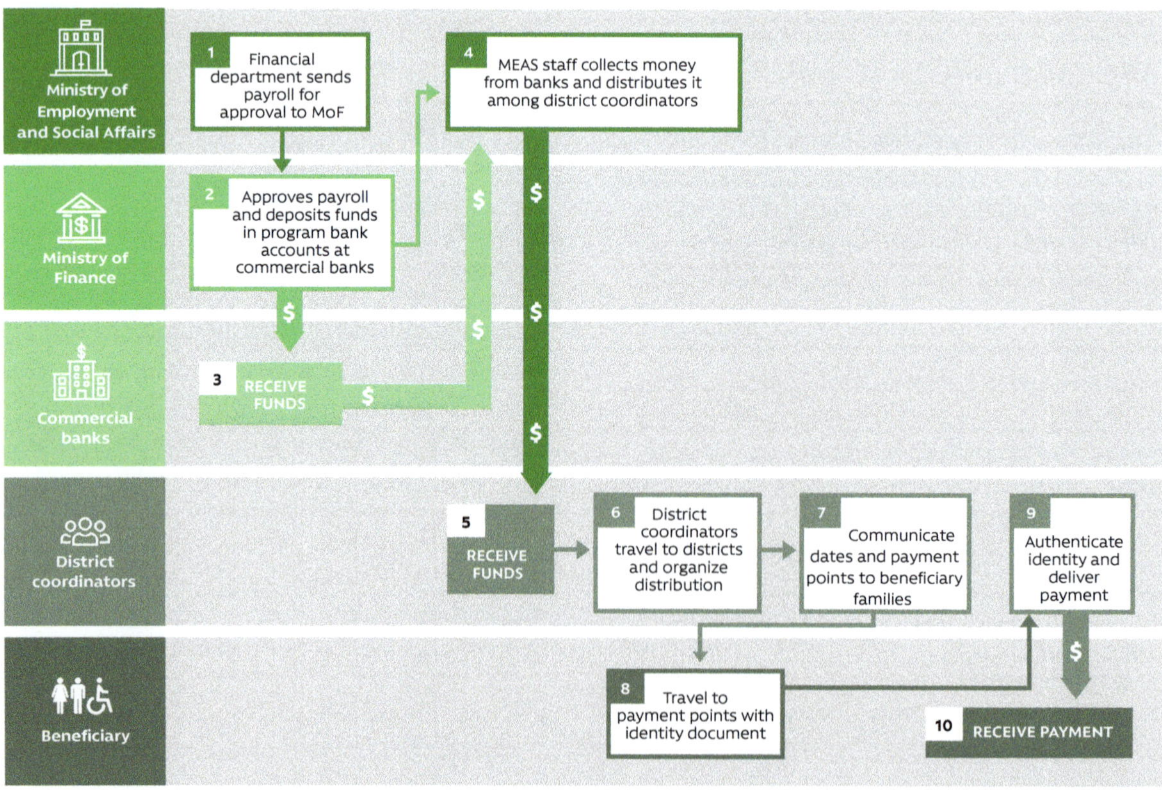

Source: Original figure for this publication.

to MEAS bank accounts at commercial banks (step 2). Commercial banks receive the funds (step 3). Once MEAS has the resources in their bank accounts, it organizes the distribution through their local coordinators (step 4). District coordinators receive funds (step 5) and travel to set up arrangements to distribute payments to beneficiaries (step 6). Payment points include district city halls and other social/community centers. District coordinators communicate payment dates, amount to be paid, and payment points to beneficiaries (step 7). For this process the government uses mainly national radio stations, district city halls, and community (local) radio stations. Beneficiaries travel to payment points and line up to collect their transfers (step 8), produce ID credentials (national or electoral card, or birth certificate) for authentication by district coordinators (step 9), and receive their payments (step 10). Once they have received their transfer, beneficiaries sign the payroll sheet or provide a stamp of their fingerprint if they cannot sign their names.[21]

Analysis of Potential Process Improvements

District coordinators often travel without security cover to distribute payments. Payment points have precarious infrastructure with inadequate conditions of service provision to the communities, with very limited privacy, connectivity, or electricity. Payments are distributed by staff on top of their additional activities, which creates considerable pressure on their day-to-day workloads. Payments security is strengthened implicitly by the presence of local control officers (*veedores*) during the payment process and community or neighborhood leaders (World Bank 2015). There are processes in place for alternate recipients to collect payments on behalf of the beneficiary. Proof of payment is not provided to beneficiaries. There is little reconciliation of accounts. In the current context, in-person provision is appropriate given the financial ecosystem. There are limited points for beneficiaries to withdraw funds (ATMs, agents, or bank branches) and limited use for mobile transactions or cards in rural areas. Envisioning the trajectory for SP G2P payments in similar contexts, automation could support payment administration processes in the production of up-to-date payrolls, information exchange between ministries, approvals, and verification of reconciliation reports. Increased coordination can improve the periodicity of payments, not only in the movement of funds but also in coordinating payment schedules. Communication channels can be reinforced to ensure that recipients are aware of payment dates. For the in-person provision sequence, there are enhancements that could improve the experience of recipients and reduce errors. Authentication standards can be instituted. Privacy protocols can be established, ensuring that when a payment is received, it is done in a separate room, or private cubicles are available. Reconciliation processes also need to be implemented, where each recipient receives a certification of receipt stating the amount that the household is entitled to as well as contact information for beneficiaries to submit questions regarding their payment.

Nigeria (G2P 1.5—Single Program to Single Provider, in Person, Electronically Assisted)

Nigeria, a lower-middle-income country in Sub-Saharan Africa with a population of 190 million, makes cash payments to beneficiaries. Of the world's 2 billion unbanked people, 2.7 percent live in Nigeria. The National Social Safety Nets Project (NASSP) has put in place a basic digital payments system. Targeted poor and vulnerable households are identified through the National Social Registry and enrolled in the cash transfer program, the Household Uplifting Programme. Regular and reliable transfers are delivered through an end-to-end electronic payments system which creates either a mobile wallet or bank account for each household. Transfers are delivered to those accounts, and then networks of payment agents tied to the different payment service providers physically distribute cash to beneficiaries at set locations every two months. Each household receives a base transfer of N5,000 (US$16) per month. This base benefit is designed to ensure a minimum, reliable payment to promote consumption smoothing, address food insecurity, and protect against economic shocks. Some households will also be eligible for an additional monthly benefit (top up) of N5,000 upon the completion of agreed co-responsibilities.

Step-by-Step Process

The beneficiary operations management system (BOMS) generates a payment schedule for each community for

Figure 6.6 Payments Administration Processes: Nigeria's HUP Cash Transfer Program

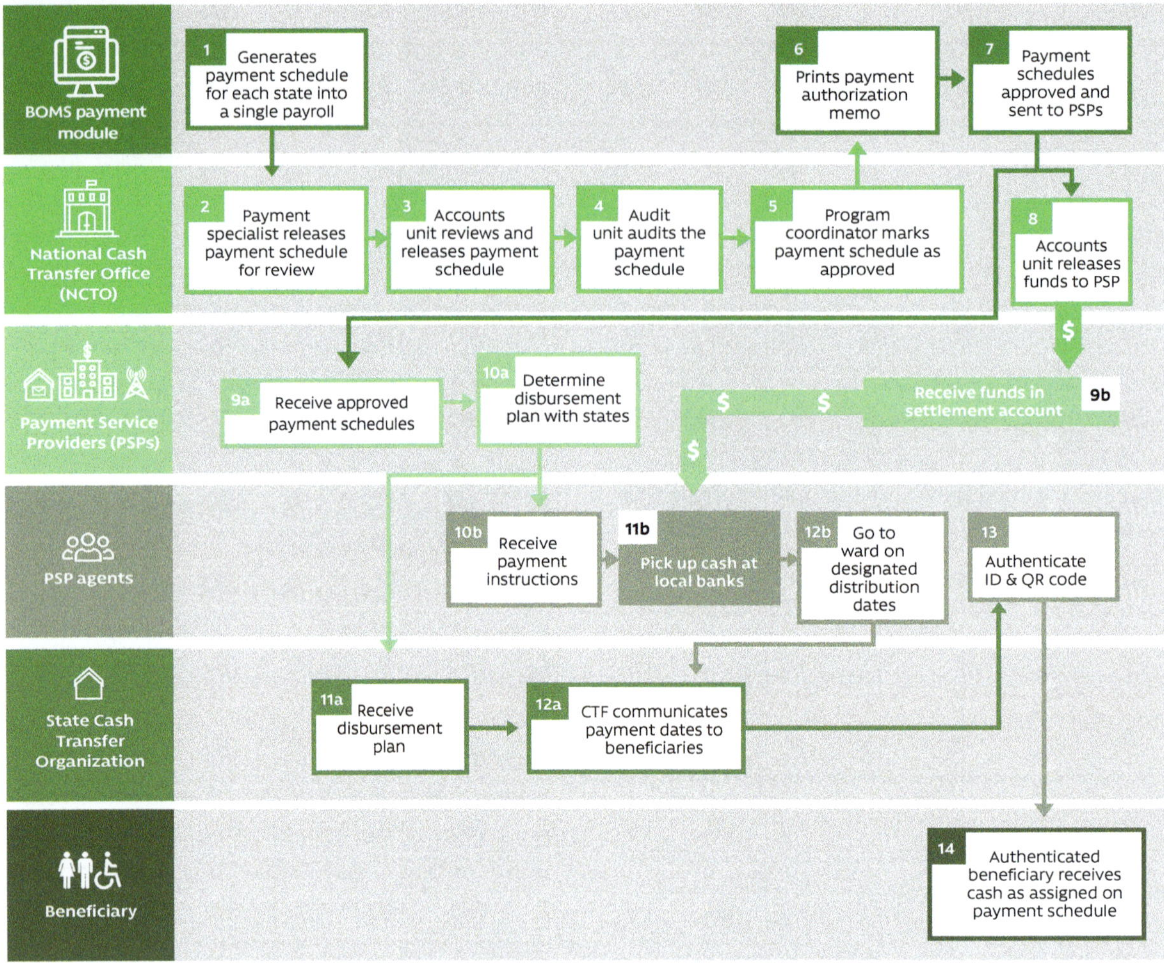

Sources: Ubah Thomas Ubah, social protection specialist, Social Protection and Jobs, World Bank; Cornelia M. Tesliuc, senior social protection specialist, Social Protection and Jobs, World Bank, 2019.
Note: BOMS = beneficiary operations management system(s); CTF = cash transfer facilitator; HUP = Household Uplifting Programme; PSP = payment service provider; QR code = matrix barcode.

base cash transfers (BCTs) and conditional cash transfers (CCTs) based on data from the conditionality monitoring system, and an ad hoc payment schedule for each community for both BCT and CCT, based on input from the grievance redress system (see step 1 in figure 6.6). A payment specialist from the federal government (NCTO) releases the payment schedule for review and approval (step 2). The accounts department reviews and releases the payment schedule (step 3). The audit unit audits the payment schedule (step 4). The NCTO program coordinator marks the payment schedule as approved (step 5). The BOMS payments module prints a payment authorization memo (step 6). The BOMS generates the payroll and sends to the PSP in parallel (step 7). The PSP receives the approved list of beneficiaries and amounts—that is, the payments schedule (step 9a). The accounts unit funds the PSP settlement amount and the funds are transferred to the PSP (step 8). The PSP receives the funds in the settlement account (step 9b). The PSP determines payment distribution schedules at the community level (step 10a). PSP agents at the community level receive payment distribution schedules from the PSP (step 10b). PSP agents then go to the local banks and pick up cash as per the schedule (step 11). Cash transfer facilitators inform beneficiaries of payment distribution schedules for each community (step 12a). Agents visit communities on the dates designated per the payment distribution schedule (step 12b). Payments are made bimonthly. The PSP disburses cash to beneficiaries at wards, which are the lowest administrative units of the Nigerian federal structure, together with the State Cash Transfer Organization (SCTO). Agents authenticate beneficiaries at payment points using laminated beneficiary ID cards with a QR code (step 13). Authenticated beneficiaries receive cash as per value and per the payment distribution schedule (step 14).

Analysis of Potential Process Improvements

Process redesign of payments administration could help simplify government processes underlying the disbursement (steps 1 through 9b in figure 6.6). Most beneficiaries dwell in rural areas with limited to no access to services, nor vital infrastructure such as roads, health care, telecommunications, financial services, and so on. For successful cash disbursements to its beneficiaries, NCTO (the National Cash Transfer Office) currently leverages a mix of technology and traditional agency banking to manage the payment life cycle. Payments are done at a reasonable distance from the beneficiaries. Due to the insecurity in some regions it is permissible for beneficiaries to be transported to the nearest safe location where payments can be carried out. Gender-intentional social protection programs such as NASSP in Nigeria can play a vital role in improving women's access to finance through digital payments; it can empower them within their households and lead to better outcomes for their families (Bill & Melinda Gates Foundation 2019). Provisioning payments through electronic means can give female recipients greater control over how the money will be used, particularly if linked to a stored-value product such as a mobile wallet (Chamberlin et al. 2019). However, poorly designed systems can also have negative consequences on women's empowerment and safety. As it stands, the last steps in provision do not provide access to transactional accounts. Geospatial mapping of existing infrastructure (mobile coverage, branches, agents, ATMs, POS) can highlight potential locations to pilot G2P 2.0 solutions, where beneficiaries can own bank accounts or mobile wallets, with flexibility to withdraw or store transfer funds, supported by guidance, financial education, and customer service. Options for including other PSPs can be explored. Some states may be better serviced by other financial institutions, which could also broaden choice for beneficiaries.

Pakistan (G2P 2.0—Single Program to Single Provider, Virtual Provision)

Pakistan, a lower-middle-income country in South Asia, with a population of 197 million, makes payments using debit and smart cards to beneficiaries. Of the world's 2 billion unbanked people, 5.2 percent live in Pakistan. The Benazir Income Support Programme (BISP) has been provided to women in poor households since 2009 and reaches more than 5 million beneficiaries. Eighty-seven percent of beneficiaries receive their transfers through a cardless system, where one can transfer funds through a mobile wallet or withdraw cash at POS or ATMs with biometric readers. Recent evaluations of the BISP have found positive effects on malnutrition for girls, food consumption, and women's empowerment: beneficiaries are more likely to have permission to travel alone in the community and are more likely to report being able to vote.

Step-by-Step Process

As shown in figure 6.7, the payroll schedule is created and cleared internally through the BISP beneficiary operations management system (step 1). The data are sent to banks in real time through web services to open bulk accounts (step 2). Funds are released to BISP LMA-1 accounts with the banks (step 2). Beneficiaries receive an SMS confirmation through a biometrically verified SIM (step 3). Partner banks receive disbursement instructions (step 4). Funds are credited from LMA-1 to LMA-2 virtual accounts for beneficiaries or branchless banking (BB) accounts (step 5). Beneficiaries receive a notification of availability of funds (step 6) and they may either withdraw funds through franchise agents or ATMs using BISP cards or transfer funds (step 7). Banks receive information on the method (step 8) and debit LMA-2 accounts (for cash withdrawal or funds transfer) or credit BB accounts

Figure 6.7 Payments Administration in Pakistan's BISP Cash Transfer Program

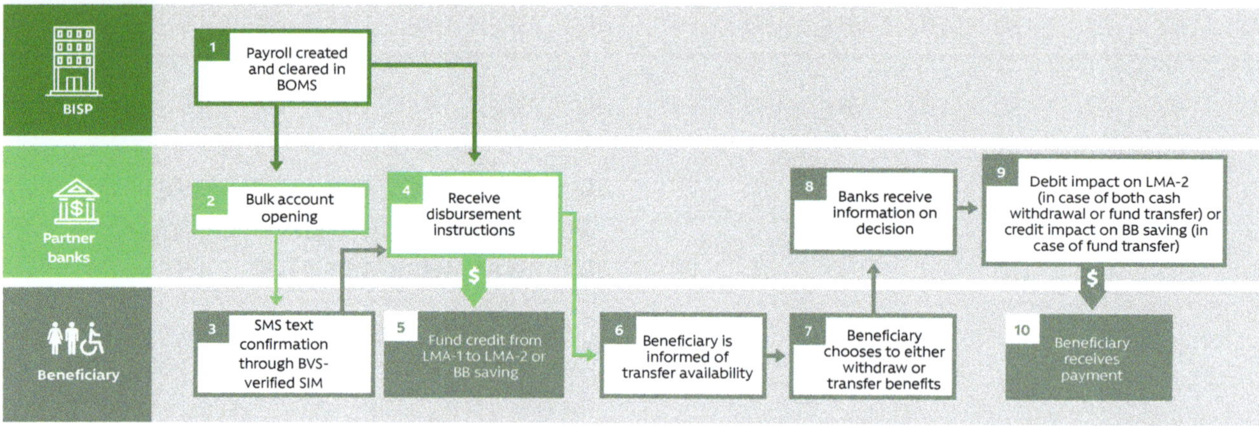

Source: Amjad Zafar Khan, senior social protection specialist, Social Protection and Jobs, World Bank.
Note: BB = branchless banking; BISP = Benazir Income Support Programme; BOMS = beneficiary operations management system; BVS = Biometric Verification System; LMA = limited mandate account.

(in case of funds transfer) (step 9), and the beneficiary receives the payment (step 10). Beneficiaries may withdraw cash or transfer funds using one of two methods: (1) Beneficiaries who are listed on the approved payment schedule in the BISP management information system are authenticated using their IDs to gain entrance into a mobile camp, where the payments service provision process is set up. NADRA, the ID agency, ensures that identity is authenticated prior to issuing a mobile handset linked to a bank account and a SIM (a mobile ID) registered to the beneficiary, at a camp. On a monthly or quarterly basis, beneficiaries receive an SMS text on their mobile phones with information that their accounts have been credited with the payment. Beneficiaries cash out the payment from franchises using a PIN code on their mobile phones. (2) Debit cards are distributed based on the payments schedule with a list of approved beneficiaries. Beneficiary identities are authenticated using their biometric national IDs in order to gain entry to a camp. A bank representative at the camp authenticates identity and distributes debit cards. Beneficiaries withdraw money at ATMs using the debit cards. Smart cards are also used for payments provision. Smart cards are linked to virtual beneficiary accounts. The ID agency (NADRA) issues those cards and shares the list of issued cards with the bank, which links it to the virtual accounts.

Analysis of Potential Process Improvements

Real-time electronic reconciliations show that 87 percent of beneficiaries withdraw payments through debit cards within 72 hours of the funds transfer to bank accounts. This could likely be a result of a requirement that funds that are not withdrawn from LMA-2 accounts be transferred back to LMA-1 accounts within 180 days of disbursement. Moreover, aside from using the debit and smart cards to withdraw the full value of the transfer, beneficiaries cannot perform any other financial transactions, including savings or peer-to-peer transactions, which limits the ability of the program to improve financial inclusion outcomes. Converting virtual accounts to transactional accounts would open access to additional financial services. Using additional payment system operators, like payment aggregators, or working toward an interoperable system that uses a national switch, opens options to other PSPs to potentially distribute BISP transfers. Competitive pricing and services can provide added incentive for existing banks to make the change to transactional accounts or allow for other solutions to be made available for recipients. Integration of G2P payments (pensions, salaries, and other social assistance transfers) could offer a business case for banks and other financial institutions to work with the bank on interoperable solutions.

6.5 TECHNOLOGIES SUPPORTING DIGITAL PAYMENTS

Rapidly evolving financial and technological advances coupled with the onset of covariate shocks such as COVID-19 are providing a new impetus to countries for leapfrogging traditional SP payments approaches to benefit people who are in urgent need of assistance.

Enabling Better SP Payments to People through Newer Technologies

Several countries are grappling with the challenge of offering ease of SP payments to the poor and to people living in situations of fragility, conflict, and violence, or to enable 100 percent digital delivery in the age of COVID-19. Notwithstanding investments in digitizing payments administration and provision, the kind of user interface that makes it easy for people to transact through internet-based private platforms such as Amazon, Alibaba, Gojek, and Jumia remains out of reach of the poor.

Meanwhile, the use of digital payments is on the rise according to the World Bank's 2017 Global Findex surveys. In developing economies, the share of adults using digital payments rose by 12 percentage points, to 44 percent.[22] Digital payment methods offer an alternative to debit and credit cards. They can be made through a mobile phone or the internet. In developing economies, 19 percent of adults (30 percent of account owners) reported making at least one direct payment using a mobile money account, a mobile phone, or the internet.

Different models of digital financial services prevail in the consumer space, two of which include digital wallets and mobile money. While digital wallet accounts may be accessed via mobile service and via web (internet), mobile money accounts are linked to a mobile number.

Digital Wallets

In the consumer space, more people are embracing digital wallet solutions based on the momentum created by Fintech innovations such as P2P (person-to-person) technologies. China has Alipay and WeChat, which by some accounts handled more than US$37 trillion in mobile payments in 2018.[23] Indonesia has Go-Pay and Ovo.[24] India has Paytm.[25] Nigeria has JumiaPay[26] and Paga, and Colombia has DaviPlata. In this model, smartphone apps are linked to an account at a bank or another type of financial institution. Users store digital credit in the app to pay for goods and services within the app or at partner merchants. The rise of Alipay and WeChat has made it possible to go a whole day without having to use cash. They use a mobile phone, a QR code (two-dimensional barcode), and biometric authentication to send and receive payments to individuals, businesses, and governments. In most contexts, digital wallets are not being used by governments to transfer SP benefits.

Mobile Money

It is widely recognized that digital financial services act as a key catalyzer of financial inclusion, offering greater convenience and the possibility of lower cost than what is allowed by traditional banking. E-money access points are the most numerous, and mobile users outnumber bank and microfinance institution (MFI) account holders, making mobile technology one of the most promising tools for expanding access to finance and achieving financial inclusion objectives. In West Africa, for example, the Central Bank of West African States adopted a new framework in 2015 allowing for the licensing of e-money issuers. Mobile phone penetration in this region represents a potential expansion of mobile payment services that can serve as a means to increase the country's financial inclusion (Guven 2019; Guven, Brodersohn, and Joubert 2018).

Mobile money is offered through mobile network operators where accounts do not necessarily need to be linked to an account at a financial institution. Examples include mobile financial services such as m-Pesa in Kenya, which are offered mainly by mobile network operators but are not necessarily used for social protection payments. In Kenya most account owners have both a financial institution account and a mobile money account. This is reflected in how people make mobile payments. One challenge is that many mobile money accounts are "closed-loop" payment systems. This means that if beneficiaries receive transfers into such accounts, they need to withdraw cash to carry out everyday transactions. Interoperability of payment systems through "open-loop" systems—that allow people to make everyday cashless transactions based on their choice and convenience—are complex and challenging to achieve but are critical to success.

Several countries in West Africa use mobile money accounts for SP payments to beneficiaries, including Côte d'Ivoire (box 6.10), Benin, Chad, Niger, Togo, and other West African Economic and Monetary Union (WAEMU) countries. Togo implemented an emergency cash transfer program called Novissi in response to the COVID-19 crisis, using a mobile money platform. Beneficiaries were encouraged to transact electronically and advised not to cash out the benefit in order to avoid overcrowding mobile money operators and to maintain social distancing. Accompanying measures such as increasing CICO agent density and proliferation of acceptance technologies such as QR codes and NFC could further incentivize beneficiaries to transact electronically and reduce the need for cash-outs, in line with the social distancing measures put in place (Boko et al., 2020).

Box 6.10 Mobile Money Payments in Côte d'Ivoire's Social Assistance Program

In Côte d'Ivoire, the World Bank has implemented a program to provide regular and predictable cash transfers to 35,000 previously excluded poor households. This marks the first time in Côte d'Ivoire that vulnerable households are receiving transfers from the government through mobile technology; and these benefits extend to some of the most remote households that had previously been invisible to the social protection system. The digital payments mechanism brought many women into the financial system for the first time. As a result, women are increasingly active in terms of farming and income-generating activities, and they have motivated greater household financial savings. Also, with the digitization, there has been an uptake in the request for birth certificates and identification for children.

Source: Hebatalla Elgazzar, program leader, Human Development, World Bank, 2017.

Internet Banking/Payments

Another way to make digital payments is using the payments infrastructure integrated with government applications into bank accounts of the users which can be accessed both through a mobile or web interface over the internet. The users can also use the normal banking channels for cashing out the payments using checks, ATMs, bank branches, and banking correspondents. The beneficiaries can also use their bank accounts for making purchases online on e-commerce websites with their bank accounts or debit cards or prepaid cards.

The Promise of Fintech for G2P Social Protection Payments

The Fintech market is growing quickly. G2P payments for social programs have the potential to reach millions of individuals, families, and households living at the base of the pyramid. When beneficiaries of social protection programs are able to use open-loop G2P payments to transact directly with other individuals and with merchants or service providers to buy food or to pay for school fees or health visits, they stand a greater chance of exercising agency over when, where, and how the money will be used. The promise of interoperability between G2P and P2P (peer-to-peer) platforms holds great potential for beneficiaries of social protection programs, particularly women, in contributing to their economic empowerment, in investing human capital outcomes for their families, and saving for old age or crises. It could be an attractive market for Fintech firms as volumes are key for their growth—it could help drive up numbers and bring people closer to financial inclusion.

The key challenge is how to allow the poor and vulnerable to own their own digital wallet or mobile money accounts and keep using them. In Indonesia, most people immediately cash out their social benefits from their e-money wallets because they do not see the value of the digital account. People are not fully aware of the program and how to do transactions and maintain their accounts.[27] In Pakistan, SP payments are made to limited mandate accounts, so most beneficiaries withdraw payments within 72 hours of the disbursement. G2P programs can enable a digital ecosystem around G2P payments; engaging merchants and other players in the value chain to become digital and to accept digital payments, to encourage people to own accounts and to keep using them.

Go-Pay, a digital wallet offshoot of the ride-hailing app called Gojek in Indonesia, permits users to add money to their Go-Pay digital wallet by going to most ATMs in most cities in Indonesia; other options include mini-markets, online bank account top-ups, and top-ups via Gojek drivers. If people do not have bank accounts, they can also add money to their wallet by giving cash to their Gojek drivers. For Gojek, every driver works as a deposit machine for Go-Pay and a walking ATM machine from whom people can withdraw cash.[28]

India and Colombia are leveraging new technologies for social protection payments, albeit in different ways. In India, the government has attempted to do so through the JAM trinity—Jan Dhan Bank accounts, Aadhaar Unique IDs, and mobile devices. In Colombia, the focus was on encouraging people to access digital wallets without the need to link to bank accounts.

In India, as part of the Direct Benefits Transfer (DBT) initiative, beneficiaries of social programs were required to open bank accounts to enable direct G2P transfers. Preceding this initiative, India mandated an affordable, zero-balance bank account (Jan Dhan Yojana [JDY], People's Wealth Scheme) with free accident and life insurance to improve financial inclusion.[29] In five years, more than 357 million accounts were opened. In this way, the G2P social program payments leveraged JDY to make transfers directly to people's accounts as the JDY could be used to receive transfers. The focus was on encouraging the recipients to save money in a bank account since savings accounts must pay interest on retail deposits. India's unique identification platform enabled accounts to be opened with an electronic KYC. It also allowed beneficiaries of social programs to link their Aadhaar number (unique identification number) to a bank account of their choosing. This made it possible for any government benefit transfer program to use just an Aadhaar number as the unique financial address. An Aadhaar Payments Bridge (APB) system, which mapped an Aadhaar-to-bank-to-account, maintained by the National Payments Corporation of India, enabled the government to initiate bulk payments for social protection programs to be directly credited into thousands of individual Aadhaar-linked accounts of beneficiaries without having to collect and update beneficiary bank account details in multiple government databases. Beneficiaries could provide their Aadhaar ID number and biometrically authenticate themselves at branches, agents, or merchant locations for proof of identification for account opening and updates, and for performing transactions. Another system, the Aadhaar-enabled Payments System (AePS) enabled the use of POS terminals and micro-ATMs to withdraw cash using an Aadhaar number and biometric authentication. If needed, beneficiaries can change their accounts and receive payments at a new account by linking the new account to their Aadhaar number, thereby mitigating the need to provide updates to social programs. Also see box 6.11.

In Colombia, Banco Davivienda has created DaviPlata, a mobile P2P payments technology that does not require individuals to have bank accounts, and offers money transfer services for free to the poor. DaviPlata allows people to set up an account online linked to their government-issued ID, and to withdraw funds at Davivienda ATMs or DaviPlata points across the country. The platform won a government contract to deliver G2P payments to more than 900,000 recipients of Familias en Acción, Colombia's largest social assistance program that provides conditional transfers to families to provide health care to children and to keep them in school. The DaviPlata app allows people to transfer money across wallets, cash in and cash out, and request their wallet balance from their phone at no cost (box 6.12).

Finally, newer technologies such as Blockchain are enabling payments administration for social services such as disability support. A recent proof-of-concept from Australia's National Disability Insurance Agency (NDIA) demonstrates how payments are enabled by creating tokens to represent promises to pay in currency for services such as disability support (box 6.13).

Box 6.11 Blue-Sky Thinking: Unified Payments Interface

The Unified Payments Interface (UPI) allows small-value retail payments from nearly any bank or digital account to any other bank or digital account in real time. In India, a Unified Payment Interface (UPI) enables mobile applications linked to bank accounts to make payments. The UPI enables individuals to make instant money transfers directly between two bank accounts, between two individuals, or between a customer and a merchant (peer-to-peer). Users can choose from multiple mobile applications that may be developed by banks or nonbanks supporting the UPI. However, nonbank providers require at least one sponsoring bank that is a participant in the National Payments Corporation of India's (NPCI's) UPI scheme, in order to provide that service. Money can be transferred by a sender to a recipient either using their UPI ID, a virtual payment address which is a unique identifier or by using the bank account number and a bank identifier (IFSC code) or using a mobile number. Once a UPI ID is created and mapped against a bank account, the UPI ID (e.g., myname@bankname) is shared with the payer, who enters the UPI ID and sends money to be directly credited to the recipient's bank account. These mobile apps can also be used to make payments to merchants by scanning their QR code at a POS device in shops. (The QR code encodes the payment address details like IFSC code and bank account, etc.) The NPCI provides the infrastructure and the implementation of the information exchange as well as clearing and settlement of funds underlying the UPI interface which enables the interoperability of different identifiers (virtual payment address, mobile number, account number + IFSC code) across multiple banks that participate in the UPI system. NPCI estimated the total number of UPI transactions in the country grew to 1.3 billion in June 2020.[a]

Source: Cook and Raman 2019.

a. https://www.npci.org.in/product-statistics/upi-product-statistics.

Box 6.12 Government-to-Person Payments in Colombia's DaviPlata

Colombia's DaviPlata offers innovative approaches to enable financial services for the poor. It does not require bank accounts and offers money transfer services for free to the poor.

Registration and activation of the product is done in an over-the-air operation in a session that is opened from the menu stored in the SIM. This happens most often without the need of external help or involvement of a third party. The electronic account number is the same as the mobile phone number, and it is opened by merely entering the name, ID number, date, and place of issue. There are no fees.

Approved transactions include withdrawals from ATMs (by requesting a PIN), transfers between DaviPlata accounts and from or to a savings or checking account in Davivienda, international remittances and payments, payments for public and private utilities, recharging of mobile phone minutes, changes in password, and queries on balances and transfers.

By regulation, deposits may not exceed a monthly limit of three monthly legal minimum salaries. Accounts are exempt from the tax on withdrawals from the financial system (called "tax on financial movements," equivalent to 4 per 1,000).

The service model was based on the premise of moving people to branchless banking. It required a call center that was separate from that of the bank, outsourced to a third party. Over time the bank adapted its interactive voice response system, incorporating a predictive solution with a specific DaviPlata for the Familias en Acción site and using social networks to expand interaction with program beneficiaries. Furthermore, to take advantage of the bank's extensive network of ATMs, it allowed withdrawals exclusively from the bank's ATMs, which were adapted to work without a card, using a one-time password. The decision to offer withdrawals exclusively at ATMs was later changed when withdrawals from commercial banks, other payment points, access points, and cash-out points were authorized.

Much has changed since the instrument was originally launched in the early 2010s, with the introduction of regulatory, technological, and operational improvements that have changed the interface and functionality of the product. DaviPlata has evolved and is now a leading instrument for person-to-person (P2P) and government-to-person (G2P) payments. The state of play in Colombia has also rapidly evolved, and it is estimated that there are currently nearly a dozen digital wallets in play.

Source: CGAP 2015.

Box 6.13 Blockchain-Based Payments for Disability Support Services in Australia

The National Disability Insurance Agency (NDIA) of Australia provides funding to people with disability, called participants, to spend on disability support services. Funds are spent in accordance with the rules set for each participant's plan. The project created programmable money by attaching smart contracts to blockchain tokens that can be redeemed for payment in Australian dollars. Once programmed, smart money can know who it can be spent by, what it can be spent on, when it can be spent, how much of it can be spent, and any other conditions that may be set by the party funding the payment. The proof-of-concept design combines blockchain token technology and Australia's New Payments Platform. The blockchain component was developed as a system using tokens to represent promises to pay in Australian dollars, smart contracts to create spending conditions based on NDIA plan rules, and registries to represent parts of the payment environment such as lists of eligible service providers for particular services. See figure B6.13.1 for a visual overview.

Figure B6.13.1 Smart Contracts and Blockchain Tokens for Service Provider Payments

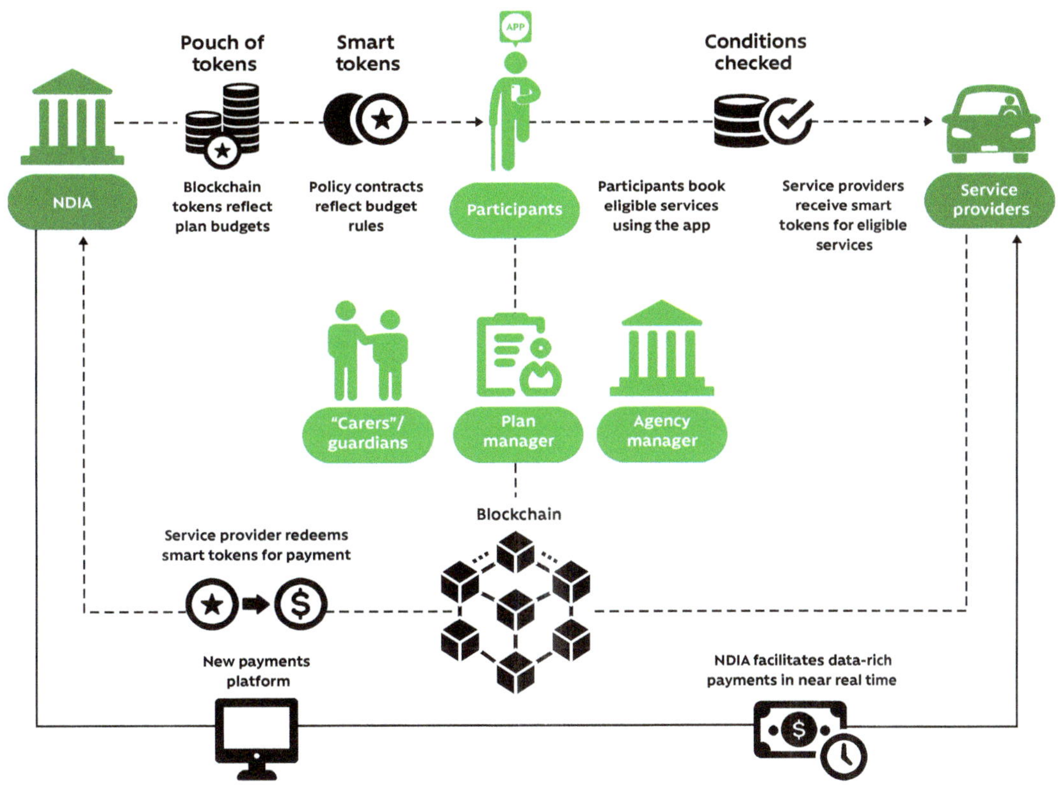

Source: Royal et al. 2018.

Note: NDIA = National Disability Insurance Agency.

6.6 SOME CONCLUDING POINTS

G2P payments to beneficiaries of social protection programs present an unmet opportunity for improving financial inclusion as well as women's economic empowerment for the "first mile." Social protection beneficiaries tend to be poor, are often women, and carry a legacy of financial exclusion. Reaching these "first mile" populations and ensuring their financial inclusion has the promise of being transformational given social protection beneficiaries receiving G2P payments outnumber civil servants 5:1. Digitization of payments for social protection programs has the potential of substantially increasing financial inclusion, particularly among the poor and vulnerable. There is a range of digitization in use in social protection program payments. The evolution from G2P 1.0 to 1.5 to 2.0 to 3.0 and 4.0 is not linear and many programs and countries have coexisting modalities. Moreover, the notion of "payments digitization" goes beyond the biometric authentication of beneficiaries or virtual provisioning of payments, both front-end processes more visible to individuals, families, and households. Payments digitization extends to the automation of payments administration, and the back-end processes that are more visible to program administrators. Modern G2P payment systems improve recipients' experiences by allowing them to choose providers and accounts to receive funds, lower delivery costs for governments, reduce leakage through integrated payment systems, and introduce incentives for payment service providers who must compete for their market share.[30]

A human-centered design approach is helpful to make adaptations to payments provision for intended populations. Efforts to digitize SP G2P payments have suffered from shortcomings. A common complaint among those receiving government transfers as digital payments is that the payment products are not designed with beneficiary contexts in mind. Risk mitigation and controls should be in place to prevent error, fraud, and corruption in payments. Security should be balanced between program objectives and people-centeredness. Delivery chain process mapping can help with analysis of current state end-to-end processes, offer opportunities for eliminating non-value-added steps for administration, and improve processes to better support the needs and expectations of end-users.

Newer technologies are enabling some countries to leapfrog traditional payment approaches, but the key challenge is how to allow the poor and marginalized to own their own digital wallet/mobile money accounts and keep using them. Countries are improving access and account ownership, while minimizing costs of administration and provision by adopting rapidly evolving financial and technological services. Nevertheless, challenges remain in the interoperability of payment systems, with many being "closed-loop" systems that do not allow people to make everyday cashless transactions based on their choice and convenience, hindering financial inclusion and women's economic empowerment. Another key challenge is the issue of data sharing, data protection, and privacy concerns. See Data Protection, Privacy, and Security in chapter 4.

ANNEX 6A: MOST COMMON PAYMENT SERVICE PROVIDERS IN SOCIAL PROTECTION PROGRAMS

Table 6A.1 Features of Common Payment Service Providers

Payment service provider	Main features
Public agencies and offices	**These are the most basic form of PSPs and are more prevalent in countries with limited financial infrastructure and lack of alternative options.** Under this modality, national or subnational/local offices of line ministries or community organizations are responsible for the manual distribution of cash, checks, or vouchers. Under this modality, the government establishes a series of payment points (taking advantage of social and community infrastructure) and organizes a payment process, usually using a paper payroll with name of recipients and amount to be paid. Identity is validated with a program or national (foundational) ID, signature, and often a fingerprint. Reconciliation is done by sending a signed payroll to the central office, frequently without major processes to prevent fraud. Benefits of this approach reside in the relatively easy process to establish payment points and the close relationship with beneficiaries. Also, payment sessions can be used to disseminate information related to the program. Examples of countries that still are using manual payments delivered by line ministries include the social pension (Programa Subsidio Social Basico) in Mozambique and the Social Cash Transfer in Zambia. Drawbacks of manual payments have been largely documented, including security issues (for both program managers and recipients), low control in authentication of identity, high costs for beneficiaries (represented in both travel and waiting time), and lack of rigorous reconciliation of payments.
Banks	**Public or private banks are the most common PSP in SP transfers.** Banks can be used not only as payment points for cash or vouchers but also to offer bank accounts to beneficiaries. Regardless of the type of bank and nature of involvement with the program, it is key that the bank has as business case to both satisfactorily deliver SP transfers and facilitate financial inclusion of program beneficiaries. This is one of the main prerequisites to guarantee sustainability of payment delivery. Banks have many advantages as PSPs, because they offer their networks to distribute payments, including branches, ATMs, branchless banking (agents), mobile banking, e-banking, and so forth. In addition, bank transactions often offer security for users and for program implementers, as well as accountability by means of implementing reconciliation and auditing processes. However, it is important to note that there are associated costs and fees with the different payments modalities that someone will need to bear. The costlier for the bank, the higher the possibility that those costs will be passed either to beneficiaries or to the program.[a] One of the disadvantages of using banks, since bank branches may sometimes be hard to reach, is the potential incremental cost of activating a payment network with a higher geographical coverage. Also, it is common that SP beneficiaries have relatively low exposure to banking products, conducting transactions, or knowledge on costs of financial services. Therefore, it is important to prepare and conduct processes to familiarize customers with financial instruments. More than half of the programs including in the inventory use banks (state or commercial) to deliver transfers of social protection programs.

continued

Table 6A.1 *(continued)*

Payment service provider	Main features
Post offices (PO)	**In many countries, POs have the responsibility, in addition to postal services, to deliver and provide basic financial services (remittances, deposits, payments, etc.) primarily to people not served by the banking system.** Among common advantages of POs are their wide geographical coverage, established delivery routes, and familiarity with all prospective clients. Common drawbacks include the transfer of funds, which are generally physically transferred to offices and then also delivered to beneficiaries in cash, introducing potential security problems. Also, given technological, infrastructure (or sometimes regulatory) limitations, POs have more difficulties offering transactional accounts that connect with other payment networks or options for storing resources. Also, payment reconciliation processes from POs could be manual and authentication of identity may face challenges. While in countries like the Arab Republic of Egypt (Takaful and Karama Program, CCT), Morocco (Tayssir, CCT), and Vietnam (Decree 136, social pension), the post office is the only authorized agency for the delivery of social protection programs, in others like Jamaica (Programme for the Advancement of Health and Education [PATH], CCT), Romania (Universal Child Allowance), and Turkey (Sartli Egitim Yardimi, CCT), the governments have opted to introduce different providers and modalities for the delivery of SP payments, which includes national post offices.
Mobile money/e-money providers	**MNO payments offer coverage advantages given the large penetration of mobile phones globally**, however, they require a regulatory framework that authorizes their operation. In addition, they should be able to guarantee a large network of retail outlets to enable beneficiaries to cash out their transfers. Examples include Orange Money that delivers transfers for the Productive Social Safety Net in Côte d'Ivoire and MTN in the SAGE program in Uganda. In certain countries, MNOs have started working in partnership with financial institutions (mainly banks) that offer mobile money applications like DaviPlata (an e-wallet) in Colombia that is one of the PSPs used for the delivery of benefits for Familias en Acción (CCT).
Microfinance institutions (MFI)	**MFIs aim to promote economic activity among low-income people with barriers to banking services.** MFIs come in all shapes and sizes; they can differ in scale, experience, legal statute, strategy, and budget. The common characteristic is that MFIs provide hard-to-find financial services to local individuals and groups. An MFI could be a good player since they typically target their services to low-income clients by means of operating locally and through financial products customized to their clients. However, regulations on the type of products that can be offered by these organizations vary considerably across countries. Evidence does not show a significant involvement of MFIs in the delivery of social protection payments, and in fact, none of the programs included in the inventory used MFIs for the delivery of social benefits.

Source: ISPA 2016.

Note: Agents and business correspondents are basically cash-out points that work with licensed PSPs rather than PSPs themselves. CCT = conditional cash transfer (program); MNO = mobile network operator; PSP = payment service provider; SAGE = Social Assistance Grants for Empowerment; SP = social protection.

a. From *For Protection and Promotion: The Design and Implementation of Effective Safety Nets* by Margaret Grosh, Carlo del Ninno, Emil Tesliuc, and Azedine Ouerghi, 2008, World Bank, Washington, DC.

ANNEX 6B: PAYMENT SERVICE CONTRACTING MODELS

There is a great degree of variation with respect to service fees and charges for delivery of electronic payments. The service level agreement (SLA) service charge structure largely depends on the maturity of the program, the payment infrastructure in the country, and the specific electronic payment instruments being utilized. Card payment models generally include a basic service charge and the cost of the card. In some cases, the SLA can also include withdrawal charges or infrastructure charges to incentivize the PSP or cover set-up costs. Mobile payments or over-the-counter payment models generally follow a service charge only model. See below for more details (Khan 2015).

Service charges only. This model is generally used by mobile payment models, where the service charge is shared by the mobile operator and the agents. Beneficiaries typically withdraw cash over the counter or perform POS-based transactions at mobile operator service points or the designated agent network. These solutions are a cost-effective way to reach beneficiaries, provided the agent network is large.

Float income only. Where governments may not have enough fiscal space to pay for service charges for payments for each of the beneficiaries explicitly, the complete lump sum payment is provided in advance to the selected PSP. The PSP can then accrue income from float before disbursing payments. This is a likely possibility in emergency programs where the cash transfer amount has been already earmarked by the government and transferred to the PSPs, while beneficiaries are still being identified and enrolled. This was the case in the emergency cash transfer programs in Pakistan.

Flat service charges and card costs only. The Philippines followed this simple SLA structure, with minimal additional services or charges, as this was a contract between two government departments. The authorizing bank charged a flat transaction-based service fee for payments to beneficiaries and separate charges for the cost of the card which could be used at any authorized ATM to withdraw cash. This arrangement is applicable if the country has a wide network of financial access points and the PSP is mandated to deliver services by the government. In the Philippines, when the government initiated payments, using the banking system it mandated a simplified SLA negotiation that kept the service charges low (under 1 percent) and enabled the program to launch account-based payments relatively quickly. Lack of additional investments in outreach can increase transaction costs for beneficiaries; especially for those in rural areas who have to travel large distances to access designated ATMs to withdraw cash.

Service charges for cash transfers and cash withdrawals. The SLAs of Bangladesh's Income Support Program for the Poorest (ISPP) with Bangladesh Post include the following: (1) a standard service fee for every cash transfer to the beneficiary account; and (2) an additional withdrawal charge when the beneficiary withdraws the cash from her account.[31] The former is a standard fee globally, but the withdrawal fee is an incentive for the PSPs to ensure and encourage beneficiaries to withdraw their payments as soon as they receive them or within a stipulated time frame. Though this deters the PSPs from developing savings or graduation products for the beneficiaries linked to their cash transfer accounts, it serves the primary function of ensuring timely payments.

Combinations of service charges for transactions and income for infrastructure setup. This is applicable for first-time adopters of electronic payments with limited initial branchless banking infrastructure. Pakistan's BISP used this approach when it started to roll out electronic payments in 2009/2010. At the time, the branchless banking network was limited, and the PSPs were a combination of private and government-owned commercial banks providing electronic payments to the extreme poor for the first time. The SLA included two components: (1) a flat service charge fee of about 2.75 percent for transactions for the transfer of cash to beneficiary accounts; and (2) infrastructure set-up costs, which included a one-time card cost, and an advance for float-based income to be utilized for setting up infrastructure to enroll beneficiaries for electronic payments. The second element provided an incentive for PSPs to participate, and to enhance the financial infrastructure footprint and outreach of BISP electronic payments for beneficiaries. This two-fold costing made the program initially expensive to implement but it was deemed necessary to provide an attractive business case for the private sector to participate (World Bank 2014). Eventually, this was discontinued as the volume of electronic G2P payments and branchless banking transactions increased (Khan 2015).[32] BISP now pays a 3 percent fee under a two-year contract. The fee was determined through consultations with the banking sector and reflects global standards (Rotman, Kumar, and Parada 2013).

Open competitive SLA model. From 2016, all payments for India's Mahatma Gandhi National Rural Employment Guarantee Scheme (MGNREGS) will be through the Direct Benefit Transfer (DBT) system for delivering electronic payments to beneficiary bank accounts; this is linked to the Aadhar where available.[33] Due to the duration of the program and various payment pilots, the government has a predefined criterion for PSPs. According to a circular from the Ministry of Finance dated May 26, 2017, the government of India pays Re 0.50 per transaction, which is to be split between the sponsor bank, the destination bank, and the National Payment Corporation of India. This makes it easier for state implementing agencies to contract PSPs, without having to individually negotiate SLAs. Also, unlike Indonesia, Pakistan, and several other countries, the SLA model is not a time-bound tender process; it is open to any PSP that chooses to participate. However, the service fee of 1 percent is likely too low for PSPs to sustainably provide this service, particularly in remote areas.

ANNEX 6C: UNDERSTANDING OPTIONS FOR STRUCTURING GOVERNMENT-TO-PERSON DISTRIBUTION FEES

Table 6C.1 Structuring Government-to-Person Distribution Fees

Things to pay for	Pay payment service provider (PSP)	Pay customer	Government covers costs or involves third party
Distribution/ cash-out fee	No cash-out fees for a limited number of transactions in a defined time period, thereby making cash-out free or cheaper to recipients	Top up transfer amount with cash-out fee to enable customer to access full benefit	N/A
Reach of recipients/ transport to access point	Tiered pricing structures for PSPs serving customers (tiering to be done based on remoteness as measured in distance from highways and population density)	Use tiered travel rebate basis: the distance of recipient's location from the nearest access point	N/A
Account opening/know your customer	Flat fee for every new qualifying account opened, spread across first six months of usage; banks can be encouraged to waive fees on account of potential deposit mobilization	Flat amount at first disbursement or spread across payments	Government supports recipients with account opening
Education and training of customers	Tiered commissions for PSPs educating customers (tiering to be done based on remoteness as measured in distance from highways and population density)	Compensate customer for their opportunity cost and travel costs	Recipients educated directly by government or through third parties
Technological requirements and devices	For acquisition of service terminals based on meeting demand	Provide mobile phones or other electronic devices to recipients	N/A
Customer support and redress	Initial set-up costs for customer support and redress	N/A	Government trains recipients on how to access support and grievance redress

Source: Baur-Yazbeck and Mdluli, forthcoming.
Note: N/A = not applicable.

Notes

1. While this Sourcebook covers provision of cash benefits (this chapter) and services (chapter 7), we do not delve deeply into the provision of in-kind benefits. The other phases of the delivery chain covered in chapters 3, 4, 5, and 8 would all pertain to in-kind benefits, but it is beyond the scope of the Sourcebook to cover the actual provision of in-kind benefits. Moreover, food-related benefits have recently been covered extensively in Alderman, Gentilini, and Yemtsov (2018).
2. A share of this is also on disability services.
3. See Global Findex Database at https://globalfindex.worldbank.org/.
4. This chapter does not include an analysis of person-to-government (P2G) SP payments for contributory SP programs.
5. World Bank Global Payment Systems Survey (GPSS) 2016, http://www.worldbank.org/en/topic/financialinclusion/brief/gpss and "Payment Systems Worldwide: A Snapshot," World Bank Group, Washington, DC, September 2018. http://pubdocs.worldbank.org/en/591241545960780368/GPSS-4-Report-Final.pdf.
6. UFA2020 strategy: https://www.worldbank.org/en/topic/financialinclusion/brief/achieving-universal-financial-access-by-2020.
7. Presentation by Silvia Baur-Yazbeck and Gregory Chen of CGAP (Consultative Group to Assist the Poor) on G2P 3.0: "Future of Government Payments," World Bank, February 2019.
8. http://www.worldbank.org/en/topic/financialinclusion/brief/gpss.
9. World Bank's Mozambique Financial Inclusion and Stability Project-Procurement Plan P166107: http://documents.worldbank.org/curated/en/626361590678996837/Mozambique-AFRICA-P166107-Mozambique-Financial-Inclusion-and-Stability-Project-Procurement-Plan.
10. Reconciliation is the process of comparing the number of transfers approved in a payroll with the number of transfers carried out. When discussing services, the process of comparing planned delivery of services to actual delivery is normally conducted as part of beneficiary progress monitoring, which forms a part of beneficiary operations management.
11. This section draws on Rodríguez et al. (forthcoming).
12. Payment provision approaches can take many structures, and intermediation of services can happen at different levels. For example, payments can be made in a one-step process from treasury to beneficiary. Similarly, the process may require two or three steps, where funds are first transferred into pooled accounts at one or multiple service providers or aggregators and then provisioned to beneficiaries.
13. Settlement finality refers to the moment in time when one party is deemed to have discharged an obligation or to have transferred an asset or financial instrument to another party, and such discharge or transfer becomes unconditional and irrevocable despite the insolvency or entrance into bankruptcy of either party. See Principles for Financial Market Infrastructures, Principle 8 (Settlement Finality). "Netting" refers to the resolution of all bank transactions at the end of the day.
14. "No-frills," simplified, or basic savings accounts provide basic banking services to low-income customers to promote financial inclusion (by means of access to financial services like microloans, savings, insurances, remittances, etc.). Typically, the services available in these accounts will include receipt of money through electronic payment channels issued by government agencies. The main characteristics of these accounts is that they do not have requirements in terms of minimum balances or nominal charges and offer a limited number of transactions at no cost. Also, they tend to require little documentation and a more relaxed KYC process. Sometimes they have additional eligibility requirements, such as being unbanked or being a recipient of social assistance. Under no-frills/basic accounts most of the facilities offered are limited. Once this limit is exceeded, the bank charges for these services.
15. GPSS 2016—Accounts and Access, http://www.worldbank.org/en/topic/financialinclusion/brief/gpss.
16. https://www.worldbank.org/en/topic/financialinclusion/brief/gpss.
17. Programs such as the GEWEL program in Zambia top up the value of the transfer to beneficiaries to compensate part of the private cost of direct transfers to beneficiaries. Specifically, the payment system compensates for the fee and provides a travel rebate.
18. In certain schemes with multiple payment service providers, a lump sum amount is transferred temporarily to payment service providers to ensure liquidity until all beneficiaries receive transfers.
19. Cash is understood to be money in the physical form of currency such as bank notes and coins.
20. Quote from the Bill & Melinda Gates Foundation's D3 criteria provided by Liz Kellison of the foundation, in 2019.
21. The payment system in São Tomé and Príncipe has changed since the drafting of this chapter.

22. See Global Findex Database at https://globalfindex.worldbank.org/.
23. Governor Lael Brainard. "The Digitalization of Payments and Currency: Some Issues for Consideration." Speech at the Symposium on the Future of Payments, Stanford, CA, February 5, 2020. https://www.federalreserve.gov/newsevents/speech/brainard20200205a.htm. However, they are not used by the government to pay benefits to eligible households.
24. Entrepreneur.com, "How Ovo Has Grown to Be Indonesia's Largest Digital Payments Platform," March 28, 2019. https://www.entrepreneur.com/article/330561.
25. However, the government of India has specifically avoided the use of digital wallets for benefits disbursements. There are several reasons for it and one major reason is the lack of interest rates on savings.
26. Toptechblitz.com, "All You Need to Know about JumiaPay," July 25, 2018. https://toptechblitz.com.ng/all-you-need-to-know-about-jumiapay/.
27. Back to Office Report (BTOR) on Fintech, December 2018.
28. Inc42.com, "We Are Banking On Our Digital Wallet Go-Pay for the Foreseeable Future—Go-Jek CTO, Ajey Gore," July 11, 2017. https://inc42.com/buzz/go-jek-go-pay-digital-wallet-indonesia/.
29. Although there is a premium on life insurance, it is borne by the government of India.
30. This idea is explored in CGAP's focus note *The Future of G2P Payments: Expanding Customer Choice*, which lays out the advantages and challenges of this model and how governments can create such a G2P system (Baur-Yazbeck, Chen, and Roest 2019).
31. ISPP is a maternal and child CCT introduced in 2014 to provide income support for the poorest of the poor.
32. Colombia took a similar route in 2009 when electronic payments were first launched for social cash transfers. The original fee included infrastructure set-up costs, by the sole bidder Union Temporal, and was almost 70 percent more costly than the earlier cash payment fee, since the PSP needed to issue debit cards, perform system upgrades, and enhance the network of financial access points. These costs were significantly reduced over time, as the share of electronic payments rose from 24 percent to 91 percent between 2009 and 2011 (Bold, Porteous, and Rotman 2012).
33. MGNREGS has always supported the electronic transfer of funds. However, the act also stipulates that anyone not wanting electronic payment may choose otherwise. There is opt-out in the system. See Financial Express, "All Wage Payments to MGNREGA Workers from April 1 through Direct Benefit Transfer: Govt," February 2, 2016, https://www.financialexpress.com/economy/all-wage-paymentstomgnrega-workers-from-april-1-through-direct-benefittransfergovt/206169/.

Bibliography

A2i. 2019. "Amplifying Beneficiary Impact and Experience in the G2P Digital Transformation." A2i, Dhaka, Bangladesh.

Aker, Jenny C. 2020. "Social Protection Programs in the Time of a Pandemic: Reevaluating What We Know." Presentation to the World Bank, Fletcher School and Department of Economics, Tufts University, Medford, MA, April.

Aker, Jenny C., Rachid Boumnijel, Amanda McClelland, and Niall Tierney. 2016. "Payment Mechanisms and Anti-Poverty Programs: Evidence from a Mobile Money Cash Transfer Experiment in Niger." Tufts University Working Paper, Fletcher School and Department of Economics, Tufts University, Medford, MA.

Alderman, Harold, Ugo Gentilini, and Ruslan Yemtsov, eds. 2018. *The 1.5 Billion People Question: Food, Vouchers, or Cash Transfers?* Washington, DC: World Bank.

Atansah, Priscilla, Masoomeh Khandan, Todd Moss, Anit Mukherjee, and Jennifer Richmond. 2017. "When Do Subsidy Reforms Stick? Lessons from Iran, Nigeria, and India." CGD Policy Paper 111, Center for Global Development, Washington, DC. https://www.cgdev.org/publication/when-do-subsidy-reforms-stick-lessons-iran-nigeria-and-india.

Bansal, Mohit, Shekhar Lele, Ashish Punjabi, and Pooja Lad. 2018. "UPI 2.0: Towards a Complete Digital Ecosystem." PricewaterhouseCoopers India. https://www.pwc.in/consulting/financial-services/fintech/fintech-insights/upi-2-0-towards-a-complete-digital-ecosystem.html.

Barrientos, Armando, and David Hulme, eds. 2008. *Social Protection for the Poor and Poorest: Concepts, Policies, and Politics.* Houndmills, Basingstoke, Hampshire, UK: Palgrave Macmillan.

Baur, Silvia. 2016. "Digital Social Payments and Financial Inclusion." Presentation at the World Bank's Social Safety Nets and Delivery Systems Core Course, Washington, DC, April 2016.

Baur-Yazbeck, Silvia, Gregory Chen, and Joep Roest. 2019. *"The Future of G2P Payments: Expanding Customer Choice."* Focus Note, Consultative Group to Assist the Poor, Washington, DC. https://www.cgap.org/sites/default/files/publications/2019_09_FocusNote_Future_G2P_Payments_1.pdf.

Baur-Yazbeck, Silvia, Craig Kilfoil, and Ioana Botea. 2019. "Case Study: The Future of G2P Payments: Expanding Customer Choice in Zambia." Consultative Group to Assist the Poor, Washington, DC.

Baur-Yazbeck, Silvia, and Gcinisizwe Mdluli. Forthcoming. "Pricing G2P Payments Distribution: Considerations for Program Designers." Consultative Group to Assist the Poor, Washington, DC.

Baur-Yazbeck, Silvia, and Joep Roest. Forthcoming. "G2P 3.0 Case Study: A2i in Bangladesh: Toward a Shared Government Payments Platform." Consultative Group to Assist the Poor, Washington, DC.

Baur-Yazbeck, Silvia, and Jamie Zimmerman. 2016. "Understanding Consumer Risks in Digital Social Payments." Consultative Group to Assist the Poor, Washington, DC. https://www.cgap.org/research/publication/understanding-consumer-risks-digital-social-payments.

Beegle, Kathleen, Aline Coudouel, and Emma Monsalve, eds. 2018. *Realizing the Full Potential of Social Safety Nets in Africa*. Africa Development Forum Series. Washington, DC: World Bank.

Berthaut, Antoine, Bertrand Ginet, Sebastian di Paola, and Tobias Thayer. 2018. "Cash Digitization: UN Collaboration, Coordination, and Harmonization Opportunities." Better than Cash Alliance, UNHCR, UNICEF, and WFP, New York.

Bill & Melinda Gates Foundation. 2019. "A G7 Partnership for Women's Digital Financial Inclusion in Africa." Report Prepared at the Request of the G7 French Presidency. https://docs.gatesfoundation.org/Documents/WomensDigitalFinancialInclusioninAfricaEnglish.pdf.

Boko, Joachim, Luis Inaki Alberro Encinas, Maimouna Gueye, Audrey Ariss, and Tina George Karippacheril. 2020. "Technical Note on Togo's Novissi Program: Technology and Innovations for Africa's Human Capital in the Face of the COVID-19 Crisis." Social Protection and Jobs Global Practice and Finance, Competitiveness, and Innovation Global Practice, World Bank, Washington, DC.

Bold, Chris, David Porteous, and Sarah Rotman. 2012. "Social Cash Transfers and Financial Inclusion: Evidence from Four Countries." Focus Note 77, Consultative Group to Assist the Poor, Washington, DC.

CaLP (Cash Learning Partnership). 2018. *The State of the World's Cash Report: Cash Transfer Programming in Humanitarian Aid*. Oxford, UK: CaLP.

CDFI (Centre for Digital Financial Inclusion). 2018. "Rethinking Benefit Delivery: Exploring the Reasons behind the Success of the Pradhan Mantri Matru Vandana Yojana (PMMVY), the Government of India's Flagship Maternity Benefit Programme." CDFI, New Delhi.

CGAP (Consultative Group to Assist the Poor). 2015. "DaviPlata: Taking Mobile G2P Payments to Scale in Colombia" (blog post), July 1, 2015. https://www.cgap.org/blog/daviplata-taking-mobile-g2p-payments-scale-colombia.

Chamberlin, Wendy, Liz Kellison, Jeni Klugman, and Jamie Zimmerman. 2019. "Enhancing Women's Economic Empowerment through Digital Cash Transfers: Digitize/Direct/Design: The D3 Criteria." Bill & Melinda Gates Foundation. Working draft. https://www.findevgateway.org/sites/default/files/publications/files/_bmgf_d3_criteria_june_1_2019.pdf.

Cho, Yoonyoung, Ashiq Aziz, and Kenichi Nishikawa Chávez. 2018. "Evolution of Safety Net Payments in Bangladesh." Presentation at the World Bank's Social Safety Nets and Delivery Systems Core Course, Washington, DC, May 7, 2018.

Coady, David, Margaret Grosh, and John Hoddinott. 2004. *Targeting of Transfers in Developing Countries: Review of Lessons and Experience*. Regional and Sectoral Studies. Washington, DC: World Bank.

Cook, William, and Anand Raman. 2019. "National Payments Corporation of India and the Remaking of Payments in India." Working paper, Consultative Group to Assist the Poor, Washington, DC.

del Ninno, Carlo. 2016. "Payment Systems: An Introduction Training Course on 'For Protection and Promotion: The Design and Implementation of Effective Social Safety Nets'" (Social Safety Nets Core Course). Presentation, World Bank, Washington, DC, April 26, 2016.

del Ninno, Carlo, and Bradford Mills, eds. 2015. *Safety Nets in Africa: Effective Mechanisms to Reach the Poor and Most Vulnerable*. Africa Development Forum Series. Washington, DC: World Bank and Agence Française de Développement.

Demirgüç-Kunt, Asli, Leora Klapper, Dorothe Singer, Saniya Ansar, and Jake Hess. 2018. *The Global Findex Database 2017: Measuring Financial Inclusion and the Fintech Revolution*. Washington, DC: World Bank.

DFID (UK Department for International Development). 2006, June. "How-to Note: Managing the Fiduciary Risk Associated with Social Cash Transfer Programmes." DFID Practice Paper ref. no. PD Info 098. http://www.gsdrc.org/docs/open/sp22.pdf.

Grosh, Margaret E. 1994. "Administering Targeted Social Programs in Latin America: From Platitudes to Practice." World Bank, Washington, DC.

Grosh, Margaret, Carlo del Ninno, Emil Tesliuc, and Azedine Ouerghi. 2008. *For Protection and Promotion: The Design and Implementation of Effective Safety Nets*. Washington, DC: World Bank.

Guven, Melis. 2019. "Extending Pension Coverage to the Informal Sector in Africa." Social Protection and Jobs Discussion Paper 1933, World Bank, Washington, DC.

Guven, Melis, Ernesto Brodersohn, and Clement Joubert. 2018. "Benin: Pension Scheme for Informal Sector Workers." Unpublished country paper, Social Protection and Jobs Global Practice, World Bank, Washington, DC.

HelpAge International. 2012. "Electronic Payment for Cash Transfer Programmes: Cutting Costs and Corruption or an Idea Ahead of Its Time?" Pension Watch Briefing No. 8, HelpAge International, London.

Hikmat, Harry. 2018. "Balancing Impact and Inclusion: Scaling Up the PKH Conditional Cash Transfer Program in Indonesia." Presentation, World Bank, Washington, DC.

Holmemo, Camilla, Pablo Acosta, Tina George, Robert J. Palacios, Juul Pinxten, Shonali Sen, and Sailesh Tiwari. 2020. *Investing in People: Social Protection for Indonesia's 2045 Vision*. Jakarta, Indonesia: World Bank. https://openknowledge.worldbank.org/handle/10986/33767.

Ibarrarán, Pablo, Nadin Medellin, Ferdinando Regalia, and Marco Stampini, eds. 2017. *How Conditional Cash Transfers Work: Good Practices after 20 Years of Implementation*. Washington, DC: Inter-American Development Bank.

ICRC (International Committee of the Red Cross). 2018. "Cash Transfer Programming in Armed Conflict: The ICRC's Experience." ICRC, Geneva, Switzerland.

IFC (International Finance Corporation). n.d. "A Sense of Inclusion: An Ethnographic Study of the Perceptions and Attitudes to Digital Financial Services in Sub-Saharan Africa." IFC, Washington, DC. https://www.ifc.org/wps/wcm/connect/industry_ext_content/ifc_external_corporate_site/financial+institutions/resources/a+sense+of+inclusion+an+ethnographic+study+of+the+perceptions+and+attitudes+to+digital+financial+services+in+sub-saharan+africa.

International Rescue Committee. 2019. "Safer Cash Toolkit: Collecting and Using Data to Make Cash Programs Safer." International Rescue Committee and United States Agency for International Development, New York. https://reliefweb.int/report/world/safer-cash-toolkit-collecting-and-using-data-make-cash-programs-safer.

ISPA (Inter-Agency Social Protection Assessments). 2016. "Social Protection Payment Delivery Mechanisms: What Matters Guidance Note." ISPA, Washington, DC. https://ispatools.org/payments/.

ISPA (Inter-Agency Social Protection Assessments). 2017. "Identification Systems for Social Protection: What Matters." Guidance Note, ISPA, Washington, DC. https://ispatools.org/id/.

Joyce, Michael, Shelley Spencer, Jordan Weinstock, and Grace Retnowati. 2015. "Qualitative Survey of Current and Alternative G2P Payment Channels in Papua and Papua Barat." TNP2K Working Paper 26-2015, Team for the Acceleration of Poverty Reduction (TNP2K), Jakarta, Indonesia.

Karippacheril, Tina George. 2018. "The 'First Mile' in Delivering Social Protection and Jobs (SPJ): Human-Centered Design." Presentation at the Plenary Session of the World Bank's Social Safety Nets and Delivery Systems Core Course, Washington, DC, April.

Karippacheril, Tina George, and Kathy Lindert. 2017. "Payments in Social Protection and Labor Delivery Systems." Presentation, World Bank, Washington, DC, March.

Khan, Quanita. 2015. "Digital Payments for Pakistan." Presentation at the World Bank's Fragility, Conflict, and Violence Forum 2015, Washington, DC, February 11–13.

Kilfoil, Craig. 2018. "Multi-Service Provider Payments: Girls' Education, Women's Empowerment, and Livelihoods (GEWEL) Project in Zambia." Presentation at the World Bank's Social Safety Nets and Delivery Systems Core Course, Washington, DC, May 7, 2018.

Leisering, Lutz. 2018. *The Global Rise of Social Cash Transfers: How States and International Organizations Constructed a New Instrument for Combating Poverty*. Oxford, UK: Oxford University Press.

Marulanda Consultores. 2015. "Going Mobile with Conditional Cash Transfers: Insights and Lessons from the Payment of Familias en Acción through DaviPlata Wallets in Colombia." Consultative Group to Assist the Poor, Washington, DC.

Muralidharan, Karthik, Paul Niehaus, and Sandip Sukhtankar. 2014. "Payment Infrastructure and the Performance of Public Programs: Evidence from Biometric Smartcards in India." Technical Paper, BREAD (Bureau for Research and Economic Analysis of Development).

Namara, Suleiman, and Christabel Dadzie. 2018. "Ghana—Paperless Public Works Program: Building Efficient Delivery Systems." Presentation at the World Bank's Social Safety Nets and Delivery Systems Core Course, Washington, DC, May 7, 2018.

OECD (Organisation for Economic Co-operation and Development). 2019. Public Spending on Unemployment Benefits, Incapacity, Pensions (indicators). Social Expenditures Database. doi: 10.1787/f35b71ed-en (accessed April 30, 2019).

OPM (Oxford Policy Management). 2012. "Disbursement of Social Assistance Cash Transfers through Bank Accounts: A Study of PKH Payment Mechanisms and Options for Social Assistance Cash Transfers." OPM in collaboration with Tim Nasional Percepatan Penanggulangan Kemiskinan (TNP2K), Jakarta, Indonesia. http://www.tnp2k.go.id/images/uploads/downloads/PKH%20payment%20study-English%20Final-1.pdf.

Palacios, Robert. 2017. "Identification and Payments." Presentation at the World Bank's Pensions and Social Insurance Core Course, Washington, DC, March 9, 2017.

Pickens, Mark, David Porteous, and Sarah Rotman. 2009. "Banking the Poor via G2P Payments." Focus Note 58, Consultative Group to Assist the Poor, Washington, DC.

Pulver, Caroline. 2019. "Driving Financial Inclusion through G2P Payments: A Literature Review and Country Landscaping Exercise." Bill & Melinda Gates Foundation, Seattle, WA.

Rawlings, Laura. 2016. "Social Protection Payments Tool." Presentation at the World Bank's Social Safety Nets and Delivery Systems Core Course, Washington, DC, April 2016.

Rawlings, Laura, and Luz Stella Rodríguez. 2018. "Social Protection Payments Delivery." Presentation at the World Bank's Social Safety Nets and Delivery Systems Core Course, Washington, DC, May 7, 2018.

Rodríguez, Luz, Laura Rawlings, Ana Verónica Lopez, Quanita Khan, Harish Natarajan, Karol Karpinski, and Anita Kumari. Forthcoming. "Cash Transfer Payment Systems: Lessons from Programs in 35 Countries." Technical Note, World Bank, Washington, DC.

Rotman, S., K. Kumar, & M. Parada. 2013. *An Overview of the G2P Sector Payments in Pakistan*. Washington, DC: CGAP (Consultative Group to Assist the Poor). https://www.cgap.org/research/publication/overview-g2p-payments-sector-pakistan.

Royal, Daniel, Paul Rimba, Mark Staples, Sophie Gilder, An Binh Tran, Ethan Williams, Alex Ponomarev, Ingo Weber, Chris Connor, and Nicole Lim. 2018. "Making Money Smart: Empowering NDIS Participants with Blockchain Technologies." Commonwealth Bank of Australia and Data61 (CSIRO), Sydney, Australia.

Sagmeister, Elias, Sara Pavanello, Maximilian Seilern, Ledia Andrawes, Paul Harvey, and Anna Kondakhchyan. 2018. "Iraq Case Study: Improving User Journeys for Humanitarian Cash Transfers." Ground Truth Solutions and the Humanitarian Policy Group (HPG), DFID. https://groundtruthsolutions.org/wp-content/uploads/2018/12/User_Journeys_Iraq_Report_2018.pdf.

Smart, Kristin. 2018. "CTP Operational Models Analytical Framework." Cash Learning Partnership, Oxford, UK.

Staschen, Stefan, and Patrick Meagher. 2018. "Basic Regulatory Enablers for Digital Financial Services." Consultative Group to Assist the Poor, Washington, DC. https://www.cgap.org/research/publication/basic-regulatory-enablers-digital-financial-services.

Tesliuc, Emil, Lucian Pop, Margaret Grosh, and Ruslan Yemtsov. 2014. *Income Support for the Poorest: A Review of Experience in Eastern Europe and Central Asia*. Directions in Development Series. Washington, DC: World Bank.

TNP2K (National Team for the Acceleration of Poverty Reduction) and World Bank. 2018. "Government-to-Person Social Assistance Payments in Indonesia: The Landscape." Report. TNP2K and World Bank, Jakarta, Indonesia.

World Bank. 2014. "Beneficiary Study on Financial Inclusion and Literacy Outcomes of Cash Transfer Beneficiaries in Pakistan." World Bank, Washington, DC.

World Bank. 2015. "ISPA Payments Assessment Report for São Tomé." Social Protection and Jobs Global Practice, World Bank, Washington, DC.

World Bank. 2016. "Social Protection Payments in the Productive Social Safety Net Program in Tanzania." Interagency Social Protection Assessment.

World Bank. 2018a. "Payment Systems Worldwide: A Snapshot." Summary Outcomes of the Fourth Global Payment Systems Survey, September. World Bank, Washington, DC.

World Bank. 2018b. "Risk-Sharing for a Diverse and Diversifying World of Work." Review draft, Social Protection and Jobs Global Practice, World Bank, Washington, DC.

World Bank. 2018c. *The State of Social Safety Nets 2018*. Washington, DC: World Bank.

WWP (Brazil Learning Initiative for a World Without Poverty). 2017. "How Are Bolsa Família Cash Benefits Granted?" http://wwp.org.br/.

Zimmerman, Jamie, and Silvia Baur. 2016. "Understanding How Consumer Risks in Digital Social Payments Can Erode Their Financial Inclusion Potential." Consultative Group to Assist the Poor, Washington, DC.

Zimmerman, Jamie, Anjana Ravi, and Nichole Tosh. 2012. "From Protection to Investment: Understanding the Global Shift to Financially-Inclusive Social Protection Payment Systems." New America Foundation, Washington, DC.

Chapter 7

Provision of Social and Labor Services

Lucía Solbes Castro, Verónica Silva Villalobos, Sara Giannozzi, María Cecilia Dedios, and Kathy Lindert

Cash benefits provide financial assistance to people and families in need, but often they are insufficient to respond to a wide variety of risks and vulnerabilities which require provision of social and labor services. "Services" implies a set of actions and activities to support individuals and their families in facing certain circumstances and contributing to their overall well-being. While cash benefits can have positive impacts on poverty reduction and living conditions of households, certain vulnerabilities not purely related to income and consumption levels are better tackled through the provision of social and labor services. Besides, people often simultaneously face several needs that may be better approached through a bundle of benefits and services. For example, the extreme poor usually suffer from multiple entangled circumstances that can be addressed through a package combining cash assistance with social services, such as early childhood interventions or disability services for specific family members. Another common example is the provision of labor activation packages for the unemployed, which combine unemployment or social assistance benefits with employment services and active labor market programs (ALMPs), usually with the guidance of an individualized action plan (IAP) and mutual responsibilities requirements.

When providing social and labor services, governments likewise face the dual challenges of inclusion and coordination. While most countries generally offer a range of social and labor services, these services are often small, disconnected, available only through donor funds, and not adequately covering the overall population or specific vulnerable groups, negatively affecting the inclusiveness and effectiveness of the social protection system. Indeed, many developing countries face the challenge of unavailability of services and/or service providers, further undermining the dynamic inclusion principle. The multiplicity of actors involved in delivering social and labor services, especially when providing a combined package of services (or of benefits and services), often result in lack of coordination, which in turn reduces efficiency. As discussed in chapter 2, to confront these dual challenges, countries count on different operating models. For instance, in countries with well-developed social services, people can generally access services on a continuous basis (on-demand approach). Otherwise, where social services are scarce or nonexistent, governments generally strengthen the foundational delivery systems of an already solid existing program, gradually linking services. For example, people tend to receive services to complement a cash benefit (administrator-driven approach), as in, for instance, cash plus programs that also offer group services (e.g., family development sessions). Similarly, if governments provide combined packages of benefits and services, there is a tendency to implement articulated strategies for the delivery, to improve coordination.

Implementation phases of the delivery chain also apply to the provision of services. The common implementation phases, including outreach, intake and registration, assessment of needs and conditions, enrollment, provision, and beneficiary operations management, apply to the delivery of most social and labor services (figure 7.1). The provision of services, however, is the most idiosyncratic phase because of the specialized nature of many services. The main objective of providing services is to ensure that enrolled beneficiaries receive appropriate services, according to service standards. The primary inputs to the provision of services are information on beneficiaries, IAPs, and service referrals. Inputs may also come from the beneficiary operations management phases of the previous implementation cycle, including any updates to the IAPs, service package, beneficiary status, or other changes. The main output is the verification that services are being provided. Although the focus of this chapter is on the provision stage, the service intervention in other phases of the delivery chain can also provide an intangible "service" to the clients. For example, the act of carrying out assessments can be a service, as can the act of developing and monitoring an individualized action plan, since there is generally some counseling involved in the process. The service-oriented nature of many phases along the delivery chain is discussed in the relevant chapters.

Given its multidimensional nature, social protection serves as a platform to link interventions and to provide integrated packages of services (or benefits and services). This chapter distinguishes between the direct provision of specific services, with a focus on care and employment, which are more directly related to social protection, and the integrated provision of services. Integrated provision of services refers to the organized delivery of a combination of social and labor services, as well as benefits, that are pertinent to the profile, needs, and conditions of a target group, to improve their overall well-being. In this sense, social protection can serve as a platform to provide individuals and families with the information, linkages, referrals, and accompanying services that are best tailored to their needs and conditions, whether as a single intervention or as an integrated package of benefits and services. The chapter does not discuss the provision of basic social services (health and education) or other specific services outside the scope of human development.

Figure 7.1 Provision of Services Phase of the Social Protection Delivery Chain

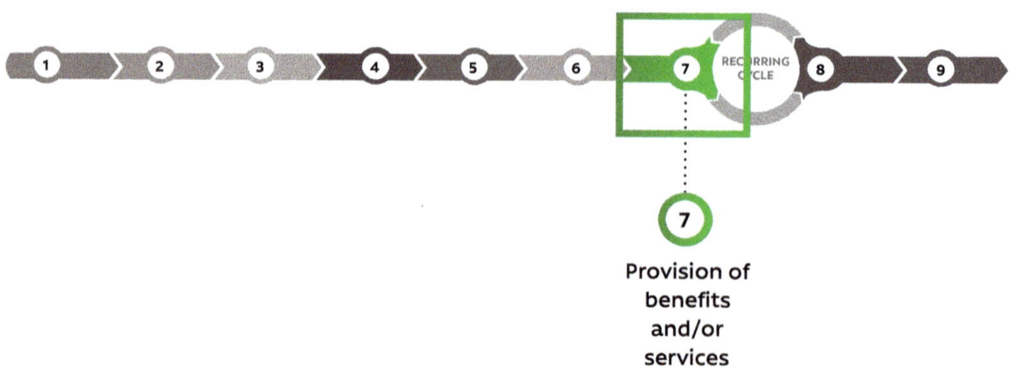

Source: Original figure for this publication.

The chapter is organized as follows:

- Section 7.1 presents typologies of both social and labor services within an organizing framework of risk groups and service modalities. This section gives a general overview of the diversity of existing services available to the population in addition to benefits, to set the stage for the discussion that follows, which focuses on provision and integration of services.
- Section 7.2 provides a brief overview of the provision of social and labor services, as well as a discussion on the quality standards expected for those specific services.
- Section 7.3 discusses the core content of the chapter: the integrated provision of social and labor services. The integrated assistance to people at the different phases of the delivery chain is a service per se, in the sense that it confers personalized attention through assessments, intermediation, and casework services. In this context, the section will review the main drivers of service integration, propose a framework for levels of integration of service provision, and discuss the main tools used to provide integrated social and labor services, as well as benefits.
- Section 7.4 provides some concluding points highlighting key aspects of the provision of social and labor services.

Various examples are discussed in this chapter, which include a wide range of social and labor services. They also include examples from each region:

- **Africa:** Burkina Faso, Madagascar, Niger, Rwanda, Senegal
- **East Asia and the Pacific:** China, Indonesia, Singapore, Vietnam
- **Europe and Central Asia:** Estonia, Finland, Germany, Ireland, the Netherlands, Norway
- **Latin America and the Caribbean:** Colombia, Costa Rica, Mexico, Nicaragua, Peru
- **Middle East and North Africa:** the Arab Republic of Egypt, Jordan, Lebanon, Morocco, Tunisia
- **South Asia:** Bangladesh
- **Other Organisation for Economic Co-operation and Development (OECD) countries:** Canada, New Zealand, the United States

7.1 TYPOLOGY OF SOCIAL AND LABOR SERVICES

The term "services" implies a set of actions and activities, generally not involving transactions of goods, which support individuals and families in overcoming certain vulnerabilities for an overall improved well-being. Social services support individuals and their families to improve their living conditions when facing various risks throughout the life cycle. Labor services support the integration of individuals into the labor market with the goal of improving their income-generating capacity. There are many types of social and labor services, too many to discuss in this Sourcebook. As such, this section aims to organize the discussion of services into a workable typology.

Typology of Social Services

Social services include a wide variety of programs made available by public or private agencies to support individuals or families in addressing their particular risks and improving their overall well-being. Such services are typically organized around individuals as the assistance unit, but they commonly involve family, household, or community members to enhance the support. Services may be voluntarily sought by individuals or families, recommended or referred by caseworkers, or required (such as through a court order or specific legal mandates).

The range of social services provided in countries around the world is vast. Even a quick scan of the lists of social services offered on the websites of municipalities or central ministries reveals thousands of social services available to the population. They may be categorized by risk groups, administrative groupings, the legal framework, areas of human development, or in other ways—often with dozens to hundreds of services listed, depending on the category.

This chapter covers the provision of social and labor services, but given the vast range, some sort of logical typology of services is helpful as background. In this chapter, we organize a typology of social services by risk group and modalities of delivery. Risk groups can include, among others, children (ages 0–18), adolescents and youth (ages 12–29), adults, the elderly, persons with disabilities, homeless individuals and families, migrants and refugees, and many others. Our typology's modalities of social service delivery include the following:

- ***Social work services***, which are those provided by social workers, caseworkers, facilitators, counselors, psychologists (in programs, municipalities, communities, etc.). They refer to services that provide information and awareness; assessments, intermediation, and referrals to other services; and counseling and mediation (also called social casework[1]).
- ***Care services***, which can be home-based, community-based, or provided within an institutional setting. They may be provided by a range of specialists, such as socio-educational specialists in the case of children and youth, and health professionals and socio-sanitary personnel in the case of elderly and people with disabilities.
- ***Other specialized services*** for specific groups and situations, which generally relate to services provided by specialized health professionals and legal counselors.

We illustrate this typology with examples of social services for specific groups and risks. It is beyond the scope of this Sourcebook to cover all types of risk groups or social services. Rather, we illustrate the typology for specific groups (and a subset of risks they may face).

Children can face a variety of risk factors and needs. These relate to neglect, abuse, orphanhood, behavioral needs, learning and stimulation, nutritional needs, and care and supervision, among others. Table 7.1 illustrates examples of just a fraction of the types of social services that may be available to children for selected risk factors. For example, with delays in a child's development, social work services could include classes and support groups for parents, specialized assessments, and various counseling services. In some developing

Table 7.1 Typology of Social Services: Examples for Children Ages 0–18

	Social work services			Care services			Other
Risk group	Information, awareness	Intermediation, referrals	Counseling, mediation	Home-based	Community-based	Institutional	Specialized
Children with disabilities or potential delays in development	Parenting and early childhood development classes, family development sessions, support groups, special instruction	Specialized assessments (learning, psycho-social, occupational, physical)	Counseling for behavioral needs, family counseling	Assistive technologies,, home adaptations, respite care, personal care	Early intervention programs; day care; learning support; tutoring; IEPs; occupational, physical, speech/language therapy; transport	Residential habilitation, residential care	Health services, medical or other specialized equipment or materials
Children at risk of neglect, abandonment, abuse	Child abuse hotline, child abuse prevention, awareness	Child abuse screening, risk assessments, service referrals	Child-family counseling, mediation, reunification planning	Home visits, in-home protective services, support to foster care families	Child protective services, crisis center, shelters, placement to foster care families	Residential centers for protective cases	Protective case management for children's protection, adoption, legal advocacy

Source: Original table for this publication.
Note: IEP = individualized education plan.

countries, parenting programs are combined with cash transfers to promote early childhood development through community-based family development sessions (box 7.1). Care services could include home-based services, such as installing adaptations for physical disabilities in the home; assistive technologies; respite care for caregivers of children with severe disabilities; personal care services; community-based services, such as early intervention programs (early stimulation programs); day care/childcare programs; learning support services (tutoring, individualized education plans, accommodations at school); various types of therapies (occupational, physical, speech-language); transport services; or institutional care, such as residential habilitation and care. A variety of specialized services may also be available (see chapter 5, section 5.3, for additional examples). When children are at risk of abuse and neglect, social work services could include a child abuse hotline, prevention and awareness services, child abuse screening and assessments, and counseling

Box 7.1 Promoting Early Childhood Development through Family Development Sessions

Parents and caregivers are crucial to the healthy development of infants, acting as the agents responsible for investing in their nutrition, health, and safety. They shape the environment in which the child develops and help ensure a safe, supportive home as well as access to key services. They also actively shape children's skills and socio-emotional development by talking to them, playing with them, reading or telling stories to them, and interactively responding to their cues.

Recognizing the importance of parents in early childhood development, many developing countries are enhancing cash transfer programs with the provision of complementary services, including parenting programs. These complementary services aim to enhance parent-child interactions, parenting knowledge, beliefs, attitudes, behaviors, and parenting practices through information and awareness building, training and classes, and coaching. The content of such services typically covers a range of topics, including health, hygiene, child stimulation, positive parenting, and nutrition. Delivery models vary, but when combined with cash transfers, a common modality is to provide such information and training through family development sessions offered to groups of families in the community. Other delivery modalities include home visits and links to primary health facilities.

Arriagada et al. (2018) identify several models in which parenting programs are combined with cash transfers:

- **Integrated approach.** The parenting intervention is managed by the cash transfer program. Examples include Jawtno (Bangladesh), Familias en Acción (Colombia), Burkin-Naong-Sa Ya (Burkina Faso), and Niger Safety Nets (Niger).
- **Convergence approach.** Different agencies explicitly combine efforts to bring the separate cash transfer and parenting programs to the same populations. Examples include Program Keluarga Harapan (PKH) (Indonesia) and Human Development Cash Transfer program (Madagascar).
- **Alignment approach.** The cash transfer and the parenting programs do not explicitly coordinate with one another but deliver interventions to the same or similar populations. One example is Juntos and Cuna Más (Peru).
- **Piggybacking approach.** The cash transfer is delivered through a separate established platform such as the primary health care network that is already delivering a parenting program. One example is a rapid response child-focused social cash transfer (Senegal).

Family development sessions are common in developing countries where the supply of social services is scarce, and as a result, it is through the platform of cash transfer programs that these interventions are delivered by program staff to a group of people, as opposed to being delivered by a social worker to a single person or family. Nonetheless, in a few countries these interventions have experienced promising results including improved parental practices and child development outcomes, with results in cognition and language.

Source: Arriagada et al. 2018.

and mediation. Care and specialized services could include a range of child-protective services, placement with a foster family, adoption, and other interventions.

Adolescence presents many risks, such as substance abuse, depression, and other mental health disorders, suicidal behaviors, dropping out of school, not in education, employment, or training (NEET), teen pregnancy, sexually transmitted diseases, physical and sexual abuse, gang violence and criminal activities, teen homelessness, and so on. While it is beyond the scope of this Sourcebook to cover all risks or services, table 7.2 illustrates the typology for some of the services that may be available for adolescents and youths facing teen pregnancy, parenting, and substance abuse. Teen pregnancy and parenting are particularly vulnerable situations, with important implications for human development both for the mother and for the child. A wide range of services can be available to provide "wraparound" support for teen parents. In Nicaragua, for example, the Ministry of Family promotes an integrated approach to providing social and health services for pregnant teens, teen parents, and their children (box 7.2). Substance abuse services can be provided either on their own or as part of integrated youth services. Specific services can include awareness and prevention, substance abuse screening and assessment, counseling, home-based support (including drug and alcohol-testing kits for daily monitoring), and other services. Since substance abuse can coexist with a wide range of other risks (dropping out of school, risky sexual behaviors, family conflict, mental health disorders, criminal activities, and teen homelessness, among others), integrated youth services often address substance abuse within a broader package of social services.

Table 7.2 Typology of Social Services: Examples for Adolescents and Youth Ages 12–19

	Social work services			Care services			Other
Risk group	Information, awareness	Inter-mediation, referrals	Counseling, mediation	Home-based	Community-based	Institutional	Specialized
Pregnant teens, teen parents	Awareness, parenting and life skills classes, healthy relationships, nutrition awareness, early years classes	Confidential pregnancy testing, service referrals	Individual, family, or group counseling	Home visits, in-home services, co-parenting support	Early years and childcare programs, support groups, school-based teen parent-child services, responsible fatherhood programs	Pre- and postnatal residential services, transitional housing	Family planning, teen prenatal care
Youth at risk of substance abuse (drugs and alcohol)	Awareness and prevention, substance abuse education classes	Substance abuse screening and assessments, referrals	Individual, family, group counseling; recovery support	Family-based interventions, in-home support, screening kits, online services	Substance abuse programs, day treatment programs, school-based programs, support groups, continuing care, relapse prevention services	In-patient services, residential treatment and rehabilitation programs	Integrated youth services, legal services when substance abuse intersects with the law

Source: Original table for this publication.

Box 7.2 An Integrated Approach to Social and Health Services for Pregnant Teens and Young Children in Nicaragua

Teen pregnancy is a challenge in Nicaragua. Among girls between 15 and 19 years of age, 25 percent have children or are pregnant (34 percent in the poorest quintile). Teen pregnancy and parenthood is also linked to the "not in education, employment, or training" (NEET) phenomenon for youth because teen moms are often not in school or work. Moreover, the importance of early childhood development and parenting programs for teen parents cannot be overstated. As such, Nicaragua has developed an integral approach to supporting pregnant teens and teen parents, spanning both health and social services. The approach includes the following:

- **The Casas Maternas (Maternal Homes).** These provide health and social services to expectant mothers and their babies. Services include (1) a strong network for outreach to pregnant teens; (2) health services and temporary shelter: prenatal care and monitoring, early intervention for at-risk pregnancies, including providing a place for expectant mothers to stay (including with family members and other children) so that they can be near the health facility before giving birth, which is particularly important for teen moms from rural areas; and (3) information, education, and awareness on early childhood development, family planning information, and so forth.
- **The Programa Amor (Love Program).** This program is an early intervention for young children. It includes multisectoral coordination at the central and local levels. Services for children include early childhood development services, nutrition, growth monitoring, child development milestones, and early stimulation and education. Services for parents include counseling, training, parenting education and awareness, and positive parenting. Poor families may be provided with income support and other integrated services. Many of those services are provided to all young children and parents in the community (including group sessions), while others are provided to specific individuals and families (including income support, counseling, and other programs). The program is not limited to teen parents, but their participation is actively promoted, including through the Casas Maternas.

Source: Montenegro 2014.

Adults can face a variety of social risks (besides disability and unemployment). Examples include gender-based violence (GBV), domestic violence (DV), or partner violence; substance abuse; homelessness; mental illness; and so on. These risks can affect their overall well-being, their ability to work and earn income, and their ability to care for their families. Social services typically include a variety of services for adults as individuals (besides those for families). Examples are included in table 7.3 for just two types of risks: GBV/DV and substance abuse.

Persons with disabilities and the elderly face a wide range of needs and risks. For people with disabilities, needs and risks can include (1) economic risk (low income, poverty, reduced work capacity, unemployment, high costs of health care and other additional costs associated with disability); (2) physical barriers; (3) mobility and transportation barriers; (4) reduced access to services; (5) learning challenges, barriers to education; (6) communication barriers; and (7) social isolation and attitudinal barriers (stigma, stereotyping, being perceived only for limitations rather than strengths). Table 7.4 presents a typology of the many services that may be available for persons with disabilities. Similarly, for the elderly, these can include, among others (1) economic risks such as low income, poverty, and the high costs of health care and medications; (2) risks of disability; (3) worsening health and wellness; (4) mental health risks (including dementia); (5) mobility and transport barriers; and (6) social isolation and a lack of activities or opportunities. Since similar care services are common for people with disabilities and the elderly, table 7.4 presents the types of social work services and care available for those two population groups.

Table 7.3 Typology of Social Services: Examples for Adults (besides Disability and Unemployment)

Risk group	Social work services			Care services			Other
	Information, awareness	Inter-mediation, referrals	Counseling, mediation	Home-based	Community-based	Institutional	Specialized
Adults at risk of gender-based violence/ domestic violence	Domestic violence hotline, gender-based violence/ domestic violence prevention, awareness, advocacy	Risk assess-ments, service referrals	Individual, couples, or family counseling	Home visits, crisis services	Protective services, crisis center, shelters	Safe housing, residential centers for protective cases	Legal services
Adults at risk of substance abuse (drugs and alcohol)	Awareness and prevention, substance abuse education classes	Substance abuse screening and assess-ments, referrals	Individual, family, group counseling, recovery support	Family-based inter-ventions, in-home support, screening kits, online services	Substance abuse programs, day treatment programs, school-based programs, support groups, continuing care, relapse prevention services	In-patient services, residential treatment and reha-bilitation programs	Legal services when substance abuse intersects with the law

Source: Original table for this publication.

Table 7.4 Typology of Social Services: Examples for Persons with Disabilities and Elderly

Risk group	Social work services			Care services			Other
	Information, awareness	Inter-mediation, referrals	Counseling, mediation	Home-based	Community-based	Institutional	Specialized
Persons with disabilities	Awareness information on services and disabilities, classes for caregivers, specialized instruction	Disability assessment, specialized assess-ments, coordi-nated care, referrals	Individual, family, or group counseling	Home-based care, support for independent living, assistive technologies, home adaptations, respite care, personal care, in-home helpers	Day centers; services for supported living; camps; learning support; occupational, physical, speech/ language therapy; transport	Residential care	Lifelong learning, health and rehabilitation services, specialized equipment or materials
Elderly	Awareness information on aging, health, well-being, prevention services; classes for caregivers; information	Disability assessment, specialized assess-ments, coordi-nated care, referrals	Counseling, geriatric social work supports	Home-based care, support for independent living, assistive technologies, home adapta-tions, respite care, personal care, in-home helpers	Community-based care, adult day care	Residential care	Active aging, lifelong learning, health and rehabilita-tion services, specialized equipment or materials

Source: Original table for this publication.

Typology of Labor Services

A review of the literature on labor services reveals a multiplicity of ways of classifying labor services.[2] In our typology, we classify labor services into two broad categories: employment services and employability-enhancing services. Both types also can be combined into an activation package that combines services with active or passive benefits, often with specific requirements expected from the beneficiaries. More specifically, they can include the following:

- ***Employment services.*** Services provided to job seekers, the underemployed, the unemployed or inactive, workers with disabilities, or others, to help them find gainful employment. They can be divided into two subtypes: services that provide information and those that offer counseling and intermediation. Examples of information-related services include (1) self-service tools with job information (websites, online service windows, kiosks, bulletins, and the like), including information on the value of education or the economic returns on technical specialties; (2) job-matching platforms (where firms post vacancies and job seekers post their profiles); and (3) other employment-promotion activities, such as job and vacancy fairs, or job clubs. Counseling and intermediation services are more proactive, usually involving direct one-to-one support between the client and a caseworker, program staff, employment counselor, employment services officer, or similar individual. Examples include job search assistance; career counseling; caseworker guidance and support; job referrals; and counseling about agricultural technology and management practices, among others. Those services are provided by public employment services (PES, also referred to as employment offices, job centers, or by other names) and labor programs where PES are scarce—or they may be outsourced to private agencies.
- ***Employability-enhancing services***. These are often called active labor market programs (ALMPs). They aim to improve clients' prospects of finding gainful employment; in other words, to enhance their employability. Examples include training to refresh or upgrade skills; entrepreneurship training; apprenticeships; job-readiness and soft-skills training; training in occupational or technical skills; basic and second-chance education; digital literacy; wage subsidies to encourage firms to hire the unemployed or first-time job seekers; public works; or job creation.
- ***Activation packages***. These are packages of benefits and services that combine some form of income support, such as unemployment insurance or assistance benefits, with a tailored combination of employment services and/or employability-enhancing ALMPs. They often also include mutual responsibilities for beneficiaries, which require their participation in the services provided plus active job search efforts. As discussed in chapter 5, section 5.3, activation packages are often detailed in an individualized action plan (IAP) that sets out a summary of the individual assessment, including profiling results; goals and agreed steps toward the goals; benefits (if any); a list of assigned services (employment services, ALMPs and other activities available to the job seeker); the actions and commitments required of both parties (the job seeker and the caseworker or employment counselor); rules and procedures regarding sanctions for noncompliance with required actions; the rights of the job seeker; and information on grievance and redress mechanism (GRM) procedures.

Labor services vary by risk group. Those risk groups are identified according to their distance from the labor market, which is established through labor profiling and caseworker assessments (as discussed in chapter 4). They can include, among others, employed job seekers (who are seeking a better job); short-term unemployed (including those looking for first job); the long-term unemployed; inactive and discouraged workers; informal sector workers; the underemployed; and temporary, seasonal, or part-time workers. In turn, a few cross-cutting characteristics (age, disability, gender) can further distance those individuals from the labor market. Among such distancing characteristics are members of groups such as youths (as first-time job-seekers or NEETS), women returning to the workforce, single parents, workers with disabilities, migrants and refugees, ex-prisoners, elderly workers, and unemployed workers with substance abuse challenges (Kuddo 2012).

Since the combinations of risk groups and types of labor services are numerous, we illustrate the typology by zeroing in on services for three general groups. Table 7.5 presents the typology for short-term and

Table 7.5 Taxonomy of Labor Services for Short- and Long-Term Unemployed, by Type of Service

Risk group	Benefits (passive or active)	Employment services: Helping people find jobs		Employability-enhancing services or ALMPs: helping people become more employable
		Information, orientation	Counseling, intermediation, activation casework	
Short-term unemployed	Short-term benefits (unemployment insurance or unemployment assistance), usually with IAPs and co-responsibilities Back-to-work incentives Start-up support for businesses, entrepreneurship	Self-service tools Job matching platforms Websites and call centers Info on returns to education	Job search assistance Caseworker guidance and monitoring, including IAPs Job referrals Career counseling Job readiness	Training to refresh or upgrade skills Entrepreneurship training Apprenticeships Wage subsidies for firms to hire unemployed or first-time job seekers Subsidies for firms to adjust working place or to purchase assistive technology for employees with disabilities
Long-term unemployed	Long-term benefits (unemployment assistance or social assistance after unemployment insurance runs out), usually with IAPs and co-responsibilities	Self-service tools Job matching platforms Outreach activities for youth, discouraged, inactive workers Information about the value of education, returns to technical specialties	Intensified counseling and caseworker guidance, including IAPs Some job search assistance, referrals Mentoring	Job-readiness and soft-skills training Occupational/technical skills training Basic and second-chance education Digital literacy Wage subsidies for firms to hire long-term unemployed Public works/job creation
Under-employed[a]	Short-term benefits (unemployment insurance or unemployment assistance), usually with IAPs and co-responsibilities Start-up support for businesses, entrepreneurship	Self-service tools Websites and call centers Information about the value of education, returns to technical specialties	Job search assistance Job referrals Career counseling Information and counseling about agricultural technology and management practices	On-the-job training Apprenticeships Entrepreneurship and business management training (finance, accounting, etc.) Financial support and micro-credits combined with technical advice Business development services with grants and technical assistance

Sources: Based on Brown and Koettl (2015); Blatman and Ralston (2015); Datta et al. (2018 a, 2018b); Kuddo (2012); and Loxha and Morgandi (2014).
Note: ALMP = active labor market program; IAP = individualized action plan.
a. The International Labour Organization defines two types of underemployment: time-related underemployment, which is due to insufficient hours of work, and inadequate employment situations, which are due to other limitations in the labor market that limit the capacities and well-being of workers. A person can be simultaneously in these two forms of underemployment (ILO 1998).

long-term unemployed and underemployed, as those are the most prominent categories in the labor literature and also the categories that are referred to throughout the Sourcebook. For instance, in most developing countries, labor programs and services focus on helping people who are already working to access more productive and better jobs or increase their productivity in the activities they are already doing. One example of this is the Youth Employment and Opportunities Project in Kenya, which combines grants with business development support. Since labor services are often provided jointly with benefits through combined activation packages, table 7.5 also presents various types of active and passive benefits. In fact, participation in employment services or ALMPs may even be a requirement for receiving benefits, as established in IAPs. The provision of benefits is covered in chapter 6 of this Sourcebook.

7.2 SERVICE PROVISION MODALITIES AND QUALITY STANDARDS

One main difference between the delivery of benefits and that of social or labor services is the different degrees of administrative intensity required for their delivery. Because of the nature of services, more face-to-face interaction with beneficiaries is required for the delivery of services than for the delivery of benefits; therefore, their institutional organization also tends to grow more complex. That complexity is also one of the reasons that a larger variety of services tend to be found in more mature social protection systems, which have had time to develop the institutional and organizational arrangements required for the service provision at the local level. A preexisting institutional organization (including administrative capacity) and quality standards are two of the key elements for successful delivery of services. While it is beyond the scope of this Sourcebook to delve into the nuances of the various modalities of financing, contracting, and service provision, we highlight a few key points.

Service Provision Modalities

It can be helpful to illustrate some of the complexities of providing services with an example that involves different modalities of delivery. We do so with an example of employment services for at-risk youth who are NEETs (figure 7.2).[3] In this scenario, a youth may enter the process via active recruitment or referral. An initial assessment will determine whether the youth can be referred directly to employment services or training, or whether the situation is more complex and additional services (social, health, or other) are required. This one service, therefore, encapsulates several different services involving multiple actors in their provision. Those actors may include governmental agencies, nongovernmental organizations, the private sector, communities, or the households themselves.

- ***Intake and assessment (social work services intermediation, in the typology of the previous section).*** During intake and registration, a caseworker not only collects information needed to understand the situation, but also uses the opportunity to build a relationship with the youth. If the initial assessment suggests that the youth is not ready for work or training, a more comprehensive assessment would be carried out, which could include specialized educational and cognitive assessments.[4] An IAP is agreed upon, and the caseworker would then also monitor the youth's progress and activities according to the IAP, adjusting service referrals as needed until the youth exits the program (which occurs when goals are met). Such social work services are typically provided through local government offices.
- ***Employment services.*** The provision of employment services varies considerably around the world.[5] While some employment services are provided solely by public agencies, many are provided through contracting or partnerships with private firms or foundations. Such public-private partnerships are administered through a wide variety of arrangements, including (1) a cooperation model, whereby public and private providers share information on vacancies and services; (2) a complementarity model, whereby a public employment service outsources some employment

Figure 7.2 Composite Example of Employment Services for At-Risk Youth (NEETs)

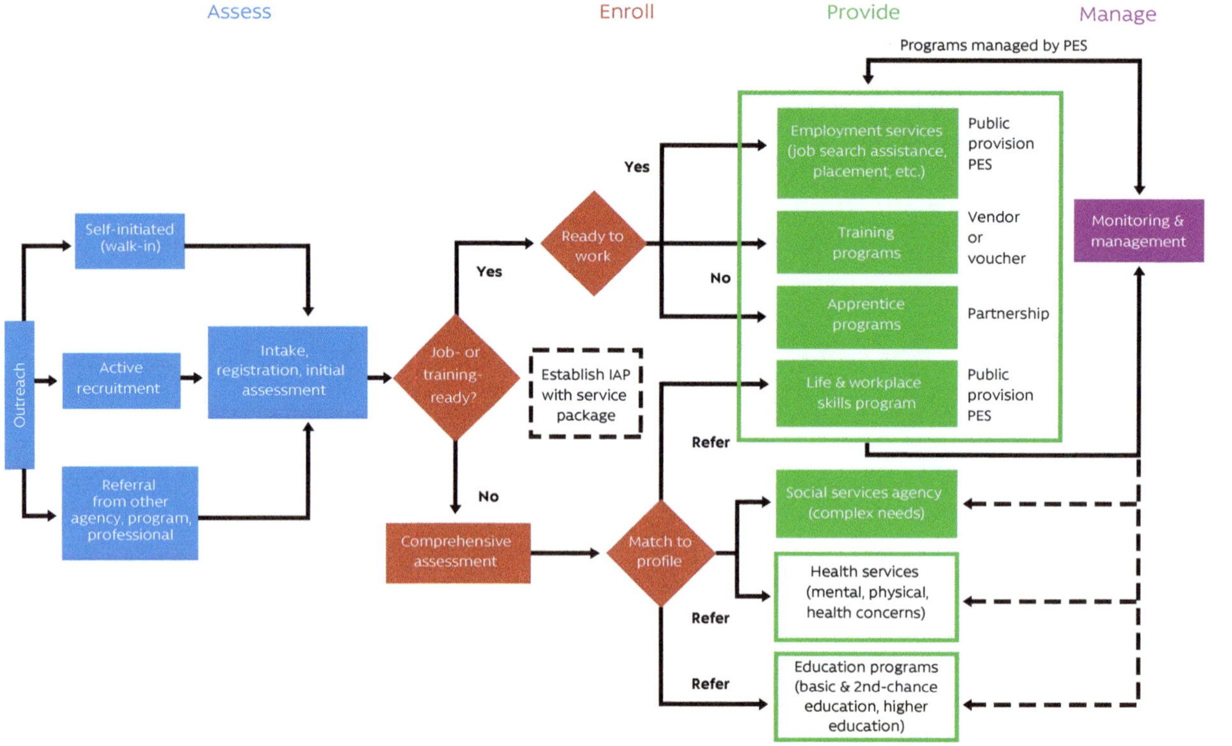

Source: Original figure for this publication, based on composite of examples.

Note: IAP = individualized action plan; NEET = not in education, employment, or training; PES = public employment services.

services or employability-enhancing services; and (3) the fully outsourced model, whereby private firms or foundations are contracted and regulated to provide services.

- ***Training services.*** If further skills or experience are needed, the IAP may focus on referrals to training programs or apprenticeships. With ALMPs, particularly training, provision is typically carried out by private entities with at least partial public financing. Private providers may include private agencies, semi-private institutes, and civil society stakeholders, as well as employers. For instance, in some circumstances, the private sector may fund efforts to train workers in skills that businesses foresee they will need in the future.
- ***Social services (social work services and counseling, in the typology of the previous section).*** The comprehensive assessment may reveal a number of complex needs, in which case the youth may be also referred to social services. Similar to intermediation services, counseling and mediation services are often provided publicly (as close to the beneficiary as possible, depending on existing administrative capacity), though in some instances of very specialized counseling or mediation they can also be outsourced. When social care services are required, they are frequently outsourced to vendors or provided by foundations or other partners.

In practice, provision modalities differ substantially by country capacity and type of service, but one can observe a tendency to outsource some services because of the complexity for the public sector to administer so many different types of services, and the details required to operate them successfully. In the case of care services, for example, managing residential care centers has proved to be a challenge for governments, due in large part to the burdens of public procurement and administration of the necessary inputs, as well as the need to hire, manage, and supervise large numbers of center-based staff, among other challenges. In an attempt to decrease cost and improve outcomes, many countries have moved away from institutionally based provision of residential care toward greater reliance on community and family-based care. Box 7.3 presents the case of deinstitutionalization in the Europe and Central Asia region.

In the case of employment services, while services related to counseling, intermediation, and activation are often still managed and provided by the PES

Box 7.3 Deinstitutionalization in Europe and Central Asia

In Europe, since the early 19th century, residential institutions have been countries' typical response to the needs of persons with disabilities requiring accommodation and assistance with daily living. In most European countries, residential institutions were also established for orphans, the elderly, chronically ill, the poor, and other groups. People who were placed in public or private institutions by expert authorities could not participate in choosing the services they required, and frequently lived their entire lives in isolation, segregated from their families, friends, and local communities. Deinstitutionalization initiatives had emerged by the mid-20th century as a human rights-based approach, advocating for the right of all people to live in the community (UN Convention on the Rights of People with Disabilities, Article 19), with access to home-based or community-based services. One of the globally recognized examples of the deinstitutionalization of persons with mental disabilities is also an example of successfully integrating social and health services in the area of the Italian city Trieste. The Mental Health Department in the province of Trieste, with 236,000 inhabitants as of 2013, is a network of institutions that consists of four community mental health centers (which are on call 24/7), a rehabilitation and residential support service, and a network of 15 social cooperatives. The department is cofinanced by the state budget for health care and by local budgets for social and health care. It consists of a well-established service in which psychiatrists, psychologists, social workers, trainers, therapists, nurses—205 employees in total—make it possible to address emergencies and prevent long-term stays in hospitals or social welfare homes.

In the transition countries of Southeast Europe and the Commonwealth of Independent States (CIS), the deinstitutionalization process started later (in the 1990s) and has been an ongoing process since the beginning of the 21st century. During socialism, the state was the exclusive provider of social services, which were predominantly organized in large residential care institutions for various groups of beneficiaries—children without parental care, persons with physical and mental disabilities, and the elderly. Therefore, the deinstitutionalization process included the diversification of social service providers, the development of community-based services, and gatekeeping (limiting or banning referrals to old institutions). Governments in transition countries are changing their legislative framework and practices in order to shift from institutional care to community-based services and to change their role from direct service provider to regulating and monitoring authority. The Ozalj Community Services Center in Croatia is an example of a successfully transformed rehabilitation center. The beneficiaries were previously placed in residences in rural areas, isolated from the local communities. In late 2014, the Zorkovac residence (with 55 beneficiaries) was closed. Thirty-two of those beneficiaries began living in supported housing in apartments in Karlovac and Ozalj, while the remaining 23 were returned to their counties of origin. As of 2019, there are no permanent residents in the institution. In addition to supported living for 80 adult beneficiaries, the institution also provides half-day care, psychosocial support, and occupational activities. Eighty-five children with developmental difficulties are covered by outreach services like early intervention and inclusion in regular educational programs and various rehabilitation programs. The former main building is used for workshops, while the other buildings house occupational activities in the area of agricultural production, product processing, and the production of natural cosmetics.

Source: Prepared by Lidija Japec, consultant, SCASO, World Bank, based on Mansell et al. (2007); https://zeroproject.org/practice/mental-health-department-whocc-italytrieste/; and https://www.centar-ozalj.hr/.

themselves, it is increasingly common to see efforts to improve outcomes for hard-to-place individuals through public-private partnerships. For example, in the United Kingdom, the long-term unemployed are referred to private organizations, which are paid based on results of labor market integration according to the IAPs established for these clients. For ALMPs and training, the combination of class-based technical and life skills training with on-the-job training through internships and apprenticeships has been proved to be more effective than class-based vocational training only, and provision of such combined services often requires the vocational and technical training programs to build alliances with the private sector. In the Middle East and North Africa (MENA) region, while some countries (Tunisia and, to some extent, Morocco) still provide labor services primarily through the public sector, others (such as Egypt, Jordan, and Lebanon) actively involve the private sector in the provision of training, job brokerage, and other labor market services.[6] Box 7.4 discusses the key issues to consider when contracting out labor and skills services based on outcomes/performance.

In any case, a significant involvement of the public sector is required to effectively manage and/or regulate the provision of social and labor services. Effectively managing outsourcing is not easy. Even when services are outsourced, public entities typically still carry out key functions along the delivery chain, such as intake, registration, assessment, enrollment, and beneficiary operations management. In addition, they manage the partnerships or contracts with firms and foundations. In several cases, those contractual relationships transfer part of the risk of achieving outcomes to service providers. Contracts that pay providers for delivering a certain number of services (output-based contracts) transfer little risk, while contracts that pay by result (outcome-based contracts) transfer most of the risk but also require increased oversight to monitor compliance.[7] An area in which outcome-based contracts have been increasingly used is the provision of labor market and training services. Sometimes, outsourcing the delivery of key services is a last-resort effort where administrative capacity is low. However, two important elements should be kept in mind when considering outsourcing, particularly in middle- and lower-income contexts: (1) the existence of a market for service providers that provides sufficient options for competition, and (2) the availability of adequate capacity within the public sector to properly set up and monitor outsourcing.

When services are entirely provided by the private sector, the government still needs to regulate the provision of services to ensure coverage and adequate services for target groups, including the hardest-to-serve groups. The regulatory process typically has three components: (1) rules that establish quality standards; (2) monitoring, inspections, or other means of assessing adherence to these standards; and (3) enforcement or other remedies to address gaps in quality. Quality standards are discussed in the next section. In both cases (outsourcing and private provision), the contracting or responsible branch of the government will have to invest meaningfully in staffing and human resources to provide adequate supervision of services.

Quality Standards in the Provision of Specific Social and Labor Services

Besides the provision modalities and institutional arrangements, the other key element for effective services is the quality of their provision.[8] Providing social and labor services is a complex management process, given the diversity of risks and barriers that the services intend to tackle, and the high degree of specialization that is therefore required. In this sense, it is crucial that countries define and enforce a set of quality standards for services. While provision of services varies significantly according to country context, there is consensus on the general quality standards for delivery. The European Union's Voluntary European Quality Framework for Social Services (2009) proposes a set of seven indicators that can be applied to ensure quality across services, mostly for social services but also for labor services. In this framework, services should aim to fulfill seven overarching principles such that they are:

- ***available***, by ensuring access to a wide range of social services for users to respond appropriately to their needs, and ideally giving users freedom of choice and a convenient location;
- ***accessible***, by facilitating access to those who require services, with information and impartial advice about available services and providers; people with

Box 7.4 Key Issues to Consider When Contracting Out Labor and Training Services

When contracting out labor or skills services, some important elements should be kept in mind:

- How to have a competitive market when there are not enough service providers of quality
- How to get a private provider to serve "high-cost" areas
- How to create the right incentives for private providers to serve difficult-to-serve populations
- How to screen potential service providers when there is not sufficient information on "quality" ex ante
- How to create incentives for service providers to deliver quality services, and how to provide quality control and standards.

It is easy to think of *performance-based contracting* as a golden rule to contract for service provision, given that it transfers the risk for nonperformance to the provider. While it is true that this type of contracting can improve efficiency (Vinson 1999), "unchecked" performance-based contracting can create perverse incentives to promote efficiency at the expense of quality in the provision of services. Part of the problem relies in the difficulty of determining and measuring quality outcomes as we have discussed throughout this chapter. For example, if the contract/outcomes are not defined correctly, contractors will likely prioritize easy-to-achieve goals over harder ones, such as with "creaming" of employment services clients, when the provider prioritizes immediate job placements over sustainable, long-term employment or orients the provision of services to more "employable" clients over those who need more assistance to find a job.

When the reward structure is designed appropriately, outcome-based funding can facilitate a significant increase in performance while allowing the risk of service delivery to be passed effectively from public procurer to outsourced provider. But finding the right balance between *performance/outcome* and *risk* for providers can be hard. The more emphasis is put on performance, the bigger the risk for the provider of nonpayment or reduced payment. In some cases, it may be more effective to offer incentives for providers to keep completion at a certain rate rather than penalizing them for dropouts.

An increasing number of experiences show the focus during the contracting and the management of contracts needs to be oriented toward outcomes (GPL 2016, 2017; Mansour and Johnson 2006). Management capacity and procurement practices ultimately will define the effectiveness of the outsourced provision. Overall, the guidance is to plan strategically, articulating clearly the goals and problems to be solved by the (social, labor) service. Include quality outcomes in the performance framework, and use data (both qualitative and quantitative) to understand the population needs and specify appropriate and realistic goals for the programs. Allow space for providers to propose new interventions and for areas lacking evidence, and set aside money for evaluation. Last, even though compliance is important, there also needs to be space for jointly tackling performance issues (between contracting governments and contractors).

Procuring services in low-capacity contexts presents additional challenges. For example, in a nascent provider market, in order for a provider market to develop, it may be necessary to reduce the risk for the provider and thus put less emphasis on performance and then gradually increase the performance element. Because monitoring activities as opposed to outputs or outcomes is easier, it may also be preferable in difficult contexts to move gradually toward monitoring outputs and outcomes.

Sources: Elaboration based on Vinson (1999); GPL (2016, 2017); and Mansour and Johnson (2006).

disabilities should be ensured access to services, information, and communication;

- ***affordable***, either free or at a reasonable cost for those in need;
- ***people-centered***, by addressing in a timely and flexible manner the changing needs and environment (physical, intellectual, cultural, and social) of the individual, aiming at improving their quality of life;
- ***comprehensive,*** attending the multiple needs, capacities, and preferences of users by integrating services;
- ***continuous***, ensuring continuity of service delivery for the duration of a need, but also responding to the developmental and long-term needs of users; and
- ***outcome-oriented,*** focusing primarily on the benefits to the users but taking into account the benefits for families and communities when appropriate, and including continuous evaluation and feedback processes (EU Social Protection Committee 2010).

Budgetary constraints and other programmatic limitations pose challenges in setting and ensuring certain quality standards. Quality standards describe the general principle to be safeguarded, and while most governments would ideally set high quality standards for all services, operationalizing them is not easily affordable in all contexts, and less so in low- and middle-income countries. In that sense, countries set quality standards according to a logic of progressive levels of quality. The tensions between service quality (and coverage) and budgetary constraints define the minimum levels in the quality ladder, and accreditation systems are often put in place to incentivize higher levels of quality in service provision. In the case of early childhood development, education, and care (ECEC) services, the minimum level of quality standards generally entails security aspects related to building structure, enough staffing and proper facilities, but each country defines these minimum standards according to their preferences and constraints. Generally, these minimum standards are required to open an ECEC facility. Challenges arise when services are not necessarily subject to formalized quality standards, like for instance the family development sessions linked to cash transfer programs. In the case of labor, when countries have unemployment insurance, there are greater incentives for governments to improve labor services to reduce the target population for the unemployment insurance. Also, the bigger the size of the informal economy in any given country, the smaller the demand for labor services and therefore the smaller incentives to improve their quality (Auer, Efendioglu, and Leschke 2008).

In addition to the overall quality standards previously presented for service provision, specific quality criteria can be highlighted for services that target a particular demographic or vulnerability group. In the following subsections, a few population groups and services are selected to identify sets of quality standards for each, describe how different countries operationalize quality standards, and offer some examples of the prioritization decisions some countries have made in trying to assure minimum levels and progressive increases in the quality of service provision. Table 7.6 summarizes key quality standards for services targeting children, youth, the elderly, and the unemployed.

Early Childhood Development, Education, and Care Services

Quality of ECEC services can be enhanced by various actions. The recruitment of well-qualified staff, along with continuous training and supportive working conditions, are key to the provision of high-quality ECEC services. In addition, adequate adult-child ratios and group sizes can facilitate the creation of reflective and innovative practices by the staff. The curriculum is another important factor in the quality of ECEC services. Good-quality curricula combine education and care for holistic development. They also respond to the needs of children at different developmental stages and facilitate engagement in active learning on the part of children, promoting both staff-initiated and child-initiated activities. Finally, good-quality ECEC services seek to engage parents, include diverse children, and establish clear roles and responsibilities for all stakeholders.

When setting quality standards for ECEC, countries focus on structural quality and process quality. In the United States, Europe, and other high-income contexts, the intuition is to have strict licensing standards for the operation of childcare centers, and accreditation systems that assure structural quality (infrastructure, safety, and curriculum). In low- and middle-income countries, stringent structural quality standards may be much harder to achieve (Araujo, Dormal, and Schady 2017;

López Bóo, Araujo, and Tomé 2016). Increasingly, evidence shows that once a minimum standard of structural quality has been achieved, ECEC services benefit more from focusing their efforts and financial resources on process quality over structural quality. In terms of process quality, the caregiver's experience and ability to foster high-quality interactions with infants is particularly important because those factors are robustly associated with better developmental outcomes among children attending ECEC programs. Experienced caregivers are

Table 7.6 Examples of Quality Standards for Specific Social and Labor Services Targeted at Certain Risk Groups

Intended population group	Specific service and criteria for quality standards
	**Early childhood development, education, and care services:** • Accessible, available, and affordable to families and children, encouraging participation, diversity, and social inclusion • Well-qualified staff with continuous training and supportive working conditions that facilitate observation, reflection, innovation, planning, and teamwork with parents • Curriculum based on pedagogical goals and values, combining education and care for holistic development, to ensure children's full potential and joint engagement of staff, children, and parents • Monitoring and evaluation processes that support continuous improvements that serve the best interest of the child • Strong governance with clear roles and responsibilities for all stakeholders
	**Services for youth at risk:** • Young people included in the design, implementation, and evaluation to ensure responsiveness to their needs • Staff training and technical assistance • Compliance with laws applicable to children and young people, including health and safety laws, and providing a supportive environment • A range of effective youth work methodologies, helping to develop technical, personal, and social skills • The practice of innovation and critical reflection
	**Home, community, and institutional care for the elderly:** • Free choice of provider • Staff qualified to provide personalized care • Low levels of bureaucracy • Structural quality including physical environment and exploitation of technologies • Central funding to at least assure minimum standards for quality of elderly care
	**Employment services for the unemployed:** • Qualified instructors who engage in a supportive relationship with the client • Accreditation and formal training of the staff • Structural factors to develop effective individualized action plans (IAPs) • Reasonable counselor-to-client ratios • Systems for complaints and grievances • Facility standards • Adequate stipends and wages for participants • Use of information and communication technologies (ICT)

Sources: Elaboration based on European Commission (2014); Barlett (2010); Ireland, Minister for Health and Children (2010); Glinskaya and Feng (2018); Auer, Efendioglu, and Leschke (2008); Honorati and McArdle (2013); and Piopiunik and Ryan (2012).

better able to foster high-quality interactions and increase the frequency of interactions when there is an adequate and manageable child-to-caregiver ratio. Importantly, a caregiver's experience is not necessarily determined by their level of education. For example, ECEC programs in Peru recruited mothers from the community who had experience with child rearing and provided them with training (Araujo, Dormal, and Schady 2017).

Services for At-Risk Youth

The quality of services provided to young people depends to a considerable extent on those services being rights-based, participatory, and cross-sectoral. The inclusion of young people in core aspects of the services, such as the design, implementation, and evaluation of the programs, assures these are responsive to their needs. Such an approach is responsive to the emerging cognitive and social capabilities of young people and to their development as individuals and citizens. However, getting young people to participate in improving service quality can be very hard. The cycles of service-quality improvement are long, usually longer than the length of time youths attend programs and services. Moreover, the social and psychological development of young people pertains to outcomes across various sectors, including education, labor, and health, to name only a few. Also, crucial to assuring higher-quality interactions and instruction practices with youths is staff training and technical assistance, as well as satisfactory employment terms (Smith et al. 2012), since they often correspond with higher levels of engagement on the part of young people in the program and its content.

An example of such an approach to quality is the Irish National Quality Standards Framework (NQSF) for Youth Work developed in 2010. In Ireland, youth services work for—and alongside—young people outside the formal education sector. Guided by the NQSF, programs for young people in Ireland have the explicit aim of "aiding and enhancing the personal and social development of young persons" and work specifically to include young people in the design, implementation, and evaluation of the services they provide. As a result, a key characteristic of the NQSF is that it promotes self-assessment as fundamental to the process of increasing the quality of youth services. To that end, youth services undergo a dual assessment, including internal and external evaluations and a "continuous improvement plan" (similar to an IAP) that includes timelines and different sources of evidence on improvement (internal and external). Seven years after its initial rollout, the NQSF was assessed in 2017. Most youth service providers considered service quality to be of significant value. However, financial cuts, reductions in the number of staff and their hours, and an increased bureaucratic burden on staff (resulting from the implementation of NQSF), mean that services are not able to engage in improving quality as fully as they would want. Indeed, one of the unintended consequences of the push to improve quality in the Irish case is that staff had to decrease the amount of time they spent with young people.

Long-Term Care Services for the Elderly

The quality standards for long-term care are generally thought to belong to two domains: quality of care and quality of life. Quality of care refers to the technical competency of medical and nonmedical services. The lack of training for long-term care workers is a major cause of low-quality services for the elderly. Most legislation is concerned with quality of care. Quality of life refers to factors such as consumer choice and autonomy, dignity, individuality, comfort, and meaningful activity. In this sense, the main elements of quality of care for the elderly are (1) the staff qualification to perform individualized care; (2) the need to maintain low levels of bureaucracy; (3) the client's ability to freely choose his or her service provider; (4) the structural quality of the services provided, including the infrastructure to assure the health and safety of elderly beneficiaries; and (5) the continuous and mandatory evaluation of service providers.

Countries around the world have developed different strategies to assure and improve the quality of care to the elderly. Those strategies are shaped by the economic resources available and the extent to which the services are outsourced or provided by the government. Australia, Japan, Sweden, the United Kingdom, and the United States are examples of countries where substantial public funds are allocated to long-term care, and therefore quality assurance systems are most developed in those countries. All five countries rely heavily on inspection and regulation of services for the elderly, an approach that puts structural quality ahead of process

Table 7.7 Requirements for Quality-Based Accreditation of Services for the Elderly

Country	Specific service and criteria for quality standards
Australia	Providers need to meet 44 outcomes, including physical environment, staffing, and management systems, and funding is conditioned upon the accreditation.
Japan	There are strict complaint-handling procedures and protections for the elderly. Staff training and qualifications are required to assure service quality.
Sweden	Requires staff to have basic competence (an upper secondary school health care education), preferably advanced competence (a university health care education). Measures the percentage of staff on full employment (preferably over 85 percent), the amount of employee turnover after one year, and management capacity (ratio of employees to first-line managers) to assure structural quality.
United Kingdom	Providers need to meet "Essential Standards of Quality and Safety" across six domains with specific indicators, and there is an accreditation process in which providers are evaluated by a third-party organization.
United States	Federal quality standards need to be met if the provider is to receive federal Medicare. Federal quality standards encompass both structural and process quality, including quality of care, quality of life, and the availability of nursing, dietary, physician, dental, and rehabilitative services.

Source: Based on Glinskaya and Feng (2018) and Stolt et al. (2011).

quality in their efforts to both set minimum standards and monitor improvement. In most of these countries, the provision of high-quality services for the elderly is sought through accreditation schemes for residential and home care providers. There is considerable variation between the countries in the requirements needed for service providers to obtain quality accreditation (Glinskaya and Feng 2018). Table 7.7 summarizes the requirements for quality accreditation in those countries.

Employment Services for the Unemployed

In addition to the aforementioned broad performance standards, several factors shape the quality of provision of employment services. One key input is staffing. Employment services require qualified instructors who are well trained and knowledgeable about the techniques and instructions they provide to the client. In addition, it is crucial that the staff can engage in a supportive relationship with the client, providing guidance and counseling when it is needed, and that staff have a positive attitude and work strategies. Accreditation and formal training of staff are desirable, but other alternatives include hiring highly skilled workers and training them to be instructors. Successful examples of this approach can be found in the Gambia, Kenya, Malawi, Mali, and Morocco. IAPs are another crucial element to assure the quality of employment services. Structural factors such as having the time and resources to develop effective IAPs with clients is of the utmost importance. The counselor-to-client ratio is also important because individual sessions to work on IAPs are more effective than group work. The existence of systems to record and respond to complaints and grievances from beneficiaries is relevant as well, to ensure the accountability of a service provider and as a source of feedback on the unmet needs of clients and opportunities for improvement. Facility standards (equipment, tools, materials, classrooms, and workshops, as well as acceptable safety standards) are another important factor to assure minimum standards of service quality. Additionally, adequate stipends and wages for participants have been shown to improve the effectiveness and quality (for example, beneficiaries' satisfaction) of training programs. Last, but not least, it is important that providers make the best use of available technology to improve the quality of employment services (Auer, Efendioglu, and Leschke 2008; Honorati and McArdle 2013; Piopiunik and Ryan 2012).

To ensure the quality of IAPs, countries have defined different measures. For example, in Germany, as a precondition for good-quality counseling interviews and IAPs, the German PES have implemented a range of general and specific quality assurance measures: (1) core counseling competencies are the basis of quality interactions with the clients and the development of an appropriate IAP; (2) caseworkers schedule the interviews without disturbances, incoming telephone calls are redirected to a service center, and caseworkers have text modules that reflect the applicable law and can be individualized; (3) the heads of the local placement teams regularly review the degree of individuality and the comprehensiveness of IAPs, discussing any problems in quality circles; and (4) monitoring activities are conducted by central units and by the internal audit unit. In Estonia, the quality of IAPs is monitored to ensure that plans are oriented to employment and are relevant to job seekers (that is, the plans account for job seekers' talents and barriers). Twice a year, a sample of IAPs that is representative of all the regional PES offices is reviewed and assessed. Also, a specialist team in the head office reviews the agreed-upon aspects of IAPs and assesses them on a scale of 1 to 4 points. Those aspects include accuracy and consistency of background information, assessment of advantages and barriers to employment; overall approach and coherence of the plan, relevance of planned activities, and reporting on progress. Points are awarded to regional employment offices according to their results (Tubb 2012).

7.3 INTEGRATED PROVISION OF SERVICES (AND BENEFITS)

Delivering services to clients effectively is critical for creating trust and shaping perceptions of the public sector. Recent global trends and changing expectations from citizens, together with opportunities derived from recent technological progress, have encouraged decision makers to prioritize service integration for specific population groups.

In this chapter, integrated provision of services refers to the organized delivery of a combination of social and labor services,[9] as well as benefits, that are pertinent to the profile and needs of a target group, to improve final outcomes. Lara Montero et al. (2016) refer to integrated services as "a range of activities implemented to achieve efficient coordination between services and improved outcomes for service users." For the European Commission, service integration refers to "all initiatives that aim to establish or strengthen systematic cooperation between employment and social services" (European Commission 2018). Munday (2007) mentions that the term integration "refers to not just one but a range of approaches or methods for achieving greater coordination and effectiveness between services, principally to achieve improved outcomes for service users." In this chapter, service integration, which is aligned to previous definitions, does not refer just to the sum of services provided, but rather to the provision of a combination of services that are most appropriate to the needs and profile of the target group, to achieve a common goal centered in the household or individual. Throughout the rest of the chapter, integration of services can also refer to the integration of services and benefits, since it is not only services that are offered in response to those multidimensional needs.

As implied in some of the definitions summarized above, two drivers of service integration efforts include the need to improve final outcomes in particularly complex cases and the desire to improve efficiency in the delivery of services themselves. Individuals can face a combination of risks and challenges at each stage of their life cycle, and those risks and challenges are connected and entangled with other needs that their families, communities, and overall environments face over time. Vulnerable and poor families are exposed to a greater number of barriers, generally for longer periods of time. In those cases, the provision of one unique service or benefit may not be enough, and the provision of several services (and possibly benefits) in parallel may not be efficient. Fragmentation in public services can lead to duplication and gaps in service provision, a heavy load for individuals trying to navigate different enrollment processes and, in turn, to increased client dissatisfaction and poor outcomes. A more effective—and, possibly, more efficient—intervention to respond to these complex situations is to provide an appropriate package of services and benefits in a combined, orderly manner, considering the family and surrounding environment.

Drivers of Service Integration

Improving final outcomes for complex cases. From the point of view of users, some global trends are increasing the need for integrated service provision to particularly vulnerable target groups. While service integration can help respond to a variety of multidimensional needs of individuals and their families, a review of international cases, with a focus on European experiences, suggests that it is possible to identify three main "hard-to-serve" target groups behind the drive for service integration: (1) **the long-term unemployed and unemployed youth**, who face higher and more complex barriers to labor market entry that require a combination of social and labor market services;[10] (2) **children**, in view of their need for specialized protection, risk prevention, and early childhood development, which by nature require integration among the service provisions targeted to each child and her/his family; and (3) **the elderly**, in the context of the increased population of the aging and structural changes in family composition globally that increase their need for health and care services, as well as active aging and lifelong learning. An additional hard-to-serve target group that is increasingly receiving integrated services, particularly in developing countries, is the **extreme poor**. It is important to work with the family as a whole, since the vulnerability affects all members, and interventions need to be concentrated in the household and follow a logical sequencing, taking all members into account. Around the globe, more and more countries are starting to link beneficiaries of social assistance with social and labor services, through productive inclusion and graduation strategies, among others.

Seeking efficiency gains. From the point of view of public agencies in charge of providing services, the same trends identified above are also responsible for increases in the volume of users of individual services, resulting in pressure on frontline staff and processes, as well as budget constraints. Structural changes in the economy have amplified volatility in the labor market, leading to rising long-term unemployment and increased youth unemployment rates. Aging, with associated increases in multiple morbidities, and structural changes in family composition increase the need for health and care services for the elderly. Those increases in the volume of users are highlighting inefficiencies in the provision of services, resulting in duplications for users and staff alike. Where many steps for accessing separate services are similar (such as assessment), integration has the potential to offer significant benefits in terms of simplified processes, reduced cost (in both time and money), and increased access for users.

Institutional Impetus. Integration efforts can be driven by either policy goals (top-down approach) or from the specific needs at the local level, often for efficiency purposes (bottom-up approach). In the first case, depending on the levels of service development and the institutional capacity of the public administration, integration reforms may be mainstreamed from the central level, with major institutional changes and tasks distributed between the state and local governments, or through a more flexible model based on less institutionalized cooperation, with considerable leeway at the local level (European Commission 2018). When the efforts are born at the local level, motivations for integration are related more to management in the face of an increasing volume of service users and the need for more efficient benefit and service provision, especially for families with complex needs. The literature suggests that integration works better when taking a "whole system approach," meaning that efforts to integrate services are accompanied by service accountability and governance arrangements. The integration of services requires the support of the higher governance level, but also needs to mobilize local governments and local programs. When assessing which services are best to integrate, key steps are to (1) identify the population groups in most need; (2) analyze which services are most needed; and (3) identify which of those services could be provided in an integrated manner for more effectiveness. In this analysis it is important to limit the exercise to a manageable number of services that are available and closely related, as well as to consider the legal and institutional contexts. Box 7.5 presents an example of institutional factors relating to integration in Peru.

A precondition for service integration is services that work properly within their scope of action. For instance,

Box 7.5 Institutional Arrangements and Key Features for Integrated Provision of Services: Performance Fund in Peru

Institutional arrangements are a key element underpinning the successful integration of service delivery. Many social protection programs require shifting some degree of program implementation responsibility to local governments, to nongovernmental public service providers, or to the private sector, while central governments typically lead in policy-setting (design) and financing. Moreover, the institutions providing the services may be set up very differently in terms of division of roles and responsibilities across government levels (that is, they may or may not be decentralized, to different degrees), meaning that the administrative level at which key functions for integration are performed can be different, adding complexity to the design of the institutional arrangements to support it. Therefore, integration—and the institutional arrangements underpinning it—must be taken into consideration at all stages of the policy cycle for provision and implementation to be successful.

To overcome vertical coordination problems in the delivery of integrated interventions, the Ministry of Social Development and Inclusion (Ministerio de Desarrollo e Inclusión Social [MIDIS]) of Peru established in 2014 a Performance Fund (Fondo de Estímulo al Desempeño y Logro de Resultados Sociales [FED]) to promote multisectoral intervention and inter-institutional coordination, with the objective of supporting early childhood development. FED acts as an incentive mechanism directed to regional governments, providing them with both technical assistance and supplementary resources to incentivize them to reach predetermined targets related to the delivery of the integrated package of services for pregnant women and children under five, such as prenatal treatments, micronutrient supplementation, vaccines, growth monitoring, early stimulation and education, and different community-level services like childcare or water and sanitation, among others. Targets are agreed upon by MIDIS, the Ministry of Finance, and each regional government in a specific Agreement of Funding for Performance (Convenio de Asignación por Desempeño [CAO]). FED has been very successful in improving the use of resources and achieving results through more coordinated work between the central and local government.

Source: Elaboration based on Peru, MIDIS (2016).

while integration can be a very good strategy to improve the quality, efficiency, and cost-effectiveness of service provision, integration may not be the top priority if social services are limited in terms of quality or accessibility (European Commission 2015a; OECD 2015). Indeed, some developing countries have tackled the challenge of service supply by complementing certain interventions that already target the most vulnerable with group services (such as productive inclusion or family development sessions). Moreover, sometimes the standardization of processes for service integration may come at the expense of lost specialization in the most complex cases. Therefore, it is important to balance integration with adequate provision of specific services (Cosmo 2017). Also, efforts for integration should consider existing conditions and processes, instead of starting from scratch.

Levels of Integration of Service Provision

The provision of services is becoming increasingly integrated around the globe, and variations between the ways they are integrated are substantial. The level of service integration can be classified according to the frequency of interactions, and their degree of intensity, between the service provider and the user. At the most basic level, the service provider or a virtual platform provides **information and orientation** to the client about the other services and benefits generally available. A second level would be that of **intermediation**, where the service provider or social worker in a community center makes an informed referral to another service through a formal channel. A higher level of integration in the provision of services, **casework**, would additionally include treatment, and entail a service provider or social worker that would act as a focal point for the client. That caseworker would track the case, providing information, undertaking assessments, working on individual action plans, doing referrals, and following the case over time until it closed (figure 7.3). Each level of integration requires the previous level, in the sense that through intermediation, the social worker also provides information and orientation, and through casework, the social worker provides information and intermediation, together with further specialized treatment. Moreover, analyzing experiences reveals that the levels of integration become a continuum, in the sense that specific examples may fall in between levels, depending on the characteristics of the service provision and instruments used.

Level 1: Information and Orientation about Available Benefits and Services

At the most basic level of integration, the individual or family accesses a service or a community center and receives general information and orientation about all the services and benefits available, without an in-depth assessment of needs. This information can include the location and schedule of services, type of support, eligibility criteria, and application requirements and deadlines, among other details. While this option offers information in a unified way, and sometimes offers the possibility for a few administrative transactions, in general services continue to be provided independent of each other and individuals access them through separate channels. For this level of integration, it is essential to have a significant number

Figure 7.3 Levels of Integration of Service Provision

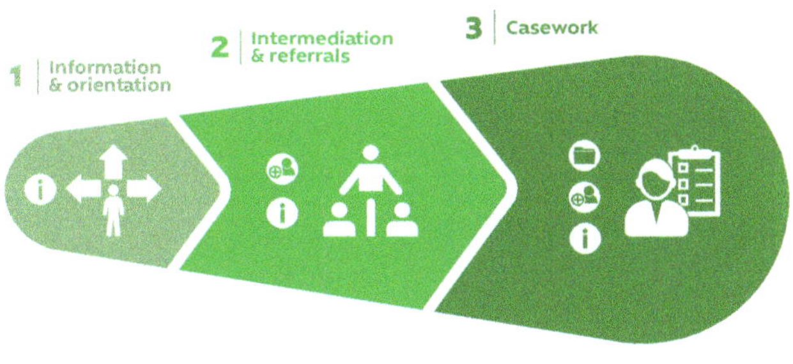

Source: Original figure for this publication.

of services contributing and updating their information to facilitate access and users' engagement. In general, such efforts reach a broader population than the next two levels of integrated provision.

This level of integration may be delivered to the client in different modalities. One alternative is virtual: a digital platform contains information about benefits and services; either all providers have access to it, or it is open to the public. Sometimes virtual sites are organized according to the most typical events that occur to people in the specific country ("I need a job," "I have a kid with a disability," "I am returning to my country," for example). Some examples of virtual platforms include Service Canada, which offers information to access a variety of services, including employment, taxes, migration, administrative records and pensions, among others, and similarly, Service Public in France and eCitizen Portal in Singapore.[11]

Virtual platforms may be complemented by on-site offices at the sector agencies or at a community center (or other information point), where clients can receive information in person, based on the information contained in the virtual platform, but also including other details. This is a particularly important modality for clients who lack access to computers or internet. For example, Vietnam has implemented a network of 11,160 one-stop service centers to offer information and conduct administrative procedures at all levels of government (provincial, district, commune, with complementary responsibilities). The coverage is high and so are the scope of services and transactions offered. Each center relies on a website that has information about the services provided, their scope, costs, time frames, and instructions for applying. Most services are offered at the district level, although the provincial level provides some additional services, and the community level generally serves as an information point. To complement, there is a dedicated telephone helpline to provide this information locally. Box 7.6 presents an innovative approach to information and family development sessions in Madagascar.

Level 2: Intermediation and Referrals

In this level, the service provider or social worker at the community center assesses the specific situation of the client and provides information and intermediation

Box 7.6 Innovative Approach to Family Development Sessions in Madagascar

In Madagascar, the conditional cash transfer (CCT) program, or "Human Development Cash Transfer," is complemented by a set of essential family and early childhood development practices, in the format of group sessions. These monthly sessions are called *espaces de bien-être* (well-being spaces), and they are delivered through trained Mother Leaders (elected by beneficiaries) to the other mothers to reinforce key messages delivered during the "well-being sessions." Behavior nudge sessions are organized during the day of payment. Those behavioral nudges have been incorporated to improve the planning skills of mothers and to develop their self-confidence. These nudges include drawing up intermediate steps for achieving their goals and putting money aside for their goals; enabling them to define what they want and to make decisions about the well-being of the family; and reinforcing their identity as guardians and their power to improve the lives of their children. The interventions are implemented in a very interactive and pictorial way for greater impact, such as drawing, playing games with cards and stones, using stickers, image cards, storybooks, and playtime with their children. Since these are all done in groups, beneficiaries are enabled to share goals and successes with each other and also to effect change in local social norms through collective action. Finally, the timing of the intervention is important. It is done right before the women (female heads of households) receive their payments, when they are primed to think of immediate needs and expenditures and not of longer-term goals. By timing the nudges right before the payments, the attempt is to break this cycle and engender longer-term thinking about expenditure, investment, and savings.

Source: Vermehren and Ravelosoa 2017.

through referrals to adequate benefits and services. A referral implies that the client will be eligible for the program or service she or he is referred to, although this is not always the case; it depends on the maturity of the referral process. Moreover, the caseworker informs the client and the program about the referral. This level of integration involves neither a specific treatment nor follow-up once the client has been referred, but it does require at least a quick screening or assessment of the person, as well as knowledge about alternative benefits and services, to make an informed referral.

This level of integration may be delivered through a network of service providers or through co-location. In the first case, every service of the network is an entry point for the client. In that sense, irrespective of where the client accesses the network, she or he is referred to the service that best responds to her or his needs. This is done in a more structured way, often through partnerships. Alternatively, services may be co-located in the same center. When the person enters the center, a professional discusses her or his needs and refers the client to the relevant service, either within that same center or elsewhere. Box 7.7 presents an example of co-location in Montgomery County, Maryland (United States).

OECD countries have sought to integrate services for children and adolescents with mental health problems. This has generally entailed multidisciplinary services that are co-located in schools. Integrated services most commonly include drug and alcohol prevention, case management, individual and group counseling, and referrals to community health services. Norway uses widespread co-location of health centers in schools. The Netherlands has special care and advice teams in the schools that help detect various problems, including mental health, in order to make referrals to health services. Co-location of such services in schools ensures that they are available where the target group spends most of its time, which is a benefit for students and their families. Moreover, both education and health agencies benefit from this situation. For education, resolving complex problems faced by students results in improving their learning. For health, a school can enable officials to locate a particular target group that would not otherwise show up in health centers. Other countries, such as France and Belgium, offer integrated services in the form of child and youth centers located in the community, which bring together service providers in one place.[12]

Level 3: Casework

In this most advanced level of integration, the interaction between the social worker and the client involves specific treatment and close monitoring and contact.

Box 7.7 Integrated Provision of Services in Health and Human Services in Maryland (US)

The Department of Health and Human Services (DHHS) of Montgomery County, Maryland, has been innovating in its efforts to integrate services. This is critical since DHHS must administer, deliver, and implement some 134 federal, state, and county programs (services and benefits) in six major service areas: programs for children, youth, and families; programs for the elderly and people with disabilities; mental health services; public health services (including Medicaid and the Affordable Care Act); services for the homeless; and programs for the community. Over time, through several reorganizations, integration efforts have been made at the political and institutional levels, in integrated case management, in personnel management, and in the infrastructure of information technology. Given that a significant percentage of department customers have three or more service needs, an integrated practice has made it easier for staff to be aware of other services the client is already receiving, and provides a mechanism to routinely coordinate delivery of services through multiple programs and systems, making it easier for staff to not only identify customer needs, but also to identify what specific services are available and how to access them.

Some key aspects of this progressive integration are as follows:

- **A single director.** The six service areas report to the same director.
- **Centralized administrative functions**. The first steps in the reorganization focused on the centralization of all administrative functions (budget, finance, contracts, and responsibility), and then greater emphasis was placed on coordination of treatment and services.
- **Single admission form (single case file).** A customer record that makes it possible to collect information about who the department serves and promotes the exchange of information across areas for service integration.
    - Challenges: (1) it is still necessary to maintain the link to other applications because of state mandates; (2) there is a continued need to maintain a paper record; (3) the various programs and disciplines have different requirements and terminology; (4) data quality is sometimes poor; (5) because of confidentiality issues, the system does not allow sharing between programs.
- **Multiservice and multipoint entry.** There is no "wrong" entry point and the assessment tool (single case file) allows early identification of multiple needs.
    - All doors are open as an entry point because the goal is to maximize inclusion.
    - Intensive teaming protocol (ITP) to support intensive and medium-level users: 20 percent of clients use multiple services and represent a significant cost to serve (using 80 percent of the resources). On the other hand, 80 percent of clients utilize only one service and use 20 percent of the resources.
- **Confidentiality.** The integration of a wide range of services requires adjustments in information management to guarantee a higher level of confidentiality.

Sources: QLess Training Guide Version 6.0: 2018 version, Department of Health and Human Services, Montgomery County, Maryland; notes from field visit and conversations with DHHS staff.

The case is assigned to a social worker who has specialized experience, and the client is accompanied and supported by that person during the time that the case is open. The caseworker analyzes in depth the situation and barriers of the client; prepares with her or him, and with other family members if required, a plan to move forward, including the services the client will be referred to, as well as additional obligations for the client; follows up on the referrals; follows the case with periodic checkups and overall support to the client; and finally, closes the case when the plan's goals have been met or when agreed with the client. In this level of integration, referred services work in full collaboration to respond to the needs of the client. Moreover, referred services are responsible for informing the social worker in charge of the case about the progress of the client, generally through a counter-referral mechanism with the corresponding procedures. While this may represent the highest level of integration in service provision, it is important to note that it is not necessary for all types of individuals or needs, but probably is necessary for the most complex cases or hard-to-serve clients. Moreover, the higher the degree of effective integration, the more specific is the target group and the fewer the variety of services offered.

While this third level has generally been delivered by social service divisions at the local level, countries are starting to create specific programs and strategies to integrate provision of services in response to recent global trends. Starting in 2011, through the Pathways to Work Strategy, Ireland sought to link benefit payments to participation in activation through early targeted interventions to return to work first, as the ultimate goal that would in turn help to prevent long-term unemployment (LTU). This strategy required services to be fully merged, for case management at the same location. The merged services included employment services, community welfare services, redundancy and insolvency services, and services for people with disabilities. Through the Intreo Centers, single points of contact for all employment and income supports, clients can receive support from functional experts to resolve their immediate needs and receive job placement support or referrals to personal development services (Kennedy 2013). Box 7.8 provides a detailed example of the Puente al Desarrollo strategy in Costa Rica, which includes casework with extremely poor families.

Box 7.8 Casework in the Puente al Desarrollo Program in Costa Rica

Puente al Desarrollo (Bridge to Development) is a national strategy for extreme poverty reduction, which deploys *cogestores sociales* (social workers) to work with extremely poor families and link them to government benefits and services to overcome poverty. The program provides a framework to improve the efficiency and efficacy of public efforts to reduce poverty through inter-institutional coordination. One of its components focuses on improving the provision of services to families in extreme poverty (in 75 prioritized districts) through a counseling intervention that produces a family development plan and facilitates their access to the main social programs provided by the government. Access by these families to complementary services is prioritized and coordinated and supports different skills to break the poverty cycle. These families must live in one of the 75 districts prioritized because of higher concentrations of poverty, extreme poverty, and deprivation. Sixty-five percent of the extremely poor in the country are residents of these districts.

To ensure a change in the approach to fighting poverty, Puente builds on five elements: (1) monitoring and coordination led by a Presidential Social Council; (2) a social registry with information on potential and actual beneficiaries of social programs; (3) a multidimensional poverty index, to take into account other barriers besides income poverty; (4) use of "social maps," maps that locate the services in the territory, to identify gaps in provision of social services; and (5) an accountability mechanism based on a set of shared goals for all agencies participating in the strategy, monitored by the Presidential Council.

The implementation of the Puente program is composed of four phases: eligibility, preparation of family plans, implementation of the plan and monitoring, and exit out of the program (see figure B7.8.1). In terms of casework, social workers bring the programmatic supply closer to the needs of the families, accompany the families in developing their skills and linkages to employment or productive opportunities, ensure that families fulfill the commitments made, and follow up on the plan for integrated support.

continued

Box 7.8 *(continued)*

Figure B7.8.1 Phases of Puente al Desarrollo Program

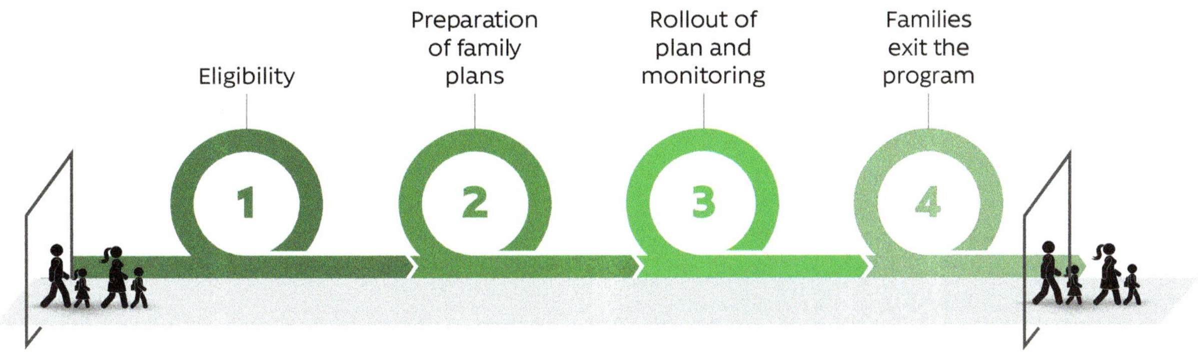

Sources: IMAS 2015, 23; Zumaeta 2016.

Instruments for Integration of Service Provision

Integration of service provision requires a set of cross-cutting tools. In order to have a certain level of integration, it is necessary to have a set of management tools that support operation and ensure achievement of integrated goals. Those tools can have different degrees of sophistication, but often simple instruments go far in supporting coordination and integrated provision of services. Some tools were discussed in box 7.7, the integrated provision of services in Montgomery County, Maryland (US).

- ***Information systems:*** Mechanisms that allow for information exchange and that vary significantly according to the type of content and the degree of information technology (IT) development. Efficient sharing of information would avoid duplications in information gathering efforts and support coordinated actions for the benefit of the client, at all stages of the service provision. See box 7.9 for a detailed example of an information system in Jordan that supports social work.
- ***Service mapping:*** A catalog or inventory of the local supply of services and benefits, both public and private, which is updated on a periodic basis. Protocols for updating the catalog should be jointly defined. The tool serves to provide information and orientation, but also is the basis for the referral and counter-referral mechanisms.
- ***Referral and counter-referral mechanisms:*** These mechanisms work based on service protocols with each of the service providers, which are formalized based on inter-agency agreements. Those protocols must define roles and responsibilities for each provider, as well as the rules for maintaining the confidentiality and privacy of information.
- ***Common comprehensive assessments:*** For social screening and joint planning, as discussed in chapter 4.
- ***Single case file:*** Dossier of information about a person that is shared by all agencies involved in the multidisciplinary intervention, and that allows keeping track of the different supports. The dossier should allow for alerts in terms of attention and case management. It requires a joint agreement among agencies about the way information is shared and updated, and it does not substitute for the specific registries that agencies keep internally for management.

Table 7.8 summarizes the minimum characteristics that tools must fulfill to best serve the different levels of integration. For instance, a basic information system and service mapping are required for the information and orientation level. For intermediation, it is important to have a referral mechanism with corresponding formalized protocols. The casework level of integration requires several

Box 7.9 Information System in Jordan to Support Management of Social Protection Cases

Jordan is implementing an Integrated Outreach Worker Program (IOWP) to lift poor and vulnerable households out of poverty, through social work services provided to each poor household. The goal is to provide a tailored package of services that address the "first mile" implementation challenges of the government and social programs to "graduate" poor households out of poverty.

A case management information system (CMIS) was developed to support the work of these outreach social workers in registering households, determining the eligibility of each household for a set of services, generating electronic referrals, and tracking updates and the provision of services to households through electronic records. The CMIS contains the demographic information about households that is required to determine their eligibility for a set of services. Moreover, it contains a database of outreach workers that allows GPS to track them, monitor their work in the field, and define financial allocation, among other features. The CMIS has an overall monitoring dashboard containing visual key performance indicators showing real-time progress.

Sources: National Unified Registry and Outreach Worker Program Project Appraisal Document (PAD), 2013. http://documents.worldbank.org/curated/en/192391467990997851/pdf/74924-PAD-P143193-PUBLIC.pdf; International Youth Foundation 2018.

Table 7.8 Instruments for Integrated Provision of Social Protection Services

Instrument	Levels of integration		
	Information and orientation	Intermediation	Casework
Information system	Service mapping with additional information for managing and improving the system (number and types of requests, etc.)	Contains specific information about the client. Ideally, the system would automatically calculate eligibility for each individual/family. It also serves for referrals	More sophisticated system that supports assessment (information gathering and eligibility calculation), planning (preparing the joint plan), and monitoring the joint plan. Serves for referrals and counter-referrals
Service mapping	Contains information on generic characteristics such as location, schedule, main eligibility criteria, type of support, and so on	Must contain detailed information on the eligibility criteria, and the specific schedule or timing for receiving new beneficiaries	Similar details as for intermediation
Referral and counter-referral mechanisms	Not applicable	Simple service protocols, often just general agreements to collaborate	More detailed service protocols specifying how referral and counter-referrals are done, and the joint monitoring of the case
Single case file	Not applicable	File including simple information, from a short screening, generally not sent to other programs	More detailed file containing information from assessment, joint plan, and activities, and monitoring of progress informed by the services themselves (not the clients)

Source: Original table for this publication.

instruments (single case file, comprehensive assessment and joint planning, referral and counter-referral mechanisms), combined with specific working techniques, characteristic of the social work sector.

At the third level of integration (casework), often the client requires the intervention from different sectors or disciplines. As such, she or he interacts not only with the social worker responsible for the case, but also with a multidisciplinary team consisting of specialists of different sectors who provide support in all phases (mainly assessment and treatment) based on their expertise. In the city of Salos (Finland), the labor-force service centers, called LAFOS, offered integrated services for the long-term unemployed (LTU). LAFOS clients go through a work ability assessment and are accompanied at all stages of the service process by a team composed of an employment officer, social worker, and national insurance worker, as well as being joined occasionally by a medical doctor. LAFOS centers try to first tackle health problems, which are one of the main problems that LTU people face (European Commission 2018). Similarly, the municipality of Asker, in Norway, developed a new concept for integrated service delivery centered on the user, in which all relevant municipal services, together with external partners, invest together in a person's welfare. The choice of wording is intentional: this multisectoral team is called an "investment team," and under this model, people with complex needs, or municipal agents who work with them, contact the Welfare Lab, which arranges a meeting with an interdisciplinary team to examine their situation. The team has training in design thinking and uses a planning matrix that has been specially developed to lead to a plan together with the user, with short- and long-term objectives.[13] The common objective is a sustainable situation and better living conditions. While the family is assigned to a caseworker who is responsible for monitoring the case, every member of the multidisciplinary team has the authority to make referrals and has the capacity to pool resources from inside or outside the public sector.[14]

While the set of tools serves to facilitate service integration, the skills and attitude of personnel working with the client, as well as institutional arrangements, are crucial for effective and efficient service provision. As discussed in previous sections of the chapter, a prerequisite to ensure quality in the integrated provision of services is staff who are well-prepared and who coordinate effectively to deliver tailored interventions, as well as sufficiently mature institutional arrangements that facilitate that integration. Moreover, while this section focused on the provision stage, integrated provision would not be possible if the integration principle was not considered at all other stages of the policy cycle. At design, it would be important to bring all stakeholders from the beginning to assess the existing institutional structure and define a clear overall goal for everyone, as well as specific goals that guide the work of the different actors. During the planning and financing stages, it would be ideal to consider a gradual implementation with progressive changes and capacity-building activities for new shared tasks, selecting partners based on their capacities as well as their contribution to the overall goal, and, most importantly, defining clear division of responsibilities with financial or administrative incentives. The monitoring and evaluation stage should be adapted to the nature of integrated services, with performance indicators adjusted for the joint efforts, within a unified monitoring system and accountability mechanisms.

7.4 SOME CONCLUDING POINTS

This chapter has reviewed the provision phase of the delivery chain for social and labor services, which involves delivering services to enrolled beneficiaries according to service standards. We conclude with the following remarks:

- Over the course of their lives, individuals and families often face a variety of risks and vulnerabilities that require specialized interventions through the provision of social and labor services, not necessarily or not only cash benefits. It is common for families to face multiple needs at the same time, which would be more appropriately tackled through a combined package of services, or of services and benefits, that are provided in a timely and structured (simultaneous or sequenced as appropriate) manner. That is what the chapter means by integrated provision of services.

- Many phases along the delivery chain perform service functions in their own right. In addition to the actual provision of specific services, many casework functions provided during the "life of the case" can confer an intrinsic service value. This value derives from many phases along the delivery chain, such as assessments, establishing a service plan or IAP, making referrals to a wide range of services, beneficiary operations management, and so on, in addition to the formal "provision of services phase."
- Social protection can serve as a platform for the integrated provision of social and labor services. Given its multidimensional nature, social protection can support the provision of integrated packages tailored to individuals and their families through multisector approaches.
- Countries offer a myriad of social and labor services, and different actors classify them based on a diversity of cross-cutting issues such as risk groups, sectors, legal frameworks, and so on. This chapter presented a typology for social services based on risk groups and modalities of social services, and a typology for labor services based on risk groups and types of labor services. Those typologies set the stage for the discussion on provision and integration of services.
- While the provision modalities differ substantially by country capacity and type of service, there is a tendency to outsource parts of the service provision to the private sector and/or nongovernmental organizations. In such cases, a significant involvement of the public sector is required to effectively manage and regulate the provision of social and labor services.
- Since providing social and labor services is a complex management process, given the diversity of vulnerabilities those services intend to tackle, countries define and enforce a set of quality standards for their provision. This chapter presented a general overview of the type of service standards proposed by countries and the tensions that emerge in defining them, complying with them, and enforcing them in a resource-constrained environment.
- In the last decade, countries have started to integrate the provision of services, in response to the need to improve final outcomes in particularly complex cases, and with the desire to improve efficiency in the delivery of services themselves. It is common to see integrated provision of services for children, for the elderly, for the unemployed, and for the extremely poor.
- This chapter summarized the three levels of integration most commonly experienced by countries: a first level of integration for information and orientation; a second level of integration for intermediation and referrals; and a third, more sophisticated, level of integration for casework. Those levels of integration demand different frequencies and degrees of intensity in interactions between the service provider (usually a social worker) and the client. The chapter also presented a set of tools that can facilitate integration in the service provision at the three levels. While the tools are helpful, the most crucial aspects of successful integration are the quality and capacity of staff or social workers interacting with clients, as well as adequate, properly aligned institutional arrangements and integrated or interoperable information systems.

Notes

1. "Casework" refers to comprehensive interventions starting with a full assessment of the situation and preparation of a work plan or project in collaboration with the user, followed by accompaniment of the individual in undertaking the project until the intervention closes. As discussed in chapter 2, in some regions, this type of intervention is also called case management.
2. Kuddo (2012), Brown and Koettl (2015), and Mazza (2017), among others. Our typology echoes that of Kuddo (2012). Brown and Koettl (2015) distinguish between (1) services for labor demand (employers); (2) services for labor supply which they further categorize as: (a) incentives for seeking and keeping a job (benefits, public works, activation and workfare, sanctions); and (b) incentives for human-capital enhancement (training); and (3) labor-market matching services that intermediate between labor demand and supply. They refer to that entire set of services as ALMPs. Mazza (2017) distinguishes between three categories of labor services: (1) "core functions," which are similar to what we call employment services and include job search assistance, counseling, job placement, and job banks for job seekers and employers; (2) "extended services—intermediation plus," which are similar to what we call employment-enhancing services, and include management or training of other ALMPs, migrant support services, microenterprise and self-employment support, as well as placement services for employers; and (3) "support services," which include labor market information systems, specialized human resource

services to employers, and social service gateway or unemployment insurance administration.

3. The example is a composite of examples of programs in various countries and settings, and illustrates various service provision modalities, as well as links to services in other sectors, such as education and health.
4. This phasing of assessments helps match the individual with a tailored package of appropriate services.
5. Some useful references on the topic of provision of labor services include Kuddo (2012); Angel-Urdinola and Leon-Solano (2013); OECD (2014); World Bank (2014); and Mazza (2017).
6. For instance, according to a recent World Bank study, there are 45 licensed private employment agencies in Jordan and 54 in Egypt (Angel-Urdinola and Leon-Solano 2013).
7. For a more complete discussion of these issues, see Bassett et al. (2012).
8. The literature on quality standards identifies three spheres of quality: (1) structural quality that relates to the stable properties of the service, including how the service is designed and organized, accreditation, staff-to-user ratios, physical requirements to meet safety and health requirements, curriculum, and so on; (2) process quality that refers to the way that the service is provided, capturing practice within the service and perceptions of the quality of service received; and (3) outcome quality that relates to the change before and after the intervention in terms of benefits for the users, their families, communities, and the broader society.
9. In the sense of timely, structured, simultaneous, or sequenced as appropriate.
10. For a review of experiences of integration of labor and social services for minimum income recipients in European Union countries, see European Commission 2018.
11. See the following platforms: https://www.canada.ca/en/employment-social-development/corporate/portfolio/service-canada.html; https://www.service-public.fr/; and https://www.gov.sg/resources.
12. OECD 2015. For additional examples of integration, particularly between social and labor services, see European Commission (2018).
13. "Design thinking" refers to the cognitive, strategic, and practical processes by which design concepts (proposals for new products, buildings, machines, etc.) are developed by designers and/or design teams (Hevner et al. 2004; IDEO 2015; Simon 1996).
14. Because of the intensity of this approach, the pilot phase (2016–2017) focused on three specific target groups: families with children experiencing "vulnerable living conditions," vulnerable youngsters ages 17 to 25, and families of children with disabilities. The Asker Welfare Lab is currently in its second phase of development involving a broader set of services and participants, and has received multiple recognitions for innovation in public service, both in Norway and internationally (OECD 2018, Norway case study on Asker Welfare Lab).

Bibliography

Angel-Urdinola, Diego F., and Rene A. Leon-Solano. 2013. "A Reform Agenda for Improving the Delivery of ALMPs in the MENA Region." *IZA Journal of Labor Policy* 2 (13). http://www.izajolp.com/content/2/1/13.

Araujo, Maria Caridad, Marta Dormal, and Norbert Schady. 2017. "Child Care Quality and Child Development." Working Paper IDB-WP-779, Inter-American Development Bank, Washington, DC.

Arriagada, Ana-Maria, Jonathan Perry, Laura Rawlings, Julieta Trias, and Melissa Zumaeta. 2018. "Promoting Early Childhood Development through Combining Cash Transfer and Parenting Programs." Policy Research Working Paper 8670, World Bank, Washington, DC.

Auer, Peter, Ümit Efendioglu, and Janine Leschke. 2008. "Active Labour Market Policies around the World: Coping with the Consequences of Globalization." 2nd ed. International Labour Office, Geneva, Switzerland.

Barlett, William. 2010. "People-Centred Analyses: The Quality of Social Services." United Nations Development Programme, London.

Bassett, Lucy, Sara Giannozzi, Lucian Pop, and Dena Ringold. 2012. "Rules, Roles, and Controls: Governance in Social Protection with an Application to Social Assistance." Social Protection and Labor Discussion Paper 1206, World Bank, Washington, DC. http://documents.worldbank.org/curated/en/301371468151778608/Rules-roles-and-controls-governance-in-social-protection-with-an-application-to-social-assistance.

Behrendt, Christina. 2013. "Building National Social Protection Floors and Social Security Systems: The ILO's Two-Dimensional Social Security Strategy." In *Social Protection in Developing Countries: Reforming Systems*, edited by Katja Bender, Markus Kaltenborn, and Christian Pfleiderer, 207–18. New York: Routledge.

Blattman, Christopher, and Laura Ralston. 2015. "Generating Employment in Poor and Fragile States: Evidence from Labor Market and Entrepreneurship Programs." https://ssrn.com/abstract=2622220.

Brown, Alessio JG, and Johannes Koettl. 2015. "Active Labor Market Programs—Employment Gain or Fiscal Drain?" *IZA Journal of Labor Economics* 4 (12): 1–36. https://doi.org/10.1186/s40172-015-0025-5.

Cosmo, Howard. 2017. "Putting One-Stop-Shops into Practice: A Systematic Review of the Drivers of Government Service Integration." *Evidence Base* 2017 (2): 1–14.

Datta, Namita, Angela Elzir Assy, Johanne Buba, Sara Johansson de Silva, Samantha Watson, et al. 2018a. "Integrated Youth Employment Programs: A Stocktake of Evidence on What Works in Youth Employment Programs." World Bank, Washington, DC.

Datta, Namita, Angela Elzir Assy, Johanne Buba, Samantha Watson, et al. 2018b. "Integration: A New Approach to Youth Employment Programs." World Bank, Washington, DC.

EU (European Union) Social Protection Committee. 2010. "A Voluntary European Quality Framework for Social Services." Report no. SPC/2010/10/8 Final, 13. Social Protection Committee, Brussels, Belgium.

European Commission. 2014. "Proposal for Key Principles of a Quality Framework for Early Childhood Education and Care." Directorate-General for Education and Culture, European Commission, Brussels, Belgium.

European Commission. 2015a. "Literature Review and Identification of Best Practices in Integrated Service Delivery: Part I—Study." Publications Office of the European Union, Luxembourg.

European Commission. 2015b. "Literature Review and Identification of Best Practices in Integrated Service Delivery: Part II—Case Studies." Publications Office of the European Union, Luxembourg.

European Commission. 2018. "Study on Integrated Delivery of Social Services Aiming at the Activation of Minimum Income Recipients in the Labour Market—Success Factors and Reform Pathways." Publications Office of the European Union, Luxembourg.

European Social Network. 2016. "Integrated Social Services in Europe: A Study Looking at How Local Public Services Are Working Together to Improve People's Lives." European Social Network, Brussels, Belgium.

European Social Network. 2017. "Investing in Later Life: A Toolkit for Social Services Providing Care for Older People." European Social Network, Brussels, Belgium.

Glinskaya, Elena, and Zhanlian Feng, eds. 2018. *Building an Efficient and Sustainable Aged Care System*. Directions in Development Series. Washington, DC: World Bank.

Golub, Stephen, and Faraz Hayat. 2014. "Employment, Unemployment, and Underemployment in Africa." United Nations University WIDER Working Paper 2014/014. World Institute for Development Economics Research, Helsinki, Finland.

GPL (Government Performance Lab). 2016. "Results-Driven Contracting: An Overview." Harvard Kennedy School, Cambridge, MA.

GPL (Government Performance Lab). 2017. "Active Contract Management: How Governments Can Collaborate More Effectively with Social Service Providers to Achieve Better Results." Harvard Kennedy School, Cambridge, MA.

Grosh, Margaret, Carlo del Ninno, Emil Tesliuc, and Azedine Ouerghi. 2008. *For Protection and Promotion: The Design and Implementation of Effective Safety Nets*. Washington, DC: World Bank.

Hevner, Alan R., Salvatore T. March, Jinsoo Park, and Sudha Ram. 2004. "Design Science in Information Systems Research." *MIS Quarterly* 28 (1): 75–105.

Honorati, Maddalena, and Thomas P. McArdle. 2013. "The Nuts and Bolts of Designing and Implementing Training Programs in Developing Countries." Social Protection and Labor Discussion Paper 1304, World Bank, Washington, DC.

IDEO.org. 2015. *The Field Guide to Human-Centered Design*. IDEO.org, San Francisco.

ILO (International Labour Organization). 1998. "Resolution Concerning the Measurement of Underemployment and Inadequate Employment Situations, Adopted by the Sixteenth International Conference of Labor Statisticians." ILO, Geneva, Switzerland.

ILO (International Labour Organization). 2012. "R202: Social Protection Floors Recommendation (n. 202)." Adopted at the 101st International Labour Conference, Geneva, Switzerland, June 14, 2012. https://www.ilo.org/dyn/normlex/en/f?p=NORMLEXPUB:12100:0::NO::P12100_INSTRUMENT_ID:3065524.

IMAS (Instituto Mixto de Ayuda Social). 2015. Puente Strategy. http://www.imas.go.cr/ayuda_social/plan_puente/Documento%20Estrategia%20Puente%20al%20Desarrollo.pdf. https://www.imas.go.cr/es/general/estrategia-nacional-para-la-reduccion-de-la-pobreza-extrema-puente-al-desarrollo; https://www.imas.go.cr/sites/default/files/custom/Documento-Estrategia-Puente-al-Desarrollo.pdf.

International Youth Foundation. 2018. "Support Implementation of a National Unified Registry and Outreach Program for Targeting Social Assistance." Slide presentation, World Bank, Amman, Jordan.

Ireland, Minister for Health and Children. 2010. "National Quality Standards Framework (NQSF) for Youth Work." Government Publications, Dublin.

Kennedy, Barry 2013. "Coordination and Integration of Institutions: Pathways to Work—Ireland." Slide presentation, World Bank workshop on Activation of Social Safety Nets Beneficiaries, Tbilisi.

Kuddo, Arvo. 2009. "Employment Services and Active Labor Market Programs in Eastern European and Central Asian Countries." Social Protection and Labor Discussion Paper 0918, Human Development Network, World Bank, Washington, DC.

Kuddo, Arvo. 2012. "Public Employment Services and Activation Policies." Social Protection and Labor Discussion Paper 1215, World Bank, Washington, DC.

Lara Montero, Alfonso, Sarah van Duijn, Nick Zonneveld, Mirella M N Minkman, and Henk Nies. 2016. *Integrated Social Services in Europe: A Study Looking at How Local Public Services Are Working Together to Improve People's Lives*. Brighton, UK: European Social Network.

López Bóo, Florencia, María Caridad Araujo, and Romina Tomé. 2016. *How Is Child Care Quality Measured? A Toolkit*. Washington, DC: Inter-American Development Bank. https://publications.iadb.org/en/how-child-care-quality-measured-toolkit.

Loxha, Artan, and Matteo Morgandi. 2014. "Profiling the Unemployed: A Review of OECD Experiences and Implications for Emerging Economies." Social Protection and Labor Discussion Paper 1424, World Bank, Washington, DC.

Malley, Juliette, and José-Luis Fernández. 2010. "Measuring Quality in Social Care Services: Theory and Practice." *Annals of Public and Cooperative Economics* 81 (4): 559–82.

Mansell, Jim, Martin Knapp, Julie Beadle-Brown, and Jennifer Beecham. 2007. *Deinstitutionalisation and Community Living—Outcomes and Costs: Report of a European Study*. Volume 2: Main Report. Canterbury, UK: University of Kent.

Mansour, Jane, and Richard Johnson. 2006. "Buying Quality Performance: Procuring Effective Employment Services." WorkDirections, UK, London.

Mazza, Jacqueline. 2017. *Labor Intermediation Services in Developing Economies: Adapting Employment Services for a Global Age*. Cham, Switzerland: Palgrave Macmillan.

Montenegro, Miriam. 2014. "Nicaragua: An Innovative Model of Community Participation and Integrated Delivery of Social Services." Slide presentation, World Bank, Washington, DC.

Munday, Brian. 2007. *Integrated Social Services in Europe*. Strasbourg, France: Council of Europe Publishing.

OECD (Organisation for Economic Co-operation and Development). 2014. *Connecting People with Jobs: Activation Policies in the United Kingdom*. Paris: OECD Publishing. https://doi.org/10.1787/9789264217188-en.

OECD (Organisation for Economic Co-operation and Development). 2015. *Integrating Social Services for Vulnerable Groups: Bridging Sectors for Better Service Delivery*. Paris: OECD Publishing. https://doi.org/10.1787/9789264233775-en.

OECD (Organisation for Economic Co-operation and Development). 2018. *Embracing Innovation in Government: Global Trends 2018*. Paris: OECD Publishing.

Peru, MIDIS (Ministerio de Desarrollo e Inclusión Social). 2016. Fondo de Estímulo al Desempeño y Logro de Resultados Sociales—FED. http://www.midis.gob.pe/fed/sobre-el-fed/el-fed.

Pfeil, Helene, Berenike Laura Schott, and Sanjay Agarwal. 2017. "Recent Developments and Key Considerations Impacting the Operations of One-Stop Shops for Citizens: A Summary of Major Trends and a Design Guide for Citizen Service Centers." Citizen Service Centers Brief No. 1, World Bank, Washington, DC. http://documents.worldbank.org/curated/en/108371498753288065/Recent-developments-and-key-considerations-impacting-the-operations-of-one-stop-shops-for-citizens-a-summary-of-major-trends-and-a-design-guide-for-citizen-service-centers.

Piopiunik, Marc, and Paul Ryan. 2012. "Improving the Transition between Education/Training and the Labour Market: What Can We Learn from Various National Approaches?" European Expert Network on Economics of Education, European Commission, Brussels, Belgium.

Scoppetta, Anette, and Arthur Buckenleib. 2018. "Tackling Long-Term Unemployment through Risk Profiling and Outreach." Technical Dossier 6, ESF Transnational Platform, European Commission, Brussels, Belgium.

Simon, Herbert A. 1996. *The Sciences of the Artificial*. 3rd ed. Cambridge, MA: MIT Press.

Smith, Charles, Tom Akiva, Samantha Sugar, Thomas Devaney, Yun-Jia Lo, Kenneth Frank, Stephen C. Peck, and Kai S. Cortina. 2012. *Continuous Quality Improvement in Afterschool Settings: Impact Findings from the Youth Program Quality Intervention Study*. Washington, DC: Forum for Youth Investment.

Stolt, Ragnar, Paula Blomqvist, and Ulrika Winblad. 2011. "Privatization of Social Services: Quality Differences in Swedish Elderly Care." *Social Science and Medicine* 72 (4): 560–67. https://doi.org/10.1016/j.socscimed.2010.11.012.

Tubb, Helen. 2012. "Activation and Integration: Working with Individual Action Plans: Toolkit for Public Employment Services." European Commission Mutual Learning Programme for Public Employment Services: DG Employment, Social Affairs, and Inclusion, Brussels, Belgium.

UNRISD (United Nations Research Institute for Social Development). 2010. "Universal Provision of Social Services." In *Combating Poverty and Inequality: Structural Change, Social Policy and Politics*, 161–84. Geneva, Switzerland: UNRISD.

Vermehren, Andrea, and R. Ravelosoa. 2017. "Behavioral Interventions: Designing and Implementing an Innovative Approach." Unpublished.

Vinson, Elisa. 1999. "Performance Contracting in Six State Human Services Agencies." Governing for Results and Accountability. Urban Institute, Washington, DC.

Waddington, Lisa, with contributions from Mark Priestley and Roy Salisbury. 2018. "Disability Assessment in European States: ANED Synthesis Report." Academic Network of European Disability Experts. https://sid.usal.es/idocs/F8/FDO27447/ANED_2017_18_Disability_assessment_synthesis_report.pdf.

Wiener, J., M. Freiman, and D. Brown. 2007. "Strategies for Improving the Quality of Long-Term Care" (p. 50). National Commission for Quality Long-Term Care, Washington, DC.

World Bank. 2014. "Experience of OECD Countries in Contracting Employment Services: Lessons for Saudi Arabia." Policy Research Paper EW-P151144-ESW-BBRTA, Social Protection and Labor Global Practice, World Bank, Washington, DC.

Zumaeta, Melissa. 2016. "Social Protection Reforms in Costa Rica: An Accelerated Process to Increase the Effectiveness of Social Interventions." Internal document, World Bank, Washington, DC.

Chapter 8

Beneficiary Operations Management

Kenichi Nishikawa Chávez, Kathy Lindert, Inés Rodríguez Caillava, John Blomquist, Saki Kumagai, Emil Tesliuc, Vasumathi Anandan, Alex Kamurase, Ahmet Fatih Ortakaya, and Juul Pinxten

One of the most overlooked stages of the delivery chain is that related to the continuous activity of beneficiary operations management. This common omission arises during the initial design period, and then continues during implementation until glitches in delivery systems and concerns about implementation quality demand attention. The typical trajectory for the focus of program administrators and policy makers is as follows. In the initial period of implementation, attention centers on the phases of intake, registration, assessment, eligibility determination, and enrollment ("getting people into" the program) as well as on the payment process (getting benefits paid out) or service provision. This could be considered the **output-focused phase**, with attention going to the number of beneficiaries enrolled plus benefits or services delivered. As the program carries out several delivery cycles, attention shifts to evaluation, with measurement of the impact of programs taking precedence. This may be considered the outcome-focused stage. In most instances, issues of implementation quality move to the top of program administrators' priority lists, often prompted by criticism from the press and other stakeholders.[1] Such concerns are typically a perceived lack of accountability and reliability of information, errors and fraud, grievance management, and inefficient processes such as long lines, waiting periods, excessive documentation, and static systems, in addition to other issues. It is at this point that the topic of beneficiary operations management finally gets the attention it deserves. It can be viewed as the **maintenance and continuous improvement stage**. Eventually, with cash transfers, as the program matures and the journey from applicant to beneficiary is improved and consolidated across implementation cycles, the attention of program administrators, as well as that of policy makers, shifts toward questions of beneficiary dependency, reassessment, and exit. This is the graduation-focused stage[2] (figure 8.1).

This chapter focuses on the beneficiary operations management stage of the delivery chain (figure 8.2). This stage is critical to all programs (benefits or services)

Figure 8.1 Evolution of Social Protection Program Administration Priorities

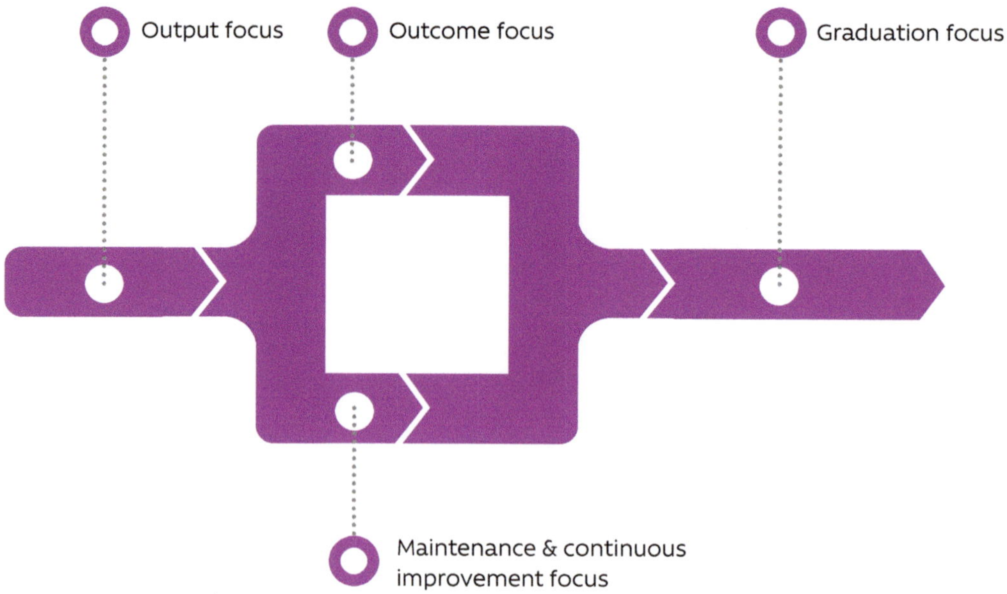

Source: Original figure for this publication.

Figure 8.2 The Beneficiary Operations Management Stage of the Social Protection Delivery Chain

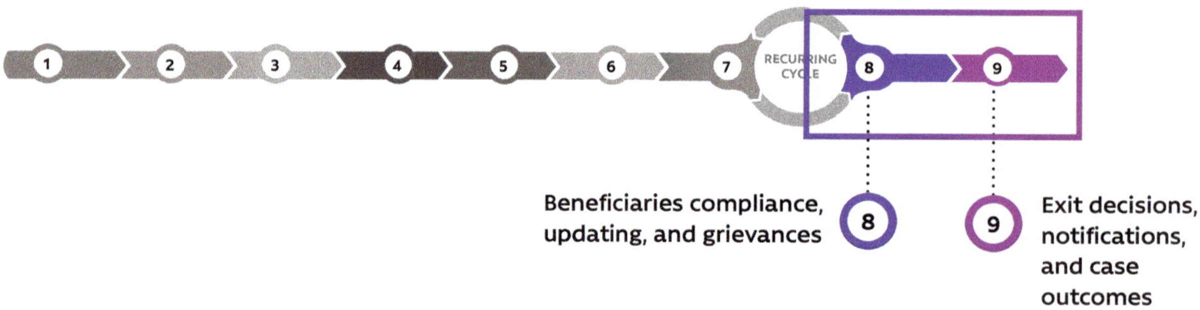

Source: Original figure for this publication.

and should ideally be considered earlier in the evolution than the common trajectory for social protection programs described above. The **inputs** to beneficiary operations management come from the provision stage of the recurring implementation cycle for beneficiaries already in the program, and from the enrollment stage of the delivery chain for those entering for the first time. Those inputs include the beneficiary registry, information on benefit amounts and services that will be delivered, and information on any conditionalities required of beneficiaries or activities that they must carry out. Other inputs include grievances filed by beneficiaries or nonbeneficiaries.[3] The **outputs** of beneficiary operations management include revisions to the beneficiary registry (record and status) as well as revisions to benefits and services to be provided. Those revisions feed back to the provision stage of the delivery chain for the next implementation cycle. Many **activities** are carried out during this stage, including beneficiary data management, monitoring of conditionalities (for education, health, and activation conditions, depending on the type of program and its requirements), and redress of grievances.

We organize the chapter into four main sections:

- Section 8.1 provides an umbrella framework for beneficiary operations management, elaborating on inputs, outputs, and activities, and how they all come together to feed back to the provision stage.
- Section 8.2 delves deeper into beneficiary data management, including the recurring cycle for updating and correcting information and reviewing beneficiaries' progress, implementation quality and logistics, and other matters. The section also touches on structural aspects of provision that occur less frequently, such as reassessment (recertification) and exit decisions.
- Sections 8.3 and 8.4 examine how countries verify and track compliance with conditionalities for education and health in conditional cash transfers (CCTs, in section 8.3) and activation requirements in labor programs (section 8.4).
- Section 8.5 discusses grievances, appeals, and complaints, as well as the management of grievance redress mechanisms.
- Section 8.6 describes a specific approach to identify and correct benefits or services affected by error, fraud, and corruption (EFC) employed by some countries.

Numerous examples are discussed in this chapter throughout the four sections. The examples include various types of social and labor services. They also include examples from each region:

- **Africa:** Ethiopia, Rwanda, Sierra Leone, Tanzania, Uganda
- **East Asia and the Pacific:** Indonesia, the Republic of Korea
- **Europe and Central Asia:** Austria, Armenia, Bulgaria, Croatia, Denmark, Estonia, Germany, Ireland, Moldova, Mongolia, the Netherlands, North Macedonia, Romania, the Russian Federation, Spain, Switzerland, Tajikistan, Turkey, the United Kingdom
- **Latin America and the Caribbean:** Brazil, Chile, Costa Rica, Colombia, Honduras, Jamaica, Mexico
- **Middle East and North Africa:** West Bank and Gaza
- **South Asia:** Bangladesh, India, Pakistan
- **Other Organisation for Economic Co-operation and Development (OECD) countries:** Australia, New Zealand, the United States

8.1 OVERALL FRAMEWORK FOR BENEFICIARY OPERATIONS MANAGEMENT

Practitioners or administrations regularly refer to these phases as "case management." As mentioned in chapter 2, the term case management is particularly problematic because it is used differently by different professions. Some practitioners use it to refer to the beneficiary operations management stage in the delivery chain, while others refer to an integrated approach to managing the complex needs of the individual or family across the entire "life of the case." For this reason, we instead use the term "beneficiary operations management." The term denotes the activity of continuously engaging and collecting information from the field or other sources (as other databases), which is then processed through a set of protocols, recorded and used to make decisions. This simple pattern of engaging, collecting, processing, and deciding is the common thread that ties together the set of activities that occur continuously in the implementation of a program.

What is beneficiary operations management? For simplicity, let us use a cash transfer program as an example. In an unconditional cash transfer (UCT) or CCT, beneficiary operations management is that black box of activities that normally takes place between payment periods, through which a set of coordinated activities are implemented to collect, validate, and decide on all the inputs needed to adequately and accurately proceed to the next payment period, assuring the right benefit is delivered to the right people at the right time through the right delivery arrangement (figure 8.3).

This stage is usually composed of three main functions, which are implemented simultaneously: beneficiary data management, monitoring of conditionalities, and implementation of a mechanism for the redress of grievances (table 8.1). This stage is an

Figure 8.3 Beneficiary Operations Management Framework

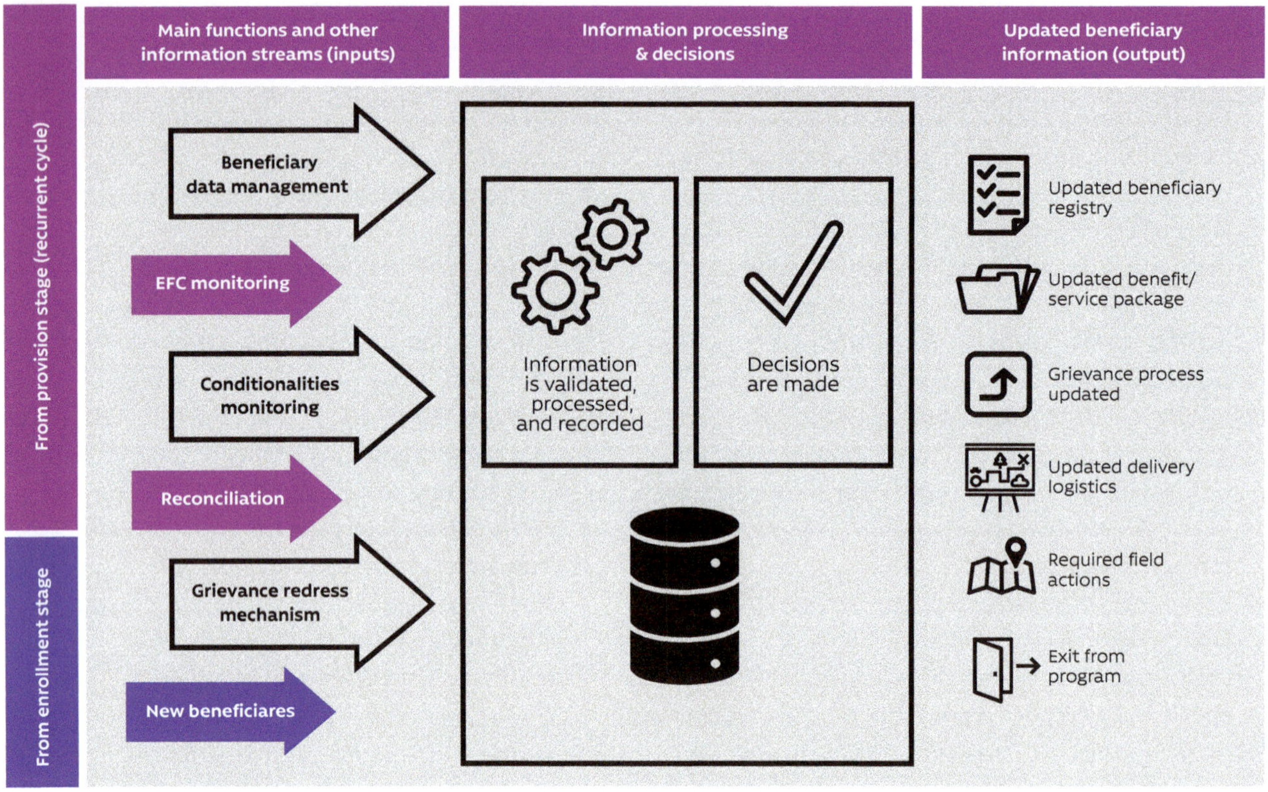

Source: Original figure for this publication.
Note: EFC = error, fraud, and corruption.

essential part of the recurring implementation cycle and has the objective of continuously updating, correcting, and verifying the beneficiaries' information, monitoring their path through the program and making decisions on their status. It covers a broad array of functions that we group into the following categories of tasks:

- ***Correcting delivery-related errors:*** identifying delivery-related issues, program inclusion or exclusion errors, incorrect information, and so on, with the objective of providing corrective, and eventually, preventive measures.
- ***Assuring adequate delivery logistics:*** assessing changes in access-related needs and/or geographic location to assure beneficiary accessibility to service or benefit delivery interface.
- ***Assuring delivery of the correct benefit or service package:*** continuously assessing the match between evolving beneficiary characteristics, needs and conditions, with the packages offered by the program.
- ***Verifying or monitoring compliance with program specific conditionalities:*** monitoring the beneficiary's observance of program co-responsibilities, which will serve as input to calculate payroll, or administer subsequent services or benefits in programs with progressive steps for beneficiaries, such as labor activation programs.
- ***Providing beneficiaries with a voice in the program's management:*** giving them and others the capacity to provide positive and negative feedback to program administrators. This includes regularly flagging mistakes in provision, potential inclusion and exclusion errors, mistreatment by frontline workers, and so on. Beneficiaries' voices may also be channeled to reinforce good delivery practices and strong personnel performance.
- ***Monitoring beneficiary status and progress:*** determining who should continue in the program and who

should exit. Some programs have developed differentiated beneficiary status to correspond with a beneficiary's progress in the program. This task also allows the program to assess the level of accompanying support required.

- ***Updating eligibility-related information*** to assess whether beneficiaries still fall under established criteria.
- ***Identifying and correcting EFC cases.*** This normally happens in countries where they have a dedicated approach to managing errors, fraud, and corruption.

Beneficiary operations management tasks are not independent of one another and do not adhere to a specific sequence. They normally occur simultaneously and the manner which they relate to one another is a function of the type of program. For example, monitoring progress may lead to changes in a beneficiary's status; correcting beneficiary information may lead to changes in the benefit or service package; and changes in the service package may result in changes in delivery logistics. Table 8.1 shows how the tasks are normally distributed among the three main procedures mentioned above.

Table 8.1 Tasks Involved in Beneficiary Operations Management

Functions	Tasks
Beneficiary data management	Correct service-related or information management errors Assure adequate delivery logistics Assure correct benefit or service package Assure correct beneficiary status and progress Maintain compliance with eligibility criteria
Monitoring of conditionalities	Verify or monitor compliance with program-specific conditionalities
Grievance redress mechanism	Correct service-related or information management errors Provide beneficiaries with a voice in the program's administration

Source: Original table for this publication.

Outputs, Information Streams, and Frequency

An essential characteristic of the beneficiary operations management phase is that it serves as a program's clearinghouse. It processes information from different streams and translates it into a single stream, allowing program administrators to make decisions to achieve the following outputs:

- Update the beneficiary operations management system (including beneficiaries who will exit the program)
- Update the benefit or service package
- Update delivery logistics
- Apply penalties or sanctions for noncompliance with conditionalities as well as fraud cases
- Provide or record resolutions to grievances
- Identify and plan additional field actions

The information streams may vary from program to program. As shown in figure 8.3, those streams may include the three main beneficiary operations management procedures: beneficiary data management, compliance monitoring, and grievance information. They may also include reconciliation of the previous cycle's provision of benefits and services as well as a list of newly enrolled beneficiaries, who are integrated into the recurring cycle for the first time.

The frequency of these tasks is a function of a program's approach and provision cycles. In programs that adhere to the administrator-driven approach, beneficiary operations management normally aligns with payment cycles. That is, if a program delivers benefits every two months, beneficiary operations management processes take place every two months. For example, in regular CCT programs such as the Philippines's Pantawid Pamilyang Pilipino Program (4Ps), Pakistan's Benazir Income Support Programme (BISP), and Bangladesh's Jawtno program, their respective beneficiary operations management information collection, digitization, and processing align with their respective provision cycles. The logic behind that alignment is straightforward. Payroll calculation and delivery logistics must be as accurate as possible every cycle, and beneficiary operations management allows for constant updating of who beneficiaries are, what they receive, and where they receive it. On the other hand, in programs that operate in an on-demand approach, beneficiary operations management normally reflects the intensity of the program's interaction with an individual or household. An example of this is Costa Rica's Puente al Desarrollo Program. That program develops a custom-made benefit and service package for each beneficiary based on a household diagnostic and an individualized action plan (IAP). The frequency of beneficiary operations management tasks is a function of the planned interactions between the social worker (known as the *cogestor*) and the household, which vary among beneficiaries.

In many administrator-driven programs, the different information streams are planned in such a manner that they all converge at a single point of time every cycle. That is, the program administrator establishes a deadline each cycle to finish grievance collection, conditionalities monitoring, and basic information updates, and then processes the information. A common tool used to manage the timing and convergence of the information streams is a master calendar, described below.

Provision cycles determine how often information needs to be updated. In programs that require a payroll, for example, those responsible for producing it may need to know whether a beneficiary is alive (in the case of social pension programs), whether a family attended a clinic for its monthly measurement (in the case of nutrition-sensitive CCT programs), or whether the beneficiary attended the work site (in the case of public works programs). Having such information on time, to continue the payroll example, allows the program administrator to conduct a precise benefit calculation and logistical planning, reflecting the changes that have taken place in the real world.

Shorter cycles require efficient beneficiary operations management mechanisms. Public works programs normally deliver payments to beneficiaries every one or two weeks. This design feature poses a challenge to program administrators as the attendance verification, grievances, and updates need to be collected, recorded, and finalized, almost on a daily basis, in order to provide payments by the end of the work period or a few days afterward.

Aligning Information Streams: The Master Calendar Tool

Managing information streams may prove to be one of the most complex activities a program undertakes during the early stages of its implementation. Among the most complex arrangements are CCTs that have health and education conditionalities. The complexity results from three main factors: multiple sources of information streams, intersectoral coordination (vertical and horizontal), as well as different processing times. Such challenges are normally met by developing a **master calendar**. This tool is an integral part of implementation planning and is used to program in a sequential and logical manner all the activities that take place in each cycle, taking into account processing time, capacity, and workload, among other variables. The process is sometimes referred to as "programming."

A master calendar facilitates coordination among different participants (inside and outside the program) and it keeps them accountable for meeting certain deadlines and outputs. For example, Mexico's social pension program, the Pension for the Elderly Program (Pensión para el Bienestar de las Personas Adultas Mayores), updates a detailed master calendar annually. The calendar is agreed upon by the relevant internal departments of the program and the payment service provider and it is communicated to all of the regional offices. The internal departments within this program that participate in finalizing the master calendar are as follows:

- ***Implementation department.*** This department is responsible for preparing the master calendar proposal. The proposal uses historical information and previously agreed-on time frames to determine periods and deadlines for each step of the process.
- ***Beneficiary registry department (responsible for the program's beneficiary operations management system).*** This department is responsible for one of the most complex activities in the program's beneficiary operations management process. The department integrates the different streams of information, assuring the consistency of the information collected in the field, providing an updated registry, and calculating the payroll.
- ***Finance Department.*** This department assures that the established payment periods align with the program's monthly budget allocations from the Ministry of Finance.

Once the master calendar is agreed upon by those three departments, it is sent to the payment service provider for review and acceptance (see chapter 6). Figure 8.4 illustrates how periods and deadlines are defined for one semester in Mexico's social pension program.

Figure 8.4 Master Calendar: Pension for the Elderly Program in Mexico

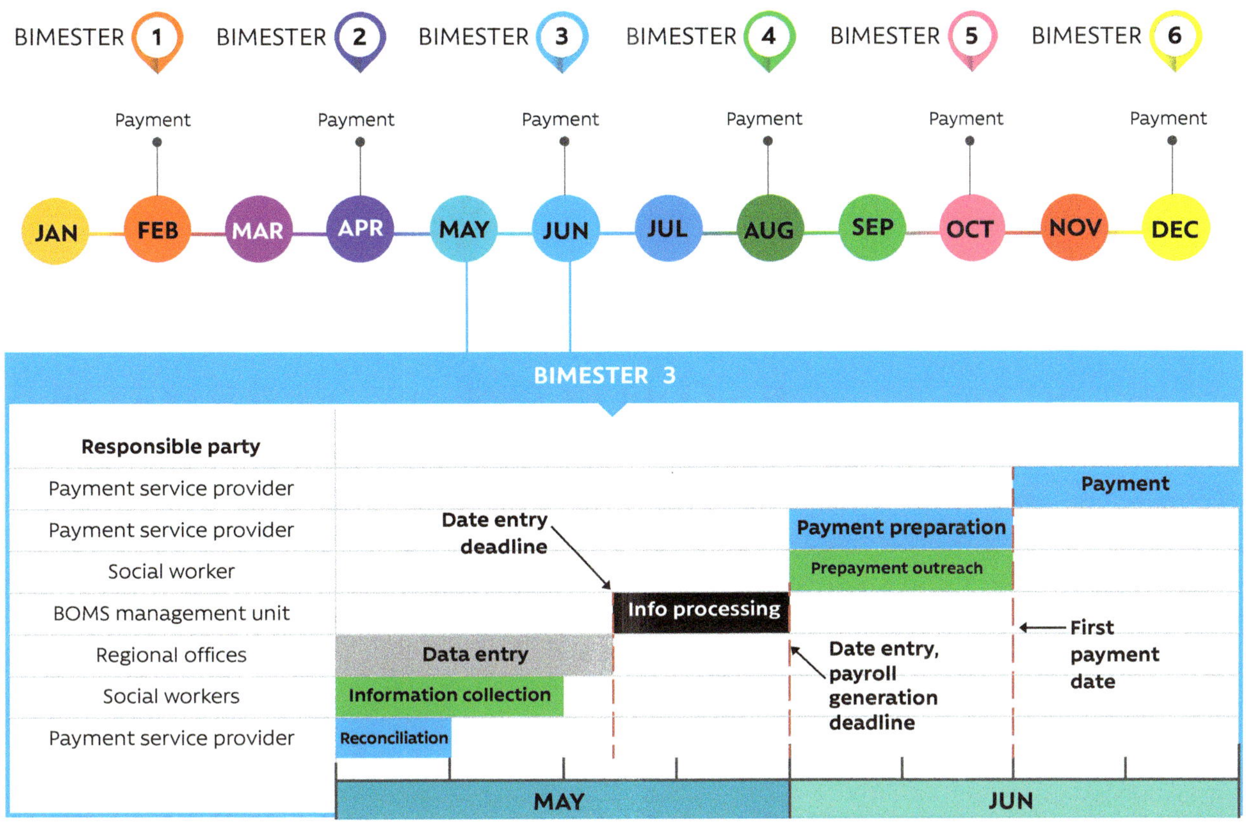

Source: Original figure for this publication.
Note: BOMS = beneficiary operations management system.

8.2 BENEFICIARY DATA MANAGEMENT

Beneficiary data management is a program's recurrent function of updating and correcting beneficiaries' information and making decisions based on these changes. As mentioned in the introductory section of chapter 8, this is one of the three main functions that programs conduct in every cycle of the delivery chain as a part of the beneficiary operations management stage (figure 8.5).

This function is an essential part of the program's day-to-day maintenance. Presently, discussions on delivery systems focus on the role technologies have on the systems' implementation. Most of those discussions center on how programs improve the provision of services, for example using advances in the financial sector through Fintech (financial technology) and other upcoming strategies like e-KYC (electronic know your customer). Other discussions look at leveraging the interoperability of administrative databases to link them with the social registry and support the assessment of needs and conditions. So the former focuses on leveraging technology to make payment systems more accessible and transparent, while the latter centers on using innovation to reduce inclusion and exclusion errors. Both innovations result in immediate efficiency gains which are easy to grasp. Consequently, it is no surprise that policy makers and program administrators tend to ride the wave of innovation related to these two areas, and neglect, to a certain degree, the applicability of new technologies in the regular process of information maintenance. One issue this section will address is how innovations can serve the function of continuously **maintaining the accuracy** of previously collected information to make timely and adequate decisions on the current beneficiary roster.

Figure 8.5 The Beneficiary Data Management Function in the Social Protection Delivery Chain

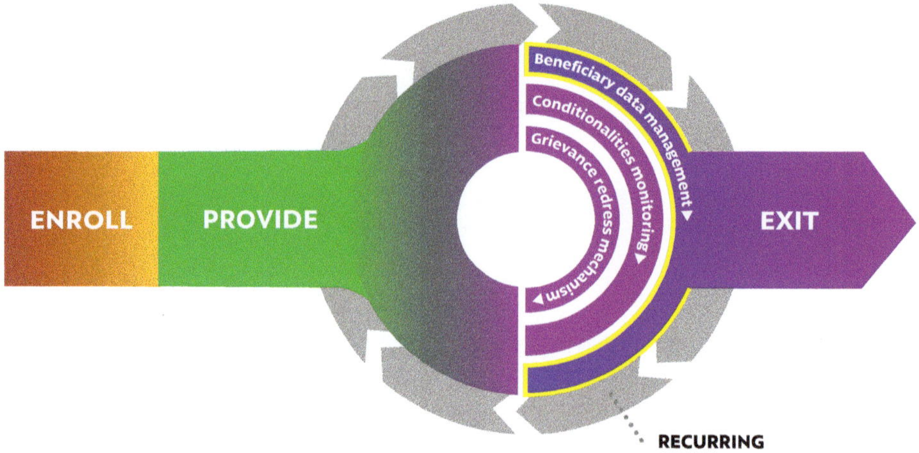

Source: Original figure for this publication.

This section also examines the process of maintaining the accuracy of beneficiaries' basic information, through updates and corrections that support a program's capacity to decide its clients' status as well as program benefits and services. There are two major reasons programs may lack the information to make necessary day-to day-decisions:

- ***Information is outdated*** because family needs and conditions are fluid. The information collected during the assessment and enrollment phases provides a snapshot of an individual's or household's needs and conditions at a certain point in time. That information will change based on vital events such as births, deaths, marriage, and migration. Other effects have to do with changes in socioeconomic condition, changes in other vulnerability factors, or other influences.
- ***Information is incorrect*** as a result of collection errors at the assessment and enrollment phases; or self-declared information was incorrect, whether provided in error or deliberately.[4]

Incorrect or outdated information may lead to a series of mistakes in the recurring cycle. For example, programs end up assigning beneficiaries to the wrong payment or service point, make payment to deceased beneficiaries (particularly social pensions), or continue providing a service package that does not reflect changes to the beneficiary household. Additionally, programs may continue providing benefits to those who for geographical or socioeconomic reasons are no longer eligible for support.

To reduce the incidence of such mistakes, programs have adopted beneficiary data management procedures. As we will see in this section, some of the updates and corrections are made as part of a program's recurring cycle. Some updating schemes make updates and corrections less frequently. That approach, which tends to be more time-consuming and resource-intensive, is not implemented within the regular program cycle, for reasons we will examine separately.

Another aspect of this section that requires special attention is "exiting." As we have previously discussed, information is updated or corrected to enable decisions, and one of the major decisions is related to beneficiaries' length of time in the program. How do programs deal with the process of moving beneficiaries out of a program? This is the final phase of the delivery chain and, outside of policy, not enough attention has been paid to protocols to terminate the beneficiary's path through a program.

We have therefore organized section 8.2 in four subsections:

- ***Types of updates and basic information.*** This subsection introduces how programs organize basic beneficiary information and how that information is tied to regular program decisions.

- ***Updating schemes.*** This subsection will analyze different strategies that are often implemented, as well as some innovations in the area.
- ***Exit decisions.*** This subsection will look at the criteria and procedures used for beneficiaries who are exiting a program.

Throughout this section, we will use country case examples to better illustrate the function of this stage. Before jumping into schemes, the next subsection will introduce basic program information and how it serves as the basis of procedures for updating and correcting information.

Types of Updates and Basic Program Information

Basic program information consists of the set of data fields that program administrators continuously verify to maintain a consistent beneficiary roster. Those fields are regularly used to assess the following potential changes:

- ***Permanence in the program.*** That is, who should remain in the program and who should exit, including who has passed away.
- ***Delivery logistics.*** This information guides the questions of where and how to deliver services and benefits.
- ***Benefit or service package.*** For programs that have differentiated packages, this type of information helps assess how the package matches up with beneficiaries' needs.

Regarding updates related to permanence, this task picks up on some of the functions that take place during the enrollment decision (discussed in chapter 5) as program administrators assess whether a change in basic information affects the beneficiary's compliance with established eligibility criteria. Furthermore, for programs that use socioeconomic status, calculated through aggregate welfare measures (described in chapter 4), as an eligibility criterion, it is not normally feasible to continuously reassess this information because collecting long household questionnaires is costly and time-consuming. For that reason, some programs have opted to implement a separate procedure outside the regular cycle.[5] That procedure, often called recertification, we term reassessment. This activity ensures that the individuals or households that comprise the current roster still fit the program's beneficiary profile. Depending on the program, this may entail reassessing socioeconomic needs and conditions or assessing employment status or social risk for vulnerable individuals and families. Although the activity is part of beneficiary data management because it applies to current beneficiaries, the mechanics of its implementation reiterates the assessment of needs and conditions described in chapter 4, and this activity is therefore described in more detail in that chapter of the book. Therefore, this section will focus on examples of the types of updates and corrections which occur regularly in the recurring cycle of the delivery chain.

Beneficiary data management focuses on different updates depending on the program and the country's administrative data characteristics. The Philippines's 4Ps has a Beneficiary Update System (BUS), which uses 12 types of updates (table 8.2). Not to be confused with software, the BUS is a procedure complete with business process, responsibilities, and criteria, used to provide beneficiaries with a mechanism to change their basic information (the process is described in detail in the next section). BUS has two types of updates that may affect permanence in the program: they are (1) moving out of the Pantawid Pamilya area, and (2) death of the beneficiary or a household family member. BUS also has nine updates that may change the beneficiary's delivery logistics: a newborn in the family, change in address, change in servicing health unit, change in school, change of designated recipient (this will entail new contact information), a biological or legally adopted child who returns home, correction of basic information, replacement of children being monitored for compliance with conditionalities, and a second or subsequent pregnancy. Finally, there are eight types of updates that may imply changes in the service package (table 8.2).

Supporting documents can be used as a validation tool. Certifying an update or correction may prove to be a challenge because administrative documentation for some vital events may not be readily available. For instance, a change of address is not always easy to certify because utility bills may not exist or may be in the name of a different household head, or people may lack basic forms of documentation. A typical supporting document that programs opt for is a letter from the

Table 8.2 Types of Beneficiary Updates for the Philippines's 4Ps

Type of update	Supporting document	Potential change
Newborn	• Birth certificate • Rural health unit/Barangay health station • Registration certificate	Delivery logistics and benefit or service package
Change of address (within Pantawid Pamilya areas)	Certification of transfer of residence from Barangay Captain	Delivery logistics
Moved out of the province, city, or municipality (to non-Pantawid Pamilya areas)	• Certification by Barangay Captains of old and new addresses • C/ML certification	Permanence in the program
Change of servicing health unit	Registration certificate from the new health center/unit signed by municipal health officer or station head	Delivery logistics
Change of school/new enrollment	Proof of enrollment signed by the principal or head teacher	Delivery logistics and benefit and service package
Change designated recipient	• Death certificate • Certification by C/ML stating reason for long absence • Medical certificate • Completed Landbank of the Philippines form on substitute beneficiary paired with other document • Incident report or case study by the Municipal Social Welfare Development Office (MSWDO). For C/MLs case study to be validated by MSWDO	Delivery logistics
Death of beneficiary or household member	Death certificate	Permanence in the program and benefit or service package
Returning biological or legally adopted child 18 years old or younger	• Birth certificate (if biological child) • Legal adoption papers (if adopted child) • School enrollment certificate (if 3–18 years old) • Certification of enrollment to health center if under 5 • C/ML certification that child is not already a Pantawid Pamilya beneficiary in their place of origin	Delivery logistics and benefit or service package
Correction of basic information, that is, name, sex, date of birth	• School enrollment certificate (if 3–18 years old) • RHU/BHS registration certificate (if 0 to 5 years old) and medical certificate (for a differently abled child) certifying the disability and incapacity	Delivery logistics and benefit or service package
Identification of indigenous people tribal membership	Certification from indigenous people tribal leaders	Benefit or service package
Replacement of child(ren) monitored for compliance with conditionalities	• Medical certificate (for a differently abled child) certifying the disability and incapacity • Death certificate if deceased • Birth certificate • Certificate of enrollment	Delivery logistics and benefit or service package
Second or subsequent pregnancy	Rural Health Units (RHU)/Barangay Heath Station (BHS) registration certificate	Delivery logistics and benefit or service package

Source: Based on information provided in the Philippines's Pantawid Pamilyang Pilipino Program Operation Manual, Department of Social Welfare and Development, December 2015.

Note: C/ML = city/municipal link; RHU/BHS = Rural Health Units/Barangay Health Station; 4Ps = Pantawid Pamilyang Pilipino Program.

local authority certifying the beneficiary's new address. Whatever documentation is chosen, defining which documents constitute proof of change ensures some level of traceability and accountability. Table 8.2 provides examples of supporting documents accepted for each type of update.

Some programs include voluntary exit from a program as one of the update types. The fluidity of a beneficiary household's needs and conditions does not necessarily mean those conditions will always worsen. In some cases, people's needs may decline and conditions improve, which may result in individuals opting out of a program because they are no longer willing to shoulder the cost of complying with program obligations. For instance, in the Waseela-e-Taleem CCT under Pakistan's Benazir Income Support Programme, one of the seven update types is voluntary exit from a household. The program's guidelines state, "Household's voluntary exit from the program: when a beneficiary voluntarily wants to exit from the program giving or without giving any justification."

Schemes for Updating and Correcting Beneficiary Information

There are several update and correction schemes that programs employ to maintain the accuracy of the basic beneficiary information. Here we will look at a spectrum of schemes currently being employed, using country cases.

Updating processes can be classified by who initiates the process and the scope of the update. We can divide updating schemes into two main groups. On the one hand, scheduled program-triggered procedures take place once every year (or two) and cover all beneficiaries in the beneficiary operations management system (BOMS). On the other hand, demand-based procedures may be triggered by the beneficiary or by a social worker, and update requests are processed for beneficiaries who have notified the program of a change, or who have been the subject of a social worker's follow-up session. As we will see in this chapter, some programs employ one of these schemes, either scheduled or demand-based, and others use a combination of schemes.

On-Demand Schemes

On-Demand, Beneficiary-Triggered Update

This is one of the most commonly used updating strategies and relies, as the name suggests, on beneficiaries proactively informing program administrators of any change that has taken place in their basic household information. Some programs set this requirement as a beneficiary obligation in their guidelines. For example, in the Philippines's 4Ps program, during onboarding, all eligible applicants who wish to join the program receive an orientation on their rights and obligations and are required to sign an "oath of commitment" where those responsibilities are laid out. The obligation related to updating states, "Attend the meetings and group sessions and coordinate with 4Ps mother-leaders on the concerns relative to 4Ps program in the community ... and changes on household information."[6]

In the same manner, the Benazir Income Support Programme contains the following beneficiary responsibility: "Present updates/grievances/claims with the required information/documents using any of the available mechanisms, in times of updates/grievances/claims."[7]

This type of on-demand scheme normally collects update and correction requests throughout the year. However, that does not necessarily mean that an update is processed immediately. Normally, programs that operate this scheme organize the procedure around the regular payment cycles. The Pension for the Elderly Program in Mexico is constantly collecting update requests, but these are processed only once every bimester or every two months (figure 8.6). Using the master calendar, local program administrators have a deadline to submit the update/correction requests to the program's beneficiary operations management system, so there is time to process the required change and the update can take effect for the immediate payment process. Use of the master calendar is essential to make this scheme operate smoothly.

Another characteristic of the on-demand beneficiary triggered schemes is that they require defined validation and approval procedures. As the update and correction requests are collected in the field, there is a need to review whether the request falls within program

Figure 8.6 Beneficiary Update Scheme for Mexico's Pension for the Elderly Program

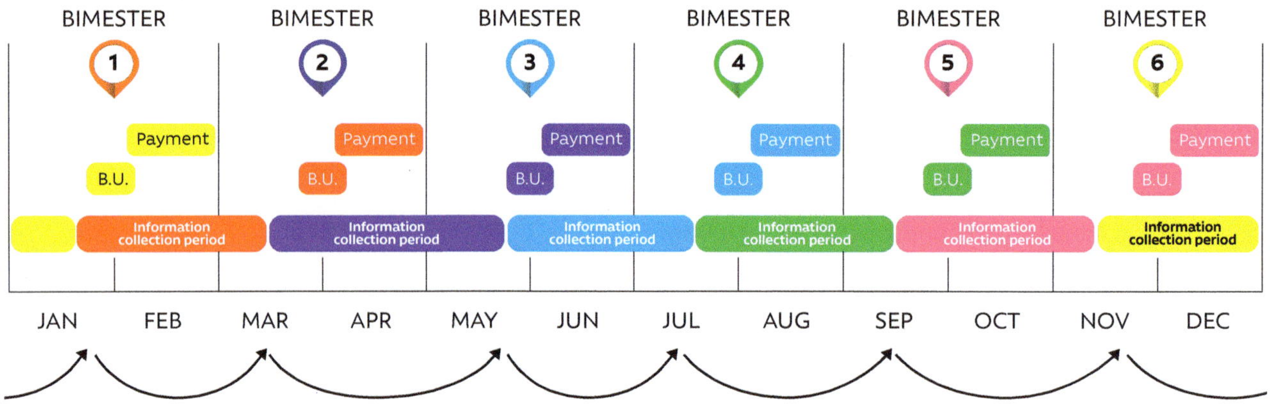

Source: Original figure for this publication.
Note: B.U. = beneficiary registry update/correction process.

guideline parameters, as well as a need to review the validity of the supporting documents. A fundamental question here is, who authorizes or approves the final changes to the beneficiary registry? In the 4Ps example, the request is collected by the parent leader. It is then received by the municipal or city link who reviews its completeness and enters it in the Pantawid Pamilyang Information System (PPIS). It is then collated with other requests for the same updating period by the provincial cluster which applies an en masse review. Finally, it is submitted to the regional director for final approval (figure 8.7).

Some programs develop controls to establish a chain of custody for the update request,[8] The Pension for the Elderly Program in Mexico uses a form (Ficha Única de Atención) that includes a unique filing number and an acknowledgment receipt that the beneficiary keeps (figure 8.8). The unique filing number allows the program to control the request through the different parts of the process. The acknowledgment receipt allows the beneficiary to follow up the updating process through the program's call centers or offices, and at the same time it serves as a paper trail or proof of the transaction for the beneficiary.[9] Additionally, both the acknowledgment and the request include the unique number of the social worker who initially received the request, which adds a level of accountability to the process. Moreover, as the process flows upstream through the program's beneficiary operations management system, all actions that affect the request include the number of the program administrator responsible for it (from the data entry specialist to the managerial staff that approves it).

On-Demand, Triggered by Social Worker

This scheme is mostly applied in social services. It is used to keep a record of a beneficiary's progress through the support phases. Its frequency is a function of the interaction between the beneficiary and the program's social workers. Costa Rica's Puente al Desarrollo Program is a family intervention program that integrates services from different disciplines and government agencies. In this program, the social worker, who develops an individualized action plan with each family, conducts regular follow-up household visits and is responsible for updating beneficiary progress and basic information after every individual family session. For this, the program developed the Personalized Family Support System (Sistema de Atención Personalizada a las Familias [SAPEF]). This system contains the beneficiary's basic information as well as each family's IAP. Unlike the beneficiary-triggered scheme, the social worker is trained and empowered to enter, validate and authorize changes to the beneficiary's information.

Figure 8.7 Beneficiary Initiated Update: Philippines's Pantawid Pamilyang Program (4Ps) Illustration

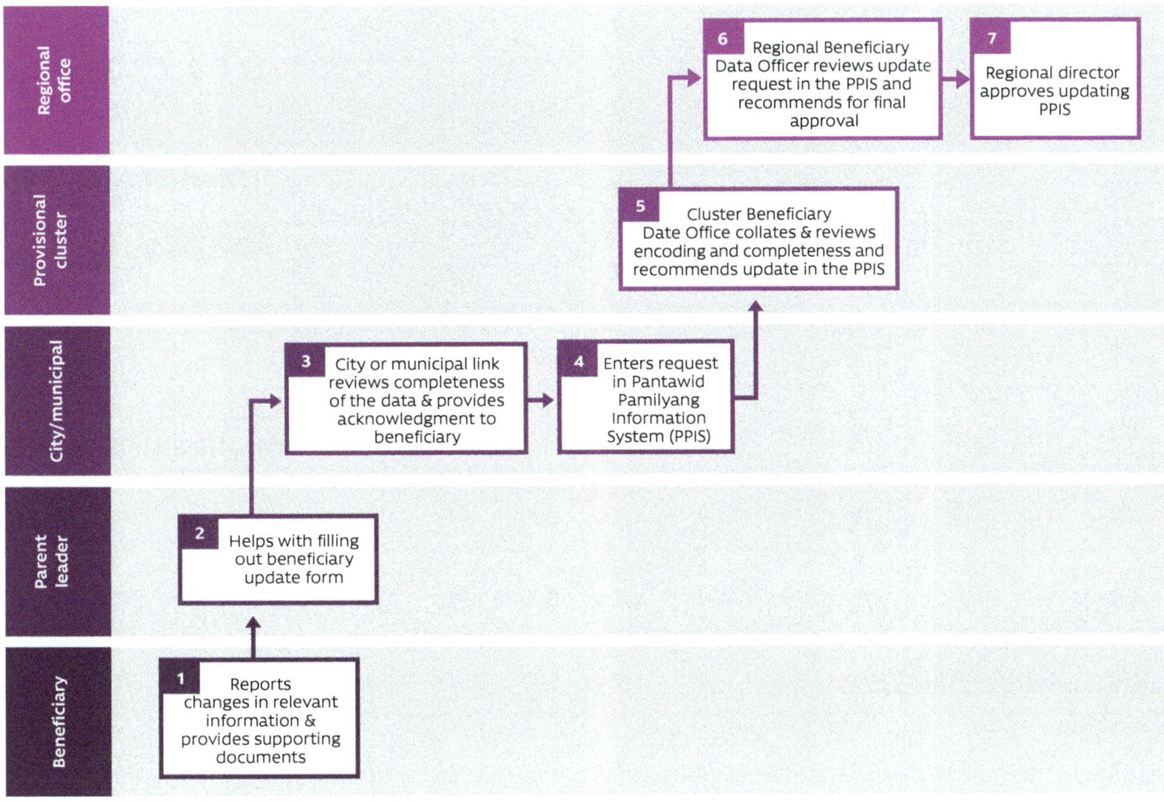

Source: Based on process descriptions in the Philippines's Pantawid Pamilyang Pilipino Program Operations Manual, Department of Social Welfare and Development, December 2015.

Scheduled Program-Triggered Schemes

The second group of update and correction schemes are those that are triggered by a scheduled procedure. Normally these procedures involve updating the complete beneficiary roster; it may also entail cross-referencing with other administrative databases. There are two main types of scheduled program-triggered schemes: (1) those that update information based on the interoperability of administrative databases; and (2) those that use field validation to update their roster.

Integrated Social Information Schemes

These schemes conduct periodic updates by pulling beneficiary data from several linked government administrative databases. Turkey's Integrated Information System for the Social Assistance Services (ISAS; see chapter 4) integrates the functions of a social registry, an integrated beneficiary registry, and integrated systems for payments and beneficiary data management.[10] One of the programs that ISAS serves is a CCT that has a roster of approximately 3 million beneficiaries. The CCT does not have a separate beneficiary operations management system. It is basically a subset of individuals in ISAS, which includes more than 10 million households and 40 million individuals. The information of all the individuals in ISAS is updated every 45 days through a web services procedure that pulls data from 24 linked government administrative databases. That information update can be conducted at any time, but in order not to burden interlinked systems, the government decided to do it as a batch process once every 45 days. In addition, local users in 1,000 Social Assistance and Solidarity Foundations (SASFs) can update their beneficiary profiles in the system any time they want (through web services). Moreover, before calculating payroll,

Figure 8.8 Beneficiary Update Form for the Pension for the Elderly Program of Mexico

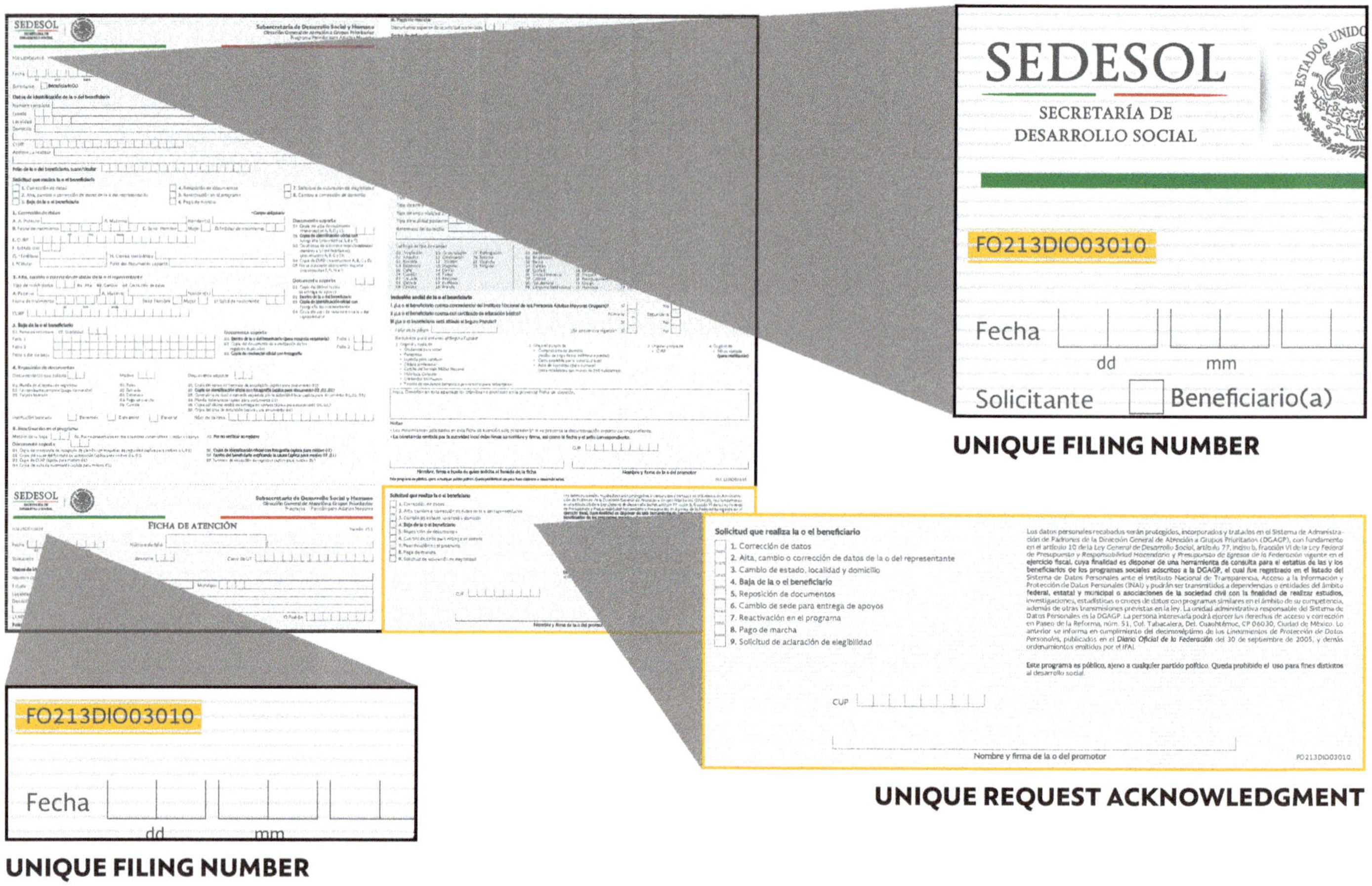

Source: "Guía para el Llenado de Fichas de Atención," Secretaría de Desarrollo Social, Mexico, Dirección General de Atención a Grupos Prioritarios, 2017.

data from all social assistance beneficiaries (including the CCT) must be updated.

Chile's Household Social Registry (RSH, for its acronym in Spanish) is also an integrated social information scheme. Once a month, the RSH pulls 18 data fields from 20 different administrative databases. The RSH uses system integration to update administrative data and, in parallel, it uses an on-demand-beneficiary triggered scheme to update self-reported data.

Scheduled Field-Validation Schemes

This scheme entails committing resources once or twice a year to validate beneficiary information in the field. For instance, the Prospera program in Mexico would use the first payment period of the year to ask beneficiaries if there have been any changes to their basic information (figure 8.9).[11] To do so, a form called F1, containing the basic information of each household, was printed out and provided to each household head so they could signal if there had been any change. If a change was identified, the program's social worker would fill out the Unique Updating Form (Ficha Única de Atención), which was managed through a process similar to the 4Ps BUS process in the Phillipines.

Turkey's updating scheme, in addition to the integrated information scheme discussed above, requires that all social assistance recipients (including CCT beneficiaries) receive an annual in-person evaluation performed by a social assistance inspection officer from the local SASF office. To do so, the social assistance inspector officer prints out a standard household visit form embedded in ISAS. The form is prepopulated by administrative data. Once the visit is completed, the form is entered into ISAS.

Similar to Turkey's ISAS, some programs combine a set of schemes to assure a higher level of reliability. Another example is the Pension for the Elderly Program in Mexico, which cross-references its beneficiary registry every bimester against the civil registration records in the National Population Registry office to verify whether any of the beneficiaries have been reported as deceased.

Integrated information schemes tend to be more efficient, both in time and cost, as it is technology enabled, and processing can take less than four hours. However, they may not be feasible in all country contexts because they are highly dependent on a foundational ID system with good coverage, standardized information across government information platforms, and digitization of the relevant administrative records.

Exit Decisions

One of the major decisions in beneficiary management is that of moving beneficiaries out of the program. Well-functioning beneficiary rosters tend to be highly dynamic tools: they are constantly incorporating new beneficiaries through the enrollment phase and moving out those who have completed the beneficiary path, as well as those who, due to a change or correction, no longer meet the program's criteria. Why do beneficiaries exit a program? One reason is that they have completed the program. Some programs have a defined set of sequential interventions and upon completion, the individual or household graduates from the program. This is normally the case with labor market interventions, particularly those that focus on improving an individual's employability through a defined set of training modules. Another common completion parameter is a time limit. This usually applies to programs that are intended to serve as a first push to achieve some level of self-reliance, or that provide a safety net to help people cope with a temporary condition, such as unemployment insurance. Another exit criterion is that of completion of an IAP. Some programs, particularly those which provide services that are built around the interaction between a beneficiary and a social worker, use a set of individualized goals that are constantly monitored and reinforced by the social worker. Costa Rica's Puente al Desarrollo uses both time limits and IAP completion as exit parameters. Beneficiary households are diagnosed individually and an individualized action plan of up to 41 goals in six improvement dimensions is formalized.[12] A beneficiary exits the program upon completion of the goals or upon completing two years in the program.

A second reason for beneficiaries to exit a program is that their beneficiary profile changes. The most commonly used criterion in this regard, particularly for safety net programs, is that of changes in socioeconomic status. As discussed above, some conditional cash transfers implement reassessment processes to continuously validate the eligibility of their roster (see chapter 4). Another common parameter is that of place of residence, particularly for programs that have some level of geographical targeting. Exit parameters based on geographical targeting are normally the result of beneficiaries' relocation to nontargeted areas. As described in table 8.2, the Philippines's 4Ps, which targets specific provinces, continuously monitors whether beneficiaries have moved to non-Pantawid Pamilya areas of the country.

A subsequent reason for program exit relates to the life cycle, in particular to aging out of a program or dying. In the Waseela-e-Taleem Program under the

Figure 8.9 Scheduled Field Validation by the Prospera Program in Mexico

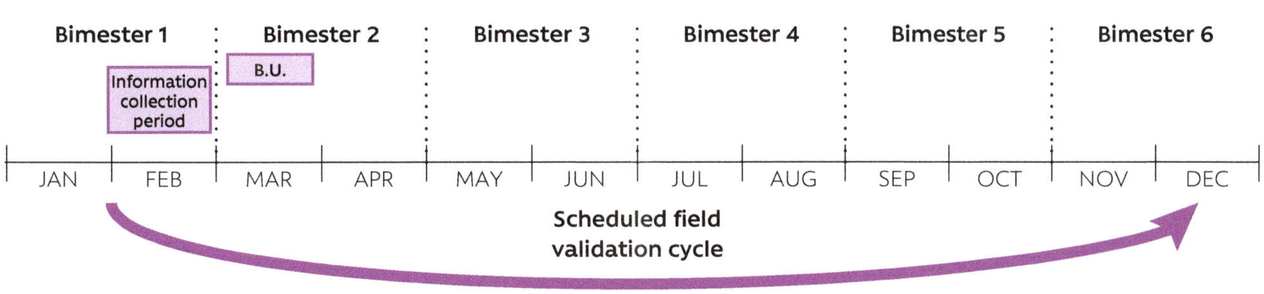

Source: Original figure for this publication.
Note: B.U. = beneficiary registry update/correction process.

Table 8.3 Reasons Beneficiaries Exit a Program

Exit categories	Exit criteria
Completion	• Time limits • Individualized action plan • Graduation
Change in beneficiary's profile	• Socioeconomic status • Vulnerability condition • Geographic location • Employment
Life cycle	• Age • Death
Noncompliance with program conditions	• Labor activation requirements • Program health or education conditionalities

Source: Original table for this publication.

BISP (WET BISP), an individual who reaches age 15 falls under what the program call "separation criteria" and is removed from the roster. Deaths are regularly monitored in social pension programs, although such monitoring is not exclusive to that type of program.

Finally, another common reason for beneficiaries to exit a program is their noncompliance with program conditions or co-responsibilities. Those conditions will be further detailed in the following sections of this chapter. Table 8.3 identifies four major reasons for beneficiaries to exit a program.

From an implementation perspective, a more relevant question is how beneficiaries exit the roster. Specifically, how does a program identify exit cases? How does it verify that the exit criteria have been met? And how does the program notify the individual or household about the decision?

Programs normally carry out four steps in the process of moving beneficiaries out of the roster, including an exit trigger, criteria validation, exit decision, and beneficiary notification. Exit triggers are changes in a beneficiary's basic information or compliance metrics, resulting from the update process (described above) and conditionalities monitoring, respectively, which indicate that a beneficiary has fallen out of program parameters. The triggers can be built in a beneficiary operations management system (BOMS; see chapter 5) or noticed easily in paper and pencil systems (Grosh et al. 2008). As described in the updating schemes section, these triggers may come from the field from on-demand update schemes or may arise from a scheduled updating scheme.

Verification of the exit criteria is rarely documented in a program's operations manual, but it is an essential part of conducting the process in an accountable manner. Particularly in safety nets where the beneficiary's participation in the program may last as long as a decade, accurately certifying that beneficiaries have met the exit criteria is a critical activity. A clear example is certifying that death has occurred for social pension programs. There may be motivation to over-hastily accept a person's death in order to open a spot on the beneficiary roster. A clear, accountable mechanism should be in place to certify, through official means (such as a death certificate) if possible, that a person has passed away and that the information is clearly matched with the one in the BOMS.

Exit decisions are better placed at bureaucracy levels that can be held accountable for high-level decision making. There are some cases, as in social service provision, where the field-level interface with the beneficiary is a trained social worker who, as part of the job description, can make exit decisions independently. There are other cases where field staff carry out a combination of enumeration and social-mobilization functions, and are not endowed with the necessary skills, training, or compensation to assume a responsibility of this nature. In those cases, establishing vertical layers of oversight to assure that exit decisions go through a more rigorous process is preferable. Such is the case with the 4Ps, illustrated in figure 8.7, through which a change in the beneficiary registry goes through the municipal link, is reviewed in the provincial cluster, and approved by the regional director.

A well-designed notification process is essential to completing the beneficiary's experience. As in any service-oriented organization, how you finalize an engagement is just as important as how you initialize it. The question here is, once the decision is made, how is that information conveyed to the beneficiary or the family? Continuing with the example of Costa Rica's Puente al Desarrollo, after each beneficiary household completes the two-year time limit set by the program, the assigned social worker will carry out a work session to review their achievements during this period to finalize the exit procedure. In contrast, most of the programs reviewed in this chapter do not explicitly describe messaging arrangements in their operations manuals. Effective methods of communicating exit decisions should be detailed and standardized and should employ appropriate channels.

8.3 MONITORING COMPLIANCE WITH EDUCATION AND HEALTH CONDITIONALITIES IN CCTs

Reasons for conditionalities. Over 60 countries operate conditional cash transfers (CCTs).[13] They aim to alleviate poverty by providing cash assistance to poor families and to reduce the intergenerational transmission of poverty by incentivizing investments in human capital (Baird et al. 2014). (Table 8A.1 in the annex provides the menus of conditionalities for nine country cases.) CCTs are probably among the most thoroughly evaluated social policy instruments, with solid evidence of their impressive impact on poverty, schooling, and health outcomes.[14]

Monitoring conditionalities along the delivery chain. A few studies have considered the implementation features of conditionalities, and one of the key findings has been that monitoring and enforcement of conditionalities matter (Baird et al. 2014; Bastagli et al. 2016; Dodleva et al. 2018; Ibarraran et al. 2017). A crucial question is: how do CCTs monitor and enforce conditionalities? This section seeks to unpack the processes and systems underpinning such monitoring, which is part of the recurring cycle of beneficiary operations management on the delivery chain. The objective of monitoring conditionalities is to provide behavioral "nudges" to beneficiaries by verifying their school attendance and utilization of health care. The primary input to conditionalities monitoring is the roster of individuals within beneficiary families who require monitoring in each implementation cycle, such as pregnant or postpartum women, children ages 0–6, children ages 6–15, and youth ages 16–18, including their assigned schools and health care facilities. Monitoring also requires institutional coordination, including collaboration with service providers (education and health facilities); human resources; compliance verification forms, protocols and processes; and beneficiary operations management systems. The primary output of conditionalities monitoring is an updated BOMS with information on compliance or noncompliance for that monitoring cycle, decisions on consequences for noncompliance, and any revisions in benefits amounts because of financial penalties. The updated beneficiary registry then loops back to update the payroll for the next payment cycle.

Nine country cases. With the aim of covering a diverse array of regional and contextual experiences around the globe, this Sourcebook includes CCTs in nine countries: Brazil's Bolsa Família Program (BFP), Colombia's Familias en Acción Program (FA), Indonesia's Family Hope Program (PKH), Jamaica's Programme for the Advancement of Health and Education (PATH), Mexico's Prospera program, Pakistan's Waseela-e-Taleem Program (WeT), the Pantawid Pamilyang Pilipino Program (4Ps) in the Philippines, Tanzania's Productive Social Safety Nets Conditional Cash Transfer (PSSN CCT) program, and Turkey's CCT Program.

Road map. The first section delves into the core questions: how do countries monitor conditionalities in CCTs and how do they link back to payments to enforce penalties for noncompliance? The second section explores how to enforce consequences and the link between conditionalities and payment cycles. The third section presents some core indicators for assessing the performance of implementation of conditionalities monitoring (with links to chapter 9). The fourth section provides a checklist summary of good practices regarding the monitoring of conditionalities.

How Do CCTs Monitor Conditionalities?

A key question is how countries monitor conditionalities in CCTs. This section seeks to unpack the black box of implementation to examine the institutional arrangements and processes for monitoring conditionalities. It also looks at the use of information systems (BOMS, commonly referred to as an "MIS"),[15] and how they are used not only to record and manage data on compliance but how they can also automate processes and improve efficiency by reducing processing times.

Institutional Arrangements and the Importance of Vertical and Horizontal Coordination

Institutional coordination—both vertical and horizontal—is a critical element of conditionalities monitoring. One of the factors that makes compliance monitoring complex is the number and diversity of actors involved, including frontline program personnel, teachers, health care workers, subnational agencies, and central agencies, including the social, education, and health ministries.

Monitoring of CCTs requires significant vertical collaboration between the central ministries, subnational, and local actors. The central social ministries typically oversee CCTs; manage information systems, including the compliance verification modules; decide on any consequences for noncompliance; and feed compliance information back to the payments department for payroll processing. Subnational (regional or local) actors typically serve as conduits for transmitting information, overseeing the process, and interacting with the service providers. Various approaches govern these vertical collaboration arrangements.

- Some CCTs rely on **deconcentrated agents at subnational levels**, with central financing and reporting arrangements. Such is the case with Indonesia's PKH, which is managed at the national level by the Family Social Security Sub-Directorate (JSK) in the Ministry of Social Affairs (MoSA); at the subnational level through 33 provincial implementation offices; and at the district, or local, level with some 36,000 program facilitators contracted by JSK or MoSA to manage operations on the front lines.[16] Similarly, the Philippines's 4Ps is managed centrally by the National Program Management Office (NPMO) in the Department for Social Welfare and Development (DSWD), subnationally through the regional program management office and the provincial operations offices, and at the front line by city and municipal links who are contracted by DSWD and report to the regional field offices.
- In countries with decentralized contexts, CCTs rely on **vertical collaboration with autonomous subnational and local government units**. In Brazil, municipal coordinators are directly involved with local implementation of conditionalities monitoring. Municipal implementation is guided by formal adhesion agreements between the Ministry of Social Development (MDS) and the municipalities, and implementation quality is closely monitored with a performance index that includes completeness of information for conditionalities verification. MDS makes significant performance-based budget transfers to the municipalities to help cover their administrative costs for these activities.
- Another approach involves **outsourcing**; Pakistan's WeT CCT contracts out some of the subnational and local responsibilities to two implementation partner firms, including compliance verification processing.[17]

Horizontally, all CCTs require cross-sectoral collaboration at the local level; some also coordinate with central and subnational education and health authorities. First, at a minimum, horizontal coordination is needed locally to involve school officials and health care workers in the process, given their frontline roles for recording school attendance and health care visits, as well as with local program personnel because of their roles in following up with the families. Given their pivotal roles, it is crucial to ensure that these frontline actors are all onboard with the program's objectives and understand their responsibilities. It is also important to keep the processes for monitoring conditionalities and filling out paperwork manageable and user-friendly (box 8.1). Second, some CCTs also involve subnational or central ministries of education and health directly in the monitoring process, in addition to local actors. In Mexico, the state-level education and health authorities were directly involved in monitoring conditionalities for Prospera, as discussed below. The CCTs in Brazil and Turkey rely heavily on direct operational cross-sectoral collaboration at the central levels (in addition to local), with the central ministries of education and health taking on direct responsibility for managing information relating to monitoring school attendance and health visits, as discussed below.

Processes for Monitoring Conditionalities

There are several key stages associated with monitoring conditionalities. They are part of a recurring conditionalities monitoring cycle, which begins with the latest roster of pertinent beneficiary family or household members and ends with a revised beneficiary registry with updated compliance information for that cycle, as well as decisions on consequences for noncompliance. That updated BOMS (output) links back to the payroll for the next payment cycle. Within each monitoring cycle, there are two key periods: (1) the compliance period, which is the period during which beneficiaries are observed for compliance (in other words,

Box 8.1 Human-Centered Design Aspects of Conditionalities Monitoring

Monitoring compliance with conditionalities can be "human-intensive," depending on the degree of automation. It is important that the processes are also "human-centered," meaning that they are agile and do not impose undue burdens on beneficiaries, school officials and health care providers, or program personnel.

For beneficiaries. Five guidelines will help beneficiaries comply with conditionalities. First, a human-centered approach means keeping conditionalities simple and synchronizing them with the requirements of schools and health clinics and recognizing their inherent limitations in local contexts, such as travel distances and supply-side limitations. Second, a human-centered approach also means communicating clearly the rights and responsibilities of beneficiaries and ensuring that they understand what is expected of them. Indonesia, Jamaica, and Pakistan all offer onboarding training to ensure that beneficiary families/households are properly inducted into their CCT programs, including understanding their rights and responsibilities and the conditionalities they are expected to comply with. Third, it means notifying beneficiaries of any observed instances of noncompliance in advance of any penalties so that they can plan accordingly. Fourth, it means ensuring that there are accessible channels and feasible processes for filing grievances, prompt investigations of them and responses to resolve them. Fifth, it is important to conduct periodic beneficiary assessments, including probing their experience with education and health services as well as their experience of conditionalities compliance.

For school officials and health workers. It is important to communicate with frontline officials about the program so that they understand its objectives, their role in implementing it, and the procedures and schedules for reporting on school attendance, health visits, growth monitoring and vaccinations of the beneficiary population. Again, minimizing paperwork and keeping conditionalities simple and synchronized with school and health systems also helps with officials' willingness to collaborate. In addition, it is important to keep them abreast of their "caseloads" and changes in the beneficiary rosters assigned to their facilities, with updated lists and compliance verification forms for each implementation cycle transmitted early enough to allow them to prepare paperwork. It also helps when local representatives of the program (such as facilitators or social workers) maintain a relationship with school officials and health workers, build trust, and cooperate with them regarding variations in schedule (such as school holidays and exam periods, or village visits by mobile health teams). Finally, it is important to conduct periodic qualitative assessments that include interviews with school officials and health care providers regarding their roles in the program.

For program personnel, such as facilitators, social workers, data enumerators, and supervisors, a human-centered approach means training personnel so they have the knowledge and skills needed to do their job, resolving problems and handling complaints; interacting with families, village heads, service providers, and local officials as the "face of the program," and so on. This approach also means providing personnel in a timely manner with the necessary tools to do their job properly, such as local office space, inputs (such as tablets, laptops, compliance verification forms, and communications materials), and safe transport or transportation allowances so they can meet with families and service providers. Efforts to minimize paperwork and transactions costs for all involved are also important. Finally, it is important to keep caseloads and workloads manageable to ensure that personnel can complete their tasks within the allotted time frames and avoid social worker burnout.

Sources: Compilation based on field visits in Brazil and Indonesia, as well as field reports, manuals, and evaluations from Brazil, Indonesia, Jamaica, and Pakistan.

the time period during which they would be expected to comply); and (2) the compliance verification period, which is the period during which compliance verification processing is carried out (note that the allotted time may differ from the actual time needed).

Most CCTs adopt a two-month compliance period for each cycle, with a few exceptions (figure 8.10). Pakistan's WeT CCT and Indonesia's PKH program both use three-month (quarterly) compliance periods.[18] Brazil's BFP uses six-month compliance periods for health conditionalities, recognizing that health visits are sporadic and allowing for a longer catchment period to capture data on compliance. Jamaica's PATH program distinguishes between different groups, with two-month compliance periods for health conditionalities for mothers and children, but six-month periods for the disabled, elderly, and adults (in line with the expectation that they will make biannual health visits).

This review reveals eight steps for compliance verification that are common among the CCTs in the sample:

1. Generating an updated beneficiary monitoring roster, with pertinent information on each individual family/household member in each category, as well as their assigned schools and health facilities (this is the key "input" to the process of conditionalities monitoring)
2. Transmitting updated beneficiary monitoring roster and distributing compliance verification forms (CVFs)
3. Recording school attendance/health care utilization at assigned facilities for each beneficiary in each category onto the CVFs
4. Collecting the CVFs from the service providers

Figure 8.10 Compliance Periods for Education and Health Conditionalities in Select Countries' CCTs

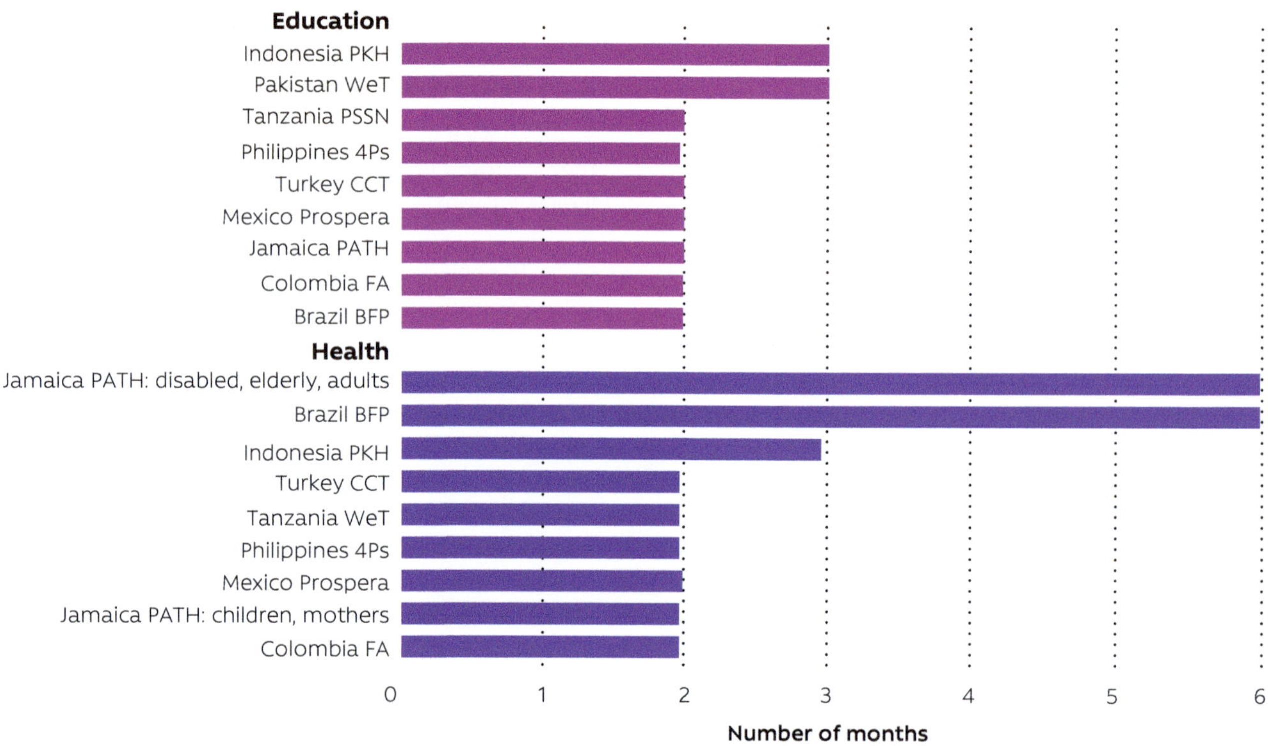

Sources: Brazil: MDS BFP Operations Manual 2017. Colombia: Prosperidad Social, FA Operational Manual, 2017. Indonesia: MoSA (2018) Ministerial Regulation on PKH, articles 3,4, and 5. Jamaica: MLSS PATH Operations Manual 2017. Mexico: Dávila Lárraga 2016. Pakistan: BISP-WeT Team, Operational Manual for Wet 2017. The Philippines: DSWD Pantawid Pamilyang Pilipino Program Operations Manual, December 2015 Edition. Tanzania: TASAF III, PSSN Operations Manual. Turkey: General Directorate of Social Assistance; Ortakaya 2018; MoH Schedule.

Note: A compliance period is the period in each monitoring cycle during which beneficiaries are required to comply with conditionalities. CCT = conditional cash transfer (program).

5. Entering and transmitting the data from the CVFs
6. Consolidating, transmitting, and receiving data
7. Reviewing information and determining compliance status for each individual beneficiary (yes or no)
8. Deciding on any consequences, as well as any follow-up actions, such as family monitoring or counseling, and updating the BOMS with revised benefit amounts associated with compliance or noncompliance by the individual family members (this is the "output" of conditionalities monitoring) and forwarding it as an input to the payroll for the next payment cycle

An important step that is not always implemented is to notify beneficiaries of compliance decisions. Effective communication practices for the CCT programs should include protocols for informing beneficiaries of noncompliance and any penalties. Many programs rely on frontline program personnel to inform beneficiaries, but the protocols are not always formalized or followed. Some CCTs do have formalized protocols and processes to notify beneficiaries of noncompliance decisions. For example, in Pakistan's WeT program, beneficiaries are notified of noncompliance status through an SMS text alert or home visit by the implementation partner firm or the BISP Beneficiary Committee. In Brazil's BFP, MDS notifies families of their noncompliance status through letters and messages on their bank statements when they withdraw their benefits. Those messages instruct the families to contact the local BFP municipal coordinator if they have any questions.

Other parallel steps include grievance redress and oversight activities. Most CCTs have grievance redress mechanisms, and these usually cover appeals regarding noncompliance status (see section 8.5). In Turkey's CCT program, appeals can be made to the local SASFs. Those appeals can be granted if the monitoring data are updated with supporting documents from the respective education or health facilities. In Brazil's BFP, families can file an appeal at the municipal office if they believe that there was an information error or that failure to meet the conditionalities was justified. There is a deadline for filing the appeal, which is then recorded and assessed (granted or denied) by the municipal administration. If the appeal is granted, the noncompliance record is canceled, and the families return to normal status to ensure a regular flow of benefits (WWP 2016a). CCTs also use oversight mechanisms, such as regular spot checks to compare compliance data with facility-level records, to support quality processes and outputs. Some programs also undertake deeper process evaluations to review conditionalities monitoring, such as the compliance assessment for Jamaica's PATH CCT (see chapter 9 for more information on process evaluations).

The process map for the Philippines's 4Ps illustrates a typical compliance verification process, with the common U-shaped pattern that we see in most countries. The process begins with the central agency generating an updated roster of all individuals to be monitored and also ends at the central level, with the central agency's decisions on compliance status and consequences fed into the updated beneficiary registry for payroll. In the Philippines's 4Ps, those central functions are undertaken by the Compliance Verification Division (CVD) in the NPMO of DSWD (see the top row of the process map in figure 8.11). In between those steps, processes occur at the subnational and local levels, including the service providers (school and health officials). In the Philippines, the subnational actors include (1) the Regional Program Management Office and the Provincial Operations Offices, which are responsible for printing and distributing compliance verification forms and then collecting them to manage data entry, consolidation, review, and transmission (the second row of the process map); and (2) local actors, including the city or municipal links (C/MLs, who are contracted by DSWD), assisted by the Social Welfare Assistants (the third row of the process map). Finally, the school officials (principals, secretaries, and teachers under the department of education) and the health care workers (who report to the local government units) are responsible for recording information on beneficiaries' school attendance and health care visits (bottom row of process map). The monitoring of conditionalities is supported by the Pantawid Pamilyang Information System (PPIS), including the Compliance Verification System (CVS) which supports data entry, processing, and consolidation, and links to the payroll generation system.

In virtually all CCTs in the sample, the processes for verifying compliance with conditionalities follow the same U-shaped pattern, from the central level down to local levels and back up to the central level. While there is some variation between countries, the eight basic steps occur at similar levels of institutional responsibility (see table 8.4).

Figure 8.11 Typical "U-Shaped" Process for Compliance Verification in the Philippines

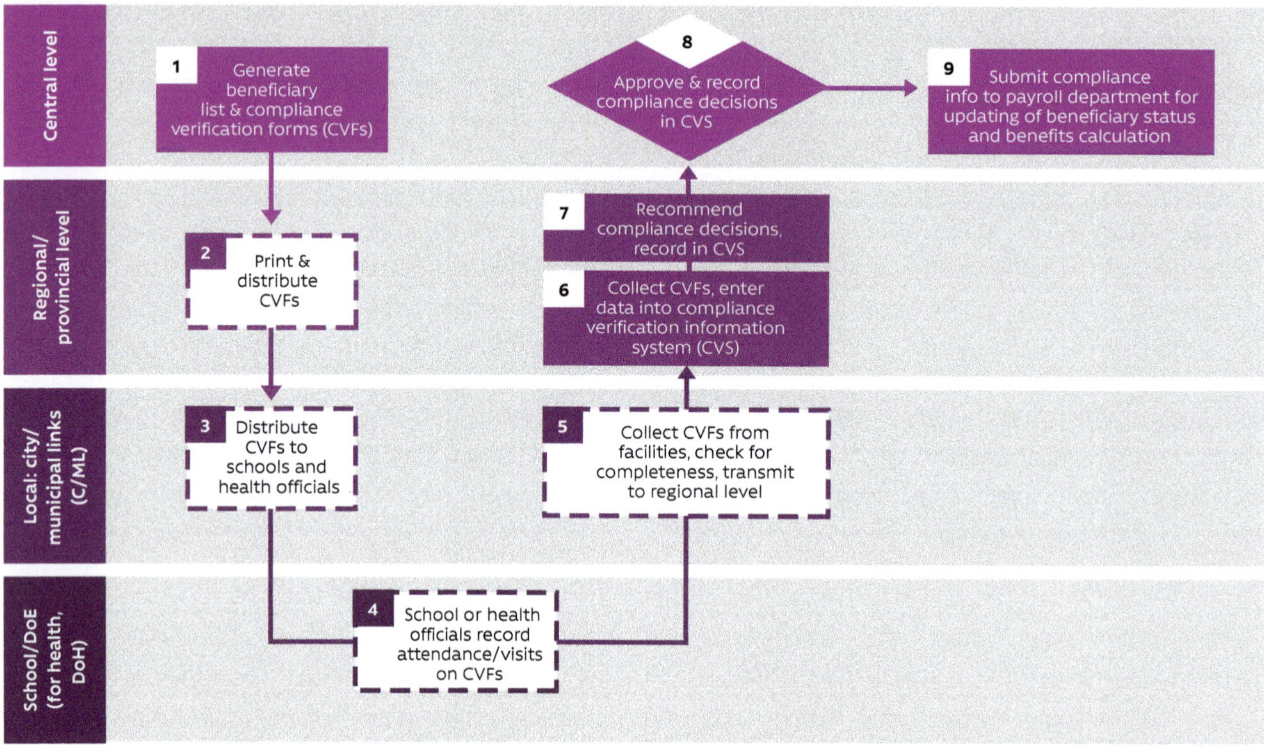

Sources: Based on processes outlined in Philippines, Department of Social Welfare and Development (2015b) and PWC (2016).
Note: Solid purple boxes indicate information system; white boxes indicate paper-based process. DoE = Department of Education; DoH = Department of Health.

Some CCTs may combine some of these steps (especially with automation), while others may have additional substeps. Table 8.4 lists the institutional arrangements for those steps for each of the nine countries in our sample. Color coding reveals similarities in the levels of vertical collaboration: blue indicates central-level responsibilities, gray represents subnational and local actors, and yellow indicates the steps that are the responsibility of the service providers (schools, health clinics). When mapped using "swim lanes" process charts (like the one for the Philippines below; see also box 2.2 in chapter 2), these steps take on a common "U-shaped" pattern, from central to local and back up to central. The variations in implementation across CCTs stem from (1) differences in institutional arrangements for vertical collaboration; (2) differences in the degree of inter-sectoral coordination with the ministries of education and health (central and local); and (3) the degree to which processes are automated or paper-based.

How long do these processes take? Data on actual processing times typically come from business process evaluations and are not readily available for all countries. In the Philippines, DSWD commissioned a business process review to assess the adequacy of processing targets for implementation of the 4Ps (see box 9.11 in chapter 9) (PWC 2016). Such a review is quite thorough. Based on the Philippine review, the total time allotted for compliance verification processing is 53 business days (figure 8.12). To save time, some steps in the process are carried out during the compliance period, such as generating, printing, and distributing CVFs, which together account for 24 days of each cycle. However, the remaining steps must occur after the end of the compliance period to represent a meaningful recording of beneficiaries' school attendance and health visits. Those steps include verifying compliance and filling out CVFs, collecting CVFs from the schools and health facilities, entering data, reviewing information and determining compliance status, making final compliance decisions, and preparing the revised benefit amounts for payroll. They require a total of 29 days, which can make for a tight turnaround if there are any slippages, because

Table 8.4 Institutional Responsibilities for Common Steps in the Verification of Conditionalities Compliance in Select Countries' CCTs

	Brazil BFP	Colombia FA	Indonesia PKH	Jamaica PATH	Mexico Prospera	Pakistan WeT	Philippines 4Ps	Tanzania PSSN	Turkey CCT
1. Generate updated beneficiary roster	MDS: SIBEC (info system), SICON (info system) + MoE/MoH	Prosperidad Social Sistema de Informacion de Familias en Acción (SIFA)	Ministry of Social Affairs (MoSA)	Ministry of Labour and Social Security (MLSS) head office	Prospera's National Coordination Office (SIIOP)	Benazir Income Support Programme (BISP)	CVD in National Program Management Office (NPMO)/DSWD	Tanzania Social Action Fund (TASAF) headquarters	District-level Social Assistance and Solitary Foundations (SASFs) update beneficiary profile into ISAS
2. Transmit roster and CVFs (or upload in system/tablets)	Municipal coordinators under MoE/MoH	Prosperidad Social/SIFA	District- or provincial-level operators	MLSS parish offices	Education and health authorities at state level, SICEC	WeT unit	RPMO/POOs, then transmit to local	Project Administrative Authority (PAA)	
3. Record school attendance/health care use	School/health officials under MoE/MOH	School/health officials enter data directly into SIFA	Facilitators visit schools/health facilities to record noncompliance data	School/health officials	School/health officials (paper-based and electronic in SICEC)	School/health officials	School/health officials	School/health officials	School officials enter student data into e-school MIS under MoE; health officials enter health data into FMIS under MoH
4. Collect and transmit CVFs	Municipal coordinators under MoE/MoH		District-level facilitators	SWs for parish offices	Prospera's state offices, SICEC	IPF teams collect info and enter on tablets	Local C/MLs collect CVFs	PAAs	
5. Enter and transmit data			District data entry operators	MLSS MIS unit			RPMO/POOs	PAAs	
6. Consolidate, transmit, receive data	MoE/MoH consolidate info	Prosperidad Social/SIFA	Provincial-level offices	Parish administrator	SIIOP	WeT MIS	RPMO		ISAS pulls data from E-school MIS and FMIS
7. Review info and determine compliance status	MDS/SICON identifies cases of noncompliance	Prosperidad Social/SIFA	PKH MIS in MoSA	MLSS PATH unit	SIIOP	BISP unit/MIS	RPMO	Productive Social Safety Net (PSSN) unit MIS	ISAS monitors compliance
8. Decide on consequences, update beneficiary roster, forward to payroll	MDS/SICON	Prosperidad Social/SIFA	PKH in MoSA	MLSS PATH unit	SIIOP	BISP unit/MIS	National project manager in NPMO	TASAF headquarters	ISAS automated decisions and links back to payroll

Sources: Brazil: MDS BFP Operations Manual 2017. Colombia: Prosperidad FA Operational Manual 2017. Indonesia: MoSA (2018) Ministerial Regulation on PKH, articles 3,4, and 5. Jamaica: MLSS PATH Operations Manual 2017. Mexico: SEDESOL 2018. Pakistan: BISP-WeT Team, Operational Manual for Wet 2017. The Philippines: DSWD Pantawid Pamilyang Pilipino Program Operations Manual, December 2015 Edition. Tanzania: TASAF III, PSSN Operations Manual. Turkey: General Directorate of Social Assistance; Ortakaya 2018; MoH Schedule.

Note: ■ = central level; ■ = subnational and local levels); ■ = service provider. CCT = conditional cash transfer (program); CVD = Compliance Verification Division; CVF = compliance verification form; DSWD = Department for Social Welfare and Development; FMIS = Family Medicine Information System; IPF = implementation partner firm; ISAS = Integrated Social Assistance System; MDS = Ministry of Social Development; MIS = management infomation system; MoE = Ministry of Education; MoH = Ministry of Health; NPMO = National Program Management Office. RPMO/POOs = regional program management office and provincial operations offices; SICEC = Electronic Certification System of Co-responsibilities.

Figure 8.12 Compliance Verification Processing Times in the Philippines's 4Ps Process Evaluation

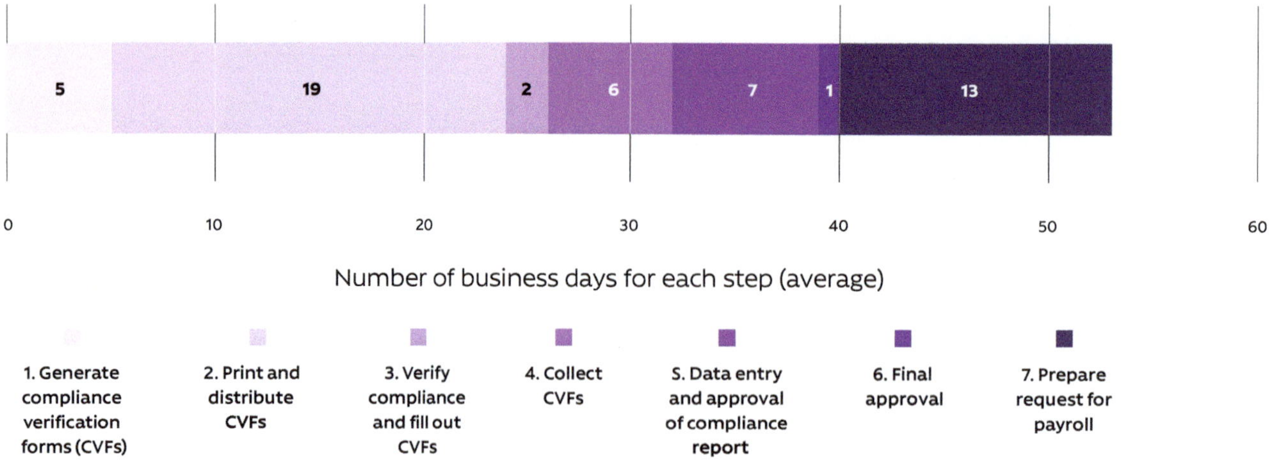

Source: PWC 2016.

Note: 4Ps = Pantawid Pamilyang Pilipino Program.

that exceeds the total number of business days in a calendar month. The review found that overtime delays occur due to bunching of processes such as data entry, given the large number of CVFs that need to be encoded per region and disparities in the number of CVFs processed per day. Underestimating the amount of time required to enter data can result in data entry operators becoming overworked, which can cause inaccuracies in the data and absenteeism (PWC 2016). In addition, processing targets need to be adapted to diverse contexts, with likely longer times in remote or geographically dispersed areas.

Information Systems to Support Conditionalities Monitoring

All CCTs rely on information systems to record data on compliance; some also use them to automate processes. For some CCTs, much of the process remains largely paper-based, with information systems serving more to record data rather than to automate processes. In those cases, there are numerous paperwork transitions, and data entry occurs late in the process, further from the point of collection. Bottlenecks can arise due to bunching of data entry for all CVFs during the compliance verification period. Other CCTs make extensive use of integrated information systems and a high degree of collaboration and interoperability with the ministries of education and health to automate and expedite compliance verification processes, as discussed below (see also chapter 5).

Information privacy and security policies and practices are particularly important for conditionalities monitoring, given the sensitive nature of personal data involved in compliance verification. Education and health conditionalities involve personal information on school attendance and health care utilization of individual beneficiaries. Whether paper-based or automated, the privacy and security of that information must be protected. Health information (pregnancy, childbirth, health visits, vaccines, growth monitoring) is particularly sensitive, and health information privacy standards must be adopted. Compliance verification processes involve passing such information from education and health providers to local program representatives (e.g., facilitators) and then into the CCT information system. In Turkey, written consent is required from the applicant indicating permission for use of personal data throughout the delivery process. The consent is explicit about the types of information to be used. In Jamaica, health workers emphasized that they would be the only ones to review the beneficiaries' health records and to fill out the CVFs. With CCTs, further complexities arise because of the individual nature of conditionalities vis-à-vis the household as the assistance unit for benefits. If one family member does not comply, CCTs (should) typically notify the household (in general, or the designated recipient) of noncompliance and any benefit-reduction consequences. That implies intrahousehold sharing of personal information (see Data Protection, Privacy, and Security in chapter 4).

In some CCTs, most steps are manual, with data entry done centrally after all CVFs are collected and consolidated. An example of this approach is Jamaica's PATH Program. The Beneficiary Management Information System (BMIS) supports the generation of monitoring rosters for each implementation cycle and the recording of compliance information at the central level. However, most processes are still manual and paper-based. Significant effort is spent generating and checking the beneficiary lists, preparing batches of CVFs, distributing them to the relevant service providers, and then collecting and transmitting them back up to the Ministry of Labor and Social Services, where the data are entered. Interestingly, as discussed below, Jamaica's monitoring rates are relatively high despite these manual paper-based processes, especially for verification of health conditionalities, which is particularly challenging in all countries.

In some CCTs, data entry occurs closer to the point of collection, thus reducing some of the paper-based handovers. In the Philippines's 4Ps, data are entered at the regional or provincial level (after being collected from schools and health facilities by the C/MLs and are then transmitted electronically to the central agency, DSWD (figure 8.11). In other CCTs, data entry is done locally immediately after compliance information is collected from the education and health facilities. In Indonesia's PKH program, for example, facilitators collect compliance information from the schools and health clinics and pass the CVFs to the data entry operators. The operators enter the data into the PKH MIS, which transmits them to the central agency. MoSA/JSK launched a software app for tablets that allows for direct entry of compliance information by facilitators on the front lines. Similarly, in Pakistan's WeT CCT, tablets have automated some processes, with frontline data entry once compliance information is collected from schools by implementation partner firm personnel.

Mexico's Prospera program transitioned to a system that automated compliance verification processes, with a coexistence of paper-based and electronic methods. Figure 8.13 illustrates both paper-based and electronic processes (solid purple boxes show the automated

Figure 8.13 Conditionalities Verification Processes in Mexico's Prospera Program

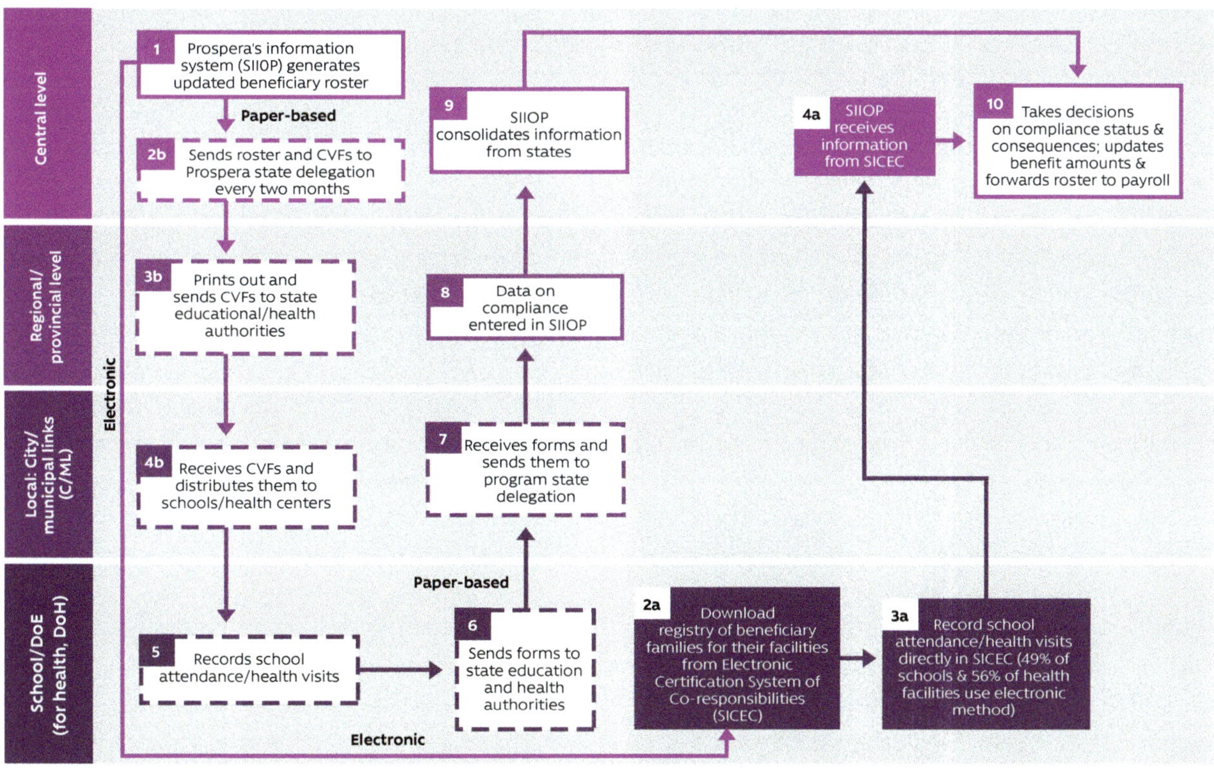

Source: Adapted from SEDESOL (Mexico, Secretaría de Desarrollo Social 2018a).

Note: Solid purple boxes indicate electronic processing through automated system; white boxes with dashed outlines indicate manual processing in paper-based system; white boxes with solid outlines indicate electronic processing in either system. CVF = compliance verification form.

Figure 8.14 Direct Collaboration with the Ministry of Education for Monitoring Education Conditionalities in Brazil

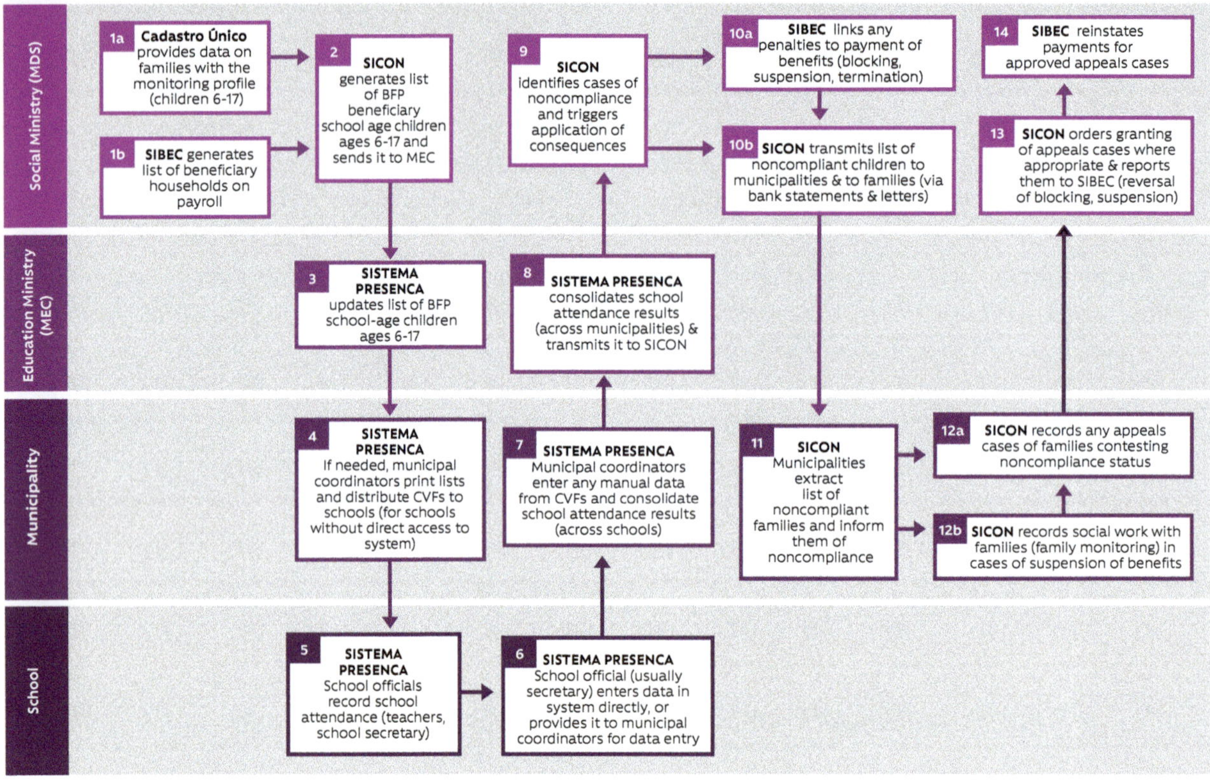

Sources: Brazil: MDS BFP Operations Manual 2017; http://wwp.org.br/ (see WWP 2016a–e).
Note: BFP = Bolsa Família Program; SIBEC = benefits management system; SICON = information system.

system). Reliance on paper-based processes involved many processing steps and document handoffs. With the development of the Electronic Certification System of Co-Responsibilities (SICEC), many of those processes were automated. As of 2018, about half of schools and health facilities entered compliance data for Prospera beneficiaries directly into SICEC, which then transmitted the data to Prospera's main institutional information system (SIIOP). SICEC significantly reduced the number of processing steps.

A high degree of intersectoral collaboration and interoperability between the BFP and the ministries of education and health pervades the processes for compliance verification in Brazil. Institutionally, responsibilities are clearly delineated across central ministries according to their sectoral responsibilities: the ministries of education and health oversee service provision and track school attendance and health care utilization with their own information systems; the social ministry has responsibility for linking that information to the systems of the BFP and making decisions on compliance or noncompliance. The specific steps and responsibilities are illustrated in the process map in figure 8.14 (although figure 8.14 relates to education, the process map is similar for health). Interoperability between three information systems supports these processes:

- ***The Ministry of Social Development (MDS) hosts SICON, the information system for monitoring BFP conditionalities.*** The key functions of SICON include (1) generating the list of beneficiary family members whose conditionalities will be monitored for each cycle through information from the BFP's benefits management system (SIBEC) with links to the social registry (Cadastro Único); (2) transmitting those lists to the ministries of education and health; (3) consolidating information from the Ministry of Education (Sistema Presença) and the Ministry of Health (Sistema PBF Saude) on families with noncomplying members (linking the individuals' noncompliance information for education and health conditionalities to each BFP family) (4) generating consequences for noncomplying families; and (5) generating analytic reports for decision making. Access to this system is online, and state and municipal BFP managers have their own passwords to login. The steps that are overseen by MDS and supported by the SICON are shown in figure 8.14, with links to partner systems such as SIBEC and the Cadastro Único, also managed by MDS.

- ***The Ministry of Education is responsible for managing the system for monitoring school attendance by all BFP children and adolescents ages 6–17.***[19] Data on school attendance by BFP beneficiaries is recorded directly into the Sistema Presença, hosted by the Ministry of Education. The key functions of the Sistema Presença include (1) receiving (from MDS's SICON) the updated roster of BFP beneficiaries whose school attendance must be monitored; (2) receiving school attendance records of each BFP beneficiary, which are entered at the municipal level based on school records; (3) making consolidated monitoring data available in concise and analytic form; and (4) transmitting school attendance monitoring data on BFP children and adolescent beneficiaries to SICON in MDS. The steps that are overseen by the Ministry of Education and supported by the Sistema Presença are shown in figure 8.14.
- ***The Ministry of Health is responsible for managing the system for monitoring health information and service utilization by BFP beneficiaries: (1) all BFP children under age 7; and (2) all women of childbearing age (ages 14–44).*** Since pregnancy is a random event from an administrator point of view, it was decided to monitor health information and service utilization for all beneficiary women of childbearing age, and to note any pregnancies and associated prenatal visits in the system. The Ministry of Health hosts the Sistema PBF Saude, a specially designed health monitoring system for the BFP, which monitors compliance with health conditionalities for all relevant family members. The key functions of that system include (1) receiving and maintaining information on all beneficiary household members who must be monitored for health visits (growth monitoring, vaccines, prenatal visits); (2) tracking information on health and nutritional status, including data on vaccinations, health visits, and anthropometric measures (height, weight), allowing for nutrition diagnostics; (3) receiving individual family members' health monitoring records; (4) transmitting information on compliance with health conditionalities for BFP beneficiaries to MDS; and (5) generating consolidated reports for beneficiary families and for analytics.

Inter-institutional collaboration, interoperability, and IT innovations have improved efficiency by reducing data processing times for compliance verification in the Bolsa Família Program.[20] Cross-sectoral collaboration and improvements in processing steps were accompanied by investments in IT solutions to facilitate compliance verification. SICON was developed with new IT solutions that centered on the installation of a Teradata relational database management system, integration of operational routines, integration of systems, and improved analytics. With these systems improvements, the time lags for core operational routines were reduced from two days, 22 hours, and 30 minutes, before the new system, to one hour, 27 minutes, for all data processing, including just 4 minutes for education conditionalities data processing, 12 minutes for health data processing, and the remainder for data transfers, validation, and other processing. Those processing times exclude the time needed for any manual transactions, such as the recording of school attendance and health visits by service providers and data entry by municipal coordinators for facilities that do not directly access the system.

Turkey takes cross-sectoral collaboration and automation even further with universal tracking of school attendance and health care use for all individuals (not just CCT beneficiaries) and interoperability of information systems. As such, the Integrated Social Assistance System (ISAS) of the General Directorate of Social Assistance (GDSA) pulls information on CCT beneficiaries from the information systems of the ministries of education and health to verify compliance, as follows:

- The **Ministry of Education** monitors school attendance, absenteeism, and grades for all school-age children from kindergarten through 12th grade through **e-school MIS**, its integrated management information system. School officials routinely capture data for all students in the e-school system.

- Similarly, the **Ministry of Health (MoH)** monitors health care services, utilization, pregnancy, vaccinations, and health visits for all individuals through the **Family Medicine Information System (FMIS)**, which is an integrated health registry hosted by the MoH. FMIS is linked to all relevant public health institutions and contains health-related information on all individuals. There are strict regulations from MoH on health monitoring for women during pregnancy and the postpartum period, and for children from birth until age six. Health officials contact all individuals if they do not show up on time for vaccinations, growth and development visits, health care follow-ups, and so on.
- With the help of systems interoperability and a unique ID, Turkey's **Integrated Social Assistance System (ISAS)**[21] (1) pulls data on the population of CCT beneficiaries whose conditionalities will be monitored for each cycle from e-school MIS and FMIS through web services; (2) monitors compliance with conditionalities; (3) links individuals to households and updates the benefit amounts included in the subsequent payroll, automatically calculating any penalties for noncompliance (with benefits being reduced on a prorated basis for noncomplying members). There is no need for ISAS to generate an updated beneficiary list and distribute it to local offices or education or health service providers because it simply pulls compliance information from e-school MIS and FMIS on the relevant beneficiaries in each conditionalities monitoring cycle.

With these systems, efficiency has greatly improved and compliance verification in Turkey's CCT program is carried out in just a few hours. Before ISAS, the CCT operated its own beneficiary operations management system, which was not linked to other administrative systems. Monitoring of conditionalities was completely paper-based. For each monitoring cycle (monthly for education and bimonthly for health), the beneficiaries themselves were responsible for obtaining compliance verification forms (in hard copy) from the local social assistance offices (SASFs) and visiting education or health facilities to have them approved by the relevant staff. Subsequently, the beneficiaries had to bring the CVFs back to the SASFs. The social workers then entered the data into the beneficiary operations management system. Due to a high volume of forms (especially in big districts), this process took up to two or three months. There were few or no random spot checks or verification of the compliance forms from relevant education and health facilities. With ISAS, the efficiency of conditionalities monitoring was greatly enhanced. With interoperability between ISAS, the Ministry of Education's e-school MIS, the Ministry of Health's FMIS, and numerous other agencies, now ISAS pulls information on education (facility name, grade, class, attendance, school success, and other information) for each beneficiary student from e-school MIS. It pulls information on health (follow-ups, health checks, vaccinations, by facility level) from FMIS for all relevant beneficiaries. ISAS then automatically identifies cases of noncompliance and adjusts benefit levels accordingly (deducting the amount for any noncomplying member). This process now takes just two or three hours.

How to Enforce Consequences? Linking Conditionalities Monitoring and Payment Cycles

CCTs typically try to coordinate the cycles of conditionalities monitoring with payments in their master implementation schedules. As discussed above, the reason is that noncompliance can trigger a reduction in benefits (partial or full; temporary or irrevocable). Therefore, the primary output from conditionalities monitoring feeds into the adjustments of benefit amounts for payroll processing. Table 8A.2 in annex 8A presents the implementation cycles for the CCTs in all nine countries in our sample. In each diagram, we plot the months for the conditionalities monitoring cycle, including the compliance period and the allotted time for the compliance verification period (CVP), recognizing that the latter may differ from actual processing times. We also plot the months corresponding to the payments schedule. Each diagram assumes that these are regular implementation cycles for which conditionalities monitoring would be required and that school is in session (not holiday months).[22] To standardize the format of the schedules across countries, we anchor each calendar with the beginning of the first compliance period.[23]

Some CCTs directly link all payments to conditionalities monitoring and consequences (for consequences of noncompliance, please see table 8A.3 in annex). One example is Turkey's CCT, which has tightly aligned its two-month compliance period with the bimonthly payment cycle. As discussed above, compliance verification takes only two to three hours thanks to continuous universal recording of school attendance and health visits by the ministries of education and health, plus a high degree of interoperability in information systems. This allows ISAS to pull the information immediately after the close of the compliance period, and automatically apply penalties in time for the next bimonthly payment (table 8.5). All six payment cycles are linked to conditionalities monitoring (though the links to education conditionalities are skipped during school holidays).

Table 8.5 Direct Linking of Payments and Conditionalities Monitoring Cycles in Turkey's Conditional Cash Transfer Program

Turkey CCT: Education and health	Month		
	1	2	3
Compliance period	CP1		Continue next cycle . . .
Compliance verification period and link to payroll			CV + links to payroll (2-3 hours)
Payments frequency	Bimonthly		Bimonthly

Sources: Turkey, General Directorate of Social Assistance 2014; Ortakaya 2018; MoH Schedule.

Other CCTs deliberately stagger their schedule so that compliance verification affects only a subset of payments during the year. Not all CCTs link all payments to conditionalities monitoring, nor should they. An example of staggered master-scheduling is Brazil's BFP. The BFP delivers 12 monthly payments per year, but benefit amounts are adjusted for noncompliance just four times per year for education and twice per year for health. That schedule allows for more frequent payments, which has the advantage of providing a regular source of income to beneficiary families, while respecting the time needed for beneficiaries to comply and for administrators to verify compliance. Table 8.6 shows the official calendar for conditionalities, while table 8.7 presents it in our standardized format as is done for other countries (see table 8A.3 in annex 8A).

Some countries have found it necessary to recalibrate their master schedules to allow more time for compliance verification and avoid delays in payments. Prior to recent reforms, a tight schedule for Indonesia's PKH program resulted in bunching of workloads for data entry operators, causing delays in payments. The schedule allotted only one month for compliance verification following the

Table 8.6 Calendar for Conditionalities Monitoring in Brazil's Bolsa Família Program

Type	Compliance period	Allotted time for compliance verification	Enforcement of consequences/links to payments
Education (duration of full cycle: 4 months)	2-month time period	One-month period	Consequences apply on 4th month of the cycle
	February-March	April	May
	April-May	June	July
	August-September	October	November
	October-November	December	March (skip January-February because schools are closed)
Health (duration of full cycle: 9 months)	Six-month time period[a]	Completion requirement	Consequences apply 3 months after the close of the monitoring period
	1st semester: January-June	By July-August	September
	2nd semester: July-December	By January-February	March

Sources: Brazil's MDS BFP Operations Manual 2017; WWP 2016a.
Note: Payments are made on a continuous basis through the banking system. The school year in Brazil runs from February-November
a. Note that when pregnancies are detected, that information is transmitted on a monthly basis as it could allow for the introduction of a new variable benefit for pregnant mothers. All other health information is transmitted on a semestral basis.

Table 8.7 Staggered Linking of Payments and Conditionalities Monitoring Cycles in Brazil's Bolsa Família Program

Brazil BFP: Education	Month 1	2	3	4
Compliance period	CP1 (2 months)		Continue next cycle . . .	
Compliance verification period and link to payroll			CVP1 (actual < 1 month)	Compliance linked to payroll
Payments frequency	Monthly	Monthly	Monthly	Monthly

Brazil BFP: Health	Month 1	2	3	4	5	6	7	8	9
Compliance period	CP1 (6 months compliance period)						Continue next cycle . . .		
Compliance verification period and link to payroll							CVP1 (actual time is less, but 2 months allotted)		Compliance linked to payroll
Payments frequency	Monthly	Monthly	Monthly	Monthly	Monthly	Monthly	Monthly	Monthly	Monthly

Sources: Brazil's MDS BFP Operations Manual 2017; WWP 2016a; Brazil Learning Initiative for a World Without Poverty, http://wwp.org.br.

Table 8.8 Delinking of Conditionalities Monitoring and Payments Cycles in Indonesia's PKH (pre- and post-reforms)

Indonesia PKH: Education and health, prereforms (before 2018)	Month 1	2	3	4	5	6
Compliance period	CP1			Continue next cycle . . .		
Compliance verification period and link to payroll				CVP1 (1 month allotted)	Compliance linked to payroll	
Payments frequency		Quarterly	Often delayed . . .		Quarterly	Often delayed . . .

Indonesia PKH: Education and health (since 2018)	Month 1	2	3	4	5	6
Compliance period	CP1 (3 months)			Continue next cycle . . .		
Compliance verification period and link to payroll				CVP1 (2 months allotted in schedule)		Compliance linked to payroll
Payments frequency			Quarterly			Quarterly

Source: Indonesia, Ministry of Social Affairs 2016.

end of the three-month compliance period (first panel of table 8.8). Facilitators would print CVFs, visit the service providers (schools, health facilities), and record compliance data for all of the individuals in their caseloads. They would bring the CVFs to the data entry operators, who would compile and enter all data into the management information system (MIS) via the e-PKH web app (or scan forms into the PKH MIS). MoSA/JSK would receive the data, check quality, enter compliance decisions into the MIS, and then update the payroll for payments processing. According to the master schedule, those conditionalities verification processes had to be carried out in one month—for millions of children (both school and health conditionalities) and hundreds of thousands of women (health conditionalities) at thousands of facilities all over the country. The tight schedule led to significant bottlenecks in terms of server overload, incomplete data submission, and low-quality data. In 2018, reforms recalibrated the cycles for conditionalities monitoring and payments to allow more time for compliance verification (second panel of table 8.8). The allotted time for compliance verification and processing is now two months instead of one, with period 1 compliance informing benefit amounts for period 2 payments.

Performance Indicators for Conditionalities Monitoring Systems

While the primary objective is to verify compliance for individual beneficiaries, metadata generated from conditionalities monitoring systems can also be used to monitor the performance of CCT programs and their delivery systems. Most CCTs focus on tracking overall compliance rates, measured as the number of beneficiaries in each category with verified compliance as a share of those who were monitored. However, as discussed below, compliance rates can be misleading if only a small share of the total number of beneficiaries in each category is monitored. Ideally, both compliance rates and monitoring rates are tracked. It is important to report these indicators for each category of beneficiaries, or at least for education and health separately, and not just at the household level since behavioral expectations vary by group (as discussed above). Some countries, such as Jamaica, even track school attendance for boys and girls separately—which is considered good practice.

Most monitored beneficiaries do comply with the required conditionalities. Compliance rates average

Figure 8.15 Compliance Rates for Education and Health Conditionalities in Select Countries' Conditional Cash Transfer Programs

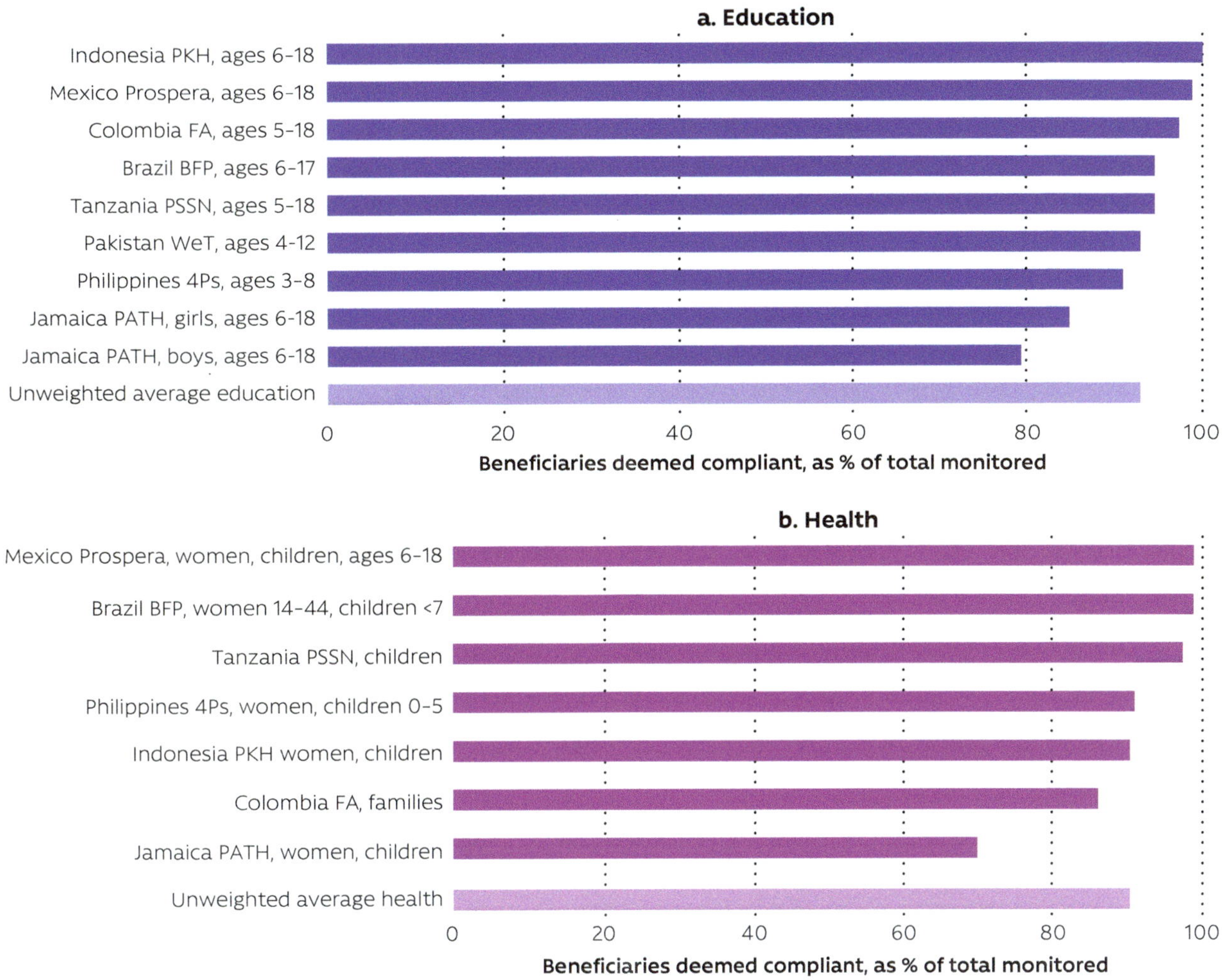

Sources: Brazil BFP: SICON—Sistema de Condicionalidades—DECON/SENARC/MDS, data for September 2018. Colombia FA: Prosperidad Social, data for August to September 2017. Indonesia PKH: MoSA PMIS, data gathered for 2nd Social Assistance Reform Supervision Report for period from April to July 2018. Jamaica PATH: MLSS Beneficiary Management Information System, data for August 2018. Mexico—Prospera: SIIOP, education data for 2017; Servicios Estatales de Salud e IMSS-Prospera, November to December 2017. Pakistan—WeT CCT: WeT MIS, data from quarter ending April 2018. The Philippines—4Ps: DSWD 4 Ps Program Implementation Status Report for First Quarter of 2018; compliance data for December 2017 to January 2018. Tanzania PSSN CCT: TASAF III PSSN MIS for 2018.

92 percent for school attendance and 90 percent for compliance with health conditionalities for the CCTs in our sample (figure 8.15). In several countries, nearly all beneficiaries complied. Compliance rates are a bit lower in Colombia (for health) and Jamaica, where a decline in compliance rates over time prompted an in-depth evaluation to delve into the factors underlying noncompliance.

However, not all programs track monitoring rates. We define monitoring rates as the number of monitored beneficiaries in each category as a share of the total number of beneficiaries in that category.[24] Some programs do not track these rates for all categories, and some adopt different definitions. Most of the challenges relate to monitoring of health conditionalities, which are more complex than conditionalities for education, as discussed below. For example, Mexico's Prospera program tracked conditionalities only for beneficiaries who had registered at health clinics. Thus, its records show the monitoring rate to be 100 percent because the program had information for all of the clinic registrants. However, because Prospera did not track beneficiaries who had not registered at clinics, those beneficiaries were not monitored. The Philippines's 4Ps tracks only children who were ages 0–5 and women who were pregnant at the time of the last Listahahan registration in 2015.[25]

Moreover, programs that track monitoring rates find that not all beneficiaries are monitored. For programs for which we have comparable data, monitoring rates average 87 percent for school attendance and 84 percent for health (figure 8.16). The variance across programs is high, ranging from 39 percent for education and 33 percent for health in some CCTs to virtually all beneficiaries in others. Those unweighted averages for health do not include data for Mexico and the Philippines because differences in reporting would overstate monitoring rates, for reasons discussed above.

Figure 8.16 Monitoring Rates for Education and Health Conditionalities in Select Countries' Conditional Cash Transfer Programs

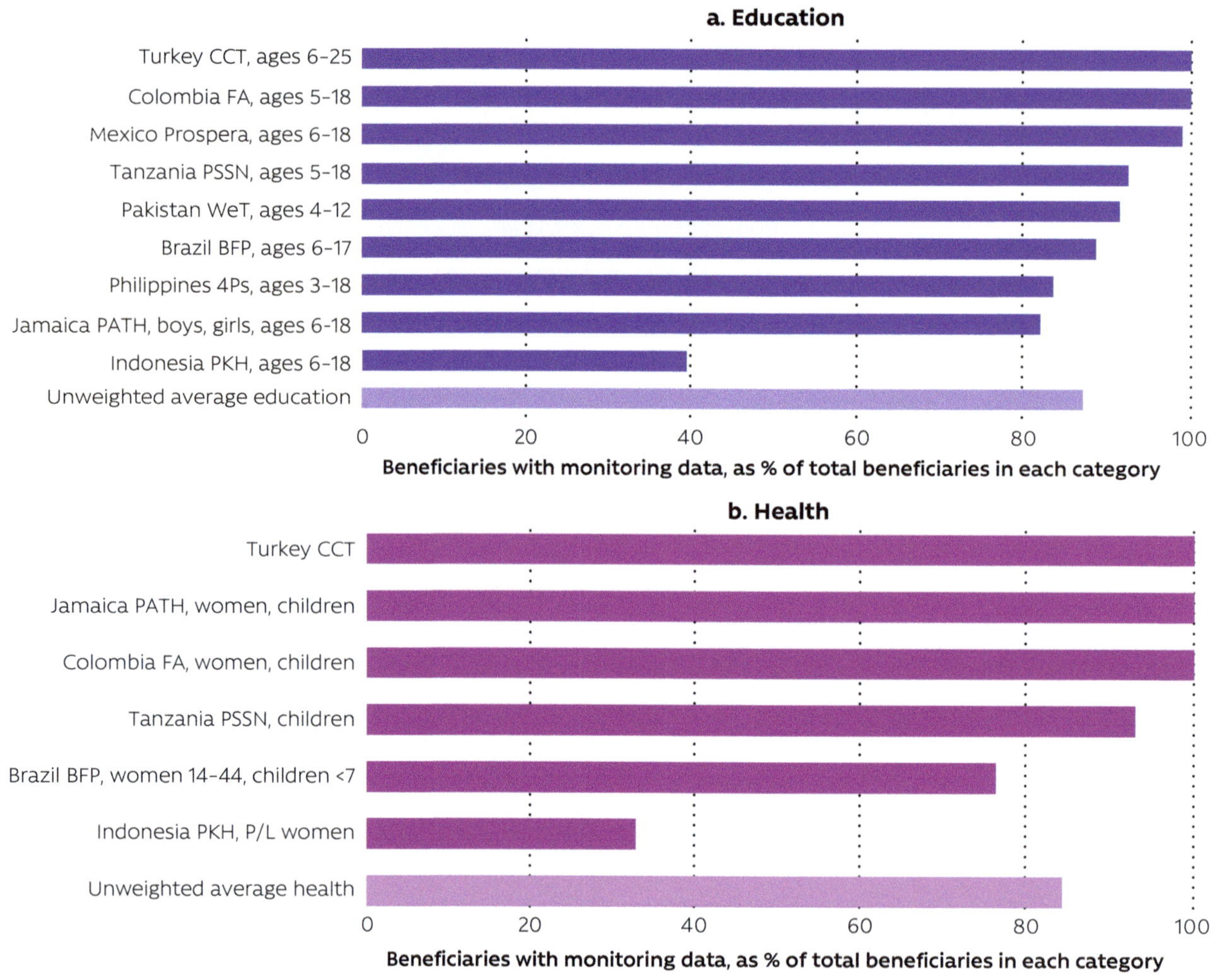

Sources: Brazil BFP: SICON—Sistema de Condicionalidades—DECON/SENARC/MDS, data for May 2018. Colombia FA: Prosperidad Social, data for August to September 2017. Indonesia PKH: MoSA PMIS, data gathered for 2nd Social Assistance Reform Supervision Report for period from April to July 2018. Jamaica PATH: MLSS Beneficiary Management Information System, data for August 2018. Mexico—Prospera: SIIOP, education data for 2017. Pakistan—WeT CCT: WeT MIS, data from quarter ending April 2018. The Philippines—4Ps: DSWD Updates on Pantawid Pamilyang Pilipino Program as of May 2018. Tanzania PSSN CCT: TASAF III PSSN MIS for 2018. Turkey CCT: Ortakaya 2018.
Note: P/L = pregnant/lactating.

Most CCTs have explicit policies to avoid penalizing beneficiaries for lack of compliance information. In Brazil, this lack of information is viewed as a potential failure on behalf of the state or service or an extreme vulnerability on behalf of the beneficiary,[26] and the policy of not penalizing beneficiaries for lack of information is consistent with their nonpunitive approach to conditionalities more generally. In Jamaica, similarly, PATH grants compliance overrides to beneficiaries in schools or health centers where the compliance listing is insufficient or incomplete for the compliance period, in order to avoid punishing beneficiaries in those facilities. In Pakistan, in the case of nonreporting schools, the BOMS generates prompts with a form for all noncompliant schools, which leads to a school follow-up with the relevant education departments and a notification of families. Beneficiary children are marked "compliant" for nonreporting schools for up to three quarters.

Why is it that CCTs do not monitor compliance for all beneficiaries? In general, the task of monitoring conditionalities is complex, requiring vertical collaboration between the central and local actors, and horizontal cooperation across sectors and agencies. It also requires management of updated information on numerous beneficiary households (whose composition, locations, and beneficiary status can change for other reasons) as well as individual members and their own use of education and health services at thousands of service points across the country on a continuous basis.

Many factors could underpin nonreporting of conditionalities compliance. One possibility is that information in beneficiary rosters, such as beneficiaries changing address or service provider or exiting the household, has not been updated. Another factor could include supply-side factors, such as the school or health facility not providing (complete) information for that implementation cycle. Or, more ominously, beneficiaries who are not monitored could have dropped out of school or failed to use the health services, suggesting important vulnerabilities that should be addressed to nudge them to comply or help remove obstacles to human capital investments.[27] Without further examination, by definition, it is impossible to know why there is no compliance information. Brazil conducted such an investigation to diagnose gaps in monitoring conditionalities in 2014. During that period, compliance information for education was not available for 10.8 percent of beneficiary school-age children. Of those, 63 percent of the children and youth were not found (the student's school was unknown), and schools failed to provide attendance information for 37 percent. For health, compliance information was not available for 26.7 percent of beneficiary families. Of those, 83 percent were not visited during that compliance period, 4 percent were visited but not monitored, 2.7 percent were partially monitored and recorded (at least one member was not recorded), and 11.2 percent were not found at the address in their record.

Monitoring conditionalities is particularly complex for health. With school attendance, a known set of beneficiaries are expected to be in a specific location at a specific time, five days a week during the school year. With health care, from a program administrator's point of view, pregnancy and childbirth are "random events" that can occur at unknown times and unknown locations. Even for children, the date when their parents bring them to the health clinic for their checkups may not coincide with the scheduled collection of compliance verification forms, especially for older children, who are required to visit the health centers less frequently. These difficulties are apparent in the incomplete monitoring data for beneficiaries of CCTs. Moreover, Tanzania's PSSN CCT has dropped conditionalities for pregnant women because of difficulties in monitoring compliance.

Brazil and Turkey have addressed these challenges by monitoring everyone. Rather than waiting until a pregnancy is reported, Brazil monitors all beneficiary women of potential childbearing age (14 to 44) continuously, to ensure that they are all connected to the health system even in advance of a pregnancy.[28] Turkey's Ministry of Health universally tracks health care use for all citizens (not just beneficiaries), and the CCT simply pulls information on program beneficiaries to check for compliance. For both countries, continuously monitoring the full (target) population has helped reduce the unpredictability surrounding health care utilization for people in specific states of being (such as pregnancy, childbirth, or aging).

The rapid expansion of CCTs' coverage also makes systematic monitoring of conditionalities challenging, especially in large countries. This has been the experience of Indonesia, where the PKH program expanded from 3.5 million families in 2016 to 6 million in 2017 and 10 million in 2018, more than tripling over those two years to become the second largest CCT in the world, after Brazil's BFP. That rapid scaling-up was not immediately matched by a strengthening of delivery systems, which were monitoring only about half of program beneficiaries even before the expansion. Full monitoring would mean tracking the daily attendance of 12.4 million school children, as well as health care visits by 3.2 million young children and nearly 200,000 pregnant or postpartum women, in a country of 13,000 inhabited islands now spanned by PKH operations in all 520 districts and more than 7,000 subdistricts.

Conditionalities monitoring was also hampered by rapid expansion in Brazil's Bolsa Família Program, requiring systems improvements. In the early years of the program, coverage increased from 3.4 million families at the time of its launch in October 2003 to 11 million families by mid-2006, and to 14 million during the economic crisis. Brazil's challenge of monitoring conditionalities while scaling up is evident in figure 8.17. During the transition year from October 2003 to October 2004, MDS temporarily stopped requiring municipalities to consolidate and transmit information for monitoring of compliance. The hiatus reflected the conceptual and legal transitions of the program during the reform period, as well as the inevitable systems challenges in transitioning from pre-reform CCTs to the BFP even as the program doubled in size. Central monitoring of compliance with education conditionalities resumed in late 2004 following a legal decree, and health conditionalities monitoring was launched in 2005. Even still, it took several years, significant systems improvements, extensive cooperation between MDS and the Ministries of Education and Health, and direct collaboration with counterparts in 5,570 municipalities before monitoring of conditionalities reached its current levels of 88 percent for school attendance and 77 percent for health care. This level of coverage is no small accomplishment in a country as large and diverse as Brazil, or for a program as large as the BFP, which tracks the daily school attendance of over 14 million children in 160,000 schools nationwide, and the health care visits of about 9 million women and young children in facilities across the country.

Monitoring and Enforcement of Conditionalities: Checklist Summary

This section sought to examine how countries monitor and enforce conditionalities for CCTs as a key phase on the delivery chain. A summary checklist of design and implementation considerations includes the following:

- ***For monitoring conditionalities.*** Use "swim lanes" process maps (see chapter 2) to chart implementation steps across actors; keep it simple: do not over-bureaucratize the processes or overburden the actors (human-centered design principles and journey mapping can help; see chapter 2); explore the possibility of leveraging interoperability and information systems to help automate and expedite processes; do not forget the importance of communicating with beneficiaries regarding changes in their compliance status; facilitate channels for grievances; consider incorporating social work accompaniment to follow up with noncomplying families to help diagnose and remove obstacles to compliance and facilitate their attendance at school and their use of health care services.
- ***For enforcing penalties.*** Coordinate the conditionalities monitoring cycle and the payment cycle in the master calendar to allow time for benefit adjustments associated with compliance verification to feed back into the payroll; consider staggering the schedule so that not all payments link to compliance verification; be realistic about the time lapses between compliance periods and the enforcement of financial penalties.
- ***Performance.*** Monitor both the compliance rates and the monitoring rates.

Finally, for those who may be deterred by the amount of effort required to monitor conditionalities, it is important to remember the significant effects that CCTs have demonstrated in countless impact evaluations. Those effects are stronger for CCTs than for UCTs, and studies suggest that both compliance monitoring and compliance enforcement matter. We conjecture that the link between incentives and behaviors may have less to do with the actual imposition of financial penalties and more to do with monitoring. Very few beneficiaries face

Figure 8.17 The Triple Challenge of Rapid Expansion: Evolving Systems and Monitoring Conditionalities in Brazil's Bolsa Família Program

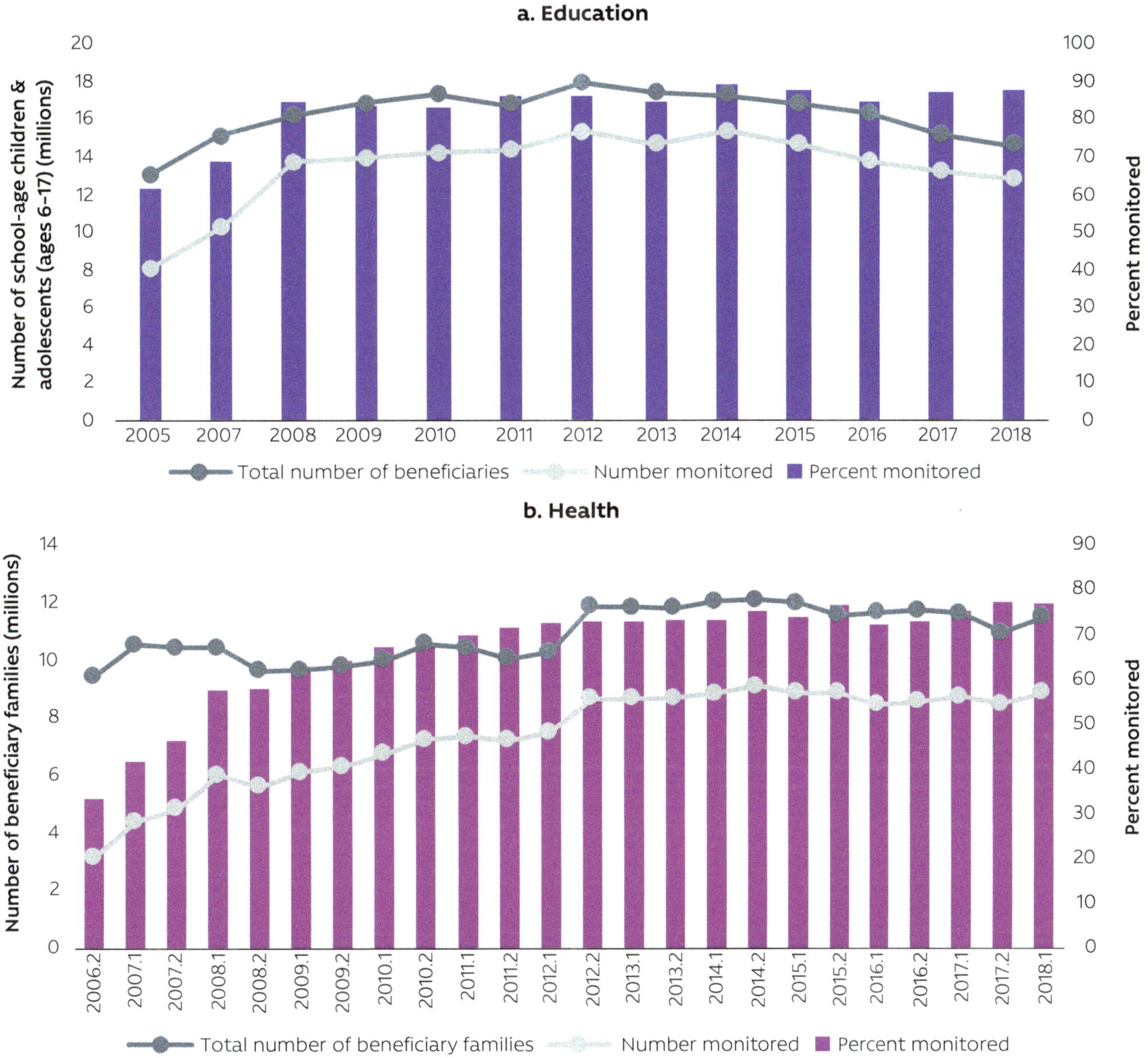

Sources: Brazilian government sources MDS/SICON/DECON/SENARC with data from the Sistema de Accompanhamento de Frecuencia Escolar (Sistema Presenca); Sistema PBF Saude.

financial penalties, and when they do the amounts are relatively small and distant from the timing of expected behaviors. Since most beneficiaries comply, it could be that the mere threat of benefit losses helps incentivize behavioral change. Given that the poor live month-to-month, however, the strength of these penalties seems rather blunt. Instead, the strong effects measured in impact evaluations for CCTs may derive from the act of monitoring.

Monitoring compliance with conditionalities provides a behavioral nudge for families to invest in human capital. Just knowing their behaviors are being monitored may incite people to comply. They receive a stream of regular nudges at critical moments: (1) by teachers and health workers who record their attendance; (2) by program personnel who accompany the families and collect that data from service providers; (3) by the "system" if it issues formal notifications or warnings when noncompliance is detected;

and (4) by social workers in programs that provide additional supports and counseling in response to the flags of persistent noncompliance that are raised. This additional support can help diagnose the reasons for noncompliance, help families remove obstacles to compliance and better connect to services, and correct information errors. These nudges bring together the benefits of social protection with the services of education and health.

Future impact evaluations could dig into the question of whether it is monitoring or enforcement of conditionalities that matters most. While it is beyond the scope of this Sourcebook to answer that question, this unpacking of "the black box of implementation" helps untangle the process or at least suggest some of the key aspects of implementation that should be assessed.

8.4 MONITORING COMPLIANCE WITH LABOR PROGRAM CONDITIONALITIES

Labor and Activation Requirements

Applying conditions for continued receipt of unemployment benefits or activation programs serves two functions. First, introducing conditionalities reduces the moral hazard problem of beneficiaries accepting cash transfers without seeking opportunities for gainful employment. Many governments and societies place significant policy weight on "co-responsibility" between the state and the individual and are concerned about the work disincentives that unconditional cash transfers may engender. The United States and the United Kingdom, for example, have both implemented policy changes over the last several decades to ensure tighter conditions on social protection transfers generally and unemployment benefits in particular. Many East Asian countries also stress productive employment and as a result have limited or nonexistent unemployment insurance programs, including Indonesia, Thailand, and until recently, Malaysia.

Second, conditionalities can function as a targeting mechanism. In theory, strict conditions that are monitored closely encourage only those people who most need assistance to apply for and receive benefits while those who can find suitable employment more quickly will not go through the effort of program compliance. Many countries also maintain a variety of cash and in-kind social safety net programs intended to assist the poor and those most vulnerable to poverty. Labor and activation interventions may complement safety nets, but they need not be considered substitutes and frequently have more intensive monitoring requirements. Many academic papers and models over the last 30 years have been devoted to determining the optimal balance between the provision of benefits and monitoring of conditions and sanctions under different labor market assumptions. Distinguishing between these cases in practice is not always easy.

The existence of this trade-off between strict enforcement of conditionalities and provision of benefits is even more salient given the changing nature of work globally, with persistent informality and more frequent changes in job profiles over workers' lives. Traditional labor programs, including unemployment insurance (UI), unemployment assistance (UA) and active labor market programs (ALMPs) such as job search assistance and training were all designed to respond to a formalized labor market. Jobs are, for the most part, expected to be long term, with regular pensionable salaries and other benefits. UI and UA are provided to bridge the relatively rare gaps in job spells, while job search assistance and training are intended to get the individual back into a job as quickly as possible, preferably in the same industry or occupation. This scenario no longer prevails in many countries, and never did in most developing countries. Most workers hold informal jobs with irregular or lump-sum wage payments and limited or no benefits offered by employers. Many young people will experience many different jobs over their working lives, often in several different occupations or industries, sometimes going from informal to formal employment or the reverse.

The nature of labor market programs will need to change to respond to the new world of work. Assistance will need to be integrated more directly with other forms of social protection, including cash transfers and safety nets and portable social insurance mechanisms. Activation strategies will need to anticipate the wide variety of employment relationships and avenues to move into productive employment. Similarly, monitoring of beneficiaries and the types of conditionalities may need to evolve as well. However, this section will focus on monitoring compliance with conditionalities as it is practiced currently.

Most labor programs have similar initial eligibility requirements. Three are commonly applied to an individual seeking benefits: (1) a minimum history in the labor force prior to unemployment. This minimum is often referred to as the period of labor force "attachment." This eligibility condition applies particularly in the case of UI, which is funded partially by payroll taxes and employer contributions. If an individual has just started working or has only had short spells of temporary employment, he or she has not contributed enough to the insurance system to warrant receiving benefits; (2) the cause of unemployment is due to an involuntary separation from the job, not as a result of firing for cause or voluntary quitting; and (3) the ability and willingness of the individual to seek and accept suitable employment.

Ongoing eligibility conditionalities follow from the initial requirements. To continue to receive benefits, the individual must demonstrate

- the ability and willingness of the individual to seek and accept suitable employment.
- participation in specified ALMPs.

This section of the chapter will focus on monitoring continuing eligibility conditionalities in labor programs. The next subsection looks at how labor conditionalities are monitored, describing both typical institutional arrangements and the processes for monitoring. The last subsection concludes with a review of selected experience with performance indicators and compliance with monitoring systems.

How Are Labor Conditionalities Monitored?

Verifying and monitoring compliance with program-specific conditionalities is a critical function of beneficiary operations management in all labor market programs. Many social safety net cash transfer programs assess initial eligibility for benefits once until a reassessment is conducted much later, sometimes after years. Labor activation programs typically involve frequent monitoring of compliance conditions on a weekly or monthly basis.

Institutional Arrangements

The public employment service (PES) is the dominant form of organization for the provision of employment services. The PES is a government agency that helps job seekers and employers by delivering job search support, counseling and placement services, labor market information, and support for improving employability of job seekers through ALMPs such as training for employment and self-employment or entrepreneurship. Not all PES provide the entire range of services, but many are expanding the types of services offered, stressing ALMPs. A global study of 73 countries found that at least half had expanded the availability of employment services to priority population groups between 2014 and 2016 (ILO 2018). Some PES also provide unemployment benefits and related subsidies, although in many cases UI/UA is managed by a separate dedicated agency in the Ministry of Labor or Social Security. In nearly all countries, the PES reports to the Ministry of Labor or other central authority, with its own organizational line structure and offices. In some cases, the PES reports directly and in others the PES is more autonomous but is supervised by the central authority. For example, in the Middle East and North Africa (MENA) region, the Arab Republic of Egypt and Jordan provide ALMPs through a department within the Ministry of Labor; while in Lebanon, Morocco, and Tunisia the programs are administered by independent public employment agencies supervised by the Ministry of Labor.

In some countries, there is a greater focus on the activation of social assistance recipients along with unemployed job seekers. In the past, and still in many countries, social safety net programs are organized and managed in separate ministries with vertical linkages to localities through safety net program offices, while national PES organizations focused on the insured unemployed and more job-ready clients (Mosley 2011). Since the early 2000s, the activation of social assistance beneficiaries has become a greater focus of labor market policy. In some countries such as Finland, Germany, North Macedonia, and Norway this has taken the form of mandated cooperation between social service agencies and the PES, or even a uniform responsibility for both insured unemployed and activated social assistance beneficiaries (e.g, Denmark and Serbia).

Historically, the number of caseworkers and counselors available to handle job seekers in activation programs has been limited. This is still the case in many developing countries. Low-income and developing countries often do not have trained caseworkers available, focusing primarily on cash transfer assistance or forms of automated job search. The International Labour Organization recommends an average staff caseload of 100. Caseloads in practice are often much higher. Recent studies of public employment services around the world have found that Europe averaged about 170 job seekers per PES staff member, with some European and Central Asian countries with caseloads exceeding 500 (Kosovo, North Macedonia, Turkey).[29] East Asian and the Pacific countries average just over 280. However, MENA, Africa, and Latin American countries each averaged between 2,100 and 5,200 job seekers per staff member. The high number of job seekers per office makes effective expansion into ALMPs and assistance to job seekers more difficult. Among high income countries, caseloads have decreased on average in recent years, potentially improving meaningful engagement with job aspirants and making the task of monitoring conditionalities more effective.

Many countries increasingly outsource employment activation services to the private sector or nongovernmental organizations (NGOs). The traditional model of a centralized PES providing all activation services is still the most common, but is changing over time, both because of the expense and inefficiency associated with government provision as well as the importance of linking training and services more closely to the employment needs of the private sector. Approximately two-thirds of PES surveyed globally in 2014 were responsible for delivery of all employment services. The remaining one-third outsourced or coordinated service delivery provided by other organizations or the private sector.[30] Only a few countries rely exclusively on private services or a combined network of public, private, and nonprofit organizations, including Australia, Colombia, Denmark, Switzerland, and the United Kingdom.

There are several examples of countries using private services extensively. In Denmark, for example, local PES offices have a high degree of autonomy to organize and contract activation services independently. In Honduras, the National Employment Service of Honduras (SENAEH) has partnered with private organizations to comanage and cofinance employment services. The staff and supplies to provide the services are also provided by the private sector.[31] India's National Skills Development Agency is a nonprofit public limited company under (and funded by) the Ministry of Skill Development and Entrepreneurship which funds private enterprises and organizations that provide skill training across the country. Jobactive Australia (JSA) relies heavily on results-based contracting for the delivery of employment services. JSA has a one-stop shop/service center concept that refers all the registered unemployed to providers based on a competitive contract paying a standard service fee plus a bonus both for results and for serving the hard-to-place job seekers. The United Kingdom's Jobcentre Plus provides payments to contractors depending on job placement outcomes and the sustainability of jobs in terms of length of retention. This is also the case in Germany, where a placement voucher entitles the job seeker to use a private agency. If the voucher leads to employment, the agency receives a predetermined percentage of the payment at insertion and the remainder six months after placement.

Box 8.2 provides a detailed example of how employment services are organized and delivered through a full-service PES for North Macedonia.

Processes for Monitoring Conditionalities

In almost all countries, monitoring of labor conditionalities starts from the development of an individualized action plan (IAP) for the job seeker.[32] The job seeker enters labor activation programs typically through a local office located near the job seeker's residence, usually the PES office, but sometimes a specialized unemployment benefits office or social welfare office. Once the job seeker has completed application formalities and is enrolled, an IAP is developed in consultation with an assigned caseworker or counselor. See chapters 4 and 5 of this Sourcebook for more on the intake, registration, needs assessment eligibility determination, and enrollment processes. The IAP sets out the activities that the job seeker will be expected to undertake, including a set of mutual obligations that the job seeker and various service providers are to fulfill over the course of participation

Box 8.2 Providing Employment Services in North Macedonia

North Macedonia offers a range of unemployment benefits and activation services. Together with the Ministry of Labor and Social Policy (MOLSP), the Employment Service Agency (ESA)—the country's public employment service—is responsible for implementing the national employment policy. The ESA is an independent public institution reporting to MOLSP responsible for (1) collecting and disseminating labor market information; (2) providing employment counseling and career guidance; (3) providing job placement; and (4) administering passive (unemployment insurance) and active labor market programs. It is funded from a combination of government budget resources (about 75 percent of the total) and contributions from unemployment insurance.

The ESA has several departments and a local presence in many areas. In 2014, ESA has one central office, one employment center in the capital, Skopje, 29 local employment centers, and 16 outreach offices with a total of 473 on staff. The ESA central office has 54 on staff and is divided into units including Unemployment Insurance, Active Employment Policies, Research and Analysis, and several administrative and supporting units such as Information Technology and Human Resources.

The mix of duties assigned to staff depends on the availability of human resources, the number of registered unemployed allocated to the local office, and the overall volume of work to be carried out. On average, there are 378 job seekers for each front office staff member, with more than 80 percent of staff designated to engage with job seekers. In practice, the administration of the unemployment benefit is managed by specialized counselors only in the larger employment centers. In most of the smaller offices, frontline staff cover all employment services (registration, counseling, guidance, vacancy registration, job placement, recording of work contracts, and administering passive and active measures).

All job seekers apply for benefits at an employment center and are listed on the ESA unemployment register. "Active" job seekers are those available to take up work and are actively looking for a job. The ESA has a well-developed set of web-based self-help services for employers and job seekers. Only active job seekers meet with a dedicated counselor or frontline staff to develop an individual employment plan and are referred for training or other services.

Unemployment insurance and social welfare recipients are required to actively search for work, and refusing a job offer or an opportunity for training/retraining twice is sanctioned with the loss of benefits. Recipients can be reinstated after demonstrating job search activities and participation in training.

Source: Summary from Corbanese (2015).

in the program. Box 8.3 highlights the requirements for a cross section of participants in the Jobactive program, Australia's primary labor activation initiative.

The obligations, or conditionalities, often vary by the type of job seeker. Individuals who have lost employment may have an emphasis placed on a short-term job search, accompanied by counselling, whereas long-term unemployed may have a larger skill training component. Younger individuals or out-of-school youth may have a combination of training elements, apprenticeship, or on-the-job training to prepare them for entry-level employment or even entrepreneurship assistance.

Based on the particular activities included in the IAP, conditionalities are tracked at various points of interaction between the job seeker and the service provider or potential employer, recorded and processed through the verification system, feeding back to the IAP and sometimes resulting in sanctions. Figure 8.18 illustrates a general compliance verification process for a typical labor activation program. It identifies key verification steps under the responsibility of each of the main actors, the job seeker; the employment service officer, caseworker, or other service provider; the social service office, and finally, the central-level ministry or department.

The verification process starts after the job seeker has agreed to an IAP with the caseworker and begins activation activities. For UI/UA programs without ALMPs, reporting is generally only on job

Box 8.3 Australia Jobactive Mutual Obligation Requirements

Under the Jobactive program, the main employment services program in Australia, after job seekers are assessed by the Job Seeker Classification Instrument and placed in a job stream, they develop a job plan that identifies activities and requirements to transition to employment. A set of "mutual obligation requirements" are shared with job seekers at the time they enroll in one of the component programs. These obligations must be fulfilled to continue to receive income support payments. Obligations include regular attendance of service provider appointments and minimum job search requirements. In addition, job seekers must meet an annual activity requirement which determines the number of hours and time frame over which activities must be undertaken. Failure to comply with the mutual obligation requirements and the job plan results in sanctioning of cash assistance and can lead to termination.

The table below details the requirements for different streams of job seekers up to 30 years of age. An individual job seeker's mutual obligation requirements will vary depending on their age and stream placement. For example, in addition to the "work for the dole" phase, a job seeker will progress through a case management phase, and those in stream A (general) will have a "self-service and job activity" phase for their first six months under the Jobactive program. Other requirements in different phases, including job search frequency and hours of annual activity, are shown in the table.

Table B8.3.1 Mutual Obligation Requirements: Job Seekers up to 30 Years of Age

<table>
<tr><th>Period of service</th><th>Stream A (general)</th><th>Stream B (general)</th><th>Stream C</th></tr>
<tr><td>0–6 months</td><td>Self-service and job activity
• appointments
• job search (20 per month)
• other suitable activities</td><td>Case management
• appointments
• job search (20 per month)
• other suitable activities</td><td>Case management
• appointments
• job search (depends on capacity)
• other suitable activities</td></tr>
<tr><td>6–12 months</td><td colspan="2">Case management
• appointments
• job search (20 per month)
• other suitable activities</td><td>Case management
• appointments
• job search (depends on capacity)
• other suitable activities</td></tr>
<tr><td>12–18 months
24–30 months
Etc.</td><td colspan="3">"Work for the dole" phase
• appointments
• job search (depends on capacity)
• Annual activity requirement: 650 hours over 26 weeks (50 hours per two weeks), work for the dole as the principle activity</td></tr>
<tr><td>18–24 months
30–36 months
Etc.</td><td colspan="2">Case management
• appointments
• job search (20 per month)
• other suitable activities</td><td>Case Management
• appointments
• job search (depends on capacity)
• other suitable activities</td></tr>
</table>

Source: ANAO Annual Report 2017–18, Australian National Audit Office, table A.2. https://www.anao.gov.au/sites/default/files/ANAO_Report_2017-18_04.pdf.

Figure 8.18 Labor Program Compliance Verification

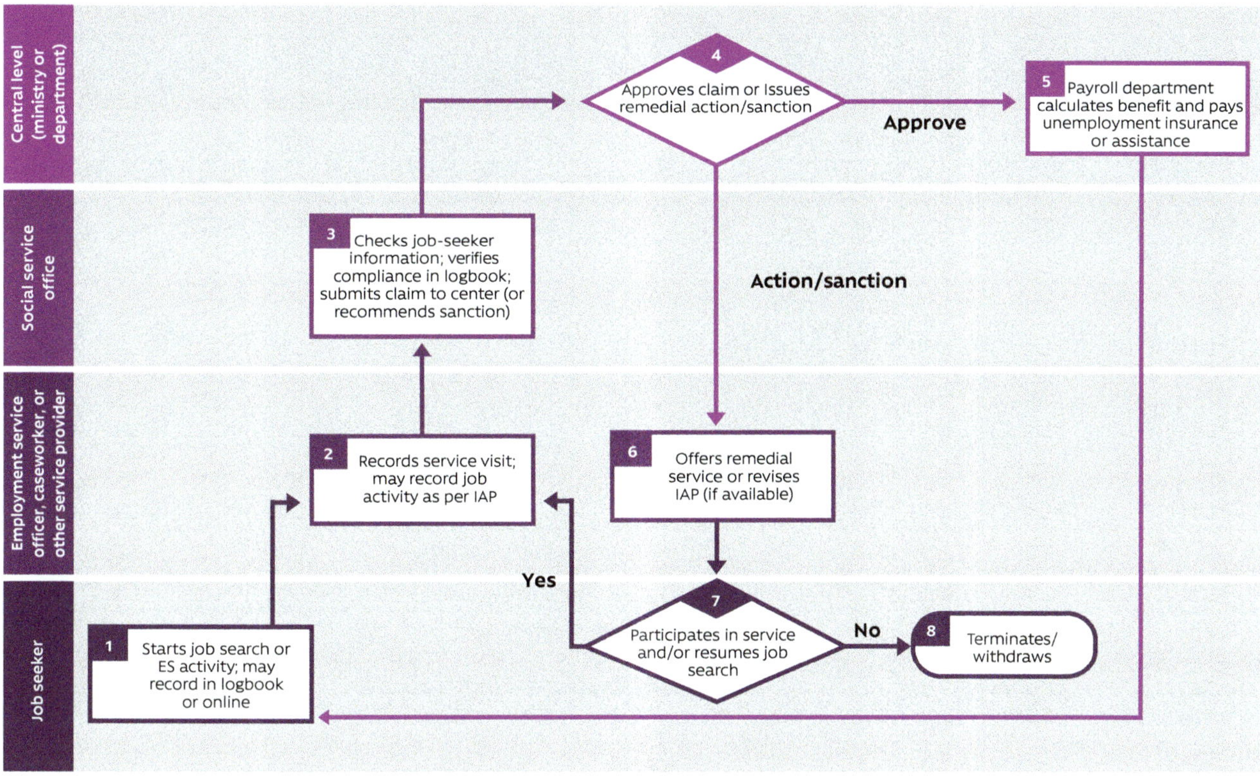

Source: Original figure for this publication.
Note: ES = employment service; IAP = individualized action plan.

search activities, including reasons for not accepting an employment offer. For ALMPs or combined activation programs, reporting would include participation in counseling and training as well as job search activities. In many countries, job seekers report their participation activities directly, either using a paper-based log book or using online software. In the case of activation services such as counseling or training, usually the service provider records participation by the job seeker. At this stage, there is no checking or verification of the veracity of job-seeker reporting.

At a predetermined interval, a meeting with the caseworker or employment service office will be scheduled. During these meetings, the caseworker reviews progress with the job seeker on IAP activities and goals and checks the log book of job interviews and services. In addition to regular meetings, there are intensive interviews with job seekers to review or adapt the IAP given the pace of employment progress. The interviews can be quite lengthy, up to an hour in some cases when the IAP is being adjusted or new activities are being incorporated.

The frequency of intensive interviews varies according to the program rules and the profile of the job seeker. Table 8.9 summarizes the interview frequency, caseload, and other characteristics of several OECD PES programs. The table suggests that many programs require an intensive interview every one to three months. In the United Kingdom, interviews are scheduled regularly after the initial claim to receive a benefit allowance, first after 13 weeks, then at 26 weeks and 52 weeks for those who remain unemployed. These dates correspond to the trigger dates for different benefits, including extended benefit payments, disability allowance, mortgage support, and others. In programs relying heavily on online reporting and follow-up, in-person interviews may be less frequent, as in the case of Denmark.

Often, individuals report directly to the local PES agency or record search and interviews individually or online on a weekly or monthly basis. This is often done in person rather than online and case officers will verify the reports by selectively calling potential employers with whom the job seeker has claimed to

Table 8.9 Timing and Follow-Up of IAPs, Caseloads, and ALMP Participation in Select OECD Public Employment Services, 2009/10

	Austria	Denmark	Germany		United Kingdom	Switzerland
			SGB II (welfare)	SGB III (insurance)		
Timing of IAP and first intensive interview	90% of cases by 4 weeks after registration	Target: IAP by start of activation phase Actual first interview: 11 weeks after registration, on average	Target: 10–15 days Actual: 15.4 days after registration, on average	5.5 days after registration, on average	Target: JSA 6 weeks after claim; ESA 8 weeks after claim	Target: 15 days Actual: 12.6 days, on average
Monitoring job search	Every job interview	Weekly, online	Every job interview		Every 2 weeks, in person	Every job interview
Frequency of interviews	Every 37 days, on average	Target: every 3 months Actual: variable	Based on client profile Job-ready and complex profiles: every 3–4 months, on average Activation clients: every 1–2 months, on average		Target: after 13, 26, and 52 weeks Actual: 86% achievement rate	Target: monthly Actual: variable
Duration of interviews	Counseling zone		Recommended:	Recommended:		
Initial	30 min. average	n.a.	60 minutes	60 minutes	40 min. average	n.a.
Follow-up	24 min. average	n.a.	Based on client profile	30–45 minutes	7 min. average	n.a.
Caseload (staff-to-client ratio)	Service zone: 1:257 Counseling zone: 1:142	n.a.	Ages <25, 1:79 Ages <25, 1:160	1:142	1:142	1:100
Participation in ALMP	Adviser decision Compulsory once agreed in IAP	Age-dependent activation Compulsory once agreed in IAP	Adviser decision Compulsory once agreed in IAP Immediate offer of work or education for welfare clients ages <25		Referral to work program conditional on type/age of benefit claim	Adviser decision Compulsory once referred by caseworker

Source: Konle-Seidl 2012.

Note: ALMP = active labor market program; ESA = employment support allowance; IAP = individualized action plan; JSA = job-seeker allowance; n.a. = not applicable; OECD = Organisation for Economic Co-operation and Development; SGB = *Sozialgesetzbuch* (Social Code).

be in contact. For example, the Temporary Assistance to Needy Families (TANF) program in the United States requires individuals to provide weekly time sheets to the caseworker to track work participation. The United Kingdom has recently intensified monitoring, checking nearly half of all unemployment benefit claimants each week instead of every two weeks, in part to investigate the effectiveness of different monitoring procedures. In the Netherlands, benefit claimants must provide full details of job search activity upon request and must document all search activities online. Countries in Latin America and the Caribbean vary in their job search requirements. Brazil's PES (Sistema Nacional de Emprego [SINE]), for example, does not have an active job search requirement, but limits receipt of UI to five months and does not allow new labor market entrants to receive benefits. In Poland, the caseworker or employment officer, rather than the individual job seeker, is responsible for documenting job search activities and identifying a violation in search compliance. The emphasis on caseworker documentation, as in Poland, is not common in most PES, however; in some countries, job search has moved toward greater use of online job portals and digital search diaries which caseworkers can check at their own discretion without requiring formal reporting by the UI recipient. Use of online portals is common in Denmark, for example, and many PES in OECD countries are moving away from in-person monitoring of all aspects of IAPs. The "e-werkcoach" in the Netherlands follows the progress of job seekers online, reminding them of agreed IAP activities and consequences of noncompliance. Only job seekers at the highest risk of long-term unemployment receive in-person case support and counseling. Germany, the Flemish Region of Belgium, and Estonia all rely to differing degrees on online systems to serve and monitor job seekers and IAP success.[33]

Where training, counseling, and perhaps other services are provided privately, a separate monitoring system is typically established between the provider and the PES or government agency. Providers may transmit a periodic file recording attendance by job seekers or may have access to an offline or online system that conveys participation details. Contracts can trigger payment to providers based on the number of job seekers completing training or services, or more appropriately, the number of job seekers who are placed or find employment in a given period. Design of performance-based contracting and monitoring for private providers is increasingly important in activation programs.

Increasingly, monitoring of job seekers also involves the private service providers. For example, in the United Kingdom's Jobcentre Plus program, private work search providers provide services according to a delivery contract, but also notify the government compliance agency when participants need additional support such as a training allowance or are suspected to be noncompliant. Similarly, in South Africa's Expanded Public Works Program (EPWP), nonprofit organizations contracted through the program must record the daily attendance of beneficiaries as well as identification and payment information, to be available for audit by the program authorities.

When a compliance failure occurs, either the caseworker or social support office will formally report it to the central ministry, PES, or department. Often, caseworkers have some degree of discretion in the frequency of reporting upward. Where staffing numbers permit, many labor programs elevate the decision to sanction to specialized staff within or outside the PES (Konle-Seidl 2012). This removes the perception of the job counselor as a policeman or bureaucrat of the system. Conversely, removing the policing role entirely can undermine the authority of the counselor. It is a difficult balance. Several PES in European Union countries provide regular training to employment counselors on stress-management, psychological self-awareness, assertiveness, and even peer group sessions to complement the technical training they receive (for example, in Ireland's PES). After a reported compliance failure, the PES or central ministry will decide whether to further examine the report, issue a remedial action through the caseworker to the job seeker, or sanction benefits along with recommended remedial actions.

Sanctioning practices vary widely. In many cases, benefits can be temporarily suspended or reduced, depending on the compliance violation. Failure to accept employment opportunities is generally the most serious violation in most systems. In Russia, unemployment benefits may be suspended for up to one month if the job seeker fails to accept two consecutive offers of suitable work or fails to participate in paid public works or training after a period of one month of unemployment.[34] In Estonia, benefits can be suspended for a period of between 10 and 30 days the first time a job seeker refuses suitable work without a valid reason, or if the individual receives income equal to 30 days of unemployment benefits (Kuddo 2012). Australia, Korea, the Netherlands, New Zealand, Spain, Sweden, and the United Kingdom all have benefit suspension periods for refusing employment. The Netherlands imposes a sliding scale of payment reductions up to 100 percent depending on the number of refusals and their nature (Immervoll and Knotz 2018).

Many PES will sanction job seekers who fail to meet obligations beyond not accepting job opportunities. Sweden sanctions benefits for not participating in the drafting of the IAP, failing to submit an "activity report" every month, missing an appointment, not accepting a job referral, and/or not actively looking for work (Garsten, Jacobsson, and Sztandar-Sztanderska 2016). The first instance of noncompliance results in a warning, while the second, third, and fourth instances lead to a suspension of benefits for 1, 5, or 10 days, respectively. The fifth instance will result in cancellation of benefits until a new work condition is met.

In Australia under the Jobactive program, once a job seeker has reached a threshold level of reporting or participation failures, an automatic assessment known as a "comprehensive compliance assessment" is triggered. The assessment is triggered by three failures to record job search activities, or nonattendance at activities or job interviews, or failure to agree on a job plan. An assessment can also be requested by the service provider or by the Department of Health Services (DHS) when they determine that a job seeker is not able to meet the mutual obligation requirements (see box 8.3 for further details). A DHS specialist conducts the assessment and produces a report with action steps for the job seeker and possibly service providers. If the assessment determines that a serious failure or fraud has occurred, an eight-week payment penalty on cash support is imposed. Further failure to complete directed compliance activities can result in further sanctions, including reduction or termination of cash support. These graduated steps are clearly identified in the mutual obligations requirements.

Monitoring beneficiaries in public works programs is somewhat different from that typical of labor activation programs. Public works are often considered self-targeting schemes, paying below or very near prevailing minimum wages, so it is assumed that beneficiaries accept work under the program only if other work is unavailable. Most programs therefore spend most administrative attention on ensuring that people who want work under the program are accommodated, together with monitoring the performance of implementing agents and contractors to complete the activities. However, it is still important to ensure that workers are present at the work sites and have not exceeded any limits placed on allowed days of participation.

The Mahatma Gandhi National Rural Employment Guarantee Act (MGNREG) program in India monitors the presence of workers on a daily basis and keeps track of days worked through the individual family's Job Card. If an individual household member is not recorded by the Gram Rozgar Sevak (a village-level official of the program) as being present at the work site on a given day, benefits are not paid for that day. If the period for which employment is sought ends and no member of the household has appeared for work, benefits are not provided and the application is terminated. If the household has received 100 days of work within the financial year, further benefits are stopped for that household. As the program has evolved, MGNREG has developed a sophisticated BOMS known as NREGAsoft that supports each workflow area of the program and records all transactions, from program registration through payment of wages. Box 8.4 provides more detail on NREGAsoft.

Some public works programs incorporate human capital-building components in addition to standard work components, requiring beneficiary monitoring similar to CCT programs. For example, El Salvador's Programa de Ingreso Temporal (PATI) provided temporary income through community projects and training to improve employability of vulnerable people including youth in urban disadvantaged areas. The Productive Safety Net Program in Ethiopia has several different elements, including a public works scheme, provision of food and cash transfers, and facilitation of livelihood opportunities, training, and credit. The public scheme incorporates participation in a community health and nutrition education and behavior change program as a core responsibility of clients. Clients are expected to participate in at least six behavior change sessions over the six months of a public works period. Attending sessions is counted as public works participation. Attendance is recorded on the "client card" by the health extension workers from the Ministry of Health, which is presented at the next public works participation day for inclusion in the public works attendance sheet. The site foreman records the attendance of public works workers twice a day, generally before starting in the morning and after completion of the day's work. Households are reassessed annually by the Community Food Security Task Forces based on several criteria, including status of household assets and income, vulnerabilities including illness, presence of elderly, and female-headed households, among others. The list of eligible households is verified by the wider community, displayed in a public place and discussed during a full general meeting of the village residents.[35]

Box 8.4 Monitoring Beneficiaries and Providers of Public Workfare: NREGAsoft in India

The Mahatma Gandhi National Rural Employment Guarantee Act (MGNREGA) is the largest public works program in the world. It guarantees 100 days of employment for households in rural areas through local public works activities. In 2018–19, 75.8 million individuals were provided work, with an average of 46 days of employment across 51.1 million households with a total program expenditure of more than US$6 billion.

Process and monitoring. The potential beneficiary applies to the Gram Panchayat (GP, village-level government) for a Job Card, and then submits a written application seeking employment. The GP or Block Development Officer prepares and submits an "e-Muster Roll" to implementing government or other agents conducting the public works activities.[a] Measurement of the work is recorded weekly based on a seven-day muster roll, with daily attendance recorded by the Gram Rozgar Sevak (village livelihood worker, an employee of MGNREG). Authenticated copies of muster rolls and expenditure vouchers will be submitted by implementing agents to block officers for online entry, with another copy to the concerned GP to update the employment register and individual Job Cards. Payment to beneficiary workers will be made within 15 days of completing work directly to individual bank accounts.

Comprehensive beneficiary operations management system (BOMS). The Ministry of Rural Development has developed a work flow-based, web-enabled BOMS application known as NREGAsoft. The software allows recording of all transaction details of different processes in the implementation of MGNREGA, making much of the information available directly to the public. NREGAsoft is available in online as well as in offline mode, addressing connectivity challenges in some remote areas of India. It supports all local languages and is available in both Microsoft-supported as well as open source technologies. The software has various modules to support each workflow area of the program. For beneficiary monitoring purposes, three are most relevant:

- **Worker management module** of the software provides backbone for the services provided to the worker, from the registration and issuance of the Job Card to the payment of wages through bank accounts.
- **Social audit module** captures the details of the social audit done in various GPs.
- **Labor budget module** helps the Gram Panchayats in planning for the next financial year and assist the ministry to decide on the amount to be released depending upon their future projections of labor demand and works to be taken up.

Other modules. (1) the fund management module, which tracks the transfer and location of funds; (2) the grievance redress system; (3) the staffing position module, which strengthens communication and coordination among various stakeholders; (4) the cost estimation module, which makes detailed estimates for the works taken up under the program; (5) knowledge network/solution exchange, which provides a common platform to all stakeholders to exchange views, pose queries, and exhibit good practices; and (6) bank/post office modules, which wage and worker information to financial institutions to credit individual accounts.

For more information, see: https://www.nrega.nic.in/netnrega/home.aspx.

Source: Summary based on the government of India's MGNREGA Master Circular-A Guide for Programme Implementation FY 2018–2019.

a. An e-Muster Roll is an electronically generated list of eligible workers for a work site. It includes names of eligible participants entered in NREGAsoft and prepopulated worker details, verified by the block officer. In some select areas, a manual muster roll is prepared where there is limited electricity and connectivity.

Labor Activation Performance Indicators and Compliance

Historically, PES have collected and disseminated labor market information to improve the targeting and effectiveness of ALMP services. Monitoring employment trends, regional and local job openings, and sectoral performance is important to increase the relevance of job counseling, placement, and training. This information is often collected through a labor market information system (LMIS), combining survey-based data on the supply and demand for jobs and skills with job vacancies posted by employers, usually restricted to the formal sector. The information in LMIS is often made available to stakeholders external to the PES to enable more informed decision making by individuals, employers, training providers, and other public and private agencies.

Many PES now go beyond monitoring of overall labor market conditions to collect and utilize a range of performance indicators more closely related to the performance of ALMP services. The data are often taken from administrative records maintained at individual employment offices or digitized and aggregated more centrally. Basic core indicators collected typically include the following:[36]

- ***Job placement rate.*** The number of registered job seekers (or those who have completed training or other ALMP) who are to be employed in a later period, often a subsequent month or quarter.
- ***Placement cost.*** Number of registered job seekers who obtained a job divided by the program budget in a given period, often a fiscal year.
- ***Job retention rate.*** The number of registered job seekers who remain employed in subsequent periods, often two quarters.
- ***Average earnings.*** Average earnings for registered job seekers who remain employed over a give period, frequently quarterly or annually.
- ***Filled vacancy rate.*** The number of registered job vacancies that are filled by registered job seekers over a period, often quarterly.
- ***Adequacy rate.*** The share of registered job seekers who complete training who are employed in a given period (often monthly or quarterly) in an occupation compatible with the training provided.
- ***Underemployment rate.*** The share of registered job seekers who complete training who are employed in a given period in an occupation that requires a lower education profile.

More comprehensive systems would include a larger number of indicators drawn from administrative data and survey data. These indicators measure the resources and inputs as well as outputs and outcomes toward assessing the actual effects of the services provided on client job seekers. Some PES use labor market data and administrative data to help assess the performance of labor programs. For example, both Denmark and Germany maintain a data warehouse used by managers in the PES. In Denmark, the data are publicly accessible through a website. Users define their own queries, choosing from different benefits, activities, expenditure categories, and individual characteristics. Data are drawn from many sources, including PES local office unemployment registration, unemployment funds, residence permits from the Danish Immigration Service, income from the Danish Ministry of Taxation, and education from the Ministry of Higher Education and Science, among others. In Germany, data are taken primarily from the operations systems in local offices.[37] Poland also monitors the performance of local PES offices, and from 2014 has linked a part of the resources from the national Labor Fund to the placement rate of job seekers into employment. This change has directly affected PES staff in local offices, as their remuneration is also linked to the performance of their PES office.[38]

Box 8.5 summarizes Austria's performance management approach, incentivizing knowledge sharing for monitoring and program improvement. The "Balanced Scorecard" allows PES offices to be assessed and compared, but the system incentivizes the use of the information for knowledge sharing and program improvement through financial rewards, as well as nonfinancial public awards for knowledge sharing behavior.

India is developing a comprehensive skill training management system that collects a wide range of information on performance and makes it available widely. The Skill Development Management System was originally designed as a transaction processing system for private training providers to be used by the National Skill Development Corporation. It is being transformed into a complete MIS and program management software. Modules are under development to register and

Box 8.5 Performance Management: Austria's Balanced Scorecard and Incentives for Knowledge Sharing

The "Balanced Scorecard" (BSC) is intended to provide an objective performance comparison of local public employment service (PES) offices and regions. It includes 25 indicators covering quantitative outcomes, process and quality-oriented targets such as reintegration rates of active measures, services to employers, call center services, and management processes. The BSC is weighted to take into account the local employment market condition, staffing and budgets.

The BSC is used to benchmark the performance of the 100 local PES offices. The performance of an office is measured with different reference points: (1) calculation of office-specific expected results; (2) benchmarking across two different types of office clusters; and (3) fixed references to compare across all offices.

The BSC is used to adjust and correct procedures directly at the office level and is also used by the regional branches and federal office to monitor local offices. Low and high performers within clusters are encouraged to share knowledge on performance improvement. In addition, a project database is maintained to create transparency and disseminate lessons. The database includes information on PES core processes, extent of implementing and meeting job market goals, and improving BSC scores.

Austria's PES prioritizes knowledge sharing across local offices to encourage the spread of good practices. Visits to other offices to discuss performance are viewed as an indicator of good performance in itself. Local offices are financially rewarded for knowledge sharing. Each year, a formal jury selects three innovative projects to be recognized at the Austrian PES awards ceremony.

Source: Summary from Bjerre, Sidelman, and Puchwein-Roberts (2016).

onboard training and job seekers, register training institutions, facilitate program notifications and reporting to job seekers and trainers, record and manage payments and costs, assess workflow processes, and other analytics through web-based applications. Job placement data are also recorded, as individuals and training institutes must report within 90 days of certification of trained candidates in the Skill Development Management System.

The United States' Benefit Accuracy Measurement (BAM) system is an example of a sample-based monitoring and performance system. The BAM program estimates the accuracy of paid and denied claims in UI programs in the United States. Each week, state workforce agencies (SWAs) select random samples from the universe of UI claims and state BAM staff review agency records, contact claimants, employers, and others to verify information relevant to the UI claim. Conclusions are entered into an automated database maintained in each SWA. The national Department of Labor uses BAM data to measure SWA performance and to receive information on UI operations and claimant characteristics. Table 8.10 details the various types of overpayments in 2017 recorded in the BAM. The left column reports the share of total overpayments attributed by cause (approximately US$3.71 billion). The right column

Table 8.10 Benefit Accuracy Measurement System: US Unemployment Insurance Overpayments, July 2016 to July 2017

Cause	Total overpayment (%)	Overpayment from fraud (%)
Work search	37.44	3.12
Earnings	26.38	54.81
Job separation (quit or fired)	17.30	26.82
Able and available to work	5.55	6.48
Other	13.33	8.77
Total	100.00	100.00

Source: U.S. Department of Labor's Benefit Accuracy Measurement Program state data summary, improper payments, performance year 2017.

shows the share of overpayments classified as fraud, again attributed by cause (about US$1.09 billion was estimated to be overpaid due to fraud). The single largest cause of overpayments results from work search issues—generally, not reporting search efforts accurately. This is followed by reported earnings in the year of UI benefit receipt. When the focus is on sources of fraud, by far the largest cause is concealed earnings. That is, nearly 55 percent of overpayments from fraud stem from individual recipients willfully not reporting earnings while continuing to receive UI benefits. The second leading source of detected fraud is misreporting the cause of job separation as involuntary, when the determined cause was either quitting or being fired. This pattern has persisted for more than a decade.[39]

8.5 GRIEVANCE REDRESS MECHANISMS IN SOCIAL PROTECTION DELIVERY SYSTEMS

Grievance redress mechanisms (GRMs) are an important component of beneficiary operations management. By giving people the capacity to provide feedback to program administrators, a GRM provides beneficiaries and the general public with a voice in the program's administration and its performance management. Grievances can be related to unclear program guidelines; lack of program awareness resulting from insufficient outreach; potential inclusion and exclusion errors; an unsatisfactory package of benefits and services; problems with the payment of benefits or the provision of services; mistreatment by frontline workers; or the GRM itself. In addition, aggregated grievance data are one data point for a program's administrators and decision makers in judging personnel performance and the efficiency and effectiveness of a program on the basis of the experiences of beneficiaries and other citizens.

It is essential that all stakeholders understand how grievances will be collected and resolved. Where do they learn about ways and means to address grievances, and programs' rules and standard processes? How do program administrators ensure that grievances, especially those affecting vulnerable groups, are addressed, and ensure that no one falls through cracks in the system? Here is a quick rundown of the what, why, who, where, and how of GRMs:

- ***What?*** GRM refers to a system by which queries, suggestions, positive feedback, and concerns about a program are responded to, problems with implementation are resolved, and complaints are addressed efficiently and effectively. In the context of social protection programs, grievances are requests for information, suggestions, feedback, complaints, and appeals about the programs from beneficiaries and stakeholders of social protection programs as well as from the general public.[40] The grievances referenced in this chapter are administrative in nature.
- ***Why?*** A GRM supports more effective institutions for social protection programs by establishing and strengthening systems for constructive sharing of information, citizens' feedback, and complaint resolution. It harnesses stronger state-client interaction and increases stakeholder involvement in a program. It helps programs achieve better development outcomes by improving service delivery and program effectiveness, achieving greater beneficiary and client satisfaction, allowing decision makers to allocate resources efficiently, reducing fraud and corruption, and improving governance. A GRM also supports increased awareness of a program and its objectives. Social protection programs are complex and usually implemented on a large scale. Hence, it is important to detect and mitigate risks and grievances at an early stage before they create massive upheaval, lead to public distrust, and damage the reputation of a program.
- ***Who?*** A well-designed and well-implemented GRM serves a program's beneficiaries, potential beneficiaries, nonbeneficiaries, and the general public, who may want to know about the program, may be affected by it, or may benefit from it.
- ***Where?*** A well-designed and well-implemented GRM is accessible through different types and locations of uptake channels. Uptake channels can include postal mail, email, call centers, a website, social media platforms, complaint forms, face-to-face interaction with

program administrators, text messaging or SMS, and complaint boxes.

- ***How?*** A well-designed and well-implemented GRM usually consists of six steps to collect and address grievances. Those steps are: uptake; sorting and processing; acknowledging and following up; verifying, investigating, and acting; monitoring and evaluation; and providing feedback. The steps will be unpacked later in this chapter.

There is no "one-size-fits-all" GRM. While well-designed and well-implemented GRMs share common features; each needs to be adjusted to fit its purpose as well as the country and program contexts. When designing or strengthening a GRM, it is important to assess existing formal and informal grievance collection and resolution practices. The following questions may guide assessment of whether the GRM associated with a program is functioning to its full potential.

- ***Structure.*** How does the program or the ministry currently collect and resolve grievances? Is there an informal structure and practice, if the program or the ministry does not have an existing formal structure? If the GRM is formalized, does the program have clear and transparent internal mechanisms, processes, and procedures to collect and address grievances (for example, a grievance unit, designated grievance redress offers or roles, or a grievance committee)? Are program officers at all levels aware of the GRM's system, processes, and procedures?
- ***Capacity to collect and address grievances.*** Are there internal processes in place to record, track, and monitor grievances and the actions taken on them? This could be a log book, an Excel spreadsheet, or an information system. If a record management system exists, who has access to it, at which level of the organization are they, and what type of access do they have?
- ***Authority.*** Do the program officers responsible for grievance collection and resolution have the authority to take or demand remedial actions?
- ***Existing practice.*** Does the GRM provide timely feedback (written or otherwise) to complainants on actions taken?
- ***Appeals.*** Is there an appeals process in place that complainants can access if they are not satisfied with how their grievance has been addressed?
- ***Potential complainants' perspective.*** Do the people affected by the program, including beneficiaries, feel comfortable lodging grievances without fear of retaliation? What are the commonly used communication and interaction channels in the country and with the target groups? What are the literacy and technology levels of potential complainants? Are project beneficiaries aware of their right to file a grievance and of the grievance redress process in general?[41]

The absence of grievances does not mean that they do not exist for a program. Such an absence could imply a number of challenges, including the lack of a formal GRM or few and irregular channels for the redress of grievances. The absence of grievances could also indicate landscape barriers and field challenges, such as being far away from GRM uptake channels and out-of-pocket expenditures an individual must incur to submit a grievance. Certain programs do not have the institutional capacity or resources to collect, document, and address grievances. Beyond the barriers that prevent the population from filing grievances, another cause could be systematic errors or fraud and corruption at one or more administrative levels. Finally, failure to use a GRM can indicate lack of accessibility for marginalized populations, including lack of awareness about GRM processes by individuals who have low or no literacy, and the anticipated cost of filing grievances, which can range from the monetary cost of accessing GRM points to fear of retaliation from local leaders.

An effective GRM provides a continuous, constructive feedback loop between people and institutions or program administrators. While grievances arise along all phases of the delivery chain, their redress is part of the beneficiary operations management stage and can feed back into earlier stages. The decisions taken in resolving grievances (for example, on errors of exclusion, errors in beneficiary data, or incorrect payment amounts) can feed back into the assessment and enrollment stages, as well as into the recurring implementation cycle for benefits and services.

GRMs also constitute an instrument for continuously improving delivery systems' effectiveness and efficiency, as well as for promoting greater transparency and accountability in social protection programs. Program administrators can incorporate lessons learned from recurring grievances to improve program design and implementation as well as the performance of delivery systems. The main intent of a GRM is to receive, assess, and resolve complaints, appeals, updates, and other grievances to improve the delivery of benefits and services. GRM systems provide program administrators with insights into the effectiveness and efficiency of delivery systems and possible improvements to them.

Grievances along the Delivery Chain

Grievances occur at every stage and phase of the delivery chain. Figure 8.19 includes examples of grievances for different phases of the delivery chain.

Grievances in the Assessment Stage

In the outreach phase, many grievances may simply be requests for information about the program. Grievances may arise because of poor outreach mechanisms and inadequate outreach modalities. As a result, outreach efforts may exclude or miss people such as minorities or those living in remote areas. Grievances may also arise due to poorly designed communication strategies, resulting in people receiving inaccurate or incomplete information as well as a lack of outreach material in the local language or lack of audiovisual material in contexts of low literacy.

Grievances at the intake and registration phase may arise from errors in beneficiary data, exclusion from the registration process, lack of knowledge (including lack of clarity on requirements for registration, such as what documents to bring), long waits at the registration office, long distances to the registration office, lack of intake and registration staff who speak the local language, and lack of assistance for individuals with disabilities. Grievances at the assessment of needs and conditions phase may arise from lack of understanding of assessment results, errors in the results, or issues with the implementation of the process.

Grievances in the Enrollment Stage

Grievances at the eligibility and enrollment phase may arise from incorrect decisions about eligibility, such as inclusion or exclusion errors, difficulty completing the actions required for enrollment, or a missed opportunity to enroll. Grievances at the benefits and service package phase might occur if there is an error in the determination of the benefits and services to be provided, including miscalculation of the benefit amount. In the notification and onboarding phase, grievances may be filed if the program fails to notify registrants about their acceptance or rejection for the program. They may also arise because onboarding is of poor quality, such as lack of clear information on program rules and beneficiaries' rights and responsibilities. In addition, grievances at the enrollment stage may arise from the vested interests of decision makers toward target beneficiaries.

Grievances at the Provision Stage

Grievances in the payment of benefits phase may arise from missed or delayed payments, payment errors, or the amount of distance or other challenges that must be overcome to reach payment points, including out-of-pocket expenses incurred for transportation, insurance, and other needs (for example, meals, for labor-intensive operations). For a cash transfer program, technical grievances relating to payment cards and automated teller or mobile money systems and failures in authentication of IDs at the point of benefits or service provision may also arise at this phase. Grievances related to the provision of services might be caused by delays and mishaps in the service, long waits, poor standards, lack of availability of a service, and mismatched services.

Grievances at the Beneficiary Operations Management Stage

Grievances related to beneficiary data management occur when the beneficiary data are incorrect or needs to be revised or updated. Grievances related to compliance with conditionalities can occur if beneficiaries face penalties, delays, or cancellation of services and benefits due to administrative errors or incorrect capturing and processing of compliance data by the institutions responsible for compliance monitoring. There may also be grievances about the grievance redress mechanism itself—if the process is lengthy, time-consuming, unclear, or not easily accessible, or if GRM officials appear to show poor behavior, discrimination, nepotism, fraud, or corruption. Finally, grievances in the exit decisions, notifications, and case outcomes phase can be related to unclear processes and decision-making rules about exits, lack of or improper notification of exit decisions, or case resolutions. Those grievances can take the form of a complaint about the processes or appeal of an exit decision.

Across the phases of the delivery chain, grievances could also result from perceived or actual fraud, as well as other types of unprofessional behavior among the staff responsible for registration, enrollment, payment, and monitoring.

Table 8.11 includes a sample of grievances along the delivery chain that were documented across three programs in Bangladesh:[42] (1) Old Age Allowance, a means-tested program that provides a monthly allowance to approximately 2.75 million poor elderly; (2) Vulnerable Group Development, which provides food security, skills development, and complementary inputs for vulnerable women; and (3) Employment Generation Program, a public works program that aims to mitigate seasonal joblessness in rural Bangladesh.[43]

The GRM Framework

A well-designed and well-implemented GRM ensures that there are principles and formalized steps for grievance collection and resolution. The framework for an effective GRM comprises a set of principles, institutional structures, rules, procedures, and processes through which queries, complaints, and appeals about a social protection program are resolved. The GRM is an important tool through which beneficiaries, potential beneficiaries, nonbeneficiaries, and implementing agencies including other stakeholders exercise their voices. It provides ways and means to mitigate, manage, and resolve grievances and ensure the transparency and accountability of social protection programs.

Principles of GRM

It is important that social protection programs adhere to international standards and principles when collecting and resolving grievances. Programs must have GRMs to remedy mistakes when implementers and decision makers become aware of them, as well as to correct the processes and systems that do not provide the quality of service promised. The following principles and attributes should normally apply to a well-functioning GRM (World Bank 2012a, 2018c):

- ***Independence.*** The GRM must be operated independently of all interested parties to guarantee fair, objective, and impartial treatment of each case.
- ***Accessibility and inclusivity.*** The GRM should be accessible by the project beneficiaries and the general public without fear of retaliation or discrimination. The resolution process should be simple enough for complainants to easily understand the general process and the timeline stipulated for resolution. The uptake channels for grievances need to be accessible to program beneficiaries and the general public regardless of the remoteness of an area, the language spoken, and the levels of education, literacy, or income. For this reason, an effective GRM often provides multiple means (such as complaint boxes, telephone, SMS texts, emails, forms, and face-to-face interaction with social workers) and locations (for example, local offices and branches, program sites, and ministries) for them to submit grievances with ease. Given that social protection programs target the most vulnerable populations, the GRM should consider its accessibility and usability by the marginalized groups (for example, women, youth, the elderly, and the disabled).
- ***Confidentiality.*** Grievances are treated confidentially—no personal information should be disclosed to third parties.
- ***Responsiveness.*** The GRM is designed to be responsive to the needs of complainants in a timely manner. Grievances should be assessed impartially and handled transparently. The actions taken, which should be proportionate, need to be communicated to complainants to close the feedback loop. Officials handling grievances therefore require appropriate training to take effective actions and respond to grievances, and all program staff should be aware of the functions and roles of a program's GRM.
- ***Effectiveness and continuous improvement.*** An effective GRM monitors and analyzes GRM data in order to utilize beneficiary and citizen feedback to improve the effectiveness and efficiency of the program and of the GRM itself. A GRM can start small and simple. It can be assessed and continuously improved throughout the life of the program as the program expands and matures.

Figure 8.19 Grievances along the Social Protection Program Delivery Chain

continued

Figure 8.19 *(continued)*

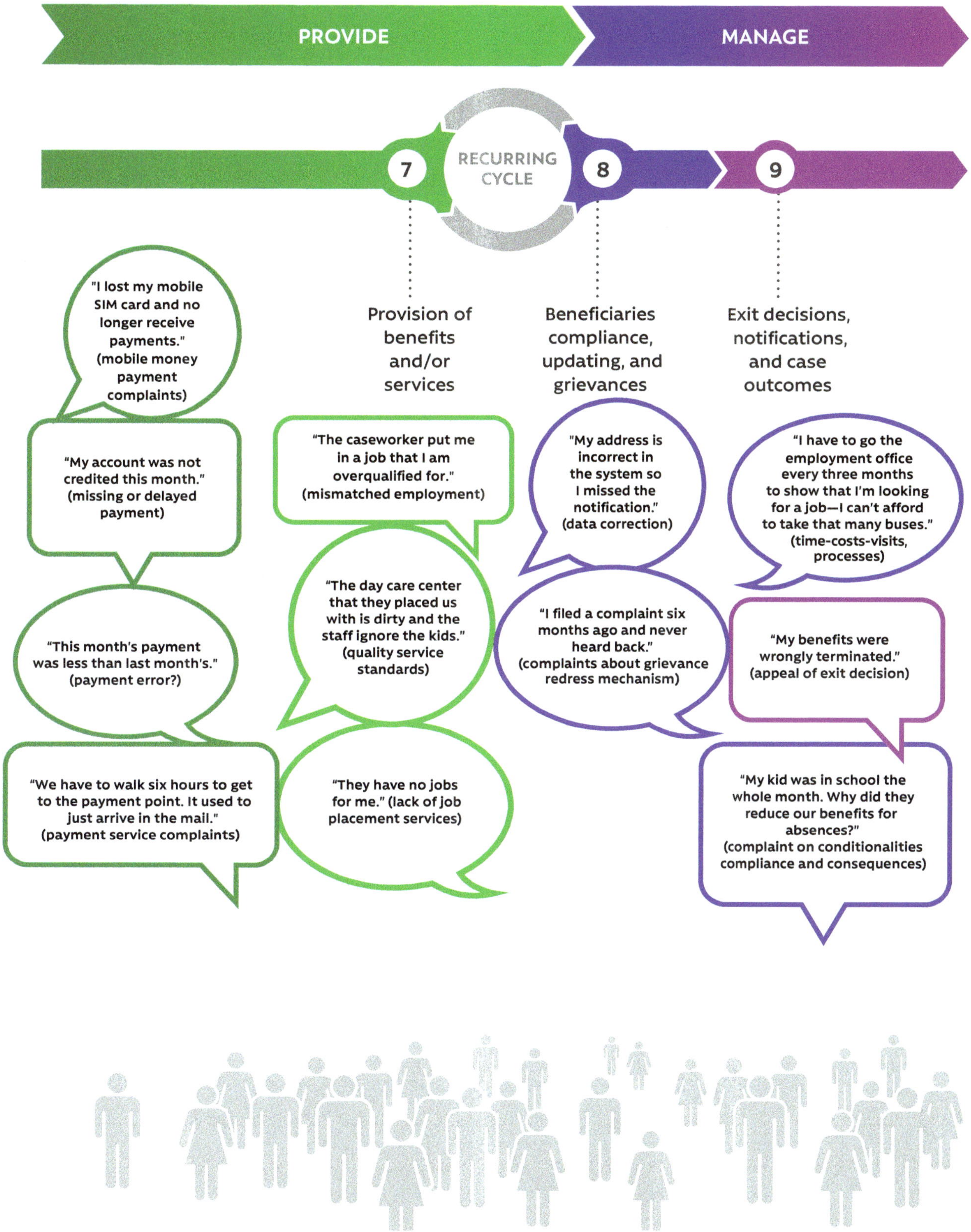

Source: Original figure for this publication.

Table 8.11 Sample of Grievances along the Delivery Chain in Three Social Protection Programs in Bangladesh

Grievances by phases of delivery chain	Old Age Allowance Program	Vulnerable Group Development Program	Employment Generation Program
Eligibility and enrollment decisions	Beneficiaries and nonbeneficiaries were unclear about eligibility and enrollment decisions. There were grievances about nepotism and inclusion of beneficiaries who are favored by the politicians.	Grievances included nepotism and bribes demanded by the program administrators to provide the Vulnerable Group Development program card.	Grievances included nepotism, bribery, and manipulation of the beneficiary registry to include ghost workers.
Determination of benefits and services package	Grievances about the size of the allocated benefits. Grievances that the benefits were insufficient to cover both food and medicine.	• Grievances about the size and quality of the allocated benefits and services. • Grievances that the food grains were of low quality, and the quantity of food grains was insufficient to serve the whole family. • Grievances about the inconsistencies in the quantity and packaging of the food benefits.	Grievances about the program's wage level.
Payment of benefits	• Grievances about the tedious collection process, and the distance to the payment point, long waiting time, and lack of facilities such as bathroom, drinking water, and so on. • Grievances about the out-of-pocket expenditure for transport. • Grievances about additional hidden cost before collecting payments (e.g., some banks charge Tk 10 per transaction). • Grievances about the delays in receiving the transfer. • Beneficiaries also reported that their treatment at the payment points was good only when *upazila* (administrative unit) staff were present, but unfortunately, they were not present regularly.	Grievances about the long waiting time, wastage, and misappropriation at the payment points.	• Grievances that the payment was made to middlemen, *Union Parishad* (UP)/ward members (politicians). • 17% of beneficiaries received payment through UP member. • 10% of beneficiaries received payments from UP office.
Beneficiary data management	Grievances about the replacement of the designated recipient in case of death not handled according to guidelines.	Grievances about poor treatment; beneficiaries reported that their treatment was smooth only when *upazila* (administrative unit) staff were present, but unfortunately, they were not present regularly.	Data not available.
Grievance redress mechanism (GRM)	Grievances about the GRM—people did not know the point of contact or GRM channel or process to file grievances.	Grievances about the GRM—people did not know the point of contact or GRM channel or process to file grievances.	Grievances about the GRM—people did not know the point of contact or GRM channel or process to file grievances.

Source: Piloting a Grievance Mechanism for Government of Bangladesh's Social Protection Programs: Final Report, 2015.

GRM principles are not prescriptive, but rather a set of generally accepted practices that are recommended for social protection programs to design effective GRMs. Box 8.6 provides an example of the principles governing the GRM of the Pantawid Pamilyang Pilipino Program (4Ps) in the Philippines.

Process of GRM[44]

Most GRMs go through similar steps. Although there might be a slight variation from system to system, most GRMs have six main steps: uptake; sort and process; acknowledge and follow up; verify, investigate, and act; monitor and evaluate; and provide feedback (figure 8.20). Grievance redress usually starts at the community level, moves through local administrative entities, and escalates to national institutions through program administrative structures or independent institutions, like the offices of ombudsman, only when grievances cannot be resolved at the local level.

The first step is uptake, which refers to the methods by which grievances are collected. An effective GRM should have multiple uptake locations (at the community, village, district, provincial or regional, and national levels) as well as multiple channels (such as mail, email, phone, SMS text, website, or complaint box). When identifying uptake channels, consider technology, funding and resources, including human resources, and constraints on capacity. Since the cost and complexity of GRMs are likely to increase with the number of uptake channels, program managers should choose channels and locations strategically. As the program and the GRM expand and mature, additional uptake channels can be added. Such an expansion plan needs to be strategically sequenced based on the goals of the program.

The second step is to sort and process grievances, because different types of grievances require different follow-up actions. For instance, some grievances require a simple explanation or sharing of program information, while others may require an investigation

Box 8.6 Principles Governing the GRM of the Philippines's 4Ps

The Philippines 4Ps features a systematic, professional, and rules-based procedure for handling grievances and appeals. The 4Ps GRM resolved nearly 500,000 grievances between 2009 and 2013. The GRM is characterized by well-designed structures, clear business processes, and robust standards, as well as well-trained staff. The GRM in the 4Ps not only resolves grievances, but also allows program management to learn from grievances to continuously refine program policies and improve implementation. The underlying principles of the 4Ps GRS are the following:

- **Simplicity and accessibility.** All the GRM procedures for filing grievances and seeking redress are simple and easy to understand; grievances can be submitted by the beneficiaries and the community in general through multiple channels and multiple modalities.
- **Transparency.** The system is publicized to a broad audience encompassing beneficiaries, potential beneficiaries, nonbeneficiaries, civil society organizations, media, and government officials—at all levels—from *barangay*/village to the national level.
- **Empowering and participatory.** Communities, program implementers, and the media are encouraged to share feedback and file grievances.
- **Timeliness.** The GRM guidelines include timelines that ensure grievances are handled in a timely manner.
- **Right of appeal.** The GRM channels for appeal are available if complainants are not satisfied with the resolution of a problem.
- **Confidentiality.** The identity of complainants remains confidential unless otherwise requested.
- **Pro-community.** The GRM aims to involve the community to address complaints.

Source: Patel et al. 2014

Note: 4Ps = Pantawid Pamilyang Pilipino Program.

Figure 8.20 Steps in the Implementation of GRM Systems

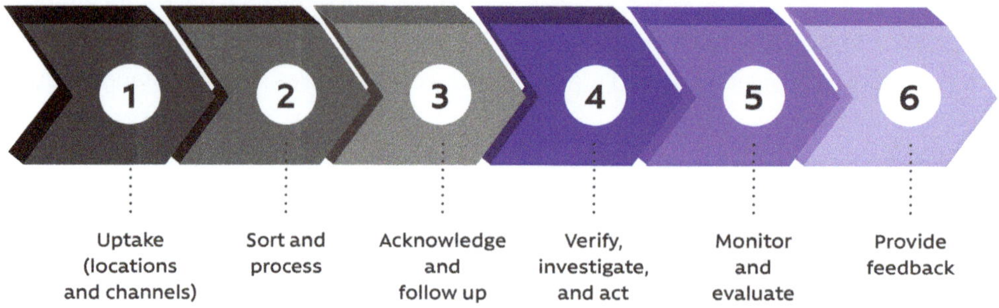

Source: World Bank 2012a.
Note: GRM = grievance redress mechanism.

and thorough follow-up. Some grievance categories are listed below. In this process, the relevant departments, units, and agencies of the program or a higher level of the program structure need to be involved or a case needs to be assigned to them. Grievances need to be logged in order for the program to keep track of referrals to other relevant units, departments, or agencies, or of escalation to a higher level when a grievance is received at a lower level. The information log helps the program monitor progress and performance on resolving grievances. This step therefore is crucial to categorize, prioritize, and assign each grievance to the relevant unit, department, or agency. An effective GRM sometimes receives grievances that are outside the scope of the social protection programs. The process of sorting also helps the program distinguish between program-related grievances and others (table 8.12).

After the grievance is sorted and processed, the third step is to acknowledge its receipt and inform the complainant of follow-up actions. This step involves clear communication to the complainant that the grievance has been received and informs them about the expected timeline for resolution and follow-up activities. At this time, an effective GRM generates a case number—automated or manual—and shares that case number, along with relevant contact details, with the complainant in case he or she would like to contact the program to follow up on a case. To enhance the GRM's transparency and accountability, information about the timeline for resolution, an easily understandable explanation of the resolution process, and details of follow-up methods should be widely disseminated to various stakeholders.

The fourth step is to verify, investigate, and take appropriate action(s) to resolve a grievance. This step requires gathering information about the grievance to determine its validity and take appropriate actions to resolve it. This step also involves referring or escalating grievances that could not be resolved at one level of the system to respectively higher officials for further investigation and follow-up. Potential actions at this step may include responding to information requests or comments, providing complainants with a status update on any resolution, requesting supporting documents as needed, verifying the supporting documents, imposing sanctions, and escalating a case to a higher level for further investigation and actions.

The fifth step, monitoring and evaluation, is critical for an effective GRM. Monitoring refers to the process of tracking grievances and assessing the extent to which progress is being made to resolve them. The social protection program tends to receive high volumes of grievances because it serves a large number of people. Ideally, it should have an electronic system for entering, tracking, and monitoring grievances and resolutions. Monitoring may involve spot checks to ensure the quality of a grievance's resolution. An effective GRM includes a set of indicators to measure grievance monitoring and resolution. Evaluation involves analyzing grievance data to inform the program management so that it can make changes in processes and procedures to minimize similar grievances in future. Regular reports should be submitted to senior program management in order for them to monitor data on resolutions and grievance trends.

Table 8.12 Indicative List of Grievance Categories

Category	Subcategory
Information request/query	• General information about the program (e.g., purpose of the program, generic information about the target population and the selection criteria, program timeline, procedures and documents required for application, types of employment opportunities available and locations, duration of the program) • Information about the registration/application and/or enrollment (e.g., application methods, time period, documentation required) • Information about payment (e.g., benefit amount, payment schedule and frequency, payment methods) • Information about the GRM
Complaint	• Grievance about enrollment (e.g., failure to enroll due to a system failure or shut down) • Grievance about eligibility (e.g., inclusion and exclusion errors) • Grievance related to payment (e.g., late payment, inaccurate payment amount, payment card malfunction, stolen or lost payment cards, malfunction of ATMs and other payment methods) • Grievance about staff and contractor performance, including unprofessional behaviors, misconduct, and fraud and corruption • Grievance about social and environmental risks and/or damage associated with the social infrastructure and public works programs • Procurement complaints by suppliers, vendors, contractors, or consultants of social infrastructure and public works programs • Grievances related to services (e.g., CCT's conditionality related service areas)[a]
Beneficiary information update	• Updates on registration/application information (e.g., address, phone number) • Updates on beneficiary information (e.g., address, phone number, family status including number of children, employment status)
Suggestions	Suggestions to improve the program and the GRM
Other feedback	Compliments on the program, program staff and contractors, and the GRM

Source: Original table for this publication.

Note: CCT = conditional cash transfer (program); GRM = grievance redress mechanism.

a. Oftentimes, education and health are the selected service sectors related to the conditionalities of cash transfer programs. Complaints relating to the availability and quality of services may be beyond the administrative jurisdiction of the implementing ministry/agency, depending on the program context.

The sixth and last step in the GRM is to provide feedback by informing complainants and the general public about the results of investigations and the actions taken. This step involves clear communication of the results of the investigations and relevant actions taken by the program to complainants to close the feedback loop. This final step is crucial in reinforcing the trust between the program, program beneficiaries, and the general public. When numerous levels of grievance resolution are available (for example, local, municipal, and national), and a complainant would like to challenge the outcome of a grievance that was resolved at a lower level, a case can be appealed to a higher level. The program GRM could potentially ask complainants about their user experience to understand how to improve the efficiency and effectiveness of the GRM. At the program level, disclosing the performance information as part of the program's regular reporting is encouraged to advance its transparency.

Figure 8.21 outlines the steps grievances go through in the Philippines's 4Ps. Box 8.7 provides a detailed look at the steps in the implementation of the GRM in Turkey.

Institutional Arrangements for GRMs

It is critical to conduct an assessment of any country systems and existing practices for grievance resolution, including informal mechanisms, to determine possible institutional arrangements when designing a GRM. The institutional arrangements for the implementation of a GRM differ from one country to another. This section summarizes some of the key elements that practitioners should consider when assessing and making decisions about a GRM's institutional arrangements.

There are two basic types of GRMs for social protection programs: in-house GRMs at the ministry, program,

Figure 8.21 Steps in the GRM for the Philippines's 4Ps

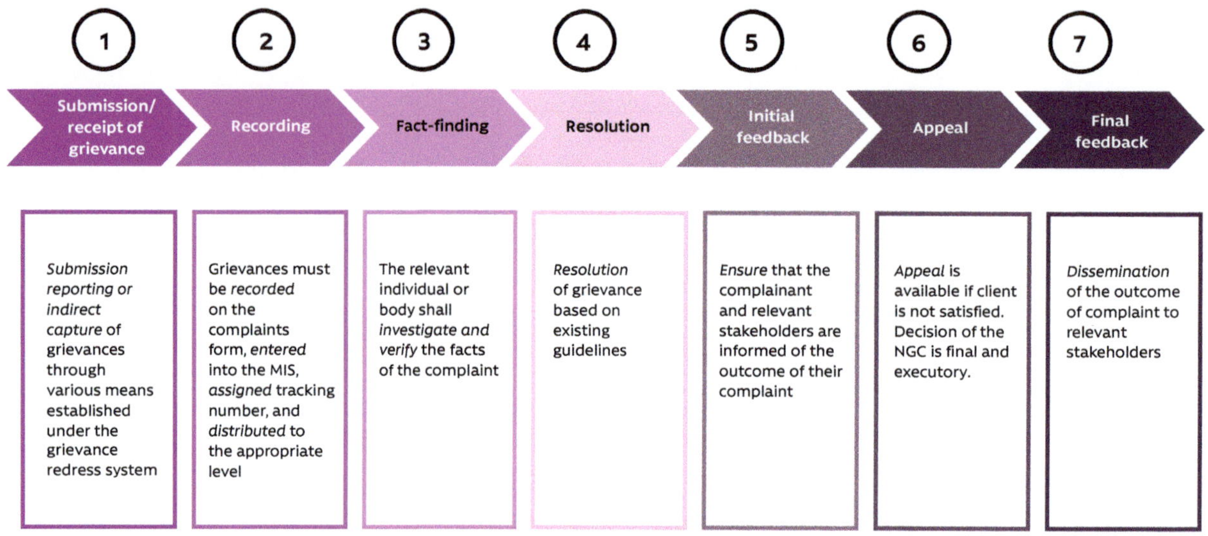

Sources: Philippines, Department of Social Welfare and Development 2015; "Grievance Redress System Overview," presentation by the Philippines's Department for Social Welfare and Development, Manila, 2015.
Note: GRM = grievance redress mechanism; MIS = management information system; NGC = National Grievance Committee; 4Ps = Pantawid Pamilyang Pilipino Program.

or project level (box 8.8) and outsourced GRMs. Many social protection programs establish and strengthen a GRM at the line ministry or program and project levels as part of the ministry and program's administrative functions, and within the mandate and the scope of the programs. These are in-house GRMs. Examples of in-house GRMs include the GRM of the Philippines's 4Ps, the GRM of Egypt's cash transfer program Takaful and Karama (T&K), the complaints-handling mechanism of Egypt's labor-intensive and youth employability programs, the complaints-handling units of West Bank and Gaza's cash transfer program, and the GRM of Sierra Leone's decentralized service delivery program, which is handled through local councils. Other GRMs involve independent institutions and outsource key grievance collection and resolution functions on behalf of the program. The independent institution model includes the ombudsman offices in Ethiopia, Uganda (called "Inspectorate of Government"), and Rwanda, and the Anti-Corruption Commission in Sierra Leone's cash transfer program. One needs to pay close attention to the institutional and legal mandates of institutions that are responsible for grievance resolution, the existing grievance collection and resolution practices, including informal practices, and institutions' local presence, because social protection programs tend to cover vast geographical areas.

Institutional mandate. A GRM can be housed within the relevant line ministries or outsourced to an independent institution. The decision often has to do with institutional mandate regarding the nature and types of grievances that programs are likely to receive. Those grievances are often administrative (see table 8.12, Indicative List of Grievance Categories). In Ethiopia, for instance, the mandate of the Institution of the ombudsman includes the resolution of administrative grievances. The institution has a local presence nationwide through its regional offices. It made sense to strengthen the grievance resolution capacity and functions of the ombudsman's offices and utilize them for social protection programs. In West Bank and Gaza, on the other hand, ministry-led complaints-handling units are legally mandated to resolve administrative complaints, while the ombudsman's office specializes in human rights complaints. The complaints-handling units of the Ministry of Social Affairs (MoSA) at the central level and in governorates are mandated to collect and address grievances related to any of MoSA's programs, including the cash transfer program. It made sense to strengthen the complaints-handling units for MoSA at the ministry and its governorate offices, so that they not only address complaints about the cash transfer program but also grievances related to other programs MoSA delivers. In some countries where the law

Box 8.7 Managing Grievances in Turkey's Integrated Social Assistance System

Turkey has several GRM channels for submitting grievances for all social assistance programs in Turkey. Those channels include, but are not limited to, the integrated GRM module in ISAS; Turkey's hotline, Alo 144; the Presidency Communication Center (CIMER); the Ombudsman Institution; the Ministry of Family, Labor, and Social Services (MFLSS); the General Directorate of Social Assistance (GDSA); and the relevant bodies of district governors. See figure B8.7.1. More information about each channel is below.

- ISAS has an integrated GRM module used for any type of grievance related to social assistance programs (including conditional cash transfers, or CCTs). Clients apply to the Social Assistance and Solidarity Foundation (SASF) in their district using a standard form provided by SASFs. Appeals are sent to ISAS for evaluation during the board of Trustees' weekly decision meetings. Depending on the relevant GSDA regulation, the board must resolve the matter and notify the client about its decision within a month. Notification is made by SMS text.
- The hotline Alo 144 is a call center that provides information and support to clients on social assistance programs.[b] Calls are free of charge. The hotline gives clients the status of program applications as well as payment information, information on new programs, and other information. It is one of the most prominent information channels for all social assistance programs in Turkey. The hotline is also commonly used for grievances. Alo 144 uses Voice-over-Internet-Protocol (VoIP) technology. It can contact any SASF about grievances and can direct citizens to an SASF, if necessary. Alo 144 receives over 1 million calls a year.
- CIMER (Présidence Communication Center) is an online portal that clients can use to file any demand, appeal, proposal, or complaint.[b] Appeals made through CIMER are directed to the relevant authorities depending on the subject matter. The law on information (law no. 4982) and the law on petition (law no. 3071) direct that those appeals must be resolved within 15 business days by the relevant public authority. In terms of CCT, appeals can be addressed to MFLSS, GDSA, and district or provincial governors through the CIMER portal.
- The Ombudsman's Institution (OI) employs an independent, efficient complaint mechanism, and investigates, researches and makes recommendations about all actions.[c] Grievances through OI can be made through an online portal or using a paper form. Usually, it takes several months for an appeal to be resolved through OI.

Figure B8.7.1 Multichannel Grievance Redress in Turkey

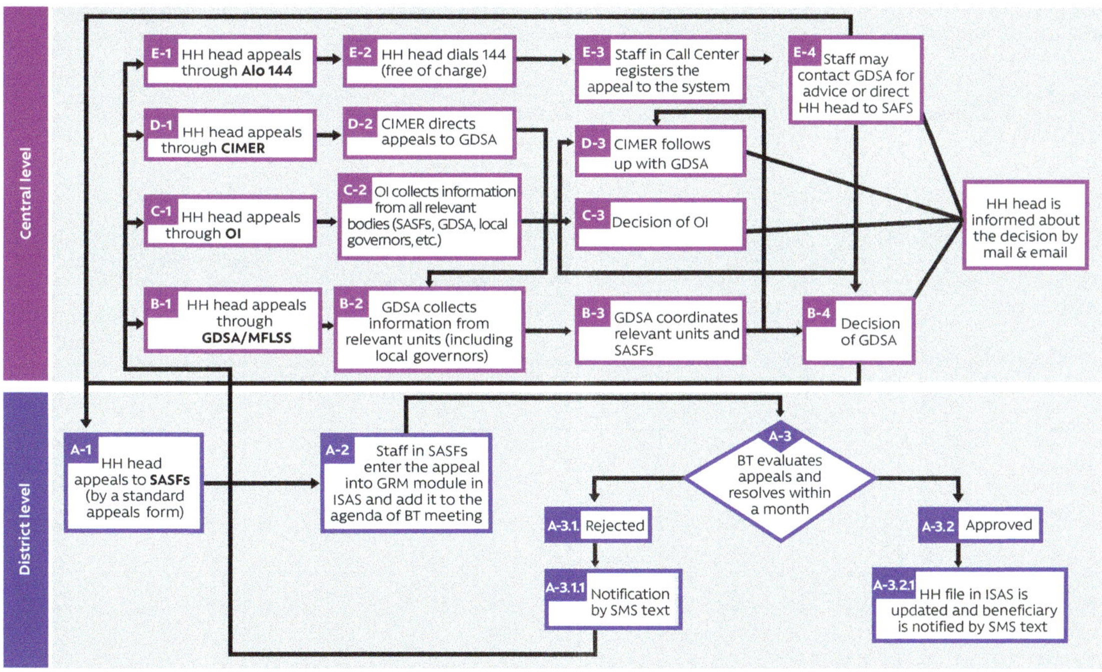

Source: Original figure for this publication.
Note: BT = Board of Trustees; CCT = conditional cash transfer (program); GDSA = General Directorate of Social Assistance; GRM = grievance redress mechanism; HH = household; ISAS = Integrated Social Assistance System; MFLSS = Ministry of Family, Labor, and Social Services; SASF = Social Assistance and Solidarity Foundations; SMS = short message service.
a. Turkey, General Directorate of Social Assistance 2016.
b. Turkey, Presidency Communication Center 2019.
c. Turkey, Ombudsman Institute 2018.

Box 8.8 Types of In-House GRMs

In-house grievance redress mechanisms (GRMs) can be categorized into three types: single program or project GRM, multiprogram or ministry-level GRM, and in-country GRM.

A single program or project GRM is a GRM that is exclusively for an individual social protection program. Examples include the following:

- In Mexico, the two major social protection programs, the conditional cash transfer program, Prospera, and the noncontributory pension program for citizens over 65, Pensión para Adultos Mayores, use a program-specific GRM.
- In the Arab Republic of Egypt, the cash transfer program T&K has its own GRM. Housed at the Ministry of Social Solidarity, which leads the implementation of T&K in coordination with the Ministries of Health and Education, among others, T&K's GRM focuses on the resolution of program grievances (for example, information requests, inclusion or exclusion complaints, and issues with cash cards), working closely with other entities such as the Medical Commission, which has its own GRM for the functional disability assessment required to enroll in Karama (an unconditional cash transfer program for disabled).

A multiprogram or ministry-level GRM refers to cases where a GRM is used for multiple programs, covering some or all of the programs in a ministry, a sector or social protection agency. Examples include the following:

- In Mexico, social protection programs other than Prospera and Pensión para Adultos Mayores use the Ministry of Social Development´s Internal Control Body (Órgano Interno de Control).
- In Rwanda, a GRM that has evolved for over five years currently serves the flagship social safety net program but has also been expanded over time to serve other local economic development programs that are run under the Local Administrative Entities Development Agency.
- Similarly, a GRM that was established under the Tanzania Social Action Fund (TASAF) has not only become a mechanism for grievance management for the Productive Social Safety Net program, but also serves other community-driven development and livelihood programs managed under TASAF. In both Rwanda's and

Figure B8.8.1 West Bank and Gaza's National Grievance Redress Mechanism

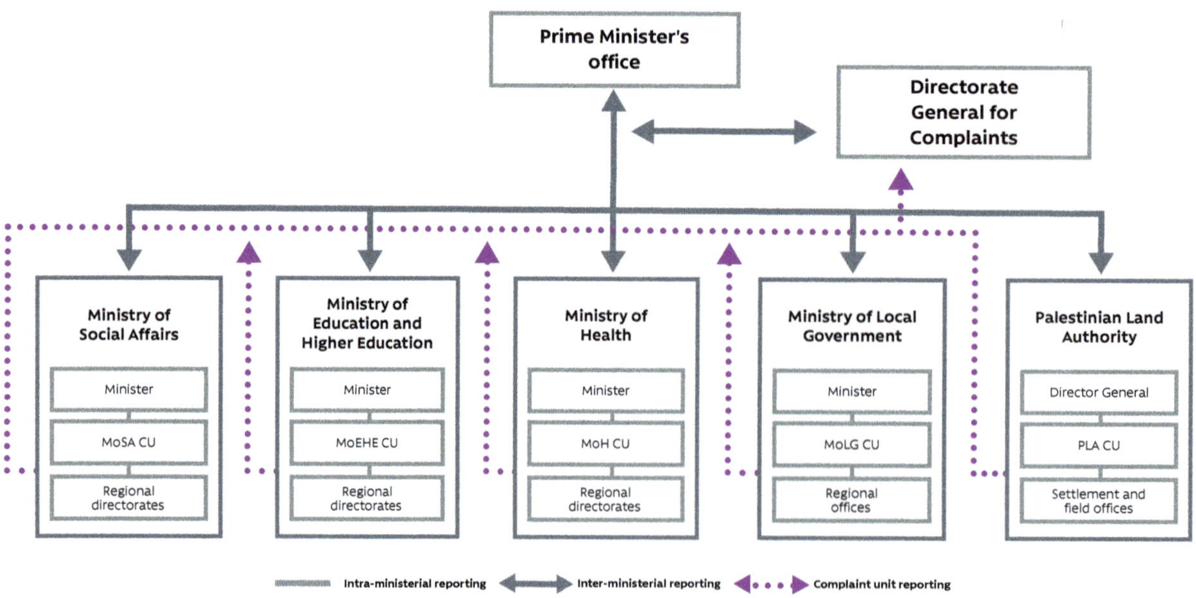

Source: Original figure for this publication.
Note: CU = complaint unit.

continued

Box 8.8 ***(continued)***

Tanzania's GRMs, variable data sets on grievances are classified by different programs, in addition to program-level details of grievances—facilitating comparative analysis across and within the programs and services.

An in-country or national GRM is an approach whereby a collective GRM for the entire government is used to file grievances for social protection and other government programs. Examples include the following:

- Costa Rica's Contraloría General de la República (Comptroller General of the Republic) serves the entire government, and complaints about social protection programs are channeled to the relevant programs through this national system.
- In West Bank and Gaza, the Directorate General for Complaints under the Prime Minister's Office envisions a national GRM, which it hopes will function as a sorting house for grievances (see figure B8.8.1). When this national-level grievance channel becomes available, each line ministry's complaints-handling unit receives relevant grievances from the national level; this can coexist with the grievance uptake channels available at each ministry's complaints-handling unit. This approach can also be effective in a larger context with a huge dispersed population.
- This is the case for Indonesia, which has a GRM called LAPOR that serves a population of about 200 million living across the 17,000 islands of the archipelago. LAPOR, which translates as "to report" in Bahasa, is Indonesia's first integrated complaint handling system for public services and programs. This GRM is built as a social platform to enable interaction between people and the government. LAPOR is accessible via mobile channels. People can initiate the GRM process by sending an SMS text to 1708, a number which is easy for citizens to remember because August 17 is the day Indonesia gained independence. LAPOR intermediates and connects people to over 80 government institutions. LAPOR allows people to submit reports on many issues, ranging from delays in welfare payments to damaged roads. It also provides a way to report fraud and corruption. It has received about 800 complaints a day, on average, from all over Indonesia since the portal's launch in 2012. However, one major drawback is that citizen feedback portals are likely to be disproportionately used by educated, digitally savvy individuals. It has also been reported that most users of LAPOR are from Jakarta, the largest city and the capital, and far fewer from the poorer and more remote regions in eastern Indonesia.

These three types of systems can coexist as different uptake channels for grievances. In Jordan, for example, the national government hosts an in-country GRM called "At Your Service." The Jordanian National Aid Fund (NAF), which is responsible for implementing an expansion cash transfer program, receives grievances relevant for NAF through that GRM. The NAF focal point for this countrywide system refers cash transfer cases to the program's complaint handling mechanism within the Complaints and Citizen Service Center.

What matters for the effective grievance resolution is that the process and roles and responsibilities for grievance resolution are clearly defined within the program administration as described above. No matter how grievances are collected, they need to be responded to in accordance with GRM principles.

allows it, such as Jordan, a complainant could potentially appeal an administrative complaint to an independent institution if he or she was not satisfied with the administrative GRM's resolution. In Rwanda, an independent institution, the ombudsman's office, oversees resolution of administrative grievances (box 8.10).

Geographic coverage and local presence. Many social protection programs provide nationwide services covering vast geographical areas. (When programs roll out in phases or waves, however, coverage is not national until the phases are complete.) As a result, many effective GRMs for social protection programs have multiple decentralized locations, making the GRM accessible to beneficiaries and the general public. When independent institutions are being considered for a program's GRM, it is essential to assess their existing geographical representation because the social protection program may have no influence on the location of the institution's local branches or offices, those offices' budget allocation, or human resource decisions. When a GRM for a

Box 8.9 The Systematic Institutional Arrangements for the Philippines's 4Ps GRM

The administration of conditional cash transfer (CCT) programs is often complex because it requires the involvement of multiple sectors (social welfare, education, and health) from national to local levels. For the Philippines's nationwide CCT program, 4Ps, the Department of Social Welfare and Development (DSWD) is the lead implementation agency. It houses over 11,000 program staff at all levels—from national to city or municipal—and serves approximately 4 million beneficiary households. The DSWD Secretary acts as the national program director and is responsible for providing the overall program direction. The National Project Management Office (NPMO)—housed in the DSWD—and its subnational offices manage the day-to-day operations of the program. The NPMO executes all plans, policies, and activities of the program and is composed of 12 divisions or units, including the Grievance Redress Division (GRD). Ninety-seven percent of the program staff is decentralized and deployed at the regional, provincial, cluster, and city/municipal levels. The program's Interagency Advisory Committees at the national, regional, provincial, and city or municipal levels serve to enhance national ownership and promote joint efforts with partner agencies (for example, the Departments of Education and Health), local implementers (local government units), and civil society organizations. These Interagency Advisory Committees at different levels function as grievance committees as well.

The program's grievance redress mechanism (GRM) follows the same program structure at the national, regional, provisional, and city/municipal levels. At the national level, the GRD, housed in the NPMO, oversees and manages the GRM with a team of dedicated staff (17 full-time staff). The GRD monitors and supervises the overall complaints handling process, coordinates monthly meetings of the National Grievance Committee, prepares monthly grievance reports, investigates and resolves grievances that have been referred to the national level, categorizes and distributes them to the appropriate level for resolution, maintains a dedicated grievance database, and builds the capacity of the grievance monitors at field levels. The GRD also analyzes trends in grievance reporting, identifies strategies to address major problems, and reviews GRM guidelines to continuously improve them.

Over 200 grievance officers are deployed in field offices to serve as focal points at regional, provincial, and cluster levels. City and municipal links are the primary focal points for grievance redress on the frontlines, entrusted with the responsibility of accepting, recording, and investigating program-related complaints. They also keep track of all grievances in their work areas. Grievances related to a particular level are addressed by the grievance unit just above that level. For instance, the national unit facilitates the resolution of serious grievances at all levels but particularly those that relate to the regional level. However, grievances that relate to the performance or behavior of the city or municipal link can be reported directly to the provincial, regional, or national 4Ps office. This multitiered structure also provides complainants with opportunities to appeal resolutions that were decided at a lower level. Decisions at the national level—by the GRD with the advice of the National Advisory Committee—are final.

Source: Patel et al. 2014.
Note: 4Ps = Pantawid Pamilyang Pilipino Program.

program is to be established or strengthened within one or more ministries, it is important to align the GRM's institutional structure with that of the program. See box 8.9 for the Philippines's 4Ps GRM, which is an example of a program-level GRM housed in a ministry—in this case, the Department of Social Welfare and Development (DSWD). Box 8.10 highlights Rwanda's GRM for social protection programs, which is operated through a more complex government system. Irrespective of which institutional arrangements countries select, it is important that roles and responsibilities for grievance redress are clearly defined so that GRMs function effectively and their objectives are achieved.

There is no one-size-fits-all GRM model that can be replicated and scaled across all programs because programs vary in complexity and maturity.

Box 8.10 Vision 2020 Umurenge Program: Localized Grievance Redress Mechanism in Rwanda

Rwanda's Vision 2020 Umurenge Program (VUP) is an integrated local development program to accelerate poverty eradication, rural growth, and social protection by (1) direct support, (2) public works, and (3) financial services. The VUP is a flagship program in Rwanda and has established a highly localized level of grievance redress mechanisms (GRMs). The Ministry of Local Government is the national-level implementing agency for the program, but the GRM system is implemented through parallel structures to promote transparency and fairness. The principles of VUP's GRM system are the following: (1) minimize risks and reduce errors and corruption; (2) strengthen transparency and accountability of service providers; and (3) strengthen trust, improve program performance, and inform relevant policy changes. The VUP program adopted a highly decentralized policy, where most of the grievances get resolved at a local level and only when absolutely necessary the grievances get escalated to the central level. The local government and the central government work cohesively to provide timely, accurate, and transparent GRM.

At the local level,

- the District Council reviews and makes decisions on grievances and complaints from the sector.
- the Sector Council reviews and makes decisions on grievances and appeals from the cells and villages.
- the Cell Council convenes to resolve cases initiated by the village and cell executives.
- the Village Assembly formally registers grievances and appeals

And at a national level,

- the Ombudsman office reviews and decides on cases from districts and provides feedback to the district administration for appropriate actions.

The business process map in figure B8.10.1 gives an overview of GRM in the VUP.

Figure B8.10.1 Summarized Process Map of GRM in Rwanda's Vision 2020 VUP

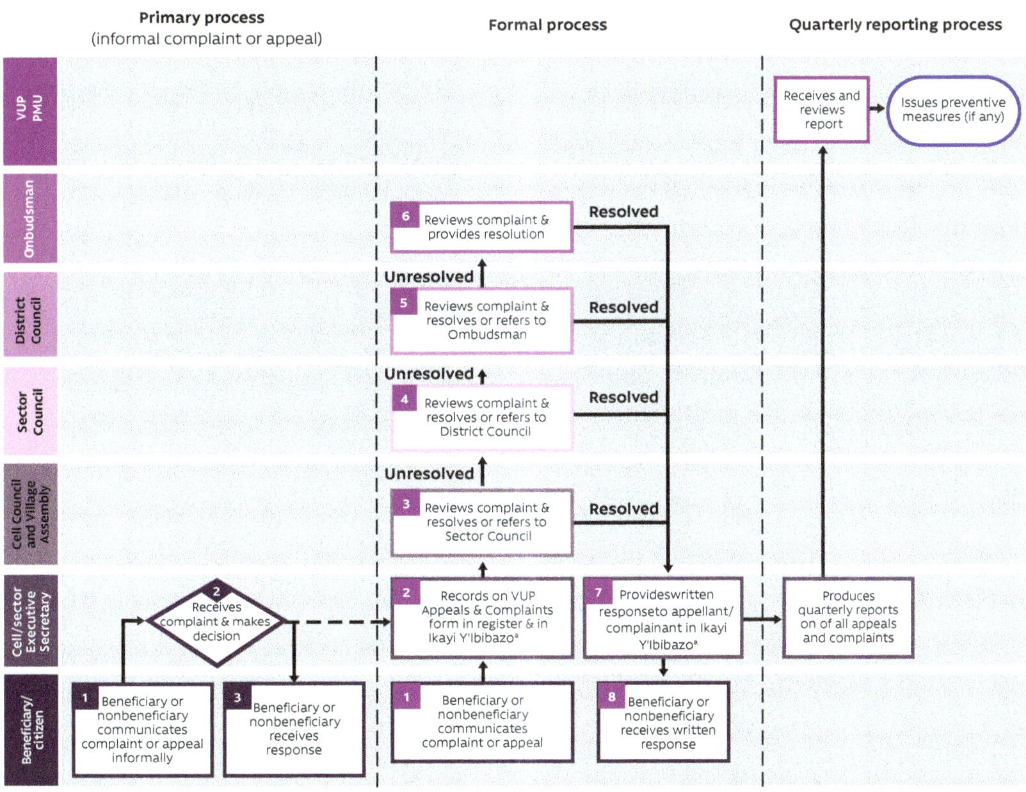

Source: Original figure for this publication.

Note: GRM = grievance redress mechanism; PMU = project management unit; VUP = Vision 2020 Umurenge Program.

a. Ikayi Y'Ibibazo is Rwanda's grievances registry.

A universal child allowance or social pension program can be relatively simple compared to a means-tested CCT program or public works program (Grosh et al. 2008). Similarly, mature programs can have more sophisticated versions of GRM supported by strong institutions, while programs in fragile, conflict, or violent contexts or low-income contexts may need to adapt to solutions that work well in resource-constrained contexts, like low-cost technology solutions that have proved to be effective. A GRM can start simply and expand and mature as the program scales and matures. The GRM's scaling and increasing functions can be planned in phases along with the program's expansion and maturity.

Common Key Features of Effective GRMs

There are several key common components for a successful GRM, including outreach and communications, uptake channels, a process for grievance resolution, information systems, performance, and institutional capacity.

Outreach and Communications

Outreach and communications are key components for a GRM. Effective outreach and communication are needed to inform people where to go, how to access the system, and how to file a grievance. People must not only understand how to access and use the GRM system, but also feel encouraged to file grievances as needed. Facilitating access and eliminating potential barriers to accessing the GRM is important for vulnerable and marginalized groups, such as people living in remote areas, members of ethnic or linguistic minorities, and indigenous populations who may have difficulty filing a complaint. Many social protection programs have utilized posters, brochures, or other media to inform beneficiaries and the general public about the GRM. For example, the Sierra Leone's Decentralized Service Delivery Program developed GRM jingles in different languages which were aired on radio programs to inform the public about the GRM that was available at their ward committees and local councils.

Uptake Channels

There are many uptake channels, both traditional and emerging. Program administrators need to establish grievance uptake locations in areas where poor and marginalized people live to reach the "first mile." Because the cost and complexity of GRMs are likely to increase with the number of uptake channels, the program should choose channels and locations strategically. As the program and the GRM expand and mature, additional uptake channels can be added. Such an expansion plan needs to be strategically sequenced based on the goals of the program (box 8.11).

The following are some traditional channels used in grievance redress mechanisms.

- ***Social workers and community agents.*** Face-to-face interaction with social workers or community agents is an effective channel for grievances, especially where literacy levels are low.
- ***Complaint boxes.*** They are a simple and accessible channel for grievances, though they are not appropriate for illiterate populations.
- ***Complaints and appeals registries or books.*** In some countries, registry books are available in program offices and other designated local offices where people can formally log complaints and appeals by entering them in the designated books. In Rwanda, this channel remains an important one for receiving grievances, even in the face of technological advances, mainly because the channel is trusted and those who cannot read or write can confide in people close to them who can write for them.
- ***Call centers.*** Providing information by phone can be efficient when the telecommunications infrastructure is well-developed and cheap. The public may find placing a call much easier than traveling to an office and waiting in line. For a large program, it may also be safer for employees, and it may be cheaper to run such a back-office function. Call centers can be helpful, although they are never enough by themselves because some part of the client base may find them impossible or uncomfortable to use. Moreover, call centers must be adequately staffed and equipped and well-monitored. Calls that are never answered, or worse, answered incorrectly, can harm a program's reputation (Grosh et al. 2008).

Box 8.11 Multichannel GRM: Mexico's Pension for the Elderly Program

Mexico's social pension program, PBPAM, implements a multichannel grievance redress mechanism (GRM):

- **Social worker.** This first channel utilizes the beneficiary update form (described in section 8.2), which is filled out by the social worker. This is a paper-based form that is later digitized in the regional office; it records the information of the requesting party, the name and number of the receiving agent (normally the social worker), and the characteristics of the grievance. Grievances managed through this channel are: clarification on noneligibility status; replacement of the payment instrument; and reinstatement into the program (for beneficiaries who were temporary suspended). Those grievances are collected bimonthly, and processed and attended to in alignment with the payment cycle.
- **Social audit committees.** According to the General Social Development Law, all social programs are required to establish a social audit committee in the localities where the programs are implemented. The social audit committee's objective is to supervise the adequate usage of public funds, guard against any political utilization of the program, and receive and channel any grievances arising in its locality. In the case of the PBPAM program, two committee members are elected by the beneficiaries in each locality. Grievances channeled through the social audit committees relate to misuse of public funds and political utilization of the program.
- **Complaint boxes in program offices.** Every Ministry of Welfare office, whether at the regional or national level, has a complaint box clearly identified, where individuals can deposit written complaints. Complaints are collated periodically and channeled to the corresponding program directorate. Grievances collected through this channel are normally service-related.
- **Call centers and internet portal.** This channel is used by the in-country GRM managed by Mexico's Comptroller General.

Sources: Mexico's Reglas de Operación de la Pensión para el Bienestar de las Personas Adultas Mayores, 2019, and Guía para el Llenado de Fichas de Atención, Secretaría de Desarrollo Social, 2017.

- ***Community grievance committees.*** Several countries have chosen to set up a community grievance committee. For example, Armenia uses local social protection councils composed of five representatives of the local government's social sector offices and five representatives of nongovernmental organizations. The councils hear appeals from those who were deemed ineligible for assistance but consider themselves in need.
- ***Mobile unit.*** This option is particularly useful for reaching vulnerable groups who are living in the streets or in remote regions. In the absence of permanent institutional structures, mobile units can help document and mitigate public grievances on a periodic basis.

The pros and cons of the GRM channels are detailed in table 8.13.

Emerging Channels: Technologies in Grievance Redress Mechanisms

There are several challenges in using traditional methods for GRMs, including cost, institutional capacity, labor-intensive processes, and resource constraints. Those challenges have led to the emergence of new, improved GRM channels that leverage new technologies. Some of the most common emerging channels are as follows:

- ***Mobile solutions for GRM.*** Mobile cell phones have proved to be remarkable instruments for improving inclusion, transparency, and accountability. The ubiquity of mobile phones means that mobile solutions work well in both urban and rural regions. In Sierra Leone, mobile technologies are being used to improve the delivery of social protection programs. An interactive GRM with an automated,

Table 8.13 Pros and Cons of Common Grievance Redress Channels

Grievance channel	Pros	Cons
Community agents, social workers	• Strong understanding of social protection programs • Accessible locally • Regular contact with the social protection program team • Can be trained easily	• Potential conflict of interest (cannot complain to them about their conduct) • Not always capable of solutions • Not anonymous or confidential • Could be biased against certain community members
Complaints box	• Easy to set up • Can be anonymous (if grievance form clearly states that name and address are not needed)	Not suitable for those who are illiterate
Call Center	• Direct • Simple • No barriers linked to illiteracy • Can be anonymous/confidential • Useful in decentralized contexts	• Poor people are less likely to have access to a phone or to be willing to pay for the call • People may not have trust in revealing their identity and problems to someone they do not know • More difficult to follow up on how the complaint is being managed • Needs to operate very well, or can backfire
Community grievance committees	• Members are from the community; widely known and trusted • Easy to access (direct and simple) • No barriers linked to illiteracy	• Not anonymous or confidential • More expensive to set up and train
Mobile unit	• Direct • Simple to access • No problems linked to illiteracy • Theoretically can be anonymous/confidential • Unbiased/external	• People may not trust in revealing their identity and problems to someone they do not know • Not easily organized throughout the country • Expensive to set up • People can complain only periodically

Source: Barca 2016.

toll-free, SMS-based (text) mechanism is currently being implemented. To access the system, the user sends an SMS to 161 and the system interacts with the user to help submit a report. SMS reporting can be used even in areas with low 3G coverage and low smartphone diffusion. The main advantages of this system are that the interaction is automated and thus no operator is needed; it is free for the user; it reaches a wider user base; and it improves inclusiveness. A human-centered adaptation for GRM via telephone, using voice-based messaging to help illiterate populations document their grievances, is currently being designed (World Bank 2018b).

- ***Social media communication channels and feedback mechanisms.*** Social media feedback mechanisms and interactive feedback involve direct two-way communication with individuals and are good for resolving specific issues. The use of social media or private messaging apps can help channel complaints and facilitate interactive feedback from beneficiaries and the population in general.[45]
- ***Natural language processing: Chatbots and virtual assistants.*** Natural language processing (NLP), in combination with artificial intelligence, can help create a new generation of GRM tools by addressing recurring queries.

Process of Grievance Resolution

A clear step-by-step process and procedure for grievance collection and resolution is a key to effective GRM. Section 8.2 provided a framework for grievance collection and resolution. This section aims to provide more detailed guidance on resolution processes.

Articulating the processes. All staff involved in grievance resolution need to have the same understanding of how to collect, document, and resolve grievances. Grievance resolution flowcharts for each category of grievance are effective tools to visualize and streamline the grievance resolution processes.

Roles and responsibilities. Each step in the process should clearly define which department at which level is going to be responsible for the action. This helps define who will need particular types of access to the grievance management system.

Resolution time frame. Some grievances (such as information requests) can be resolved on the spot, while others (such as potential inclusion/exclusion errors or staff performance) could take longer to resolve and require procedures to address them. Programs may have different time frames for resolving each complaint category because the administrative procedures and length of investigation may vary. Each of the resolution processes should have a designated time frame for action.

Information Systems

A GRM's information system can be as simple as a log book or as sophisticated as a dedicated information management system. Given the complexity and scale of the social protection programs, it is highly recommended that programs invest in a GRM module within the program's information system (as did Egypt, Jordan, and West Bank and Gaza) or as an independent system that speaks to the program information system (as does the Philippines's 4Ps Unified Information and Communication System–Client Relationship Management). The common features of effective GRM information systems are listed in table 8.14.

Table 8.14 Common Features of Effective GRM Information Systems

Key Feature	Description
Real-time data collection	Grievance data are collected in real time from various uptake channels, including website, SMS text, and social media
Automated response	Where applicable, automated response is issued to acknowledge the receipt of a grievance, generate a case number, and inform a stipulated resolution time and follow-up methods
Consolidated data repository	Collected data are stored, including data through informal grievance channels
Dashboard: Internal interface	• Allows real-time tracking and monitoring of resolution status per case and allows viewing assigned officer information • Allows the monitors of the GRM to see flags when resolution time frame is nearer, and issues automated reminders to an assigned officer and his/her supervisor(s) • Decision makers have access to real-time evidence for evidence-based policy and program decision making with data visualization and/or geotagging features
Dashboard: External interface	• Allows real-time tracking of resolution status with a case number • Allows the public to view the aggregated grievance resolution status of the program, along with the regular reports (e.g., annual reports)
Rapid custom reporting	• Automated reporting feature allows decision makers and other stakeholders to have program/project information as frequently as they want • Various reporting types—pie and bar charts, maps, and so on—can be chosen • Customization allows selecting which data are to be analyzed at which level and how frequently
Language	Multiple languages can be used or different language options can be chosen
Security	Data encryptions, firewalls, and the like safeguard the grievance and personal data collected
API	Maximizes compatibility with other applications

Source: Kumagai 2013.

Note: API = application programming interface; GRM = grievance redress mechanism.

Performance of GRM Systems

Tracking the performance of GRMs is a critical step to their success, whether they are program-specific, multiprogram or in-country. Tracking and assessing the extent to which grievances are received, processed, and resolved includes regular analysis of the frequency, patterns, and causes of grievance; strategies and processes used for grievance resolution; and their effectiveness.

An effective GRM includes grievance-redress performance indicators and monitors the GRM's performance, as well as using grievance data to improve a program's effectiveness and efficiency. Analyzing GRM monitoring data allows governments and program administrators to assess the performance of the GRM system and identify potential areas of improvement so as to minimize similar grievances in the future. Analysis of grievance data can also help identify processes within a program or delivery system that can be improved. For instance, if there are recurring grievances on a specific subject, such as delayed payments, poor service quality, or errors in the determination of eligibility, program administrators might need to improve the program's business processes.

Given the complexity and scale of social protection programs, there should ideally be an electronic system for entering, tracking, and monitoring grievance logging and resolution. When an electronic system is available, it is critical that it include rapid custom reporting. That feature should allow the implementation teams and the programs' decision makers to have real-time or near real-time data management and monitoring of grievance resolution. Analysis of grievance resolution should also be integrated into the regular reports to program management. The list below presents examples of indicators, which can be auto-generated and analyzed at different levels (national, regional, provincial, or local), and include other characteristics of interest (such as gender), on a regular basis.

- Number of complaints collected (in a given time period [e.g., monthly, quarterly, annually])
  - Number (and percentage) of complaints relevant to each program
  - Number (and percentage) of complaints, by uptake channels
  - Number (and percentage) of complaints, by types of complaints
  - Number (and percentage) of complaints submitted by women
  - Number (and percentage) of complaints, by resolution status (open, referred, or closed)
  - Number of open complaints, by type and age of complaint (e.g., one, two, or three months from the date of receipt)
  - Number of open and outstanding complaints, by type and age of complaint (e.g., one, two, or three months overdue per the stipulated resolution timeline)
- Number and percentage of complaints resolved within the stipulated time frame
- Number and percentage of complainants satisfied with complaint handling process
- Number and percentage of complainants satisfied with action(s) taken

Additionally, table 8.15 includes a list of possible performance indicators for GRM, which may require surveying complainants.

Institutional Capacity

Institutional capacity can play a significant role in the effectiveness of a GRM. Social protection programs require dedicated, trained staff. A shortage of frontline workers might affect certain phases of the delivery chain, including the management of grievances. Some programs adapt to this challenge by taking advantage of existing public systems outside the social protection institutions, contracting with an external firm, or simplifying the GRM's design.

Other factors that affect institutional capacity are the program budget and political will. Regular reporting of GRM data may provide an incentive for program staff to take grievance management seriously. Integration of the GRM training module in program training can be an effective way to increase awareness of the importance of grievance resolution. Raising awareness of GRM is useful not only for beneficiaries and clients, but also for program staff.

Table 8.15 Performance Indicators for Grievance Redress Mechanisms (GRMs)

GRM indicator categories	Performance indicators
Client awareness	Percentage of clients who are able to name at least one complaint uptake channel*
Access	Percentage of clients with access barriers who are receiving adequate accommodation for voicing grievances*
Potential use	Percentage of clients who would complain in case of poor quality in the delivery of benefits and services*
Actual use	• Percentage of clients who considered quality to be low and used the established procedures to complain about it* • Percentage of clients who have provided feedback
Sorting and processing	Percentage of registered grievances disaggregated by type (e.g., eligibility, payments, etc.)
Resolution	Percentage of grievances resolved within stipulated time frame
Quality standards	Percentage of registered grievances that have been placed in the process of resolution according to quality standards
Processing/resolution time	Average time required to resolve grievances
Client satisfaction	Percentage of complainants satisfied with response and grievance redress process*
Notification/feedback	Percentage of grievances for which the beneficiary is notified of status according to quality standards

Source: Original table for this publication.
Note: * = requires beneficiary or complainant survey(s).

8.6 ERROR, FRAUD, AND CORRUPTION MONITORING

Social protection systems include programs delivering benefits and services to thousands or millions of beneficiaries. While the value of benefits or services may be relatively low, on aggregate, social protection spending is a substantial part of the national budget. Thus, it is important to make sure that benefits and services reach the intended beneficiaries, in the right amount, at the right time, with the correct logistical arrangements. Error, fraud, and corruption (EFC) reduces the economic efficiency of interventions by decreasing the amount of benefits and services that go to the intended beneficiaries, and subsequently, may erode the political support for the program. Hence, monitoring and curbing the level of EFC in these programs is an essential task.

This section will describe how a deliberate monitoring approach to identify and correct benefits or services affected by EFC can help social protection programs curb EFC all along the delivery chain of a program.

As such, we have organized section 8.6 in four subsections:

- ***Definitions, prevalence, and factors affecting the level of EFC.*** This subsection will introduce the main concepts and relevance, as well as incidence, of EFC.
- ***EFC mitigation strategies.*** Here, an EFC monitoring implementation framework, built around four pillars (prevention, detection, deterrence, and monitoring), is described.
- ***Measuring EFC.*** This subsection explains how to measure EFC at the systems level as well as at the individual program level.
- ***Building a system to reduce the rate of EFC.*** Finally, this subsection provides a summarized road map of establishing the building blocks to achieve an end-to-end EFC monitoring system.

Definitions, Prevalence, and Factors Affecting the Level of EFC in Social Protection Programs

Definitions

Any social protection program would like to transfer all its resources to the right beneficiaries, in the right amount, at the right time, and with the correct logistical arrangements. Unavoidably, a fraction of these transfers or services is lost to EFC (figure 8.22). As a starting point, let us discuss the central concepts. First, **error** is the unintentional deviation from program or benefit rules, resulting in the wrong benefit package or benefits to an ineligible applicant. Errors may be the result of unintentional mistakes by program administrators, or the product of applicants or beneficiaries inadvertently providing incorrect information. Intentional abuses of the program by beneficiaries are termed as fraud, and by program administrators, as corruption. **Fraud** occurs when a client or beneficiary deliberately makes a false statement or conceals or distorts relevant information regarding program eligibility or level of benefits. Finally, **corruption** commonly involves manipulation of beneficiary rosters (e.g., registering potential beneficiaries for clientelist purposes to garner political support); staff accepting illegal payments from applicants or beneficiaries; or diversion of funds to ghost or illegal channels.

The rate of losses due to EFC (overpayments or underpayments over the program budget, excessive or inadequate provision of services) shows the degree to which the program is compliant with its own rules. When a program is not implemented in full compliance with its rules, there are losses due to EFC. For example, when a part of the beneficiaries' caseload will be admitted in the program based on inaccurate information, it will result in overpayments due to errors or fraud. Similarly, some applicants will be either rejected or receive lower benefits due to inaccurate provision of or handling of information, resulting in underpayments due, most likely, to some form of error. Conversely, if program officials ask beneficiaries for kickbacks, thus reducing their benefits, this is a case of corruption. For poverty-targeted programs, EFC losses will add up to the design-based inclusion and exclusion error and will further erode the degree to which the program is achieving its ultimate objective.

Figure 8.22 Visual Depiction of Error, Fraud, and Corruption (EFC) Concepts

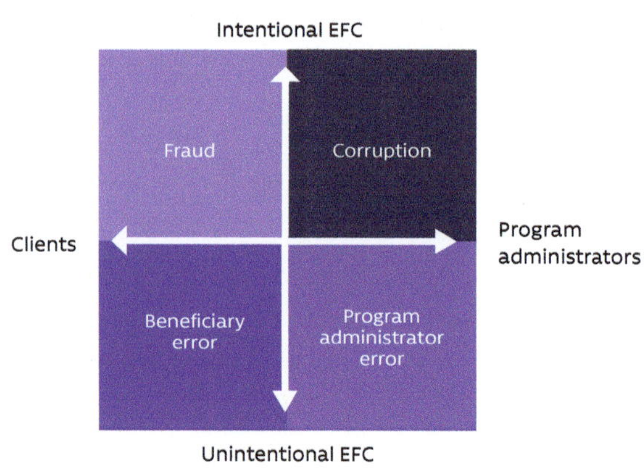

Source: Original figure for this publication.

Why Do We Care about EFC in Social Protection Programs?

These programs channel a large amount of public resources to beneficiaries, and even a small fraction of misappropriated benefits may add up to large sums of money with high opportunity costs. On average, social protection spending represents 16 percent of GDP in developed countries, 7 percent in middle-income countries, and 4 percent in lower-income countries. While EFC statistics are not always available in many countries, the evidence from countries monitoring EFC shows that significant amounts are lost to EFC. Even in countries that devote a large amount of resources to prevent, deter, detect, and recover money lost to EFC, this amount can be large. For example, in five OECD countries reviewed by the United Kingdom National Audit Office in 2006, this fraction varied between 2 and 5 percent of the total social protection spending. The rate of EFC varied by type of program, being higher in those programs with more complex eligibility criteria and/or reassessment requirements, such as poverty-targeted programs (in this case, means-tested welfare programs), disability insurance, or unemployment supports. For means-tested programs, the rate of EFC climbed up to about 10 percent. The information from developing countries is scarcer, as only a few programs and countries have taken measures to combat and/or measure the incidence of EFC. However, it is plausible to expect the share of funds affected by EFC be larger compared to developed countries. Romania carried out benefit inspections of six large and EFC risk-prone safety net programs during 2011–13 and found rates of irregularities between 8 and 20 percent.

Why the Rate of EFC Losses Varies across Social Protection Programs

The share of funds lost to EFC will go up with increasing program generosity and complexity,[46] and go down with greater institutional capacity, in general, and with the level of resources devoted to prevention, detection, deterrence, and monitoring, in particular.

First, let us examine the benefits from fraud or corruption and what type of social protection programs will have higher a priori EFC risks. The programs most "profitable" to defraud are those which offer higher benefits for a longer period (e.g., income replacement programs with longer recertification periods). Among two safety net programs that offer X and 10X in benefits while all other conditions are the same, one can expect the EFC rate to be higher in the second program. Among two identical safety net programs, one with annual reassessment policy and the second with no reassessment policy, the second will have a higher EFC rate.

Apart from program generosity, complexity increases the EFC risk as it affects the ease of defrauding the program. Among programs, poverty-targeted safety net programs are more complex, hence more prone to EFC. Eligibility for these programs is often based on the welfare position of the household, which is more difficult to assess and harder to verify than, for example, for an old-age pension where all that is needed is proof of past contribution and age. Because welfare status of a beneficiary changes over time, eligibility also changes over time, which increases the risk of EFC. Disability programs, be it pensions or social assistance, are also more prone to EFC risk, due to complex certification requirements. This risk will be higher for the beneficiaries with temporary, as opposed to permanent, disabilities. Moreover, the responsibilities for implementing safety net programs are often shared across different departments, agencies, and levels of government—another factor that can facilitate EFC to creep in the program. Having the right instruments and tools to minimize EFC is thus more important for safety net and disability programs.

Developing the institutional capacity of the program will reduce EFC losses. In general, this means moving toward a good practice implementation mode as described in the previous chapters. For example, improving the assessment of clients' needs and conditions by linking the roster of beneficiaries with a reliable ID database would eliminate ghost and duplicate beneficiaries. Moving away from cash to payments in bank accounts or digital modalities would also reduce EFC losses. Having a system of sanctions that are proportional with the value of the loss as well as with its repeated or collusive character would prevent and deter EFC, as well as getting the message to the public that most cases affected by EFC are caught by the program staff. More specifically, program administrators could invest in the specific measures that are detailed in the next and final subsections.

EFC Mitigation Strategies

The standard mitigation strategies consist of prevention, detection, and deterrence (figure 8.23).

Preventive measures reduce the likelihood of EFC occurrences. These measures are implemented early in the delivery chain, during the assessment and enrollment phases. They are aimed both at deliberate dishonesty on behalf of the applicant (e.g., undeclared income or other economic circumstance during eligibility, failing to report changes in material circumstances, multiple program claims, misrepresentation of material circumstances, and identity fraud) and cutting out corruption by officials (e.g., collusion with beneficiaries and theft from program resources) and error. They could include a range of activities focusing on the design and governance of a social protection program, such as (1) streamlining the administrative steps involved

Figure 8.23 Standard Mitigation Strategies

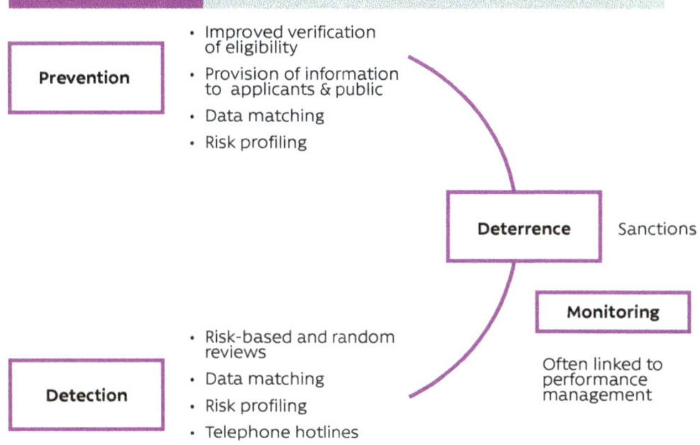

Source: Original figure for this publication.

in administering the benefit; (2) simplifying eligibility criteria; and (3) reducing the complexity of the whole benefit system (e.g., by moving from program-by-program eligibility determination to a harmonized assessment, through a social registry). EFC prevention may also look at staff caseloads, wider administrative capacity, and the systems used to administer a program. System weakness (e.g., lack of interoperability between IT systems) is a common cause of EFC in many programs. Tighter eligibility verification and cross-checks at the outset of a claim may also be considered. Some prevention looks at the information campaigns to inform beneficiaries of rights and responsibilities during the assessment phase

"Detection" refers to finding EFC within the social protection system or program. These measures are implemented during the recurrent delivery cycle. Detection includes several ways to identify cases where there is a suspicion of EFC, which can then be handed over to a specialized unit (compliance unit, review unit, inspection unit, fraud unit) for further verification. The modalities of identifying cases suspected of EFC can include data matching using databases across the public sector (e.g., identity, asset registries, tax and benefit registries, utility consumption records), risk profiling, tip-offs from the public through a telephone hotline, and referrals from officials, one the frontline—units that have direct contact with applicants and beneficiaries. The inspection of cases with suspicions of EFC can be either random, time-based (after a specific time of being on the benefit), or risk-based. The latter would focus the inspection efforts on specific subpopulations, based on algorithms that predict EFC risk based on the characteristics of a particular beneficiary and claim.

"Deterrence" refers mostly to sanctions against the applicant, beneficiary, or program administrators. Sanctions impose a cost of committing EFC and create a disincentive for the individual involved in EFC. Sanctions can include the loss of an entitlement (or, in the case of a program administrator, loss of a job), recovery of overpayments, an administrative sanction (financial penalty), or criminal prosecution. These measures occur during the recurrent service delivery cycle. Some countries, especially in the OECD, use media campaigns to deter applicants from EFC, or to influence public opinion about EFC (either as part of the assessment or the recurring cycle).

Good practice also requires the monitoring and evaluation of the actions put in place to reduce EFC. As these actions typically cost money, it would make sense to monitor the recovered overpayments or misappropriated benefits, to show they are cost-effective or at least cost-neutral. Evidence from Australia, Romania, the United Kingdom, and the United States suggests that well-designed interventions can recover more than the investment in mitigation (see annex 8B, Measuring EFC).

Building a System to Reduce EFC Rate in Social Protection Programs: Strategy and Tools

While no program is immune to EFC, evidence from developed countries demonstrates EFC losses can be brought to negligible levels. A first step is to develop a strategy and an action plan to put in place a comprehensive, end-to-end EFC control system. This was the first step taken both by the United Kingdom and Romania, in 2000 and 2010, respectively.

Second, given the limited resources to combat EFC and their cost, the social protection system should focus its efforts on high-budget, risk-prone programs such as disability pensions, income-replacement programs, and proxy- or means-tested benefits. In the United Kingdom, as a result of the solid monitoring system, the government was able to rank the different programs in terms of their EFC losses and budget and focus the mitigation measures on the largest ones. Romania applied this strategy by 2010–11, at two levels. The country had an investigative unit in charge of compliance of about 300 social inspectors, but they were almost exclusively used to verify the compliance with standards in the provision of residential social services (for children deprived of parental care, persons with disability, or elderly). These services represented, at the time, only 5 percent of the social protection spending, and the EFC losses were probably proportionate. A first strategic move of the government at that time was to shift the focus on the inspection toward social protection benefits, accounting for 95 percent of the spending. Within those, the government further prioritized five safety net programs as well as disability pensions, programs with the highest a priori EFC risk.

Figure 8.24 Comprehensive End-to-End Error, Fraud, and Corruption System

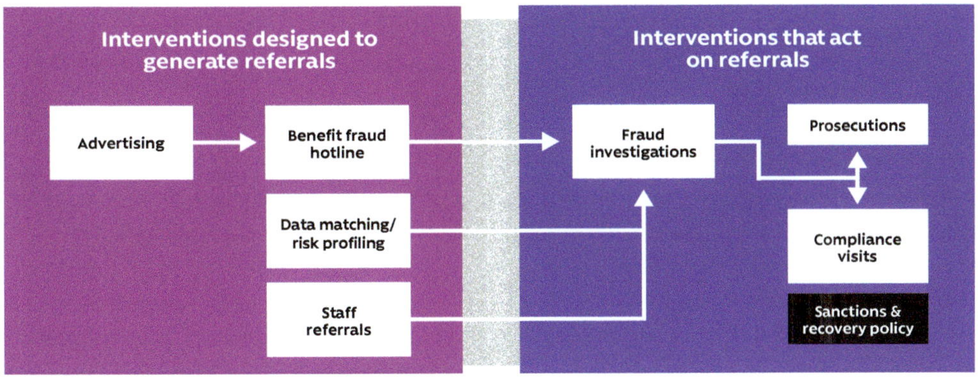

Source: Original figure for this publication.

Third, the social protection ministry or the program administration should develop, on top of the existing and likely fragmented measures to reduce EFC, a comprehensive, end-to-end system. Such a system would comprise, generally, two parts (figure 8.24). One part would collect information about cases that are likely affected by EFC (suspicious cases). Such information may come from frontline staff, from a hotline (telephone, email, website), or from systematic intelligence gathering efforts such as data matching or risk profiling. Second, this information would then be used by the units and staff to attempt to correct the claims. The volume of such referrals can be larger than the human capacity to handle such referrals. In such cases, a triage is typically done, when checks or inspections are focused toward the cases with the higher potential losses, multiplied by the ability to correct them.

The development of an end-to-end system would entail measures across a range of instruments or policies (box 8.12): development of a harmonized, effective sanction policy and recovery system; development of a professional workforce for compliance reviews and inspections; developing the analytical capacity of the system (e.g., capacity to carry regular database cross-checks and risk-profiling models); and moving from random or experience-based inspection to analytically informed risk-based inspections. The development of such a system would take some time, especially if reducing EFC in social protection programs is not a major priority. A typical transition can take anywhere from three or more years, and a functional system will include the elements outlined in table B8.12.1 (in box 8.12).

The Role of Analytics

Traditionally, the identification of cases suspicious for EFC has relied on the experience of the "control" staff: inspectors, investigators, or auditors. This specialized staff selects the cases they believe have a high probability of EFC and inspects them. Often, after a certain period, the control staff gets together, shares their insights, and subjectively ranks the factors associated with or circumstances indicative of EFC. This knowledge is used in the second round of inspections. Post-inspections, the subjective risk profiling can be updated. The social inspections of Moldova and Romania used this approach in their early days.

Increasingly, the identification of cases with high likelihood of EFC is carried out with the use of analytical models using ICT, such as data cross-checks and risk profiling.

- Data cross-checks are used to identify cases where the information reported by the applicant and recorded by the frontline staff is different than identical information stored in other public databases. For example, an applicant family might report that they do not own a car, but a cross-check with the vehicle registry shows they do own one. The results of such data cross-checks would identify a case with EFC: an official error if the information was not properly recorded by the frontline staff, or a case of fraud if the applicant has intentionally concealed this information. Sometimes, the cross-checks would use logical rules to determine incompatible situations. One such example is of applicants for permanent disability

Box 8.12 Developing an Effective EFC Control System in Three Years in Romania

By 2010 Romania was spending twice as much on social assistance compared to 2005, without a commensurate improvement in the welfare of the poor and vulnerable. The number of social assistance programs and the complexity of applying for benefits also increased, but not the frontline staff who had to deal with an increased level of paperwork. Policy makers were convinced that the losses due to EFC had increased as well. Reducing EFC was set as a policy priority by the line ministry in charge of social protection.

To curb the level of EFC, Romania gradually developed an end-to-end EFC mitigation system by 2013/14, with good results.

- **Professional workforce for compliance reviews and inspections.** By mid-2013, the country had established a professional team of social inspectors, part of the National Agency for Social Benefits and Inspection (NASBI). The size of the team was increased from about 130 persons to more than 300 from 2010 to 2013. A special training module was developed and delivered by the NASBI to its staff by April 2013.
- **Strategic focus of compliance reviews on large budget and EFC risk-prone programs.** After 2010, the Social Inspection (SI) team carried out annual large-scale compliance reviews (named "thematic inspections" in Romania) for all its large, risk-prone programs (Child Raising Benefit, or CRB; Guaranteed Minimum Income, or GMI; Family Benefit, or FB; Heating Benefit, or HB; and disability allowance benefits, or DA). Without a system of referrals for high-risk cases, these inspections were carried on at random up to the end of 2012.
- **An end-to-end monitoring system** was developed by mid-2012, that encompass thematic inspection planning (selection of files and beneficiaries to be reviewed); documenting the findings of the thematic inspection, including the proposed remedial actions and the sanctions that have been applied; and follow-up of the implementation status of the recommendations.

Table B8.12.1 Moving from Isolated EFC Monitoring to a Monitoring System in Romania, circa 2011–14

Thematic areas	Situation at baseline	After 3+ years
Sanction and recovery policy	Each social protection benefit has its own sanctions policy Sanction/inspection not based on cost-benefit or severity Weak recovery policy	Same sanction for the same offence across programs Larger sanctions for larger offenses, repeated offenses Effective recovery policy
Investigative powers for the social inspector/ compliance worker	Incomplete powers Focused on the service provider, not on suspect beneficiaries	Stronger powers Clear oversight mechanisms to prevent abuse
Database cross-checks	Occasional, ad hoc	Routine, regular, clear procedures to detect irregularities
Risk profiling and risk-based inspections	Based on the experience of the social inspectors	Derived from analytic models

Source: "Reducing Fraud, Error, and Corruption (EFC) in Social Protection Programs," a slide presentation by Vlad Grigoras and Emil Daniel Tesliuc, World Bank Group, 2017.
Note: EFC = error, fraud, and corruption.

benefits due to blindness, who subsequently have obtained a driving license. Again, these logical checks would result in the identification of cases with EFC.

- Risk profiling is used to estimate the probability of a case suspicious for EFC. A simple way to build such analytically based risk profiles is to (1) use the results of an inspection of a random set of benefits; (2) build a regression model that predicts the level or occurrence of overpayments using the information that is typically found in the program database of beneficiaries; (3) use the model to predict/assign a probability of EFC to all cases or beneficiaries; and (4) inspect those with the highest probability of EFC, multiplied by the value of the estimated loss (if available). This type of model is likely to outperform the traditional identification model based on the experience of the staff in charge of control.

The use of analytics to step out the effort to curb EFC in social protection programs is a promising path for all countries, including lower- and middle-income countries. These techniques can be implemented at a small overall cost. In the case of Romania, the team in charge of analytics included five persons, a small addition to about 300 social inspectors, which resulted in a large increase in the cost-effectiveness of the resources used. For cross-checks, the cost of verification and identification of an extra case is close to zero.

These techniques would reduce the discretion of the control staff and limit the possibility of collusive or corrupt practices, while producing more accurate referrals of suspect cases. The experience of the social inspection of Moldova in introducing analytically based risk profiles is illustrative. A specialized team of nine inspectors and two supervisors was in charge of inspecting about 3 percent of the total caseload of a last-resort program called Social Aid, to reduce EFC losses. Between 2013 and 2015, Moldova used the traditional model of identifying the cases for EFC inspection, based on rules derived from the experience of social inspectors. Over time, this approach proved its value. When the social inspection commenced its work in 2013, only about 7 percent of the inspected cases were affected by EFC. This ratio increased to 10 percent in 2014 and to 64 percent in 2015. By 2016, using the result of past inspections and information from the client files, a statistician has determined an analytically based risk-profiling model. The social inspectors, whose identification rate was already quite high, were reluctant to use the statistical model. To see its worth, the cases to be inspected in 2016 were selected using both methods, 266 selected based on inspectors' experience, and 508 using the new statistical risk-profiling model. The two modalities offered good identification rates: the one based on experience identified correctly 68 percent of the cases, while the statistical model had an accurate hit rate of 90 percent. The statistical model proved its worth and was there to stay.

The Role of Technology

Increasingly, social protection delivery uses modern technologies to transfer cash or in-kind benefits or services to the beneficiaries. Some of these technologies could be used to reduce EFC in programs, and to reduce the cost of inspections. India's Andhra Pradesh Rural Employment Guarantee program used a host of methods and technologies to reduce EFC in the programs. The EFC risks were many, from ghost beneficiaries or relatives inserted on the muster roll (daily attendance sheet of laborers), to inflated reporting of the work done or poor quality or ghost work (resulting in theft of materials), to forged checks by program staff. To curb EFC along the delivery chain, the program deployed several technologies (table 8.16) to curb abuse and corruption. All these techniques can be applied more broadly to middle- and lower-income countries.

To conclude, programs or social protection systems that want to curb EFC should put in place an end-to-end system. Mitigating the risk of EFC is not something that is done after the benefit or service is provided. It is a system that cuts across the whole delivery chain (for example, it could be embedded in the eligibility test itself if income test is combined with risk profiling); a system that is not costly when you use modern tools and pays for itself many times relative to leakages saved. Such a system will boost political acceptability of redistributive programs and would not impose costs on legitimate beneficiaries if they are accompanied by a well-designed risk-profiling system.

Table 8.16 Technology-Supported Tools to Minimize EFC in a Workfare Program in India

Tool	Description
Quality control (QC) teams	Four civil engineers + two horticulture experts Conduct random inspections and check paid work quantities and specifications of works; power to recover loss and apply sanctions
Internal audit	Visit every administrative block once in every two-month period and check the accounts; head office takes follow-up actions
Electronic muster and measurement system	Upload data from worksites to a website on day to day basis through mobiles e-Muster, e-Measurement, e-muster verification and e-check measurement Addresses muster fudging and measurements distortions
Comprehensive IT software that provides end-to-end IT solutions	The transaction-based software issues job cards; generates estimates; issues work commencement letters updates muster rolls and measurements and generates pay orders
Wage payments through Biometric Technology	Wage payments are done in the village using biometric fingerprint identification; the right worker receives his rightful payment

Source: "Reducing Fraud, Error, and Corruption (EFC) in Social Protection Programs," a slide presentation by Vlad Grigoras and Emil Daniel Tesliuc, World Bank Group, 2017.
Note: EFC = error, fraud, and corruption; IT = information technology.

8.7 SOME CONCLUDING POINTS

This chapter has unpacked one of the most complex parts of the delivery chain. It involves the recurring cyclical task of managing the continuous flow of information each program undertakes in achieving its policy objectives as well as assuring that the right benefit or service is provided to the right person, at the right time, and with the appropriate logistical arrangements.

As discussed in the introduction to this chapter, most discussions on delivery systems focus mainly on the entry point, that is, the assessment and enrollment stages, and on the actual delivery of the service or payment. When program administrators implement a program for the first time, these two stages absorb the greater part of interest and resources as they provide some of the key outputs a program needs to demonstrate its functioning. As the program stabilizes in terms of coverage, that is, it has single digit annual growth, the issues unpacked in this chapter become the bread and butter of a program administrator, and as such, is where most of the continuous improvements of programs occur.

Here, in the arduous yet creative task of identifying continuous improvements, it is useful to approach them in two complementary dimensions: technique—the way something is done—on the one hand, and technology—the instrument used to do it—on the other.

Technology is an enabler and allows for previously unimaginable results. For example, if a person has a grievance, he or she does not need to wait for the next visit of the program staff to submit it; they can call a hotline or use a mobile phone application and begin the redressal process immediately. Mobile technology provided a solution to assure that a person can contact the program instantly. Similarly, program administrators are supported by information systems, such as beneficiary operations management systems, in their daily tasks of data update, monitoring of conditionalities, and grievance redress. They are also supported by technological tools in their efforts to reduce error, fraud, and corruption.

On the other hand, technique is the informed procedure that allows a program administrator to know that, in order to effectively empower a person in his or her complaint, each person needs to be provided with a unique case number to allow follow-up.

Technique tells us that grievances should be preclassified to allow for effective triaging and efficient redressal. It also tells us that keeping a record of grievances will allow the program to analyze aggregate information and identify grievance hot spots or procedures that need additional improvements. Technique is also key in the programming and planning of all the activities that take place in each implementation cycle through the use of a master calendar, which allows management of the timing and convergence of the information streams, to take into account processing time, capacity, and workload, as well as to coordinate among different agencies involved in beneficiary operations management. Similarly, technique is also key in embedding end-to-end EFC systems all along the delivery chain to help mitigate the risk of EFC processes being run after the benefit or service is provided. These systems contribute to cost savings, curb leakages, and engender greater trust and acceptability of redistributive programs.

The distinction between technology and technique is fundamental, as technology will provide solutions, as long as it has a well-informed technique or set of techniques to employ it. The human-centered approach discussed in chapter 2 gives us methods to listen to people and to better understand their needs and constraints. On the supply side, it is always good to talk to field implementers and incorporate their voices and understand their contexts. This should be done in a systematic manner, through workshops and organized discussions with central-level decision makers, and not limited to the simple anecdotal information obtained in a field visit.

ANNEX 8A: ASPECTS OF CONDITIONALITIES IN NINE SELECT CONDITIONAL CASH TRANSFER PROGRAMS

Table 8A.1 Menus of Conditionalities in Select CCTs

	Education		Health care				
			Women		Children		
	School enrollment ages	School attendance % by age	Pregnant	Postpartum	Health visits[a] children 0–6	Other	Conditionalities for other household members
Brazil BFP	6–17	>85% for 6–15 >75% for 16–17	MoH schedule[b] 4 visits	MoH schedule 3 visits	MoH schedule[c] 0–1: 7 visits 1–2: 2 visits 2–3: 1 visit 3–4: 1 visit 4–5: 1 visit 5–6: 1 visit	n.a.	n.a.
Colombia FA	5–18	>80% for 5–18	n.a.	MoH schedule 4 visits	MoH schedule 0–1: 6 visits 1–2: 3 visits 2–3: 2 visits 3–4: 1 visit 4–5: 1 visit 5–6: 2 visits	n.a.	n.a.

continued

Table 8A.1 *(continued)*

	Education		Health care				
			Women		Children		
	School enrollment ages	School attendance % by age	Pregnant	Postpartum	Health visits[a] children 0–6	Other	Conditionalities for other household members
Indonesia PKH	6–21	>85% for 6–21	4 visits; take iron tablets; birth assisted by trained professional	2 visits	0–1: 12 visits 1–2: 4 visits 2–3: 4 visits 3–4: 4 visits 4–5: 4 visits 5–6: 4 visits	Children 0–6 take vitamin A capsules twice/year	Disabled: yearly health checkup Elderly: attend social welfare activities, where available
Jamaica PATH	6–18	>85% for 6–18	4 visits	2 visits	0–1: 6 visits 1–2: 2 visits 2–3: 2 visits 3–4: 2 visits 4–5: 2 visits 5–6: 2 visits	n.a.	Disabled, elderly, adults: 2 health visits per year
Mexico Prospera	6–22	>80% for 3–22	5 visits	3 visits	0–1: 9 visits 1–2: 2 visits 2–3: 2 visits 3–4: 2 visits 4–5: 2 visits 5–6: 2 visits	Children and teens age 5–19: health care visits twice/year	Adults ages 20+: 2 health care visits per year Pregnant and lactating women and women with children 6–59 months: pick up nutritional supplements every two months in health clinics
Pakistan WeT	4–12	>70% for 4–12	n.a.	n.a.	n.a.	n.a.	n.a.
Philippines 4Ps	3–5 and 6–18 Parents select up to three children to be included and monitored	>85% for 3–5 >85% for 6–18	Visit every 2 months; at least one prenatal/trimester; professionally assisted birth	At least one visit in first six weeks	0–1: 12 visits 1–2: 12 visits 2–3: 2 visits 3–4: 2 visits 4–5: 2 visits 5–6: 2 visits	Ages 6–14 take deworming pills twice/year	Designated recipient for household

continued

Table 8A.1 *(continued)*

	Education		Health care				Conditionalities for other household members
			Women		Children		
	School enrollment ages	School attendance % by age	Pregnant	Postpartum	Health visits[a] children 0–6	Other	
Tanzania PSSN	5–18 Up to 4 primary-age school-children, 3 lower-secondary, and 2 upper secondary	>80% for 5–18	4 visits Conditionalities for pregnant women were dropped due to difficulties in monitoring compliance	n.a.	If no services available, primary care givers of children <60 months must attend health and nutrition sessions every 2 months	n.a.	n.a.
Turkey CCT	6–25 (12 years of schooling mandatory)[d]	>80% for 6–25[e]	MoH schedule Before 14 weeks 18–24 weeks 28–32 weeks 36–38 weeks Birth in hospital (extra benefit)	MoH schedule 3 checkups at hospital, plus 3 more before 42 days	MoH schedule 0–1: 9 visits 1–2: 3 visits 2–3: 2 visits 3–4: 1 visit 4–5: 1 visit	n.a.	n.a.

Sources: Brazil: MDS BFP Operations Manual 2017; Ministry of Health. Colombia: Prosperidad FA Operational Manual 2017. Indonesia: MoSA (2018) Ministerial Regulation on PKH, articles 3, 4 and 5. Jamaica: MLSS PATH Operations Manual 2017. Mexico: Dávila Lárraga 2016. Pakistan: BISP-WeT Team, Operational Manual for Wet 2017. The Philippines: DSWD Pantawid Pamilyang Pilipino Program Operations Manual, December 2015 Edition. Tanzania: TASAF III, PSSN Operations Manual. Turkey: General Directorate of Social Assistance; Ortakaya 2018; MoH Schedule.

Note: CCT: conditional cash transfer; MoH = Ministry of Health; n.a. = not applicable; PSSN = Productive Social Safety Net.

a. Child health visits typically include check-ups, growth and development monitoring, and vaccines according to schedule.

b. Brazil's Ministry of Health schedule includes prenatal visits at least every 8 weeks; postnatal visits during first week, between 7th and 10th days, and another between 42 and 60 days for lactating mothers, and between 30 and 42 days for nonlactating mothers (Manual de Assistencia Pre-Natal, Normas e Manuais Tecnicos, 3rd addition; and Cronograma Sugerido para o Acompanhamento Pre-natal e Puerperio).

c. Brazil's Ministry of Health schedule for young children: 1st week, 1st month, 2nd month, 4th month, 6th month, 9th month, 12th month, 18th month, 24th month, then once per year. Visits would include vaccines, plus monitoring of growth and development.

d. Children in state boarding schools and open schools (primary, secondary, and high schools that have distance learning) are out of the scope of CCT.

e. Conditional education assistance might start as early as 48 months with enrollment in preschool (if there is an interlink between preschool and the Ministry of Education) and might continue up to age of 25 (if the child is enrolled in formal education).

Table 8A.2 Calibration of Conditionalities Monitoring Cycles and Payment Cycles in Select CCTs

Brazil BFP: Education	Month			
	1	2	3	4
Compliance period	CP1 (2 months)		Continue next cycle . . .	
Compliance verification period and link to payroll			CVP1 (actual <1 month)	Compliance linked to payroll
Payments frequency	Monthly	Monthly	Monthly	Monthly

Brazil BFP: Health	Month								
	1	2	3	4	5	6	7	8	9
Compliance period	CP1 (6 months)						Continue next cycle . . .		
Compliance verification period and link to payroll							CVP1 (actual time is less, but 2 months allotted)		Compliance linked to payroll
Payments frequency	Monthly	Monthly	Monthly	Monthly	Monthly	Monthly	Monthly	Monthly	Monthly

Colombia MFA: Education and health	Month					
	1	2	3	4	5	6
Compliance period	CP1 (2 months)		Continue next cycle . . .			
Compliance verification period and link to payroll			CVP1 (2 months allotted in schedule)			Compliance linked to payroll
Payments frequency	Bimonthly		Bimonthly		Bimonthly	

Indonesia PKH: Education and health (since 2018)	Month					
	1	2	3	4	5	6
Compliance period	CP1 (3 months)			Continue next cycle . . .		
Compliance verification period and link to payroll				CVP1 (2 months allotted in schedule)		Compliance linked to payroll
Payments frequency			Quarterly			Quarterly

Jamaica PATH: Education and health for women and children	Month			
	1	2	3	4
Compliance period	CP1 (2 months)		Continue next cycle . . .	
Compliance verification period and link to payroll	Distribute CVFs	CVP1 (collect forms, processing)		Compliance linked to payroll
Payments frequency		Bimonthly		Bimonthly

Jamaica PATH: For disabled, adults, elderly	Month							
	1	2	3	4	5	6	7	8
Compliance period	CP1 (6 months)						Continue next cycle . . .	
Compliance verification period and link to payroll	Distribute CVFs					CVP1 (collect forms, processing)		Compliance linked to payroll
Payments frequency		Bimonthly		Bimonthly		Bimonthly		Bimonthly

Mexico Prospera: Education and health	Month					
	1	2	3	4	5	6
Compliance period	CP1 (2 months)		Continue next cycle . . .			
Compliance verification period and link to payroll			CVP1 (2 months allotted in schedule)			Compliance linked to payroll
Payments frequency	Bimonthly		Bimonthly		Bimonthly	

Pakistan WeT: Education	Month						
	1	2	3	4	5	6	7
Compliance period	CP1 (school quarter)			Continue next cycle . . .			
Compliance verification period and link to payroll				CVP1 (3 months allotted in schedule)			Compliance linked to payroll
Payments frequency	Quarterly			Quarterly			Quarterly

Philippines 4Ps: Education and health	Month			
	1	2	3	4
Compliance period	CP1 (2 months)		Continue next cycle . . .	
Compliance verification period and link to payroll		Distribute CVFs	Verify compliance (CVP1)	Compliance linked to payroll
Payments frequency		Bimonthly		Bimonthly

Tanzania PSSN: Education and health	Month				
	1	2	3	4	5
Compliance period	CP1		Continue next cycle . . .		
Compliance verification period and link to payroll			CVP1 (2 months allotted in schedule)		Compliance linked to payroll
Payments frequency	Bimonthly		Bimonthly		Bimonthly

continued

Table 8A.2 *(continued)*

Turkey CCT: Education and health	Month		
	1	2	3
Compliance period	CP1		Continue next cycle . . .
Compliance verification period and link to payroll			CV + links to payroll (2-3 hours)
Payments frequency	Bimonthly		Bimonthly

Sources: Compilation based on program operational manuals and related documents for each country. To standardize the presentation across countries, the months in these schedules are anchored with month 1 in the beginning of the initial compliance period. As such, these months do not correspond to calendar months (January, February, March). Brazil: MDS BFP Operations Manual 2017. Colombia: Prosperidad FA Operational Manual 2017. Indonesia: MoSA (2018) Ministerial Regulation on PKH, articles 3, 4, and 5. Jamaica: MLSS PATH Operations Manual 2017. Mexico: Dávila Lárraga 2016. Pakistan: BISP-WeT Team, Operational Manual for Wet 2017. The Philippines: DSWD Pantawid Pamilyang Pilipino Program Operations Manual, December 2015 Edition. Tanzania: TASAF III, PSSN Operations Manual. Turkey: General Directorate of Social Assistance; Ortakaya 2018; MoH Schedule.

Table 8A.3 Consequences for Noncompliance with Conditionalities in Select CCTs

	Consequences	Follow-up actions
Brazil BFP	• 1st instance: warning • 2nd instance: temporary block for one month, but not irrevocable—the benefit can be withdrawn the following month if no further instances of noncompliance • 3rd instance: irrevocable full benefit reduction for two months (called a "suspension") • After continued noncompliance even with one year of family monitoring: termination from the program	• 3 periods of noncompliance triggers "suspension" status (irrevocable benefit reduction) and the family is placed in family monitoring, which is undertaken by social workers and recorded in SICON (information system). • Appeals allowed
Colombia FA	Partial benefit reduction for the noncompliance period	
Indonesia PKH	• 1st instance: warning (no penalty) • 2nd instance: Until 2017, family faced a 10% reduction in benefits on 2nd/continued instance of noncompliance; since 2017, current policy withholds the entire family benefit after two consecutive periods of noncompliance (by any family member); family can recuperate that benefit if compliance resumes; after 3 periods of noncompliance, the benefits are suspended, and after the 6th period, the family is terminated from the program	Facilitator visits noncomplying families to try to resolve the causes of noncompliance; families can submit grievances via the Ministry of Social Affairs contact center
Jamaica PATH	• 1st instance: irrevocable partial reduction of family benefit (to the minimum base benefit amount of J$800) • 2nd instance: irrevocable partial benefit reduction (same as 1st) • 3rd instance: termination of the beneficiary from program	Social worker must follow up after 2 instances of noncompliance to find out the reasons for noncompliance, to identify if there are special circumstances, and to nudge noncomplying members to comply
Mexico Prospera	• 1st instance: temporary (monthly) partial suspension • 2nd instance with health co-responsibility (4 consecutive months or 6 nonconsecutive months): indefinite full but revocable suspension	The full suspension of benefits is communicated through a suspension notice, which includes the reason, the circumstances, and the legal basis for the suspension; the notification also contains the procedures and deadlines for requesting a reactivation of the benefit, if applicable
Pakistan WeT	• 1st instance: warning (no penalty) • 2nd instance: irrevocable partial benefit reduction; the part of the benefit that corresponds to the noncomplying child is not paid • 3rd instance: child is suspended from the program, but can return to WeT if compliance resumes	The child is followed up after 2 noncompliance quarters and families are informed by BISP or IPF and encouraged to resume compliance
Philippines 4Ps	• 1st (and subsequent) instances: Irrevocable partial benefit reduction; the part that is reduced corresponds to grant amount for the noncomplying family member • 4th instance: termination with written notice to the family	Appeals within 15 days, and grievance must be acted upon within 3 months of receipt of appeal

continued

Table 8A.3 *(continued)*

	Consequences	Follow-up actions
Tanzania PSSN	• 1st instance: warning • 2nd instance: irrevocable partial benefit reduction (reduced on pro-rated basis)[a]	Follow-up warning with counseling from CCT management committee
Turkey CCT	• Deduction of the benefit amount associated with the noncomplying member of the household	None

Sources: Brazil: MDS BFP Operations Manual 2017. Colombia: Prosperidad FA Operational Manual 2017. Indonesia: MoSA (2018) Ministerial Regulation on PKH, articles 3, 4 and 5. Jamaica: MLSS PATH Operations Manual 2017. Mexico: Dávila Lárraga 2016. Pakistan: BISP-WeT Team, Operational Manual for Wet 2017. The Philippines: DSWD Pantawid Pamilyang Pilipino Program Operations Manual, December 2015 Edition; Tanzania: TASAF III, PSSN Operations Manual. Turkey: General Directorate of Social Assistance; Ortakaya 2018; MoH Schedule.
Note: BISP = Benazir Income Support Programme; CCT = conditional cash transfer (program); IPF = implementation partner firm; PSSN = Productive Social Safety Net.
a. The Tanzania PSSN program has a pro-rata system of penalties, that is, if there are two beneficiaries in a household and one of them is noncompliant for two consecutive months, the benefit is reduced in half as a penalty. Similarly, when there are five beneficiaries in a household and one of them is noncompliant for two consecutive months, then one-fifth of the benefit is deducted as a penalty.

ANNEX 8B: MEASURING EFC

Measuring the level of EFC is hard, but not impossible. Measuring the full amount of losses to EFC is as elusive as an attempt to measure precisely the level of gray economy. Nonetheless, there are techniques that produce good estimates of these losses. Broadly, there are two types of monitoring approaches: (1) estimating and monitoring the overall level of EFC in the social protection system; or (2) estimating and monitoring the level of EFC in a single program.

A good practice is to estimate and monitor the total fraud and error in the social protection (SP) system. Although complex, this methodology generates an unbiased representative estimate of the level of fraud and error in each SP program, that is aggregated for the whole SP system. In practice, this means the assignment of the monitoring and evaluation functions at the ministry level, across many or all SP programs. The level of EFC is expressed as a percentage of program funds affected by error and fraud, or the number of cases, or both.

To arrive at an unbiased EFC estimate, a representative (random) sample of cases (client files) is drawn from the active caseload for each program.[47] The program will provide the (electronic and written) records to a review team that would check each case for mistakes or inaccuracies in the data and, where appropriate, would visit and reinterview the applicant. For each case, the review team will estimate the amount of money under- and overpaid, and whether the difference is due to error or fraud. These figures are summed up to estimate the total level of error and fraud. These estimates are qualified by confidence intervals that consider the fact that a relatively small sample is used in relation to the size of the actual caseload. Estimating EFC based on representative sampling of beneficiary files gives administrators an indication of the overall problem of EFC in a social protection system, as well as information on where EFC is the most prevalent (in what programs), the types of beneficiary or staff behavior most associated with EFC (main causes of EFC), and additional characteristics (or profile) associated with EFC (profession, marital status, age, etc.).

Few countries measure the level of total fraud and error across social protection programs. From the nine countries reviewed in a National Audit Office study (United Kingdom, NAO 2006), only Australia, Ireland and the United Kingdom measure overall level of fraud and error based on "rolling measurement" and/or "snapshots." This is considered best practice. The United Kingdom developed this approach and it is broadly perceived to be the best practice for assessing the total volume of fraud and error in a system. About 500 staff in the United Kingdom review benefit files on a rolling basis (figure 8B.1).

Another common approach found in practice is to estimate fraud and error in a specific program, using a random-sample approach. The program is likely chosen because it is considered high risk and/or has a large budget. The methodology is the same as in the first measurement type outlined above. Greece, Ireland, Moldova, New Zealand, Sweden, and the United States use this approach. Romania used an intermediate approach with EFC rates estimated from six

Figure 8B.1 Tracking the Overall Level, Composition, and Causes of EFC in the United Kingdom

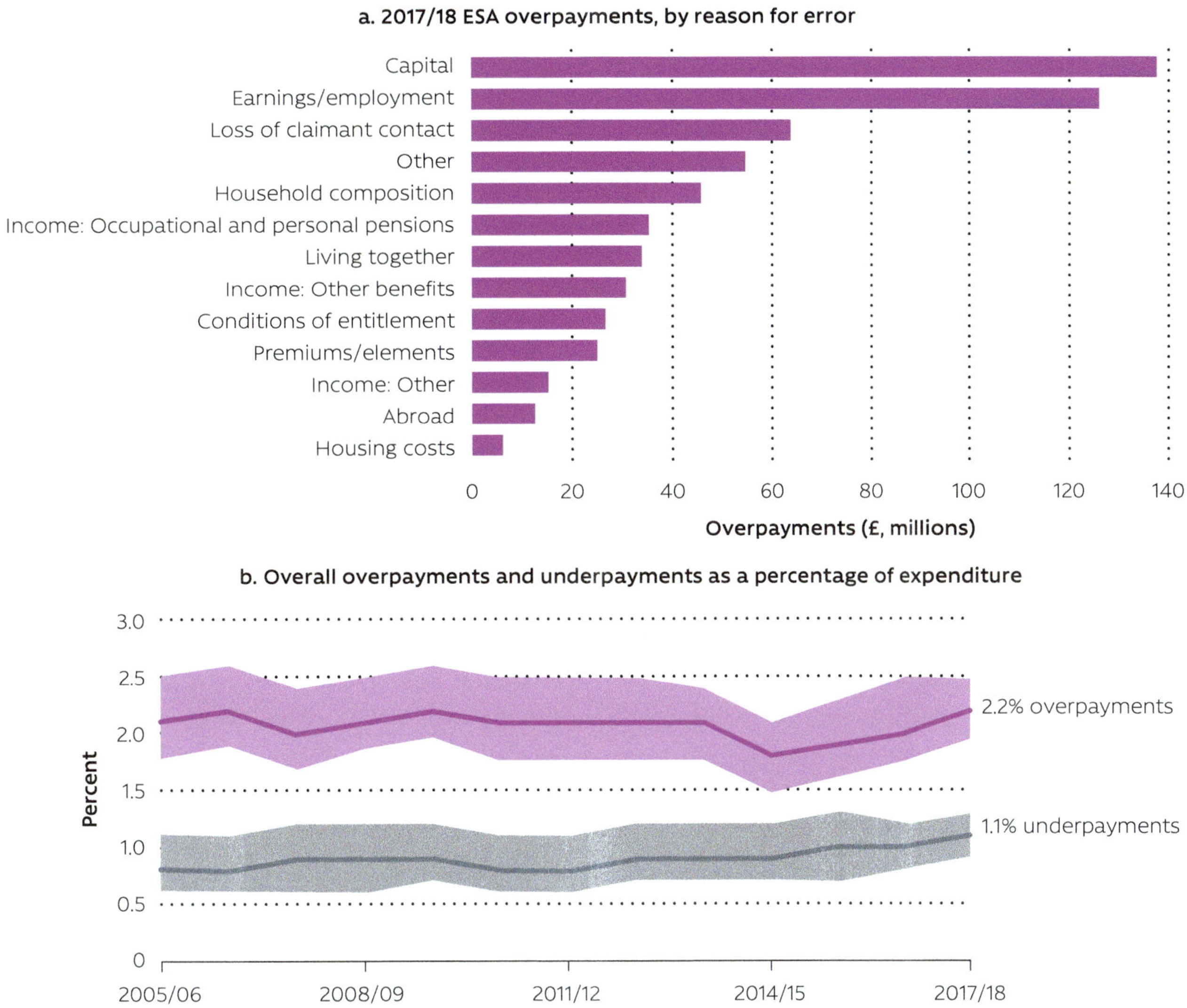

Source: Department for Work and Pensions, Great Britain, 2018. https://assets.publishing.service.gov.uk/government/uploads/system/uploads/attachment_data/file/762141/fraud-and-error-stats-release-2017-2018-final-estimates.pdf.
Note: EFC = error, fraud, and corruption; ESA = employment support allowance.

risk-prone social assistance programs. For example, the US SNAP (former "food stamps") uses the estimation of the EFC rates of each state as a criterion linked with performance-based incentives.

Evaluation of the cost-benefit of anti-fraud initiatives. The advantage of EFC mitigation measures is that, when done effectively, a measure would recover more in overpayments than is spent on the initiative. Some countries have started using this as a yardstick. Australia establishes specific cost-benefit ratios for each anti-fraud initiative it introduces. If the intervention does not prove cost-effective (i.e., does not recover more overpayments than its cost), it may be reviewed or aborted. In the United Kingdom, studies have also looked at this ratio for different types of intervention to understand the trade-offs between approaches. The Romanian benefit administration is also tracking overpayments identified as a result of data matching, and their associated costs (table 8B.1). The purpose of these evaluations is to create an understanding of what works and to gain knowledge of how different mitigation measures compare against each other. The latter could lead to strategic decisions on the portfolio of EFC interventions, for instance, to do more prevention than detection or use more of one approach in detection compared to the others (within a given budget).

Table 8B.1 Cost-Benefit Ratio of the First Data-Matching Exercise in Romania, 2013

	Number of cases with suspicions: data matching	Number of cases investigated, 2013	Number of cases with EFC, 2013	Total over-payments (debts), 2013	Recovered debts by March 31, 2014	Costs: December 31, 2013
CRB	36,818	27,720	5,650	11,569,170	5,117,824	115,692
FA	51,664	34,123	15,151	2,643,421	1,690,999	1,129,939
GMI	15,964	9,676	2,959	1,730,223	877,075	
SCA	541,502	27,308	2,549	1,189,902	692,476	74,964
Heating	35,851	24,030	4,874	755,368	241,046	490,989
Disabilities	5,457	5,457	2,724	1,301,069	551,914	143,118
Total		128,314	33,907	19,189,153	9,171,334	1,954,701
Cost-benefit ratio on overpayments (estimated debts)						9.58
Cost-benefit ratio on recovered debts						4.69

Source: "Reducing Fraud, Error, and Corruption (EFC) in Social Protection Programs," a slide presentation by Vlad Grigoras and Emil Daniel Tesliuc, World Bank Group, 2017.

Note: CRB = Child Raising Benefit (program); EFC = error, fraud, and corruption; FB = Family Benefit (program); GMI = Guaranteed Minimum Income (program); SCA = state child allowance.

These monitoring and evaluation approaches serve two purposes: accountability and learning lessons. The latter may involve ways to target initiatives more effectively or even cost-effectively. Those purposes are mostly driven by the wider political context in which the EFC mitigation takes place. In the United Kingdom for instance, the measurement of the total volume of EFC in the system was mostly driven by accountability pressures emanating from the lower chamber of Parliament. In Romania, concerns about EFC emerged after the 2008 crisis after a period of steep increases in social safety net spending.

Reducing EFC is not only a question of reducing overpayments. Maintaining the integrity of a social protection system is not only about reducing overpayments in a system. Intrinsically, an underpayment is an error that a social protection system should address with the same vigor as errors that lead to overpayment, fraud, and corruption. This will ensure a fairer social protection system. There can be a variety of reasons why individuals do not receive the benefits that they are entitled to. Typically, there can be administrative errors, meaning that beneficiaries do not receive their full entitlement. There may also be more systemic issues around discrimination and disenfranchisement that help explain why certain groups may not receive benefits. Finally, there may be cultural and personal reasons for people not claiming their benefits. In the United Kingdom, underpayments are estimated to be potentially higher than overpayments due to fraud. The few measurements that are available internationally again suggest that error can be a more substantial issue than fraud itself.

Notes

1. This pattern is echoed in the findings of a paper by Lindert and Vincensini (2010), who trace the evolution of such focus by the press and the priorities of administrators of Brazil's Bolsa Família Program over six years.
2. Some policy makers, however, bring the focus on graduation into the design phase up-front, particularly with cash transfers and often due to political-economy pressures. From an implementation standpoint, however, they should be careful not to overload the design of a new program, since capacity is limited, and the learning curve is steep. The principle of "keep it simple" (or "do simple well") should reign before complex "cash-plus enhancements" are introduced.
3. Although we call this phase beneficiary operations management, we recognize that grievances (complaints and appeals) may be filed by both beneficiaries and nonbeneficiaries. In some instances, the decision on the appeal or grievance may result in a nonbeneficiary being enrolled in the program

and becoming a beneficiary. We include grievance redress in the beneficiary management and monitoring stage of the delivery chain because it feeds back into the recurring implementation cycle. Such grievances may be filed regarding any phase along the delivery chain (or during the program more generally).

4. Additionally, in some cases, information is incomplete due to changes in procedures or new requirements.
5. Other reasons have to do with a program's minimum program permanence rules.
6. Pantawid Pamilyang Pilipino Program Operation Manual, Department of Social Welfare and Development, government of Philippines, December 2015.
7. Operation Manual Waseela-e-Taleem, Benazir Income Support Programme, government of Pakistan, 2017.
8. "Chain of custody" is understood as the chronological documentation or paper trail that records the sequence of custody, control, transfer, analysis, and disposition of physical or electronic information.
9. Guía para el Llenado de Fichas de Atención, Secretaría de Desarrollo Social, 2017.
10. Turkey, General Directorate of Social Assistance 2016.
11. The program has recently been transformed and no longer exists as a CCT due to shifts in the social policy in Mexico.
12. The six dimensions are social protection, family dynamics, education and training, health, employment, and housing.
13. World Bank's ASPIRE database and World Bank 2018b).
14. See meta reviews by Fiszbein and Schady (2009). Baird, et al. (2014), Bastagli et al. (2016), Bastagli et al. (2018), and many other studies.
15. Refer to chapter 2, box 2.1, on terminology confusion.
16. The number rises to 40,000 including facilitators, operators, supervisors, and district coordinators.
17. In Pakistan, BISP hired two implementation partner firms (one private and one NGO) to undertake social mobilization, enrollment, admission support, and compliance verification for the WeT CCT. They were selected through a competitive bidding process and report to BISP (WeT director). The rationale for outsourcing such functions included the lack of implementation capacity of provincial and local actors, as well as the fact that BISP could not pay such authorities for services rendered due to complex procurement regulations governing federal-provincial budget transfers.
18. In Pakistan, one of the compliance periods is not enforced due to the vacation/holiday period.
19. The Ministry of Education monitors school enrollment for all students in Brazil on a yearly basis in the annual school census (Censo Escolar), but daily and monthly school attendance is systematically monitored only for BFP beneficiaries (in the Sistema Presença).
20. Based on presentation by the government of Brazil's SENARC/MDS in October 2015.
21. As discussed in chapter 4, in 2009, GDSA launched ISAS, which is an integrated e-government information system that links information from 24 different public authorities to facilitate the management of social protection programs, including for applications, determination of eligibility, enrollment decisions, payments, beneficiary monitoring, automated accounting, and auditing.
22. In some CCTs, the first payments are not linked to verification of compliance with conditionalities (those "grace payments" are not shown here).
23. As such, these months refer to average 30-day periods from the start of the first phase of the monitoring cycle. They do not necessarily correspond to the numbering of calendar months (in other words, month 1 ≠ January, month 2 ≠ February, month 1 ≠ March, etc.).
24. By monitored, we mean beneficiaries in each category for whom monitoring data are available (whether or not they comply).
25. This is a drawback for the 4Ps, since clearly women who were pregnant in 2015 are not still pregnant, and others who were not pregnant at that time may have become pregnant since then. Similarly, children ages 0–5 have grown older since 2015, and others have been born into beneficiary families.
26. Brazil, Ministerio do Desenvolvimento Social 2017.
27. This is also related to our concern with Mexico's monitoring only those beneficiaries who have registered at health clinics in the Prospera program.
28. Brazil also starts tracking data if any pregnancy is reported outside of that age band. Moreover, while most CCT program compliance periods are two months, Brazil's BFP extended the compliance period for health care monitoring to six months to increase the probabilities that it would be able to capture data on health care use.
29. WAPES-IDB 2014 survey, reported in *The World of Public Employment Services* (IDB/WAPES/OECD 2015). See also Konle-Seidle (2012) and Kuddo (2009).
30. WAPES-IDB 2014 survey, reported in IDB/WAPES/OECD (2015).
31. IDB/WAPES/OECD 2015.

32. "IAP" goes by different names in different countries and contexts. It can be known as a job plan (Australia), job search plan (Hungary), employment plan (North Macedonia), career plan, or use other related terminology. The general contents are similar and we will refer to these generically as IAPs.
33. Malta has biometric fingerprint scanning machines in each PES job center. On the basis of the scan, each job seeker receives a printed record with relevant aspects of their IAP, including services that may be available to them. See Tubb (2012).
34. This reflects recent amendments to the Federal Law on Employment of Population in the Russian Federation effective since January 1, 2019.
35. From Ethiopia's Ministry of Agriculture's Productive Safety Net Programme-Phase IV-Programme Implementation Manual (December 2014).
36. See Angel-Urdinola and Leon-Solano (2013) and Betcherman (2012).
37. Danish information is available at www.jobinsats.dk. See Bjerre, Sidelmann, and Puchwein-Roberts (2016).
38. World Bank 2016a.
39. Fuller et al. 2014. Concealed earnings was the dominant source of fraud-related overpayments from 2005–09.
40. The Social Insurance Administrative Diagnostic (SIAD) defines grievances with two distinct categories: complaints and appeals. Complaints are classified as complaints about the manner or quality of services given by the Social Security Agencies (SSA), while appeals are classified as complaints about the correctness of decisions made by the SSA (World Bank 2019).
41. Adapted from World Bank's "Feedback Matters" (World Bank 2012a).
42. Shelley 2015.
43. The Old Age Allowance Program is one of the longest running and large-scale social protection programs in Bangladesh. The Vulnerable Group Development Program was developed as a humanitarian response to food insecurity in Bangladesh. The Employment Generation Program is one of the biggest public works programs. It provides 100 days of employment (unskilled manual labor) to individuals in rural areas during the flood and famine seasons.
44. World Bank 2012a.
45. The process for using social media to gather user feedback in social protection can include (1) requesting beneficiary feedback on programs using social media and messaging platforms; (2) beneficiaries sending feedback using social media or messaging platforms; (3) beneficiaries receiving automated responses that feedback has been received; (4) plugging feedback into customer-relationship management (CRM) platforms with analytical and visualization capabilities; and (5) personalizing responses sent to the beneficiary, thanking them for their feedback and on action taken if appropriate.
46. In general, this complexity pays off. Programs that are narrowly targeted toward their target group cost less than categorical or universal programs. The reduction of inclusion error due to more complex eligibility criteria would result in savings that are several times higher than the remaining cases affected by EFC.
47. Some countries or programs try to monitor EFC without using random sampling of beneficiary files, using, for example, the number of prosecutions or number of fraudulent cases detected. This normally underestimates the level of fraud and error in the social security system as much fraud and error is unlikely to show up in these measures. This type of measurement leads to a partial and noncomparable estimate of the level of error and fraud in the system. Given the small marginal cost involved to carry on an unbiased inspection or review, we recommend the use of the first two approaches.

Bibliography

Agarwal, Sanjay. 2011. "Beneficiary and Civil Society Engagement in SSN Programs." Slide presentation, World Bank, Kuwait City.

Andersen, Torben M., Mark Strom Kristoffersen, and Michael Svarer. 2015. "Benefit Reentitlement Conditions in Unemployment Insurance Schemes." IZA Discussion Paper 8991, Institute for the Study of Labor, Bonn, Germany.

Angel-Urdinola, Diego F., and Rene A. Leon-Solano. 2013. "A Reform Agenda for Improving the Delivery of ALMPs in the MENA Region." *IZA Journal of Labor Policy* 2 (13). http://www.izajolp.com/content/2/1/13.

Arulpragasam, Jehan, Luisa Fernandez, Yasuhiko Matsuda, Rosechin Olfindo, and Matt Stephens. 2011. "Building Governance and Anti-Corruption in the Philippines' Conditional Cash Transfer Program." Philippine Social Protection Note No. 1, World Bank, Washington DC. http://documents.worldbank.org/curated/en/279051468093836088/Building-governance-and-anti-corruption-in-the-Philippines-conditional-cash-transfer-program.

Ashenfelter, Orley, David Ashmore, and Olivier Deschenes. 2005. "Do Unemployment Insurance Recipients Actively Seek Work? Evidence from Randomized Trials in Four US States." *Journal of Econometrics* 125 (1–2): 53–75.

Asian Development Bank. 2012. "The KALAHI-CIDSS Project in the Philippines: Sharing Knowledge on Community-Driven Development." Asian Development Bank, Mandaluyong City, Philippines. https://www.adb.org/sites/default/files/publication/29878/kalahi-cidss-project-philippines.pdf.

Australia, Department of Human Services. 2018. https://www.humanservices.gov.au/.

Baird, Sarah, Francisco H. G. Ferreira, Berk Ozler, and Michael Woolcock. 2014. "Conditional, Unconditional, and Everything in Between: A Systematic Review of the Effects of Cash Transfer Programmes on Schooling Outcomes." *Journal of Development Effectiveness* 6 (1): 1–43.

Barca, Valentina. 2016. "Grievance Mechanisms for Social Protection Programmes: Stumbling Blocks and Best Practice." International Policy Centre for Inclusive Growth, Brasilia, Brazil. https://ipcig.org/pub/eng/OP320_Grievance_mechanisms_for_social_protection_programmes_stumbling_blocks_and_best_practice.pdf.

Bassett, Lucy, Sara Giannozzi, Lucian Pop, and Dena Ringold. 2012. "Rules, Roles, and Controls: Governance in Social Protection with an Application to Social Assistance." Social Protection and Labor Discussion Paper 1206, World Bank, Washington, DC. http://documents.worldbank.org/curated/en/301371468151778608/Rules-roles-and-controls-governance-in-social-protection-with-an-application-to-social-assistance.

Bastagli, Francesca, Jessica Hagen-Zanker, Luke Harman, Valentina Barca, Georgina Sturge, and Tanja Schmidt. 2018. "The Impact of Cash Transfers: A Review of the Evidence from Low- and Middle-Income Countries." *Journal of Social Policy* 48 (3): 569–94.

Bastagli, Francesca, Jessica Hagen-Zanker, Luke Harman, Valentina Barca, Georgina Sturge, and Tanja Schmidt, with Luca Pellerano. 2016. *Cash Transfers: What Does the Evidence Say? A Rigorous Review of Programme Impact and of the Role of Design and Implementation Features*. London: Overseas Development Institute.

Begum, Mahmuda. 2018. "Bangladesh's Vulnerable Group Development (VGD) Program." Slide presentation at the South-South Learning Forum 2018, Frankfurt, Germany, February 19–22. http://pubdocs.worldbank.org/en/804111520537796819/SSLF18-Building-Resilience-Bangladesh.pdf.

Benhassine, Najy, Florencia Devoto, Esther Dulfo, Pascaline Dupas, and Victor Pouliquen. 2013. "Turning a Shove into a Nudge? The 'Labeled Cash Transfer' for Education." NBER Working Paper 19227, National Bureau of Economic Research, Cambridge, MA.

Betcherman, Gordon. 2012. "Labor Market Institutions: A Review of the Literature." Background paper for the World Development Report 2013, World Bank, Washington, DC. © World Bank. https://openknowledge.worldbank.org/handle/10986/12139 License: CC BY 3.0 IGO.

Bjerre, Karsten, and Peter Sidelmann, with Isabelle Puchwein-Roberts. 2016. "Practitioner's Toolkit: Performance Management in PES." Ramboll Management Consulting and ICF International, prepared for the European Network of Public Employment Services, European Commission, Brussels, Belgium.

Boone, Jan, Peter Fredriksson, Bertil Holmlund, and Jan C. van Ours. 2001. "Optimal Unemployment Insurance with Monitoring and Sanctions." IZA Discussion Paper 401, Institute of Labor Economics, Bonn, Germany.

Brazil, Ministerio do Desenvolvimento Social (MDS), Secretaria Nacional de Renda da Cidadania (SENARC). 2017. Manual de Gestao do Programa Bolsa Família. 3a Edicao.

Brown, Alessio JG, and Johannes Koettl. 2015. "Active Labor Market Programs—Employment Gain or Fiscal Drain?" *IZA Journal of Labor Economics* 4 (12): 1–36. https://doi.org/10.1186/s40172-015-0025-5.

Caixa Economica Federal and Ministerio do Desenvolvimento Social e Agrario (MDSA), Secretaria Nacional de Renda de Cidadania (Senarc). 2016. Manual do SIBEC: Sistema de Beneficios ao Cidadao: Programa Bolsa Família.

Campello, Tereza, and Marcelo Cortes Neri, eds. 2014. "Bolsa Família Program: A Decade of Social Inclusión in Brazil" (executive summary in English, full report in Portuguese). Institute for Applied Economic Research, Federal Government of Brazil, Brasilia.

Cecchini, Simone, and Aldo Madariaga. 2011. "Conditional Cash Transfer Programmes: The Recent Experience in Latin America and the Caribbean." *Cuadernos de la CEPAL* 95 (September/November). https://ssrn.com/abstract=1962666.

Chile, Ministerio de Desarrollo Social. 2018. Registro Social de Hogares de Chile, World Bank.

Colombia, Departamento Administrativo para la Prosperidad Social. 2018a. "Dirección Transferencias Monetarias Condicionadas: Informe de Gestión, Julio-Diciembre de 2017." Departamento Administrativo para la Prosperidad Social, Bogotá. https://www.prosperidadsocial.gov.co/inf/doc/Documentos%20compartidos/Informe%20de%20Gestio%CC%81n%20II%20semestre%202017%20DTMC-nov29.pdf.

Colombia, Departamento Administrativo para la Prosperidad Social. 2018b. "Guía Operativa para la Verificación de Compromisos en Educación: Más Familias en Acción." Departamento Administrativo para la Prosperidad Social, Bogotá. https://www.prosperidadsocial.gov.co

/inf/doc/Documentos%20compartidos/G-GI-TM-7%20GUI%CC%81A%20OPERATIVA%20PARA%20LA%20VERIFICACIO%CC%81N%20DE%20COMPROMISOS%20EN%20EDUCACIO%CC%81N%20VERSIO%CC%81N%205.pdf.

Colombia, Departamento Administrativo para la Prosperidad Social. 2018c. "Guía Operativa para la Verificación de Compromisos en Salud: Más Familias en Acción." Departamento Administrativo para la Prosperidad Social, Bogotá. https://www.prosperidadsocial.gov.co/inf/doc/Documentos%20compartidos/G-GI-TM-8%20GUI%CC%81A%20OPERATIVA%20PARA%20LA%20VERIFICACIO%CC%81N%20DE%20%20SALUD%20VERSION%205.pdf.

Colombia, Departamento Nacional de Planeación. 2016. "Declaración de Importancia Estratégica del Sistema de Identificación de Potenciales Beneficiarios (Sisbén IV)." Documento CONPES 3877, Departamento Nacional de Planeación, Bogotá. https://colaboracion.dnp.gov.co/CDT/Conpes/Econ%C3%B3micos/3877.pdf.

Colombia, Departamento para la Prosperidad Social. 2017. "Manual Operativo: Más Familias en Acción."

Corbanese, Valli. 2015. "Assessment of Delivery of Employment Services and Programmes for Youth by the Employment Service Agency of the FYR of Macedonia." Decent Work Technical Support Team and Country Office for Central and Eastern Europe, International Labour Organization, Budapest.

Costa Rica, Gobierno de, Instituto Mixto de Ayuda Social. 2015. Puente al Desarrollo, Estrategia Nacional para la Reducción de la Pobreza, Gobierno de Costa Rica.

Dávila Lárraga, Laura G. 2016. "How Does Prospera Work? Best Practices in the Implementation of Conditional Cash Transfer Programs in Latin America and the Caribbean." Technical Note IDB-TN-971, Inter-American Development Bank, Washington, DC.

Dodlova, Marian, Anne Giolbas, and Jann Lay. 2018. "Non-contributory Social Transfer Programs in Developing Countries: A New Dataset and Research Agenda." *Data Brief* 16: 51–64.

Fiszbein, Ariel, and Norbert Schady, with Francisco H. G. Ferreira, Margaret Grosh, Niall Keleher, Pedro Olinto, and Emmanuel Skoufias. 2009. *Conditional Cash Transfers: Reducing Present and Future Poverty.* Washington, DC: World Bank.

Fuller, David L., B. Ravikumar, and Yuzhe Zhang. 2014. "Unemployment Insurance Fraud and Optimal Monitoring." Working Paper 2012-024D, Research Division, Federal Reserve Bank of St. Louis, St. Louis, MO.

Garsten, C., K. Jacobsson, and K. Sztandar-Sztanderska. 2016. "Negotiating Social Citizenship at the Street-Level: Local Activation Policies and Individualization in Sweden and Poland." In *Integrating Social and Employment Policies in Europe: Active Inclusion and Challenges for Local Welfare Governance*, edited by M. Heidenrich and D. Rice, 265–94. Cheltenham, U.K., and Northhampton, Massachusetts: Edward Elgar Publishing.

Gomez Hermosillo M., Rogelio. 2016. "Mission Accomplished: The Accelerated Scale Up of the Productive Social Safety Net in Tanzania Achieved by TASAF." Consultant report.

GovTech Singapore. 2019. Government of Singapore. https://www.tech.gov.sg/.

Grigoras, Vlad, and Emil Daniel Tesliuc. 2017. "Reducing Error, Fraud, and Corruption (EFC) in Social Protection Programs." Slide presentation, World Bank, Washington, DC.

Grosh, Margaret, Carlo del Ninno, Emil Tesliuc, and Azedine Ouerghi. 2008. *For Protection and Promotion: The Design and Implementation of Effective Safety Nets.* Washington, DC: World Bank.

Ibarrarán, Pablo, Nadin Medellin, Ferdinando Regalia, and Marco Stampini, eds. 2017. *How Conditional Cash Transfers Work: Good Practices after 20 Years of Implementation.* Washington, DC: Inter-American Development Bank.

IDB/WAPES/OECD (Inter-American Development Bank/World Association of Public Employment Services/Organization for Economic Co-operation and Development). 2015. *The World of Public Employment Services.* IDB/WAPES/OECD. https://publications.iadb.org/en/world-public-employment-services.

ILO (International Labour Organization). 2018. "Public Employment Services: Joined-up Services for People Facing Labour Market Disadvantage." Working paper, ILO, Geneva, Switzerland. https://www.ilo.org/employment/Whatwedo/Publications/policy-briefs/WCMS_632629/lang--en/index.htm.

Immervoll, Herwig, and Carlo Knotz. 2018. "How Demanding Are Activation Requirements for Jobseekers?" IZA Discussion Paper 11704, Institute of Labor Economics, Bonn, Germany.

Indonesia, Ministry of Social Affairs. 2016. Implementation Guideline Program Keluarga Harapan (Family Hope Program, PKH).

International Labour Organization. 2016. *What Works: Active Labor Market Policies in Latin America and the Caribbean.* Geneva: International Labour Office.

Jamaica, Ministry of Labour and Social Security—PATH Team. 2017. Programme of Advancement through Health and Education (PATH): Operations Manual.

Kamurase, Alex. 2018. "Grievance Redressal Mechanism: Checklist." Internal document, World Bank, Washington, DC.

Klepinger, Daniel H., Terry R. Johnson, Jutta M. Joesch, and Jacob M. Benus. 1997. "Evaluation of the Maryland Unemployment Insurance Work Search Demonstration." Abt Associates Inc. and Battelle Memorial Institute, prepared for the Maryland Department of Labor, Licensing, and Regulation, Baltimore.

Konle-Seidl, Regina. 2012. "Activation and Integration: Working with Individual Action Plans: Monitoring and Follow-Up of IAPs and Their Outcomes in Selected EU Countries." European Commission Mutual Learning Programme for Public Employment Services: DG Employment, Social Affairs, and Inclusion, Brussels, Belgium.

Kuddo, Arvo. 2009. "Employment Services and Active Labor Market Programs in Eastern European and Central Asian Countries." Social Protection and Labor Discussion Paper 0918, Human Development Network, World Bank, Washington, DC.

Kuddo, Arvo. 2012. "Public Employment Services and Activation Policies." Social Protection and Labor Discussion Paper 1215, World Bank, Washington, DC.

Kumagai, Saki. 2013. "Platforms for Grievance Management." Presentation, Social Development Grievance Redress Mechanism Working Group Meeting, World Bank, Washington, DC, October 30, 2013.

Kumagai, Saki. 2016. "Sierra Leone Decentralized Service Delivery Project 2 (DSDP2): Activity Summary Report 1: Grievance Redress Mechanism." World Bank, Washington, DC. http://documents.worldbank.org/curated/en/523421467995644865/Sierra-Leone-decentralized-service-delivery-project-2-DSDP-2-activity-summary-report-1-grievance-redress-mechanism.

Leite, Phillippe, Tina George, Changqing Sun, Theresa Jones, and Kathy Lindert. 2017. "Social Registries for Social Assistance and Beyond: A Guidance Note and Assessment Tool." Social Protection and Labor Discussion Paper 1704, World Bank, Washington, DC. http://documents.worldbank.org/curated/en/698441502095248081/Social-registries-for-social-assistance-and-beyond-a-guidance-note-and-assessment-tool.

Lindert, Kathy, Anja Linder, Jason Hobbs, and Benedicte de la Briere. 2007. "The Nuts and Bolts of Brazil's Bolsa Família Program: Implementing Conditional Cash Transfers in a Decentralized Context." Social Protection Discussion Paper 0709, World Bank, Washington, DC.

Lindert, Kathy, and Vanina Vincensini. 2010. "Social Policy, Perceptions, and the Press: An Analysis of the Media's Treatment of Conditional Cash Transfers in Brazil." Social Protection Discussion Paper 1008, World Bank, Washington, DC.

Loxha, Artan, and Matteo Morgandi. 2014. "Profiling the Unemployed: A Review of OECD Experiences and Implications for Emerging Economies." Social Protection and Labor Discussion Paper 1424, World Bank, Washington, DC.

Maragh, Daynia T. 2017. "Analysis of Current Compliance Situation: Programme of Advancement through Health and Education (PATH)." Ministry of Labor and Social Security, Kingston, Jamaica.

McKenzie, David. 2017. "How Effective Are Active Labor Market Policies in Developing Countries? A Critical Review of Recent Evidence." Policy Research Working Paper 8011, World Bank, Washington, DC.

Mexico. 2019. Reglas de Operación de la Pensión para el Bienestar de las Personas Adultas Mayores.

Mexico, Secretaría de Desarrollo Social. 2017. "Guía para el Llenado de Fichas de Atención." Secretaría de Desarrollo Social, Dirección General de Atención a Grupos Prioritarios.

Mexico, Secretaría de Desarrollo Social. 2017. Reglas de Operación del Programa Pensión para Adultos Mayores, para el ejercicio fiscal 2018.

Mexico, Secretaría de Desarrollo Social. 2018a. Prospera's current process in verification of co-responsibilities (Mexico): Responding to challenges leveraging new and emerging technologies. http://socialprotection.org/discover/publications/Prosperas-current-process-verification-co-responsibilities-mexico-responding.

Mexico, Secretaría de Desarrollo Social. 2018b. Reglas de Operación de Prospera Programa de Inclusión Social.http://socialprotection.org/discover/publications/Prosperas-current-process-verification-co-responsibilities-mexico-responding.

Mosley, Hugh G. 2011. "Decentralisation of Public Employment Services." European Commission, Social Affairs and Inclusion, Brussels, Belgium.

Ortakaya, Ahmet Fatih. 2018. "Monitoring Conditionalities in Turkey's CCT Program." Internal background note, Delivery Systems Global Solutions Group, Social Protection and Jobs Global Practice, World Bank, Washington, DC.

Paes-Sousa, Romulo, Ferdinando Regalia, and Marco Stampini. 2013. "Conditions for Success in Implementing CCT Programs: Lessons for Asia from Latin America and the Caribbean." Social Protection and Health Division Policy Brief IDB-PB-192, Inter-American Development Bank, Washington, DC.

Pakistan, Government of, Benazir Income Support Programme. 2017. Operation Manual Waseela-e-Taleem.

Patel, Darshana, Yuko Okamura, Shanna Elaine B. Rogan, and Sanjay Agarwal. 2014. "Grievance Redress System of the Conditional Cash Transfer Program in the Philippines." Social Development Department and East Asia Social Protection Unit Case Study, World Bank, Washington, DC. http://documents.worldbank.org/curated/en/111391468325445074/Grievance-redress-system-of-the-conditional-cash-transfer-program-in-the-Philippines.

Pearce, Rohan. 2017. "Department of Human Services Plans Next Generation of Virtual Assistants." *Computerworld*, October 11, 2017. https://www.computerworld.com.au/article/628424/department-human-services-plans-next-generation-virtual-assistants/.

Peixoto, Tiago, and Micah L. Sifry, eds. 2017. *Civic Tech in the Global South: Assessing Technology for the Public Good*. Washington, DC: World Bank and Personal Democracy Press. https://openknowledge.worldbank.org/handle/10986/27947.

Pellerano, Luca, and Valentina Barca. 2014. "Does One Size Fit All? The Conditions for Conditionality in Cash Transfers." Oxford Policy Management, Oxford, UK.

Pfeil, Hélène, Saki Kumagai, Sanjay Agarwal, and Alfredo Gonzalez-Briseno. 2016. *Strengthening the Citizen-State Compact through Feedback: Effective Complaint Management as a Pathway for Articulating Citizen Voice and Improving State Response*. Washington, DC: World Bank. http://documents.worldbank.org/curated/en/265311467007229719/Strengthening-the-citizen-state-compact-through-feedback-effective-complaint-management-as-a-pathway-to-articulate-citizen-voice-and-improve-state-response.

Philippines, Department of Social Welfare and Development. 2015a. "Grievance Redress System Overview." Presentation, June.

Philippines, Department of Social Welfare and Development. 2015b. GRS flowcharts—examples.

Philippines, Department of Social Welfare and Development. 2015c. Pantawid Pamilyang Pilipino Program Operations Manual, 2015 Edition.

Pinxten, Juul. 2018. "Background Note: Monitoring Conditionalities in Indonesia's PKH Program." Delivery Systems Global Solutions Group, Social Protection and Jobs Global Practice, World Bank, Washington, DC.

PWC (PricewaterhouseCoopers). 2016. "Comprehensive Assessment and Benchmarking Report of the Pantawid Pamilyang Pilipino Program Business Processes and Information Systems: Assessment and Benchmarking of the DSWD Pantawid Pamilyang Pilipino Program, Final Report." Consultant report.

Ranganathan, Malini. 2012. "Re-engineering Citizenship: Municipal Reforms and the Politics of 'e-Grievance Redressal' in Karnataka's Cities." In *Urbanizing Citizenship: Contested Spaces in Indian Cities*, edited by Renu Desai and Romola Sanyal, 109–32. Thousand Oaks and New Delhi: Sage.

Shelley, Selina. 2015. "Piloting a Grievance Mechanism for Government of Bangladesh's Social Protection Programmes: Final Report." Manusher Jonno Foundation, Dhaka, Bangladesh. http://nfspbd.org/wp-content/uploads/2018/07/GM-Scoping-Report.pdf.

Singapore, Inland Revenue Authority. 2019. https://www.iras.gov.sg/irashome/default.aspx.

Social Security Administration. n.d. *Social Security Programs throughout the World*. Various regions and years. Washington, DC: Social Security Administration. https://www.ssa.gov/policy/docs/progdesc/ssptw/.

Tanzania, President's Office. 2013. Tanzania Third Social Action Fund/Productive Social Safety Net (PSSN): Operational Manual.

Transparency International. 2016. "Complaint Mechanisms: Reference Guide for Good Practice." Transparency International, Berlin, Germany.

Tubb, Helen. 2012. "Activation and Integration: Working with Individual Action Plans: Toolkit for Public Employment Services." European Commission Mutual Learning Programme for Public Employment Services: DG Employment, Social Affairs, and Inclusion, European Commission, Brussels, Belgium.

Turkey, General Directorate of Social Assistance. 2014. Operational Manual on Central Regular Assistance Programs.

Turkey, General Directorate of Social Assistance. 2016. Turkey's Integrated Social Assistance System.

Turkey, Ministry of Family, Labor, and Social Services. 2019. https://alo144.aile.gov.tr/alo-144.

Turkey, Ombudsman Institution. 2018. https://www.ombudsman.gov.tr/English/about-us/index.html.

Turkey, Presidency Communication Center. 2019. https://www.cimer.gov.tr/.

UNDP (United Nations Development Programme) and UNDP-APRC (Asia-Pacific Regional Centre). 2013. "Strengthening the Governance of Social Protection: The Role of Local Government: Regional Analysis." UNDP, Bangkok, Thailand. http://www.asiapacific.undp.org/content/dam/rbap/docs/Research%20&%20Publications/democratic_governance/RBAP-DG-2014-Strengthening-Governance-of-Social-Protection.pdf.

United Kingdom, NAO (National Audit Office). 2006. "International Benchmark of Fraud and Error in Social Security Systems." NAO, London.

Van den Berg, Gerard, and Bas van der Klaauw. 2006. "Counseling and Monitoring of Unemployed Workers:

Theory and Evidence from a Controlled Social Experiment." *International Economic Review* 47 (3): 895–936.

van Stolk, Christian, and Emil D. Tesliuc. 2010. "Toolkit on Tackling Error, Fraud, and Corruption in Social Protection Programs." Social Protection Discussion Paper 1002, World Bank, Washington, DC.

Velarde, Rashiel B. 2018. "The Philippines' Targeting System for the Poor: Successes, Lessons, and Ways Forward." Social Protection Policy Note 16, World Bank and Australian Aid, Washington, DC.

Venn, Danielle. 2012. "Eligibility Criteria for Unemployment Benefits: Quantitative Indicators for OECD and EU Countries." OECD Social, Employment, and Migration Working Paper 131, Organisation for Economic Co-operation and Development Publishing, Paris.

Villa, Juan M., and Miguel Niño-Zarazua. 2017. "Poverty Dynamics and Graduation from Conditional Cash Transfers: A Transition Model for Mexico's Progresa-Oportunidades-Prospera Program." *Journal of Economic Inequality* 17: 219–51. https://doi.org/10.1007/s10888-018-9399-5.

Wazed, Mohammed A. 2010. "Employment Generation Program of Bangladesh." Presentation by the Bangladesh Ministry of Food and Disaster Management at the South-South Learning Forum 2010, Arusha, Tanzania, June 14–18, 2010.

World Bank. 2012a. "Feedback Matters: Designing Effective Grievance Redress Mechanisms for Bank-Financed Projects. Part 1. The Theory of Grievance Redress." World Bank, Washington, DC. https://openknowledge.worldbank.org/handle/10986/12524.

World Bank. 2012b. *World Development Report 2013: Jobs.* Washington, DC: World Bank.

World Bank. 2013. "A Rapid Assessment Report of the Grievance Redress System (GRS) for the Conditional Cash Transfer Program in the Philippines: Pantawid Pamilyang Pilipino Program (Pantawid Pamilya)." World Bank, Washington DC.

World Bank. 2016a. "Activation and Public Employment Services in Poland: Enhancing Labor Market Policies for the Out-of-Work Population." World Bank, Washington, DC. https://openknowledge.worldbank.org/handle/10986/29831.

World Bank. 2016b. "World Development Report 2016: Digital Dividends." Overview booklet. World Bank, Washington, DC. http://documents.worldbank.org/curated/en/961621467994698644/World-development-report-2016-digital-dividends-overview.

World Bank. 2018a. "Grievance Redress Mechanisms: Responsible Agricultural Investment (RAI) Knowledge into Action Notes." RAI KN 19, World Bank, Washington, DC. http://documents.worldbank.org/curated/en/145491521090890782/Grievance-redress-mechanisms.

World Bank. 2018b. "Mobile Technology in Sierra Leone: Improving Inclusiveness, Transparency, and Accountability." Slide presentation, World Bank, Washington, DC.

World Bank. 2018c. "Stakeholder Engagement and Information Disclosure." Guidance Note for Borrowers ESS10, World Bank, Washington, DC. http://documents.worldbank.org/curated/en/476161530217390609/ESF-Guidance-Note-10-Stakeholder-Engagement-and-Information-Disclosure-English.pdf.

World Bank. 2018d. *The State of Social Safety Nets 2018.* Washington, DC: World Bank.

World Bank. 2018e. "Tanzania—Progress Review and Implementation Support of PSSN I and Preparation of Proposed New Phase Operation (PSSN II)." World Bank, Washington, DC.

World Bank. 2019. "Social Insurance Administrative Diagnostics (SIAD): Guidance Note." Working draft, World Bank, Washington, DC.

World Bank, Office of the Compliance Advisor Ombudsman. 2008. "A Guide to Designing and Implementing Grievance Mechanisms for Development Projects: Advisory Note." World Bank, Washington, DC. http://www.cao-ombudsman.org/howwework/advisor/documents/implemgrieveng.pdf.

WWP (Brazil Learning Initiative for a World Without Poverty). 2016a. "Bolsa Família Program Conditionalities: How Does It Work?" http://wwp.org.br/.

WWP (Brazil Learning Initiative for a World Without Poverty). 2016b. "Breach of Bolsa Família Program Conditionalities." http://wwp.org.br/.

WWP (Brazil Learning Initiative for a World Without Poverty). 2016c. "Results and Impacts of the Bolsa Família Educational Conditionalities Monitoring." http://wwp.org.br/.

WWP (Brazil Learning Initiative for a World Without Poverty). 2016d. "Results and Impacts of the Health Conditionalities of the Bolsa Família." http://wwp.org.br/.

WWP (Brazil Learning Initiative for a World Without Poverty). 2016e. "Results of Monitoring the Bolsa Família Conditionalities." http://wwp.org.br/.

Chapter 9

Assessing the Performance of Social Protection Delivery Systems

Estelle Raimondo, Briana Wilson, Inés Rodríguez Caillava, and Kathy Lindert

This chapter provides an evaluative framework to assess the performance of the core building blocks of delivery systems for social protection programs, as well as to evaluate how these systems can promote inclusion and strengthen coordination. The chapter is organized as follows:

- Section 9.1 gives an overview of the results chain for delivery systems in the context of a theory of change.
- Section 9.2 identifies key dimensions of performance as well as performance indicators for delivery systems along the delivery chain.
- Section 9.3 provides a review of the types of assessments that are commonly used to evaluate delivery systems.
- Section 9.4 concludes with some thoughts on how to operationalize this performance measurement framework to move from performance measurement to performance management.

Various country examples are discussed in this chapter, as listed below:

- **Africa:** Malawi
- **East Asia and the Pacific:** the Philippines
- **Europe and Central Asia:** Greece, Moldova, North Macedonia, Romania, and Serbia
- **Latin America and the Caribbean:** Brazil, Chile, Colombia, Costa Rica, the Dominican Republic, Peru
- **Middle East and North Africa:** the Arab Republic of Egypt, West Bank and Gaza
- **South Asia:** Pakistan
- **Other Organisation for Economic Co-operation and Development (OECD) countries:** the United States

9.1 CONNECTING DELIVERY SYSTEMS TO PROGRAM OUTCOMES: A RESULTS CHAIN

How Do Delivery Systems Contribute to Social Protection Program Results?

Results chains typically focus on linking program activities to high-level outcomes. The focus of conventional theories of change tends to be on the causal chain linking activities of the program, such as cash transfers or job training, to high-level outcomes, such as the graduation of vulnerable populations from extreme poverty, or their enhanced resilience to shocks. In traditional theories of change, a set of underlying assumptions about delivery systems are usually spelled out including the accuracy of targeting and the ability of vulnerable populations to access the program's benefits or services. Other assumptions might include the effectiveness of the referral system.

However, theories of change are rarely explicit about how delivery systems contribute to effective and efficient social protection programs. In other words, those theories do not elaborate on what it takes for their assumptions to be fulfilled. Yet, as this Sourcebook has shown, delivery systems involve many processes, actors, and enabling factors to implement social protection programs. Without delivery systems, there is no implementation. Without implementation, there are no program activities. Without program activities, there are no outcomes.

Delivery systems merit a results chain with a performance logic of its own, underlying the program's theory of change. This chapter intends to fill the gap by synthesizing a performance framework that captures this often ignored yet essential part of effective social protection programs. Figure 9.1 shows graphically where the

Figure 9.1 Connecting the Layers of the Theory of Change in Social Protection Programs

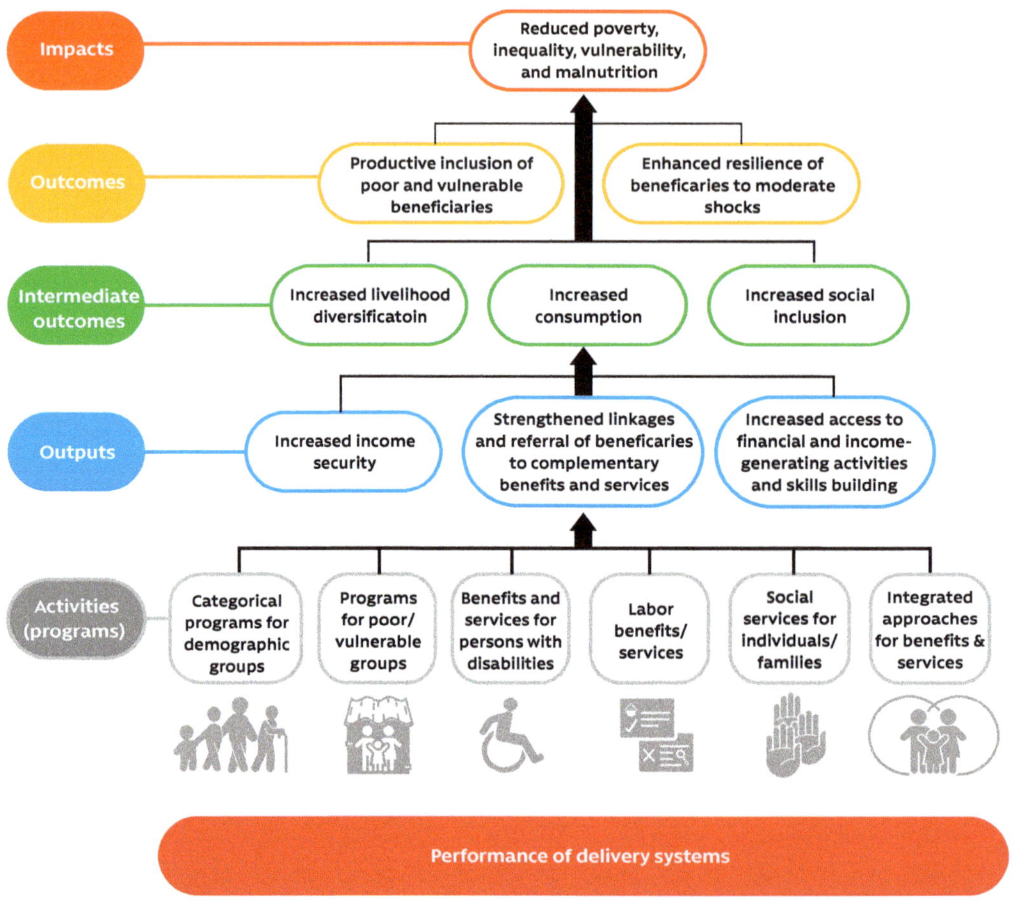

Source: Original figure for this publication.

performance focus of this chapter operates compared with traditional theories of change.

Performance along the Delivery Chain

Delivery systems are the backbone of social protection programs because they constitute the operating environment for implementing social protection benefits and services. That operating environment includes the core implementation phases and processes along the delivery chain (figure 9.2), the main actors (people and institutions), and enabling factors (communications, information systems, and technology).

A well-performing delivery chain supports the dual objectives of effective and efficient delivery of benefits and services to the intended population. ***Effective*** delivery systems are by essence inclusive. They not only reach the intended population, but they do so in part by overcoming the challenge of including vulnerable groups and those who face specific access barriers. Delivery systems that function well also promote ***efficient*** program delivery: that is, clients and administrators can go through each phase of the delivery chain at a reasonable cost in terms of time and money. Thus, an efficient delivery system has necessarily overcome the challenges of coordination and fragmentation. Such a system exploits synergies within and between programs to minimize costs for administrators and integrates systems and delivery chains across programs to minimize costs for clients. Well-performing delivery systems ensure ***effectiveness*** and ***efficiency*** throughout the delivery chain, from outreach to routine oversight, and are supported by effective and efficient information systems, client interfaces, and institutions. The performance narrative along the delivery chain is laid out graphically in the upper tier of figure 9.3.

Each part of the delivery chain builds on the others.[1] For example, effective outreach ensures that intended populations and vulnerable groups are informed of and understand the interventions, and are willing to apply to programs, and provide information about themselves. Those outputs feed into the intake and registration phase. Other important elements need to come together to enable effective intake and registration, including a well-functioning client interface as well as a robust information system that accurately records clients' information in the social registry. The outputs of that phase would then include complete, validated, and verified information on applicants. Those outputs, along with various assessment tools, feed into the assessment of needs and conditions. The outputs of the assessment phase are the profiles of assessed applicants/registrants. Registrants' profiles along with program-specific eligibility criteria are the inputs to the determination of eligibility. Enrollment decisions are further informed by programs' budgets and protocols for wait-listing eligible individuals if there are insufficient slots. Registrants'

Figure 9.2 The Social Protection Delivery Chain

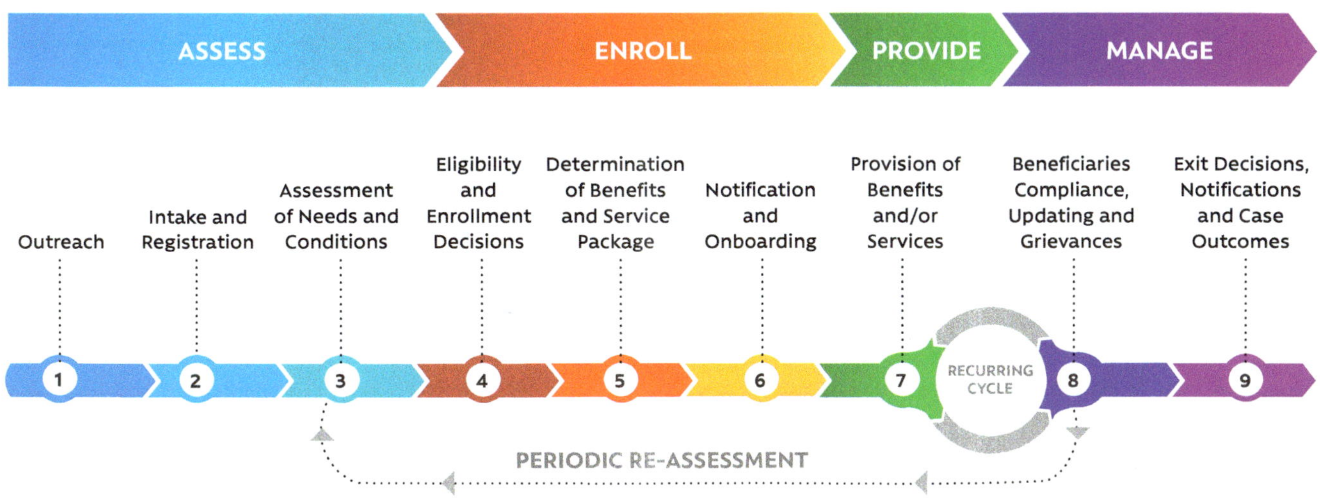

Source: Original figure for this publication.

profiles also inform decisions on the package of benefits and services that will be offered. Those decisions are made according to program rules and caseworkers' discretion. Applicants are notified of their status (eligible or ineligible, and enrolled or wait-listed), and enrolled beneficiaries are onboarded, including an explanation of rules, activities, expectations, and the rights and responsibilities of beneficiaries. After beneficiaries are notified and onboarded, the beneficiary registry is updated. The beneficiary registry in turn provides information that feeds into the payment of benefits and the provision of services. In the recurring implementation cycle, the next stage, beneficiary operations management, results in updates to the beneficiary registry, changes in the benefit-service packages, decisions on any penalties or sanctions for noncompliance with conditions, and resolution of grievances (in some cases leading to the addition of new beneficiaries or changes in benefit-service packages). These outputs feed back to the provision of benefits and the provision of services.

Communication, especially within the client interface, as well as information systems and the technology that support them, enables an effective and efficient delivery chain. The contribution of these enabling factors to the performance of delivery systems is represented at the bottom of figure 9.3. The performance of the delivery

Figure 9.3 The Results Chain of Social Protection Delivery Systems

Source: Original figure for this publication.

chain also depends on whether key actors and enabling factors such as institutions, communications, and information systems are doing their part effectively and efficiently. More specifically, well-performing delivery systems rely on the following:

- ***Institutions*** that are well-governed by a robust legal framework, with clear roles and responsibilities and appropriate oversight. They must also be well-resourced, with skilled human resources, and appropriate budgets and incentives. They must be well-coordinated with each other, to ensure proper information and data sharing.
- ***Effective communication and client interface*** that facilitate the interaction and feedback loops between the program and the clients it serves. A well-performing interface provides appropriate information to clients, supports them throughout the various phases of the program, from application to enrollment, and helps them navigate various tasks. Specific attention to clients with access barriers is critical to ensure that social protection programs are inclusive.
- ***Information systems*** that support the social protection program throughout the delivery chain by providing accurate information. Information systems need to provide complete and accurate information; and to be well secured, to protect the data privacy of the clients and ensure the safety of payments and other transactions. In addition, they need to be efficient, to minimize the time and money involved in entering, retrieving, curating, and accessing information. The most efficient systems are dynamic: they can evolve with the program's changes and are interoperable with other information systems, within or outside the program. In that sense, interoperable systems are a quintessential feature of good coordination.

Rationale for Assessing the Performance of Delivery Systems

One of the objectives of the Sourcebook is to open up the black box of implementation. This includes understanding the inner working of delivery systems, identifying good practices that make the various parts of the system work, and delineating processes that ensure fluidity in the delivery chain and minimize its cost. Measuring the performance of delivery systems is an essential part of this endeavor. A performance measurement framework serves three main purposes that echo the core objectives of monitoring and evaluation, performance management, learning, and accountability:

- First, performance indicators that are monitored regularly can help diagnose bottlenecks in the delivery chain early on and help correct course to prevent systemic challenges. Generating performance information is necessary for the effective management of the system. By regularly taking the pulse of the system, a performance measurement framework can emit signals that the system is running effectively to reach the intended population, providing accommodating access to vulnerable groups to ensure inclusion, and efficiently minimizing costs for administrators and clients. Conversely, when a part of the delivery chain is not working as intended, a performance measurement framework can raise red flags. Program managers can then act to course-correct.
- Second, paired with other evaluative techniques (see Data Sources in section 9.2), performance indicator frameworks can also help identify alternative channels, processes, or practices that enable the system to be more effective or save clients time or money. Performance measures of delivery systems can feed into a broader set of evaluative evidence on the program, including impact evaluations, and contribute to a broader learning agenda to refine and improve a program's impact.
- Third, a performance measurement system is an important part of a wider oversight function for social protection programs, ensuring that public funds are allocated effectively. Strategic decisions at the program/policy level can also benefit from up-to-date and timely performance information on delivery systems and enable adjustments to key parameters of the program on the basis of real-time information. Moreover, if performance information is made available in usable form to a broad range of stakeholders, it can help preserve the program's integrity and reputation.

9.2 MEASURING PERFORMANCE OF DELIVERY SYSTEMS: INDICATORS

A performance indicator framework is a useful management tool to monitor the progress and contribution of delivery systems. This chapter proposes several options for measuring performance along the delivery chain. Annex 9A categorizes 100-plus indicators that capture various dimensions of performance. The compilation is not meant to suggest that a program should adopt the entire framework, but rather to offer a list of options for social protection programs to choose from and adapt to their specific circumstances. Indeed, parsimony is an important feature of a quality indicator framework. Only those indicators that are measurable, monitorable, and above all, useful for making decisions should be integrated. This section highlights the logic behind the indicator framework, which is presented in annex 9A.

Key Dimensions of Performance: Effectiveness and Efficiency

The Sourcebook focuses on two broader categories of performance: effectiveness and efficiency. There are many dimensions to the performance of delivery systems, but most fit under the broad objectives of effectiveness and efficiency. For example, inclusion is explicitly included as a key component of effectiveness. Performance can also be assessed by other criteria, depending on the objectives of the programs the delivery systems support. In addition, the performance of information systems, communications, institutions, and people are included in annex 9A.

Effectiveness is central to the performance of delivery systems. As defined by the OECD/DAC (Development Assistance Committee) evaluation criteria, "effectiveness is a measure of the extent to which a program or activity attains its objective" (OECD/DAC Network on Development Evaluation 2019). In this Sourcebook, an effective system is not only one that reaches, registers, and provides benefits and services to most of the intended population, but it is also a system that is inclusive because it accommodates the specific needs of vulnerable populations and those who face access barriers. Consequently, the evaluation criterion of inclusion is embedded within effectiveness to reflect this logic. However, dedicated performance indicators to measure the extent to which each part of the delivery chain reaches vulnerable groups and those who face access barriers are integrated in annex 9A. Without its own set of measurements, inclusion is likely to "evaporate" along the way. This phenomenon is well-evidenced in the literature on gender mainstreaming.

Efficiency is another important dimension, albeit one that is difficult to measure. Ensuring that outcomes are achieved at reasonable costs, including moving clients through the various stages of the delivery chain at minimal cost in terms of time and money both for administrators and clients, is critical to evaluating performance. Alternative measures of efficiency include processing times for various phases or stages along the delivery chain.

Performance indicators can help track the effectiveness and the efficiency of delivery systems. The choice of indicators depends on the system's level of maturity as well as on the overarching objectives of the program and how the system is intended to contribute to the program. Therefore, there is no ideal set of indicators that could be replicated for all programs. Nevertheless, this chapter proposes a set of indicators that are considered important to capture performance along the delivery chain. Figure 9.4 highlights those key performance indicators. This chapter's companion indicator framework (annex 9A) provides a wide range of options to track performance and to monitor inputs throughout the delivery chain.

When deciding which indicators to integrate in a delivery system's performance measurement framework, a few principles should be kept in mind. First, performance indicators are only as good as their use. It can be costly to generate performance measurement data and to make sense of them through reporting. Thus, when deciding which performance indicators to track, consultation with the intended users should take place to ensure the indicators will be used. Second, generating the most useful and valid indicators might be costlier than collecting routine indicators that are less useful but are automatically generated by the system. Thus, being selective about indicators also means considering the value of each indicator against its cost. Third, to track performance over time, it is helpful to generate longitudinal data. Some core performance indicators should not change every year. Others can be adopted for shorter periods to track the short-term effects of an innovation in the delivery system or to verify whether performance is improving after a problem in the delivery chain has been fixed. Fourth, the performance indicator framework should evolve with the delivery systems. More mature delivery systems will be able to generate and absorb more advanced data sources. Given these four considerations, programs should make careful choices about which indicators to adopt for performance management.

Examples of Common Indicators

To measure the effectiveness of outreach, it is useful to survey whether people are informed about a program or social registry. Indicators for this phase would have to come from specific surveys or public opinion polls. In terms of user experience and rights, some programs track whether people are informed about program objectives, eligibility criteria, and rights and responsibilities. For example, in North Macedonia's conditional cash transfer (CCT) program, the results framework includes

Figure 9.4 Key Performance Indicators along the Social Protection Delivery Chain

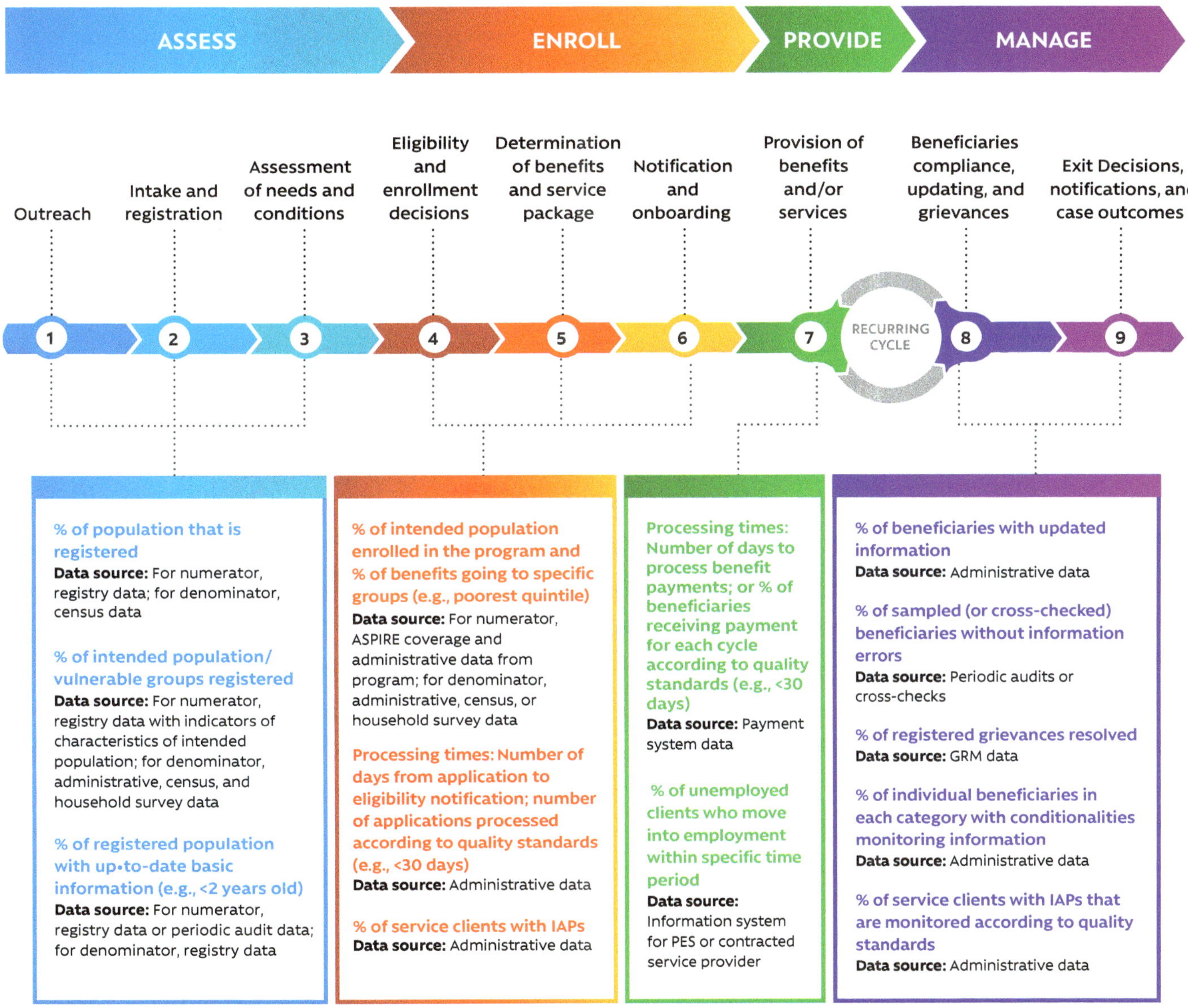

Source: Original figure for this publication.

Note: ASPIRE = Atlas of Social Protection Indicators of Resilience and Equity (World Bank); GRM = grievance redress mechanism; IAP = individualized action plan; PES = public employment service.

a performance indicator on the percentage of prospective beneficiaries (households that are potentially eligible for CCT) who were informed of their eligibility status and the requirements of the application process as part of the program's monitoring system.

There are several performance indicators to measure effectiveness for **intake and registration.** Let us look at four indicators that can be useful for this phase of the delivery chain:

- The simplest indicator, and one that is frequently tracked, is the share of the population that is registered in a social registry. Figure 9.5 provides such data for various countries, and also notes whether intake and registration were carried out using on-demand or administrator-driven approaches (see chapters 2 and 4). This indicator is an easy way to categorize how large a social registry is and is particularly relevant if the registry serves multiple programs (in social protection and beyond).[2] It might also be important to track the share of the population that is registered where the social registry has actually been rolled out. This would allow taking into account the geographical targeting that might exist in a country. For labor-related programs, this indicator could be the total number of (unemployed) people who have registered at the public employment service (PES) office.
- The second indicator that could be useful is the share of the ***intended*** beneficiary population that is registered. The data needed for this indicator is more complex. If the intended population is the poor, then the indicator would be the number of poor people in the social registry as a share of the total number of poor people in the country. For labor-related programs, this indicator could be measured as the share of unemployed who are registered at the PES office.[3]
- The third indicator is the number or share of people (or families) from vulnerable groups who are registered, a variation of the second indicator.

Figure 9.5 Share of the Population in Social Registries in Select Countries, circa 2015–17

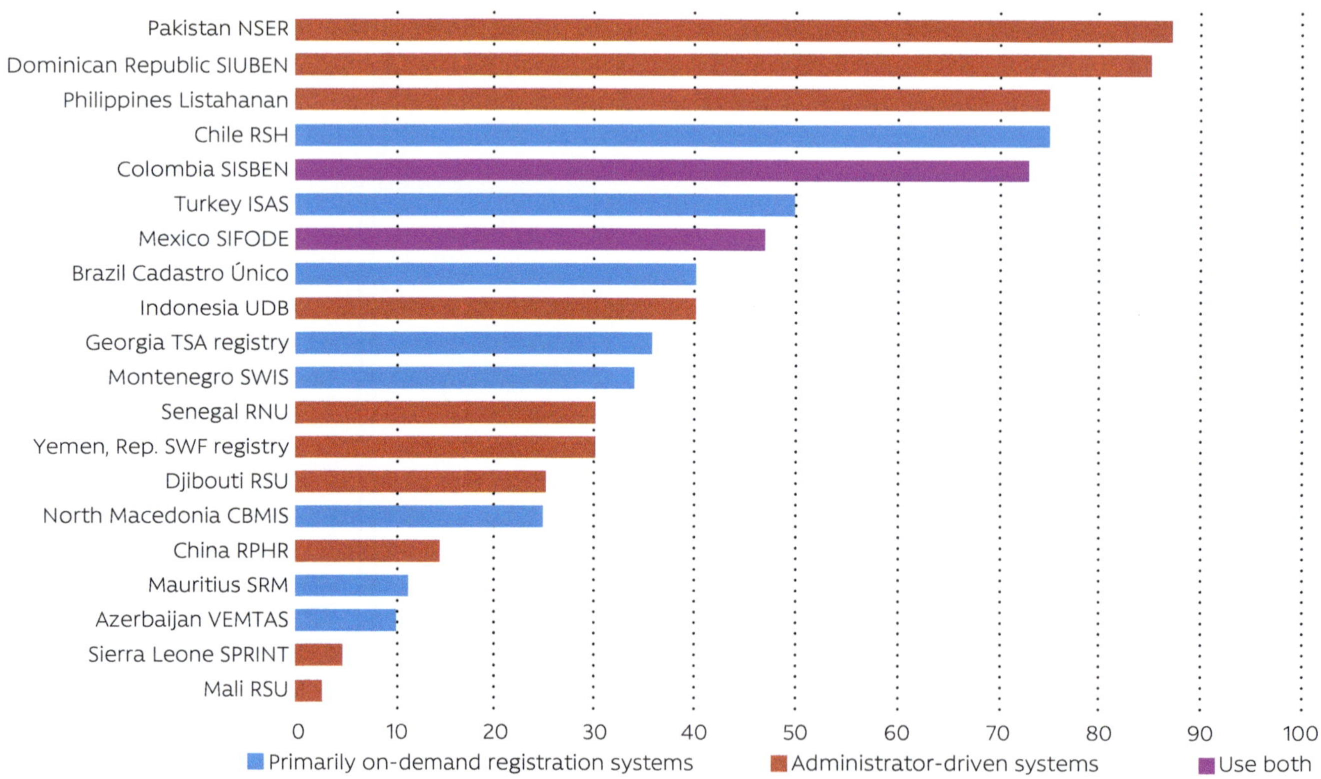

Source: Leite et al. 2017.

- Finally, the fourth indicator is the share of registered people (or households) whose information is up to date (say, less than two years old). For on-demand social registries, this indicator is likely something less than 100 percent, since not everyone continues to seek the support of social protection programs and may not return for reassessment. For static administrator-driven social registries, this indicator is likely to be similar for cohorts of households. If the registration wave was recently carried out, this indicator could be close to 100 percent (for that cohort). If registration has not been carried out in several years, that indicator would be zero. All of these indicators are illustrated for Brazil's Cadastro Único social registry in box 9.1, which also highlights some of the data challenges involved in calculating the second indicator.

Most programs track indicators pertaining to program **enrollment**. Indeed, because of the traditional focus of results chains on program activities, data on number of beneficiaries are generally readily available. A key performance indicator for the enrollment stage is the coverage of the intended population based on administrative data. The numerator would be the number of people or households enrolled (based on program data) and the denominator would be the size of the intended population (from either household surveys or census). Another variation on that indicator could be the number of enrolled individuals or households covered as a share of targets, particularly if a program is scaling up to meet a national target. For various services, an important part of the enrollment stage is the development of Individualized action plans (IAPs), which set out goals, referred service activities, and so on (see chapters 5 and 7). An indicator could thus be the share of beneficiaries with IAPs established as part of the onboarding phase.

At the **provision** stage, tracking effectiveness depends on whether the program is providing benefits or services, but many indicators can apply to both. The following sample indicators can be used or adapted to measure services or benefits: coverage of intended population, frequency of services/benefits, timeliness or quality of payment or service receipt, and access to benefits or services (disaggregated by specific groups). Two key performance indicators are detailed as follows:

- ***Share of the intended population that receives benefits and/or services ("coverage").*** For demographic categorical programs, that could be the share of all elderly (ages 65 or older) receiving a social pension, or the share of all children ages 0–18 receiving a child allowance. This indicator can be estimated using administrative or household survey data. For poverty-targeted programs, the indicator could look at the share of those in the poorest quintile (or some other income range) who are receiving benefits or services. In this case, the numerator would be the number of beneficiaries receiving benefits or services in the poorest quintile (or some other income range) and the denominator would be the total population of the poorest quintile. To calculate coverage by quintiles or deciles of per capita welfare would usually require household survey data. Coverage is a core indicator in the World Bank's ASPIRE database (figure 9.6).[4] For labor programs, such indicators can be used to measure the share of the unemployed receiving unemployment benefits or services (sometimes disaggregating by specific group). Similarly, for disability benefits or services, coverage can measure the share of the disabled population receiving disability benefits or services.
- ***Benefits or beneficiary incidence.*** This indicator is commonly used in poverty-targeted programs to assess the distribution of program benefits or beneficiaries along the welfare distribution. Thus, this indicator will determine if a program is pro-poor by looking at the share of total benefits or services going to the poorest quintile (or any other measure of poverty). In this case, the numerator is the number of beneficiaries receiving benefits or services (or amount of benefits) in the poorest quintile and the denominator is the total number of beneficiaries (or amount of benefits). This is another core indicator in the World Bank's ASPIRE database (figure 9.7).

Provision of benefits. The Inter-Agency Social Protection Assessments (ISPA) tool for payment systems provides rich guidance on how to assess the performance of payment systems for social protection, including tools and guidelines.[5] Box 9.2 illustrates how the effectiveness of payment systems can be tracked. There are a few key performance indicators for benefit payments that apply to all types of benefits (social assistance, unemployment

Box 9.1 Indicators for Intake and Registration in Brazil's Cadastro Único Social Registry

Brazil's Cadastro Único is a social registry that provides information gathered during intake and registration to the Bolsa Família Program as well as numerous other programs. It is an on-demand system, so data in the registry are fluid. The General Secretariat for Evaluation and Information (SAGI) of the Ministry of Social Development (MDS) publishes monthly reports on key indicators drawn from the Cadastro Único. Using those, plus some other data from the Brazilian Institute of Geography and Statistics (IBGE), we can illustrate how to calculate three key indicators for the intake and registration phase of the delivery chain:

Indicator 1: The percentage of the population that is registered. This indicator is relatively straightforward because SAGI reports on the number of households (27,313,209 as of January 2019) and individuals (74,437,980) registered in the Cadastro Único, and IBGE maintains population data (209,626,347 people estimated for 2019). That indicator was 74,437,980/209,626,347 = 36 percent registered in the Cadastro Único as of January 2019.

Indicator 2: The percentage of the intended population that is registered. This indicator is more complicated because it requires additional data from the social registry as well as poverty estimates from IBGE. It also requires aligning the social registry's characterization of "poor" as closely as possible to the national definition of poverty. Data from the SAGI report indicate that, of those registered in the Cadastro Único,

- 38.3 million people lived in families with incomes of less than R$89 per month.[a]
- 9.7 million people lived in families with incomes of R$89–178 per month.[b]
- 17.1 million people lived in families with incomes between R$178 and half the monthly minimum wage, R$499.[c]
- In all, 65.1 million (88 percent of those registered) were living in families with incomes <R$499, meaning that 31 percent of the total national population was low-income and registered in the Cadastro Único.

The latest poverty data from IBGE are for 2017. They suggest that 58.4 million people lived on less than R$406 per month, representing about 28 percent of the total population in 2017. Unfortunately, poverty data for 2019 are not available. Further adjustments would be needed for proper conversions into the same cutoff point (R$406) and for the same point in time. This would be possible with additional data beyond the monthly report for SAGI. Importantly, however, it seems pretty clear that virtually all of those considered "poor" are registered in the Cadastro Único.[d] That suggests strong performance of this "on-demand" system in achieving nearly universal coverage of lower-income groups, which is important since the Cadastro Único, serves many programs.

Indicator 3: Number or share of people or families from vulnerable groups that are registered**.** Importantly, SAGI/MDS tracks this indicator in their monthly reports, with information on the number of families who are registered (and the subset who are beneficiaries of Bolsa Família) from various vulnerable groups, such as the indigenous, quilombolo, and cigana populations; those with specific status relating to the environment or agriculture; and those living in various types of precarious situations (such as the homeless).

Indicator 4: Share of registered households with up-to-date information**.** This is a core performance indicator that is actively monitored and reported by MDS because it also feeds into their index of decentralized implementation (IGD), as discussed in chapter 4. In the monthly SAGI report, the data for 85 percent of registered households were less than two years old (their reassessment period) in the Cadastro Único in January 2019. This makes sense because not everyone who previously registered is still seeking support. MDS also monitors this indicator for each of the 5,570 municipalities, which helps track variations in performance at the subnational level.

Sources: Relatorio Bolsa Família e Cadastro Único, a monthly report from SAGI/MDS (https://aplicacoes.mds.gov.br/sagi/RIv3/geral/index.php?relatorio=153&file=entrada), consulted in 2019. Population and poverty data from IBGE (https://www.ibge.gov.br/).

a. R$89 is the monthly income threshold for the extreme poor to be eligible for benefits under the Bolsa Família Program. They receive the highest benefit amounts, which are calculated on the basis of incomes and household composition.

b. R$178 is the monthly income threshold for the moderate poor to be eligible for benefits under the Bolsa Família Program. Those with incomes of R$89–R$178 receive more moderate benefits, as per the benefits menu.

c. As of January 2019, the monthly minimum wage income was R$998, so half of that is R$499.

d. Besides the differences in the year and thresholds used, data in a social registry are not exactly comparable to annual poverty statistics since the social registry captures both a stock (of those registered over time) and a flow (more recent registrants).

assistance or insurance, disability benefits, or pensions). The first is the *share of individuals, families, or households paid in each payment cycle.* This indicator is usually disaggregated by geographic area, target group (including specific vulnerable groups), payment modality, and payment provider (see box 9.2 on Colombia). This indicator can be taken one step further to measure the *share of beneficiaries receiving payments according to quality standards for each cycle.* This would require not only tracking payments made to beneficiaries, but also payments made according to quality standards, which usually include an indication of their frequency (monthly or quarterly, for example) and punctuality (within the first five days of the month, first two weeks, etc.). A related key indicator is the *frequency and extent of arrears in benefit payments,* as well as the *percentage of delayed payments or the percentage of individuals, families, or households receiving delayed payments.*

Figure 9.6 Share of the Population in the Poorest Quintile Receiving Social Assistance Benefits

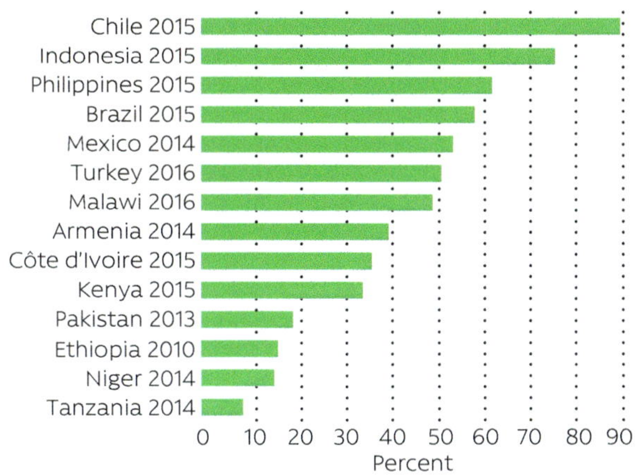

Source: ASPIRE database, World Bank, http://datatopics.worldbank.org/aspire/.

Note: The indicator is calculated as follows: (number of individuals in the poorest quintile who live in a household where at least one member receives the transfer) / (number of individuals in the poorest quintile). This figure underestimates total social protection and labor coverage because household surveys do not include all programs that exist in each country. The indicator includes direct and indirect beneficiaries (all the individuals who live in a household where at least one member receives the transfer). In the case of Kenya, a public expenditure review (Sundaram and Pape 2019) found that the total coverage of the poorest quintile is 12.5 percent when core social protection programs are considered. When school feeding programs (which accrue to students across the income quintile) are added (in ASPIRE), this leads to the difference in coverage when compared to the public expenditure review.

Provision of services. For service provision, the indicators would be more heterogeneous, given the specialization and diversity of labor and social services. The key measure of effectiveness in service provision is the quality of the service being provided. Countries define and enforce sets of quality standards per service to measure the performance of service provision.

- ***All services.*** As discussed in chapter 7, various quality standards exist for social services, including the European Union's Voluntary European Quality Framework for Social Services (2009). Those standards establish key principles (available, accessible,

Figure 9.7 Share of Social Assistance Benefits Going to the Poorest Quintiles in Select Countries

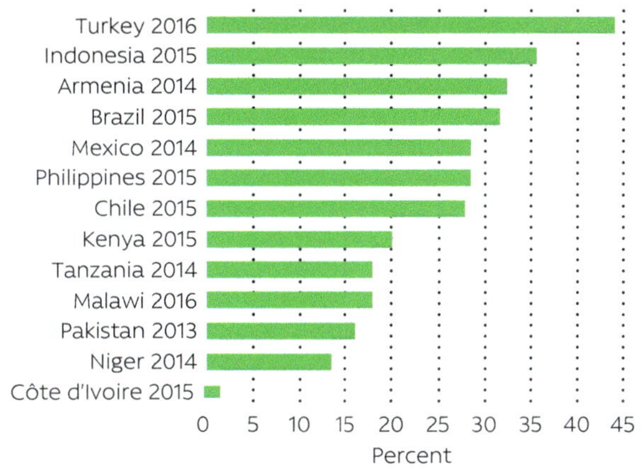

Source: ASPIRE database, World Bank, http://datatopics.worldbank.org/aspire/.

Note: The indicator is calculated as follows: (sum of all transfers received by all individuals in the poorest quintile) / (sum of all transfers received by all individuals in the population). In the case of Kenya, a public expenditure review (Sundaram and Pape 2019) found that targeting accuracy is 32.4 percent when core social protection programs are considered. When school feeding programs (which accrue to students across the income quintile) are added (in ASPIRE), this leads to lower targeting accuracy when compared to the public expenditure review. This is because the school feeding programs have lower targeting accuracy when compared to the core social assistance programs.

Box 9.2 Indicators for Payment of Benefits in Colombia's Familias en Acción

Colombia's Familias en Acción is a cash transfer program that pays benefits in six payment cycles. Two payment modalities are used: deposits in bank accounts or mobile wallets, and delivery of benefits at payment points for families without a bank account or mobile wallet. The program measures the effectiveness of its payment system by tracking several indicators:

- **Percentage of families paid by payment cycle.** This indicator measures the number of families paid as a share of the total number of families enrolled in the program. For the three last payment cycles of 2018, the numbers were as follows:
  - September 2018: 74.07%
  - November 2018: 74.71%
  - December 2018: 74.65%

- **Percentage of families paid by target group.** This indicator disaggregates families by target group, including SISBEN (families assessed through the country's social registry, which has the same name), displaced populations, UNIDOS (families living in extreme poverty), and indigenous populations. The data from the last payment cycle of 2018 are as follows:
  - SISBEN: 89.22%
  - Displaced populations: 90.82%
  - UNIDOS: 90.82%
  - Indigenous populations: 46.32%

- **Percentage of families who receive their benefits through bank accounts or mobile wallets.** This indicator tracks families receiving payments through the first modality. The percentages for the last three payment cycles were as follows:
  - September 2018: 74.50%
  - November 2018: 85.41%
  - December 2018: 84.83%

This indicator is also disaggregated by payment provider and by municipality group.

- **Percentage of families who have collected their benefits at the payment point.** This indicator is tracked for families who do not have a bank account and is disaggregated by municipality group (municipalities are grouped by four). For the fifth payment cycle of 2018, the percentages were as follows:
  - Group 1: 50.68%
  - Group 2: 48.19%
  - Group 3: 69.63%
  - Group 4: 73.11%

The source of the data needed to track all these indicators is the program's beneficiary operations management information system, or MIS.

Source: Colombia's Prosperidad Social, Dirección Transferencias Monetarias Condicionadas, Informe de Gestión, Julio-Diciembre de 2018, 2019.

affordable, human-centered, comprehensive, continuous, and outcome-oriented) to ensure quality in the provision of services. Not all of the principles are relevant for the provision stage, such as affordability (which is a question of program design). However, those key principles that are relevant can be measured, for example, by the following indicators: percentage of beneficiaries reporting that services meet their needs; percentage of beneficiaries who face access barriers and are receiving accommodation according to national standards; percentage of clients who benefit from integrated provision of services; percentage of services delivered according to quality standards; and percentage of beneficiaries or clients satisfied with the quality of services.

- ***Social services.*** To assess the provision of social services, it can be useful to track the number of referrals, the share of beneficiaries receiving intermediation services. More importantly, quality standards can also be specific to the type of service being provided. These standards are usually established nationally by service category (elderly care, early childhood care, etc.), are monitored and inspected for compliance, and, when gaps exist, corrective measures or enforcement are taken. Those standards typically govern such things as workers' performance, effectiveness of worker management, ratios of workers to clients, workers' qualifications, staff working conditions, and beneficiaries' freedom to choose their care provider. Those standards can be measured by adapting the following generic indicators to specific services:

- *Percentage of clients who were provided intermediation services who now access their referred service; percentage of clients who enter other social services through social assistance referrals;* number of targeted households reached by intermediation services (an indicator measured in West Bank and Gaza)
- *Percentage of staff or service providers with appropriate accreditation/certification/higher-level accreditation; percentage of assessed clients receiving services*

- ***Labor services.*** Various indicators are used to measure the quality or performance of employment services, both for those that are publicly provided (by PES offices) and for privately provided services. As discussed in chapter 7, many types of employment- or employability-enhancing services are outsourced to contractors. The indicators are often used as pay-for-performance contracts when services are outsourced to private providers. The Jobs Monitoring and Evaluation (M&E) Toolkit has a number of useful indicators for provision of labor services (European Commission 2012), which incude the following:
  - *Number of job seekers registered per PES employee; average number of monthly contacts with registered job seekers per PES employee; number of applications for types of services per PES employee; number of applications for unemployment benefits per PES employee; number of specific types of training referrals; percentage of clients with individual action plans; percentage of unemployed clients who move into work within a specific time period* (an indicator tracked by U.K. Jobcentre Plus); and percentage of women clients reentering the workforce (after childbirth) who are placed in training or placed in employment after training (an indicator measured in Austria). Other useful indicators could include *filled vacancy rates,* and *jobs placement per number of job counselors.*

There are many performance indicators for assessing the effectiveness of **beneficiary operations management.** Some of the key indicators include:

- ***Updating.*** An important indicator is the percentage of registered individuals with updated information. This information is important for all types of programs. Updated information can be basic information or more specific information on beneficiary status (see chapter 8). Some programs are more fluid than others in terms of the potential changes for beneficiaries. For example, unemployment status may change much more rapidly than disability or household socioeconomic status, and mechanisms for regular updating are particularly important for unemployment programs. Unemployment status is also relevant for maintaining updated job banks where the unemployed register.
- ***Error rates.*** The share of sampled beneficiaries whose status has been cross-checked and do not have any information error.
- ***Conditionalities monitoring.*** As discussed in chapter 8, two key indicators should be tracked to monitor the performance of delivery systems: (1) the compliance monitoring rate (individual beneficiaries with monitoring information as a share of the total number of beneficiaries, for each category); and (2) the compliance rate (share of those monitored who comply). Most CCTs track the latter, but the data lacks meaning if the former is not also reported (see chapter 8 for country examples).
- ***Monitoring IAPs for service clients.*** For services, one indicator that could be tracked is the share of service clients with updated information in their IAPS. The data source would be administrative information.
- ***Grievance redress.*** The efficacy of grievance redress mechanisms (GRMs) can be gauged in part by tracking the share of registered grievances that were resolved, along with some indications that the GRM is used adequately (box 9.3). Note that it is very important to provide a definition of "resolution" when measuring the performance of a GRM.

Box 9.3 Performance of GRM Systems in the Dominican Republic and the Philippines

Tracking the effectiveness of grievance redress mechanism (GRM) systems requires a combination of multiple indicators that track whether the GRM system is used, whether grievances are acted upon and resolved, and whether clients are informed of the actions taken to address their grievances.

In the **Dominican Republic,** a community report card is embedded in the Progresando con Solidaridad (PROSOLI) cash transfer program. A participatory monitoring and grievance redress mechanism is in place to identify issues with the cash transfer as well as with the local services associated with the conditionalities. After a meeting between beneficiaries and service providers, action plans to address the grievances are agreed upon between community members. Those action plans are monitored by the implementing agencies with key performance indicators that track the rate of grievances for which a solution has been found or that have been escalated to a higher administrative level. Additionally, the system also tracks the extent to which the feedback loop has been closed with community members regarding the status of their grievances. In addition, through a client survey that fed into a process evaluation, the program sought client feedback on the extent to which they were satisfied with the grievance redress mechanism and the participatory monitoring. Survey questions asked clients whether they were satisfied with the mechanisms to identify and resolve problems, and whether the mechanisms were adequate to voice their concerns and opinions. Other questions sought to gauge whether the GRM was effective in identifying the most pressing issues and addressing them in a timely manner.

In **the Philippines** Pantawid Pamilyang Pilipino Program (4Ps), the GRM system tracks very closely the effectiveness and the efficiency of grievance resolution.

- Feedback can be received through multiple channels such as email, mail, faxes, phone calls, complaint boxes, text messages, and face-to-face.
- Grievances are input into a database as they are received, and their status is tracked until they are resolved. The database is maintained at the city or municipal level and aggregated at a higher level.
- The system monitors the number of grievances received, the number resolved (resolution is defined based on the complainant's satisfaction), and the number resolved "on time" (which varies depending on the type of complaint—for example, a maximum of 60 days to resolve payment issues).
- The grievance resolution rate in 2014 was almost 100 percent, with an average resolution time of 32 days. The total number of grievances received between 2010 and 2014 was over 485,000, with a steep increase from 50,000 in 2010 to about 217,000 in 2013, or 5.5 percent of total beneficiaries.[a] Those numbers did not include complaints related to exclusion errors, which are tracked separately.

Sources: The Dominican Republic: Vicepresidencia de la República Dominicana, 2014, Progresando con Solidaridad, Tema 7, Monitoreo Participativo de Servicios Sociales Mediante Reportes Comunitarios, Santo Domingo, https://www.scribd.com/document/248086281/Manual-7-Programa-Prosoli#download&from_embed; the Philippines: Patel et al. 2014.

a. According to Patel et al. (2014), this is a high percentage, "indicating that the GRS is well known and being widely utilized." It is unclear, however, on what basis this is considered a high percentage, as it is well known that the payment process, for example, is particularly taxing on recipients, who in most cases need to spend more than half a day to collect their payment.

Examples of Common Indicators, Identification of Costs, Challenges, and Good Practices

Efficiency at its most simple level is measured by the time or cost it takes to deliver an output or an outcome and whether those costs are reasonable. As with any public service, cost-efficiency metrics are critical to evaluating the performance of the system. Cost efficiency can be measured throughout the delivery chain using various indicators. Efficiency should be measured both from the ***client perspective*** and from the ***administrator perspective***. It is more difficult to measure efficiency at some phases in the delivery chain than others. Accurate collection and estimation of costs is essential to track indicators, and the indicators themselves must be evaluated carefully to avoid cutting costs at the expense of quality. Good practices are shared at the end of this section to address some common challenges.

Efficiency Indicators along the Delivery Chain

Intake and registration. The efficiency of this phase for clients can be measured by calculating the client's time, costs, and visits (TCV) to complete the process. The time, costs, and visits (TCV) metric measures the amount of time the client spends on intake and registration, the financial costs the client incurs, and the number of visits the client is required to complete an application. For administrators, the relevant indicators include the following:

- ***Processing time for applications.*** The number of calendar or business days from the date of application to the date of notification. This metric is mainly relevant for on-demand systems. It is a crucial indicator, particularly from the point of view of the clients who have applied for benefits or services to fill a particular need. (See composite example in chapter 2 for a discussion of this indicator.)
- ***Percentage of applicants who are notified of eligibility status or enrollment decisions according to quality standards (such as <30 days).*** This indicator can allow administrators to track how well such standards are met. An alternative is to measure the volume of applications that go through the system per day, week, or month. The alternative indicator needs to be paired with another indicator to ensure that quality is incentivized as well as speed (such as the percentage of applications without information errors). The combined measurement would help find the optimum efficiency while maintaining quality.
- ***The cost of an intake and registration modality.*** This measures the cost of the modality over time, or cost of one type of modality compared with another (such as paper-based versus electronic-based). See the next subsection, Data Sources, for examples of how the latter indicator can be assessed, including the return on investment (ROI) methodology. Pakistan's National Socioeconomic Registry (NSER) tested the efficiency of different methods for intake and registration (box 9.4).

During the ***assessment of needs and conditions*** phase, efficiency *for administrators* can be measured by looking at the costs of assessment (or reassessment). This could be compared either to targeting effectiveness outcomes, or to the share of applicants screened for relevant risks, to ensure quality is being maintained. The costs of assessments could be defined in various ways: the administrative costs of operating a social registry, for on-demand systems; the total cost of a mass registration wave, for administrator-driven systems; or the cost of various risk or needs assessments, for services. (Steps on how to identify costs are listed below.) For clients, the performance system can track the time from application to notification of eligibility.

For ***eligibility and enrollment decisions and notification and onboarding***, tracking the TCV to apply to a program, enrollment transaction costs or reassessment costs are useful to evaluate efficiency *for clients*, while the processing times from intake and registration to eligibility and enrolment decisions, or to notification and onboarding, are useful *for administrators*.

To assess the efficiency of ***benefits and services packages decisions***, indicators that measure effectiveness can also be used to measure efficiency *for administrators*. Those indicators can be compared to administrative costs or overall program costs to determine how much the performance of the indicator would decrease or increase on the basis of a decrease or increase in administrative resources. Among the indicators for decisions are:

- inclusion errors (percentage of recipients who are not members of the intended population),
- exclusion errors (percentage of intended population not receiving transfers),
- targeting effectiveness (percentage of total transfers reaching target group[s]), and
- adequacy of benefits (total transfer amount as a share of household consumption or income for eligible groups).

For example, higher rates of inclusion or exclusion errors indicate that a system is ineffective, because benefits accrue to some people outside of the intended population and do not reach some members of the target group, thus reducing the program's overall impact on poverty reduction. But higher rates of error can also indicate inefficiency in providing benefits or services, depending on how much of the administrative or program costs are spent transferring benefits that would not have any impact on poverty reduction. Finally, low benefit levels may be inefficient if they do not spur changes in household spending or consumption.

For *clients*, the main measure of the efficiency in the provision of benefits and services is the TCV to arrive at a benefit or service package decision.

Various indicators and performance ratios are useful in analyzing the efficiency of ***providing benefits and services***. For *administrators*, they would include the following:

Box 9.4 Value-for-Money Study to Test Different Modalities for Mass Registration in Pakistan's NSER

In 2017, Pakistan began updating its National Socioeconomic Registry (NSER), which contains data on household, socioeconomic characteristics for more than 25 million households (which is more than 85 percent of the population). For the 2017 registration wave, Pakistan decided to experiment with two modalities to compare their effectiveness and efficiency: the traditional door-to-door (D2D) approach and a pilot temporary-desk approach (see chapter 4).

The NSER team carried out a value-for-money study to assess each modality's pros and cons and to compare their effectiveness and efficiency. The findings suggest that **overall cost effectiveness** was better with the traditional D2D approach. Total costs were slightly higher per household interviewed under the temporary-desk approach at US$2.70 per household (PRe 287), compared to US$2.30 per household for D2D (PRe 246). The temporary-desk approach had higher **design and setup** costs but lower **operational costs** (operational costs were US$1.34 per household for desks compared to US$1.83 for D2D). When considering simulated targeting errors (errors of exclusion and inclusion), the costs of the desk approach were higher. For every US$1,000 spent, the desk approach mistargeted 10 households more than the D2D method. However, inclusion errors were lower for the desk modality, largely due to lower coverage and self-selection.

The temporary-desk approach faced some challenges in **quality during implementation**, which were likely due in part to the fact that it was a pilot with less experience behind it. The lessons learned are instructive. The quality of service at desks was high overall, with some challenges due to overcrowding and waiting times. Over two-fifths of households revisited the desk to complete the process. On average, women had a longer waiting period than men (3 hours versus 2.3 hours). Impoverished households that had limited exposure to information were least likely to use the desks. Some of the main barriers to the desk approach were higher out-of-pocket costs, travel distance to a temporary desk, lack of information about the modality, and barriers to accessing the location. There were also a significant number of errors reported at the desk: some 5 to 20 percent of households (up to 40 percent in some regions) did not register all of their family members. Additionally, some households misreported key variables, some households reported fewer children than they had, and some assets were underreported or overreported, which led to 18 percent of households being misclassified. Nonetheless, two-thirds of households were satisfied with the registration process, and most households (73 percent) indicated that they thought that the process was transparent.

continued

Box 9.4 (continued)

In terms of **communications and outreach,** several approaches were used to promote awareness of the desk approach. Most people were aware of the temporary-desk centers, and most of those who were aware of them used the desks (75 percent). However, awareness was relatively low in some regions. Most of the people who were aware of the temporary desks had heard about them through family or friends (60 percent) or mosques (27 percent). Those were also the most trusted sources. In general, mosque announcements have wide reach, reaching 81 percent of households. Interestingly, existing beneficiaries of the Benazir Income Support Programme (BISP) cash transfer program were more likely to use a desk than were households that had not previously been beneficiaries (77 percent versus 50 percent). Poor households with limited exposure to BISP were even less likely to use a desk: 30 percent of those who did not know a BISP beneficiary went to a desk, compared to 70 percent of those who knew a beneficiary (or who were already beneficiaries).

Nonetheless, the value-for-money study suggested that the temporary-desk approach could be **useful in some settings.** Productivity at temporary desks was much higher in urban areas compared to rural areas: 24 questionnaires per day versus 12 per day at rural centers (productivity measures are still not available for the D2D approach). Moving the location of the temporary desks proved to be an effective way to increase coverage in low-density rural areas but was also costly.

The study concluded that the D2D approach is more cost-effective for mass registration census sweeps. However, it also showed that the temporary-desk approach could be promising for smaller, dynamic, and targeted registration waves because inclusion errors are lower. The temporary-desk approach could also be improved with a strategy to optimize desk location and quantity to attract the poorest households, as well as communication and queuing tools to manage visitor flow. Overall, the program team concluded that the temporary-desk approach can be advantageous only if the poor can be drawn to use the registration process, for which the team needs to refine its communications, especially the messaging. In future, the team hopes to use GPS data in addition to piloting data and qualitative work to better understand why some of the poor did not get registered at the temporary desks.

Source: Rosas, Jamy, and Khan 2017.

- ***Time taken to process benefit payments*** (in calendar or business days). The data source is the information system for benefits management. Defining the start and end points is key to the measurement. The start point could be the day on which the benefits claim was filed (for on-demand systems) or the date the final payroll was established for that pay period. The end point might be the date on which benefits are transferred to beneficiaries. Alternatively, a more complete view of the delivery chain could be obtained by tracking the number of days from the date of registration and/or enrollment to the first benefit claim. See box 9.5 for an example of payments of social assistance and disability benefits in Egypt.
- ***Cost per payment,*** measurable in a number of ways, as follows:

Box 9.5 Efficiency Measures for the Provision of Social Assistance and Disability Benefits in the Arab Republic of Egypt

Egypt's Takaful and Karama is a cash transfer program that provides benefits to poor families with young children, the elderly, and persons with severe disabilities. The program tracks the number of days after the payment due date it takes for funds to be deposited in beneficiaries' individual accounts as a measure of the payment system's efficiency. The original target indicator was a maximum of 10 days after payment due date that the deposit was made. The program has been improving its processes, resulting in an efficiency gain. All payments are now made by the due date and there are no delays.

- *Cost-transfer ratio (CTR).* The share of administrative costs in the total program budget (administrative costs / total program costs) or the administrative cost of making a one-unit transfer to a beneficiary (Tesliuc et al. 2014)
- *Total cost-transfer ratio (TCTR).* The total cost, including transfers, of delivering a one-unit transfer to a beneficiary (total program cost / total value of transfers). The more TCTR exceeds parity, the less cost-efficient the program is (White, Hodges, and Greenslade 2013).

- ***Unit cost.*** Program cost per household, per client, or per transfer package or service (White, Hodges, and Greenslade 2013)
- ***Administrative cost per beneficiary.***
- ***Direct delivery cost as a percentage of transfers.*** Focuses specifically on the cost-efficiency of payment service providers (White, Hodges, and Greenslade 2013)
- ***Time taken to develop an individualized action plan.*** This indicator is used to measure the efficiency of the provision of social and labor services. See box 9.6 on Costa Rica.
  - *Unit cost per service or client; caseload per worker.*
  - *Time taken for a job seeker to secure employment.* For example, Australia measures actual outcomes against regression-based predicted measures to take into account job seekers' characteristics and local labor market conditions (European Commission 2012).

For clients, indicators of the efficiency with which benefits and services are provided would include the following:

- *The TCV for beneficiaries to receive a payment*
- *The payment collection cost as a percentage of the value of the transfer*

Box 9.6 Measuring the Efficiency of the Provision of Social Services in Costa Rica's Puente al Desarrollo

Costa Rica's Puente al Desarrollo is a national strategy that aims to address poverty using a multisectoral and inter-institutional approach, by providing poor households with access to the social protection system, skills development, employment and entrepreneurship opportunities, and decent housing, while reducing inequality and promoting human development and social inclusion. The program entails the development, implementation, and monitoring of Family Intervention Plans, as well as referrals to benefits and services. The key performance indicators used by the program to measure its efficiency in the provision of social services are the following:

- **Time taken to develop Family Intervention Plans.** This indicator is also disaggregated by province. Between January 2015 and June 2016, the average time for the development of Family Intervention Plans was 89 days.
- **Time taken to approve referrals.** This indicator is also disaggregated by service provider. Between January 2015 and June 2016, the data was as follows:
  - 44% of referrals took fewer than 30 days to be approved
  - 29% took between 31 and 60 days
  - 12% were approved between 61 and 90 days
  - 15% took more than 90 days
- **Percentage of families who have achieved the objectives established in their plans.** This indicator is also disaggregated by the number of goals achieved. Between January 2015 and June 2016, 47 percent of families had not achieved any of the objectives in their plans and had an average of six objectives to be achieved.

Source: Operational audit on the effectiveness and efficiency of the National Strategy Puente al Desarrollo para la Reducción de la Pobreza 2015–2018, in relation to the achievement of its objectives, Costa Rica's Division of Operational and Evaluative Audit, December 2016.

The following are useful and common indicators to measure administrator efficiency for ***beneficiary operations management***:

- *Processing times for beneficiary information updating/grievance redress/conditionalities monitoring.* This indicator is typically measured by staff surveys using self-assessment, workload analysis, or administrative data.
- *Time taken to address a complaint.*
- *Caseload per staff member.* For this indicator, it is good practice to compare caseload to some reasonable norm (established via a workload analysis, for example) to determine who may be over- or underprogrammed.
- *Administrative cost* of conditionalities monitoring/compliance rate (though these costs are very difficult to disentangle from other types of administrative costs). Again, this information could be collected via a workload analysis or staff self-report.
- *Cost of detecting errors, fraud, and corruption (EFC) versus the amount of erroneous benefits recovered.* This metric is very important for EFC work to ensure that the value of recovered funds always exceeds the cost to recover those funds.

Identifying Costs

Accurate cost data are essential to measure the majority of efficiency indicators. Several tools and methods can assist institutions in collecting and measuring cost data.[6] It is important to plan for and regularly collect cost data to be able to analyze any cost-efficiency metrics. Cost data collection is often neglected and not prioritized. A simple framework is proposed here, based on recent costing tools developed by the World Bank (IRC, SIEF, and World Bank 2019; World Bank 2018). When collecting cost data to measure the efficiency of social protection delivery systems, the following steps are useful (World Bank 2018):

1. **Determine the universe of activities to be costed.** What interventions and activities should be included (for example, the full phase of the delivery chain or just one or two phases)? What are line items in their current budgets? What geographic areas or beneficiary groups will be included (for example, the cost of delivery systems for one district or the cost of delivery systems for just one benefit type)? (For an example of a cost assessment of intake and registration modalities, see box 9.4.)
2. **Define cost categories.** For the purposes of this framework and Sourcebook, the cost categories will follow the main actors (people and institutions), and enabling factors (communications, information systems, and technology) along the delivery chain. In other exercises, such as costing an identification system, the cost categories may include human resources, software development, central IT infrastructure and help desks. It is also important to distinguish between development or start-up costs and recurring implementation costs. This can be accomplished by adding another layer of categories or by developing two different costing sheets, one for start-up and one for implementation.
3. **Define cost ingredients within cost categories.** Reviewing the existing budgets, expenditures, and available administrative data from the various agencies, institutions and organizations involved in delivering social protection benefits can help define cost elements. Examples of cost items include staff (by title, location, function, etc.), materials, fuel, vehicles, facility rental, and maintenance. The perspective of the costing exercise must also be determined. The most common perspectives are fiscal or financial, private, and social cost. Fiscal or financial costs include only the monetary resources required to run a program. Private cost refers to the monetary and time costs incurred by beneficiaries when applying to a program, complying with co-responsibilities, reassessing needs and conditions, and cashing in benefits, as well as time spent by volunteers in the community and use of community space. Social costs combine financial and private costs and include all the resources required to run the program, including those directly budgeted or expended by the program and its staff as well as costs to beneficiaries, communities, and society. See table 9.1 for an example of financial costs.
4. **Determine the share of cost ingredients dedicated to each step of the delivery chain.** This step pertains mostly to resources that are shared or spread across the delivery chain, such as staff, hardware, or facilities. The share is most often determined through staff interviews and surveys (box 9.7).

Table 9.1 Example of a Cost Estimate

Delivery chain phase	Cost category	Cost ingredient	Unit	Unit price (currency)	Number of units	Level of effort (%)	Total cost (currency)
Outreach	Communications	Local staff	Number of staff	20,000	100	20	400,000
Outreach	Communications	Fuel costs	Miles	0.70	1,000	100	700
Outreach	Communications	Contract vehicles	Vehicle days	20	20	100	400
Outreach	Communications	Outreach materials	Number of packages	0.50	1,000	100	500
Outreach	Communications	Lodging	Days	100	10	100	1,000
Outreach	Communications	Volunteer time	Days	75	2	100	150
Outreach	Communications	Citizen time	Days	75	1	100	75
Outreach	Institutions	Central staff	Number of staff	30,000	3	10	9,000
Outreach	Information systems	Tablets	Ammortized annual per tablet cost	75	50	10	375
Total annual cost of outreach phase							**412,200**

Source: Original table for this publication.

Box 9.7 Tips for Improving Staff Time Estimates

- **Asking for estimates of time spent on an activity,** rather than population served or time spent in a certain geographic area, is generally easier for staff to assess.
- **Monthly or quarterly estimates of how staff spend time** will generate relatively precise data about how shared resources are used across activities. Asking staff to capture data at higher frequency can pose a significant burden with little increase in data quality.
- **In order to estimate how a resource is shared across activities, staff need training and practice in allocating shared costs.** Clarifying to program staff what program activities are/are not part of your universe is key for accurate allocations.

Source: IRC, SIEF, and World Bank 2019.

5. **Collect costs for each element.** Cost data should be from multiple sources (such as expenditure and other financial data, interviews, surveys, M&E, and administrative data); disaggregated (by type of staff and number of staff, for example); intervention-specific (by phase of the delivery chain); and captured in real time before and during implementation, if possible. The following are key steps to collecting cost information (IRC, SIEF, and World Bank 2019; World Bank 2018):
   - Decide on a time frame for the costing. In the example in table 9.1, it is one year.
   - Determine the quantities, prices, and frequency of purchase for cost elements. Surveys and interviews of program staff, budgets, expenditure data, and historical administrative data can be useful methods to identify elements and estimate their cost.
   - Determine what cost data are missing and develop a data collection plan for the missing data.
6. **Finalize cost estimate.** After carrying out these steps, one can estimate the cost of delivering one phase or multiple phases of the delivery chain or the cost of one category, such as outreach across the delivery chain. An example of a cost estimate is in table 9.1. The ingredients for each cost category that are relevant to the outreach phase of the delivery chain are included. Ingredients such as central facilities, hardware maintenance, or a help desk, for example, are not included because their use during the outreach phase is very limited.

Cost data, once collected, must then be analyzed to produce data for indicator monitoring, performance evaluation, or the selection of design options. Costs, as discussed below, should never be used as stand-alone data to make decisions and must always be compared to the value of what they are purchasing (the benefits) to determine the best course of action. Once cost data are collected, they should be used to develop ***cost-efficiency ratios*** (divide cost by output data, such as number of program applicants) or ***cost-effectiveness ratios*** (divide costs by outcome data, such as the inclusion error rate over time). (See next section, Data Sources). A note on collecting time data is included in box 9.8.

Challenges and good practices

Delivery systems often include multiple types of costs spread across the delivery chain without a central system to track and manage them (Tesliuc et al. 2014; White, Hodges, and Greenslade 2013). Challenges include the following:

- ***Identifying and tracking the costs of delivery systems can be challenging.*** For example, information systems alone involve many different types of costs. At the front end, set-up costs may include human resources, software development costs, hardware procurement, training, and capacity building. Implementation and rollout also have costs, including maintenance, system upgrades, help desk staffing, administration facilities, and human resources, among others.

Box 9.8 A Note on Collecting Time Data

Time is a key metric to evaluate efficiency. Time data are often a byproduct of collecting cost data (for example, to come up with staff costs, there needs to be a reasonable estimate of their level of effort per activity), and time data can be distilled from cost data. If a financial perspective is taken in the costing exercise, but there is a need to report on time, costs, and visits for beneficiaries, for example, surveys of a sample of beneficiaries can collect estimates of these values. These can be one-time surveys or quick surveys of beneficiaries during their application, registration, or benefit collection visits.

- ***Costs are spread across various stages in the delivery chain, across central and local governments and across various donors.*** In addition, costs are spread out over time. As such, the types and amount of costs change.
- ***Usually there is no central accounting system to keep track of all costs across various implementing entities, donors, and time.*** Implementation modalities may differ by implementer, there is often no standard or centralized budgeting method or system, and many costs are not captured in budgets or expenditures, such as costs incurred by the beneficiary or in-kind costs.

One way to address the problem of collecting costs spread across multiple sources, given the challenges of collecting and categorizing all the various costs involved, is to use a sample district or region to come up with average costs, rather than calculating the exact national cost (figure 9.8). Other methods of limiting the universe include bounding the exercise by a very specific time interval, phase of the delivery chain, or program type.

Another challenge is the scarcity of data. Scarcity of data can result from (1) the complexity of the delivery chain (it can be spread across different levels of government, and among multiple programs within units, or there can be a disconnect between budgeting and between cost administration and program administration); (2) insufficient knowledge of the methodology for quantifying administrative costs at the program or subnational level; (3) limited understanding of the usefulness of administrative cost information for monitoring and evaluation (M&E); (4) lack of consistency and transparency in indirect costs, such as shared staff time or facilities; (5) difficulty in separating costs between set-up and rollout (or across the delivery chain), especially when rolling out programs geographically means setting them up in an expanding number of regions or districts (Tesliuc et al. 2014; White, Hodges, and Greenslade 2013); and (6) reluctance to share cost data, either because the information is sensitive, such as government salaries, or because there are concerns about how the data will be used, for example, to cut program budgets (Holla 2019).

One way to address the problem of data scarcity is to plan data collection in advance. Systems should be established, or annual efforts programmed, for real-time collection of cost data to avoid retrospective

Figure 9.8 Cost per District by Cost Item in Malawi's Social Registry

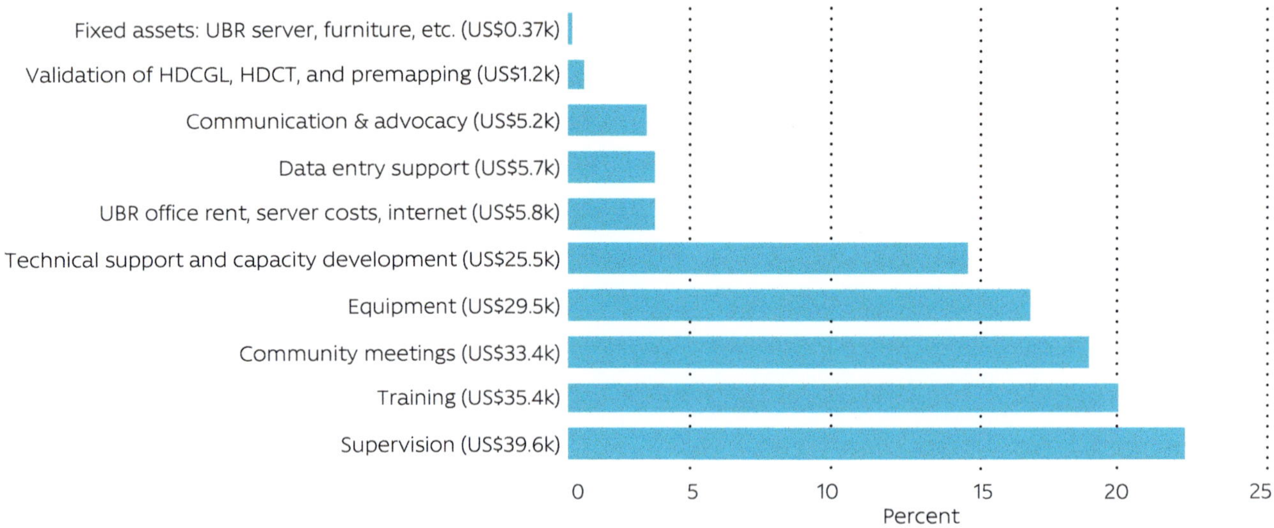

Source: Lindert et al. 2018.

Note: HDCGL= harmonized data collection guidelines; HDCT = harmonized data collection tool; UBR = Unified Beneficiary Registry (Malawi's social registry).

and costly collection exercises. Advance planning will increase the accuracy of cost data and the efficiency of collecting it.

Another key challenge is that data can be interpreted incorrectly.

- First, program features affect many cost-benefit metrics, including the maturity and coverage of the program, the size and type (cash or in-kind) of the transfer, and other design elements such as the targeting method, frequency of reassessment, and the type of payments system. For example, a program with more generous benefits will have—other things being equal—a lower share of administrative costs than a similar program with smaller transfer amounts per beneficiary (Tesliuc et al. 2014).
- Second, low administrative costs per unit of output do not necessarily mean a program is performing efficiently and effectively. TCTR and CTR do not tell us anything about what outcomes they are buying or the quality of delivery. A high TCTR, for example, may imply waste, or it may imply the beneficiary is receiving complementary services, thus increasing the effectiveness of the intervention.
- Third, administrative costs may be high in a context of limited budget and high demand for benefits and services. Costs do not depend only on the actual size or coverage of a program, but also on the number of applicants, or take-up rate, which actually determines the amount of administrative effort devoted to interviews, verification of beneficiaries' self-reported incomes, cross-checks, and so on (Tesliuc et al. 2014).
- Fourth, administrative costs may be high due to inefficiencies (in which case business processes should be optimized) but often costs are higher because certain functions require higher costs to be effective. For example, job seekers who are hard-to-place require more intense support and resources than ready-to-work job seekers, hence some job-placement branches may spend more relative to outcomes achieved, and performance management is needed to target more resources to difficult cases. Similarly, social work is much more intense and costlier (number and intensity of visits) with families with complex needs than others. It is important to keep this in mind when interpreting cost indicators.

- Fifth, there may be trade-offs between costs, for example, low administrative costs may imply high TCV for beneficiaries, as costs can be shifted from the program to beneficiaries—so both categories need to be tracked concomitantly.
- Finally, upgrading systems can be costly in the beginning but have significant payoffs.[7] During the first seven years of Mexico's Prospera program, for example, administrative costs fell from 51 percent of the program's overall budget to 6 percent. This was because of large upfront investments in systems—the purchase of equipment, the design of systems, the definition of procedures, and so on—that yielded benefits for multiple years, as well as a gradual increase in the number of beneficiaries served by the systems (Lindert, Skoufias, and Shapiro 2006).

One way to ensure data are interpreted correctly is to not use cost data and efficiency metrics in isolation, but rather as relative measures, compared to an alternative or to progress over time. Related good practices include the following:

- Only cost-effectiveness ratios can tell us about quality and outcome achievement, but even those ratios must be interpreted in relative terms and measured against trade-offs. A pilot or start-up program will have a higher CTR than a mature program because of the fixed costs (such as large upfront administrative expenditures for systems such as purchase of equipment, design of systems, and definitions of procedures), which are high initially but not strictly proportionate to program size and tend to fall over time as programs increase in size (Beegle, Coudouel, and Monsalve 2018; Tesliuc et al. 2014).
- The costs of reducing EFC should be compared to the value of the recovered benefits.
- The start-up costs of developing information systems should be compared to the potential cost savings over the useful life of the system.
- By benchmarking performance over time, comparing a country in different periods tends to be more valuable than cross-country comparisons. Cross-country comparisons are most useful when the comparator countries have similar systems and are of a similar size and development level. International comparisons of the TCTR without adjusting for program size or development level, for example, are not appropriate given differences across systems.
- For pilot or nascent programs, projecting the return to investment over time can be useful to demonstrate the value of the initial high start-up costs. The most important thing to ensure proper interpretation of data are to present the content in which they exist.

Data Sources

There are three primary sources of data that can be used to measure the main indicators of the delivery systems, performance framework: (1) delivery systems administrative data; (2) national data sources (from periodic surveys); and (3) data that require a separate dedicated collection effort. Note that there can be some pitfalls in combining various sources of data to craft performance indicators. One of these pitfalls is that of time discrepancy: while program data are potentially collected routinely, household and census data are much more infrequent. The results framework in annex 9A indicates which data sources are appropriate to use for each suggested indicator.

Data generated by delivery systems

Most social protection programs routinely collect and process administrative data for the purpose of program implementation and monitoring. Information systems track data about different processes performed along the phases of the delivery chain. Administrative data also includes information about program staff and accounting as well as financial information, including administrative costs and the value of program benefits. Another important source of performance data can be the GRM, as shown in chapter 8 and in box 9.9.

Existing administrative data on delivery systems will be a primary data source for evaluating the delivery systems' performance. These data are a rich source, particularly for information on indicators related to the quality of the registry, efficiency performance (such as the processing time at various steps of the delivery chain), compliance with operational procedures and program rules, grievance and redress performance, and information management and control mechanisms. For example, indicators such as staff turnover rates, budget execution, the percentage of cash transfers made directly to recipients' accounts, administration costs, and time between benefit determination, notification, and delivery can be measured through administrative data. Similarly, the percentage of

Box 9.9 Using Grievance Data to Assess Performance in Mexico's Pension for the Elderly Program

In Mexico, the Ministry of Social Welfare uses data generated through the grievance redress mechanism (GRM) to track the performance of the Pension for the Elderly Program (Pension para el Adulto Mayor, or PAM). This requires dedicated institutional capacity and effective reporting. The role of the General Directorate of Vulnerable Groups Support (DGAGP) within the Ministry of Social Welfare is crucial. This directorate is responsible for the implementation and performance management of the pension program. The DGAGP established a dedicated Monitoring Directorate whose primary responsibility is to manage all the performance indicators for the PAM program as well as to collate all GRM requests, appeals, or complaints, and follow up on their resolution. Another important function of this directorate is to identify grievance patterns and provide feedback to the Implementation Directorate. Since the program revises the program's operations manual once a year (to be published in the Federal Government Gazette before the beginning of the next fiscal year), the Monitoring Directorate provides a compendium of recurring problems detected through the GRM, along with a set of suggestions on how to address them.

Source: Mexico, Secretaria de Desarrollo Social, "Lineamientos Específicos del Programa Pensión para Adultos Mayores 2017," Mexico City, January 2017.

clients receiving payments in line with quality standards for each cycle can be obtained through transaction data generated by the payment system. Given the varied quality of these data, it is important to cross-check them with other data sources (see below).

Other administrative data and national statistics

Data can also be extracted from national statistics and other sources. Rich data that can be drawn from other national data sources, such as censuses, national household surveys (particularly living standards measurement surveys), or administrative data from other sectors or delivery systems (such as health, education, and agriculture). Data from those other sources is particularly valuable to validate the accuracy of the administrative data from delivery systems. For example, cross-checking that data with health and education data helps verify the accuracy of conditionalities monitoring; and validating the registry's socioeconomic classifications against a sample of social protection beneficiaries in a national living standards measurement survey can result in a much more accurate assessment of how well the program is reaching the intended population. Census data or household survey data can also measure the size of the intended population and be combined with registry data to determine coverage rates.

Data that require separate dedicated data collection

Some indicators and assessments require standalone surveys and evaluations. Examples are discussed below (e.g., performance audit, sample recheck, process/performance evaluation, workload assessment, business process review, institutional review, etc.). These surveys will be needed to evaluate performance on indicators related to compliance with quality standards, client understanding and satisfaction, estimating TCV metrics and administrator processing times, and access for vulnerable groups, among others.

9.3 EVALUATING DELIVERY SYSTEMS: TYPES OF ASSESSMENTS

Different types of assessments can be used to evaluate the performance of delivery systems. Such assessments range from more general, comprehensive approaches to more focused, specific ones. Some assessments are interrelated and provide inputs for others. For example, business process reviews are usually an input for information systems reviews because they allow the mapping of processes that need to be automated by the information system. Similarly, some assessments, especially the more focused ones, can be part of larger, more general assessments. For example, while business process reviews can be conducted as a stand-alone evaluation, they can also be part of a larger process evaluation. For each of the assessments, multiple sources of data and information can be used to answer specific assessment questions. The choice between the various types of reviews and the methods used to conduct them should always be driven by the key performance questions that the program needs answered. In this section we briefly describe eight types of assessments, their objectives, the types of questions they can answer, and the methods that can be used to answer those questions. Table 9.2 recaps the reviews covered in this chapter.

Client-Focused Performance Assessment

Several assessments seek to gauge the effectiveness and efficiency of delivery systems from the client's perspective. The objective is to evaluate how well the delivery chain is working for clients, whether it meets clients' expectations, and whether there are specific bottlenecks that should be addressed.

Scope and Questions

The perspective of clients on the performance of the delivery chain can encompass all the stages to gauge the overall experience of clients, or it can focus on specific parts of the chain and look in depth at specific obstacles. Such a review can seek the "average" client experience by resorting to (stratified) random sampling, or it can seek the views of specific groups of clients for whom access barriers might exist. Assessment questions could encompass the following:

- How do vulnerable groups experience the process of registration to the program? What obstacles do they face and why?
- To what extent does the program meet clients' expectations with regard to the payment system? What is working and not working from the clients' point of view?
- How satisfied are specific groups of clients with the program's communications on benefits and services?
- How well does the program meet the information needs of the clients? What expectations were not met? Why not?

Methods

A number of assessment tools and techniques can be used to systematically gather clients' perspectives on the effectiveness and efficiency of the delivery chain. There is a large literature on participatory monitoring and evaluation and on how to involve a program's clients in the evaluation process (e.g., Chambers 2009; Guijt and Gaventa 1998; Holland 2013). Here, we highlight

Table 9.2 Types of Assessments to Gauge the Performance of Social Protection Delivery Systems

Type of assessment	Intended use
Client-focused performance assessment	Assess the performance of the delivery chain from the clients' perspective
Process evaluation	Assess what works and what does not work in the implementation of the program and find options to improve implementation
Business process review	Assess the effectiveness of specific business processes that are used in the delivery chain
Compliance audit	Assess whether the rules, guidelines, and protocols are followed
Efficiency analysis	Assess the relative costs to the outcomes of various systems or processes
Benchmarking	Compare the performance of two or more delivery systems
Information systems review	Assess whether information systems are appropriate and maintain data integrity and use
Institutional review	Assess whether the organizational structure, management systems, and staff are adequate

Source: Original table for this publication.

two specific tools that are widely used in analyzing the performance of social protection delivery chains:

- ***Journey maps*** are a tool that helps lay out the end-to-end client experience when navigating the different phases of the delivery chain. They trace the client's experiences, expectations, behaviors, and emotions (highs, lows, pain points) along that journey. They can also assess how well performance targets and quality standards meet client expectations. (See chapter 2.) The data underlying journey maps can come from various sources, including interviews with clients, shadowing or observing clients as they go through the various steps of the delivery chain, or from specific time-stamped data that are generated by the information systems underlying the delivery chain.
- ***User satisfaction or beneficiary feedback surveys*** also provide useful performance information. They aim to measure providers' performance through the lens of the client's experience with benefit and service delivery. These surveys collect data on individuals' behaviors, knowledge, perceptions, and practices, all of which are relevant for assessing service quality and demand-side indicators. Examples of indicators measured through household and beneficiary surveys include the level of satisfaction with benefits and services, transaction costs (in terms of money and time spent and the number of visits) involved in program participation, the amount and frequency of social assistance transfers, service accessibility, awareness of rights and obligations, and program engagement. National household surveys are also useful for targeting measures and for independent measurement of service coverage.

Process Evaluations

Process evaluations focus on assessing the processes underlying implementation and they are sometimes also called "implementation evaluations." Their main objectives are to identify what works and what does not work, as well as to identify ways to improve implementation. They assess the efficacy of specific phases of the delivery chain, while identifying constraints that clients or administrators might face with procedures. These evaluations are primarily formative, insofar as they apply evaluation methods to try to improve the way programs are delivered. If the evaluation questions focus primarily on assessing outcomes or results, the assessments are more commonly called "program evaluations."

Scope and Questions

Identification of the key evaluation questions is a vital element. Individual studies may focus on one or several evaluation questions. The following are examples of relevant questions that could be addressed by these types of evaluation:

- What processes have been used, what was the intent, what happened, and what can we learn?
- How have administrators and clients adjusted their behavior to the new process, procedure, or innovation?
- To what extent are agencies coordinating throughout the delivery chain? Why or why not?
- Have resources been secured and made available at the right time and in an optimal quantity, and have costs been minimized?
- How do vulnerable groups experience the process of intake and registration in the program? What obstacles do they face and why?

Methods

The field of program evaluation has evolved dramatically over the past decade and is becoming increasingly sophisticated, tapping into new sources of data and techniques to unpack the black box of social protection delivery systems. To understand the inner workings of delivery systems, mixed methods that draw on both quantitative and qualitative data tend to be warranted. Qualitative data collection methods—such as interviews, surveys, and focus groups—can elicit the clients' and administrators' perceptions of certain aspects of delivery systems, including client interface. Using agency records or monitoring data to identify patterns of behaviors or issues is also a typical part of a program evaluation. Other research methods can be used to answer specific evaluation questions, such as network analysis (to assess coordination), or behavioral experiments, such as discreet choice modeling. Finally, direct observations can be another useful resource (box 9.10).

Box 9.10 Greece's GMI Process Evaluation

A process evaluation of the first phase of the national rollout of Greece's Guaranteed Minimum Income (GMI) program, called "Social Solidarity Income" (SSI), was conducted in 2016. The first phase implemented the program from July through December 2016 in 30 municipalities in Greece.

The evaluation aimed at understanding how business processes were carried out with respect to the procedures detailed in the operations manual and in the Joint Ministerial Decision (JMD), which provided the legal foundation for the implementation of the first phase of the SSI. The evaluation was based on several sources of information in addition to the operations manual and the JMD. First, interviews were held with SSI Program Unit members, staff from the e-government agency (IDIKA) responsible for the implementation of the SSI-Phase 1, and officials from the Ministry of Labor, Social Insurance, and Social Solidarity (MoLSISS) to understand how the program was implemented and supervised at the central level. Second, focus groups were held at 18 Phase 1 municipalities among municipal staff involved with the SSI implementation at the local level. Third, focus groups with SSI beneficiaries were carried out in 17 municipalities.

The evaluation's results confirmed that the program was implemented smoothly and was very well accepted by both beneficiaries and municipal staff. The majority of beneficiaries and municipal staff appreciated the clarity of the application form and the fact that the applicants were informed of the outcome immediately after submission. The information system supporting the program coped very well with the volume of applications. Municipalities were able to organize a comprehensive communication campaign using the material distributed ahead of the launch of the program, therefore exploiting the program's take-up. However, the evaluation also found that the program still missed the definition and implementation of critical components that could significantly increase the success of the full rollout. These included (1) a full-time SSI program unit with clear roles and responsibilities, including a specialized and dedicated IT team; (2) timely and extensive communication at the local level as well as a full-fledged training and retraining strategy for the remaining municipalities; and (3) a grievance redress mechanism.

The program was further refined based on the results of the process evaluation, and in February 2017 the SSI was finally launched nationally. The program currently reaches over 300,000 households and well over 600,000 individuals (6.5 percent of population) and is widely considered an important and successful means of public basic income support for the poor.

Sources: Marini et al. 2017.

Business Process Reviews

Business process reviews (BPRs) constitute a subset of process evaluations (see delivery chain process mapping in chapter 2). BPRs can be stand-alone studies or embedded in other assessments. Their objective is to assess the effectiveness of current business processes and procedures, to identify gaps, and to find opportunities for improvement. These types of reviews are also useful to identify potential areas for cost savings. BPRs should identify both the benefits and drawbacks of each option they present.

Scope and Questions

A BPR can be comprehensive and cover all of the major processes underlying the delivery chain, or it can focus on only some of them. Typically, BPRs review the following processes: outreach and communications, intake and registration, enrollment, benefit or service provision, grievance handling, and monitoring of compliance with conditionalities. Questions of interest may include the following:

- Who are the key actors involved in the process and what are their roles and responsibilities?
- Are the key processes implemented by the relevant actors as intended by the program and laid out in the operation manual (fidelity)?
- What bottlenecks emerge during implementation of the processes?
- What practices work better than others?
- How did clients and other key stakeholders experience the process?

- What are feasible options for adjusting (course-correcting) the process, and what would be the likely result in improved efficiency or effectiveness if they were adopted?

Methods

A range of tools, methods, and data sources can be leveraged in a BPR, including interviews or focus groups with the administrators and clients. Process maps are a useful tool to graphically represent a series of tasks or activities that constitute the process under review. Process mapping promotes understanding and better communication of the process examined, including gaps, bottlenecks, redundant steps, or inefficiencies. Process maps can also be used to visualize and communicate what an improved process might look like. Maps can take various forms, such as flowcharts to demonstrate the sequences of tasks performed within a process. They can also be complemented by a process definition chart, which shows the applied input, resources for each activity, and the resulting output. Using "swim lanes" can be particularly helpful, as discussed in chapter 2. (See box 9.11.)

Compliance Audits/Checks

The primary purpose of compliance audits is to determine whether the rules, processes, and procedures are being followed in accordance with the requirements of the program and the standard operating procedures. Audits can be carried out for any part of the delivery chain, as well as for the information systems underlying them. Compliance audits are used to verify whether information received by the program matches the actual client, the information stored in the information system, and information registered in other places (for example, school records for compliance monitoring). When applied to payments specifically, compliance audits

Box 9.11 The Philippines's 4Ps Business Processes and Information Systems Review

A review of the Philippines's Pantawid Pamilyang Pilipino Program (4Ps) business processes and information systems was conducted in 2016 to identify areas for improvement that would make the program more efficient and responsive to emerging needs. The assessment was conducted in the context of changes in program rules, which included a proposed shift from household to family beneficiaries, the implementation of the Department of Social Welfare and Development (DSWD) data warehouse project and the decentralization of program transactions to DSWD Regional Offices.

Seven business processes were reviewed: (1) intake, registration, and updates; (2) compliance monitoring and verification; (3) benefit computation and payment; (4) grievance reporting, processing, and resolution; (5) supply-side assessment; (6) data management and generation of summaries and reports; and (7) formulation and processing of change requests for policies and business processes.

In addition, seven information systems were reviewed: (1) Eligibility Check Routine; (2) Community Assembly Registration System (CARS); (3) Beneficiary Update System (BUS); (4) Compliance Verification System (CVS); (5) Payment System; (6) Grievance Redress System (GRS); and (7) Supply Side Assessment System (SSAS).

As-is and to-be swim-lane flowcharts were created to understand both current and future business processes. Similarly, as-is and to-be data flow diagrams were created to assess current and future information systems.

The review concluded that the 4Ps is able to accomplish its objectives by effectively reaching out to more than 4.4 million beneficiaries, but that there is still significant room for improvement in terms of enhancing controls and in ensuring data integrity and accuracy. The key vulnerabilities of the program related to the multiple tasks that were conducted manually across the 4Ps processes, coupled with its unintegrated information systems. The review recommended further automation of processes and integrated information systems. Those steps entailed improving the 4Ps technological infrastructure, with primary focus on upgrading the 4Ps database.

Source: PWC 2016.

aim to verify whether the payments are directed to the right clients and whether payments are made in accordance with what was established by the benefit/service package, according to the operations manual. In social protection delivery systems, these audits are more frequently referred to as social inspections (including compliance checks and fraud investigations).

Scope and Questions

Possible audit questions include the following:

- To what extent does the implementation of the program comply with the guidelines and procedures defined in the operations manual?
- Are the eligibility criteria being assessed in accordance with the parameters of the program?
- Is the payment process being undertaken in accordance with the requirements of the program? Are payments directed to the right beneficiaries in the right time frame?
- To what extent are data entry, data quality verifications, and the production of reports in line with the program's data policy? What areas of data management need adjustments?
- Is the complaints handling system managed transparently and ethically and does it ensure that the loop between the program clients and the program administrators is closed?
- If there are discrepancies, why did they occur and what effects did they have on the program overall?
- How efficient are the defined processes and guidelines? Is there room for efficiency gains?

Methods

By using spot checks or sample rechecks, compliance audits validate the accuracy of information received and recorded by the program systems, for example with respect to the actual delivery of payments to clients (see box 9.12).

Efficiency Analysis

Some performance assessments primarily seek to compare the costs of alternative systems, processes, or courses of action. There are different types of efficiency analyses. ***Cost-effectiveness analyses (CEA)*** aim to relate the costs of a program or delivery systems to its key outcome(s) of interest. When those outcomes or benefits are monetized, the assessments are usually called ***cost-benefit analyses (CBA)***. When the objective of the review is primarily to identify areas for cost savings or ensure compliance with specific budgeting guidelines, audits would be warranted.

Methods[8]

We discussed above how to collect and analyze specific efficiency indicators. These indicators can be combined to produce a larger or more holistic efficiency analysis of delivery systems or one of its components, such as conducting a ***return on investment (ROI) analysis*** on the costs of upgrading an information system (see the Montgomery County example in box 9.13 and figure 9.9). Typically, such analyses consider all the costs and benefits that accrue to taxpayers, participants, or any number of other groups that are affected by the program under study, taking a broad perspective. A financial efficiency analysis considers only the monetary costs and benefits accruing to the particular program, organization, ministry, or department, whereas a broader social efficiency analysis would include social costs as well, such as costs to applicants, communities, and so on. The approach to CEA or CBA consists of setting out a baseline scenario against which the marginal or incremental costs or benefits will be measured. Decisions must be made about whose costs and benefits should be recognized and estimated. When evaluating the performance of social protection delivery systems, it is good practice to also consider the social costs and benefits and either benchmark performance over time within the same program or against other countries of similar development levels with similar types of programs. The quantification (CEA) or monetization (CBA) of benefits is essential. A discount rate should be used to obtain the present value of the program over a certain period.

Other efficiency analyses might consist of benchmarking various entities of a program in charge of doing the same tasks. For example, comparing multiple one-stop shops/service centers or multiple registration entities. The reviews consist of comparing the entities across a certain number of attributes (including input/output ratio) and ranking them. The ranking allows

Box 9.12 Compliance Audit: Checking Benefits Based on Risk Profiles in Moldova

Moldova's Guaranteed Minimum Income Program of cash transfers, Ajutor Social, uses proxy means testing (PMT) to assess needs and conditions and determine the eligibility of poor households to receive benefits. The program demonstrated good targeting accuracy, yet according to estimates, about 35 percent of recipients did not qualify for benefits. To reduce the program's inclusion errors, in 2011 the government launched the Social Inspection Agency (SPA), whose mandate is to minimize the risk of error, fraud, and corruption (EFC) in the social assistance system. The SPA performs ex post control of social assistance benefits to verify whether the payments are directed to the right clients, in the right amount, and according to the rules and regulations.[a] A team of about five staff members are assigned to do field-based checks of the benefits received by over 50,000 households across the entire country.

In the 2012–14 period, the SPA ran an initial screening by reviewing all active benefit cases, district by district. At the time, the agency was establishing its operational rules and procedures, and the EFC detection rate, defined as the number of detected irregularities per 100 inspected cases, barely exceeded 10 percent. In the 2014–15 period, the SPA developed its first comprehensive operational manual with standardized steps for benefit inspection campaigns, clear rules for identifying and following up on various types of irregularities, and improved procedures for recording and monitoring the results of campaigns. The SPA applied the new procedures to the first round of risk-based inspections. First, in 2015, inspections were run on a random sample and revealed overpayment and underpayment in 64 percent of the benefit cases inspected. Then, statistically significant characteristics from cases with overpayments and underpayments in the random sample were used to develop risk profiles and target cases with a higher probability of EFC. By applying those risk profiles, the SPA was able to increase the fraud and error detection rate by 20 percent in 2016 compared to 2015, while the monetary value of the identified irregularities was five times higher than in the previous campaign.

Since then, the SPA has been working to turn the risk-based inspection experience into a sustainable operational practice. In 2016, the SPA began to use a module in the social assistance management information system, which is connected with the beneficiary database as well as various public registries, to plan EFC campaigns, to carry out field checks, and to monitor their results. The data collected through a random-sample EFC campaign in 2018 helped develop new risk profiles that were used to select cases for another round of risk-based inspections in 2019.

The SPA's work has helped improve the performance of the Ajutor Social program. Inclusion errors reduced from 60 percent in 2011 to 40 percent in 2016, while benefits coverage doubled during the same period. The percentage of different errors identified through random-sample campaigns decreased significantly, from 64 percent in 2015 to 38 percent in 2018 (the most significant decrease was in income-related errors). To ensure the sustainability of the processes, the SPA is building the risk-profiling algorithms into their operational rules and information system to generate continuous adjustments of the algorithms based on real-time inspection outputs. To maximize the inspection's results for EFC deterrence and the benefit-cost ratio of the campaigns, the SPA is also strengthening its enforcement function to enable recovery of the benefits that were paid to ineligible households.

Source: Yulia Smolyar, senior social protection specialist, World Bank.

a. Ex ante control of benefits is done at the stage of eligibility assessment by cross-checking the applicant's self-declared information with data from public registries, which subsequently leads to the qualification decision.

Box 9.13 Return on Taxpayer Investment Analysis in Montgomery County, Maryland (US)

In 2013–14, the Department of Human and Health Services (DHHS) in Montgomery County (Maryland, US) conducted a return on taxpayer investment analysis (ROTI) to provide a business case that demonstrated the return on investment of taxpayer dollars from the implementation of an interoperable technology and an intensive teaming protocol for a targeted subset of the intended population.

Montgomery County DHHS provides a broad range of public health and human services to support the needs of the community's most vulnerable children, adults, and seniors through five key service areas: Aging and Disability Services; Behavioral Health and Crisis Services; Children, Youth, and Family Services; Public Health Services; and Special Needs Housing. At that time, those services operated in silos, making it challenging to meet client needs from a holistic perspective. To overcome this challenge, the department decided to invest in an interoperable technology and integrated case management process that enabled collaboration across multiple functions, increased operational efficiency across agencies, and ultimately led to better client service and outcomes.

The ROTI model focused on the costs and benefits of the application of an interoperable system and an intensive teaming protocol (ITP) to the "intensive support users" in two target populations: Transition Age Youth and Homeless. Intensive support users are the most expensive clients and represent a small percentage of the Montgomery County DHHS service population (approximately 5 percent). Transition Age Youth and Homeless categories account for 80 percent of all intensive support users.

The methodology focused on four key steps to analyze the value of the county's investment: (1) identify the target user groups using a set of defined criteria and create a "persona" profile for each target group; (2) develop a list of service bundles that are most commonly used by the target user group "persona"; (3) identify key cost elements associated with the investment, including one-time costs, fixed costs, and variable costs; (4) identify the key benefit elements associated with the investment, including cost-savings calculation (figure 9.5).

The analysis concluded that an investment in a "double intervention" of an interoperable system and intensive teaming protocol applied to "intensive support users" within the Transition Age Youth and Homeless subgroups would yield a positive ROTI.

Source: Interoperability and Intensive Teaming Protocol Business Case—Return on Taxpayer Investment Analysis, Department of Human and Health Services, Montgomery County, Maryland, 2014.

identifying which parts of the system are particularly efficient (for example, among decentralized branches) and which branches are lagging behind. The reviews capture staffing input across categories of staff (e.g., administrative staff, caseworkers, IT specialists), and budget (including salaries and operational costs), as well as outputs (e.g., number of employers contacted, schools verified, or cases monitored). Good practice would be to also assess outcomes (e.g., successful job matching, placement rates, etc.) so that there is a measure of quality against the efficiency figures (as mentioned before, lower costs do not always result in better outcomes).

Benchmarking

Benchmarking can either be a dedicated exercise or a method used in other types of assessments. It consists of comparing performance or processes across organizations or branches, within an organization, or across countries. The objective is to identify and learn from good practices through a structured process of comparison.

Scope and Questions

Performance or processes can be compared. If the objective is to compare the overall performance of delivery systems, then performance benchmarking is

Figure 9.9 Cost and Cost-Saving Calculation in Montgomery County, Maryland (US)

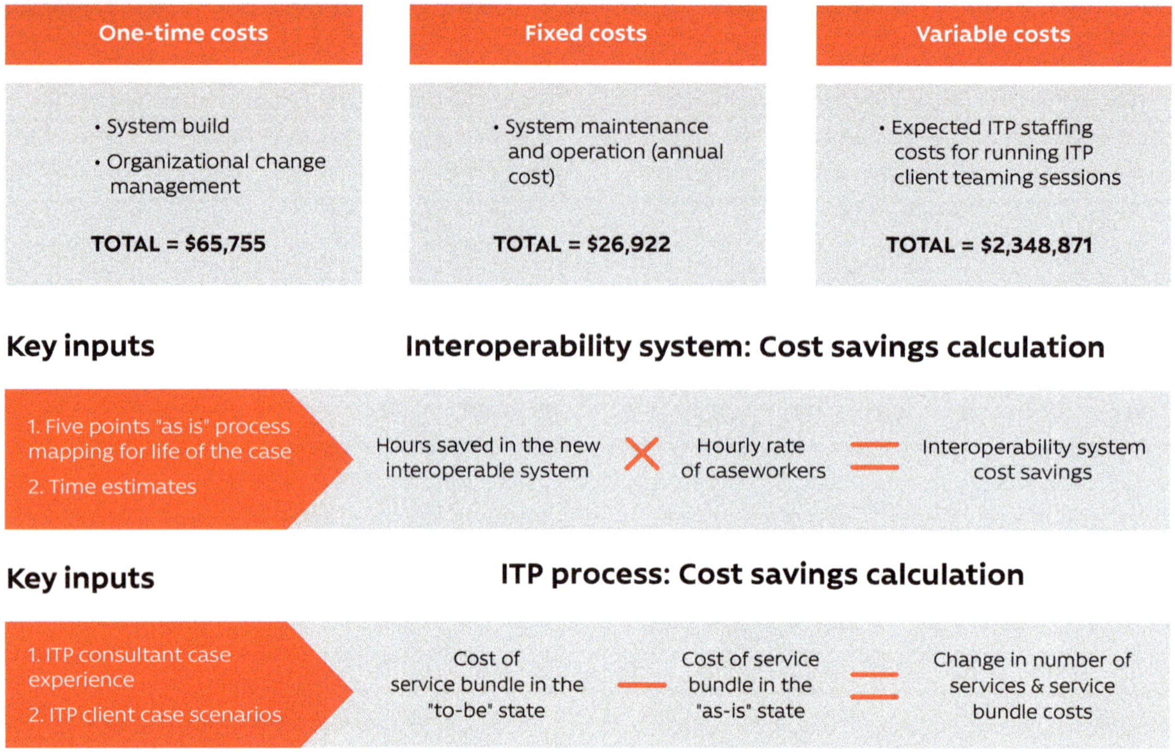

Source: Interoperability and Intensive Teaming Protocol Business Case—Return on Taxpayer Investment Analysis, Department of Human and Health Services, Montgomery County, Maryland, 2014.
Note: ITP = intensive teaming protocol.

preferable. Conversely, if the objective is to learn from other experiences for specific processes or procedures along the delivery chain, then process benchmarking should be favored. The processes and procedures of different social protection programs or entities are analyzed and compared because they are likely to lead to different outputs or outcomes. For instance, it might be instrumental to examine and compare how grievances are handled across different types of entities within a given country or across countries. The key questions motivating a benchmarking study are as follows:

- What are the similarities and differences between delivery systems?
- What factors can explain these differences?
- What changes are likely to lead to improvements in delivery systems?
- How do costs compare?

Methods

To carry out a benchmarking exercise, the first step is to identify comparators: other programs, organizations, or delivery systems that carry out similar activities or have similar functions and can be deemed suitable comparators. The availability of relevant and reliable comparative information is an important consideration in choosing the comparator. In addition, given that it is unlikely that a single comparator is superior in all dimensions, the number of comparators should increase as the complexity of delivery systems or processes increases (see box 9.14).

Information Systems Reviews

Information systems reviews seek to determine whether the information systems, related resources, and the environment are appropriate, adequately

Box 9.14 Serbia Functional Review: Efficiency Benchmarking Analysis of the National Employment Service

In 2017, as part of a larger exercise to conduct vertical functional reviews of three service sectors in Serbia (education, health, and labor), the World Bank carried out an analysis of the staffing and relative efficiency of the branch offices of the National Employment Service (NES). The objective was to provide recommendations on how to increase the overall efficiency and effectiveness of their services. The work was cofinanced by the World Bank and the European Commission.

The methodology used data envelopment analysis (DEA) and developed a quantitative benchmarking of best practices of NES branch offices at the national level, comparing different branch offices in terms of how efficiently they used their resources to produce different services and the impact of their activities on the number of unemployed who found jobs in the formal sector after using the services.[a] The methodology provided each branch office with an analysis of weaknesses and strengths, as well as recommendations to become more efficient.

The DEA was limited in that it only provided benchmarking of relative efficiency among Serbia's different regional NES offices and did not allow comparison with employment offices in other countries. It also could not account for the role of environmental factors such as regional labor market conditions and challenges (the overall skills levels and age of the unemployed, the number and kind of job offers available, dominant economic sectors, etc.).

The results showed that the local NES branch offices became more effective at placing unemployed people in jobs during 2012–14. There was scope, however, to increase job placements while reducing resources. If all branch offices could become as effective as the best offices in terms of how they used resources to achieve jobs placements, between 23,000 and 34,000 additional job matches could be achieved per year, while at the same time, between SRD 48 and SRD 53 million could be saved. To achieve those efficiency gains, the analysis recommended (1) setting individual performance targets for each branch office; (2) reviewing each office's current mix of inputs and activities; (3) increasing contacts with employers and the number of job counselors; and (4) increasing peer-to-peer learning among job counselors.

Source: Serbia Functional Review: Efficiency Analysis of the National Employment Service, World Bank and the European Commission, 2017.

a. First developed for nonprofit organizations, DEA is a nonparametric frontier estimation technique that is used to benchmark performance. The "frontier" that is estimated consists of the most efficient organizations within a group, that are used as a standard against which the performance of the other organizations is evaluated. The DEA hence verifies whether a specific unit is efficient relative to others, and identifies an "ideal" unit, which other units can imitate to achieve higher efficiency. As such, the DEA focuses on relative, not absolute efficiency—the "best" unit can still be inefficient in absolute terms. Compared to parametric methods for data analysis, such as ordinary least square regressions, the DEA method requires fewer data, allows for combining multiple inputs and multiple outputs into a single summary measure of efficiency without a priori weights, and allows for comparisons of the performance when prices of inputs or outputs are not known. DEA can also be used for both static and dynamic analysis. Progress over time can be separated into technological progress (everybody is getting better due to technical progress or changes in processes, applied methodologies, and the political environment) versus convergence (poor performing offices approach the better performing ones).

safeguard assets, maintain data and system integrity, provide relevant and reliable information efficiently, achieve organizational/information system goals, and consume resources efficiently, and have internal controls that provide reasonable assurance that operational and control objectives will be met and undesired events will be prevented, or detected and rectified, in a timely manner.

These reviews identify needs and areas for improvement to ensure alignment with best practices or compliance with program policies. They are also meant to take stock of emerging requirements and changes linked to major program and process reforms, such as the decentralization of transaction or changes in data analytics platforms.

Scope and Questions

Information systems reviews can be applied to all major information systems, such as social registries, beneficiary operations management systems, payment systems, grievance redress systems, conditionality compliance systems, and so on. The reviews should be executed by qualified IT consulting firms or service providers (see box 9.15).

Methods

Typical elements of such reviews include the following:

- Review of data management policies and procedures
- Review of data entry, data quality and integrity verifications, and productions of formats and reports
- Review of security and confidentiality of data
- Review of the IT/information system infrastructure and organization in terms of technology and HR capacity, and IT risk assessment using frameworks such as COBIT

Box 9.15 Malawi Social Registry Assessment

One type of information systems review is a social registry assessment. The World Bank conducted a rapid assessment of Malawi's social registry, known as the Unified Beneficiary Registry (UBR). The Malawi UBR was created to serve as a consolidated source of harmonized information on the socioeconomic status of households to determine their potential eligibility for social programs. The UBR was planning an expansion and a shift in registration targets (from 50 percent to 100 percent of households). The objectives of this assessment were thus to (1) review the UBR experience to date; (2) identify strengths and areas for improvement; (3) provide short-term recommendations to support the upcoming expansion, including implementation adaptations that would be needed to accommodate the revised registration targets; and (4) support the longer-term strengthening of the UBR.

The conceptual framework (methodology) for the assessment took a functional approach based on a paper on social registries by the World Bank (Leite et al. 2017) and covered the following topics: institutional arrangements, processes and implementation, data quality checks, information systems aspects, monitoring and evaluation of the UBR, user programs and the potential of the UBR as a powerful social policy tool, strategic and operational communications, and projected cost of implementing the UBR expansion.

Data was collected through (1) an extensive review of documents related to the UBR; (2) interviews with numerous stakeholders (including the UBR Taskforce, associated ministries and agencies, district and community officials, user programs, and development partners); and (3) a field visit. The assessment was "rapid" in that it was timed to be executed in a relatively short time and focused on identifying strengths, challenges, and opportunities for improvement to provide recommendations for the short and long term. The review focused on practical aspects of the UBR's implementation and its associated institutional structures, processes, systems, data quality, and uses.

The results showed that Malawi's UBR has many strong fundamentals. The government has taken the lead in designing, managing, and implementing the UBR with strong ownership across the core agencies involved. Implementation is carried out by existing decentralized institutional structures, which is a major strength. Implementation processes and information systems are effective, and most importantly, data quality is robust and registration coverage is rapidly expanding. Nonetheless, the report identifies key short-term and longer-term actions that could address challenges and strengthen the effectiveness of the UBR, including in the areas of institutional arrangements, implementation processes, information systems, data quality, links to user programs, communications, and a possible rebranding of the UBR to support better understanding of this powerful tool for inclusion and coordination in social protection and beyond.

Source: Lindert et al. 2018.

Institutional Reviews

Institutional reviews aim to assess the performance of institutions involved in the delivery of social protection benefits and services. They include different subtypes of assessments, two of which are functional reviews and staffing reviews.

Functional reviews are diagnostics of the operational environment of the agency or program(s). They seek to establish whether the management systems, policies, staffing, organizational structure, and other critical parts of a delivery system are appropriate to meet their specific objectives. A subset of functional review is to assess the adequacy of the staffing, which includes skills, training, compensation, incentives, performance evaluation, and whether the staffing is adequate in relation to the volume and nature of activities of the program. These reviews may also assess the extent to which collaboration, communication, and teamwork are adequate.

Scope and Questions

Institutional reviews encompass an assessment of the organizational structure and management practices: the extent to which roles and responsibilities are clear, and do not overlap, together with effective coordination. They may also assess whether the resources and financial management are adequate, and whether human resource management is adequate to ensure the functioning of delivery systems. Analysis of costs is also a key part of this kind of review.

Methods

Depending on the exact focus of the institutional reviews, various assessment tools and techniques can be applied. Functional reviews that seek to identify whether a specific organizational structure is fit for its purpose could include surveys of staff and management, as well as various network mapping assessments to gauge the level of coordination and cooperation across teams and pinpoint gaps in the organizational network. When conducting a staffing review, for example, a workload analysis can be a useful tool. It consists of establishing workload baselines using past data on total working time, efficiency level of various positions, and needs of employees. It can also include questionnaires for employees to determine whether they have met their key performance indicators, whether they are performing additional activities outside their job description, or whether their workload is appropriate (see box 9.16).

Box 9.16 Romania's Labor and Social Protection Sector Functional Review

A labor and social protection sector functional review was conducted in Romania in 2011. Its objective was to review the situation of the sector, assess its functioning, and develop an action plan to strengthen the effectiveness of Romania's public administration. In particular, the review examined (1) whether the policy goals and objectives of the Ministry of Labor and Social Protection (MoLFSP) and its agencies were clearly defined in measurable and achievable terms; (2) whether the information systems, policies, staffing, and organizational structure were appropriate to meet their objectives; and (3) whether there were external factors that might have impeded their ability to meet their objectives.

The main findings and recommendations of the review included recommendations around (1) integrating the management, coordination, and implementation of the labor and social protection sector in a more effective manner; and (2) rebalancing the distribution of resources in the sector, in terms of budget and spending, human resources, and information and communications technology, as well as financial management, oversight, and control.

The review recognized many advances and reforms undertaken within the sector to advance and reform the sector and proposed recommendations to strengthen implementation of these reforms. Recommended cross-cutting priority actions included (1) developing a strategy unit in the MoLFSP; (2) developing an overall umbrella information system that connects the subsectoral registries for improved policy making and

continued

Box 9.16 *(continued)*

operational functioning; (3) consolidating certain benefits (e.g., low-income benefits), eligibility criteria (e.g., for disability pensions and allowances), and payment functions (into a single payments agency); (4) strengthening cooperation between agencies involved in oversight and controls; and (5) developing an optimization plan for human resources and business processes to identify areas for improved efficiency, including possibilities for reassigning staff to improve the balance of human resources in the sector.

With the support of a €500 million World Bank loan under the Social Assistance System Modernization Project, these recommendations were turned into an action plan to improve performance management within the sector. To date, many important actions have been taken to implement these recommendations, including passage of legislation to consolidate certain benefits, implementation of new eligibility criteria, and strengthening cooperation among the oversight and control agencies. The MoLFSP continues to work on implementing the remaining recommendations.

Source: World Bank 2011, 2018.

9.4 SOME CONCLUDING POINTS

Tracking the performance of delivery systems is essential to ensure that social protection programs and delivery systems are effective and efficient. Yet a performance measurement framework is only as good as its use. In a well-functioning system, some performance information is used continuously to make course adjustments to processes, parameters, and implementation. Other performance indicators are monitored at specific time intervals, when key decisions are to be made about specific parts of the delivery chain. A third category of indicators are produced and used less frequently, when the program has to give account for its performance to an outside decision body, such as a parliament. Once a performance measurement framework is established, it is critical that it be operationalized through a performance management plan (typically referred to as a national strategy or action plan). Ideally, the delivery systems' performance management plan would not be stand-alone but would be integrated into national social protection strategies or plans. Various options exist for operationalizing a framework, but key elements include

- a dedicated working group or unit;[9]
- an action plan or operational strategy, which would highlight the results chain (main objectives, outcomes and/or output, and associated indicators), annual targets, data sources, and accountable institutions; and
- the main method for implementation, such as an annual objectives and target-setting exercise, combined with performance contracts, annual reviews and evaluations, or a combination, to measure progress, evaluate successes and failures, and propose course corrections or changes in strategies.

Approaches to performance management vary from country to country. For example, in the Philippines's Pantawid Pamilyang Pilipino Program (4Ps) there is a specific function dedicated to performance management. The Planning, Monitoring, and Evaluation Division (PMED) is in charge of data management and generation of program summaries and reports, which involves acquiring, protecting, and processing of information for different audiences or users. This includes preparing the program's status reports, sharing data, and storing of information. The division also has a coordination role and relies on five other divisions for information on each of their respective processes, including the social registry update and grievance redress system. PMED acts as the compiler, producer, and sharer of reports. On a weekly, monthly, quarterly, and annual basis, PMED produces updates on geographic and household coverage, released grants, system updates, and human resource updates. A national oversight body is in charge of reviewing and approving all periodic reports produced by PMED. For the technical annual report, the Management Committee reviews and provides comments that must be reflected prior to the approval of the National Program Manager. Besides these report-related tasks, the National Program Manager also promotes and supports data management initiatives (PWC 2016). In Chile, the Ministry of Social Development has the responsibility of enhancing complementarities across different social programs, while ensuring efficiency and effectiveness in their execution. For that purpose, during the 2014-17 period the ministry consolidated tools for the monitoring and evaluation of social programs. Those tools mainly include monitoring reports, process evaluations, and the Ministry's Integrated Database of Social Programs (Banco Integrado de Programas Sociales [BIPS]). Within the ministry, the undersecretariat of Social Evaluation is in charge of performance management. Within the undersecretariat, the Department of Monitoring of Social Programs performs a biannual monitoring of the management and implementation of social programs that are being executed by different government agencies. Each program is required to prepare a monitoring report, which includes information regarding coverage (the intended population and beneficiaries), as well as performance indicators and other information related to implementation. In addition, the Ministry of Social Development's efforts are complemented by the Budget Office of the Ministry of Finance (Dirección de Presupuesto [DIPRES]) evaluative agenda, which, among others, conducts process evaluations of government programs. BIPS constitutes an additional performance management tool of the Ministry of Social Development that allows public access to information on the performance of the different social programs. BIPS includes a list of each active social program and its description, as well as each program's monitoring reports and process evaluations.[10]

In sum, the performance management plan can take various forms and there is no "one size fits all" model. The adopted model will mainly depend on the country context, the maturity of the delivery systems, and the performance measurement capacity.

ANNEX 9A: PERFORMANCE INDICATOR FRAMEWORK FOR SOCIAL PROTECTION DELIVERY SYSTEMS

This indicator framework has been built through a bottom-up process. Indicator selection has been informed by a review of World Bank project documents, results frameworks, and self-evaluation reports and their validation by the World Bank's Independent Evaluation Group. Given the scarcity of appropriate indicators to cover the various dimensions of delivery systems, other sources of information were consulted, including government programs' own M&E systems, the literature on measuring performance of service delivery in sections other than social protection. Where there were gaps, the team created new indicators that were reviewed and crowd-sourced with experts in the field of social protection delivery systems.

No existing program currently tracks all of these indicators, nor should they. The goal of this comprehensive set of indicators is to provide a menu of good measurement options for each part of the delivery chain. The most advanced programs may hit on most of the performance categories and can aim for increased completeness, frequency, and disaggregation of the data they collect. Less mature programs may have only a partial list of indicators and can strive to incorporate more as the delivery systems develop.

This framework seeks to provide options for social protection program management units, as well as World Bank Project teams, to enrich their existing monitoring framework and capture the effectiveness and efficiency of delivery systems along the delivery chain.

Potential data sources are also proposed. They tend to fall into three categories: data generated by delivery systems themselves; data generated by other administrative systems or by the national statistical office on a somewhat routine basis; and data that require a separate dedicated data collection effort. The numbering system correlates the effectiveness and efficiency indicators with the type of data source: [a] indicates data generated by delivery systems; [b] indicates other administrative data and national statistics; and [c] indicates data that require a separate dedicated data collection effort. (See Data Sources in section 9.2 for a fuller discussion of these.)

"Intended Population" means the specific groups that the program seeks to reach and cover, depending on the program. The intended population can be the unemployed, the disabled, poor people in the bottom quintile of the income distribution, single-parents, women, the elderly, and so on. Data should be disaggregated by these subgroups as much as possible.

The indicator framework captures performance along two main criteria: effectiveness and efficiency. In the effectiveness column, specific indicators target the extent to which the delivery systems promote the inclusion of the vulnerable population, including populations that face access barriers. While these two groups are generally part of the intended population, identifying whether they are truly included requires dedicated attention and a specific set of indicators. In addition, key indicators should ideally be disaggregated by relevant demographic and social markers (e.g., gender).

Depending on the program, the relevant assistance unit of population can be individuals, families, and households. It can also refer to applicants (registrants) and/or beneficiaries.

Some indicators are appropriate only for on-demand registration systems, whereas others would be appropriate only for administrator-driven systems. The majority of indicators apply to both system types.

Table 9A.1 Social Protection Delivery Systems Performance Indicators

Delivery systems indicators	Effectiveness	Data sources for effectiveness indicators	Efficiency	Data sources for efficiency indicators
	Assesses whether the delivery chain supports the effective delivery of benefits and services to the intended population, and promotes the inclusion of vulnerable groups, including populations with access barriers		Assesses whether the various steps of the delivery chain can be achieved in a cost-efficient way (in terms of time and money) for both the administrators and the clients	
Part 1: Delivery chain				
1. Outreach	**(1)** % of intended population who understand the program **(2)** % of intended population who apply to the program **(3)** % of vulnerable groups or populations with access barriers who have applied to the program	**(1, 2, 3)** Periodic survey [c][a]		
2. Intake and registration	**(4) % of population that is registered (included in social registry) [KPI]** **(5) % of intended population that is registered (included in social registry) [KPI]** **(6)** % of vulnerable groups and population with access barriers in the social registry **(7) % of applicants/registered population with up-to-date basic information [KPI]** **(8)** % of (sampled) applicants without information errors	**(4, 5, 6)** Numerator: Social registry data [a] Denominator: Census data or household surveys with oversample of program beneficiaries [b] **(7, 8)** Periodic audit data [c]	**For clients:** **(9)** Time, costs, and visits (TCV) for applicants[b] **For administrators:** **(10)** Processing time **(11)** Volume of applications processed through the system per day/week/month	**(9)** Client survey [c] **(10, 11)** Social registry data or periodic performance audits [a] and [c]
3. Assessment of needs and conditions	**(12)** % of applicants assessed against eligibility criteria **(13)** % of applicants with complete data **(14)** % of applicants whose categorization/classification is done according to program rules **(15)** % of (sampled) applicants whose classification in the social registry (e.g., as moderately poor, extreme poor) is comparable to those in the same categories in household surveys (using similar welfare measures) **(16)** % of exclusion errors based on this sample recheck **(17)** % of grievances received that are related to assessment issues[c] **(18)** % of vulnerable groups or intended population applicants screened for risks and/or with completed risk assessment reports	**(15, 16)** Periodic audits [c] **(12, 13, 14, 18)** Social registry data [a] and household survey data [b] **(17)** GRM data [a]	**For clients:** **(19)** Time from application to notification of eligibility **For administrators:** **(20)** Number and frequency of cross-checking and pulling data with other administrative systems **(21)** Number of other programs using information from social registry	**(19)** Social registry data [a] **(20, 21)** Social registry data [a] or periodic audits [c]
4. Eligibility and enrollment decisions	**(22) % of intended population enrolled in the program [KPI]** **(23)** % of enrolled who are part of the poorest quintiles **(24)** % of applicants whose eligibility is determined according to program rules **(25)** % of applicants who are notified of the eligibility determination according to service standards **(26)** Number of calendar or business days from the date of application to the date of notification	**(22, 23)** Administrative data or household survey data [a] and [b] **(24, 25, 26)** Beneficiary registry data [a] or periodic audits [c]	**For clients:** **(27)** Program application and enrollment transaction costs (TCV for enrollment) **(28)** Program recertification transaction costs **For administrators:** **(29) Processing time (number of days) from intake and registration to eligibility and enrollment decisions [KPI]** **(30)** % of eligibility and enrollment decisions processed electronically	**(27, 28)** Client survey [c] **(29, 30)** BOMS data [a]

continued

Table 9A.1 *(continued)*

Delivery systems indicators	Effectiveness	Data sources for effectiveness indicators	Efficiency	Data sources for efficiency indicators
5. Decision on benefits and service package	**(31) % of benefits going to specific vulnerable groups (e.g., poorest quintile) [KPI]** **(32)** % of beneficiaries whose benefit and service packages are determined according to program parameters and benefit calculators **(33)** % of beneficiaries in sample re-review with accurately calculated benefits **(34) % of service clients with individualized action plans [KPI]** **(35)** % of grievances related to discrimination/exclusion[c] **(36)** Inclusion errors (% of recipients who do not belong to the intended population) and exclusion errors (% of intended population not receiving transfers) **(37)** Targeting effectiveness (% of total transfers reaching target group[s]) **(38)** Adequacy of transfers per direct recipient and wider beneficiary (% of household consumption for eligible groups, % of GDP per capita, % of poverty line)	**(31, 35–38)** Household survey data or household surveys with oversample of program beneficiaries [b] **(32, 33)** Periodic audit or sample recheck [c] **(34)** GRM data [a]	**For clients:** **(39)** TCV to arrive at a benefit or service package decision **For administrators:** **(40)** Administrative or program costs compared to inclusion error; exclusion error; targeting effectiveness; or adequacy of transfers per direct recipient and wider beneficiary (% of household consumption for eligible groups, % of GDP per capita, % of poverty line); number of beneficiaries of services	**(39)** Client survey [c] **(40)** Household survey data [b] and BOMS data [a]
6. Notification and onboarding	**(41)** % of eligible enrolled applicants notified of their benefit and service package according to service standards **(42)** % of beneficiaries onboarded according to service standards **(43)** % of beneficiaries with access barriers whose needs have been accommodated for onboarding	**(41–43)** BOMS data [a] or periodic audit/survey [c]	**(44)** Processing time from intake and registration to notification and onboarding	**(44)** BOMS data [a]
7a. Provision of benefits (payments)	**(45) % of beneficiaries receiving payments according to quality standards for each cycle [KPI]** **(46)** Frequency and extent of benefit payments arrears **(47)** % of beneficiaries with access barriers who are receiving adequate accommodation to collect payments **(48)** % of service centers which are accessible to beneficiaries according to national standards	**(45, 46)** Payment system data [a] or periodic audits/information system review [c] **(47, 48)** Administrative data [b] or periodic surveys [c]	**For clients** **(49)** TCV for beneficiaries to collect payments **(50)** Cost for beneficiary as % value of the transfer **For administrators:** **(51)** Cost per payment (CTR or TCTR) **(52)** Unit cost (program cost per household, per client, or per transfer package) **(53)** Administrative cost per beneficiary **(54)** Direct delivery cost as a % of transfers **(55)** Processing times from payroll to cash out **(56)** % of payments unclaimed **(57)** Time to reconciliation **(58)** Average number of beneficiaries per payment point	**(49, 50)** Client surveys [c] **(51–58)** Payment system data [a] or periodic performance audits [c]

continued

Table 9A.1 *(continued)*

Delivery systems indicators	Effectiveness	Data sources for effectiveness indicators	Efficiency	Data sources for efficiency indicators
7b. Provision of services	**All services** **(59)** % of clients who benefit from integrated packages of services **(60)** % of services delivered according to quality standards **(61)** % of beneficiaries reporting services meet their needs **(62)** % of beneficiaries with access barriers who are receiving accommodation according to national standards **(63)** % of beneficiaries/clients satisfied with the quality of services provided **Social services** **(64)** % of clients who were provided intermediation services who are now accessing their referred service **(65)** % of clients who access social services through social assistance referrals **(66)** Number of targeted households reached by case management services **(67)** % of assessed clients receiving services **(68)** % of staff/service providers with appropriate accreditation/certification/higher-level accreditation **Labor services** **(69)** Average number of monthly contacts with registered job seekers per PES employee **(70)** Number of applications for types of services per PES employee **(71)** Number of applications for unemployment benefits per PES employee **(72) % of unemployed clients who move into employment within specific time frame [KPI]** **(73)** Number of specific types of training referrals **(74)** % of unemployed clients who move into work within a specific time period **(75)** % of women clients reentering workforce (after childbirth) who are placed in training or into employment after training	**All services** **(59, 60, 63)** BOMS data [a] **(61)** Periodic surveys/client surveys [c] **(62)** Periodic surveys/client surveys [c] or BOMS data [a] **Social services** **(64, 65)** Periodic surveys/client surveys [c] or BOMS data [a] **(66)** Numerator: BOMS data [a] Denominator: Census data or household surveys with oversample of program beneficiaries [b] **(67)** BOMS data [a] **(68)** Administrative data [a] (human resources data) or institutional review [c] **Labor services** **(69–73)** BOMS or administrative data [a] **(74–75)** BOMS or administrative data [a] or periodic surveys/client surveys [c]	**For administrators:** **All services** **(76)** Unit cost per service or per client **(77)** Caseload per worker **Social services** **(78)** Average time to open a personalized project **(79)** Average lifetime of the project **Labor services** **(80)** Time taken to achieve employment outcome for job seeker **For clients:** **All services** **(81)** TCV to receive a service	**For administrators:** **All Services** **(76–77)** BOMS or administrative data [a] **Social services** **(78–79)** BOMS data [a] **Labor services** **(80)** BOMS data [a] **For clients:** **All services** **(80)** Client surveys [c] **(81)** BOMS or administrative data [a]

continued

Table 9A.1 *(continued)*

Delivery systems indicators	Effectiveness	Data sources for effectiveness indicators	Efficiency	Data sources for efficiency indicators
8. Beneficiary operations management	**Beneficiary data management** **(82)** % of beneficiaries whose benefit/service package is up-to-date in the BOMS **(83)** % of beneficiaries working with caseworkers **(84) % of beneficiaries with up-to-date basic information [KPI]** **(85)** % of sampled (or cross-checked) beneficiaries without information errors **Error, Fraud, and Corruption (EFC)** **(86)** % of benefits with detected EFC (by type) (error rate) **(87)** Errors in eligibility as share of total enrolled (error rate) **(88)** % of detected EFC cases that are resolved **(89)** % of irregular payments recovered **Grievance redress** **(90)** Client awareness: % of clients who are able to mention at least one complaints mechanism **(91)** Potential use: % of clients who would complain in case of poor service quality **(92)** Actual use: % of clients who considered service quality bad and used the established procedures to complain about it, % of clients who have provided feedback **(93)** % of beneficiaries with access barriers who are receiving adequate accommodation for voicing grievances **(94)** % of registered grievances that have been placed in the process of resolution according to service standards **(95)** % of registered grievances resolved **(96)** % of grievances for which the beneficiary is notified of status according to service standards **Monitoring of conditionalities** **(97) % of individual beneficiaries in each category (e.g., school-age children, lactating women, children <6 years)[d] with conditionalities monitoring information (monitoring rate) [KPI]** **(98)** % of beneficiaries with access barriers with conditionalities monitoring information **(99)** % of beneficiaries in each category with monitoring information who are complying (compliance rate)[e] **(100)** % of noncompliant beneficiaries for whom a decision on warning or penalty has been made **(101)** % of noncompliant beneficiaries notified of the decision of warning or penalty.	**Beneficiary data management** **(82 to 84)** BOMS data [a] **(86)** Periodic institutional reviews [c] **EFC** **(86–89)** Periodic audits [c]; or EFC data review [a] and BOMS data as updated post-EFC review [a] **Grievance redress** **(90 to 93)** Periodic survey [c] **(94 to 96)** GRM data [a] **Monitoring of conditionalities** **(97 to 101)** BOMS data [a] or periodic survey [c]	**For clients:** **(102)** TCV for beneficiary information updating **For administrators:** **(103)** Processing times for beneficiary information updating/grievance redress/ conditionalities monitoring **(104)** Caseload per staff member **(105)** Cost of monitoring: actual time for compliance verification **(106)** Cost of EFC detection versus erroneous benefit amounts recovered	**(102)** Periodic survey [c] **(103 to 106)** Periodic performance audit [c] or BOMS/administrative data [a]
Part 2: Enabling factors				
1. Client interface/ communication	**(107)** % of (surveyed) population satisfied with the ease and support for completing a specific task (e.g., the registration process, the possibility of voicing grievances, etc.) **(108)** % of intended population with access barriers who report having received accommodations according to national standards throughout the delivery chain **(109)** % of (surveyed) population who apply for benefits and services based on self-reporting **(110)** % of (surveyed) beneficiaries who are satisfied with the service standards	**(107 to 110)** Periodic client surveys [c]		

continued

Table 9A.1 *(continued)*

Delivery systems indicators	Effectiveness	Data sources for effectiveness indicators	Efficiency	Data sources for efficiency indicators
2. Institutions	**(111)** Staff minimum knowledge of application process/eligibility/information system/targeting framework **(112)** % of staff trained on outreach to vulnerable populations or who speak the language of vulnerable populations or who have diversity and inclusion training **(113)** Size of case load (number of cases per staff) **(114)** % of scheduled hours worked by staff **(115)** % of key positions filled **(116)** Staff turnover rate **(117)** Frequency and extent of wage (and travel reimbursement) arrears for frontline office staff (those with direct contact with clients) **(118)** Level of staff compliance with operational procedures and processing times	**(111 to 118)** Periodic performance and process evaluation or institutional review of the program and staff audits [c]	**(119)** Executed social assistance budget as % of approved budget (aggregate and by budget line) at the central and subnational government levels **(120)** CTR (cost of making one-unit transfer to a beneficiary)	**(119, 120)** Efficiency analysis or business review [c]
3. Information systems	**(121)** % of registered population/beneficiaries (in the sample recheck) whose information is complete, accurate, unique, and up-to-date **(122)** Number of security incidents that could have breached the privacy of the data	**(121, 122)** Periodic information system review [c]	**(123)** Total cost of ownership of the system **(124)** Cost of the system relative to population served/number of applicants OR total cost-transfer ratio (TCTR), which is the ratio of total costs to value of transfers at delivery **(125)** % of information that is shared with other government programs	**(123, 124)** Periodic performance audits and budget reviews [c] **(125)** Social information system data [a]

Source: Original table for this publication.

Note: BOMS = beneficiary operations management system(s); CTR = cost-transfer ratio; EFC = error(s), fraud, and corruption; GRM = grievance redress mechanism; KPI = key performance indicator; PES = public employment service(s); TCTR = total cost-transfer ratio; TCV = time, costs, and visits.

a. The numbering system correlates the effectiveness and efficiency indicators with the type of data source: [a] indicates data generated by delivery systems; [b] indicates other administrative data and national statistics; and [c] indicates data that require a separate dedicated data collection effort. (See Data Sources in section 9.2 for a fuller discussion of these.)

b. Private costs can be measured as "time costs," "financial costs, "or "number of visits" that clients have to make to achieve the task.

c. This indicator must be interpreted in the light of other indicators capturing the access and use of GRM. For more information on GRM, please refer to chapter 8, section 8.5.

d. If monitoring at the individual level is not feasible, then second-best would be to disaggregate beneficiaries by gender. A minimum would be to monitor the % of beneficiary households with conditionalities monitoring information for at least one member of the household.

e. Compliance rate and monitoring rate should be monitored jointly, not in isolation.

Notes

1. For a more detailed discussion on these input-output aspects across the phases of the delivery chain, please refer to section 2.1 (chapter 2).
2. However, the indicator is nonlinear in the sense that more coverage does not necessarily mean better performance (and some of the larger social registries are static, not dynamic, with on-demand capabilities).
3. Kuddo (2012), however, points out that the number of people claiming to be unemployed who are registered at PES offices often exceeds the total number of unemployed. Some job seekers may register to get services to help them find a better job (without being unemployed), while others may register for the purpose of obtaining benefits, including informal sector workers who register to continue receiving subsidized health insurance.
4. ASPIRE = Atlas of Social Protection Indicators of Resilience and Equity. Users should keep in mind the following disclaimers and data caveats when interpreting ASPIRE performance indicators. Household surveys have their own limitations. It is important to note that the extent to which information on specific transfers and programs is captured in the household surveys can vary a lot across countries. Often household surveys do not capture the universe of social protection programs in the country; in best practice cases, just the largest programs. Therefore information on country social protection programs included in ASPIRE is limited to what is captured in the respective national household survey and does not necessarily represent the universe of programs existing in the country. In addition, the availability of ASPIRE indicators depends on the type of questions included in the survey.
5. The ISPA Social Protection Payments tool (https://ispatools.org/payments/) lists key performance indicators to measure both effectiveness and efficiency of payment systems. The indicators cover five main criteria, including accessibility, robustness, integration, and costs.
6. See https://ghcosting.org/pages/standards/reference_case and Vassall et al. (2017).
7. Introducing technology does not guarantee cost savings, however. In a cash-for-assets program in Kenya, electronic cash payments were 15 percent less costly to implement than the distribution of food of equivalent value (CGAP/World Bank 2013). However, in the Malawi Cash and Food for Livelihoods Pilot Program, cash was more expensive to administer than food (though it assured greater food security) because the program was able to purchase food at much lower, more stable prices in the context of weak food market integration (Audsley, Halme, and Balzer 2010).
8. Good resources for carrying out CBA and CEA include Dhaliwal et al. (2012) and Levin and McEwan (2017).
9. The working group can be composed of staff designated as performance management focal points across various institutions, ministries, implementing agencies, or local government units involved in program implementation. A working group should have one or two full-time staff for coordination and follow-up. A dedicated unit might be a monitoring evaluation unit in the national ministry or lead institution. Assigning one individual responsible for performance management is not recommended, as this silos performance management and results in viewing performance management as one individual's responsibility, rather than the responsibility of all those involved in the implementation of different phases of the delivery chain.
10. Chile, Ministry of Social Development 2017a and 2017b; websites of Ministry of Social Development (http://www.desarrollosocialyfamilia.gob.cl/) and DIPRES (https://www.dipres.gob.cl/).

Bibliography

Audsley, Blake, Riikka Halme, and Niels Balzer. 2010. "Comparing Cash and Food Transfers: A Cost-Benefit Analysis from Rural Malawi." In *Revolution: From Food Aid to Food Assistance: Innovations in Overcoming Hunger*, edited by Steven Were Omamo, Ugo Gentilini, and Susanna Sandström, chapter 7. Rome: World Food Programme. https://www.wfp.org/publications/revolution-food-aid-food-assistance-innovations-overcoming-hunger#:~:text=Revolution%3A%20From%20Food%20Aid%20to%20Food%20Assistance%20%2D%20Innovations%20in%20Overcoming%20Hunger,-Publication%20type%3A%20Books&text=It%20lays%20out%20both%20new,country%2Dled%20food%20security%20strategies.

Beegle, Kathleen, Aline Coudouel, and Emma Monsalve, eds. 2018. *Realizing the Full Potential of Social Safety Nets in Africa*. Africa Development Forum Series. Washington, DC: World Bank.

CGAP (Consultative Group to Assist the Poor)/World Bank. 2013. "Cash for Assets: World Food Programme's Exploration of the In-Kind to E-Payments Shift for Food Assistance in Kenya." Working paper, CGAP, Washington, DC. http://www.cgap.org/sites/default/files/eG2P_Kenya.pdf.

Chambers, Robert. 2009. "Making the Poor Count: Using Participatory Options for Impact Evaluation." In *Designing Impact Evaluations: Different Perspectives* (International Initiative for Impact Evaluation [3ie]

Working Paper 4), edited by Robert Chambers, Dean Karlan, Martin Ravallion, and Patricia Rogers. New Delhi, India. http://www.3ieimpact.org/media/filer_public/2012/05/07/Working_Paper_4.pdf.

Chile, Ministry of Social Development. 2017a. "Informe de Desarrollo Social 2017." Ministerio de Desarrollo Social, Santiago. http://www.desarrollosocialyfamilia.gob.cl/storage/docs/Informe_de_Desarrollo_Social_2017.pdf.

Chile, Ministry of Social Development. 2017b. "Manual de Seguimiento de Programas e Iniciativas Sociales: Año 2017." Departamento de Monitoreo de Programas Sociales, División Políticas Sociales, Subsecretaría de Evaluación Social, Ministerio de Desarrollo Social, Santiago.

Costa Rica, Government of, Division of Operational and Evaluative Audit. 2016. "Auditoría Operativa sobre la Eficacia y Eficiencia de la Estrategia Nacional Puente al Desarrollo para la Reducción de la Pobreza 2015-2018, en Relación con el Cumplimiento de sus Objetivos," December 2016.

Dhaliwal, Iqbal, Esther Duflo, Rachel Glennerster, and Caitlin Tullock. 2012. "Comparative Cost-Effectiveness Analysis to Inform Policy in Developing Countries: A General Framework with Applications for Education." Abdul Latif Jameel Poverty Action Lab (J-PAL), Cambridge, MA.

European Commission. 2012. "Performance Management in Public Employment Services. https://www.google.com/url?sa=t&rct=j&q=&esrc=s&source=web&cd=&ved=2ahUKEwiv75Dp2ObpAhVTmHIEHdB_AmMQFjAAegQIBxAB&url=https%3A%2F%2Fec.europa.eu%2Fsocial%2FBlobServlet%3FdocId%3D10310%26langId%3Den&usg=AOvVaw2nmZvL41HBFS-RmmQ1WChy.

Grosh, Margaret, Carlo del Ninno, Emil Tesliuc, and Azedine Ouerghi. 2008. *For Protection and Promotion: The Design and Implementation of Effective Safety Nets.* Washington, DC: World Bank.

Guijt, Irene, and John Gaventa. 1998. "Participatory Monitoring and Evaluation: Learning from Change." IDS Policy Briefing 12, University of Sussex, Brighton, UK. http://www.ids.ac.uk/files/dmfile/PB12.pdf.

Holla, Alaka. 2019. "Capturing Cost Data: A First-Mile Problem." World Bank Blogs, April 29, 2019. http://blogs.worldbank.org/impactevaluations/capturing-cost-data-first-mile-problem?deliveryName=DM12088.

Holland, Jeremy, ed. 2013. *Who Counts? The Power of Participatory Statistics.* Warwickshire, UK: Practical Action Publishing.

IRC (International Rescue Committee), SIEF (Strategic Impact Evaluation Fund), and World Bank. 2019. "Capturing Cost Data." 2019. http://pubdocs.worldbank.org/en/994671553617734574/Capturing-Cost-Data-190314.pdf.

J-PAL (Abdul Latif Jameel Poverty Action Lab). n.d. Basic cost collection template. https://www.povertyactionlab.org/sites/default/files/resources/basic-costing-template.xls.

J-PAL (Abdul Latif Jameel Poverty Action Lab). n.d. Costing template. https://www.povertyactionlab.org/sites/default/files/resources/detailed-costing-template.xls.

J-PAL (Abdul Latif Jameel Poverty Action Lab). n.d. "J-PAL Costing Guidelines." https://www.povertyactionlab.org/sites/default/files/resources/costing-guidelines.pdf.

Kuddo, Arvo. 2012. "Public Employment Services and Activation Policies." Social Protection and Labor Discussion Paper 1215, World Bank, Washington, DC.

Leite, Phillippe, Tina George, Changqing Sun, Theresa Jones, and Kathy Lindert. 2017. "Social Registries for Social Assistance and Beyond: A Guidance Note and Assessment Tool." Social Protection and Labor Discussion Paper 1704, World Bank, Washington, DC. http://documents.worldbank.org/curated/en/698441502095248081/Social-registries-for-social-assistance-and-beyond-a-guidance-note-and-assessment-tool.

Levin, Henry M., Patrick McEwan, Clive Belfield, A. Brooks Bowden, and Robert Shand. 2017. *Economic Evaluation in Education: Cost-Effectiveness and Benefit-Cost Analysis.* 3rd ed. Los Angeles: Sage.

Lindert, Kathy, Colin Andrews, Chipo Msowoya, Boban Varghese Paul, Elijah Chirwa, and Anita Mittal. 2018. "Rapid Social Registry Assessment: Malawi's Unified Beneficiary Registry (UBR)." Social Protection and Jobs Discussion Paper 1803, World Bank, Washington, DC.

Lindert, Kathy, Skoufias, Emmanuel, and Shapiro, Joseph. 2006. *Redistributing Income to the Poor and the Rich: Public Transfers in Latin America and the Caribbean (English).* SP discussion paper no. 605, Washington, DC: World Bank Group. http://documents.worldbank.org/curated/en/413331468300691124/Redistributing-income-to-the-poor-and-the-rich-public-transfers-in-Latin-America-and-the-Caribbean.

Marini, Alessandra, Michele Zini, Eleni Kanavits, and Alexandros Karakitsios. 2017. "Process Evaluation of the First Phase of the GMI Rollout." World Bank, Washington, DC.

OECD/DAC (Organisation for Economic Co-operation and Development/Development Assistance Committee) Network on Development Evaluation. 2019. "Better Criteria for Better Evaluation: Revised Evaluation Criteria Definitions and Principles for Use." OECD, Paris. https://www.oecd.org/dac/evaluation/revised-evaluation-criteria-dec-2019.pdf.

Patel, Darshana, Yuko Okamura, Shanna Elaine B. Rogan, and Sanjay Agarwal. 2014. "Grievance Redress System of the Conditional Cash Transfer Program in the Philippines." Social Development Department and East Asia Social Protection Unit Case Study, World Bank, Washington, DC. http://documents.worldbank.org/curated/en/111391468325445074/Grievance-redress-system-of-the-conditional-cash-transfer-program-in-the-Philippines

PWC (PricewaterhouseCoopers). 2016. "Comprehensive Assessment and Benchmarking Report of the Pantawid Pamilyang Pilipino Program Business Processes and Information Systems." Consultant report.

Rosas, Nina, Gul Najam Jamy, and Amjad Zafar Khan. 2017. "Value for Money of Different Registration Approaches—Preliminary Findings: Pakistan's National Socioeconomic Registry Update." Slide presentation.

Sundaram, Ramya, and Utz Johann Pape. 2019. *Kenya Social Protection and Jobs Programs: Public Expenditure Review*. Washington, DC: World Bank. https://hubs.worldbank.org/docs/ImageBank/Pages/DocProfile.aspx?nodeid=31272661.

Tesliuc, Emil, Lucian Pop, Margaret Grosh, and Ruslan Yemtsov. 2014. *Income Support for the Poorest: A Review of Experience in Eastern Europe and Central Asia*. Directions in Development Series. Washington, DC: World Bank.

Vassall, Anna, Sedona Sweeney, Jim Kahn, Gabriela B. Gomez, Lori Bollinger, Elliot Marseille, Ben Herzel, Willyanne DeCormier Plosky, Lucy Cunnama, Edina Sinanovic, Sergio Bautista-Arredondo, GHCC Technical Advisory Group, GHCC Stakeholder Group, Kate Harris, and Carol Levin. 2017. "Reference Case for Estimating the Costs of Global Health Services and Interventions." Global Health Cost Consortium. https://ghcosting.org/pages/standards/reference_case.

White, Philip, Anthony Hodges, and Matthew Greenslade. 2013. *Guidance on Measuring and Maximising Value for Money in Social Transfer Programmes: Toolkit and Explanatory Text*. 2nd ed. London: UK Department for International Development and UKAID.

World Bank. 2011. "Romania: Functional Review." Social Protection, World Bank, Washington, DC.

World Bank. 2018. "Cost of Identification Systems: Model Guidance Note: Assumptions and Methodology." World Bank, Washington, DC.

Chapter 10

A Continuing Journey

Margaret Grosh, Tina George Karippacheril, and Inés Rodríguez Caillava

The development of social protection delivery systems has evolved enormously in the last twenty-five or so years. Contributory pensions and labor protections have long roots, with some countries having programs a hundred years old, but social assistance started growing in developing countries in the last couple of decades, reformulations in labor programs being equally recent. Countries have rolled out new programs, expanded budgets, formed new ministries, written strategies and legislation. To carry out all these efforts, they need modern social protection delivery systems.

Virtually all governments in developing countries are working to improve one or more of the core building blocks of social protection delivery systems discussed throughout the Sourcebook—including communications and outreach, identification, social registries, social protection (SP) payments, provision of services, beneficiary operations management, grievance redress, and so on.

Standards in social protection delivery systems are rising, in part due to technology and connectivity. Once it seemed a step forward to have a program at all, even if that meant bringing cash and security officers in mobile vans to payment points where people lined up (often for many hours) for their payments that came in little envelopes of round-numbered bills. Then it seemed modern to pay through the banking sector, giving people ATM cards so that they could withdraw cash at the time and place of their choosing, lowering transaction costs for many and reducing the potential for rake-offs or politicization at pay points, but with attendant limitations on the accessibility of ATM machines. Now the vision is to pay benefits from a range of programs into a single financial or a nonfinancial account held by an individual, one that can serve as a store of value and means of virtual transaction—so that funds can be transferred to pay utility bills, used in shops with point-of-sale devices or in markets where vendors accept digital payments, or for savings for old age, for human capital investments for their families, or for access to finance and credit for economic activity.

Growing aspirations in delivery systems also result from the rising institutional and governance capacities in the social protection sector. A number of countries are building networks of people-interface points and service centers to interact with individuals and families in neighborhoods, municipalities, towns, districts, and urban and rural areas. They are developing program procedures, inter-institutional rules of the game, data sharing agreements, and legal frameworks. As these come into play, ambitions rise. Occasional census-survey sweeps to register a rationed share of the needy begin to seem not like a glass half-full, but of one half-empty. Now the sector aspires to be fully dynamic, on-demand, and even self-service. The specter of clients having to present variants of the same information over and over again to different offices to access different social protection benefits and services makes less sense. One-stop service centers, foundational unique IDs, social registries, mobile payments, and coordinated bundles of benefits and services have become the new goal.

Mounting expectations about delivery systems come from more sophisticated experiences with digital platforms. The relationship of trust between the state and its peoples is being renewed and demands transparency and reasonable quality in delivery across key sectors. Technology has provided more sophisticated experiences to people as consumers and producers, which raises their expectations for government. As people pay for grid electricity (via pay-as-you-go, or PAYGO) using their mobile phones in Rwanda, Tanzania or Uganda (Adegoke 2019); as consumers shop on Alibaba in China, Flipkart in India, Tokopedia in Indonesia or MercadoLibre in Latin America (Economist 2019); hail rides on motorbikes via Grab in Malaysia or Gojek in Indonesia (Chandler 2019); make payments via Alipay or Wepay in China, Go-Pay or Ovo in Indonesia, Paytm in India, and Paga or Flutterwave in Nigeria, the notion that they ought also to be able to interact and transact easily with government gains force.

The move toward better delivery systems matters for the impact of the programs. At one level this is intuitive—if people do not get admitted to the program, if they do not get the support or services due, if they do not get them at critical moments, then the hoped-for good effects cannot happen. If a poor pregnant woman does not get the voucher for free hospital delivery before she gives birth, it will be valueless, she will have delivered at home. If the wrong people get benefits, then the effects will be smaller than hoped for. Job search assistance to a person with a reasonable job instead of to an unemployed person may improve their situation somewhat but be less transformative than intended. At another level this is imperative. Income support that comes after a child has gone hungry for weeks or a family evicted from their dwelling or lands comes too late to prevent harm. In the wake of the COVID-19 (coronavirus) pandemic, governments around the world are responding to the socio-economic shocks with social safety nets for millions of households. Nearly 200 countries worldwide have introduced various forms of social protection to compensate workers for lost income from extensive lockdowns and the broader economic downturn and to mitigate adverse impacts on the poor and the vulnerable. The end-to-end digital delivery of these programs, with safety, security, and speed, are helping programs comply with social distancing requirements (Financial Times 2020). Examples of the power of effective and efficient delivery systems for social protection have been sprinkled throughout the Sourcebook: how they ensure timely assistance; how they lower transactions costs, facilitating access and benefit; how they may lower administrative costs, error, and fraud; how they can improve program impacts by reducing unhelpful overlaps and enable joint programming when synergies are needed.

The move toward better delivery systems probably also matters for public support and budget for the programs delivered, and more broadly for trust in the social contract. The job of the individual or family, technocrat or politician, in advocating for a social protection program or for investments in modern delivery systems is presumably easier when the general public experience of the program is one of good client service, when there are pertinent statistics that show performance and impact, and where these can help defuse blemishes on the program's reputation when an occasional incident of bad service or fraud happens. The ability of the individual/family to trust in government and to be willing to pay taxes or participate in grassroots crisis-response activities (MIT Technology Review 2020) will depend on receiving or seeing others receive benefits and services worthy of the trust.

The enormous policy agenda driving continuing development of the social protection sector will require further development of delivery systems in various ways. We sketch here just a few examples:

- ***The drive toward universal social protection implies, in many countries, serving many more people than at present, especially in lower-income countries and the poorest populations.*** Thus, the basics of extending foundational IDs, social registries, beneficiary operations management systems, and SP payment systems (person-to-government [P2G] and government-to-person [G2P]) will be important, as we saw in chapters 4, 5, and 6.
- ***In middle- and upper-income countries the decline in absolute poverty implies that innovation and expansion in the sector may move from programs whose intended target groups are the chronic poor to those serving other groups***—the rising middle class or vulnerable, for example. To the extent that this means benefits extend up the income distribution from say, the 15th percentile to the 40th or 60th or even the 80th, it means larger social registries and that, for eligibility determination, they may be able to rely more on data already held elsewhere in government than new data collection; so data matching, interoperability, and integrated social information systems may be the modus operandi more than stand-alone systems. Also, it may be that the supports are spread through many sectors—assistance with childcare, college tuition, health care, maybe mortgage subsidies, and so on—raising the need for coordination among diverse agencies in policy development, in shared information systems to support registration, cross-referrals, and possibly coordination of benefit and service delivery.
- ***Social protection systems may begin to address the social services agenda***—coverage for disability, elder care, and other social services is woefully incomplete. As we saw in chapter 7, each set of services is complex in and of themselves, with eligibility determination and standard-setting processes full of challenges in finding a balance between what is feasible and what is desirable. The services are often provided by subordinate agencies, nonprofits, or for-profit agencies, and thus paid by contract, often with some results-based features in the payment determination, which means that the contracting agency must have the ability to issue sophisticated contracts and supervise and monitor specialty services provided. There is often also a complex bundle of services that may need coordination—a disabled adult might qualify for medical or therapeutic services, sheltered employment, safe transport to employment and medical care, as well as income support. Thus, the need for coordination and information sharing for intermediation and referrals is very high and will demand interoperable and integrated information systems, and possibly skilled social workers with caseloads that permit significant attention to each client.
- ***The (un)changing nature of work means that work outside of long-term formal labor contracts*** is likely to remain high in places where it has been high, and to increase in places where it has been low, and among upper-income groups. Thus, coverage of social insurance for the informal sector, heightened in the wake of the COVID-19 crisis, becomes an ever more salient issue. To provide it requires delivery systems that replace reliance on employers/firms as recordkeepers and contributions collectors or payers with direct interaction among workers, government, and payment service providers. Again, sophisticated information systems wil be needed, with the ability to track contributions (P2G SP payments) over long time periods, with service interfaces and benefit bundles that inspire trust among workers who contribute voluntarily, and transaction costs low enough to accommodate flexible and frequent small contributions.
- ***Demographic, technological, and climate changes all contribute to demand for labor programs*** that help people skill and re-skill and find successive entrepreneurship opportunities, gigs, or job placements over the course of a lifetime, and possibly in different kinds of jobs and locations. This implies innovation and expansion in labor market programs of many sorts. For delivery systems, it implies the need for institutions and information systems that can connect government funding, information, workers, and the private sector.
- ***Climate change and the COVID-19 pandemic have put disaster risk management and shock responsive social protection systems squarely in the limelight.*** Shock responsive systems involve complex multisectoral information for planning and put enormous emphasis on dynamism in assessing and serving post-shock needs, often with a combination of expanded or topped-up benefits for long-term programs as well as coordination with special emergency response programming. For delivery systems this implies both ex ante sophistication and means of agile response, at least in locally affected areas.

- ***Productive economic inclusion programming is also much in the fore of social protection thinking*** both for its goal of reducing chronic extreme poverty and for its ability to raise the resilience of households and prepare them for disaster. These programs may have initial eligibility requirements that can be served by relatively simple static systems, but delivering the complex package of income support, coaching, skill-building, and asset transfer can be quite a complex challenge, done at scale in very few places, as yet. Numerous programs and countries are working on variations of such programs and we should see in relatively short order the results of varied attempts to provide simpler packages, harness technology in delivery, and discover whether delivery is best done by a single agent/agency on all aspects or coordinated among actors of diverse specialties.
- ***The expansion of social protection work into countries with fragility or forced displacement, as well as into disaster risk management***, puts the social protection sector, working with a long-term vision of development and through government systems, working increasingly often in the same spaces and with the same instruments as humanitarian relief agencies working with shorter-term relief objectives, and often through parallel systems. This can create some duplications or contradictions, but can also foster some detailed and constructive thinking about the details of delivery systems and how joint capacities can be shared or built—for example, purpose and therefore benefit levels may differ between programs for host communities where families' livelihoods and housing assets are intact, and displaced populations facing loss of both of those, but payment modality may be shared.

Technologies can continue to improve front-office delivery of social protection programs. Tools such as mobile technologies, chatbots, digital service windows for self-service, natural language processing, and rules engine policy automation help screen for potential eligibility, schedule appointments, and address queries. Payment authentication via speech recognition, or other biometrics (e.g., fingerprint, iris, facial recognition) and with remote imaging can simplify the beneficiary-authentication process. Artificial intelligence could provide personalized delivery and virtual assistants for the disabled, elderly, remote, and other vulnerable populations. Georeferenced apps can link beneficiaries to distributors, payment points, retailers, public services, nongovernmental organizations, and other resources. Mobile technologies, and chatbots can help people with queries and grievances in an efficient manner. Digital technologies allow people to provide regular feedback on the provision of services, which can improve the quality of delivery. Online application websites are being designed and adapted to suit the disabled and elderly, increasing morale by supporting autonomy (Coyne 2016).

Technologies can continue to improve back-office administration of social protection programs. Machine learning and predictive modeling with satellite imagery facilitate geographic targeting. Georeferencing technologies can help locate, track, and follow-up with applicants and beneficiaries continuously, and are potentially of utility for crisis response. Automated, accurate benefits calculation in compliance with often complex program rules for multiple programs can be completed with greater rapidity. Machine learning can facilitate detection of error, fraud, and corruption (EFC), prevention, risk profiling, prioritizing resources for inspections, and spot checks. In contexts of crisis, shocks, fragility, and natural disasters, the use of these technologies can reduce the time of response and increase the efficiency in the delivery of benefits and services. Robotic process automation (RPA) solutions can automate predictable, repetitive, time-consuming processes to reduce the administrative burden and time lag. Such developments would be particularly beneficial for government agencies and programs operating with a lean team stretched across various functions (Weisinger 2017). RPA can help reduce the time taken for grievance redress and for resolving user queries; the artificial intelligence on which RPA relies has the potential to transform social protection by changing the ways in which work gets done.

Managing the personnel and contractors that build technology is a significant challenge. The skills to capture the benefits of technology for social protection delivery systems and to safeguard them well are specialized, scarce within social protection agencies, and highly remunerated, so often hard to attract on civil service salaries. However, investing in information systems developed using open standards, that are interoperable and modular, can help build capacity within social protection agencies in developing, operating, and maintaining these systems. It can also help mitigate the risk of buying or developing vendor-locked-in systems that pose barriers to the adoption of newer, more innovative, or cheaper technologies and architectural elements.

Among the game-changing effects of technology is how it can transform the jobs of those who work in the sector. Because it can automate functions that previously took enormous administrative time—gathering, recording, collating, verifying information that is now much more available in shared databases—releases some of that time. We can now deploy more staff time to engage in more sophisticated interactions with people— seeking to understand the range of challenges that each faces and thus what services will be helpful, developing individualized action plans, offering coaching and psychosocial support, or the like.

Protecting personal data is a critical aspect of the design of systems and needs much more attention. Ideally, the development of technology is informed by the legal and regulatory provisions and institutional frameworks, such as strong data protection laws and autonomous data protection agencies. Already the possibilities and uses of data in social registries are challenging regulations. Many countries have not modernized their laws and protocols around data sharing and data privacy. Data sharing protocols sometimes rigidly prohibit potentially fruitful use, and sometimes they allow such extensive sharing that privacy concerns are warranted. Data privacy is more commonly underdeveloped with challenges growing ever greater as more governments hold more data, with more points of connection and ever more sophisticated data threats. Many social protection delivery systems are quite inadequate today at addressing these data issues. The protection of data includes protecting people's privacy by design and safeguarding data privacy, security, and user rights in the governance of a system.

Safeguarding the poor in a brave new world becomes a priority. The adoption of digital technologies for delivering social programs is a complex endeavor. Exponential technologies are converging and changing the way people live, work, and organize. On the one hand, this makes them disruptive and presents a unique opportunity to solve intractable development challenges. On the other hand, they point to emerging issues of inclusion and protection for the very people they are meant to serve. The "virtual" space, though parallel to the "real" world, has implications for particularly vulnerable people (Pilkington 2019). The United Nations' Special Rapporteur on extreme poverty and human rights said in 2019 to the UN General Assembly that "as humankind moves, perhaps inexorably, toward the digital welfare future it needs to alter course significantly and rapidly to avoid stumbling zombie-like into a digital welfare dystopia" (United Nations Human Rights Council 2019). The risks of surveillance, poor public accountability, entrenchment of inequality, and discrimination are a real concern (Eubanks 2018). Social protection delivery systems contribute to engendering trust in government by facilitating access to human capital and financial inclusion benefits and services. Experience has shown that that trust is fragile and could be undermined where weak governance and institutional capacity allow abuses to occur. It is therefore even more important to build in protections and safeguards that go well beyond a "do no harm" approach in designing delivery systems for social protection.

Adequate staffing and definition of institutional roles and responsibilities will be critical in developing delivery systems to support the larger policy agendas. These processes can take flexibility and political will. Just addressing both dynamic inclusion and coordination of basic programs, not even considering the increasingly ambitious range of programming as the sector develops, requires improvements of many sorts. There must be adequate staffing—either of deconcentrated social protection agencies or local governments with clear responsibilities—to reach people nationwide. It requires that the staff be present in adequate number, with adequate skills. Staff in turn need adequate tools and rules to guide them. To develop these requires significant technical capacity to develop inter-institutional operation agreements, and oversee development of technology and data protections.

Significant political will is also needed to encourage or mandate different programs to work together toward high quality standards, and to make the case to the legislature, to taxpayers, and to the general public that social protection is an important part of the social contract and that the government is committed to it. Virtuous circles may be possible, with new starts showing fruit and building support; indeed, that may be the story of the last twenty years of social assistance development in low income countries. But support for social protection seems in many places, including in a number of high-income countries, to be always in need of reinforcement.

Inclusion and dynamism will remain perennial challenges. A lot of social protection is about helping people in the moment they need help. The particular individual that may need help at any moment is hard to know, as is the number of those individuals. Who will be unemployed? When? How many will be unemployed in a downturn? Who will have a disabling accident? Which pregnant women will be poor enough to qualify for vouchers for free hospital deliveries? Which families will qualify for income support? Which youth will transition from school to work by themselves? Who will need assistance? Which elderly will need social care assistance? Which of their families will need help to provide it? These questions mean that delivery systems will always be trying to serve new clients, being more and more dynamic, agile, and nimble in the process. We have seen in the prior chapters examples of how some countries can move in this direction, by building permanent staff capacity, by opening online registrations, by active outreach among different populations who may need benefits or services, by connecting beneficiaries of one benefit or service to information about others that may be pertinent, and so on. There is progress, but much work still to do to reach the present frontier, and then to move the frontier further.

Coordination will remain a challenge. The current state of social protection is one of enormous fragmentation. Some reasons may become less pertinent over time—for example, if a flagship program is providing adequate levels of income support, it may be less important for each sectoral ministry to provide fee waivers. But policy is path-dependent and constituencies for programs—among either the clients or the administrators—may continue to support individual programs or distrust reform processes that involve multiple agencies. Integration of administrative functions—as in social registries or multiprogram payments—may be a partial substitute for reduced fragmentation in programming. It may be an important engine of coordination—the secular change in technology means information systems can get better—but there is no concomitantly inexorable drive to institutional reform. Thus, themes around coordination—among sectors, among levels of government and between government and for-profit or not-for-profit contractors—seem likely to stay on the reform agenda with incremental progress here and there, but often with fruitful agendas still to be pursued.

Diversity will continue. One of the things that has made it challenging to write the Sourcebook is that there is so much diversity in social protection delivery systems. The range of programs, of intended populations, and in-country contexts are each inherently wide. But so too is the way in which common challenges can be addressed. The mix of technology and people; the mix of institutions; the mix of policy reform versus implementation work-arounds; the varying emphasis put on different aspects of social protection—solidarity versus independence, customization versus transparency, economy versus impact, and so on. All these mean that social protection delivery systems, while sharing the same framework, will be different from place to place, use different tools for different clients, and change over time. Thus, while countries work toward high coverage of more comprehensive social protection systems, we expect that there will be an abundance of opportunities for countries to learn from each other with respect to their delivery systems.

The "first mile" and human-centered design will continue to be important. Because many of the needs attended to by social protection programs come from a change in people's circumstances, the potential beneficiaries may not be well versed in the benefits and services offered. Because the change in circumstance (unemployment, poverty, incapacity, illness) may carry stigma or new limitations, people may be less willing and able to seek out or accept benefits and services than for those things that are universal parts of a life course. The challenges of inclusion and coordination are significant, and as many examples in the book have shown, human-centered design is a valuable tool to improve social protection delivery systems. It is also entirely consonant with the view of social protection as a human right, a view not much taken decades ago, but a touchpoint for policy development now and as the world works toward sustainable development goals in a post-COVID-19 age.

Bibliography

Adegoke, Yinka. 2019. "Solar's Big Promise for Lighting Africa Is Tied to the Continent's Mobile Money Advantage." Quartz Africa, June 30, 2019. https://qz.com/africa/1655648/solar-power-in-africa-and-the-mobile-money-advantage/.

Chandler, Clay. 2019. "Grab vs. Go-Jek: Inside Asia's Battle of the 'Super Apps'." *Fortune*, March 20, 2019. https://fortune.com/longform/grab-gojek-super-apps/.

Coyne, Allie. 2016. "DHS' New Front-Line Will Be Virtual Assistants." iTnews, December 19, 2016. https://www.itnews.com.au/news/dhs-new-front-line-will-be-virtual-assistants-444926.

Economist. 2019. "How to Beat Bezos: Baby Amazons Take On Their American Role Model." August 1, 2019. https://www.economist.com/business/2019/08/01/baby-amazons-take-on-their-american-role-model.

Eubanks, Virginia. 2018. *Automating Inequality: How High-Tech Tools Profile, Police, and Punish the Poor.* New York: St. Martin's Press.

Financial Times. 2020. "Mobile Cash is the Best Way to Help Africa Fight COVID-19." April 12, 2020. https://www.ft.com/content/adc604f6-7999-11ea-bd25-7fd923850377.

MIT Technology Review. 2020. "What the World Can Learn from Kerala about How to Fight COVID-19." April 13, 2020. https://www.technologyreview.com/2020/04/13/999313/kerala-fight-covid-19-india-coronavirus/.

Pilkington, Ed. 2019. "Digital Dystopia: How Algorithms Punish the Poor." *Guardian*, October 14, 2019. https://www.theguardian.com/technology/2019/oct/14/automating-poverty-algorithms-punish-poor.

United Nations Human Rights Council. 2019. "Report of the Special Rapporteur on Extreme Poverty and Human Rights." A/74/493. https://undocs.org/A/74/493.

Weisinger, Dick. 2017. "Robotic Process Automation (RPA): Closer to a Rules Engine than to Artificial Intelligence (AI)?" Formtek blog post, October 3, 2017. http://formtek.com/blog/robotic-process-automation-rpa-closer-to-a-rules-engine-than-to-artificial-intelligence-ai/.

Glossary*

Social Protection

Activation casework. Casework services provided by employment officers, counselors, or specialists, usually at local employment offices, often with individualized action plans (IAPs), co-responsibilities, and monitoring of progress on IAPs and compliance with co-responsibilities.

Activation programs (aka workfare programs). Programs that typically provide cash benefits (such as unemployment benefits or social assistance) with monitored individualized action plans and co-responsibilities (such as availability to work, job search, participation in ALMPs).

Active labor market programs (ALMPs). Interventions aimed at the improvement of the beneficiaries' prospects of finding gainful employment, in other words, to enhance their employability. They typically include training, services and incentives to promote entrepreneurships or start-ups, job creation (including public works), wage subsidies to incentivize hiring of unemployed workers, first-time job seekers, disabled workers, or other target groups.

Active search. An approach to *outreach* whereby program administrators, local officials, foundation representatives, or others deliberately and proactively reach out to population groups (such as those living in remote areas or marginalized populations) who may otherwise be missed by, or unaware of, their potential eligibility for social protection programs.

Administrator-driven approach for intake and registration (aka supply-driven approach or en masse registration approach). Approaches sometimes used to register groups of households to be assessed and considered for potential inclusion in one or more programs. Three key features characterize administrator-driven approaches: (1) the impetus for initiating the engagement is driven by administrators, not the people being registered (state ≥ people); (2) registration is usually carried out en masse (groups or cohorts of households); and (3) timing: the timetable for administrator-driven approaches is typically driven by financing and capacity, not by the timing or needs of specific households. See also on-demand approach.

Appeals. Grievances about the correctness of decisions made by the programs. It may be a simple administrative error by the program, or involve fundamental issues of eligibility and entitlement, which can involve misinterpretation of the law by program; refusal of benefit or service; miscalculation of entitlements; or wrong categorization of the potential beneficiaries.

Applicants. Individuals, families, or households who apply for benefits and services at their own initiative. See also registrants.

Assessment of needs and conditions. Systematic processes for determining the needs and conditions of registered individuals, families, or households for the purposes of (1) determining potential eligibility for specific programs and/or (2) informing the determination of benefits and services that may be rendered by the programs.

Assistance unit. The focus of an intervention. It can be an individual, a family, or a household.

Authentication. Process of establishing confidence that a person is who they claim to be. Digital authentication generally involves a person electronically presenting one or more "authentication factors" to "assert" their identity—that is, to prove that they are the same person to whom the identity or credential was originally issued.[1]

* Compiled by World Bank Social Protection Delivery Systems Global Solutions Group.

Beneficiary, beneficiaries. Individuals, families, or households who are enrolled in a program who are recipients of a benefit or service.

Beneficiary operations management. A stage along the social protection delivery chain that involves the activity of continuously engaging and collecting information from the field or other sources (such as other databases), which is then processed through a set of protocols, recorded, and used to make decisions. This simple pattern of engaging, collecting, processing, and deciding is the common thread that ties together the set of activities that occur continuously in the implementation of a program. Beneficiary operations management includes three main functions, which are implemented simultaneously: beneficiary data management, monitoring of conditionalities, and implementation of a mechanism for the redress of grievances.

Beneficiary operations management system (BOMS). Information technology system that automates information processing for eligibility and enrollment decisions, decisions on the benefits and service package, the provision of benefits and services, and beneficiary operations management (including beneficiary data management, monitoring of compliance with conditionalities, grievance redress, and decisions on exit). Often referred to as an "MIS." See box 2.1.

Beneficiary registry. A database of beneficiaries of a social protection program. It is also a component of the beneficiary operations management system. These beneficiary registries contain information on program beneficiaries. Registries that contain information on beneficiaries of multiple programs are known as integrated beneficiary registries.

Benefits. Something tangible that is given by social protection programs to individuals, families, or households. They may be in the form of cash transfers or in-kind (such as food stamps, food rations, and subsidies). They may be noncontributory social assistance programs that are financed by general revenues, or they may be financed by direct contributions as a form of social insurance.

Biometrics or biometric data. Physiological or behavioral characteristics that are unique to an individual (e.g., fingerprints, voice patterns) and that can be used as a means of automatic verification of identity.

Biometric identification. Process of searching against a biometric enrollment database to find and return the biometric reference identifier(s) attributable to a single individual. The comparison may be either a one-to-one (1:1) matching—commonly referred to as "biometric verification"—where comparison is done against a single template, or one-to-many (1:N) matching, where comparison is done against multiple templates.[2]

Block grants. Federal or central government funds given to state or local government that must be spent for a general purpose specified by the grant. Block grants do not require preapproval for individual projects or programs so long as they are spent in the agreed-upon area, such as some aspects of health, education, personal social services, and now, public assistance for the poor. (State governments may also give funds to municipalities or other local jurisdictions in the form of block grants.)

Case management. The term "case management" is particularly problematic as it is used differently by various professions (for example, by social workers, health care workers, and IT specialists). Further, some may use the term "case management" to mean what we call beneficiary operations management. Some practitioners use the term case management to mean social work (covering awareness, intermediation, referrals, and counseling). Others use the term to refer to an integrated approach to managing clients all along the delivery chain (through the entire "life of the case," as some practitioners call it). To avoid confusion, we avoid the term.

Cash transfers. Money distributed to individuals, families, or households. Cash transfers are direct, regular, and predictable noncontributory cash payments that help beneficiaries to raise and smooth incomes. The term encompasses a range of instruments (e.g., social pensions, child grants, public works programs, unconditional or conditional cash transfers, etc.) and a spectrum of design, implementation, and financing options.

Categorical targeting. A targeting mechanism in which eligibility is defined for groups of the population on the basis of specific observable characteristics, such as age. Examples include social pensions for the elderly, child allowances, birth allowances, family allowances, and orphan benefits.

Census-sweep registration method. Mass registration of households into the social registry. With the census sweep approach, all or most households in specific areas (or the entire country) are registered en masse. In contrast to the on-demand approach (see below), with the census-sweep approach, enumerator teams go to the communities and conduct intake and registration using door-to-door methods.

Child allowance. A cash benefit provided to families based on the presence and number of children in the family. The benefit may vary by the ordinal position of the child, the age of the child, or the employment status of the parent. Eligibility can be universal or based on an assessment of socioeconomic status (such as means testing).

Childcare services. Out-of-home care of children, usually for children under compulsory school age, or of primary-school age children when school is not in session. Childcare services include preschool, childcare centers, day care in providers' homes, and before- and after-school services.

Child protective services (CPS). Services provided for the protection of children who are at risk of, or experiencing, neglect (physical or emotional) or abuse (physical, sexual, or emotional). The focus is on the safety of the child, but support may also be provided to parents or other family members to strengthen families and promote safe, nurturing homes for the children.

Child support. Financial support provided by a nonresident, noncustodial parent for the support of a child.

Child welfare services. Social services for children at-risk and their families, including child protective services, adoption and foster care, family preservation, and care services (home, community, or residential/institutional care).

Civil registration. The continuous, permanent, compulsory, and universal recording of the occurrence and characteristics of vital events (e.g., live births, deaths, fetal deaths, marriages, and divorces) and other civil status events pertaining to the population as provided by decree, law, or regulation, in accordance with the legal requirements in each country.

Client interface. The physical or digital access point or interaction between people (individuals, families, and households) and social protection delivery systems.

Collection of contributions for social insurance. The process of collecting worker- or employer-paid contributions for eligibility and accumulation of benefits for social insurance, such as social security pensions, unemployment insurance, maternity and sick leave, and so forth. In some countries, collection of social security contributions is unified with tax collection; in other countries it is carried out via a separate process and agency.

Community-based targeting. A mechanism by which local communities are given discretion to determine which individuals, families, or households will be selected as beneficiaries of a particular program—or to determine which would be registered into a social registry for further assessment of their needs and conditions and eventual consideration for potential eligibility in social programs.

Complaint. Grievances about the quality or type of processes for delivering benefits and/or services. They can arise due to delays, wait times, long lines, excessive documentation requirements, program staff behavior, public office accommodation, lack of information about the program decisions, difficulty accessing social protection benefits and/or services, and so on.

Compliance and noncompliance (of conditionalities). Compliance refers to the carrying out of specific conditionalities or co-responsibilities required for participation in the program by beneficiaries. Noncompliance refers to the failure to carry out said conditionalities.

Compliance period. The period in each conditionalities monitoring cycle during which beneficiaries would be observed for compliance monitoring (in other words, when they would be expected to comply).

Compliance rates. A performance indicator that measures the number of individuals complying with required conditionalities for a program (numerator) as a share (%) of total individuals monitored (denominator). This indicator is usually monitored for individuals within a specific categorical group, such as school-age children, pregnant/lactating mothers, and so on.

Compliance verification period. The time period during which compliance verification processing is carried out within each conditionalities monitoring cycle. The allotted period may differ from the actual time taken to carry out all the steps, which would be measured through a process evaluation (and could be more or less than the time allotted).

Compliance verification processing. The process of verifying that beneficiaries have complied with program conditionalities. This process could include preparation and distribution of beneficiary lists; gathering, recording, entering, processing, and transmittal of data on compliance (or on noncompliance); and taking decisions as to whether beneficiaries have complied with the conditionalities.

Conditional cash transfers (CCTs). Social assistance programs that make receipt of benefits conditional upon beneficiary actions (such as school attendance or health care visits), typically with the objectives of reducing poverty and providing incentives for investing in human capital.

Conditionalities (aka "co-responsibilities"). The set of obligations that each beneficiary household must comply with in order to continue receiving cash benefits. Common examples include school attendance, health visits, and labor/work efforts.

Conditionalities monitoring. The monitoring of beneficiary household members' compliance with conditionalities and processing of associated data. This is the "umbrella term" that covers compliance monitoring periods and compliance verification periods/processes.

Conditionalities monitoring cycle. The recurring period that begins with the latest roster of beneficiary households, with information on pertinent family members (inputs), and ends with a revised beneficiary roster that updates with information on compliance for that cycle, as well as any decisions on consequences for noncompliance (outputs), which would link back to the payroll for the next payment cycle (outputs). The conditionalities monitoring cycle includes both the compliance period and the compliance verification period.

Conditionalities monitoring rates. A performance indicator that measures the number of individuals for which the program monitors conditionalities compliance information (numerator) as a share (percent) of total individuals in that category (denominator). This indicator is usually monitored for individuals within a specific categorical group, such as school-age children, pregnant/lactating mothers, and so on.

Corruption. Commonly involves manipulation of beneficiary rosters, for example, registering ineligible beneficiaries to garner political support, staff accepting illegal payments from eligible or ineligible beneficiaries, or diversion of funds to ghost beneficiaries or other illegal channels.

Creaming. An informal practice in public employment services whereby employment officers focus job placement efforts on people with high employment probabilities (more likely to be placed) rather than disadvantaged clients (harder to serve). (The term derives from the sweetest cream that rises to the top of milk.)

Data. A value or set of values representing a specific concept or concepts. Data become "information" when analyzed and possibly combined with other data in order to extract meaning and to provide context. The meaning of data can vary depending on its context and is often used interchangeably with information.

Data privacy. The appropriate and permissioned use and governance of personal data.

Data protection. The securing of collected information. Data protection is fundamental to ensuring data privacy. *Data privacy*, a process and legal matter, focuses on who has authorized access, whereas data protection is more a technical matter.

Data validation. Quality control processes to ensure that data are valid (complete, accurate, and consistent). It is the process of comparing data with a set of rules to find out if data are reasonable. There are many types of data validation, including the following:

- ***Format check.*** Data are formatted correctly (e.g., date format of dd/mm/yyyy).
- ***Presence check.*** Data have been entered into a field.
- ***Range check.*** Value falls within the specified range (e.g., IB grades can only range between 0 and 7).
- ***Type check.*** Correct data type has been entered (e.g., age should be a number).

Data verification. Quality control processes to ensure that data values match information in other administrative systems (via cross-checking). It is the process of checking that the data entered exactly matches the original/authoritative source to find out if data are accurate.

Decentralization, or decentralized. Assignment of policy responsibility and/or decision-making authority to a subnational (state, regional) or local (municipality, county) level of government from a higher level of government (including a transfer of such responsibilities from central to subnational or from subnational to local).

Decisions on benefits and service packages. Setting benefit levels (for cash or in-kind benefits) and/or defining the service package (for services) that will be provided to eligible beneficiaries of social program(s) and establishing and notifying beneficiaries of such decisions (and any associated conditions on their participation).

Deconcentration, or deconcentrated. The process whereby a central organization transfers some of its responsibilities to lower-level units within its jurisdiction.

De-duplication. A technique to detect duplicate identity records. Biometric data—including fingerprints and iris scans—are commonly used to de-duplicate identities in order to identify false or inconsistent identity claims and to establish uniqueness.

Delivery chain. Social protection (including labor) benefits and services pass through common implementation phases along the delivery chain, including outreach, intake and registration, assessment of needs and conditions, eligibility and enrollment decisions, determination of benefits or service package, notification and onboarding, provision of payments or services, and beneficiary operations management.

Delivery chain process mapping. A management tool for mapping the sequencing of implementation processes across actors (institutions) or levels of government. Important for establishing uniqueness and clarity of roles, and useful for mapping the "as-is" processes and potential "to-be" vision for reforms. In addition to mapping the sequencing by actor, there may be a time dimension (calendar of implementation cycles).

Delivery systems. see social protection delivery systems.

Designated recipient. The individual in the beneficiary family or household who is designated as the grantee or recipient of benefits when they are paid out (for authentication and payment purposes). A designated recipient should be named for all benefits for which the assistance unit is a group (family or household). A designated recipient may also be needed for individual-based benefits if the beneficiary requires some guardian to act on their behalf (such as with orphans or severely disabled individuals).

Disabled. Persons with disabilities include those who have long-term physical, mental, intellectual, or sensory impairments which, in interaction with various barriers, may hinder their full and effective participation in society on an equal basis with others (International Labour Organization). An individual with a disability is defined as a person who (1) has a physical or mental impairment that substantially limits one or more major life activities; (2) has a record of such an impairment; or (3) is regarded as having such an impairment.[3]

Discouraged workers (aka available potential job seekers). Persons not currently in the labor market who want to work but do not actively seek work because they view job opportunities as limited, or because they have restricted labor mobility, or face discrimination, or face structural, social, or cultural barriers. They are also called "available potential job seekers," or "hidden unemployed," and are considered part of the potential labor force.[4]

Effectiveness. It is central to the performance of delivery systems. As defined by the OECD/DAC (Organisation for Economic Co-operation and Develelopment/ Development Assistance Committee) evaluation criteria, *effectiveness* is a measure of the extent to which a program or activity attains its objective. In this Sourcebook, an effective system is not only one that reaches, registers, and provides benefits and services to most of the intended population, but is also a system that is inclusive because it accommodates the specific needs of vulnerable populations and those who face access barriers. Consequently, the evaluation criterion of inclusion is embedded within effectiveness to reflect this logic.

Efficiency. Another important dimension of the performance of delivery systems, albeit one that is difficult to measure. Ensuring that outcomes are achieved at reasonable costs, including moving clients through the various phases of the delivery chain at minimal cost in terms of time and money both for administrators and clients, is critical to evaluating performance. Alternative measures of efficiency include processing times for various phases or stages along the delivery chain.

Eligibility. A state in which individuals, families, or households are entitled or qualified to receive a benefit or service because they satisfy certain criteria.

Eligibility criteria. Factors used to determine whether an individual, family, or household is eligible (inclusion criteria) or not eligible (exclusion criteria) to participate in a program.

Employment incentives. Measures that facilitate the recruitment of unemployed persons, first-time job seekers, and other intended populations, or help to ensure the continued employment of persons at risk of involuntary job loss. Employment incentives refer to subsidies for open market jobs which might exist or might be created without the public subsidy, and which will hopefully be sustainable after the end of the subsidy period. The jobs that may be subsidized are usually in the private sector, but public or nonprofit sector jobs are eligible, too, and no distinction is requested.

Employment opportunities and rehabilitation for persons with disabilities. Measures aimed at enabling people with disabilities to secure, retain, and advance in suitable employment and thereby to further such person's integration or reintegration into society. Rehabilitation covers measures providing rehabilitation for persons with a reduced working capacity (temporary or permanent) and that aim to help participants adjust to their disability or condition and develop competencies that prepare them to move on to work. Rehabilitation refers to vocational rehabilitation only.

Employment services. Services provided to job seekers, the unemployed or inactive, disabled workers, or others to help them find gainful employment. They typically include: (1) self-service online tools; (2) job search and placement services; (3) casework and career coaching services often guided by: Individual Action Plans (IAPs); (3) career counseling services and vocational advice; (4) other specialized services.

End-to-end implementation planning. Takes delivery chain process mapping to an even deeper level by mapping the sequence of all process steps (detailed) plus the actors, inputs, and resources, and time taken for each step—for all phases along the delivery chain (end to end).

Enrollment decisions. Decisions taken by social program administrators to admit individuals, families, and/or households into that specific program. Those decisions usually consider the assessment of needs and conditions, eligibility criteria, as well as other program-specific factors (such as fiscal space).

Error. Error is an unintentional violation of program or benefit rules that results in the wrong benefit amount being paid or in payment to an ineligible applicant.

Family. A family is defined for operational purposes as "a group of two people or more related by birth, marriage, or adoption and residing together; all such people (including related subfamily members) are considered as members of one family."

Family allowance. See child allowance.

Foundational identification system. A system for proving (or "authenticating") an individual's unique identity. It uses a minimal set of attributes, such as biographic and biometric data, to exclusively describe an individual and, on that basis, to provide government-recognized identity credentials. It is "foundational" relative to various functional systems and databases (e.g., education, health) on which it relies, but it is a parallel and complementary component (along with, for instance, the civil registration system) of the larger ecosystem.

Fraud. Occurs when a claimant deliberately makes a false statement or conceals or distorts relevant information regarding program eligibility or level of benefits.

Geographic targeting mechanisms. A means of focusing interventions on individuals, families, or households living in a certain area.

Grievance. Refers to two distinct categories: (1) complaints, and (2) appeals, and any other feedback from the general population, the intended population, registrants, applicants, beneficiaries, or other stakeholders of the social protection program.

Grievance redress mechanism (GRM). A formalized way to accept, sort, assess, and resolve complaints, appeals, and queries from the program beneficiaries and other stakeholders. The GRM is composed of a set of institutional structures, mandated rules, procedures, and processes through which complaints, appeals, and queries about the social protection program(s) are resolved.

Guaranteed minimum income (GMI) programs. Social assistance programs that differentiate benefit amounts according to the difference between specific incomes of each beneficiary household and an established amount, with the objective of ensuring at least that "guaranteed minimum income" level.

Hard-to-serve individuals or families. In general, hard-to-serve individuals or families face multiple risks and constraints, and the complexity that arises with that multiplicity makes it hard to serve them with labor and social services, requiring coordinated or integrated service approaches to help them reduce their social risks and narrow their distance to the labor market.

Home care services. Supportive care services that are provided to individuals or families in the home. Care may be provided by professional caregivers who provide daily assistance to ensure the activities of daily living are met, or by licensed healthcare professionals who provide medical treatment needs.

Horizontal and vertical coordination. Horizontal coordination involves multiple actors at the same hierarchical administrative level (e.g., coordination across peer-level central agencies or coordination across local actors). Vertical collaboration involves multiple actors across administrative levels (e.g., between central- and local-level actors).

Household. Any individual or group of individuals who are living as one economic unit, who buy food and make meals together.

Human-centered design. The continual process of understanding and meeting user needs. More specifically, human-centered design is a multidisciplinary approach to solving the needs and problems of the end-user (people) and the government's capabilities for transformation.

Hybrid means testing (HMT). A type of socioeconomic assessment that combines means testing with proxy means testing by gathering information on a household's observable income as verifiable welfare (as in means testing) and information on certain household assets to predict nonverifiable welfare (as in proxy means testing).

Identification. Action or process of identifying a person (cf. "authentication"). In its initial occurrence, it typically involves the assignation of an identity number (which is often unique) and the issuance of an identity credential which, alone or with the support of some other authentication factor (e.g., biometrics), is subsequently used to prove or authenticate a person's identity.[5]

Identity. Attribute, or set of attributes, that uniquely describe(s) a subject within a given context.[6]

Identity assurance. Ability to determine with a degree of certainty—or level of assurance (LoA)—that a claim to a particular identity made by some person or entity can be trusted to actually be the claimant's "true" identity.[7]

Identity proofing. Process of establishing that a subject is who he or she claims to be.[8]

Inactive. Individuals considered "outside the labor force," neither employed nor unemployed, that is, not actively seeking work. There are a variety of reasons why some individuals do not participate in the labor force; such persons may be occupied in caring for family members; they may be retired, sick, disabled, or attending school; they may believe no jobs are available; or they may simply not want to work.[9]

Individualized action plan (IAP). Also referred to as a service plan, family action plan, mutual responsibilities agreement, or personal progression plan, it is an agreement between a caseworker and beneficiary that typically includes a summary of the individual assessment including profiling results; goals and agreed steps toward the goals; benefits (if any); the list of services assigned or referred; required actions and commitments of both parties (the beneficiary and the caseworker); rules and procedures regarding sanctions for noncompliance with required actions; beneficiary rights and responsibilities; and information on grievance redress mechanism (GRM) procedures. During the enrollment onboarding phase, the IAP would be signed by both the beneficiary and the caseworker.

Information. Data become "information" when analyzed and possibly combined with other data in order to extract meaning and to provide context.

Information security. The practice of defending electronic or physical information from unauthorized access, use, disclosure, disruption, modification, perusal, inspection, recording, or destruction. Information security relates to the preservation of confidentiality, integrity, and availability of information, in addition to other properties such as authenticity, accountability, nonrepudiation and reliability (ISO/IEC 27000:2009). Information security ensures that only authorized users (confidentiality) have access to accurate and complete information (integrity) when required (availability).[10]

Information systems. A discrete set of information resources, such as personnel, equipment, funds, and information technology, organized for the collection, processing, maintenance, use, sharing, dissemination, or disposition of information.

Information technology. Any equipment or interconnected system or subsystem of equipment that is used in the automatic acquisition, storage, manipulation, management, movement, control, display, switching, interchange, transmission, or reception of data or information by the executive agency.

Institutional care services. A type of treatment provided to an individual in a formal residential environment by an institute, other family, or other organized form aiming at providing care services (social or health services).

Intake. The process of initiating contact, engaging with the client(s), and gathering information for the purposes of assessing their needs and conditions for potential eligibility for benefits or services. The point of entry may be via a specific program or a multiprogram access point (such as a social welfare agency, public employment service, or social registry).

Integrated information management framework. A framework that integrates all of an organization's systems and processes, enabling an organization to work as a single unit with unified objective. It links information across different services/systems and integrates information across agencies for a given user.

Intended population. The group of individuals, families, or households who are meant to be included as potential beneficiaries of a program. Also referred to as a "target group."

Intermediation. An integrated service-provision approach used in both labor and social services. Intermediation is a service in its own right—and it also connects people (workers) to other services. It is the process of informing clients about a range of benefits and services relevant to their needs, and directing them to the corresponding access point, based on agreed protocols with service provider agencies, sometimes with individualized action plans (IAPs), to help them overcome multiple socioeconomic barriers. Intermediation connects the demand and supply of social or labor services. The role of the mediator (social caseworker or public employment officer) is to correctly identify the needs of the participant (demand side—through risk screening and profiling) and then to identify the availability of services and service providers (supply side) and then connect them with referrals and counter-referrals (monitoring and follow-up) on the basis of an action plan, protocols, service contracts, and service standards.

Job search and placement services. A class of employment services that typically include job search assistance, job search skills, CV/application and interview skills, job fairs/clubs, employer contacts, and job referrals. Often provided by public employment services (PES), but sometimes contracted out to private employment service providers.

Labor force status. Share of population that is employed, unemployed, and inactive, for all 15+ population. "Employed" is defined as anyone who has worked at least one hour during the previous week for pay, profit, or family gain. A person is defined as unemployed if he or she is presently not working but is actively seeking a job or ways to start an enterprise. Those who are neither employed nor unemployed are inactive. A person is defined "inactive nonstudent" if he or she is inactive and not attending school.

Labor markets. Actual pools of skilled or unskilled labor available within local, national, or global economies, and activities intended to reduce risk and to improve the efficiency of the labor market and to increase the employability of workers, including employment security and protection. Includes employment and advisory services, training and retraining, and labor market information systems, including the design, purchase, and implementation of computer software and hardware.

Labor profiling. Job-seeker profiling is a diagnostic method to assess the prospects of unemployed people to resume work. Profiling can help public employment services (PES) to segment job seekers into groups with similar likelihoods of work-resumption, and in turn to determine their level of access to different levels of treatment. In addition, profiling can guide the resource allocation process within PES and assigning of appropriate packages of benefits, employment services and ALMPs.

Legal framework (in social protection). A legislative or legal framework that sheds light on the use and governance of laws—as well as decrees, regulations, and other legal or policy documents—and provides a foundation for the implementation of policies and programs undertaken to achieve strategic plans and outcomes.

Long-term care services (LTC). Refers to the range of services designed to support people who are unable to perform physical and cognitive functions, measured through ability to perform activities of daily living (ADLs) and instrumental activities of daily living (IADLs). Individuals may need LTC due to limited functional ability, chronic conditions, trauma, or illness that limit their ability to carry out basic self-care or personal tasks that must be performed each day. LTC refers to family-based care in the home and community, as well as institutional care. It is quite distinct from health care, in that while health care services seek to change the health condition (from unwell to well), LTC services seek to make the current condition (unwell) more bearable.

Long-term unemployment. Refers to those who have been unemployed for more than a certain time period, such as 52 weeks (1 year, International Labour Organization, Organisation for Economic Co-operation and Development) or 27 weeks (US Bureau of Labor Statistics).

Means testing (MT). A methodology that determines potential eligibility or computes benefit levels based upon some assessment of the incomes and assets of a family or household.

Migrant worker. A person who is to be engaged, is engaged, or has been engaged in remunerated activity in a state or country of which he or she is not a citizen.[11]

Notification and onboarding. Notification involves informing applicants of their enrollment decisions (in, wait-listed, or out), and onboarding involves finalizing the enrollment process for those who have been selected (conducting orientation, collecting additional information, providing option to opt-out, etc.).

On-demand approach for intake and registration. Approach that allows anyone to apply and register their information to be considered for potential inclusion in one or more programs. Three key features characterize on-demand approaches: (1) the impetus for initiating the engagement is driven by the clients (not the "state"), who take the initiative to apply; (2) specific clients engage on their own; and (3) timing: with the on-demand approach, specific clients engage in intake and registration on their own timing. While on-demand approaches are driven largely by the way intake and registration is carried out, they also influence other phases of the delivery chain. See also administrator-driven approach.

One-stop shops/service centers. One form of "integrated service provision" whereby all services are co-located, so the client needs to go to only one place for support. In some cases, these may be for both labor and social benefits and services together. In other cases, they may be for labor services separately (e.g., job centers). Other modalities combine social and health benefits and services (such as the "department of health and human services" that is common in the United States and Australia).

Outreach. Deliberate efforts to reach and inform intended populations and vulnerable groups about social protection programs and delivery systems so that they are aware, informed, able, and encouraged to engage.

Outsourcing. An arrangement where an entity decides to contract out the supply of services (sometimes goods) necessary to its operation to another entity, which then carries out the work using its own staff and equipment.

Oversight and controls. Measures, tools, and systems to prevent, detect, deter, and monitor error, fraud, and corruption (EFC).

Passive labor market programs. Programs that provide income replacement to unemployed workers without requiring any job-search or work-related activation efforts.

Payments administration. The required steps to transfer cash to beneficiaries or into the beneficiaries' accounts. Payments administration includes establishing and verifying the payroll and setting up the payment schedule, requesting the inter-account transfer (by the overseeing ministry to the treasury), issuing the inter-account payment order (by the treasury to the payment service provider), issuing the payment instruction (by the overseeing ministry to the payment service provider), and providing the payments to the beneficiaries (by the payment service provider).

Payment service provider. The public or private sector organization tasked with delivering the social protection program's payments, such as a bank, post office, mobile network operator, nongovernmental organization, savings and credit cooperative organization, or microfinance institution.

Payments provision. Processes to transfer and deliver benefits to recipients.

Payments reconciliation. An accounting process that uses two sets of records to ensure figures are correct and in agreement. It confirms whether the money leaving an account matches the amount that has been spent and makes sure the two are balanced at the end of the recording period. For cash benefits, reconciliation confirms whether the funds transferred to the service provider match the amounts paid out to beneficiaries for that implementation cycle, and identifies any amounts not disbursed.

Performance measurement framework. Serves three main purposes. First, performance indicators that are monitored regularly can help diagnose bottlenecks in the delivery chain early on and help correct course to prevent systemic challenges. Second, paired with other evaluative techniques, performance indicator frameworks can also help identify alternative channels, processes, or practices that enable the system to be more effective or save clients time or money. Performance measures of delivery systems can feed into a broader set of evaluative evidence on the program, including impact evaluations, and contribute to a broader learning agenda to refine and improve a program's impact. Third, a performance measurement system is an important part of a wider oversight function for social protection programs, ensuring that public funds are allocated effectively.

Personal data. Any information relating to an individual who can be identified, directly or indirectly, in particular by reference to an identifier (e.g., name, identification number, location data, online identifier, or one or more factors specific to the physical, physiological, genetic, mental, economic, cultural, or social identity of that individual).

Private employment services. Any natural or legal person, independent of the public authorities, who provides one or more of the following services: (1) services for matching offers of and applications for employment, without the private employment agency becoming a party to the employment relationships which may arise therefrom; (2) services consisting of employing workers with a view to making them available to a third party; and (3) other services relating to job search.

Provision of services. See service provision.

Proxy means testing. A tool used to assess a family's socioeconomic status using a composite measure that calculates a weighted score based on observable household characteristics, such as demographic structures, education levels, location and quality of the household's dwelling, and ownership of durable goods and other assets. These variables are all considered "proxies" for incomes or consumption, which may be more difficult to measure and observe in situations of high informality.

Public employment services. See employment services.

Recruitment incentives/wage subsidies. Measures providing incentives for the creation and take-up of new jobs or that promote opportunities for improving employability through work experience, and which are payable for a limited period only. Recruitment incentives may include benefits provided exclusively to persons from labor market program target group and that are conditional upon the take-up of a new job (back-to-work bonus, mobility/relocation allowance, or the like).

Reduction of benefits for noncompliance with conditionalities. When a beneficiary repeatedly fails to comply with conditionalities or co-responsibilities in a conditional cash transfer program, some countries impose a penalty on benefits, meaning that the beneficiary will lose all or part of the household benefits for some period until compliance resumes.

Refugee. Someone who has been forced to flee their country because of persecution, war, or violence.[12]

Registrants. Individuals, families, or households who have provided their information during the intake and registration phase of the delivery chain. They may have provided their information at their own initiative (on demand; see applicants) or at the initiative of a public agency or program (as in the case of en masse registration/census sweeps). In the latter case, we do not call them applicants because they did not technically "apply" for benefits and services.

Registration. The process of recording and verifying the information collected from the intake process. It can also involve pulling additional information from other administrative systems. Intake and registration usually happen simultaneously.

Registration quotas. Explicit caps (limits) on the number of households that can be registered in a specific district.

Registration targets. Planned number of households that would be registered in a specific district, but without operating as a fixed or rigid quota (cap or limit).

Self-employment/entrepreneurship. Work carried out as a business, rather than as an employee. Income from self-employment is a mixture of rewards for work and returns on private capital employed. Self-employment can be undertaken as a result of an entrepreneurial endeavor or lack of job availability.

Service provision. Provision of social or labor services to individuals, families, or households—either as individual services or as integrated service packages.

Services. Intangible acts, activities, or works provided to, or with the participation of, beneficiaries as a contribution to their well-being (such as to reduce poverty, provide opportunities, enhance employability, reduce social risks, etc.). They may be administered by public agencies or outsourced to third parties using government funding. See also definitions of employment services, active labor market programs, and social services.

Social assistance. Social safety net programs that are noncontributory transfers in cash or in-kind and are usually targeted to the poor and vulnerable but may also support other groups (such as the long-term unemployed, disabled, etc.). Some programs are focused on improving chronic poverty or providing equality of opportunity; others more on protecting families from shocks and longstanding losses they can inflict for the unprotected poor. These programs, also known as social welfare, include cash transfers (conditional and unconditional), in-kind transfers, such as school feeding and targeted food assistance, and near cash benefits such as fee waivers and food vouchers.

Social insurance. Composed of programs that minimize the negative impact of economic shocks on individuals and families. They include publicly provided or mandated insurance schemes against old age, disability, death of the main household provider, maternity leave and sickness cash benefits, and social health insurance. Social insurance programs are contributory, and beneficiaries receive benefits or services in recognition of contributions to an insurance scheme.

Social pensions. Social assistance (noncontributory) benefits paid to categorical groups of the population, such as the elderly or disabled. They may be universal (paid to all in that category) or targeted (paid to those in that category who are also poor).

Social protection. Systems that help individuals, families, and households, especially the poor and vulnerable, cope with crises and shocks, find jobs, invest in the health and education of their children, and protect the aging population.

Social protection delivery systems. The operating environment for implementing social protection (including labor) benefits and services, including the implementation phases and processes along the delivery chain, main actors (people and institutions), and enabling factors (communications, information systems, and technology).

Social protection (SP) payments. The transfer of cash or near cash to social protection program recipients (whether contributory or noncontributory programs). They include government-to-person (G2P) and person-to-government (P2G) payments.

Social registry. Information systems that support the processes of outreach, intake and registration, and assessment of needs and conditions to determine potential eligibility for social programs. They maintain information on all registered households regardless of whether they eventually benefit from a social program. As such, we do not refer to households in social registries as "beneficiaries" but as "registered households."

Social services. A wide variety of programs made available by public or private agencies to support individuals or families in addressing their particular risks and improving their overall well-being.

Start-up incentives. Measures that promote entrepreneurship by encouraging the unemployed and other target groups to start their own business or to become self-employed. Assistance may take the form of direct cash benefits or indirect support including loans, provision of facilities, business advice, and so on.

Target group. See intended population.

Targeting. A policy that seeks to direct an intervention (benefit or service) to the intended population, to minimize the coverage of those not intended to be beneficiaries (errors of inclusion) and the noncoverage of intended beneficiaries (errors of exclusion). (We prefer to avoid using the term targeting in relation to an act of implementation.)

Targeting criteria. See eligibility criteria.

Termination of benefits for conditionalities noncompliance. When a beneficiary continuously fails to comply with conditionalities or co-responsibilities over a longer period, some countries cancel or terminate benefits and exit the family from the program (usually permanently or for a significant duration of time before one can reapply, barring appeals).

Time, costs, visits (TCV). An indicator of the amount of time people spend on the process, the amount of money they spend to participate (such as transport costs, childcare costs, missed work, and notary fees), and the number of visits they must make to the local office or other agencies.

Training. Measures that aim to improve employability and are financed by public bodies. All training measures should include some evidence of classroom teaching, or if in the workplace, supervision specifically for the purpose of instruction. Includes institutional training, and workplace training, alternate training, and apprenticeships.

Unconditional cash transfers (UCTs). Programs that provide cash transfer benefits to individuals, families, or households without imposing any conditions on the beneficiaries.

Unemployment, unemployed. People who are jobless, actively looking for work, and currently available for work. See also long-term unemployment.

Unemployment benefits. All forms of cash benefit to compensate for unemployment, including unemployment assistance (noncontributory) or unemployment insurance (based on contributions and earning history). Benefits may be included as components of activation programs.

Wage subsidies. Government payments to employers offering work to the unemployed and other vulnerable groups in the labor market. See also recruitment incentives.

Warning for conditionalities noncompliance. A notification transmitted to beneficiaries if one or more family members are recorded as not complying with the conditionalities or co-responsibilities of a program (such as a conditional cash transfer program).

Work disincentives. Adverse incentives for able-bodied adults to engage in work or employment arising from benefits eligibility or tax policies.

Workfare programs (similar to activation programs). Programs that provide benefits to individuals (unemployed or poor) and require some proof of engagement in work or work-related activities (such as job search, training, intermediation, or job-readiness courses).

IT Cheat Sheet

Data. A value or set of values representing a specific concept or concepts. Data can become "information" when analyzed and possibly combined with other data in order to extract meaning and to provide context. The meaning of data can vary depending on its context and is often used interchangeably with information.

- ***Data dictionary.*** A repository that contains descriptions of all data objects consumed or produced by the software. An organized listing of all data elements that are pertinent to the system, with precise, rigorous definitions so that both user and system analyst will have a common understanding of inputs, outputs, components of stores, and (even) intermediate calculations.
- ***Dynamic data or transactional data.*** Data that change as a result of an event (a transaction). The data have a time dimension, a numerical value, and refer to one or more reference data objects such as orders, invoices, and payments.

- ***Master data.*** A single source of common business data that are agreed upon and shared across the organization, and are used across multiple systems, applications, and processes. Examples include data about customers, products, employees, suppliers, materials, vendors, and so on.
- ***Metadata.*** Data that describes other data.
- ***Semi-structured data.*** A form of unstructured data that do not conform with the formal structure of data models but contain tags, metadata, or markers to separate semantic elements and to enforce hierarchies of records and fields within the data. Examples include XML (extensible markup language) data and JSON (JavaScript Object Notation).
- ***Structured data.*** Information with a high degree of organization, such that it can be stored in a relational database and is readily searchable using algorithms or operations. An example is data in spreadsheets.
- ***Unstructured data.*** Data that do not have a predefined data model and are not organized in a predefined format. Examples include text documents, video, audio, mobile activity, social media activity, and satellite imagery.

Data analytics, business intelligence. Helps you find answers to a set of defined questions. It includes the generation, aggregation, analysis, and visualization of data to inform and facilitate business management and strategy. Includes data visualization, data mining, reporting, time series analysis (including predictive techniques), online analytical processing (OLAP), and statistical analysis.

- ***Big data.*** Helps find the questions you do not know you want to ask. This is the technology that stores and processes data from sources both internal and external to your company. Big data usually refers to the immense volume of data available online and in the cloud, which requires ever more computing power to gather and analyze. Because the sources are so diverse, and you'll probably be using this data for purposes it was not originally intended to serve, the data are often completely raw and unstructured and will need to be cleaned up before any useful insights can be garnered.
- ***Data mining.*** Helps find answers you did not know you were looking for beforehand. An analytical process that attempts to find correlations or patterns in large data sets for the purpose of data or knowledge discovery.[13] A famous legend from the retail industry was the discovery that men between ages 30 and 40 who purchased diapers on a Friday night would most likely also have beer in their cart, which led the retailer to move diapers and beer closer to each other. Data mining has now upgraded to "big data."
- ***Data scientists.*** Experts in statistics and computer science who know the tricks for finding the signals hidden in the noise of big data.
- ***Online analytical processing (OLAP).*** A data structure that allows fast analytical processing from multiple perspectives, usually using star or snowflake schema, stored as metadata, from which one can pivot the data in many ways.

Database. A large organized collection of information that is accessed via software.

- ***Database management system (DBMS).*** A software package designed to define, manipulate, retrieve, and manage data in a database.[14] It has four components: an application programming interface (API), a query interface, an administrative interface, and an underlying set of data access programs and subroutines. Application programs never access the physical data store directly. They tell an appropriate DBMS interface what data they need to read and write, using names defined in the schema.
- ***Data warehouse.*** A subject-oriented, nonvolatile, time-variant collection of data in support of management's decisions. It typically draws its content from a large number of operational and external databases and uses a federated architecture approach for implementation.
- ***Distributed database (DDB).*** An integrated collection of databases that is physically distributed across sites in a computer network. A distributed database management system (DDBMS) is the software system that manages a distributed database such that the distribution aspects are transparent to the users.[15]

- ***NoSQL.*** A class of database management systems (DBMS) that do not follow all of the rules of a relational DBMS and cannot use traditional SQL to query data.[16] In the 21st century, NoSQL database management systems have evolved, where data is modeled in means other than tabular relations, which is particularly useful for real-time web applications and for big data. NoSQL-based systems are typically used in very large databases, which are particularly prone to performance problems caused by the limitations of SQL and the relational model of databases. Many think of NoSQL as the modern database of choice that scales with web requirements. Some notable implementations of NoSQL are Facebook's Cassandra database, Google's BigTable, and Amazon's SimpleDB and Dynamo.
- ***Relational database management system (RDBMS).*** First developed in the 1970s, it is a DBMS that organizes stored data into structures called tables, or relations. The common difference between DBMS and RDBMS is that DBMS just provide an environment where people can conveniently store and retrieve information with the presence of redundant data. On the other hand, RDBMS uses normalization to eliminate the data redundancy. Examples include MS SQL Server, IBM DB2, ORACLE, My-SQL, and Microsoft Access.
- ***Virtual database.*** Information systems are developed over time using different DBMSs and may be owned by different parts of an organization. As a result, data are fragmented across a number of systems, organizational, and geographic boundaries. A virtual database is a type of database management system that serves as a container to transparently view and query several other databases through a uniform application programming interface (API) that culls from multiple sources as if they were a single entity. These databases are connected via a computer network and then accessed as if they are from a single database. The goal for a virtual database is to be able to view and access data in a unified way without needing to copy and duplicate it in several databases or manually combine the results from many queries. They are also known as federated databases.[17]

Information systems. Interdependent groups of elements that function together to accomplish some predefined goal (or to solve an organizational problem) by collecting, organizing, storing, processing, creating, and distributing information. To accomplish that goal, an information system makes use of a variety of system elements, namely, the following:

- ***Database.*** A large organized collection of information that is accessed via software.
- ***Documentation.*** Manuals, forms, and other descriptive information that portray the use and/or operation of the system.
- ***Hardware.*** A comprehensive term for electronic and electromechanical devices that comprise the physical parts of a computer. The internal parts of a computer (CPU, hard drive, RAM) are referred to as components and the external parts (mouse, keyboard, printers, scanners) are referred to as peripherals.
- ***People.*** Users or operators of elements of the system.
- ***Procedures.*** The steps that define the specific use of each system element or the procedural context in which the system resides.
- ***Software.*** Characterized by (1) a set of machine-readable instructions (lines of code) that when executed provide desired features, functions, and performance; (2) data structures that enable the instructions to manipulate information; and (3) descriptive information in both hard copy and virtual forms that describe the operation and use of the instructions. Application software are stand-alone programs that solve a specific business need. Such applications process business and technical data in a way that facilitates business operations or management/technical decision making.

Integration and Interoperability

- ***Application programming interface (API).*** A set of functions and procedures for integrating application components. APIs allow softward applications to communicate with each other without having to know how they are implemented.
- ***Data integration.*** Combines data from different sources and provides users with a unified view of these data for service integration. When services are provided by multiple suppliers, the service integration challenge is to seamlessly integrate them into

end-to-end services that operate as a single IT service delivery model. Data integration involves the practice of applying architectural techniques and tools to provide access and delivery of data with varied data types and structures in order to meet the data needs of the applications and business processes within an organization.

- ***Integration.*** Integration and interoperability are often conflated, but they mean two different things. Integration is the process of linking independently designed applications to work together as one system, so that the data contained in each becomes part of a larger, more comprehensive system that quickly and easily shares data when needed. Integration also enables access to data and functionality from such independent applications through a single interface or service.
- ***Interoperability.*** The ability of organizations to interact toward mutually beneficial goals, involving the sharing of information and knowledge between organizations, through the business processes they support, by means of exchange of data with other systems using common standards.[18] Interoperability also includes the ability of systems to provide and receive services from other systems and to use the services so interchanged to enable them to operate effectively together.
- ***Interoperability framework.*** An agreed approach for interoperability for organizations that wish to work together toward the joint delivery of public services (without having to integrate all of their subsystems into one large system).

Software. See also "Information systems" list, above.

- ***Commercial off-the-shelf (COTS).*** Packaged, commercially available software solutions that are adapted to meet the requirements of the purchasing organization.
- ***Custom, locally developed software (LDSW) or homegrown software or bespoke software.*** Software developed specifically for an organization or user.
- ***Customization.*** Includes configuration, modification, and enhancements made to the software application.
  - ***Configuration.*** The process of selecting from an assortment of options, such as defining values of parameters in a software package, without writing specific code to meet requirements of the application.
  - ***Enhancement.*** The process of adding program code or program modules to provide additional functionality to software. It does not alter existing processes. It adds to them.
  - ***Modification.*** The process of changing program code to alter the existing form of processing. Modifications may be discouraged and unsupported by packaged software vendors, and in many cases the code may not be accessible. It can cause problems when the organization decides to install an upgraded version of the software.
- ***Maintenance.*** Modification of a software after delivery to correct faults, to improve performance or other attributes, or to adapt the application to a changed environment.
- ***Mobile apps.*** The term "app" has evolved to specifically connote software that is designed to reside on a mobile platform such as a tablet or mobile phone. It encompasses a user interface that interoperates with web-based resources that provide access to a wide array of information that is relevant to the app and local processing capabilities that collect, analyze, and format information in a manner best suited to the mobile platform. Additionally, a mobile app provides persistent storage capabilities within the platform. Mobile apps are generally downloaded from application distribution platforms that are operated by the owner of the mobile operating system, such as the Apple App Store (iOS) or Google Play Store.
- ***Open-source software.*** Software developed by informal collaborative networks of programmers and are usually free. Anyone is freely licensed to use, copy, study, distribute, and change the software in any way, and the source code is openly shared so that people are encouraged to voluntarily improve the design of the software.[19] For more details and examples of open-source software, visit https://opensource.com/resources/what-open-source.
  - ***Free and open source (FOSS).*** Refers to user's freedom to copy and reuse the software.

- ***Free/libre open source software (FLOSS).*** Emphasizes the value of *libre* (free), that is, with few or no restrictions.

- ***Proprietary software.*** Software protected by intellectual property rights; generally requires purchase of a license to use by payment of a one-time fee or recurring fees, and the source code is typically hidden from users.

- ***Turnkey system.*** A complete system solution, including software and hardware, that is sold to the purchasing organization as a complete product without the need for additional configuration and can be used immediately once installed or implemented.

Systems architecture

- ***Enterprise architecture:*** *Can be considered as a superset of business, data, application, and technology architecture.* See TOGAF for more detail.[20]
    - ***Application architecture.*** A description of the structure and interaction of the applications as groups of capabilities that provide key business functions and manage the data assets.
    - ***Data architecture.*** A description of the structure and interaction of the enterprise's major types and sources of data, logical data assets, physical data assets, and data management resources.
    - ***Technology architecture.*** A description of the structure and interaction of the technology services and technology components.

- ***Microservice architecture.*** Or simply microservices, is a variant of service-oriented architecture that has grown in popularity in recent years. Microservices are an architectural and organizational approach to software development where software is composed of small independent services that communicate over well-defined application programming interfaces (APIs). These services are owned by small, self-contained teams. Microservices architectures make applications easier to scale and faster to develop, enabling innovation and accelerating time-to-market for new features. It is a method of developing software applications as a suite of loosely coupled, independently deployable, modular services in which each service runs a unique process and communicates through a well-defined, lightweight mechanism to serve a business goal. The opposite of this is the monolithic architectural style. For example, Amazon has migrated to microservice architecture. Amazon gets countless calls from a variety of applications—including applications that manage the web service API as well as the website itself—which would have been simply impossible for their old, two-tiered architecture to handle. In a microservice application, each service usually manages its unique database. See Werner Vogels video for more detail.[21]

- ***Monolithic architecture.*** Unlike microservices, a monolith application is always built as a single, autonomous unit. In a client-server model, the server-side application is a monolith that handles the HTTP requests, executes logic, and retrieves/updates the data in the underlying database. The problem with a monolithic architecture, though, is that all change cycles usually end up being tied to one another. A modification made to a small section of an application might require building and deploying an entirely new version. If you need to scale specific functions of an application, you may have to scale the entire application instead of just the desired components. Monolithic systems use a single logical database across different applications.

- ***Service-oriented architecture (SOA).*** An architectural style based on the use of services to produce interoperable, modular systems that are easier to use and maintain. These services carry out a small function such as data validation that can be reused by software applications or combined with a number of other services to provide the functionality of a large software application.

- ***Three-tier architecture.*** A client-server architecture that is made up of three layers: the data layer, business logic layer, and presentation layer. This is also known as model view controller (MVC) architecture.
    - ***Business logic layer.*** The layer that contains the programs (lines of code) that implement the logic of the application's core functionality.
    - ***Data layer.*** The layer that contains the database in which information is stored and from which it is retrieved. Data in this layer is kept independent of business logic.

- ***Presentation layer.*** The part that constitutes the front-end layer of the application and contains the user interface with which end-users interact through a web-based application to access the information system.

Notes

1. As defined in the World Bank's *ID4D Practitioner's Guide*, Version 1.0, Washington, DC, 2019, https://id4d.worldbank.org/guide.
2. As defined in International Standard ISO/IEC: Information technology—Vocabulary—Part 37, Biometrics, 2382-37, 2017, https://www.iso.org/standard/66693.html. See also *Introduction to Biometrics*, by Anil Jain, Arun Ross, and Karthik Nandakumar, New York, Springer Publishing, 2011.
3. As defined by the US Department of Labor.
4. As defined by the International Labour Organization.
5. As defined in the World Bank's *ID4D Practitioner's Guide*.
6. As defined by the National Institute of Standards and Technology (NIST).
7. As defined in the World Bank's *ID4D Practitioner's Guide*.
8. As defined by the International Labour Organization.
9. ISACA (Information Systems Audit and Control Association), 2008.
10. As defined by the United Nations.
11. As defined by the United Nations.
12. As defined by the United Nations.
13. As defined in the NIST Computer Security Resource Center, https://csrc.nist.gov/glossary/term/data_mining (accessed July 2020).
14. As defined in Techopedia.com, https://www.techopedia.com/definition/24361/database-management-systems-dbms (accessed July 2020).
15. As defined in *Encyclopedia of Database Systems* ("Distributed Database Systems" entry by KL Tan), edited by L. Liu and M.T. Ozsu, Springer, Boston, MA, 2009.
16. As defined in Techopedia.com.
17. As defined in Techopedia.com..
18 As defined in the European Union's "New European Interoperability Framework," 2017, https://ec.europa.eu/isa2/sites/isa/files/eif_brochure_final.pdf.
19. See *Open Source for Global Public Goods (English)* by Tina George (Karippacheril), Anita Mittal, Vasumathi Anandan, and Maria Inés Rodríguez Caillava, Identification for Development, World Bank Group, Washington, DC, 2019, http://documents.worldbank.org/curated/en/672901582561140400/Open-Source-for-Global-Public-Goods.
20. TOGAF Standard for Enterprise Architecture, Version 9.2, https://pubs.opengroup.org/architecture/togaf9-doc/arch/index.html.
21. Werner Vogels' "Amazon, Microservices, and the Lean Cloud," HackFwd Build 0.7, Berlin, https://vimeo.com/29719577.